Hong Kong
Macau & Canton

a Lonely Planet travel survival kit
Robert Storey

Hong Kong, Macau & Canton

7th edition

Published by
Lonely Planet Publications
Head Office: PO Box 617, Hawthorn, Vic 3122, Australia
Branches: 155 Filbert Steet, Suite 251, Oakland CA 94607, USA
10 Barley Mow Passage, Chiswick, London W4 4PH, UK
71 bis rue du Cardinal Lemoine, 75005 Paris, France

Printed by
Singapore National Printers Ltd, Singapore

Photographs by
Robert Storey (RS)
Tony Wheeler (TW)
Roger Hunter (RH)
Paul Steel (PS)
Graham Imeson (GI)
Front cover: Man Mo Temple Incense Burning – Scoopix Dallas & John Heaton

First Published
1978

This Edition
November 1994

National Library of Australia Cataloguing in Publication Data

Storey, Robert
Hong Kong, Macau & Canton – a travel survival kit.

7th ed.
Includes index.
ISBN 0 86442 247 4.

1. Hong Kong – Guidebooks. 2. Macau – Guidebooks. 3. Canton (China) – Guidebooks. I. Title. II. Title: Hong Kong, Macau & Canton. (Series: Lonely Planet travel survival kit).

915.12504

text & maps © Lonely Planet 1994
photos © photographers as indicated 1994
climate charts compiled from information supplied by Patrick J Tyson, © Patrick J Tyson, 1994

colour map facing page 128 courtesy of Kowloon-Canton Railway Corporation
cartoon copyright Larry Feign

Robert Storey

Devoted mountain climber and computer hacker, Robert has had a number of distinguished careers, including monkeykeeper at a zoo and slot machine repairman in a Las Vegas casino. After running out of money while travelling, Robert finally got a decent job as an English teacher in Taiwan. Robert then diligently learned Chinese, wrote Lonely Planet's *Taiwan* guide and became a respectable citizen and a pillar of the community. With his Las Vegas past still in his blood, Robert was lured into a Macau casino during one crazed weekend, and was thus inspired to write the current edition of this book so he could pay his way back to Taiwan. Now safely at home, Robert has devoted the rest of his life to serious pursuits such as studying Chinese calligraphy and writing a computer program that will allow him to win at the roulette tables.

From the Author

I am deeply grateful to a number of residents (both permanent and temporary) in Hong Kong, Macau and Guangzhou (Canton) who generously donated their time and energy to help me research this book. In Hong Kong, special thanks go to Jenny Chan, to Cora Juan (Philippines), Douglas Silva (Sri Lanka) and to Mary & Craig Briggs (USA). I am also indebted to Alice Chan of Macau for her valuable assistance. My contacts in Guangzhou, survivors of the Cultural Revolution, prefer to remain anonymous, but I am especially grateful to them. Also thanks to Liao Yuanxuan of Taiwan for help with the Chinese calligraphy.

This Book

The first edition of this book was researched and written by Carol Clewlow, and since then has gone through several incarnations under the influence of a number of people. The second edition was updated by Jim Hart, with a Guangzhou section added by an Australian student who had lived and studied in China for some time. The third and fourth editions were updated by Alan Samagalski. The fifth and sixth editions were major rewrites done by Robert Storey. The seventh edition is an update by the same author.

From the Publisher

The 7th edition of *Hong Kong, Macau & Canton* was edited at the Lonely Planet headquarters in Melbourne, Australia by Stephen Townshend. Rachel Black was responsible for mapping, illustrations, design and layout. The Chinese script was produced by Robert Storey and Lonely Planet. Thanks to Sharan Kaur for proofing the text, Ian Ward for proofing the Chinese script and Valerie Tellini for her assistance and advice regarding the script. And special thanks go to Rob Flynn, Dan Levin and Ric Barker for their unfailing help with computers.

Thanks

We've had a number of letters carrying useful information from people 'out there', even the odd letter from citizens of the People's Republic of China. With thanks to everyone, and with apologies to anyone who's been left out (and any name we've misspelt), I'd like to mention:

Matin Allies (HK), Mark Andersen, Gerald Barnes (USA), Andreas Beilken (D), Ross Berglund (AUS), Glenn Berkey (USA), R P Bews (UK), Lola Bjorkquist (USA), Stuart Britton (UK), Barbara Camfield (AUS), Arthur R Campbell (USA), C Cardell (S), Craig Chapman, Chung Hsin Chu (USA), Gordon Clint, John Connell (AUS), Nigel Corbett (UK), B Michelle Dewey (USA), Mary Drennan (AUS), Helen Eriksson (S), John Fairall, Brian Finch (AUS), Y Foong (SIN), Gwen Gahagan (C), Dan Gaiser, Geoff Garside, Richard Gibbs (UK), Rupert Gildenhuys (USA), Rene Granacher (D), Carrie Greig (AUS), D Haastrup, Petri Hakiwen (FIN), Ric Harcourt, Philip Hawks (UK), Christopher Hay, John Hocking, Michelle Hoctor (IRL), Kari Hoff, Annika Johannson (S), Gabrielle Keep, Gaye Keep, Mark King (UK), Alexander Lee (TAI), Hubert Maab, Iain Maciver (C), Joe J Marquez (USA), Danny McCann (C), Geoff McGowan, Scotty McNutt (USA), Mr & Mrs I Messider (UK), Ed Moylan (USA), Victoria Muise (C), Bryan Murphy, David Myron (USA), Patrick O'Dwyer (UK), Donald Oldham (UK), E Olsson (S), Gayle Parry, Michel Porro, B Powell (USA), Subreata Qas (IND), Vincent G Reidy (UK), Mark & Jeanne Rowan (USA), Johann Sander, Rick Sarre (AUS), Graham Sneddon, Kate Sharpe, Simon Smith (UK), Sam's Tailor, Jean Teixeira (F), Frank Theissen (D), F Trevascus (AUS), Bob Turner (UK), Julle Tuulianen (FIN), Hans Verhoef, Hein Van Den Wildenberg (NL), Jan Wilkman (F), Susan Wright (USA), Barbara Zimny, Tim Penney (NZ)

AUS – Australia, C – Canada, D – Germany, F – France, FIN – Finland, IND – India, IRL – Ireland, NL – Netherlands, NZ – New Zealand, S – Sweden, TAI – Taiwan, UK – United Kingdom, USA – United States of America

Warning & Request

No place in the world changes more rapidly than Hong Kong. Every time you turn around, the local street market becomes a shopping mall, a cheap youth hostel changes into a 60-storey skyscraper, and even the beach is transformed into 'reclaimed land'. In Hong Kong they build like there's no tomorrow – and perhaps there won't be after 1997. So if you find things better or worse, recently opened or long since closed, please write and tell us and help make the next edition better.

Your letters will be used to help update future editions and, where possible, important changes will also be included in a Stop Press section in reprints.

We greatly appreciate all information that is sent to us by travellers. Back at Lonely Planet we employ a hard-working readers' letters team to sort through the many letters we receive. The best ones will be rewarded with a free copy of the next edition or another Lonely Planet guide if you prefer. We give away lots of books, but, unfortunately, not every letter/postcard receives one.

Contents

INTRODUCTION...9

HONG KONG

FACTS ABOUT HONG KONG 12

History 12
Geography 18
Climate 19
Flora & Fauna................. 21
Government 22
Economy 23
Population 24
People 25
Education 25
Arts................................. 26
Culture............................ 27
Religion........................... 31
Language......................... 36

FACTS FOR THE VISITOR 42

Visas & Embassies 42
Documents................................ 43
Customs 44
Money...................................... 44
When to Go 46
What to Bring 47
Tourist Offices 47
Useful Organisations 48
Business Hours & Holidays 49
Cultural Events 50
Post & Telecommunications..... 54
Time.. 59
Electricity............................... 60
Laundry................................... 60
Weights & Measures............... 60
Cultural Centres...................... 60
Books & Maps 61
Media 63
Film & Photography 64
Health...................................... 65
Women Travellers 73
Dangers & Annoyances 73
Work.. 74
Activities................................. 76
Highlights................................ 85
Accommodation....................... 85
Food 89
Drinks...................................... 97
Tobacco................................... 99
Entertainment.......................... 99
Things to Buy........................ 102

GETTING THERE & AWAY 113

Air.. 113
Land..................................... 119
Sea....................................... 120
Leaving Hong Kong 120

GETTING AROUND...122

Bus....................................... 122
Train..................................... 125
Tram..................................... 127
Taxi...................................... 128
Car & Motorbike 129
Bicycle 129
Walking................................ 129
Escalator 130
Boat...................................... 130
Rickshaw 131
Helicopter............................. 132
Local Transport..................... 132
Tours..................................... 132

KOWLOON 134

Tsimshatsui 134
Tsimshatsui East 137
Hunghom.............................. 140
Yaumatei 140
Mongkok 142
New Kowloon 142
Places to Stay – bottom end ... 145
Places to Stay – middle........... 150
Places to Stay – top end 152
Places to Eat......................... 153
Entertainment....................... 157
Things to Buy....................... 159

HONG KONG ISLAND 163

Central 163
Sheung Wan 170
Hong Kong University 171
Victoria Peak 171
Hong Kong Trail 173
Wanchai 173
Causeway Bay 175
Happy Valley 177
Quarry Bay 177
Shek O 177
Stanley................................... 177
Repulse Bay 179
Ocean Park 179
Water World 180
Aberdeen 180
Places to Stay – bottom end.... 182
Places to Stay – middle.......... 183
Places to Stay – top end 183
Places to Eat.......................... 184
Entertainment........................ 190
Things to Buy........................ 195

THE NEW TERRITORIES 198

Tsuen Wan 199
Tai Mo Shan 202
Maclehose Trail 204
Ma Wan 205
Tuen Mun 205
Miu Fat Monastery 207

Yuen Long 207
Laufaushan 207
Mai Po Marsh 207
Kam Tin 207
Shek Kong Airfield 208
Sheung Shui 208
Fanling 208

Tai Po 208
Plover Cove Reservoir......210
Tai Po Kau 210
Chinese University 210
Shatin 211
Clearwater Bay 213
Sai Kung Peninsula 213

Tolo Harbour & Tap Mun
Chau 215
Ping Chau 215
Places to Stay 216
Places to Eat...................217

OUTLYING ISLANDS 218

Orientation & Information 219
Accommodation 219
Getting There & Away 219
Cheung Chau 220
Cheung Chau Village 220
Pak Tai Temple 220
Tin Hau Temples 222
Tung Wan 222
Other Beaches......................222
Cheung Po Tsai Cave 222
Bun Festival 223
Places to Stay.......................223
Places to Eat 223
Entertainment......................224
Getting There & Away 224
Getting Around....................226
Lamma 226

Yung Shue Wan 227
Hung Shing Ye 228
Sok Kwu Wan 229
Lo So Shing Beach 229
Mo Tat Wan 229
Shek Pai Wan & Sham Wan ... 229
Mt Stenhouse 229
Getting There & Away......... 229
Getting Around 231
Lantau 231
Accommodation 234
Mui Wo (Silvermine Bay) 235
Trappist Haven Monastery ... 235
Ngong Ping 237
Lantau Trail 238
Tai O 239
Fan Lau 239

Cheung Sha Beach & Tong
Fuk 239
Shek Pik Reservoir 239
Chi Ma Wan 240
Tung Chung 240
Discovery Bay...................240
Penny's Bay & Yam O Wan ...242
Getting There & Away 242
Getting Around 245
Peng Chau.......................245
Places to Eat....................245
Getting There & Away 245
Tung Lung Chau 249
Getting There & Away 250
Poi Toi 250
Getting There & Away 251

MACAU

FACTS ABOUT MACAU 254

History 254
Geography 258
Climate 259
Government......................259

Economy 259
Population 261
People 261
Education 261

Arts..................................261
Culture..............................262
Religion............................262
Language...........................262

FACTS FOR THE VISITOR 264

Visas & Embassies 264
Customs 264
Money...................................264
When to Go 266
What to Bring 266
Tourist Offices 266
Business Hours & Holidays 267
Cultural Events 267
Post & Telecommunications...268

Time 269
Electricity.............................269
Weights & Measures..............270
Books & Maps 270
Media 271
Film & Photography 271
Health..................................271
Emergency...........................271
Women Travellers.................271

Dangers & Annoyances 271
Work....................................272
Activities.............................272
Highlights............................272
Accommodation....................272
Food 273
Drinks.................................273
Entertainment......................274
Things to Buy......................278

GETTING THERE & AWAY 279

Air.......................................279

Land 279

Sea......................................279

GETTING AROUND..281

Bus......................................281
Taxi.....................................281
Car & Motorbike 281

Bicycle 282
Walking................................282
Pedicabs..............................282

Tour Machine 282
Tours...................................283

MACAU PENINSULA 285

Central Macau 285
The South.............................291
The North.............................296

Places to Stay 297
Places to Eat.........................300
Entertainment.......................302

Things to Buy.......................304

MACAU ISLANDS 305
Getting There & Away 305   Taipa Island 305
Getting Around 305   Coloane Island 310

GUANGZHOU (CANTON)

FACTS ABOUT GUANGZHOU (CANTON) 316
History 316   Economy 320   Religion....................................323
Geography 319   Population 322   Language..................................323
Climate 319   People 322
Government 319   Arts..323

FACTS FOR THE VISITOR 329
Visas & Embassies 329   Time 342   Work 354
Documents...............................330   Electricity................................342   Activities.................................356
Customs...................................331   Laundry...................................342   Highlights................................356
Money......................................331   Weights & Measures 342   Accommodation......................357
When to Go 333   Books & Maps 342   Food 358
What to Bring 333   Media 344   Drinks......................................362
Tourist Offices 334   Film & Photography 347   Tobacco...................................363
Useful Organisations 337   Health......................................348   Entertainment.........................363
Business Hours & Holidays 337   Women Travellers...................353   Things to Buy.........................364
Post & Telecommunications....338   Dangers & Annoyances 353

GETTING THERE & AWAY 366
Air..366   Sea...367   Leaving China.........................368
Land...367   Tours 367

GETTING AROUND.. 369
Air..369   Train 369   Motorcycle Taxis 369
Bus...369   Taxi..369

GUANGZHOU 371
Orientation...............................371   Nanhu Amusement Park 402   Foshan 405
Information 371   Lotus Mountain 403   Xiqiao Hills............................409
Around Guangzhou 402   Jinsha Park 404   Zhaoqing 409
White Cloud Hills 402   Conghua Hot Springs 404   Luofushan 417

SHENZHEN.. 418
Orientation...............................420   Overseas Chinese Town 425   Entertainment.........................428
Information 420   Places to Stay – bottom end ..425   Getting There & Away 428
Shenzhen City 421   Places to Stay – middle..........426   Getting Around 430
Splendid China 421   Places to Stay – top end.........427   Shekou 430
China Folk Culture Villages ...425   Places to Eat............................428   Around Shenzhen....................432

ZHUHAI... 433
Orientation...............................433   Places to Stay – top end 437   **Around Zhuhai................. 441**
Information 433   Places to Eat............................439   Sun Yatsen's Residence 441
Things to See 434   Things to Buy 439   Zhongshan City 441
Places to Stay – bottom end 435   Getting There & Away............440   Zhongshan Hot Springs 443
Places to Stay – middle 437   Getting Around 440   Lingding Island.......................445

GLOSSARY 446

INDEX 447
Maps 447   Text 447

Map Legend

BOUNDARIES

International Boundary
Internal Boundary

ROUTES

Freeway
Highway
Major Road
Unsealed Road or Track
City Road
City Street
Railway
Underground Railway
Tram
Walking Track
Walking Tour
Ferry Route
Cable Car or Chairlift

AREA FEATURES

Park, Gardens
National Park
Forest
Built-Up Area
Pedestrian Mall
Market
Cemetery
Reef
Rocks

HYDROGRAPHIC FEATURES

Coastline
River, Creek
Intermittent River or Creek
Lake, Intermittent Lake
Canal
Swamp

SYMBOLS

CAPITAL	National Capital			Hospital, Police Station
Capital	State Capital			Airport, Airfield
CITY	Major City			Cafe, Bicycle Hire
City	City			Swimming Pool, Gardens
Town	Town			Shopping Centre, Zoo
Village	Village			Winery or Vineyard, Picnic Site
	Place to Stay			Archaeological Site or Ruins
	Place to Eat			Stately Home, Monument
	Pub, Bar			Castle, Tomb
	Post Office, Telephone			Cave, Hut or Chalet
	Tourist Information, Bank			Mountain or Hill, Lookout
	Transport, Parking			Lighthouse, Shipwreck
	Museum, Youth Hostel			Pass, Spring
	Caravan Park, Camping Ground			Ancient or City Wall
	Church, Cathedral			Rapids, Waterfalls
	Mosque, Synagogue			Cliff or Escarpment, Tunnel
	Buddhist Temple, Hindu Temple			Railway Station

Note: not all symbols displayed above appear in this book

Introduction

Hong Kong is the last British-occupied corner of China, the final chapter of a colonial saga that began almost 150 years ago and will end when the colony is handed back to its former owner in 1997. The momentous conclusion is being watched with much interest and much trepidation – all hotel rooms in Hong Kong for 1 July 1997 have been booked solid since 1990!

Most people think of Hong Kong as an island. It is, but not just one. There are 235 islands plus a chunk of mainland bordering the Chinese province of Guangdong – a mere dot on the map compared to the rest of China. Much of it is uninhabited while other parts, especially Hong Kong Island itself, are among the most densely populated areas in the world.

Hong Kong
Macau & Guangzhou

Hong Kong Island is the heart of it all, and the oldest part in terms of British history (the British acquired it in 1841). The centre of Hong Kong Island is the business district of Central where the greater part of the colony's business life goes on. New office blocks, and the rents, shoot up almost daily to accommodate the ever-growing financial elite who want to be part of the Asian Wall St.

From Central it's a seven-minute ferry ride across one of the world's great harbours to the Kowloon Peninsula on the mainland. The tip of Kowloon is the shopping and tourist ghetto of Tsimshatsui, and beyond that are the high-rise commercial and industrial estates.

Beyond Kowloon lie the New Territories, which include not only the mainland area bordering China but also the other 234 islands which make up Hong Kong. Together the New Territories form the bulk of Hong Kong territory.

Why go to Hong Kong? Contrary to popular belief, it's more than just a place to buy a duty-free musical wristwatch. Hong Kong is one of the world's great trading ports and provides an eye-opener on how to make the most from every sq km, since space is Hong Kong's most precious commodity.

Hong Kong supports an almost intact traditional Chinese culture, in contrast to the rest of the mainland where the old culture was attacked and weakened by the Cultural Revolution of the 1960s. There are quiet, empty hills where you can walk for an afternoon and barely see another person, and there are remote villages where the locals still lead rural lives that have changed little over many generations.

Most travel agents and package tours allow a week at the most for visiting Hong Kong – enough time for a whistle-stop tour of a half-dozen attractions plus the obligatory shopping jaunt. But if you give yourself longer and make the effort to get out of Central and Tsimshatsui, you will find a lot more. Hong Kong is only the start.

An hour's hydrofoil ride away is the 500-year-old Portuguese colony of Macau. To the north of Hong Kong and adjoining the New Territories is the Special Economic Zone of Shenzhen where the People's Republic has been packing foreign money into development schemes designed to help modernise the entire country. Another Special Economic Zone, Zhuhai, is adjacent to Macau and has turned into a pricey resort playground for Hong Kong Chinese.

Northwards up the Pearl River is Guangzhou (formerly Canton), the chief city of Guangdong Province, the home of the Cantonese people and the most accessible part of China.

HONG KONG

Facts about Hong Kong

HISTORY

'Albert is so amused at my having got the island of Hong Kong', wrote Queen Victoria to King Leopold of Belgium in 1841. But while her husband could see the funny side of this apparently useless little island off the south coast of China, considerably less amused was the British Foreign Secretary, Lord Palmerston. He considered the acquisition of Hong Kong a massive bungle by Captain Charles Elliot, Britain's Superintendent of Trade in China, who had negotiated the deal. 'A barren island with hardly a house upon it!', he raged in a letter to the unfortunate Elliot.

Western Traders

The story of Hong Kong really begins upriver, in the city of Guangzhou, where the British had begun trading with China on a regular basis in the late 17th century.

The British were not the first Westerners on the scene, as regular Chinese contact with the modern European nations began in 1557 when the Portuguese were given permission to set up base in nearby Macau. Jesuit priests also arrived and in 1582 were allowed to establish themselves at Zhaoqing, a town north-west of Guangzhou. Their scientific and technical knowledge aroused the interest of the imperial court and a few priests were permitted to reside in Beijing.

The first trade overtures from the British were rebuffed by the Chinese but Guangzhou was finally opened to trade with Europeans in 1685. From then on, British ships began to arrive regularly from the East India Company bases on the Indian coast, and traders were allowed to establish warehouses (factories or trading stations) near Guangzhou as a base to export tea and silk.

From the end of the 17th century the British and French started trading regularly at Guangzhou, followed by the Dutch, Danes, Swedes and Americans.

Even so, the opening of Guangzhou was an indication of how little importance was placed on trade with the Western barbarians. Guangzhou was considered to exist on the edge of a wilderness, far from Nanjing (Nanking) and Beijing (Peking) which were the centres of power under the isolationist Ming (1368-1644) and Qing (1644-1911) dynasties. As far as the Chinese were concerned, only the Chinese empire was civilised and the people beyond its frontiers were barbarians. The Qing could not have foreseen the dramatic impact which the Europeans were about to have on the country.

In 1757 the fuse to the Opium Wars was lit when, by imperial edict, a Guangzhou merchants' guild called the Co Hong gained exclusive rights to China's foreign trade, paid for with royalties, fees, kickbacks and bribes.

Numerous restrictions were forced on the Western traders: they could reside in Guangzhou from about September to March only; they were restricted to Shamian Island on Guangzhou's Pearl River, where they had their factories; and they had to leave their wives and families downriver in Macau (though not all found this a hardship). Also, it was illegal for foreigners to learn Chinese or to deal with anyone except the Co Hong. The traders complained about the restrictions and the trading regulations which changed daily. Nevertheless trade flourished, mainly in China's favour because the tea and silk had to be paid for in cash (usually silver).

Trade in favour of China was not what the Western merchants had in mind and in 1773 the British unloaded a thousand chests at Guangzhou, each containing almost 70 kg of Bengal opium. The intention was to balance, and eventually more than balance, their purchases of Chinese goods. The Chinese taste for opium or 'foreign mud' as it was called, grew exponentially.

Emperor Dao Guang, alarmed at the drain

of silver from the country and the increasing number of opium addicts, issued an edict in 1796 banning the drug trade. But the foreigners had different ideas, and with the help of the Co Hong and corrupt Chinese officials the trade flourished.

Opium Wars & Treaties

Two decades later, in 1839, the emperor appointed Lin Zexu as Commissioner of Guangzhou with orders to stamp out the opium trade. Furthermore, Captain Charles Elliot was under instructions from Lord Palmerston to solve the trade problems with China.

It took Lin just a week to surround the British in Guangzhou, cut off their food supplies and demand they surrender all the opium in their possession. The British stuck it out for six weeks until they were ordered by their own Captain Elliot to surrender 20,000 chests of opium – an act which earned him their undying hatred. Lin then had the 'foreign mud' destroyed in public at the small city of Humen by the Pearl River.

Having surrendered the opium, Elliot tried unsuccessfully to negotiate with Lin's representative. The British then sent an expeditionary force to China under Rear Admiral George Elliot (a cousin of Captain Charles Elliot) to exact reprisals, secure favourable trade arrangements and obtain the use of some islands as a British base.

The force arrived in June 1840, blockaded Guangzhou and then sailed north, occupying or blockading a number of ports and cities on the coast and the Yangtze River, ultimately threatening Beijing itself. The emperor, alarmed, lost confidence in Lin and authorised Qi Shan to negotiate with the two Elliots whom he persuaded to withdraw from northern China. In January 1841, after further military actions and threats, Qi Shan agreed to the Convention of Chuan Bi. Amongst other concessions, this ceded Hong Kong Island to the British 'in perpetuity'.

The convention was repudiated by both sides. Qi Shan, it is said, was hauled back to Beijing in chains for selling out the emperor. Despite the British repudiation of the treaty,

Commodore Gordon Bremmer led a contingent of naval men ashore and claimed Hong Kong Island for Britain on 26 January 1841.

In late February, Captain Charles Elliot successfully attacked the Bogue forts at Humen (where the opium had earlier been destroyed), took control of the Pearl River and laid siege to Guangzhou, withdrawing in May after extracting $6 million and other concessions from the Guangzhou merchants.

In August 1841, a powerful British force sailed north and seized Xiamen, Ningbo, Shanghai and other ports. With Nanjing under immediate threat, the Chinese were forced to accept the Treaty of Nanking which, among other things, again ceded Hong Kong to the British 'in perpetuity', this time officially.

That wasn't the end of the fighting. In 1856 war broke out again over the interpretation of earlier treaties and over the boarding of a British-owned merchant ship, the *Arrow*, by Chinese soldiers searching for pirates. French troops joined the British in this war and the Russians and Americans lent naval support. The war was brought to an end by the Treaty of Tientsin (Tianjin) which permitted the British to establish diplomatic representation in China.

In 1859 a flotilla carrying the first 'British Envoy and Minister Plenipotentiary' to Beijing attempted to force its way up the Pei Ho River, contrary to Chinese requests and warnings. It was fired upon by the Chinese forts on the two shores and sustained heavy losses. With this excuse, a combined British and French force invaded China and marched on Beijing. Another treaty, the Convention of Peking (Beijing) was forced on the Chinese. Along with other concessions, this ceded to the British the Kowloon Peninsula plus nearby Stonecutters Island.

Hong Kong made its last land grab in a moment of panic 40 years later when China was on the verge of being parcelled out into 'spheres of influence' by the Western powers and Japan, all of which had sunk their claws into the country. The British army felt it needed more land to protect the colony, and in June 1898 the Second Convention of

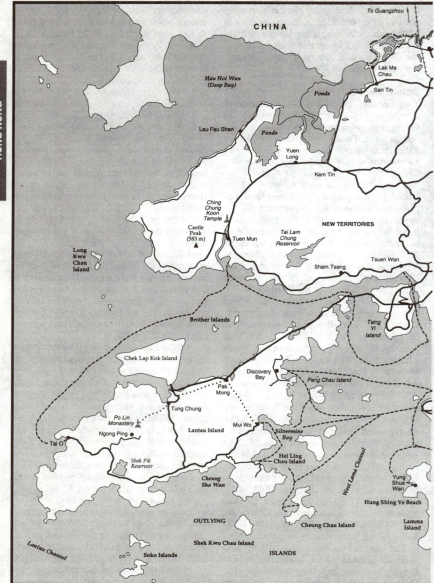

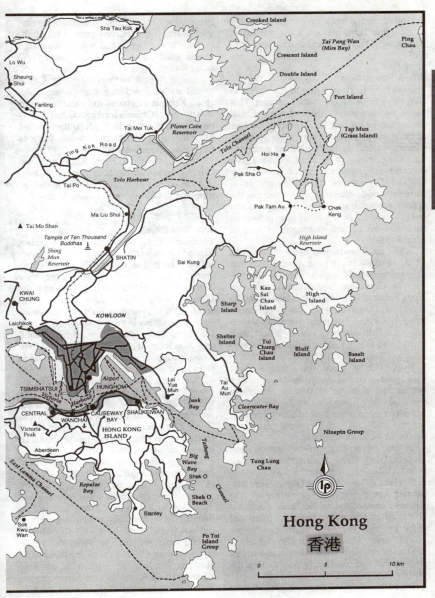

Hong Kong
香港

0   5   10 km

Peking presented Britain with what is known as the New Territories on a 99-year lease, beginning 1 July 1898 and ending on 1 July 1997.

War & Revolution

Prior to WW II, Hong Kong began a gradual shift away from trade to manufacturing. This move was hastened by the civil war in China during the 1920s and 1930s and by the Japanese invasion of the country in the 1930s as Chinese capitalists fled with their money to the safer confines of the British colony. The crunch finally came during the Korean War (1950-1953) when the American embargo on Chinese goods threatened to strangle the colony economically. In order to survive, the colony had to develop service industries such as banking and insurance, as well as manufacturing.

When the Communists came to power in China in 1949 many people were sure that Hong Kong would soon be overrun. Militarily, the Communists could have overrun Hong Kong in less time than it takes to make fried rice. However, while the Communists denounced the 'unequal treaties' which created a British territory on their soil, they recognised Hong Kong's economic importance to China.

Even without force, the Chinese could simply have ripped down the fence on the border and sent the masses to peacefully settle on Hong Kong territory. In 1962 China actually staged what looked like a trial run for this and sent 70,000 people across the border in a couple of weeks.

In 1967, at the height of the Cultural Revolution, Hong Kong again seemed doomed when riots inspired by the Red Guards rocked the colony. Several bombs were detonated. On 8 July 1967 a militia of 300 Chinese crossed the border with automatic rifles, killed five policemen and penetrated three km into the New Territories before pulling back. The governor, David Trench, kept an aircraft at Kai Tak Airport on standby in case he and his family had to flee the colony.

Property values in Hong Kong fell sharply and so did China's foreign exchange earnings as trade and tourism ground to a halt. Perhaps it was the loss of foreign exchange that sobered China, for by the end of 1967 order was restored.

Now it seems unthinkable that China would undermine Hong Kong's economy. Hong Kong is estimated to be the source of about 30% of China's foreign exchange. It is probably more than that, given the amount of technical know-how which flows across the border from Hong Kong.

At the same time, Hong Kong relies on China's goodwill. Without the cheap land and labour of China, Hong Kong manufacturers would have to move elsewhere.

The 1997 Blues

Economically, Hong Kong and China depend on each other. Yet the problem faced by both the British and the Chinese was the colony's fate when the lease on the New Territories expires in 1997. At that time the Chinese border would theoretically move south as far as Boundary Rd on the Kowloon Peninsula, taking in the whole colony except for Hong Kong Island, Stonecutters Island and Kowloon. It's hard to see how Hong Kong could remain viable when severed from most of the population.

Dynamic and well-versed in private enterprise, Hong Kong should ideally take over from China in 1997. But for the Chinese, the problem is not economics but saving face: Hong Kong remains the last reminder of foreign imperialism on mother soil (Macau is a somewhat different story).

In September 1984 the British agreed to hand the entire colony – lock, stock and skyscrapers – back to China in 1997. An alternative was to divide the colony leaving each side with a useless piece, and Britain hanging on to a colony which, arguably, it did not want. Some have said that Britain should have just shut up about the whole issue, forcing China to seek a Macau-style solution – allow the British to continue running Hong Kong with no formal agreement. However, the British were keen to

The ceremony following the signing of the Sino-British Joint Declaration in 1984 after the British had agreed to hand Hong Kong back to China in 1997

have something on paper, and now they've got it though few are proud of it.

The agreement, enshrined in a document known as the Sino-British Joint Declaration, will theoretically allow Hong Kong to retain its present social, economic and legal systems for at least 50 years after 1997. Hong Kong will cease to be a British colony and will become a Special Administrative Region (SAR) of China. The Chinese catch phrase for this is 'One country, two systems', whereby Hong Kong will be permitted to retain its capitalist system after 1997 while across the border the Chinese continue with a system which they label socialist.

As a follow-up to the Joint Declaration, in 1988 Beijing published *The Basic Law for Hong Kong*, a hefty document not unlike a constitution. The Basic Law permits the preservation of Hong Kong's legal system and guarantees the right of property and ownership, allows Hong Kong residents to retain the right to travel in and out of the colony, permits Hong Kong to remain a free port and to continue independent membership of international organisations and guarantees continuing employment after 1997 for the colony's civil servants (both Chinese and foreigners). The rights of assembly, free speech, association, travel and movement, correspondence, choice of occupation, academic research, religious belief and the right to strike are all included.

However, few Hong Kongers have much faith in the agreement. China's own constitution also makes lofty guarantees of individual freedoms and respect for human rights. Such guarantees have proved hollow. Beijing has made it abundantly clear that it will not allow Hong Kong to establish its own democratically elected government, not even on a municipal level. Although some low-level officials will be chosen by election, Hong Kong's new leaders are to be appointed. The Basic Law provides Beijing with options to interfere in Hong Kong's internal affairs to preserve public order, public morals or in the interests of national security. Beijing has also stated that Britain must remove its Gurkha battalion, which will be replaced by the People's Liberation Army (PLA).

This last issue has generated both fear and scepticism. China says it's a matter of 'national sovereignty', but sceptics say it's pure greed. The British military and Gurkha battalion currently sit on some extremely valuable chunks of real estate such as the HMS Tamar Naval Centre in Central. Attempts to transfer these bases to civilian use before 1997 have been adamantly rejected by Beijing – the PLA stands to gain real estate worth billions of US dollars overnight. Furthermore, the PLA presence will be useful to intimidate any potential political dissidents.

Hong Kong's fledgling pro-democracy movement has denounced the Joint Declaration as the new 'unequal treaty' and the Basic Law as a 'basic flaw'. Britain stands accused of selling out the best interests of Hong Kong people in order to keep good economic relations with China. It's also been pointed out that Hong Kong residents never had any opportunity to vote for or against these agreements – the negotiations were held entirely behind closed doors.

China's pro-democracy movement reached its zenith in the latter half of May

1989, when about one million people took part in protests in and around Beijing's Tiananmen Square. Hong Kong responded with its own demonstrations, with 500,000 people marching through the streets of Hong Kong supporting democracy. On 4 June, the PLA gave its response: tanks were sent into Tiananmen Square, protesters were gunned down and a wave of arrests followed.

In Hong Kong, more than one million people attended rallies to protest the massacre in Beijing. Confidence plummeted – the Hong Kong stock market fell 22% in one day, and a great deal of capital headed to safer havens overseas. In 1991, Beijing shattered confidence again by indicating it might rescind Hong Kong's recently-passed Bill of Rights.

The final five years of British rule have been characterised by increasing Chinese hostility towards Britain. The Basic Law is very unclear on the issue of democracy, but the British have belatedly recognised that it would be wise to clarify just how Hong Kong's future leaders will be chosen. Christopher Patten, who will probably be Hong Kong's last British governor, has been adamant that Hong Kong should have at least limited democracy. China has reacted by issuing threats – that public debts could be repudiated after 1997, that China might decide to 'take back' Hong Kong before 1997, etc. China is also using its 'trade weapon' to make the British shut up about democracy – the result is that British companies are finding it increasingly difficult to do business in China. This is ironic indeed, since Britain's earlier 'cooperation' with China was supposed to help improve trade relations. Now it appears that the only reward the British get for handing over Hong Kong is that China will thumb its nose at the UK.

Of course, not all Hong Kongers have to become citizens of the People's Republic in 1997. Those with money and good technological skills have little difficulty emigrating. Ironically, the outward migration of money and talent is creating a vacuum which is being filled by foreigners. Beijing has said it wants Hong Kong to be run by 'Hong Kong people'. Increasingly, it is being run by foreigners.

In its brief 160 years Hong Kong has been transformed. What was originally a 'barren island with hardly a house upon it' is now a highly developed city-state. And yet, a cloud of pessimism hangs over the city. Ultimately, Hong Kong's fate will be determined by the political dramas that unfold in Beijing.

And what of the opium trade that started it all? It folded by mutual consent in 1907, by which time the trading companies had diversified sufficiently to put their sordid pasts behind them without fear of financial ruin. Ironically, Hong Kong now has a serious dope problem, with about 38,000 addicts – a constant reminder of the colony's less than creditable beginnings.

GEOGRAPHY

Hong Kong's 1070 sq km is divided into four main areas – Kowloon, Hong Kong Island, the New Territories and the Outlying Islands.

Kowloon is a peninsula on the north side of the harbour. The southern tip of this peninsula (Tsimshatsui) is the biggest tourist area and where most of the hotels are. Kowloon proper only includes the land south of Boundary Rd, a mere 12 sq km. North of Boundary Rd is New Kowloon which is part of the New Territories.

Hong Kong Island covers 78 sq km or just 7% of Hong Kong's land area. The island is on the south side of the harbour and is the main business area, with numerous tourist hotels and sightseeing spots. Towering above the skyscrapers is the Peak, Hong Kong's premier scenic viewpoint.

The New Territories occupy 980 sq km, or 91% of Hong Kong's land area, and are sandwiched between Kowloon and the Chinese border. Foreign visitors rarely make the effort to visit the New Territories even though they have much to offer. About one-third of Hong Kong's population lives here.

The Outlying Islands simply means any island apart from Hong Kong Island. Officially, the Outlying Islands are part of the New Territories and make up about 20% of Hong

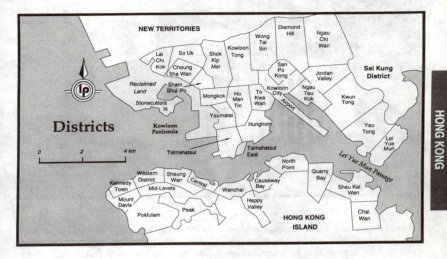

Districts

NEW TERRITORIES

Sai Kung District

Kowloon Peninsula

HONG KONG ISLAND

HONG KONG

Kong's total land area. There are actually 234 islands and while many are tiny rocks, the largest (Lantau Island) is nearly twice the size of Hong Kong Island. Previously, there were 235 islands until Stonecutters Island got absorbed by the Kowloon peninsula due to reclamation. Most tourists never make it to any of these islands, which is a shame since they offer a taste of tranquil village life and in some ways are the best part of Hong Kong.

Within these four main areas are numerous neighbourhoods. Hong Kong Island is divided into Central, Wanchai, Causeway Bay, Quarry Bay and so on, while Kowloon districts include Tsimshatsui, Yaumatei, Mongkok, Hunghom, etc.

CLIMATE
Hong Kong is perched on the south-east coast of China just a little to the south of the Tropic of Cancer. This puts the colony on much the same latitude as Hawaii or Calcutta, but the climate is not tropical. This is because the huge land mass of Asia generates powerful blasts of arctic wind that blow from the north during winter. In summer, the seasonal wind (monsoon) reverses and blows from the south bringing hot, humid tropical air.

Winter is chilly. It never snows or freezes, but it's cold enough to require a warm sweater or coat. Many travellers arrive at the airport in shorts and T-shirt, totally unprepared. Winter weather also tends to be windy and frequently cloudy. Not much rain falls, but when it does, it's usually a chilly, depressing drizzle that lasts for days on end. Because of a low cloud ceiling, the mountains are often shrouded in mist, which means it isn't too good for visiting the Peak and other scenic outlooks. Winter weather usually continues into March and often ends abruptly when the arctic wind stops blowing. Even during winter, there are windless days when the weather gets amazingly balmy.

Autumn, from October until early December, is the best time to visit. The weather is generally sunny and dry. Typhoons sometimes occur in October, but not often, and November usually has ideal weather.

Spring is a short season in Hong Kong, but it's also a good time to visit. It's generally warm by the end of March and stays pleasant until the end of May. In March or April, an occasional wind will swoop out of the north

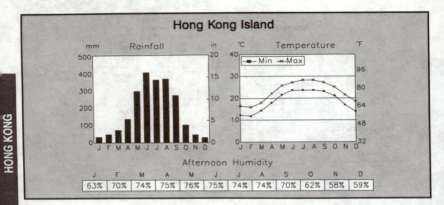

and send temperatures plummeting for a few days. Big thundershowers become more frequent as June approaches. June tends to be the wettest month, with the beginning of the summer monsoon. The Chinese call this the plum rain.

Summer is hot and humid. The weather is sunny, but big thundershowers can occur suddenly.

Typhoons

Typhoon is the Chinese word for big wind. Hong Kong's deadliest typhoon struck on 2 September 1937 when more than 1000 boats sank and about 2500 people drowned. Since then, many other severe typhoons have lashed Hong Kong, but in this age of weather satellites typhoons no longer arrive without warning.

Typhoons can hit as early as May, but the peak season is from mid-July to mid-October. Typhoons vary in size from tropical storms to severe super-typhoons. If the typhoon just brushes past Hong Kong, it will bring a little rain and wind that might only last for half a day. If it scores a direct hit, the winds can be deadly and it may rain for days on end.

Typhoons are really not much fun even if you are safely entrenched in a hotel room. You can't go outside during a bad typhoon and most businesses shut down. Sitting around a hotel with nothing to do might not

be the worst fate, but if the electric power is cut it can be rather unpleasant. In the worst-case scenario, the water pumps will fail too because of no electricity to run them. Given these possibilities, it would be prudent to stock up on food, water, candles, matches and a torch if a big typhoon is heading your way. A battery-operated radio or tape player helps to pass the time. Keep extra batteries on hand.

When a typhoon becomes a possibility, warnings are broadcast continuously on TV and radio. Signal one goes out when there is a tropical storm centred within 800 km of Hong Kong. This is followed by signals three and eight, by which time offices are closed and everyone goes home while there is still public transport. There used to be other in-between signals with consecutive numbers, but this got too confusing so a simplified system was introduced, hence the odd jumps in the numbering.

Signals nine and 10 are rare. Nine means that the storm is expected to increase significantly in strength. Ten means that hurricane-force winds are expected. This signal indicates that the centre of the storm will come close to Hong Kong.

Warning bulletins are broadcast at two minutes to every hour and half-past every hour whenever any of the signals eight, nine or 10 are displayed. If you are without a radio, or miss a bulletin, there is a number you can call (☎ 208351473).

Signals are hoisted at various vantage points throughout Hong Kong, particularly on both sides of the harbour. There's also a system of white, green and red lights. See the telephone directory for details.

FLORA & FAUNA

Back in 1841, British Foreign Secretary Lord Palmerston disparaged Hong Kong as a 'barren island with hardly a house upon it'. While the lack of houses was nothing unusual, the barrenness certainly was. With abundant rainfall and a warm climate, the British might well have expected to find a dense jungle on the shores of south China. Instead, they found Hong Kong to be devoid of trees, a situation that persists today.

The simple reason for this is that Hong Kong's earlier inhabitants cut down all the trees. Massive tree cutting by settlers started as long ago as the Song Dynasty (960-1279) and continued until the hills were stripped bare. Green politics were not fashionable in those days, and no effort was made to replant the trees. With the forests removed, heavy summer thundershowers quickly eroded Hong Kong's steep slopes, and the lack of topsoil has prevented the forests from regenerating.

These days, most uninhabited regions of Hong Kong are grasslands. Somewhat ironically, the only areas of Hong Kong that have seen any reafforestation efforts are those inhabited by humans. The British were never happy about the lack of shade trees during the scorching summers, and thus planted quick-growing species around their colonial residences. As for the Chinese, some have planted groves in an attempt to please the spirits of the deceased. Trees with commercial value like bamboo have been planted in small groves in agricultural regions. However, Hong Kong today has precious little to offer in the way of forests.

The loss of so much vegetation has also meant the loss of habitat for animals, and very few large creatures survive. Weighing in at over 100 kg are wild boars, found in some rural spots and regarded as pests because they dig up crops. Much more aesthetic are barking deers (also called muntjaks), found even on the high slopes of Hong Kong Island. Early British settlers encountered leopards and tigers, but the last tiger seen in the New Territories was shot in 1915. However, the Chinese leopard cat (weighing only two to five kg) is still found breeding in remote parts of the territory. Small mammals thought to survive include ferret badgers, otters, masked palm civets, porcupines, shrews and bats. Wild monkeys survive but are thought to be the descendants of escaped pets. The rat population of Hong Kong has apparently benefitted from the arrival of humans.

An interesting creature is the Chinese pangolin, a scaly mammal that resembles an armadillo. When attacked, it rolls itself up into an unappetising ball. Unfortunately, its existence is threatened because the Chinese regard its flesh as a tonic medicine and aphrodisiac.

Environment

Hong Kong is an urbanised, consumer-oriented, throw-away society. For years people have been throwing their rubbish into Victoria Harbour and now the harbour is starting to throw it back. Water pollution has become one of Hong Kong's most serious ecological problems. After watching fishing boats plucking fish out of the chemical-laden harbour, many foreigners have given up eating fresh seafood in Hong Kong (the locals seem indifferent).

In the past, little or no attention was paid to environmental protection, but the concept is beginning to take root, albeit slowly. The Hong Kong government has established an Environmental Protection Department (EPD) with a staff of nearly 1000 persons. The bulk of the funding goes for programmes to improve waste disposal and curb water pollution.

In spite of some mild waste-disposal regulations and environmental-awareness publicity campaigns, Hong Kong's increasing population and growing standard of living will probably lead to more ecological degradation. Many feel that after 1997, even the now-existing weak regulations will not be enforced.

Green Power is a relatively new environmental group which has established itself in Hong Kong. It appears that members of this organisation will have their work cut out for them.

Country Parks & Reserves

It surprises many visitors to learn that 40% of Hong Kong's total land area is protected by 21 country parks. Watershed protection was the major reason for putting these areas off-limits to development and private motor vehicles – all of Hong Kong's 17 freshwater reservoirs lie within park boundaries. Nevertheless, hikers, campers, bird-watchers and other nature-lovers all benefit. Most of the country parks are in the New Territories and the Outlying Islands, but even the higher mountainous slopes of Hong Kong Island are protected.

GOVERNMENT

Hong Kong is not a democracy, and the ruling elite in Beijing is determined to make sure it doesn't become one. Hong Kong is a British colony, and after 1997 it will be a Chinese colony.

Heading Hong Kong's administration is a governor who presides over meetings of both the Executive Council (EXCO) and the Legislative Council (LEGCO). EXCO is technically the top policy-making body of the government. It's composed of top-ranking officials such as the Attorney General and the Commander of the British Armed Forces in the colony, together with other members who are appointed either by the governor or on the instructions of the British government. One rung down the ladder is LEGCO, which frames legislation, enacts laws and controls government expenditure.

The Urban Council is in charge of the day-to-day running of services in Hong Kong Island and Kowloon, including street cleaning, garbage collection, food hygiene,

Hong Kong Coat of Arms

hawkers' licences and the like. In the New Territories, the Regional Council has much the same function as the Urban Council.

On the next rung down are the District Boards, set up in 1982 to give Hong Kong residents a degree of control over their local area. The boards consist of government officials and elected representatives from the local area. The problem is that these boards have little (if any) real power. The seats are sought after by only a small number of candidates who are voted in by the small proportion of the electorate who bothered to vote.

Staff in all government departments and other areas of administration are under the umbrella of the Hong Kong Civil Service which employs 173,000 people, of whom about 3500 are expatriates filling nearly all the top policy-making positions. The officer corps in the 27,000-strong police force also has a high proportion of expatriates.

However, it has been decided to stop recruiting British professionals for top administrative posts and to gradually replace them with Chinese in preparation for handing over the colony to China in 1997. The Joint Declaration decrees that expatriates cannot be heads of major government departments or deputy heads of some departments, although below these levels expatriates may still be employed after China takes over.

The colonial government is generally efficient and mostly free of corruption, but it wasn't always so. Hong Kong's police and civil service were a disgrace until 1974 when the British established the Independent Commission Against Corruption (ICAC). The ICAC was given draconian powers, and within three years of its founding nearly crushed corruption in Hong Kong. To prosecute a case, the ICAC only needs to show that a civil servant has wealth disproportional to his or her income – it's not necessary to prove that the unexplained wealth was obtained illegally. Not only can it imprison the defendant, it can also force the defendant to turn over the ill-gotten gains to the Hong Kong government.

Unfortunately, China has no independent judiciary and corrupt senior officials openly thumb their nose at the law. After 1997, many believe that the ICAC will be intimidated by Communist Party officials and corruption will once again flourish in Hong Kong. The ICAC has already seen a sharp increase in the number of cases it prosecutes, as quality civil servants emigrate abroad while their new replacements easily succumb to graft.

The Chinese Communist Party has a long history in Hong Kong, going back at least to 1949 when the Communists came to power in China. Officially the CCP is called the Hong Kong Macau Work Committee (HMWC) and has always been headed by the director of the PRC's Xinhua news agency's Hong Kong branch, which is Beijing's official mouthpiece in the colony.

Another connection between Hong Kong and China is the 50 or so Hong Kong delegates to the National People's Congress or NPC (China's rubber-stamp parliament) and to that other peculiar body, the Chinese People's Political Consultative Conference (CPPCC). The job of the CPPCC delegates seems to be to confer and consult among each other and provide an image of a united front between China, Macau, Hong Kong and Taiwan. The NPC has 16 Hong Kong delegates, all top people from banking, business, commerce, education, trade unions, media and other professional walks – and all reliably pro-Beijing.

ECONOMY

Regarded by many as a paragon of the virtues of capitalism, Hong Kong is a hard-working, competitive, money-oriented society. Its laissez-faire economic policies are a capitalist's dream: free enterprise and free trade, low taxes, a hard-working labour force, modern and efficient seaport and airport, excellent worldwide communications, and a government famous for low taxes and a hands-off approach to private business. When it comes to regulating business, the slogan of the Hong Kong government has always been 'positive non-intervention'.

Generally, Hong Kong has been moving towards capital-intensive rather than labour-intensive industries. Most of the manual labour is now being performed across the border in China. Within Hong Kong itself, service industries like telecommunications, banking, insurance, tourism and retail sales have pushed manufacturing to the background. About 75% of the workforce is now employed in service industries, a higher percentage than found in Western countries. The shift from manufacturing to services has been accompanied by a dramatic increase in wages. Hong Kong actually enjoys the best of both worlds – a high standard of living, a well-educated workforce, sophisticated service industries, and a nearby pool of sweatshop labour to do the dirty work.

The basic philosophy of Hong Kong's manufacturers has been 'export or die'. While the domestic market certainly does not get ignored, around 90% of manufactured goods head to other lands. The largest proportion of Hong Kong's exports go to the USA (45%). Other large export markets are in China, the UK, Germany, Japan, Canada, Australia and Singapore. With an official unemployment rate under 2%, Hong Kong suffers from a labour shortage. Much of the lower level work (domestic labour, construction, etc) is performed by imported labour, chiefly from the Philippines, but many think after 1997, Chinese labour will be brought in and unskilled foreigners kicked out.

In stark contrast to many other Asian states which have populations engaged mainly in agricultural production, Hong Kong has a very small agricultural base with a rapidly shrinking 9% of the total land area suitable for crop farming. Less than 2% of the total population is engaged in agriculture or fishing. Even these small numbers continue to decline.

Most food is imported, although Hong Kong's farming and fishing industries are efficient. Hong Kong has a sizeable ocean fishing industry which employs about 29,000 people working 5000 fishing vessels. However, most of Hong Kong's food supply is imported from just across the border – even McDonald's gets its potatoes and veggies from China.

In fact, because of its limited natural resources, Hong Kong depends on imports for virtually all its requirements, including water – more than 50% is pumped from China. To pay for all these imports Hong Kong has to generate enough foreign exchange through exports, tourism and overseas investments. So far, the city has had no problem paying its bills, and one of the government's 'problems' has been what to do with the revenue surpluses!

Only about 350,000 people of the 2.5 million workforce are unionised, which appears to suit Hong Kong capitalists as much as it does the Chinese government. It's argued that the People's Republic believes that a strong independent union movement could become the focus of mass political discontent, which cannot be allowed because it will upset Hong Kong's 'stability and prosperity', a favourite slogan of the Chinese government.

The living standards and wages of most people in Hong Kong are much higher than those in China and most other Asian countries – only Japan ranks higher in the statistics. Hong Kong is one of Asia's 'four little tigers' (also called 'four little dragons'), which also includes the economic power-houses of South Korea, Singapore and Taiwan. While China's per capita income is around US$400, in Hong Kong it's about US$15,000 a year and growing fast.

Maximum personal income tax is no more than 15%, company profits tax does not exceed 16.5% and there are no capital gains or transfer taxes. But the money is not close to being evenly spread and the government supports only meagre spending on social welfare. Nevertheless, even people at the bottom of Hong Kong's economic ladder are better off than the bulk of China's citizens.

Hong Kong's importance to China is manifold. For the first three decades after the Communist takeover in China in 1949, China was largely content to sell Hong Kong foodstuffs, raw materials and fuel. Hong Kong bought the produce and in return provided China with a large proportion of its foreign-exchange earnings, as it continues to do. Chinese investments in Hong Kong now amount to possibly a third of all direct foreign investment in the colony. Hong Kong has even served as a useful funnel for Taiwanese investors, who are prohibited by their government from directly trading and doing business with the communist mainland.

Finally, one should not forget tourism, Hong Kong's second largest earner of foreign exchange after textiles. And it's no longer just Westerners who make tourism such a lucrative business – Hong Kong is a favourite destination of visitors from China.

POPULATION

It was recently announced that Hong Kong's population is now officially six million, making it one of the most densely populated places in the world. The overall density of the population works out to about 5000 people per sq km, but this figure is deceiving since there is a wide variation in density from area to area. Some urban areas have tens of thousands of people per sq km, stacked in multiblock high-rise housing estates, while many areas are rural. Many of the Outlying Islands are uninhabited.

In 1851 the colony's population was a mere 33,000. The colony's dense population is largely a product of the events in China in the first half of this century.

With the collapse of the Qing Dynasty in 1911 and the wars during the 1920s and 1930s between the Kuomintang, the war-lords, the Communists and the Japanese, the Chinese were forced to flee to the safer confines of Hong Kong. By 1931 there were 880,000 people living there. When full-scale war between China and Japan erupted in 1937 (the Japanese having occupied Manchuria several years before) and after Guangzhou fell in 1938, another 700,000 people fled to Hong Kong.

The Japanese attacked the colony on 8 December 1941, the same day as the attack on Pearl Harbour, and occupied it for the next 3½ years. Mass deportations of Chinese civilians, aimed at relieving the colony's food shortage, reduced the population to 600,000 by 1945 but the displaced people began returning after the war. When Chiang Kaishek's Kuomintang forces were defeated by the Communists in 1949, another 750,000 followed, bringing the total population to about 2.5 million.

During the 1950s, 1960s and 1970s there was a varying flow of immigrants (they're no longer called refugees) across the border from China. In two years alone at the end of the 1970s, the population rose by a quarter of a million as a result of Chinese immigration, some of it legal but most of it not.

PEOPLE

About 98% of Hong Kong's population is ethnic Chinese, most of whom have their origins in China's Guangdong Province. About 60% were born in the colony. About 35% of the population lives in Kowloon, 21% on Hong Kong Island, 42% in the New Territories and 2% in the Outlying Islands.

If any groups can truly claim to belong to Hong Kong, they are the Tankas, the nomadic boat people who have fished the local waters for centuries, and the Hakka, who farmed the New Territories long before

Charles Elliot thought about running the Union Jack up a flagpole. The Hakka are a distinct group which emigrated from north to south China centuries ago to flee persecution. Hakka means 'guest'. Hakka women can be recognised in the New Territories by their distinctive spliced-bamboo hats with wide brims and black-cloth fringes.

Over 300,000 foreign expats permanently reside (legally) in Hong Kong, plus an unknown number of illegals who usually don't stay for long. In descending order, the break-down of expats living in Hong Kong (both legally and illegally) is as follows: Filipinos 106,000; US citizens 27,000; UK 22,000; Thai 20,000; Canadians 20,000; Indians 19,000; Australians 17,000; Japanese 15,000; Malaysians 13,000; others 65,000.

A very touchy issue is what will happen in 1997 to 'foreigners' who were born in Hong Kong and hold Hong Kong passports. Some are half or quarter Chinese, but Beijing has indicated that citizenship can only be endowed on those Hong Kongers of pure 'Chinese descent'. In other words, racial purity is the deciding factor, not place of birth, and this threatens to render many people stateless in 1997. Some countries, such as India, have indicated they will accept back their 'citizens' even though these people were born in Hong Kong and never set foot in the country of their ancestors. However, many Hong Kong-born Indians have said they consider this solution unacceptable, and believe the Chinese government will expel them after 1997 when they suddenly become 'foreigners'. Nor has the issue been settled of just what will happen to people of 'mixed blood' – so far, the Chinese government has given the impression that racial purity is a prerequisite for citizenship. Many also wonder if the British and other expatriates will suddenly become unwelcome and face mass expulsion – the Chinese government has been very tight-lipped on the whole issue.

EDUCATION

Hong Kong's education system closely follows the British model. Primary education is free and compulsory. At secondary level students begin to specialise, some going into a college preparatory programme while others select vocational education combined with apprenticeships.

At tertiary level education is fiercely competitive. Practically all Chinese parents push their children hard to go to university. The result is that there are insufficient university places to meet demand. Only about 5% of students who sit university entrance exams actually gain admission. This is less of a problem for wealthy families who simply send their children abroad to study.

Hong Kong has three universities. Hong Kong University, established in 1911, is the oldest and has about 8500 students. The campus is on the west side of Hong Kong Island in the Mid-Levels area. The language of instruction is English.

The Chinese University of Hong Kong is at Ma Liu Shui in the New Territories. It was officially established in 1963 on a beautiful campus. Enrolment is 7700 students.

The newest is Hong Kong University of Science & Technology, which admitted its first students in 1991. The campus is in Tai Po Tsai in the south-east of the New Territories.

Hong Kong Polytechnic was established in 1972 in the Hunghom area and has 7800 students. City Polytechnic of Hong Kong has 4800 students and is soon to move to a permanent campus in Kowloon Tong. Hong Kong Baptist College, a private school in Kowloon Tong with 2600 students, receives some government support.

ARTS
Dance
Lion Dances Chinese festivals are never sombre occasions – when the religious rites are over at any festival there is generally a lion dance, some opera or a show by a visiting puppeteer.

Celebrations in Chinatowns throughout the world have made the lion dance synonymous with Chinese culture. There is no reason why it should be. The lion is not indigenous to China and the Chinese lion is a strictly mythical animal.

Lion dance

Music
Hong Kong's home-grown variety of music consists of soft-rock love melodies. The songs are sung in Cantonese and are collectively known as 'Canto-Pop'. Pop songs sung in Mandarin are also imported from Taiwan and sometimes even mainland China. Most Chinese find Western-style hard rock, heavy metal and punk too harsh and grating.

Theatre Arts
Chinese Opera Few festivals are complete without an opera performance. There are probably more than 500 opera performers in Hong Kong and opera troupes from China make regular appearances.

Chinese opera is a world away from the Western variety. It is a mixture of singing, speaking, mime, acrobatics and dancing that can go on for five or six hours.

There are three types of Chinese opera performed in Hong Kong. Top of the line among Chinese culture buffs is reckoned to be the Beijing variety, a highly refined style which uses almost no scenery but a variety of traditional props. More 'music hall' is the Cantonese variety, usually with a 'boy meets girl' theme,

Chinese opera

and often incorporating modern and foreign references. The most traditional is Chaozhou, now the least performed of the three. It is staged almost as it was in the Ming Dynasty, with stories from Chaozhou legends and folklore, and always containing a moral.

There are at least two venues to look for opera performances. One is the theatre in City Hall near the Star Ferry in Central. The other is Laichikok Amusement Park in Kowloon. Check with the Hong Kong Tourist Association (HKTA) for the schedules.

Puppets Puppets are the oldest of the Chinese theatre arts. You can see rod, glove, string and shadow puppets. The rod puppets, visible only from waist up, are fixed to a long pole with short sticks for hand movements.

The puppets are made from camphorwood and the important characters have larger heads than the minor roles. Chinese puppets are made from leather and cast shadows on to a silk screen. The skills of the puppeteer are passed on from the parents, and the performances relate tales of past dynasties. The most likely place to see performances are on TV – live shows are somewhat rare these days.

CULTURE
Traditional Lifestyle
Face Having 'big face' is synonymous with prestige, and prestige is important in the Orient. All families, even poor ones, are expected to have big wedding parties and throw around money like water, in order to gain face.

Much of the Chinese obsession with materialism is really to do with gaining face. Owning nice clothes, a big car (even if you can't drive), a piano (even if you can't play it), imported cigarettes and liquor (even if you don't smoke or drink), will all cause one to gain face. Therefore, when taking a gift to a Chinese friend, try to give something with snob appeal such as a bottle of imported liquor, perfume, cigarettes or chocolate. This will please your host and help win you points in the face game.

The whole concept of face seems very childish to Westerners and most never learn to understand it, but it is important in the Orient.

Chinese Zodiac Astrology has a long history in China and is integrated with religious beliefs. As in the Western system of astrology, there are 12 zodiac signs. However, unlike the Western system, your sign is based on the year rather than the month in which you were born. Still, this is a simplification. The exact day and time of birth is also carefully considered in charting an astrological path.

If you want to know your sign in the Chinese zodiac, look up your year of birth in the chart. However, it's a little more complicated than this because Chinese astrology goes by the lunar calendar. The Chinese Lunar New Year usually falls in late January or early February, so the first month will be included in the year before.

It is said that the animal year chart originated when Buddha commanded all the beasts of the earth to assemble before him. Only 12 animals came and they were rewarded by having their names given to a specific year. Buddha also decided to name each year in the order in which the animals arrived – the first was the rat, then the ox, tiger, rabbit and so on.

Many festivals are held throughout the year in accordance with the lunar calendar. Some festivals only occur every 12 years at the end of every cycle of the 12 lunar animals. Some festivals occur only once in 60 years. This is because each of the 12 animals is associated with five elements: metal, wood, earth, water and fire. The full cycle takes 60 years (5 x 12) and at the end of this time there is a 'super festival'.

Being born or married in a particular year is believed to determine one's fortune. In this era of modern birth-control techniques and abortion, Chinese parents will often carefully manipulate the birth times of their children. The year of the dragon sees the biggest jump in the birth rate, closely followed by the year of the tiger. A girl born in the year of the pig could have trouble getting married!

Fortune Tellers Having your fortune told can be fun. It can also be dangerous. The danger is the psychological problems that can occur when someone's fortune is bleak.

Chinese Zodiac							
Rat	1924	1936	1948	1960	1972	1984	1996
Ox/Cow	1925	1937	1949	1961	1973	1985	1997
Tiger	1926	1938	1950	1962	1974	1986	1998
Rabbit	1927	1939	1951	1963	1975	1987	1999
Dragon	1928	1940	1952	1964	1976	1988	2000
Snake	1929	1941	1953	1965	1977	1989	2001
Horse	1930	1942	1954	1966	1978	1990	2002
Goat	1931	1943	1955	1967	1979	1991	2003
Monkey	1932	1944	1956	1968	1980	1992	2004
Rooster	1933	1945	1957	1969	1981	1993	2005
Dog	1934	1946	1958	1970	1982	1994	2006
Pig	1935	1947	1959	1971	1983	1995	2007

One good friend was told that she would die by the age of 23. Three fortune tellers made the same prediction. She became very depressed and nearly gave up trying to live. It almost became a self-fulfilling prophecy, but the last time I saw her she was 26 and still very much alive. She swears that she will never see another fortune teller again.

How did three fortune tellers manage to make the same alarming prediction? Quite simply, they used the same methods. For example, one line on your palm is your life line – a short one indicates a short life. Other lines indicate the number of spouses, children, your health, wealth and happiness. Also, astrologers use the same reference works when charting an astrological path. Some people do their own fortune telling at home using the Chinese *Almanac*, a sort of annual horoscope.

The lucrative business of fortune telling is how many of Hong Kong's temples pay their bills. The major venue for finding fortune tellers is the Wong Tai Sin Temple in Kowloon, but other possibilities include the Tin Hau Temple in Yaumatei and several smaller temples in Wanchai. Palmists (who also read your face) set up at the Temple St night market in Yaumatei. But if you decide, as many tourists do, to take the plunge and find out what fate has in store for you, keep the preceding warning in mind.

Your Age Are you sure that you know just how old you are? You might be less than certain after seeing how the Chinese calculate age. Since the Chinese believe that life begins at the moment of conception, a baby is already one year old when it leaves the mother's womb. The seventh day of the lunar New Year is 'everyone's birthday', so somebody born on New Year's eve is already two years old just eight days after birth. Some more modern Chinese follow the solar calendar, so they have yet another birthday. Then, of course, there is the conventional birthday that most Westerners celebrate.

Fungshui (Geomancy) The Chinese word *fungshui* literally means wind-water. Westerners call it geomancy, the art (or science if you prefer) of manipulating or judging the environment to produce good fortune. If you want to build a house or find a suitable site for a grave then you call in a geomancer. The Chinese warn that violating the principles of good fungshui can have serious consequences. Therefore, geomancers are routinely consulted before an apartment block can be built, a highway is laid, telephone poles erected or trees chopped down.

Trees may have a spirit living inside, and for this reason some villages and temples in the New Territories still have fungshui groves to provide a place for the good spirits to live. Attempts to cut down fungshui groves to construct new buildings has sometimes led to massive protests and even violent confrontations – the solution may be a large cash payment to the village to 'placate the spirits'. Even then, it's a delicate situation and the help of a professional geomancer will undoubtedly be required to avoid trouble.

Businesses that are failing may call in a geomancer. Sometimes the solution is to move the door or a window. If this doesn't do the trick, it might be necessary to move an ancestor's grave. The location of an ancestor's grave is an especially serious matter. If the grave is in the wrong spot, or facing the wrong way, then there is no telling what trouble the spirits might cause. If a geomancer is not consulted, and the family of the deceased suddenly runs into an episode of bad luck, then it's time to see a Taoist priest who knows how to deal with the ghosts who are causing all the trouble.

Hong Kong produces some architectural wonders – the Lippo Centre on Hong Kong Island, for example, is all lumps and bumps and mirrored glass. But no matter how attractive or innovative, any office tower built without consulting a fungshui expert could be a financial disaster – no one but gwailos will rent offices there. One prominent building in Hong Kong had to be completely renovated and worked over by Taoist priests after it was 'discovered' that the faces of wolves could be seen in the marble decor. Evidently, the spirits of wolves had been trapped in the marble and the tenants quickly moved out of this haunted place. Fortunately, the priests were able to save the building and prevent the landlord from going bankrupt, but it was a close call indeed.

Construction of Hong Kong's underground Mass Transit Railway began with an invocation by a group of Taoist priests who paid respects to the spirits of the earth whose domain was about to be violated.

Taboos

Colour Codes Every colour symbolises something to the Chinese, and red is normally a happy colour. However, a grand exception is made for red ink. Just why is it subject to speculation – perhaps red ink looks like blood? Regardless of the long-forgotten reason, do not write a note in red. If you want to give someone your address or telephone, write in any colour but red. Messages written in red convey anger, hostility or unfriendliness.

White is the colour of death, and it's not appropriate to give white flowers except at funerals. A man should never wear a green hat since this indicates that his wife is having an affair!

Killer Chopsticks Leaving chopsticks sticking vertically into the bowl is a bad omen. This resembles incense sticks in a bowl of ashes, a sure death sign.

Avoiding Offence

Clothing Hong Kong is a very fashion-conscious city. The Chinese generally judge a person by their clothing far more than a Westerner would. Still, Hong Kong is cosmopolitan – they've seen it all, so you can get away with wearing almost anything. Revealing clothing is OK – shorts, miniskirts and bikinis (at the beach only) are common. However, nude bathing at beaches is a definite no-no.

Although Hong Kongers are usually tolerant when it comes to dress, there is one exception – thongs (flip-flop sandals). Thongs are OK to wear in hotel rooms or maybe the corridor of your hotel, but not in its lobby and most definitely not outdoors (except around a swimming pool or beach). Many restaurants and hotels will not let you in the door wearing thongs. Many Westerners ignore this unwritten rule, and although the police won't arrest you for wearing thongs in public, you will be looked upon with contempt.

Ironically, sandals are perfectly acceptable. The difference between sandals and thongs is the strap across the back of the ankle. As long as the strap is there, it's OK. No strap, and you're dressed indecently.

Handling Paper Always hand a piece of paper to somebody using both hands. This shows respect. This is especially true if that person is somebody important, like a public official, your landlord or a business associate. If you only use one hand, you will be considered rude.

Sport

Taijiquan Formerly spelled 'taichichuan', this form of slow motion shadow boxing has been popular in China for centuries. It is basically a form of exercise, but it's also an art form.

Taijiquan is very popular among old people and also with young women who believe it will help keep their bodies beautiful. The movements are supposed to develop the breathing muscles, promote digestion and improve muscle tone. A modern innovation is to perform taijiquan movements to the thump of disco music supplied by a portable cassette tape player.

If you want to participate in taijiquan with a group, or if you just want to watch, you must get up early. The Chinese traditionally do this exercise at the crack of dawn. Parks are the place to go. The most popular park for taijiquan is Victoria Park in Causeway Bay, Hong Kong Island. Other popular venues include the Zoological and Botanical Gardens in Central, and Kowloon Park in Tsimshatsui.

To participate in this sport, contact the Hong Kong Taichi Association (☎ 203954884), 11th floor, 60 Argyle St, Mongkok, Kowloon.

Martial Arts Many forms of martial arts *(wushu)* were developed in East Asia, but most are based on Chinese *gongfu* (formerly spelled kungfu). Gongfu differs from taijiquan in that the former is performed at much higher speed and with the intention of doing bodily harm. Gongfu also employs weapons. Taijiquan is not a form of self-defence but the movements are similar to gongfu.

To study or participate in martial arts, you can try contacting the following associations:

Judo Association
    Room 902, Queen Elizabeth Stadium, 18 Oi Kwan Rd, Wanchai (☎ 208913879; fax 8348935)
Karatedo Association
    Room 1006, Queen Elizabeth Stadium, 18 Oi Kwan Rd, Wanchai (☎ 208919705; fax 8346264)
South China Athletic Association
    88 Caroline Hill Rd, Causeway Bay (☎ 205776932; fax 8909304)
Taekwondo Association
    Room 1004, Queen Elizabeth Stadium, 18 Oi Kwan Rd, Wanchai (☎ 208912036, 8912104)
YMCA
    Salisbury Rd, Tsimshatsui (☎ 203692211)

Qigong Gongfu meditation, known as *qigong*, is used both for self-defence and as a form of traditional Chinese medicine. *Qi* represents life's vital energy, and *gong* is from gongfu. Qigong can be thought of as energy management – practitioners try to project their qi to perform seemingly magical acts.

Qigong practitioners occasionally give impressive demonstrations, driving nails through boards with their fingers or putting their fists through brick walls. Less spectacular but potentially more useful is the ability to heal others, and it's interesting to watch them do it. Typically, they place their hands above or next to the patient's body without actually making physical contact. To many foreigners this looks like a circus act, and indeed even many Chinese suspect that it's nothing but quackery. However, there are many who claim that they have been cured of serious illness without any other treatment but qigong, even after more

conventional doctors have told them that their condition is hopeless.

In China during the Cultural Revolution of the 1960s, qigong practitioners were denounced as a superstitious link to the bourgeois past. Many were arrested and all were forced to stop the practice. It is only recently that qigong has made a comeback, but many of the highly-skilled practitioners are no longer alive.

Does qigong work? It isn't easy to say, but there is a theory in medicine that all doctors can cure one-third of their patients regardless of what method is used. So perhaps qigong gets its one-third cure rate too.

RELIGION
In Chinese religion now, Taoism, Confucianism and Buddhism have become inextricably entwined. Ancestor worship and ancient animist beliefs have also been incorporated into the religious milieu.

In Hong Kong there are approximately 600 temples, monasteries and shrines. Most are tiny but there are some enormous ones such as the Po Lin Monastery on Lantau Island, the Temple of Ten Thousand Buddhas at Shatin and Wong Tai Sin in Kowloon.

Buddhism
Buddhism was founded in India in the 6th century BC by Siddhartha Gautama of the Sakya clan. Siddhartha was a prince brought up in luxury, but he became discontented with the physical world when he was confronted with the sights of old age, sickness and death. He despaired of finding fulfilment on the physical level, since the body was inescapably subject to these weaknesses.

Around the age of 30 Siddhartha broke from the material world and sought 'enlightenment' by following various yogic disciplines. After several failed attempts he devoted the final phase of his search to intensive contemplation. One evening as he sat beneath a banyan tree, he slipped into a deep meditation and emerged having achieved enlightenment. His title 'Buddha' means 'the awakened' or 'the enlightened one'.

Buddha founded an order of monks and preached his ideas for the next four decades until his death around 480 BC. To his followers he was known as Sakyamuni, the 'silent sage of the Sakya clan'. It is said that Gautama Buddha was not the only Buddha, but the fourth, and is not expected to be the last.

The cornerstone of Buddhist philosophy is the view that all life is suffering. Everyone is subject to the traumas of birth, sickness, decrepitude, fear and death. The cause of suffering is desire – the desires of the body and the desire for personal fulfilment. Happiness can only be achieved if these desires are overcome.

Buddhism developed in China during the 3rd to 6th centuries AD. In the middle of the 1st century AD the religion had gained the interest of the Han Emperor Ming, who sent a mission to the west; the mission returned in 67 AD with Buddhist scriptures, two Indian monks and images of the Buddha. Centuries later, other Chinese monks like Xuan Zang journeyed to India and returned with Buddhist scriptures which were then translated from the original Sanskrit to Chinese.

Buddha wrote nothing, and the writings that have come down to us date from about 150 years after his death. By the time these texts came out, divisions had already appeared within Buddhism. At some stage Buddhism split into two major schools: *Theravada* and *Mahayana*.

The *Theravada* or 'doctrine of the elders' school holds that the path to nirvana is an individual pursuit. It centres on monks and nuns who make the search for nirvana a full-time profession. This school maintains that people are alone in the world and must tread the path to nirvana on their own; Buddhas can only show the way. The Theravada school is the Buddhism of Sri Lanka, Burma, Thailand, Laos and Cambodia.

The *Mahayana* school holds that since all existence is one, the fate of the individual is linked to the fate of others. The Buddha did not just point the way and float off into his own nirvana, but continues to offer spiritual help to others seeking nirvana. The Mahay-

Buddha

ana school is the Buddhism of Vietnam, Japan, Tibet, Korea, Mongolia and China.

Tibetans practice a form of the Mahayana school known as Tantric or Lamaist Buddhism. It is much more mystical than other forms of Buddhism, relying heavily on *mudras* (ritual postures), *mantras* (sacred speech), *yantras* (sacred art) and secret initiation rites. Priests called *lamas* are believed to be reincarnations of highly evolved beings; the Dalai Lama is the supreme patriarch of Tibetan Buddhism.

Taoism

Originally a philosophy, Taoism evolved into a religion. Unlike Buddhism, which was imported from India, Taoism is truly a Chinese home-grown religion. While Buddhism is found throughout East Asia, Taoism is seldom practised by non-Chinese.

View from Victoria Peak (PS)

Top Left: Street vendor, Statue Square, Hong Kong Island (RS)
Top Right: Indoor fish market, Hong Kong Island (RS)
Bottom Left: Indoor fish market, Hong Kong Island (RS)
Bottom Right: Indoor meat market, Hong Kong Island (RS)

The philosophy of Taoism originated with Laozi (Laotse), who lived in the 6th century BC. Very little is known about Laozi and some have questioned whether or not he existed. His name simply means the old one. Laozi is believed to have been the custodian of the imperial archives for the Chinese government and Confucius is supposed to have consulted him.

Laozi (or someone else) left behind a record of his beliefs, a slim volume entitled the *Dao De Qing* or *The Way and its Power*. It is doubtful that Laozi ever intended his philosophy to become a religion. Chang Ling is more or less credited with formally establishing the Taoist religion in 143 BC.

Understanding Taoism is not simple. The word *tao*, pronounced *dao*, means 'the way'. It is considered indescribable, but might be interpreted as the guiding path, the truth or the principle of the universe.

One of the main principles of Taoism is the concept of *wuwei* or doing nothing. A quote, attributed to Laozi: 'Do nothing, and nothing will not be done', emphasises this principle. The idea is to remain humble, passive, non-assertive and non-interventionist. Qian Sima, a Chinese historian who lived from 145 BC to 90 BC, put it another way: 'Do not take the lead in planning affairs or you may be held responsible'.

Non-intervention or 'live and let live' ideals are the keystones of Tao. Harmony and patience are needed, and action is obtained through inaction. Taoists like to note that water, the softest substance, will wear away stone, the hardest substance.

Just as there have been different interpretations of Tao, there have been different interpretations of *De* – 'the power', which has led to three distinct kinds of Taoism in China.

Unlike philosophical Taoism, which has many Western followers, Chinese Taoism is a religion. It has been associated with alchemy and the search for immortality, which partly led Taoists to often attract the patronage of Chinese rulers before Confucianism gained the upper hand.

As time passed, Taoism increasingly became wrapped up in the supernatural, self-mutilation, hot coal dances, witchcraft, fortune telling and magic. All this is very evident if you visit a Taoist temple during the ghost month or certain other religious festivals (see the Facts for the Visitor chapter).

Confucianism

Confucius is regarded as China's greatest philosopher and teacher. The philosophy of Confucius has been borrowed by Japan, Korea, Vietnam and other neighbours of China. Confucius never claimed to be a religious leader, prophet or god, but his influence has been so great in China that Confucianism is regarded as a religion by many.

Confucius (551 BC-479 BC) lived through a time of great chaos known as the Warring States Period. He emphasised devotion to parents and family, loyalty to friends, justice, peace, education, reform and humanitarianism. Confucius was a great reformer and humanitarian. He preached the virtues of good government. His philosophy led to China's renowned bureaucracy and the system of civil service and university entrance examinations, where a person gained position through ability and merit rather than through noble birth and connections.

Confucius preached against such evils as corruption, war, torture and excessive taxation. He was the first teacher to open his school to all students on the basis of their eagerness to learn rather than their noble birth and ability to pay for tuition.

The philosophy of Confucius can be found in the *Lunyu* or the *Analects of Confucius*. Many quotes have been taken from these works, the most famous perhaps being the Golden Rule. The Western version of this rule is 'Do others as you would have them do unto you'. The Confucian version is written in the negative, 'Do not do unto others what you would not have them do unto you'. The Chinese who are influenced by Confucius and the Tao are not so aggressive as to wish to 'do unto' anybody.

The glorification of Confucius began only after his death, but eventually his ideas permeated every level of Chinese society – government offices presupposed a knowledge of the Confucian classics and spoken proverbs trickled down to the illiterate masses.

During the Han Dynasty (206 BC-220 AD), Confucianism effectively became the state religion. In 130 BC, Confucianism was made the basic discipline for training government officials, and remained so until the end of the Qing Dynasty in 1911.

In 59 AD, sacrifices were ordered for Confucius in all urban schools. In the 7th and 8th centuries, during the Tang Dynasty, temples and shrines were built to him and his original disciples. During the Song Dynasty the *Analects of Confucius* became the basis of all education.

Not all aspects of Confucianism have been universally praised. It's clear that Confucius was a male chauvinist. Indeed, Confucianism was eventually used to justify the binding of womens' feet. Ironically, though Confucius was a radical in his time, his philosophy later came to embody conservatism and feudal practices.

Although Confucius died 2500 years ago, his influence remains strong in China. The Chinese remain solidly loyal to friends, family and teachers and much of Confucian thought has become Chinese culture as we know it.

Chinese Religion Today

On a daily level the Chinese are much less concerned with the high-minded philosophies and asceticism of Buddha, Confucius or Laozi than they are with the pursuit of worldly success, the appeasement of the dead and the spirits, and the seeking of hidden knowledge about the future.

Of most importance is *joss*, meaning 'luck'. The Chinese are too astute to leave something as important as luck to chance. Gods have to be appeased, bad spirits blown away and sleeping dragons soothed to keep joss on your side. No house, wall or shrine is built until an auspicious date for the start of construction is chosen and the most propitious location is selected. Incense has to be burned, gifts presented and prayers said to appease the spirits who might inhabit the future construction site.

Integral parts of Chinese religion are death, the after-life and ancestor worship. Chinese funerals are usually lavish events and a drawn-out process since the body can only be buried on an auspicious day. When the day finally comes, it's signalled first by the clash of cymbals and the moan of oboes. Next comes the clover-shaped coffin and grief-stricken mourners, some paid to weep and many wearing ghost-like outfits with white hoods. A fine spread of roast pig and other foods, not to be eaten but offered to the gods for the one gone beyond, accompanies the funeral.

A grave site is chosen on the side of hills with a good view for the loved one who must lie there. At the grave the mourners burn paper models of material treasures like cars and boats, as well as bundles of paper money, to ensure that the dead person is getting the good things of the first life in the great beyond. Just as during the Shang Dynasty, when the dead continue to look after the welfare of the living, the living continue to take care of the dead.

Other Religions

Hong Kong has a cosmopolitan population, and many religious denominations, other than the traditional Chinese ones, are represented. There are about 500,000 Christians (about 55% Catholic, 45% Protestant), Sikhs from India, around 50,000 Muslims and over 1000 Jews.

If you want to pursue the matter of Hong Kong's non-Buddhist and non-Taoist religions, you can contact one of the following places of worship:

Anglican
    St John's Cathedral, 4-8 Garden Rd, Central (☎ 205234157)
Bahai
    Flat C-6, 11th floor, Hankow Centre, Middle Rd, Tsimshatsui (☎ 203676407)
Christian Scientist
    31 MacDonnell Rd, Central (☎ 205242701)
Hindu
    Happy Valley (☎ 205725284)
Jewish
    Synagogue Ohel Leah, 70 Robinson Rd, Mid-Levels (☎ 208015440)

Chinese Gods

Chinese religion is polytheistic, having many divinities. Every Chinese house has its kitchen or house god, and trades have their gods too. Students worship Wan Chung, the deified scholar. Shopkeepers pray to Tsai Shin, god of riches. Every profession also has its own god, and numerous temples in Hong Kong and Macau are dedicated to certain gods or goddesses. The following are some of the important local divinities.

Tin Hau Queen of Heaven and Protector of Seafarers, Tin Hau is one of the most popular goddesses in Hong Kong. In Macau she is known as Ah Ma or Mother and in Taiwan she is known as Matsu. In Singapore she is Ma Chu Po or Respected Great Aunt.

In Hong Kong, Tin Hau has about 250,000 fishing people as followers and there are about two dozen temples dedicated to her dotted around the colony. The most famous is the Tai Miu (Great Temple) at Joss House Bay near Fat Tong Mun. Others are on Cheung Chau Island, at Sok Kwu Wan on Lamma Island, on Market St in Kowloon's Yaumatei district, on Tin Hau Temple Rd in Causeway Bay and at Stanley in Hong Kong Island.

Tin Hau is a classic case of the deification of a real person. She was born on an island in Fujian Province between 900 AD and 1000 AD. After her death the cult of Tin Hau spread along the coast of China and she became the patron goddess of fishing people.

Kuanyin The Buddhist equivalent of Tin Hau, primarily a Taoist deity, is Kuanyin, the Goddess of Mercy, who stands for tenderness and compassion for the unhappy lot of mortals. In Cantonese she is known as Kwun Yum in Hong Kong and as Kuan Iam in Macau. Kuanyin temples are at Repulse Bay and Stanley on Hong Kong Island, and at Cheung Chau in the Outlying Islands. There are some in Macau also.

Kuanti Soldiers pray to Kuanti, the red-faced God of War. Prior to his deification, Kuanti was a great warrior who lived at the end of the Han Dynasty (206 BC-220 AD) and is worshipped not only for his might in battle but because he is the embodiment of right action, integrity and loyalty. The life of Kuanti is told in an old Chinese legend called *The Story of the Three Kingdoms*.

However, Kuanti is not a cruel tyrant delighting in battle and the slaying of enemies. Rather, he can avert war and protect people from its horrors.

Kuanti is also the patron god of restaurants, pawn shops and literature, as well as the Hong Kong police force and secret societies such as the Triad organisations.

Kuanti temples are at Tai O on Lantau Island and the Man Mo (literally civil and military) Temple on Hollywood Rd, Hong Kong Island.

Pak Tai Like all gods for special localities, Pak Tai keeps an eye out for his area, Cheung Chau Island.

Like Kuanti, Pak Tai is a military protector of the state and there are various stories about his origins. Chinese ancestors are the spiritual guardians of their descendants, and Pak Tai is the Guardian of Society. When chaos reigns and there is destruction he is believed to descend from heaven to restore peace and order.

On the island of Cheung Chau, Pak Tai is revered as a life-giver, having intervened to end a plague which hit the island at the end of the last century. A large temple on Cheung Chau, the Temple of Jade Vacuity, is dedicated to him.

Tam Kung This god is worshipped only along a small stretch of the southern Chinese coast which includes Macau and Hong Kong. One theory is that he was actually the last emperor of the Southern Song Dynasty (1127 AD-1279 AD) which was overrun by Kublai Khan's Mongol armies. The emperor was a boy of eight or nine years and is now worshipped under the pseudonym of Tam Kung. A temple for Tam Kung can be seen in Coloane Village in Macau.

Wong Tai Sin This god watches over the housing settlement of the same name in Kowloon. Wong Tai Sin had a meteoric rise to success in the colony, having been brought to Hong Kong in 1915 by a man and his son who came from Guangdong Province carrying a painting of him. They installed the painting and an altar in a small temple in Wanchai. A temple was built in Kowloon in 1921 and his popularity grew. ■

Methodist
  271 Queen's Rd East, Wanchai (☎ 205757817)
Mormon
  Church of the Latter Day Saints, 7 Castle Rd,
  Mid-Levels, Central (☎ 205593325)
Muslim
  Islamic Union, 40 Oi Kwan Rd, Wanchai
  (☎ 205752218)
Quaker
  Society of Friends, 3rd floor, Conference Room,
  Mariners Club, Middle Rd, Tsimshatsui
  (☎ 206977283)
Roman Catholic
  St Joseph's, 37 Garden Rd, Central
  (☎ 205523992)
Sikh
  371 Queen's Rd East, Wanchai (☎ 205749837)

LANGUAGE

While the Chinese have about eight main dialects, about 70% of the population of China speaks the Beijing dialect (commonly known as Mandarin) which is the official language of the People's Republic. For details see the Facts About Guangzhou chapter. Hong Kong's two official languages are English and Cantonese. Cantonese is a southern Chinese dialect spoken in Guangzhou and the surrounding Guangdong Province, Hong Kong and Macau.

While in Hong Kong Cantonese is used in everyday life, English is the primary language of commerce, banking and international trade, and is also used in the law courts. However, as 1997 draws near, many have noticed a sharp decline in the level of English-speaking proficiency. Those Hong Kong Chinese who speak excellent English are usually the most educated and wealthiest, and these are the people who can emigrate most easily. As English speakers emigrate in droves, those left behind are the working classes who speak primarily Cantonese.

On the other hand, the ability to speak Mandarin is on the increase. There has been a large percentage of Mandarin speakers in Hong Kong since the 1950s because so many refugees fled from China. Until recently, the younger generation has generally not bothered studying Mandarin, preferring instead English as a second language. The new political realities are now changing attitudes.

Despite China's promises that virtually nothing will change after 1997, most Hong Kongers believe that Mandarin will soon be the official language. Furthermore, Mandarin is far easier to learn for a Cantonese native speaker than English.

Short-term visitors can get along fine in Hong Kong without a word of Cantonese. Especially in the tourist zones, there are still plenty of English speakers. All street signs and signs on public transport are bilingual, so there is no problem getting around.

Most expatriates living in Hong Kong for many years never learn the local language. This is possible mainly because they spend their time in the company of other expats. Of course, the few foreigners willing to make the considerable effort required to learn Cantonese are rewarded with a level of understanding and camaraderie not achievable otherwise.

The Spoken Language

Cantonese differs from Mandarin as much as French differs from Spanish. Speakers of both dialects can read Chinese characters, but a Cantonese speaker will pronounce many of the characters differently from a Mandarin speaker. For example, when Mr Ng from Hong Kong goes to Beijing the Mandarin-speakers will call him Mr Wu. If Mr Wong goes from Hong Kong to Fujian Province the character for his name will be read as Mr Wee, and in Beijing he is Mr Huang.

Tones

A linguist once described the Chinese language as being notable for its 'phonetic poverty'. This should not be taken to mean that Chinese lacks a rich or expressive vocabulary – indeed, it's just the contrary. What the linguist meant is that the number of possible sounds which can be uttered in Chinese is very limited. In Mandarin Chinese there are just 410 possible sounds that can make up a syllable, and in Cantonese only slightly more. Compared to most other languages, this is phonetic poverty indeed. This results in many homonyms (sound-alike words). Thus, the Cantonese word for 'four' sounds just like the words for 'death', 'silk', 'lion', 'private', 'master', and 'affair'. While the abundant homonyms are great for making puns and word plays, the sound-alike words are terribly confusing to the foreign student of Cantonese.

The Chinese language compensates for the lack of phonetic variety with tones. Mandarin has four tones but Cantonese has at least six (linguists argue about the seventh). Adding tone to a syllable has the effect of multiplying the number of phonetic possibilities several times over. This is sufficient to make Chinese just as linguistically rich as any modern language.

While intonation is not always crucial, in most cases the difference in tone will be a deciding factor in the meaning of a word. If you get the tones mixed, you can say something entirely different from what was intended. The seven tones of Cantonese are illustrated by the following example, using the vowel *a* and the syllable *wan*:

Tone	Name	Vowel	Syllable	Meaning
1	high-falling	à	wàn	to review
2	high-rising	á	wán	look for
3	middle-level	a	wan	to hold
4	high-level	ā	wān	to review
5	low-falling	àh	wàhn	cloud
6	low-rising	á	wán	to license
7	low-level	ah	wahn	to transport

In the preceding example it's worth noting that Nos 1 and 4 have the same meaning. This is the source of dispute between linguists. These two tones do not seem to differentiate anything, and in Hong Kong most people cannot distinguish the two. However, in parts of Guangdong Province there does seem to be a difference. Unless your Cantonese becomes extremely fluent, you shouldn't concern yourself with this.

You may run into a few old language textbooks which claim that Cantonese actually has 10 tones, the additional three being called 'clipped tones'. Linguists have generally rubbished this argument, and the 'clipped tones' are now referred to as

'clipped sounds'. What happens is that the final consonants *m, n* and *ng* are 'clipped' under certain circumstances. That is, they change pronunciation to become *p, t* and *k* respectively. Thus, the Cantonese word *sam* can be transformed into *sap* in certain contexts. To use an example from English, *burned* is often pronounced *burnt*.

The Written Language

Officially, written Chinese has about 50,000 pictographs or characters which symbolise objects or actions. However, most of these have become archaic, but about 5000 remain in common use. There are at least 2000 essential characters which you would need to know to read a newspaper.

It is often said that Chinese is a monosyllabic language. That is, each word is only one syllable long. However, the point is hotly debated by linguists and I don't accept it myself. It is true that each character is only one syllable long and each character has meaning, but the dispute is over what constitutes a word. For example, the spoken Cantonese word for 'coral' is *shaan-woo*, which is clearly two syllables. In written form, both the first syllable *shaan* and the second syllable *woo* are represented by individual characters. While a literate Chinese speaker would understand either of these two characters to mean coral, as a practical matter both syllables are always used together in conversation. It might be more accurate to say that Chinese uses a monosyllabic writing system.

All Chinese use mostly the same characters though the Cantonese have invented about 150 which are not understood by Mandarin speakers. And even though both Cantonese and Mandarin speakers can read the same newspaper, they pronounce all the characters differently. All Chinese can read the same newspaper, but with some difficulty. One problem is that a Cantonese word might be two syllables which would require two characters to write, whereas the equivalent in Mandarin might require three characters. This really becomes a problem when foreign words are borrowed

– the Cantonese borrowed the English word for 'taxi' *(diksi)* which is two characters, whereas Mandarin speakers have kept the three-character traditional form *(chuzuche)*.

There is another complication. In the 1950s, the Chinese government introduced a system of simplified characters in an effort to make the written script easier to learn and increase literacy in the country. Unfortunately, apart from China, only Singapore has adopted these simplified forms. The result is that many of the characters you'll see in Hong Kong are written quite differently from the same ones in China. The simplified characters should have made Chinese easier to learn, but have actually made it more difficult for students since they end up having to study both systems.

In Hong Kong, Chinese characters can be read from left to right, right to left, or top to bottom. In China itself the government has been trying to get everyone to read and write from left to right.

Romanisation

The People's Republic uses a romanisation system known as *pinyin* which, while very accurate once you learn its peculiarities, only works for the Mandarin dialect. You cannot use it to romanise Cantonese. An explanation of the pinyin system is in the Guangzhou section.

As for Cantonese, the situation is far messier. Unfortunately, several competing systems of romanisation exist and no single one has emerged as an official standard. Hong Kongers are not forced to learn romanisation in school, so asking a Cantonese native speaker to romanise a Chinese character produces mixed results. The lack of an established standard creates a good deal of confusion for foreigners trying to master the vagaries of Cantonese pronunciation.

A number of romanisation schemes have come and gone, but at least three have survived and are currently used in Hong Kong. The three are called Meyer-Wempe, Sidney Lau and Yale, and you are likely to encounter all of them if you make any serious study of the language.

The Meyer-Wempe system is the oldest in current use. Until Sidney Lau came along, it was the one most likely to appear on maps, street signs and in books about Hong Kong. The reason for its popularity is simply its age – the first past the post usually has the best chance of becoming the standard because people resist change. Unfortunately, Meyer-Wempe is also highly confusing. One of its oddities is the use of apostrophes in words to distinguish aspirated sounds (pronounced with a puff of air, such as *p*) from unaspirated (such as *b*). Map and book publishers tend to drop the apostrophes, thus leaving readers unable to distinguish *p* from *b* and *t* from *d*.

The Sidney Lau system fixed this defect and several others. Sidney Lau was the principal of the Government Language School for civil servants, and he also broadcast the popular 'Cantonese by Radio' teaching series which started in 1961. The Sidney Lau system has been widely adopted by publishers.

The Yale system is the most phonetically accurate and the one generally preferred by foreign students. It's the system adopted by the Chinese University of Hong Kong for the New Asia Yale in the China Language Institute. There are a number of textbooks and dictionaries based on this system. Unfortunately, it's the least used of the romanisation schemes.

There is in fact a fourth romanisation system, called the International Phonetic Alphabet (IPA). However, this is a purely academic system and adds some special symbols which are not part of the Roman alphabet. Linguists are fond of the system, but you are not likely to encounter it outside of academia.

The following table illustrates the notable differences between the three major romanisation systems:

Meyer-Wempe	Sydney Lau	Yale
p'	p	p
p	b	b
t'	t	t
t	d	d
k'	k	k
k	g	g

ch'	ch	ch
ts	j	j
k'w	kw	kw
kw	gw	gw
s, sh	s	s
i, y	y	y
oo, w	w	w
oeh	euh	eu
ui	ui	eui
un	un	eun
ut	ut	eut
o	o	ou
oo	oo	u
ue	ue	yu

Some have wondered about the placement of spaces and hyphens in Chinese words. 'Hong Kong' is sometimes written 'Hongkong', though you will probably not see 'Shanghai' as 'Shang Hai' or 'Beijing' as 'Bei Jing'. Chinese often hyphenate their given names, so you may find Sun Yatsen written as Sun Yat-sen. The confusion comes from the fact that every syllable in Chinese is written with a separate character, but when transcribed into romanised form a name is usually written as a multi-syllable word. In Mandarin there is a standard rule – names are kept as one word (thus 'Shanghai' and 'Beijing'). However, Cantonese has not adopted any such standard, so in this book we use what is most commonly accepted (thus 'Hong Kong'). The hyphenation of names is falling into disuse and is therefore best avoided. A reader will, therefore, become confused if Ping Chau is read as P'ing Chau or Bing Chau'.

Learning Chinese

If you want to study Chinese seriously, the Chinese University in Hong Kong offers regular courses in Cantonese and Mandarin. Classes can be arranged through the New Asia Yale in the China Language Institute, associated with the university. There are three terms a year – one 10-week summer term and two regular 15-week terms. The university does not provide dormitories, so you must make your own living arrangements.

Somewhat less popular but still OK is the course at Hong Kong University, School of Professional & Continuing Education (☎ 208592787, 8592791), Pokfulam, Hong Kong Island. There is a branch (☎ 205472225) on the 9th floor, West Tower, Shun Tak Centre, Sheung Wan.

There are a number of private language schools which cater to individuals or companies. These informal schools offer more flexibility and will even despatch a teacher to a company to teach the whole staff if need be. Some to consider include:

British Institute, also known as Chinese Language Institute of Hong Kong, Room 1701, Yue Shing Commercial Building, 15 Queen Victoria St, Central (☎ 205238455)

Personal Education, 3rd floor, One Hysan Ave, Causeway Bay (☎ 205778002)

Staff Service Hong Kong Ltd, Room 3702B, Peregrine Tower, Lippo Centre, 89 Queensway, Central (☎ 208109822)

Phrase List

Even if you never gain fluency, knowing a few simple Cantonese phrases can be useful. Hong Kong is not known as a very friendly place, yet even a small attempt to speak the local vernacular will bring smiles to the faces of Chinese people you meet. Here are a few phrases to get you started:

Pronouns

I
 ngo 我
you
 nei 你
he, she, it
 keui 他
we, us
 ngodei 我們
you (plural)
 neidei 你們
they, them
 keuidei 他們

Greetings & Civilities

hello, how are you?
 nei hou 你好
good morning
 jou san 早晨

goodbye
joi gin 再見
thank you
m goido zei 唔該/多謝
you're welcome
m saihaakhei 不客氣
I'm sorry/excuse me
deuimjyu 對不起

Useful Expressions

I want...
ngo yiu... 我要
I want to buy...
ngo yiu maai... 我要買...
yes, have
yau 有
no, don't have
m yau 沒有
How much does it cost?
gei siu chin 多少錢
too expensive
taai gwaige 太貴
Waiter, the bill
fogei, maai daan 伙記埋單
I don't understand
ngo m meng ba 我聽不懂
Wait a moment
deng chan 等一下

Necessities

toilet paper
chi ji 廁紙
tissue paper
ji gan 紙巾
tampons
wai sang ming tiu 衛生棉條
sanitary pads (Kotex)
wai seng gan 衛生巾
sunscreen (UV) lotion
tai you yau 太陽油
laundry service
sai yee chung sum 洗衣中心

Getting Around

I want to go to the...
ngo you hoi 我要去...
airport
fei gei chang 飛機場
MTR station
dei tip zam 地鐵站

KCR station
fo chei zam 火車站
LRT station
heng bin ti lou 輕便鐵路
Star Ferry
ting seng ma tau 天星碼頭
I'm lost
ngo dong sat lou 我蕩失路
Where is the...?
...hai bin dou 在那裡
telephone
din wah 電話
post office
yau go 郵局
toilet
ji sou 廁所
Turn right
yau jwin 右轉
Turn left
jwo jwin 左轉
Go straight
yet zet zau 一直走
Turn around
jwin gou wan 轉個彎
I want to hire a bicycle
ngo yu jo daan chei 我要租單車

Emergencies

I'm sick
ngo beng la 我生病
I'm injured
ngo sau cheung 我受傷
hospital
yi yun 醫院
police
geng cha 警察
Fire!
fo jok 火燭
Help!
gau meng ah 救命啊
Thief!
siu tau 小偷
pickpocket
pa sau 扒手
rapist
keng gan ze 強姦者

Numbers

0	*leng*	零
1	*yet*	一

2	*yi, leung*	二, 兩
3	*sam*	三
4	*sei*	四
5	*m*	五
6	*lok*	六
7	*chat*	七
8	*ba*	八
9	*gau*	九
10	*sap*	十
11	*sap yet*	十一
12	*sap yi*	十二
20	*yi sap*	二十
21	*yi sam yet*	二十一
100	*yet ba*	一百
200	*leung ba*	兩百
1000	*yet chin*	一千
2000	*leung chin*	兩千
10,000	*yet man*	一萬
20,000	*leung man*	兩萬
100,000	*sap man*	十萬
200,000	*yi sap man*	二十萬

Time

What is the time?
 gei dim 幾點
hour
 dim 點
minute
 fan 分

Language Footnote While Hong Kong's expatriate community tries to speak the Queen's English, some Chinese words have been incorporated into the local vernacular. *Taipan* means a 'big boss', usually in a large company, which is referred to as a *hong*. *Godown* means 'warehouse'. An *amah* is a 'servant', usually a woman who babysits and takes care of the house.

A *cheongsam* (*qipao* in Mandarin) is a fashionable, tight-fitting Chinese dress with a slit up the side. You may well see receptionists at upmarket restaurants wearing one, and it's also the favoured gown worn by a woman on her honeymoon. The dress originated in Shanghai and was banned in China during the Cultural Revolution.

A foreigner is often referred to as a *gwailo* – a Cantonese word which literally means 'ghost person' but which is more accurately translated as 'foreign devil'. It used to have a negative connotation, but these days many foreigners call themselves gwailos without giving it a second thought.

The word *shroff*, frequently used in Hong Kong, is not derived from Chinese – it's an Anglo-Indian word meaning 'cashier'.

And finally there is the word *junk*. It might be rubbish in English, but to the Chinese it's a mid-sized fishing boat. The traditional models had sails, but these days diesel engines do the job.

HONG KONG

Facts for the Visitor

VISAS & EMBASSIES

For most visitors to Hong Kong a passport is all that's required.

UK citizens (or Commonwealth citizens who were born in the UK or in Hong Kong) can normally stay for up to 12 months without a visa, and it's possible to stay longer. Australians, Canadians and New Zealanders get a visa-free stay for three months. Citizens of most Western European countries are also permitted to stay for three months without a visa, depending on which country they're from. Americans can stay for one month without a visa.

Officially, visitors have to show that they have adequate funds for their stay and that they have an onward ticket or a return ticket to their own country. In practice, this rule is seldom enforced, except in the case when a visa is required. Visitors from the following countries *must* have a visa:

Afghanistan, Albania, Bulgaria, Burma (Myanmar), Cambodia, China, CIS (former USSR), Cuba, Czech Republic, Hungary, Iran, Iraq, Laos, Lebanon, Libya, Mongolia, North Korea, Oman, Romania, Slovakia, Somalia, Sudan, Syria, Taiwan, Tonga, Vietnam, Yemen, Yugoslavia and all stateless persons.

If you do need a visa, apply at any British embassy, consulate or high commission.

Visitors are not permitted to take up employment, establish any business or enrol as students. If you want to enter for employment, education or residence you must have a work visa unless you are a UK citizen, and even then you officially have to show means of support in Hong Kong.

Visa Extensions

In Hong Kong, inquire at the Immigration Department (☎ 8246111), 2nd floor, Wanchai Tower Two, 7 Gloucester Rd, Wanchai, Hong Kong Island.

In general, visa extensions are not readily granted unless there are special circum-stances – cancelled flights, illness, registration in a legitimate course of study, legal employment, marriage to a local, etc.

Foreign Embassies in Hong Kong

Below are some of the diplomatic missions in Hong Kong. There's a complete list in the Yellow Pages Buying Guide under Consulates. Some of the small countries are represented by honorary consuls who are normally business people employed in commercial firms – so it's advisable to phone beforehand to find out if they're available.

Australia
    23rd & 24th floor, Harbour Centre, 25 Harbour Rd, Wanchai (☎ 8278881)
Austria
    14th floor, Diamond Exchange Building, 8-10 Duddell St, Central (☎ 5222388)
Burma (Myanmar)
    Room 2421-2425, Sung Hung Kai Centre, 30 Harbour Rd, Wanchai (☎ 8913329)
Canada
    11th-14th floors, Tower One, Exchange Square, 8 Connaught Place, Central (☎ 8104321)
China
    Visa Office of the Ministry of Foreign Affairs, 5th floor, Lower Block, 26 Harbour Rd, Wanchai (☎ 8353794)
Denmark
    Room 2402B, Great Eagle Centre, 23 Harbour Rd, Wanchai (☎ 8936252)
Finland
    Room 1818, Hutchison House, 10 Harcourt Rd, Central (☎ 5255385)
France
    26th floor, Admiralty Centre, Tower Two, 18 Harcourt Rd, Admiralty (☎ 5294351)
Germany
    21st floor, United Centre, 95 Queensway, Admiralty (☎ 5298855)
India
    Room D, 16th floor, United Centre, 95 Queensway, Central (☎ 5275821)
Indonesia
    6-8 Keswick St, Causeway Bay (☎ 8904421)
Israel
    Room 702, Tower Two, Admiralty Centre, 18 Harcourt Rd, Central (☎ 5296091)

Italy
     Room 805, Hutchison House, 10 Harcourt Rd,
     Central (☎ 5220033)
Japan
     24th floor, Bank of America Tower, 12 Harcourt
     Rd, Central (☎ 5221184)
Korea (South)
     5th floor, Far East Finance Centre, 16 Harcourt
     Rd, Central (☎ 5294141)
Malaysia
     24th floor, Malaysia Building, 50 Gloucester Rd,
     Wanchai (☎ 5270921)
Nepalese Liaison Office
     c/o HQ Brigade of Gurkhas, HMS Tamar, Prince
     of Wales Building, Harcourt Rd, Central
     (☎ 8633253, 8633111). Office hours are from 10
     am to noon, Monday to Friday
Netherlands
     Room 301, 3rd floor, China Building, 29 Queen's
     Rd, Central (☎ 5225120)
New Zealand
     Room 3414, Jardine House, Connaught Rd,
     Central (☎ 5255044)
Norway
     Room 1401, AIA Building, 1 Stubbs Rd,
     Wanchai (☎ 3749253)
Pakistan
     Room 307, Asian House, 1 Hennessy Rd,
     Wanchai (☎ 5274623)
Philippines
     21st floor, Wah Kwong Agent Centre, 88 Queen's
     Rd, Central (☎ 8100183)
Portugal
     10th floor, Tower Two, Exchange Square,
     Central (☎ 5231338)
Singapore
     Room 901, 9th floor, Tower One, Admiralty
     Centre, 18 Harcourt Rd, Admiralty (☎ 5272212)
South Africa
     27th floor, Sunning Plaza, 10 Hysan Ave, Cause-
     way Bay (☎ 5773279)
Spain
     8th floor, Printing House, 18 Ice House St,
     Central (☎ 5253041)
Sri Lanka
     8th floor, Loke Yew Building, 50-52 Queen's Rd,
     Central (☎ 5238810)
Sweden
     Room 804, Hong Kong Club Building, Chater
     Rd, Central (☎ 5211212)
Switzerland
     Room 3703, Gloucester Tower, The Landmark,
     11 Pedder St, Central (☎ 5227147)
Taiwan
     Chung Hwa Travel Service, 4th floor, Lippo
     Centre, 89 Queensway, Central (☎ 5258315)
Thailand
     8th floor, Fairmont House, 8 Cotton Tree Drive,
     Central (☎ 5216481)

UK
     c/o Overseas Visa Section, Hong Kong Immigra-
     tion Department, 2nd floor, Wanchai Tower Two,
     7 Gloucester Rd, Wanchai (☎ 8246111)
USA
     26 Garden Rd, Central (☎ 5239011)

DOCUMENTS

Visitors and residents are advised to carry identification at all times in Hong Kong. It doesn't need to be a passport – anything with a photo on it will do. This is because the immigration authorities do frequent spot checks to catch illegal workers and those who overstay their visas. If you have no ID, you could find yourself being 'rounded up'.

A passport is essential for visiting Hong Kong, and if yours is within a few months of expiration, get a new one now. Losing your passport is very bad news – getting a new one means a trip to your embassy or consulate and usually a long wait while they send faxes or telexes (at your expense) to confirm that you exist. If you'll be staying a long time in Hong Kong, it's wise to register your passport with your consulate or embassy – this makes the replacement process much simpler.

If you plan to be driving abroad get an International Driving Permit from your local automobile association. These are valid for one year only so there's no sense getting one far in advance of departure.

Useful (though not essential) is an International Health Certificate to record any vaccinations you've had. These can also be issued in Hong Kong.

If you qualify as a student or if you're 27 years or under, you can get an STA Youth Card. An International Student Identity Card (ISIC) entitles the holder to a number of discounts on airfares, trains, museums, etc. To get this card, inquire at your campus. These can also be issued by the Hong Kong Student Travel Bureau.

Another useful card is the STA Youth Card. To obtain one, you must be between 13 and 26 years of age. You do not need to be a student and you do not need to be from Australia.

If you're travelling with your spouse, a photocopy of your marriage licence might come in handy should you become involved with the law, hospitals or other bureaucratic authorities.

If you're planning on working or studying in Hong Kong, it could be helpful to have copies of transcripts, diplomas, letters of reference and other professional qualifications.

The Chinese are very impressed by namecards, so bring some along. Alternatively, make use of the 'Express Card' machines which can whip out customised namecards in less than 10 minutes. The machines are found mostly in MTR and KCR stations – Central MTR Station has several. For HK$20 you get 40 namecards.

CUSTOMS

Even though Hong Kong is a duty-free port, there are still items on which duty is charged. In particular, there are high import taxes on cigarettes and alcohol. The duty-free allowance for visitors is 200 cigarettes (or 50 cigars or 250g of tobacco) and one litre of alcohol. Apart from these limits there are no other import tax worries, so you can bring in reasonable quantities of almost anything without paying taxes or obtaining permits. An exception is ivory, which requires a bureaucratic tangle of permits.

Of course, you can't bring in anything which is illegal in Hong Kong. This includes fireworks. Hong Kongers returning from Macau and China are often vigorously searched for this reason. Not surprisingly, firearms are strictly controlled and special permits are needed to import one. Non-lethal weapons like chemical mace and stun guns are also prohibited – a few female travellers have run afoul of this rule.

Most importantly, dope is highly illegal. It makes no difference whether it's heroin, opium or marijuana – the law makes no distinction. If customs officials find dope or the equipment for smoking it in your possession, you can expect to be arrested immediately. Being a foreigner doesn't get you off the hook. Depending on the quantity found, the sentence for possession or smug-gling of narcotics can be several years jail in addition to large fines. If you're arriving from a suspect place such as Thailand or Vietnam, expect a more rigorous examination of luggage.

Have some sympathy for the enormous job that customs officials must perform. Aside from air passengers, more than 700 ships a day pass through Hong Kong's harbour. Obviously, not all ships can be inspected. One customs official told me that the biggest problems are with ships from South-East Asia (carrying heroin) and from the USA (smuggling guns and ammunition). This is in addition to small speedboats from China which bring in guns, drugs and illegal immigrants.

MONEY

As Asia's leading financial centre, Hong Kong is one of the easiest places to cash travellers' cheques, replace stolen cheques and have money wired to you. There are no exchange control regulations and money can be freely transferred into and out of Hong Kong. There is no foreign currency black market. Banks and moneychangers can exchange all major trading currencies and many minor ones as well.

Avoid changing money at the airport! At the time of this writing, the moneychangers at the airport were giving an exchange rate of US$1 to HK$7.24, equivalent to a 5.6% commission.

Banks give the best exchange rates, but some banks give much better rates than others. Two banks are famous for giving excellent exchange rates. One is the Hang Seng Bank which will also change many odd currencies that other banks won't touch (Macau patacas, for example). The main Tsimshatsui branch of Hang Seng Bank is at 18 Carnarvon Rd; on Hong Kong Island the main branch is at 83 Des Voeux Rd, Central. Similarly excellent exchange rates can be found at the Wing Lung Bank, 4 Carnarvon Rd (next to New Astor Hotel), Tsimshatsui; 45 Des Voeux Rd, Central; on Harbour Rd (next to the Convention Centre) in Wanchai; and at 45 Jardine's Bazaar in Causeway Bay.

The Hongkong Bank gives poor rates and tacks on a HK$30 service charge for each transaction. It also charges a hefty HK$100 to cash a bank draft, while the Hang Seng Bank does it for free.

Licenced moneychangers are abundant in tourist areas like Tsimshatsui. Their chief advantage is that they stay open on Sundays, holidays and late into the evening when banks are closed. They claim to charge no commission, but instead give lousy exchange rates equivalent to a 5% commission. These rates are clearly posted. The moneychangers stand in booths behind bars and unbreakable glass, not so much to protect themselves from robbers as from irate tourists. The best exchange rates I've seen from moneychangers are inside Chungking Mansions on Nathan Rd in Tsimshatsui.

You can bargain with moneychangers just as you do with shopkeepers. I've never been cheated by a Hong Kong moneychanger. They've always given me whatever rate was agreed on beforehand. But if you don't ask first, they will always give you the posted rate which is generally lousy.

The only other place that you can change money is at the big hotels, all of which give unfavourable rates.

Before the actual exchange is made, the moneychanger is required by law to give you a form to sign clearly showing the amount, exchange rate and any service charges.

ATM cards from a number of foreign banks will work in Hong Kong auto-teller machines. You'll have to ask the banks which machines and which cards are acceptable – there is no universal system. Payment is, of course, in Hong Kong dollars only.

Credit cards accepted by most places are American Express, Bank Americard (Visa), Carte Blanche, Diners Club, JCB, MasterCard and Air Travel. Major charge and credit cards are accepted by many restaurants and shops in Hong Kong.

Some shops may try to add a surcharge to the cost of the item if you charge your purchase against your card. In theory this is prohibited by the credit card companies, but in this case I have some sympathy for the shops. Credit card companies normally charge the shops a commission on each purchase, up to 5%, but they insist that this charge not be passed on to the customer for the obvious reason that it would hurt the credit card business. To get around this, many shops say that there is no commission charged if you use a credit card, but there is a 5% discount if you pay cash.

Currency
When making a large purchase such as a camera, many shops will accept payment in American dollars (and sometimes other currencies) but may give you slightly less than the official rate. However, for most of your everyday needs, you'll have to pay in Hong Kong dollars (HK$).

The Hong Kong dollar is divided into 100 cents. There are different banknote designs in circulation, although the notes are interchangeable.

Bills are issued in denominations of HK$10 (green), HK$20 (grey), HK$50 (blue), HK$100 (red), HK$500 (brown) and HK$1000 (yellow). Coins are issued in denominations of HK$5, HK$2, HK$1, 50 cents, 20 cents and 10 cents. China has recently insisted that the 'colonial' image of Queen Elizabeth be removed from all newly-minted Hong Kong coins. This was done and the coins look pretty drab now – just whose face goes on the coins after 1997 is anybody's guess.

Exchange Rates
Since 1983, the Hong Kong dollar has been rigidly tied to the US dollar at a rate of US$1 to HK$7.80. However, the Hong Kong dollar is permitted to float within a very narrow range of this level and has now risen to its maximum permitted value. This has led to criticism from Hong Kong's trading partners, most vocally the USA – if Hong Kong is truly a free market, why does that exclude its currency? The following exchange rates were current at the time of publication:

HONG KONG

Australia	A$1	=	HK$5.62
Canada	C$1	=	HK$5.63
China	Y1	=	HK$0.90
France	Ffr1	=	HK$1.46
Germany	DM1	=	HK$5.00
Japan	¥100	=	HK$7.86
New Zealand	NZ$1	=	HK$4.63
Singapore	S$1	=	HK$5.12
Switzerland	Sfr1	=	HK$5.87
Taiwan	NT$1	=	HK$0.29
Thailand	B1	=	HK$0.31
UK	UK£1	=	HK$12.09
USA	US$1	=	HK$7.73

Costs

Hong Kong is certainly not cheap – it's a result of the continuing economic boom and too little space to build. Nevertheless, you can still find dorm beds for around HK$70 but it takes effort to find a double room for less than HK$200 these days.

On the other hand food is reasonably priced – you can keep the eating bill under HK$60 a day if you eat fast food or buy your own from supermarkets. Transport is cheap and distances are short – you can hardly buy an expensive bus, boat or railway ticket unless you travel deluxe class and take tours.

The main way to cut costs is to control yourself – shopping in Hong Kong can be addictive. Many people find all those cameras and electronic goodies on sale irresistible and suddenly decide they need to buy all sorts of things they don't need at all! Nightlife is also a temptation – discos, pubs and pricey restaurants have been the downfall of many budget travellers.

Tipping

The good news is that historically the Chinese never had the habit of tipping. The bad news is that Westerners have introduced this vulgar custom to Hong Kong. Feel no obligation to tip taxi drivers (they make plenty as it is), but it's almost mandatory to tip hotel porters (bellhops) at least HK$10. If you make use of the porters at the airport, HK$2 per suitcase is normally expected.

Fancy hotels and restaurants stick you with a mandatory 10% service charge which is supposedly your tip. Nevertheless, many waiters, waitresses and chambermaids expect more, especially from free-spending tourists. It is said that Japanese tourists are the best tippers, Westerners the worst. Let your conscience be your guide. If you think the service was great, you might want to leave them something. Otherwise don't bother – there's no need to reward rotten service.

Bargaining

Bargaining is expected in Hong Kong's tourist districts, but less so elsewhere. Sadly, some people (both Chinese and foreigners) turn it into a ruthless contest of 'in your face' East-West rivalry. Some tourists operate on the theory that you can always get the goods for half the price originally quoted. My philosophy is that if you can bargain something down to half price, then you shouldn't buy in that shop anyway because they were trying to rip you off in the first place. If they're that crooked (and many are, particularly in the Tsimshatsui tourist ghetto), they will probably find other ways to cheat you, like selling electronics with missing components, or a secondhand camera instead of a new one. In an honest shop, you shouldn't be able to bargain more than a 10% discount, if they'll bargain at all.

Price tags should be displayed on all goods. If they aren't, you've undoubtedly entered one of those business establishments with 'flexible' (read rip-off) prices. For more details, see the Things to Buy section in this chapter, and the Things to Buy sections for Kowloon and Hong Kong Island.

WHEN TO GO

Anytime is OK, but summer is the peak season, which means higher airfares and sometimes a shortage of hotel rooms. This is not to mention the hot and humid weather. The Chinese New Year is also a crunch time, and ditto for Christmas and Easter. The ideal time is autumn, when the weather is at it's best and tourists relatively scarce.

WHAT TO BRING

As little as possible. Many travellers try to bring everything *and* the kitchen sink. Keep in mind that you can and will buy things in Hong Kong and elsewhere, so don't burden yourself with a lot of unnecessary junk.

That advice having been given, there are some things you will want to bring from home. But the first thing to consider is what kind of bag you will use to carry all your goods.

Backpacks are the easiest type of bag to carry and a frameless or internal-frame pack is the easiest to manage on buses and trains. Packs that close with a zipper can usually be secured with a padlock. Of course, any pack can be slit open with a razor blade, but a padlock will usually prevent pilfering by hotel staff and baggage handlers at airports.

A daypack can be handy. Leave your main luggage at the hotel or left-luggage room in the railway stations. A beltpack is OK for maps, extra film and other miscellanea, but don't use it for valuables such as your travellers' cheques and passport, as it's an easy target for pickpockets.

If you don't want to use a backpack, a shoulder bag is much easier to carry than a suitcase. Some cleverly designed shoulder bags can also double as backpacks by rearranging a few straps. Forget suitcases.

Inside? Lightweight and compact are two words that should be etched in your mind when you're deciding what to bring. Saw the handle off your toothbrush if you have to – anything to keep the weight down! You only need two sets of clothes – one to wear and one to wash. You will, no doubt, be buying clothes along the way – you can find some real bargains in Hong Kong, Macau and China. However, don't believe sizes – 'large' in Asia is often equivalent to 'medium' in the West. Asian clothing manufacturers would be wise to visit a Western tourist hotel to see what 'large' really means.

Nylon running or sports shoes are best – comfortable, washable and lightweight. If you're going to be in cold weather, buy them oversized and wear with heavy wool socks – it's better than carrying a pair of boots. A pair of thongs are useful footwear for indoors and shower rooms.

A Swiss army knife (even if not made in Switzerland) comes in handy, but you don't need one with 27 separate functions. Basically, you need one small sharp blade, a can opener and bottle opener – a built-in magnifying glass or backscratcher isn't necessary.

The secret of successful packing is plastic bags or nylon 'stuff bags' – they keep things not only separate and clean but also dry.

The following is a checklist of things you might consider packing, but don't feel obligated to pack everything on this list – you can buy them in Hong Kong:

Address book, alarm clock, air ticket, birth control and any special medications you may use, camera & accessories, comb, compass, cup, daypack, dental floss, deodorant, electric immersion coil (for making hot water), laxative, leakproof water bottle, Lomotil, long pants, long shirt, money, money belt, mosquito repellent, nail clipper, namecards, nylon jacket, overcoat, Panadol (Tylenol), passport, raincoat for backpack, rainsuit or poncho, razor and blades, sewing kit, shampoo, shaving cream, short pants, socks, spoon, sunglasses, sunhat, sunscreen (UV lotion), sweater, Swiss army knife, tampons, thongs, toilet paper, toothbrush & toothpaste, torch (flashlight with batteries), T-shirt, tweezers, underwear, visa photos and vitamins.

If you're planning on working or studying abroad, it could be helpful to have copies of transcripts, diplomas, letters of reference and other professional qualifications.

A final thought: airlines do lose bags from time to time – you've got much better chance of it not being yours if it is tagged with your name and address *inside* the bag as well as outside. Other tags can always fall off or be removed.

TOURIST OFFICES
Local Tourist Offices

The enterprising Hong Kong Tourist Association (HKTA) is definitely worth a visit. They're efficient and helpful and have reams of printed information, free or fairly cheap.

You can call the HKTA hotline (☎ 8017177) from 8 am to 6 pm from Monday to Friday, or from 9 am to 5 pm on weekends and holidays. For shopping advice and inquiries on HKTA members, there's a different phone (☎ 8017278) staffed from 9 am to 5 pm Monday to Friday, and 9 am to 12.45 pm on Saturday (closed Sundays and holidays).

If you have access to a fax, you can take advantage of the HKTA's almost unique fax information service. The data available includes HKTA member hotels, restaurants, places to shop and so on. To do this, if your fax machine has a handset, pick it up first and dial (☎ 1771128); if the machine has no handset, set it to polling mode before dialling. After you connect you'll receive a list of available topics and the appropriate fax numbers to call to receive the data. You can call this service from abroad and there is no additional charge beyond what you pay for an international phone connection. If calling from within Hong Kong, the local phone company tacks on a charge of HK$2 per minute between 8 am and 9 pm, reduced to HK$1 from 9 pm to 8 am.

The HKTA office at Kai Tak Airport operates a hotel booking service. They don't deal with the real cheapies but they will probably find you a room at a reasonable mid-range hotel. If you arrive very late in the evening, this might be the only option to avoid hauling heavy bags around the streets, especially as many of the smaller places don't open their doors after midnight. You'll find HKTA offices at:

Star Ferry Terminal, Tsimshatsui, Kowloon. Open 8 am to 6 pm Monday through Friday, and from 9 am to 5 pm weekends and holidays.
Shop 8, Basement, Jardine House, 1 Connaught Place, Central. Open 9 am to 6 pm weekdays, and 9 am to 1 pm on Saturdays. Closed on Sundays and holidays.
Buffer Hall, Kai Tak Airport, Kowloon. Open 8 am to 10.30 pm daily. Information is provided for arriving passengers only.
Head Office, 35th floor, Jardine House, 1 Connaught Place, Central (☎ 8017111). This is a business office – not for normal tourist inquiries.

Overseas Reps
Australia
Level 5, 55 Harrington St, The Rocks, Sydney (☎ (02) 2512855, outside Sydney (008) 251071)

Canada
347 Bay St, Suite 909, Toronto, Ontario M5H 2R7 (☎ (416) 3662389)
France
Escalier C, 8ème étage, 53 Rue Francois 1er, 75008, Paris (☎ (01) 47203954)
Germany
Weisenau 1, 60323 Frankfurt am Main (☎ (069) 722841)
Italy
c/o Sergat Italia Srl, Casella Postale 620, 00100 Roma Centro (☎ (06) 68801336)
Japan
4th floor, Toho Twin Tower Building, 1-5-2 Yurakucho, Chiyoda-ku, Tokyo 100 (☎ (03) 35030735)
8th floor, Osaka Saitama Building, 3-5-13 Awaji-machi, Chuo-ku, Osaka 541 (☎ (06) 2299240)
Korea
c/o HK PR, Suite 1204, Sungji Building, 538 Dowha-Dong, Mapo-gu, Seoul (☎ (02) 7065818)
New Zealand
PO Box 2120, Auckland (☎ (09) 5203316)
South Africa
c/o Development Promotions Pty Ltd, PO Box 9874, Johannesburg 2000 (☎ (011) 3394865)
Singapore
13th floor, 13-08 Ocean Building, 10 Collyer Quay, Singapore 0104 (☎ 5323668)
Taiwan
7th floor, 18 Chang'an E Rd, Section 1, Taipei (☎ (02) 5812967)
Hong Kong Information Service (☎ (02) 5816061)
Spain
c/o Sergat Espana SL, Pau Casals 4, 08021 Barcelona (☎ (3) 141794)
UK
5th floor, 125 Pall Mall, London, SW1Y 5EA (☎ (071) 9304775)
USA
333 North Michigan Ave, Suite 2400, Chicago, IL 60601-3966 (☎ (312) 7823872)
5th floor, 590 Fifth Ave, New York, NY 10036-4706 (☎ (212) 8695008)
10940 Wilshire Blvd, Suite 1220, Los Angeles, CA 90024 (☎ (213) 2084582)

USEFUL ORGANISATIONS
The Hong Kong Information Services Department (☎ 8428777) is on the ground, 1st, 4th, 5th and 6th floors of Beaconsfield House, 4 Queen's Rd, Central. They can answer specific questions or direct you to other government agencies that can handle your inquiry. It's best to try the HKTA before

resorting to the Information Services Department.

Since the likelihood of getting ripped off by shopkeepers is high, it's good to know about the Hong Kong Consumer Council (☎ 7363322). The main office is in China Hong Kong City, Canton Rd, Tsimshatsui, Kowloon. It has a complaints and advice hot line (☎ 7363636) and an Advice Centre (☎ 5411422) at 38 Pier Rd, Central.

If you get genuinely ripped off by robbers, you can obtain a loss report for insurance purposes at the Central Police Station, 10 Hollywood Rd (at Pottinger St) in Central. There are always English-speaking staff here.

The Royal Asiatic Society (☎ 5510300), GPO Box 3864, is dedicated to helping its members or visitors learn more about the history and culture of Hong Kong. The RAS organises lectures and field trips, operates a lending library and puts out publications of its own. The RAS was founded in London in 1823 and has branches in several Asian countries.

St John's Cathedral Counselling Service (☎ 5257202) provides help to all those in need.

If you're interested in doing business in Hong Kong, you might want to consult the Hong Kong Chamber of Commerce (☎ 5237177), 902 Swire House, 9-25 Chater Rd, Central. Even more to the point is the Hong Kong Trade Development Council (☎ 5844333), 38th floor, Office Tower Convention Plaza, 1 Harbour Rd, Wanchai.

Know any dishonest government officials? Call the Report Centre of the Independent Commission Against Corruption (☎ 5266366).

Other organisations which could prove helpful include the American Chamber of Commerce (☎ 5260165), 1030 Swire House, Central, and the British Council (☎ 8795138), Ground floor, Easey Commercial Building, 255 Hennessy Rd, Wanchai.

BUSINESS HOURS & HOLIDAYS

Office hours are Monday through Friday from 9 am to 5 pm, and on Saturday from 9 am to noon. Lunch hour is from 1 pm to 2 pm and many offices simply shut down and lock the door at this time. Banks are open Monday through Friday from 9 am to 4.30 pm and do not close for lunch – on Saturday they are open from 9 am to 12.30 pm.

Stores and restaurants that cater to the tourist trade keep longer hours, but almost nothing opens before 9 am. Even tourist-related businesses shut down by 9 or 10 pm, and many will close for major holidays, especially Chinese New Year.

Western and Chinese culture combine to create an interesting mix of holidays. Trying to determine the exact date of each holiday is a bit tricky since there are two calendars in use in Hong Kong – the Gregorian solar calendar and the Chinese lunar calendar. The two calendars do not correspond exactly because a lunar month is 29 or 30 days (the average lunar month is 29.5 days while the solar average is 30.5 days). To keep the two calendars from becoming totally out of harmony, an extra month is added to the lunar calendar once every 30 months. The result is that the Lunar New Year, the most important Chinese holiday, can fall anywhere between 21 January and 28 February on the Gregorian calendar.

Many of the Chinese festivals go back hundreds, perhaps thousands of years, their true origins often lost in the mists of time. The reasons for each festival vary and you will generally find there are a couple of tales to choose from. The HKTA's free leaflet, *Chinese Festivals & Special Events*, will tell you the exact dates that festivals are celebrated that year. Some of the more important holidays are as follows:

New Year – the first weekday in January is a public holiday.

Easter – in Hong Kong, Easter is a three-day public holiday starting from Good Friday and running through Easter Sunday. Although many Westerners don't realise it, the date of Easter is fixed by the lunar calendar, falling somewhere in March or April.

Queen's Birthday – this public holiday is normally held on a Saturday in June. The Monday after is also a public holiday.

Liberation Day – celebrated on the last Monday in August, this public holiday commemorates the liberation of Hong Kong from Japan after WW II. The preceding Saturday is also a public holiday.

Christmas & Boxing Day – Christmas (25 December) and the day after (Boxing Day) are, of course, public holidays.

The dates of important Lunar holidays and festivals from 1995 to 2000 include:

Lunar New Year – the 1st day of the first moon, this holiday falls on the following dates: 31 January 1995; 19 February 1996; 7 February 1997; 28 January 1998; 16 February 1999; 5 February 2000.

Lantern Festival – the 15th day of the first moon, this holiday falls on the following dates: 14 February 1995; 4 March 1996; 21 February 1997; 11 February 1998; 2 March 1999; 19 February 2000.

Tin Hau Festival – the 23rd day of the third moon, this holiday falls on the following dates: 22 April 1995; 10 May 1996; 29 April 1997; 19 April 1998; 8 May 1999; 27 April 2000.

Birthday of Lord Buddha – the 8th day of the fourth moon, this holiday falls on the following dates: 7 May 1995; 24 May 1996; 14 May 1997; 3 May 1998; 22 May 1999; 11 May 2000.

Dragon Boat Festival – the 5th day of the fifth moon, this holiday falls on the following dates: 2 June 1995; 20 June 1996; 9 June 1997; 28 June 1998; 18 June 1999; 6 June 2000.

Mid-Autumn Festival – the 15th day of the eighth moon, this holiday falls on the following dates: 9 September 1995; 27 September 1996; 16 September 1997; 5 October 1998; 24 September 1999; 12 September 2000.

CULTURAL EVENTS

There are literally hundreds of cultural events throughout the year, but the exact dates vary. The HKTA publishes a complete schedule every month. If you want to time your visit to Hong Kong to coincide with a particular event, it would be wise to contact the HKTA beforehand. A brief rundown of important annual events includes:

HK Arts Festival – an assortment of exhibitions and shows usually held in January.

Orientation Competition – sponsored by the Urban Council, this event is usually staged in January in Tai Tam Country Park.

HK Festival Fringe – the Fringe Club supports upcoming artists and performers from Hong Kong and elsewhere. This three-week festival occurs from late January to February.

HK Golf Open – this is held at the Royal Hong Kong Golf Club, usually in February.

HK International Marathon – organised by the Hong Kong Amateur Athletic Association, this major event is held in Shatin, usually in March.

HK Food Festival – sponsored by the HKTA and usually held in March.

HK International Film Festival – organised by the Urban Council, this event usually occurs in March or April.

HK International Handball Invitation Tournament – organised by the Hong Kong Amateur Handball Association, this event is in March or April.

Sotheby's Auction – this usually occurs in April.

International Dragon Boat Festival – usually falling in June, the international festival is usually held the week after the Chinese dragon boat races.

Davis Cup – this tennis tournament is usually held in July.

International Arts Carnival – this unusual summer festival promotes performances by childrens' groups. The carnival usually falls in July or August.

Asian Regatta – organised by the Hong Kong Yachting Association, this event usually occurs in October.

Festival of Asian Arts – this is one of Asia's major international events, attracting performers from Australia as well as nearby countries. This festival usually occurs in October or November.

Chinese (Lunar) New Year

The first, second and third day of the Lunar New Year are public holidays. Almost everything closes but you won't starve in the tourist areas. The first day of the first moon usually falls at the end of January or the beginning of February.

The festival is a family one, with little for the visitor to see except a fireworks display on New Year's Eve. To start the New Year properly can determine ones fortune for the entire year. Therefore, houses are cleaned, debts paid off and feuds, no matter how bitter, are ended – even if it's only for the day. Pictures of gods are pasted around the front doors of houses to scare off bad spirits, along with messages of welcome on red paper to encourage the good ones.

By tradition, everyone asks for double wages. The garbage collector, the milkman and so on get *lai see* (lucky money) in red envelopes as tips, which are good reasons for the traditional Chinese New Year greeting *kung hey fat choi* – literally 'good wishes, good fortune'.

It costs double to get your hair cut in the week leading up to the New Year. Even cinemas put their prices up.

It's not the time to go to China, as hordes of Hong Kongers cram the trains and every other form of transport to get there.

It is worth seeing the huge flower fairs where, on the night before New Year's Day, the Chinese buy lucky peach blossoms, cumquat trees and narcissi from the hundreds of flower sellers. Victoria Park in Causeway Bay, Hong Kong Island, is the place to go for this, although it's jam-packed. Other than that, there isn't much else to see at Chinese New Year. You might catch a lion dance in a street, but if not, you will certainly see one specially laid on in the top tourist hotels.

Lantern Festival

Also known by its Chinese name *Yuen Siu*, this is not a public holiday but is more interesting than the Lunar New Year. At the end of the Chinese New Year celebrations, customarily the 15th day of the first moon (middle or end of February), lanterns in traditional designs are lit in homes, restaurants and temples. Out in the residential areas, you'll see people carrying lanterns through the streets. The Lantern Festival is also a holiday for lovers.

Kuanyin's Birthday

While there is no festival as such, modest ceremonies are held at the various temples around Hong Kong dedicated to Kuanyin (Kwun Yum), the Goddess of Mercy. Kuanyin's birthday is the 19th day of the second moon, and this holiday falls on the following dates: 19 March 1995; 6 April 1996; 27 March 1997; 17 March 1998; 5 April 1999; and 24 March 2000.

Ching Ming

Celebrated at the beginning of the third moon, usually in April, Ching Ming is very much a family affair. It is a time for visiting graves, traditionally to call up ancestors to ask if they are satisfied with their descendants. Graves are cleaned and food and wine left for the spirits, while incense and paper money are burned for the dead. Some people follow the custom of pasting long strips of red and white paper to the graves to indicate that the rituals have been performed. The festival is thought to have its origins during the Han period about 2000 years ago, when ancestors' tombs were swept, washed and repaired.

Ching Ming is a public holiday and is not a particularly good time to visit Hong Kong, though not nearly so bad as the Chinese New Year. Many people take a three or four-day holiday. Banks and many other businesses close for Ching Ming, public transport is extremely crowded and the border crossing into China turns host to a near riot.

Tin Hau Festival

While not a public holiday, this is one of Hong Kong's most colourful occasions. The Taoist festival is traditionally held on the 23rd day of the third moon, usually in May, and about three weeks after Ching Ming. Tin Hau, patroness of fishing people, is one of the colony's most popular goddesses.

Junks on the water are decorated with flags and sail in long rows to Tin Hau's temples around the colony to pray for clear skies and good catches. Often her image is taken from the temple and paraded through the streets. Shrines from the junks are carried to the shore to be blessed by Taoist priests.

The best place to see the festival and the fortune telling, lion dances and Chinese opera that follow is at the site of Tin Hau's best-known temple, the Tai Miu Temple in Joss House Bay. It's not accessible by road and is not on the normal ferry route but at festival time the ferry company puts on excursion trips, which are usually packed.

Another main Tin Hau temple is at Sok Kwu Wan on Lamma Island. The Tin Hau temple at Stanley on the south coast of Hong Kong Island was built before the mid-18th century and is the oldest building standing in Hong Kong.

Cheung Chau Bun Festival

The Bun Festival of Tai Chiu is held in May on Cheung Chau Island, traditionally on the sixth day of the fourth moon. Precise dates are decided by village elders on the island about three weeks before it starts. A Taoist festival, it is one of the festival calendar highlights, and there are three or four days of religious observances.

While not a public holiday, it is definitely worth getting to Cheung Chau for. Festival information is in the Outlying Islands chapter.

Birthday of Lord Buddha

Also referred to as the Bathing of Lord Buddha, this festival is celebrated on the eighth day of the fourth moon, usually in late May. It's not a public holiday and, like most Buddhist festivals, it's rather more sedate than Taoist holidays.

The Buddha's statue is taken from monasteries and temples and ceremoniously bathed in water scented with sandalwood, ambergris (a waxy substance secreted from the intestine of a sperm whale and often found floating in the sea), garu wood, turmeric and aloes (a drug used for clearing the bowels, made from the fleshy, spiny-toothed leaves of the aloe tree). Afterwards the water is drunk by the faithful, who believe it has great curative powers.

While Lantau Island is the best place to observe this event because of its many Buddhist monasteries, most people visit only Po Lin, the largest and best known of the monasteries. Extra ferries operate for the crowds.

The New Territories has several good Buddhist temples worth visiting at this time, such as the Temple of Ten Thousand Buddhas in Shatin or the Miu Fat Monastery at Lam Tei.

Dragon Boat Festival

A main public holiday, *Tuen Ng* – Double Fifth (fifth day, fifth moon) or the Dragon Boat Festival – is normally held in June. It's a lot of fun despite the fact that it commemorates the sad tale of Chu Yuan.

Chu Yuan was a 3rd-century BC poet-statesman who hurled himself into the Mi Lo River in Hunan Province to protest against the corrupt government. The people who lived on the banks of the river raced to the scene in their boats in an attempt to save him but were too late. Not unmindful of his sacrifice, the people later threw dumplings into the water to keep the hungry fish away from his body.

Traditional rice dumplings are still eaten in memory of the event and dragon boat races are held in Hong Kong, Kowloon and the Outlying Islands. See the races at Shaukeiwan, Aberdeen, Yaumatei, Tai Po and Stanley, and on Lantau and Cheung Chau Islands. The boats are rowed by teams from Hong Kong's sports and social clubs. International dragon boat races are held at Yaumatei.

Birthday of Lu Pan, Master Builder

Legends say that Lu Pan was a real person, born around 507 BC and later deified. A master architect, magician, engineer, inventor and designer, Lu Pan is worshipped by anyone connected with the building trade. Ceremonies sponsored by the Builders' Guilds are held at Lu Pan Temple in Kennedy Town, Hong Kong Island. The celebration occurs around mid to late-July. It's a minor holiday.

Maidens' Festival
This is a minor holiday and you might not even notice anything special taking place. Also known as the Seven Sisters Festival, this celebration for girls and young lovers is held on the seventh day of the seventh moon (about mid-August).

The festival has its origins in an ancient Chinese story about two celestial lovers, Chien Niu the cowherd and Chih Nu the spinner and weaver. One version says that they became so engrossed in each other that they forgot their work. As a punishment for this, the Queen of Heaven decided that they should be separated from each other by being placed on either side of a river which she cut through the heavens with her hairpin. The King of Heaven took pity on the lovers and said they could meet once a year, but provided no bridge across the river, so magpies (regarded as birds of good omen) flocked together, spread their wings and formed a bridge so the two lovers could be reunited.

At midnight on the day of this festival prayers are offered by unmarried girls and young men to Chien Niu and Chih Nu. Prayers are also directed to Chih Nu's six sisters who appear in another version of the story. The main offerings made to the seven sisters are cosmetics and flowers.

Ghost Month
On the first day of the seventh moon (late August or early September), the gates of hell are opened and 'hungry ghosts' are free for two weeks to walk the earth. Hungry ghosts are the spirits of those who were unloved, abandoned or forgotten by the family, or suffered a violent death. On the 14th day, called the Yue Lan Festival, hungry ghosts receive offerings of food from the living before returning down below.

Paper cars, paper houses and paper money are burnt, and once this occurs these goodies become the property of the ghosts.

People whose relatives suffered a violent death are particularly concerned to placate the spirits. Many people will not swim, travel, get married, move house or indulge in other risky activities during this time.

The ghost month is an excellent time to visit Taoist temples in Hong Kong, as these are usually packed with worshippers burning incense and making offerings. There are also lots of Cantonese opera performances – presumably to give the ghosts one good night out before they go back down below for another year. This is not a public holiday, so there aren't any problems with crowded buses, trains and hotels.

Mid-Autumn (Moon) Festival
The Mid-Autumn Festival is held in September, on the 15th night of the eighth moon. Because the festival begins at night, the day after is a public holiday.

Although the observance of the moon is thought to date back to much earlier times, today the festival recalls an uprising against the Mongols in the 14th century when plans for the revolution were passed around in cakes.

Moon cakes are still eaten and there are many varieties – all delicious. The various fillings include coconut, dates, nuts, lotus, sesame seeds and sometimes an egg.

Everyone heads for the hilltops, where they light special lanterns with candles inside and watch the moon rise. The Peak Tram is crammed, as is all transport to the New Territories, where hillsides abound. For young couples, it's a romantic holiday – a time to be together and watch the moon.

Birthday of Confucius
Confucius' birthday is in early October and religious observances are held by the Confucian Society in the Confucius Temple at Causeway Bay. It's a minor holiday that usually passes unnoticed by most Hong Kongers.

Cheung Yeung Festival
While not an especially interesting occasion, the Cheung Yeung Festival is a public holiday.

The story goes that back in the Eastern Han Dynasty (in the first two centuries AD), an old soothsayer advised a man to take his family away to a high place for 24 hours to avoid disaster. When the man returned to his village he found every living thing had been destroyed and only he and his family had survived.

Many people head for the high spots again to remember the old man's advice. The Cheung Yeung Festival is held in mid to late October.

POST & TELECOMMUNICATIONS
Postal Rates
Local Mail Rates for Hong Kong mail are as follows:

Weight Not Over	Letters & Postcards	Printed Matter
30 g	HK$1.00	HK$0.90
50 g	HK$1.70	HK$1.30
100 g	HK$2.40	HK$1.90
250 g	HK$3.50	HK$2.80
500 g	HK$7.10	HK$5.70
1 kg	HK$15.00	HK$9.00
2 kg	HK$25.00	

International Airmail The Hong Kong postal service divides the world into two distinct zones. Zone 1 is China, Japan, Taiwan, South Korea, South-East Asia, Indonesia and India. The rates are as follows:

Letters & Postcards	Zone 1	Zone 2
first 10 g	HK$1.90	HK$2.40
each additional 10 g	HK$1.00	HK$1.10
Aerogrammes	HK$1.90	HK$1.90
Printed Matter		
first 10 g	HK$1.30	HK$1.80
each additional 10 g	HK$0.60	HK$0.80

Speedpost The rates for international express mail service vary enormously according to destination country but there is little relation to actual distance. For example, a 250 g Speedpost letter to Australia costs HK$85 but to China it's HK$90 and to Singapore HK$65! The main factors seem to be the availability of air transport and efficiency of mail handling at the destination country. Every post office has a schedule of fees and timetable for Speedpost delivery available on request.

International Surface Mail The postal service also divides the world in two parts, but not the same zones as for airmail. Area 1 is China, Macau and Taiwan. Area 2 is all other countries. The rates for Area 2 are as follows:

Weight Not Over	Letters & Postcards	Printed Matter	Small Packet
30 g	HK$2.00	HK$1.80	HK$4.20
50 g	HK$3.60	HK$3.20	HK$4.20
100 g	HK$4.80	HK$4.20	HK$4.20
250 g	HK$9.50	HK$8.60	HK$8.60
500 g	HK$18.00	HK$16.00	HK$16.00
1 kg	HK$32.00	HK$29.00	HK$29.00
2 kg	HK$52.00	HK$42.00	HK$42.00

Sending Mail

On the Hong Kong Island side, the General Post Office (GPO) is on your right as you alight the Star Ferry. On the Kowloon side, one of the most convenient post offices is at 10 Middle Rd, east of the Ambassador Hotel and Nathan Rd, Tsimshatsui (this one has a stamp vending machine outside, a big convenience after hours). Another good post office (and less crowded) is in the basement of the Albion Plaza, 2-6 Granville Rd, just off Nathan Rd, Tsimshatsui. All post offices are open Monday to Saturday from 8 am to 6 pm, and are closed on Sunday and public holidays.

Allow five days for delivery of letters, postcards and aerogrammes to the UK and the USA. Speedpost reduces delivery time by about half. Sea mail is slow, so allow from six to 10 weeks for delivery to the UK and the USA.

Receiving Mail

There are poste-restante services at the GPO and other large post offices. Mail will be held for two months. Simply address an envelope c/o Poste Restante, GPO Hong Kong, and it will go to the Hong Kong Island side. If you want letters to go to the Kowloon side, they should be addressed to Poste Restante, 10 Middle Rd, Tsimshatsui, Kowloon.

Private Carriers Rapid document and small parcel service (32-kg limit) is offered by express courier companies. Well-known competitors in this market include DHL (☎ 7658111), Federal Express (☎ 7303333) and TNT Express (☎ 3895279). All three companies have numerous pickup points, so call for the one nearest you.

For larger items, you need the services of a freight forwarder. Foremost in this market is United Parcel Service (UPS), Rooms 602-610, North Tower, Harbour City, World Finance Centre, Tsimshatsui. UPS also offers small parcel courier service, so ring them (☎ 7353535) for pick-up.

Telephone

From 2 January 1995, a '2' will be added to the beginning of all existing seven-digit telephone numbers. This applies to all telephone numbers listed in this book.

Hongkong Telecom, a joint-venture more than 50% owned by Britain's Cable & Wireless, has until recently enjoyed a total monopoly over all phone service (but not pagers). Since 1994 three other companies have been permitted into the local market, but the lucrative long-distance monopoly will continue until the year 2006. Monopolies usually charge high rates for poor service, but Hongkong Telecom is something of an exception – service is good and long-distance rates are the lowest in Asia.

All calls made within Hong Kong are local calls and therefore free, except for public pay phones which cost HK$1 per local call with no extra charges for chatting a long time. The pay phones normally accept HK$2 coins but do *not* give change, though you can make a second call by pressing the 'FC' (Follow-on Call) button before hanging up.

There are free public phones in the arrival area of the airport. You can find public pay phones in the airport, ferry terminals, post offices and hotel lobbies. On the street they are relatively rare, though perhaps the new competition will cause an increase.

IDD Calls If you want to phone overseas, it's cheapest to use an IDD (International Direct Dialling) telephone. You can place an IDD call from most phone boxes, but you'll need a stack of HK$5 coins handy if your call is going to be anything but very brief. An alternative is to buy a 'Phonecard', which comes in denominations of HK$50, HK$100 or HK$250. You can find Phonecards in shops, at all 7-Eleven stores, on the street or at a Hongkong Telecom office. 'Duet' phones accept both coins and Phonecards.

To make an IDD call from Hong Kong, first dial 001, then the country code, area code and number. If the area code begins with a zero, you must omit that zero when dialling from abroad. So to call Melbourne (area code 03) in Australia (country code 61), you would dial 001-61-3-XXXXXXX. If you're using someone else's phone and you want to know how much is the price of the call, dial 003 instead of 001 and the operator will call back to report the cost.

At the time of writing, it was discovered significant changes to UK area codes will take place on Sunday, 16 April 1995. On this date *all* UK area code numbers change by the addition of the digit 1 following the lead 0. For example, the code for Manchester changes from 061 to 0161. And Leeds, Sheffield, Nottingham, Leicester and Bristol have been given new codes and an extra digit will be inserted in front of the existing telephone number. The UK will also fall into line with the Uniform European Access Code at the same time – all international calls will be prefixed by 00 instead of the current 010. If you live in the UK and want to find out more about the code changes, you can call the free helpline on ☎ 0800 010101.

If you go to Hongkong Telecom, there are three options for overseas phone calls: operator-connected calls, paid in advance with a minimum of three minutes; international direct dialling (IDD) which you dial yourself after paying a deposit – the unused portion of your deposit is refunded; and reverse charges, which requires a small deposit refundable if the charge is accepted or if the call doesn't get through. The cost of long-distance calls is listed in the Business Telephone Directory. You can place international calls at the following Hongkong Telecom offices (listed more-or-less in order of convenience for travellers):

Hermes House, 10 Middle Rd, Tsimshatsui, Kowloon. Open 24 hours a day, including public holidays.
Unit 102A, One Exchange Square, Central, open 24 hours daily including holidays.
Unit D-37, Passenger Terminal Building, Kai Tak Airport, Kowloon. Open 8 am to 11 pm daily, including public holidays.
Ground floor, 761 Nathan Rd, Mongkok, Kowloon. Open 8 am to 8 pm Monday to Saturday, closed Sundays and holidays.
3 Hennessy Rd, Wanchai, Hong Kong Island. Open 9 am to 6 pm Monday to Friday, 9 am to 4 pm Saturdays, closed Sundays and holidays.
3 Gloucester Rd, Wanchai. Open 8 am to 9 pm Mondays to Friday, 8 am to 3 pm Saturdays, closed Sundays and holidays.

Ground floor, 143 Castle Peak Rd, Tsuen Wan, New Territories. Open 9 am to 6 pm Monday to Friday, 9 am to 3 pm Saturdays, closed Sundays and holidays.
Shop 12, 1st floor, Wo Che Commercial Complex, Shatin, New Territories. Open 10 am to 5 pm Monday to Friday, 9 am to 3 pm Saturdays, closed Sundays and holidays.

Some useful phone numbers and prefixes include the following:

Ambulance, Fire, Police, Emergency	☎ 999
Calls to China	☎ 012
Credit Card Billing	☎ 011
Crime Report, Police Business	☎ 5277177
Directory Assistance	☎ 1081
Hong Kong's Country Code	☎ 852
IDD Prefix	☎ 001
International Dialling Assistance	☎ 013
Reverse Billing	☎ 010
Taxi Complaints	☎ 5277177
Time & Weather	☎ 18501

If you don't have the cash on hand, an easy way to make collect calls or bill to a credit card is to use a service called Home Direct. This service is not offered to every country. One way to make a Home Direct call is to use a special telephone on which you simply push a button and you are immediately connected to an operator in that country – these special phones are found in airports and a few major hotels. You can also make a Home Direct call on an ordinary telephone by dialling one of the following numbers:

Australia	☎ (800) 0061
Canada	☎ (800) 1100
France	☎ (800) 0033
Germany	☎ (800) 0049
Hawaii	☎ (800) 1188
Indonesia	☎ (800) 0062
Italy	☎ (800) 0039
Japan (IDC)	☎ (800) 0181
(KDD)	☎ (800) 0081
Macau	☎ (800) 0853
Malaysia	☎ (800) 0060
Netherlands	☎ (800) 0031
New Zealand	☎ (800) 0064
Norway	☎ (800) 0047
Portugal	☎ (800) 0351
Singapore	☎ (800) 0065
South Korea	☎ (800) 0082
Spain	☎ (800) 0034

Sweden	☎ (800) 0046
Taiwan	☎ (800) 0886
Thailand	☎ (800) 0066
UK	☎ (800) 0090
USA (AT&T)	☎ (800) 1111
(MCI)	☎ (800) 1121
(Sprint)	☎ (800) 1877

Phone Directories There are more phone directories than you would expect! Currently, there are four types: the Yellow Pages Buying Guide (three volumes, all bilingual); the Yellow Pages Commercial/Industrial Guide (one volume, English only); the Business Telephone Directory (one volume each in English and Chinese); and Residential Directories (three volumes each in English and Chinese).

If you're staying any length of time in the colony, you should at least pick up the Business Telephone Directory and the Yellow Pages Buying Guide. If you're looking for a job in a particular line of work, you might want to get the Yellow Pages Commercial/Industrial Guide since it would list such things as modelling or advertising agencies. These are available from Telecom CSL shops.

Cellular Phones & Pagers Hong Kong boasts the world's highest per capita usage of cellular phones and pagers. Even if you don't take up residence, it might be worth knowing that you can rent this equipment too. And to answer an often asked question; yes, cellular phones and pagers *do* work inside the MTR.

Cellular phones can be rented from Rentel (☎ 8286600), 5th floor, Allied Kajima Building, 138 Gloucester Rd, Wanchai. Hongkong Telecom does not rent cellular phones, but will happily sell you one.

Hanging on the Telephone

It's hard to spend long in Hong Kong without noticing how much the telephone is an essential part of city life. Traffic jams aren't simply the result of cars – they're also caused by all the mobile phone users standing out in the road in search of better reception.

By almost any measuring stick Hong Kong is a world leader in telephone usage. You thought Americans talk a lot on the phone? Per capita usage of phones in the USA may be four times as much as Japan but it's nothing compared to Hong Kong where phones are used an incredible five times as much as in the States.

Hong Kong has four competing cellular phone companies and one in every six Hong Kongers has a pager. They also have access to the new CT2 technology which is a cheaper form of mobile phone. These phones can make but not receive calls. Unsurprisingly, Hong Kong is the world leader.

Why all the talking? Partly it's due to the intense competition for business in Hong Kong. And partly it's due to the free-wheeling business environment with so many competing phone companies. It could also be the prospect of expanding phone business into China. Or the large population reducing the number of base stations required for cellular operation. But the main reason is the simple fact that Hong Kongers love to talk. ■

Pagers can be rented from a wide variety of sources. Hongkong Telecom charges a HK$10 per month rental fee plus a usage fee of HK$230 for the service. The bad part is that there is a HK$500 deposit which is *not* refundable unless you use the pager for more than six months.

Some other companies rent and sell pagers at slightly lower prices. Look in the Yellow Pages under 'pagers' to find an extensive list. Cheapest of the lot is said to be ABC Communications (☎ 7100333), 40 Waterloo Rd, Kowloon Tong, but there are more convenient branches in the MTR stations at Central and Tsimshatsui. In Mongkok you can contact Star Paging (☎ 7711111), 602 Nathan Rd, or New World Paging (☎ 7816688), 558 Nathan Rd. Hutchison Paging is the largest in the Hong Kong paging market and has service centres in the following locations:

51 Des Voeux Rd, Central; 10 Harcourt Rd, Central; 133 Thomson Rd, Wanchai; 294 Hennessy Rd, Wanchai; 480 Hennessy Rd, Wanchai; 7 Paterson St, Causeway Bay; Peninsula Centre, Tsimshatsui East; 16 Carnarvon Rd, Tsimshatsui

Telecom CSL Shops This is where you go to apply for service, pay bills, rent pagers, purchase equipment and phone directories. The list of these shops is too extensive to reproduce here, but some of the major ones are as follows:

Shop 60, Lower ground floor, Silvercord Shopping Centre, 30 Canton Rd, Tsimshatsui; 221 Nathan Rd, Yaumatei; 501 Nathan Rd, Yaumatei; Shop 116, Prince's Building, Chater Rd & Ice House St, Central; Shop B, Ground floor, International Building, 141 Des Voeux Rd, Central; 46 Hennessy Rd, Wanchai; 66 Percival St, Causeway Bay

Fax, Telex & Telegraph
All your telecommunication needs can be taken care of at Hongkong Telecom. To send a one page fax (A4 size) they charge HK$10 within Hong Kong; HK$30 for South-East Asia; HK$35 to Australia, New Zealand, Canada, USA and UK; and HK$45 to all other countries. For HK$10 per page, you

can also receive a fax here. Be sure the sending party puts your name and your Hong Kong telephone number on the top of the page.

Most hotels and even many youth hostels allow their guests to send and receive faxes. The surcharge for sending is usually 10% above cost, and receiving is normally HK$10 per page.

Hongkong Telecom's fully digital fibre-optic lines ensure good quality transmission within Hong Kong. However, if dialling your own fax for an overseas transmission, you should use the international prefix 002 (for a data line) rather than 001 (for a voice line).

CallFax 1783 Determined to stay at the forefront of fax technology, Hong Kong Telecom has introduced CallFax 1783, a hi-tech version of the Yellow Pages. By dialling a certain code, you can have designated Yellow Pages listings sent directly to a fax machine. Besides catering to those who are too lazy to look things up in the phonebook, the system has the one advantage of always having the most current listings. This service is free. There are three basic steps to using the system:

1) Using a touchtone phone or fax machine with handset (or if no handset, set to polling mode), dial the CallFax gateway number, which is 1783. You will then hear instructions on how to receive your fax.
2) Enter the five-digit CallFax code for the Yellow Pages classification you need. You must look up this number in the printed CallFax index available from the phone company, or in the printed Yellow Pages Fast Find index. If you don't have either of these, the index is also available by fax – dial 1783 followed by CallFax code 20000.
3) If you're using a fax machine, press the 'start' button. If you're using a touchtone telephone, enter your fax number and hang up. Either way, the information you've requested should be sent to your fax machine within minutes.

Telex is old technology and is falling into disuse in the West. However, there are still a number of countries which use it, and you can send or receive telexes at Hongkong

Telecom branch offices. The cost for sending is HK$51 for three minutes, and there is a three minute minimum. Receiving a telex is free, but you must go to Hongkong Telecom House at 3 Hennessy Rd in Wanchai to pick it up.

Electronic Mail

If you're daunted by bits, bytes and keyboards, don't bother reading this section – it's for computer buffs only. Electronic mail (E-mail) offers a number of advantages over fax machines, but you need a computer, modem, a bit of spare cash and enough free time to learn the in-and-outs of telecomputing.

Internet is not an E-mail service as such, but a conglomeration of hundreds (or thousands?) of other information services linked together. The Internet is so vast that no one really knows the size of it. It's different parts belong to various governments, universities and private companies. Since no one really owns it, no one can control it. For this reason, paranoid governments like China prohibit public access to Internet. Through Internet you can access the *China News Digest*, an 'electronic magazine' with uncensored news about China, Hong Kong and Taiwan. The big problem with Internet is that it's cumbersome to use. Compared to other systems available in Hong Kong, it's the cheapest of the lot. To gain access, call Hong Kong Internet & Gateway Services (☎ 5274888; fax 5274848) or send an E-mail message to aaron@hk.net. You can also visit the company at Room 1286, Telecom House, 3 Gloucester Rd, Wanchai. There is a basic setup charge of HK$100, followed by a monthly subscription fee of HK$100 plus a connect-time fee of HK$20 per hour.

The most prestigious of the E-mail and data services is CompuServe, but using it will cost you significantly more than Internet. CompuServe is a private company based in the USA with worldwide representatives, and offers a gateway to Internet. This is the only E-mail service in Hong Kong that has automatic reverse billing, thus tourists can connect without having a local billing

address. If you want to subscribe to CompuServe or need help getting connected, CompuServe's representative in Hong Kong is Hutchison Information Services (☎ 8670102, 8670118; fax 8774523). If you already are a CompuServe subscriber, just connect your modem to a phone line and dial up the Hong Kong data node (☎ 3041332). Connect time from Hong Kong is HK$117 (US$15) per hour in addition to CompuServe's basic monthly charge of HK$62. There are surcharges for special services like stockmarket reports.

Another American-based data communication service is GEnie, owned by General Electric. At HK$4 per minute, connect time is much higher than CompuServe's, but there are no additional surcharges. Hongkong Telecom (☎ 8036888) is GEnie's local representative.

Hongkong Telecom's own home-grown E-mail service is Dialcom (☎ 8036888). It offers such niceties as a telex gateway, local stockmarket reports (for a hefty surcharge) and a China database (also surcharged), but overall I give Dialcom the thumbs down. The chief disadvantage of Dialcom is that there is no Internet gateway, which in effect means it's almost useless as a tool to communicate internationally. The 'Spectrum' software which the company supplies seems designed to keep you on line as long as possible, thus running up your phone bill. And finally, the numerous surcharges add up quickly, making it absurdly expensive for the generally poor service.

If you want to dial direct to other overseas E-mail services, it's probably cheapest to communicate via Datapak, Hongkong Telecom's packet-switching network.

TIME

Hong Kong Standard Time is eight hours ahead of GMT. Hong Kong does not have daylight-saving time.

When it is noon in Hong Kong it is also noon in Singapore, Hong Kong and Perth; 2 pm in Sydney; 8 pm the previous day in Los Angeles; 11 pm the previous day in New York; and 4 am in London.

ELECTRICITY

The standard is 220 V, 50 Hz (cycles per second) AC. Electrical shops in Hong Kong and elsewhere sell handy pocket-sized transformers which will step down the electricity to 110 V, but most mini-transformers are only rated for 50 watts. This is sufficient for an electric razor or laptop computer but *not* for those electric heater coils that some travellers carry to make tea and coffee. If in doubt, most appliances have a wattage rating printed somewhere on the bottom. Overloading a transformer can cause it to melt. Luxury tourist hotels often have razor outlets with multi-fittings to suit different plugs and voltages.

In Hong Kong, the electric outlets are designed to accommodate three round prongs, though some newer buildings are wired with three square pins of the British design. Inexpensive plug adaptors are widely available in Hong Kong supermarkets. Remember that adaptors are *not* transformers. If you ignore this warning and plug a 110 V appliance into a 220 V outlet, it will be sparks and fireworks.

Apart from needing the right voltage, a few electric motors need the right frequency of current to work properly. For example, your 60 Hz clock will run slow on 50 Hz current, but it shouldn't harm the motor.

PLUG DESIGNS IN HONG KONG

OR

LAUNDRY

There is no need to hide your dirty laundry as there are plenty of places in Hong Kong which will clean it cheaply. Many hotels, even the cheap youth hostels, have a laundry service. If they don't, just ask where one is. Prices are normally HK$25 for three kg. If less than three kg, you still pay the same, so you might want to throw in your clothes together with a friend's.

Two convenient laundry services in Tsimshatsui include Carlye Steam Laundry, Golden Crown Court, 66-70 Nathan Rd and Purity Laundry, 25 Chungking Arcade, Chungking Mansions, 30 Nathan Rd.

For dry-cleaning needs, you can try the chain store with the unforgettable name of Clean Living. There are branches all around, but convenient ones are in the MTR stations.

WEIGHTS & MEASURES

The international metric system is in official use in Hong Kong. In practice, traditional Chinese weights and measures are still common.

If you want to shop in the local markets, become familiar with Chinese units of weight. Things are sold by the *leung*, which is equivalent to 37.5 grams, or in *catty*, where one catty is about 600 grams. There are 16 leung to the catty.

Gold is sold by the *tael* which is exactly the same as a leung, and you will find many banks selling gold in Hong Kong. The Chinese have a long history of putting their wealth into gold as they generally have little faith in paper money. The rapid inflation that China has experienced in the past makes it easy to understand why.

CULTURAL CENTRES

You can ring up these places to ask about upcoming performances. However, it would seem that this doesn't always work well – I once rang up to find out who was playing at the evening concert and was told 'a bunch of gwailos with guitars'.

Kowloon

The main venue for cultural events is the glittering Hong Kong Cultural Centre (☎ 7342009), 10 Salisbury Rd, Tsimshatsui, Kowloon. The Philharmonic Orchestra and Chinese Orchestra, among others, have regular performances here.

Big events like rock concerts are held at the Hong Kong Coliseum (☎ 7659234), 9

Cheong Wan Rd, Hunghom, Kowloon, a 12,500-seat indoor facility next to the Kowloon-Canton Railway Station. A few performances are also booked at the Ko Shan Theatre (☎ 3342331) on Ko Shan Rd, Hunghom, Kowloon.

Hong Kong Island

The Hong Kong Stadium at So Kan Po, is situated about 300 metres due east of the horse racetrack at Happy Valley. It is the largest of the venues for cultural and sporting events.

What used to be the main centre for cultural events on Hong Kong Island is the Academy for the Performing Arts (☎ 5841500), 1 Gloucester Rd, Wanchai. Just across the street is the Arts Centre (☎ 5820200), 2 Harbour Rd, Wanchai. Some groups book performances at City Hall Theatre (☎ 5229928), Edinburgh Place, right next to the Star Ferry Terminal in Central. Queen Elizabeth Stadium (☎ 5756793), 18 Oi Kwan Rd, Wanchai, is the site for both sporting events and large rock concerts.

Lesser known is the Institute for Promotion of Chinese Culture (☎ 5594904), Rooms 1001-5, 5 Shun Tak Centre, 200 Connaught Rd, Sheung Wan. Not far away is the Sheung Wan Civic Centre (☎ 8532678), 5th floor, 345 Queen's Rd, Sheung Wan. There is also the Sai Wan Ho Civic Centre (☎ 5683721), 111 Shau Kei Wan Rd (adjacent to Sai Wan Ho MTR Station).

New Territories

There are three large cultural centres in the New Territories: Shatin Town Hall (☎ 6942511), 1 Yuen Ho Rd, Shatin; Tuen Mun Town Hall (☎ 4527300), 3 Tuen Hi Rd, Tuen Mun; Tsuen Wan Town Hall (☎ 4140144), Yuen Tun Circuit, Tsuen Wan.

BOOKS & MAPS
History

The classic history of Hong Kong is *A History of Hong Kong* (Oxford University Press, London, 1958) by G B Endacott,

which has everything you ever wanted to know about Hong Kong and more.

The foregoing is not to be confused with *A History of Hong Kong* (Harper Collins) by Frank Welsh – same title but different author and publisher. This monumental hardback is recent (1993) and also very thorough.

Maurice Collin's *Foreign Mud* (Faber & Faber, UK, 1946) tells the sordid story of the opium wars. Another version of the same story is *The Opium War* by the Foreign Language Press in Beijing.

The Taipans – Hong Kong's Merchant Princes (Oxford University Press, Hong Kong, 1981) tells the story of the Westerners – the Taipans (big managers) who profiteered during the opium wars.

A prolific writer and respected magistrate, Austin Coates wrote *Whampoa – Ships on the Shore* (South China Morning Post, 1980), a history of the Hong Kong & Whampoa Dock Company, formed in 1863 and the first great company to be founded in Hong Kong. He also wrote *Myself a Mandarin*.

Coffee-Table Books

The government's annual report is entitled *Hong Kong 1990, Hong Kong 1991*, etc. In addition to the excellent photographs, the text is full of information about the government, politics, economy, history, arts and just about any other topic relevant to Hong Kong.

Hong Kong, part of the series of Insight Guides by Apa Productions, has outstanding photographs and very readable text.

Fragrant Harbour by John Warner has many early photographs of Hong Kong.

The Taipan Traders by Anthony Lawrence is one of the Formasia series of books. A large sketchbook, it depicts many portraits by Asia's finest painters. *Great Cities of the World – Old Hong Kong* is another interesting Formasia book.

Hong Kong Illustrated, Views & News 1840-1890, compiled by John Warner, is a large sketchbook and history of the colony.

Hong Kong by Ian Lloyd and Russell Spurr is a good pictorial and part of the series of Times Editions.

Politics

The Other Hong Kong Report (Chinese University Press) is a fascinating and somewhat cynical rebuttal to the government's optimistic annual report.

Some of the gloom and doom surrounding that ominous year, 1997, is captured in *City on the Rocks – Hong Kong's Uncertain Future* (Viking, 1989) by Kevin Rafferty.

Fiction

Certainly the most famous fiction set in Hong Kong is *The World of Suzie Wong* by Richard Mason. Written in 1957 with the movie filmed in Hong Kong in 1960, it still makes an excellent read.

Spy-thriller author John Le Carre wrote a fascinating tale, *The Honourable Schoolboy* (Coronet Books). It's a story of espionage in Hong Kong and Indochina set in the early 1970s.

The marathon-length *Tai-Pan* by James Clavell will certainly help pass away your idle hours, although it's not a very realistic version of Hong Kong's early days of ships and traders. The sequel to *Tai-Pan* is another epic-length book, *Noble House*.

Also set in Hong Kong and China are Robert Elegant's *Dynasty* (McGraw-Hill, UK, 1977) and *Mandarin* (Hamish Hamilton, UK, 1983).

Triad by Derek Lambert (Hamish Hamilton, London) is a violent fictional account of the Chinese underworld.

Humour

Larry Feign doesn't pull any punches with his poignant political cartoons which have graced the pages of the *South China Morning Post* and the *Hong Kong Standard*. His best works have been released in a series of books published by Macmillan (HK) Ltd. Some titles to look for include *The World of Lily Wong* and *The Adventures of Superlily*.

Guides

There are some special-interest guide books which you might want to look into if you stay in Hong Kong awhile.

The American Chamber of Commerce publishes *Living in Hong Kong*, somewhat useful for those planning a long stay.

Associations and Societies in Hong Kong has a self-explanatory title. It's published by the HKTA.

If you're looking for obscure consulates (how about Lesotho, Monaco or St Kitts?), the Government Publications Centre publishes *Consular Posts, Officially Recognised Representatives and Bodies Established under the Sino-British Joint Declaration*.

The Best of Hong Kong & Macau, compiled and edited by Harry Rolnick, is a connoisseur's guide to the restaurants, nightclubs, discos and even shoe repair shops in Hong Kong.

The Hong Kong Guide, 1893 is available as a reprint and makes fascinating reading. The travel information is somewhat out-of-date.

Lonely Planet publishes other guides to the region, including *North-East Asia on a shoestring*, *South-East Asia on a shoestring*, *China – a travel survival kit* and the *Mandarin Chinese Phrasebook*.

Extras

The *Journal of the Royal Asiatic Society* is published annually by the RAS (☎ 5510300), GPO Box 3864, Hong Kong. Each volume delves into different topics – everything from history to flora and fauna.

Hong Kong Animals by Dennis Hill and Karen Phillipps is the definitive work on Hong Kong's fauna. The book is available from the Government Publications Office.

Hong Kong Country Parks by Stella L Thrower is an excellent government publication if you want to hike in the backwaters of Hong Kong.

The Occult World of Hong Kong by Frena Bloomfield may fascinate you or give you nightmares.

If you want to socialise with the masses then you might want to read *Let's Play Mahjong* by Benny Constantino (Federal Publications, Hong Kong).

Bookshops

One of the biggest and best bookshops is Swindon Books (☎ 3668001), 13 Lock Rd,

Tsimshatsui. There are also smaller branches: Shop 346, 3rd floor, Ocean Terminal, Tsimshatsui; and at the Star Ferry Pier, Tsimshatsui.

Times Books (☎ 3110301) gives its address as Shop C, 96 Nathan Rd, but the entrance is around the corner on Granville Rd in Tsimshatsui. There is a branch (☎ 7226583) in Tsimshatsui East in Houston Centre, Lower ground floor, Shop No LG-23. Another Times Books (☎ 5258797) is at Hutchison House, Shop G-31, Central. Hutchison House is at the corner of Murray Rd and Lambeth Walk.

Wanderlust Books (☎ 5232042), 30 Hollywood Rd, Central, is well worth visiting for its collections of travel books, maps and books about Hong Kong. The staff is extremely helpful and friendly, a rarity in Hong Kong bookshops. It can be found at the corner of Hollywood Rd and Shelley St.

There is a South China Morning Post Family Bookshop (☎ 5221012) at the Star Ferry Terminal on Hong Kong Island. There is another in Times Square, Matheson St, Causeway Bay. On the Kowloon side there is a branch on the 3rd floor, Ocean Terminal in Tsimshatsui and on the ground floor of the Tung Ying Building, Granville Rd (at Nathan Rd).

There is a very wide selection of books at The Book Centre (☎ 5227064) in the basement at 25 Des Voeux Rd, Central.

Peace Book Company (☎ 3672201), 35 Kimberly Rd, Tsimshatsui, has many books about China and Chinese magazines in English.

Bookazine Company has a fine little bookshop directly opposite the HKTA office in the basement of Jardine House in Central.

Joint Publishing Company (☎ 5250102), 9 Queen Victoria St (opposite the Central Market) is an outstanding store to find books about China or books and tapes for studying the Chinese language.

Chung Hwa Book Company (☎ 7825054), 450 Nathan Rd, Yaumatei, stocks many books in Chinese as well as in other languages.

Not to be overlooked is the Government Publications Centre in the GPO building next to the Star Ferry. 2537 – 1910 → 9-6 m-fri, 9-1 Sat

Libraries
The main library is at City Hall, High Block, Central, just one street to the east of the Star Ferry Terminal. However, they will not let you make photocopies of anything which is copyrighted (which means just about everything). As a result, most of their reference books have pages ripped out of them by frustrated students.

The American Library (☎ 5299661), 1st floor, United Centre, 95 Queensway, Admiralty, has good research facilities and *does* allow you to make photocopies.

Maps
There are a couple of good maps of Hong Kong worth picking up. Some of the best city maps are the *Kowloon Street Plan* and its companion *The Hong Kong Street Plan*, which you can buy in the bookshops.

Even more detailed and highly recommended is a small atlas called the *Hong Kong Guide – Streets & Places*, which has complete maps and an index of all the buildings and streets in Hong Kong. It's available at the Government Publications Centre in the GPO building next to the Star Ferry on Hong Kong Island. This is also the place to pick up the useful *Countryside* series of maps.

The map most people use is the freebie put out by the HKTA and private sponsors. It's covered with advertisements but is very good for finding your way around the lower Kowloon and Hong Kong urban areas.

MEDIA
Newspapers & Magazines
Hong Kong is the leading information and news centre in Asia. It's got to be that way largely because the government mostly keeps its hands off the media. The colonial government has the power to censor newspapers and occasionally uses it to avoid upsetting China. In 1989, a documentary entitled *Mainland China 1989* was censored because it was likely 'to seriously damage good relations with other territories'.

However, the power of censorship is used very sparingly in Hong Kong. What will happen after 1997 is the big question on every publisher's mind. No one believes that freedom of the press is uppermost in the minds of Beijing bureaucrats, but everyone is hoping that those same bureaucrats will understand that Hong Kong's prosperity is partially based on the free flow of information.

The three main local English-language newspapers are the *South China Morning Post*, *Hong Kong Standard* and *Eastern Express*. All three are of reasonably good quality and there is no real equivalent to the scandalous tabloids produced in many Western countries.

Three international newspapers produce Asian editions which are printed in Hong Kong. These are the *Asian Wall Street Journal*, *USA Today* and the *International Herald Tribune*, which is put together by the *New York Times* and the *Washington Post* but is only available outside the USA.

There are many magazines published in Hong Kong, including *Asiaweek*, the *Far Eastern Economic Review*, and the Asian editions of *Time* and *Newsweek*.

Hong Kong Magazine is the final word in nightlife and entertainment in this city. The magazine is published once every two weeks and is free. The best place to find it is around pubs frequented by gwailos. For subscription information, ring up the office (☎ 5755065; fax 5730914).

There are nearly 50 Chinese language newspapers in Hong Kong, giving the city the world's highest ratio of newspapers per capita.

Radio & TV
The most popular English-language radio stations are Radio 3 (AM 567 kHz), Radio 4 (classical music, FM 97.6 to 98.9 mHz), Commercial Radio (AM 864 kHz), Metro News (AM 1044 kHz), Hit Radio (FM 99.7 mHz), FM Select (FM 104 mHz), BBC World Service (AM 675 kHz, 4 am to 12.15 am). The English-language newspapers publish a daily guide to radio programmes.

TV broadcasts are only in the mornings and evenings during weekdays. On weekends and holidays, programmes run all day. Hong Kong's TV stations are run by two companies, Television Broadcasts Ltd (TVB) and Asia Television Ltd (ATV). Each company operates one English-language and one Cantonese-language channel, making a total of four stations in Hong Kong. The two English stations are TVB Pearl (channel 3) and ATV World (channel 4). The two Cantonese stations are called TVB Jade (channel 1) and ATV Home (channel 2). The programme schedule is listed daily in the English-language newspapers.

Since people in Macau also read Hong Kong newspapers, programmes from the Macau station (TdM) are listed, but the signal is too weak to be received in Hong Kong. TdM has wanted to broadcast to Hong Kong for years, but the Hong Kong government has strenuously objected, claiming that this would cause interference. Many suspect the real reason is that Hong Kong's two stations would prefer not to have any competition.

If your hotel is connected to a satellite dish, you'll be able to receive Star TV. This is broadcast from Hong Kong to East Asia in a variety of languages, including English. Other satellite stations which can be received in Hong Kong include Japan's NHK and WOWWOW.

FILM & PHOTOGRAPHY
Almost everything you could possibly need in the way of film, camera and photographic accessories is available in Hong Kong. Stanley St on Hong Kong Island is the place to look for reputable camera stores.

For security reasons (terrorism?), you cannot take photographs of the runways at Kai Tak Airport or of the security procedures (X-ray machines, metal detectors, machine gun-toting airport police, etc).

A good deal was buying Kodachrome slide film in Hong Kong that included the processing (valid in Europe only, I think). The price was HK$50 and as

Top: Night view of Central, Hong Kong Island (RH)
Left: Exchange Square, Hong Kong Island (RS)
Right: Tram (Streetcar), Central, Hong Kong Island (RS)

Top: Hong Kong Harbour (GI)
Bottom: Hong Kong Harbour at sunset (RH)

processing in Europe is very expensive it turned out to be worthwhile.

HEALTH

In general, health conditions in Hong Kong are good. Nevertheless, there are a few special problem areas and some precautions are worth knowing about.

Predeparture Preparations

Vaccinations No special vaccinations are required for Hong Kong. However, that doesn't mean you shouldn't get any. For Hong Kong, the most useful vaccinations are for hepatitis B, tetanus and influenza (during winter).

If you need vaccinations while in Hong Kong, the Port Health office can give you a low-cost jab for cholera and typhoid. They occasionally stock other vaccines depending on which epidemics are ravaging this part of Asia. Port Health has two branch offices: Kowloon (☎ 3683361), Room 905, Government Offices, Canton Rd, Yaumatei; Hong Kong Island (☎ 5722056), 2nd floor, Centre Point Building, 181-185 Gloucester Rd, Wanchai.

Health Insurance Hong Kong has no national health service and all medical treatment has to be paid for by the patient. Although not absolutely necessary, it is a good idea to take out travellers' health insurance. The policies are usually available from travel agents, including student travel services. Some policies specifically exclude 'dangerous activities', which may include motorcycling, scuba diving and even hiking. Obviously, you'll want a policy that covers you in all the circumstances you're likely to find yourself in.

Hopefully you won't need medical care, but do keep in mind that any health insurance policy you have at home is probably not valid outside your country. The usual procedure with travellers' health insurance is that you pay in cash first for services rendered and then later present the receipts to the insurance company for reimbursement after you return home. Other policies stipulate that

you call collect to a centre in your home country, where an immediate assessment of your problem is made.

You can, of course, purchase an insurance policy after arrival in Hong Kong. Some of the banks are in the business of selling medical and travellers' insurance – the Hong Kong & Shanghai Bank is one such place. If interested, drop by the banks and pick up their brochures in English describing what sort of policies are available.

If you are unfortunate enough to get very ill while travelling in Hong Kong, at least you can be grateful for one thing – medical care is cheaper in Hong Kong than in most Western countries. On the negative side, many of the best medical staff are emigrating in droves to Western countries, leading some cynics to suggest that perhaps the best place to get sick in Hong Kong is the airport.

Medical Kit You can buy almost any medication across the counter in Hong Kong or get it by prescription. If you're going to spend time hiking in the mountains or exploring remote islands, a basic medical kit would be handy. It could include panadol for pain and fever, a pin and tweezers for removing splinters, plaster for blisters, band-aids, an antiseptic, rehydration salts (for heat exhaustion), insect repellent, sunscreen and chapstick.

If you wear glasses, bring an extra pair of spectacles and/or a copy of your lens prescription with you. Sunglasses come in useful, and a hat will help protect you from getting burned.

Basic Rules

Food & Water Hong Kong is a very healthy place and no special precautions are needed. Chinese cooking relies heavily on fresh ingredients so the food is fairly safe, even from the street stalls despite their dubious appearance.

The government says it's perfectly safe to drink Hong Kong's tap water. However, traditions die hard and most Chinese will boil it anyway because they always did so in China (for good reason). In some agricultural backwaters in the New Territories and Outlying Islands, surface water may be contaminated by fertiliser. If you're going to be hiking in the countryside, be sure to bring a sufficient water supply and avoid drinking unboiled surface water.

If you suffer health problems, it's usually due to difficulty adapting to the hot summer climate. If you're sweating profusely, you're going to lose a lot of salt and that can lead to fatigue and muscle cramps for some people. If necessary you can make it up by putting extra salt in your food (a teaspoon a day is plenty), but don't increase your salt intake unless you also increase your water intake. Soy sauce will also do the trick.

Medical Problems & Treatments

Skin Problems Sunburn can be more than just uncomfortable. Among the undesirable effects of frying your hide are premature skin ageing and possible skin cancer in later years. Bring sunscreen lotion and wear something to cover your head.

Sunburn is not the only hazard to your skin. Indeed, the most common summertime afflictions that visitors to Hong Kong suffer from are skin diseases. This is because of the hot, humid climate. The most common varieties are 'jock itch' (a fungal infection around the groin), athlete's foot (known to the Chinese as 'Hong Kong feet'), contact dermatitis (caused by a necklace or watch-band rubbing the skin) and prickly heat (caused by excessive sweating). Prevention and treatment of these skin ailments is often a matter of good hygiene.

For fungal infections, bathe twice daily and thoroughly dry yourself before getting dressed. Standing in front of an electric fan is a good way to get dry. An antifungal ointment or powder should be applied to the affected area. It's more effective to use both an ointment and a powder in combination. Some popular fungicides available in Western countries include Desenex, Tinactin and Mycota. Whatever ointment and/or powder you use, it should include the ingredients undecylenic acid and zinc undecylenate. Wear light cotton underwear

or very thin nylon that is 'breathable'. Wear the lightest outer clothing possible when the weather is really hot and humid. For athlete's foot, wearing open-toed sandals will often solve the problem without further treatment. It also helps to clean between the toes with a warm soapy water and an old toothbrush.

Treat contact dermatitis by removing the offending necklace, bracelet or wristwatch. Avoid anything that chafes the skin, such as tight clothing, especially elastic. If your skin develops little painful red 'pin pricks', you probably have prickly heat. This is the result of excessive sweating which blocks the sweat ducts, causing inflammation. The treatment is the same as for fungal infections: drying and cooling the skin. Bathe often, soak and scrub with hot soapy water to get the skin pores open and dust yourself with talcum powder after drying off. Hong Kong is one of the most thoroughly air-conditioned places on earth, and sleeping in a room that has air-con will help.

Diarrhoea Even though the tap water is safe, some people rapidly develop that well-known ailment, 'travellers' diarrhoea'. Should it happen to you, don't automatically assume that you've caught some dread disease. It's more likely that your body needs a few days to adjust to the change of diet and the mineral content of the local water supply. Diarrhoea is caused by irritation or inflamation of the intestine. First try a simple cure by switching to a light, roughage-free diet for a few days. White rice, bananas, pudding and boiled eggs will usually see you through. Further relief can be obtained by chewing tablets of activated charcoal. Tea, coffee, cola and other caffeinated drinks are irritants and may worsen the diarrhoea. Ditto for spices and alcohol.

More serious cases can be treated with drugs such as Lomotil and Imodium. These drugs only treat the symptoms, not the underlying problem. Your intestine will still remain irritated or inflamed. Use anti-diarrhoeal drugs with caution because they can cause nasty side effects. Also, you don't want to take so many drugs that you become plugged up, because the diarrhoea serves a function – your body is trying to expel unwanted bacteria or irritants. Only take the minimum dose needed to control yourself. However, if you continue to suffer, you may have a serious infection that requires antibiotics or anti-amoebic drugs. If you get to this stage, you should visit a hospital or clinic and get some medical tests to determine just what the problem is.

Although you are not likely to pick up serious intestinal tract infections like dysentery and giardia in Hong Kong, you could easily do so elsewhere in Asia. More than a few travellers have arrived in Hong Kong and suddenly collapsed, but their illnesses were contracted in places like China, the Philippines or Vietnam. If you fall seriously ill after arrival in Hong Kong, it's a good idea to tell the doctor just where you've been travelling during the past few months.

Tuberculosis The infection rate for TB is surprisingly high in Hong Kong – more than 7000 cases are reported annually. While there is no reason to be unduly alarmed, if you're travelling with children it might be wise to have them vaccinated. These days, nearly all children born in Hong Kong are immunised at birth, but not so in Western countries. See the Guangzhou section.

Hepatitis More than 1500 cases of hepatitis are reported in Hong Kong annually, but the unreported number of cases is probably several times that. Also, many cases are probably first contracted in China. Some strains of hepatitis are transmitted sexually and through dirty needles used by amateur acupuncturists and drug abusers. Hepatitis is not a serious problem in Hong Kong, so don't dwell on it. Refer to the China section for more details.

Eye Problems Sunglasses not only give you that fashionable 'Hollywood look' but will protect your eyes. Amber and grey are said to be the two most effective colours for filtering out harmful ultraviolet rays.

Conjunctivitis is a common eye infection which is easily spread by contaminated towels which are handed out by restaurants and even airlines. The best advice about wiping your face is to use disposable tissue paper or moist towelettes ('Wet Ones' or similar brands). If you think you have trachoma, you need to see a doctor – the disease can damage your vision if untreated. Trachoma is normally treated with antibiotic eye ointments for about four to six weeks. Don't attempt to diagnose and treat yourself.

Sexually Transmitted Diseases The sexual revolution reached Hong Kong years ago, along with the 'social diseases' that go with it. While abstinence is the only 100% preventative, using condoms helps. Gonorrhoea and syphilis are the most common of these diseases; sores, blisters or rashes around the genitals, discharges or pain when urinating are common symptoms. Symptoms may be less marked or not observed at all in women. Syphilis symptoms eventually disappear but the disease continues and can be fatal. Gonorrhoea is not fatal but can lead to sterility and other problems. Both diseases can be cured by antibiotics.

There are a number of sexually transmitted diseases, with effective treatment available for nearly all of them. However, there is no cure for herpes and there is also no cure for AIDS. Using condoms is the most effective preventative.

AIDS can be spread through infected blood transfusions and dirty needles – vaccinations, acupuncture and tattooing can potentially be as dangerous as intravenous drug use if the equipment is not clean. If you do need an injection, ask to see the syringe unwrapped in front of you, or better still, take a needle and syringe pack with you overseas – it is a cheap insurance package against infection.

Hong Kong is a good place to get an AIDS test. Not only are the testing facilities reliable, but the government does *not* deport people who test positive for the disease. The policy is much the opposite in China, and some fear that after 1997 AIDS carriers could be deported en masse.

However, fear of infection should never preclude treatment for serious medical conditions. Although there may be a risk of infection, it is very small indeed.

Cuts & Bites

Snakes The term 'snake' is what the Cantonese call somebody who smuggles illegal aliens into Hong Kong. However, I speak here of the non-human kind.

The countryside areas of Hong Kong are home to some poisonous snakes which you'd be wise to avoid. Most dangerous are the cobras, and some species show very little shyness about living near areas inhabited by people. The king cobra is the nastiest by far, but fortunately it avoids contact with humans. Two other common poisonous snakes include the green-coloured bamboo pit viper and coral snake. There are a number of poisonous freshwater snakes and sea snakes. Non-poisonous snakes include rat snakes (which find plenty to eat in Hong Kong), copperhead racers, pythons and boas.

Don't be a fool and attack a snake with a stick – that's the most likely way to get bitten. The best technique is to make some noise, as most snakes will retreat from humans. However, cornering a snake will surely cause it to coil up into striking position. Cobras can even spit their venom – most dangerous if it hits you in the eyes.

If by some chance you do get bitten, the important thing to remember is to remain calm and not run around (sounds easier than it is). Authorities differ widely on how to treat a snake bite in emergencies without a specific antivenin, but the conventional wisdom is to rest and allow the poison to be absorbed slowly. A constricting band (tourniquet) can be useful for slowing down the poison, but it's also very dangerous – if too tight, a tourniquet can cut off circulation and cause gangrene, a possibly fatal complication. If a tourniquet is applied, be sure you *do not* use a narrow band like a shoelace. Use something wide and soft, like strips of cloth or a T-shirt. Furthermore, be sure that you can feel the pulse below the tourniquet – if

you've cut off the pulse, it's too tight! Keep the affected limb below the heart level.

The old 'boy scout' method of treating snakebite – cutting the skin and sucking out the poison – has also been widely discredited. It theoretically can help if done properly, but most people do not know how to do it and the result is often a deep cut, loss of blood (sending the patient into shock) and an infection. Even if done by an expert, only about 20% of the poison can be removed this way. Immersion in cold water is also considered useless.

Treatment in a hospital with an antivenin would be ideal. The Hong Kong police will dispatch a helicopter to pluck snake-bite victims off remote mountaintops and they don't even charge for the service. However, you are advised that this is an emergency service, so don't call for a helicopter because you're tired and would like a lift into town.

Although I hate to say it, there isn't a whole lot you can do for a snakebite victim if you are far from civilisation. To minimise your chances of being bitten always wear boots, socks and long trousers when walking through undergrowth where snakes might be present. Don't put your hands into holes and crevices, and be careful when collecting firewood. Fortunately, the vast majority of snakebite victims survive even without medical treatment.

Sharks In addition to the shopkeepers along Nathan Rd, there are several other species of sharks in Hong Kong. The tiger shark seems particularly nasty – there is about one fatal attack on humans every year. Most of these attacks have occurred at beaches in the Sai Kung area of the New Territories.

Insects & Stings Wasps, which are common in the subtropics, are a more serious hazard than snakes because they are more aggressive and will chase humans when stirred up. If you see a wasp nest, the best advice is to move away quietly. They won't attack unless they feel threatened, so don't do anything foolish like seeing how close you can get to their nest. Should you be so unfortunate as to be attacked by wasps, the only sensible thing to do is run like hell.

It would take perhaps 100 wasp or bee stings to kill a normal adult, but a single sting can be fatal to someone who is allergic. In fact, death from wasp and bee stings is more common than death from snakebites. People who are allergic to wasp and bee stings are also allergic to bites by red ants. People who have this sort of allergy usually know it. If this includes you, throw an antihistamine and epinephrine into your first-aid kit and keep it with you when exploring the countryside areas. Epinephrine is most effective when injected, but taking it in pill form is better than nothing.

Except during the dead of winter, mosquitos are a year-round annoyance in Hong Kong, even in the urban jungles of Kowloon and Central. They are especially annoying at night when you're trying to sleep. Electric mosquito zappers are useful, but are too heavy for travelling. A portable innovation is 'electric mosquito incense', also known as 'vape mats' or 'mosquito mats'. Mosquito mats and the mosquito mat electric heater are sold in grocery stores and supermarkets all over Hong Kong. The mats do emit a poison – breathing it over the long-term may have unknown health effects, though all the manufacturers of this stuff insist that it is safe.

Mosquito incense coils accomplish the same thing as the vape mats and require no electricity, but the smoke is nasty. Mosquito repellent is somewhat less effective than incense, but is probably less toxic and gives protection outdoors where incense is impractical. Look for brands that contain 'deet' (diethyl toluamide). Some effective brands include Autan and Off! Sleeping under a blowing electric fan all night (not recommended during winter) will also keep the mosquitos away.

Hospitals Public hospitals charge low fees, but Hong Kong residents pay less than foreign visitors. Private doctors usually charge reasonable fees, but fees vary and it pays to make some inquiries first. Most large hotels have resident doctors.

Hong Kong has a shortage of dentists and fees are consequently very high. If the next stop on your itinerary is Taiwan, you might want to wait because the cost for dental treatment is much lower there.

Most pharmacies in Hong Kong are open 9 am to 6 pm, with some until 8 pm. Watson's has branches all over Hong Kong and can supply most pharmaceutical needs.

Public hospitals include: Queen Elizabeth Hospital (☎ 7102111), Wylie Rd, Yaumatei, Kowloon; Princess Margaret Hospital (☎ 3103111), Laichikok, Kowloon; Queen Mary Hospital (☎ 8192111), Pokfulam Rd; Prince of Wales Hospital (☎ 6362211), 30-32 Ngan Shing St, Shatin, New Territories.

There are some excellent private hospitals in Hong Kong, but their prices reflect the fact that they must operate at a profit. Some of the better private hospitals in Hong Kong include:

Adventist
    40 Stubbs Rd, Wanchai, Hong Kong Island
    (☎ 5746211)
Baptist
    222 Waterloo Rd, Kowloon Tong (☎ 3374141)
Canossa
    1 Old Peak Rd, Mid-Levels, Hong Kong Island
    (☎ 5222181)
Grantham
    125 Wong Chuk Hang Rd, Deep Water Bay,
    Hong Kong Island (☎ 5546471)
Hong Kong Central
    1B Lower Albert Rd, Central, Hong Kong Island
    (☎ 5223141)
Matilda & War Memorial
    41 Mt Kellett Rd, The Peak, Hong Kong Island
    (☎ 8496301)
St Paul's
    2 Eastern Hospital Rd, Causeway Bay, Hong
    Kong Island (☎ 8906008)

Herbal Medicine Western visitors to Hong Kong often become so engrossed buying cameras and electronic goods that they never realise Hong Kong is well known for something else – herbal medicine.

Nearby Guangzhou is less expensive for buying Chinese medicines, but in Hong Kong there are more chemists who can speak English, and Hong Kong's prices really aren't much higher. Also, in Hong Kong it's easier to find everything you want in one place and there's less problem with counterfeit medicines.

Having experimented with Chinese medicine for several years, I'm convinced that it has something to offer, but several warnings are in order. Chinese herbalists have all sorts of treatments for stomach aches, headaches, colds, flu and sore throat. They also have herbs to treat long-term problems like asthma. Many of these herbs seem to work. But whether or not Chinese medicine can cure more serious illnesses like cancer and heart disease is uncertain. All sorts of overblown claims have been made for herbal medicines, especially by those who make and sell them. Some gullible Westerners have persuaded themselves that Chinese doctors can cure any disease. A visit to any of China's hospitals will quickly shatter this myth.

In general, Chinese medicine works best for the relief of unpleasant symptoms (pain, sore throat, etc) and for some serious long-term conditions which resist Western medicines, such as migraine headaches, asthma and chronic backache. I've personally had much success treating a chronic intestinal problem of my own with the ganoderma mushroom, a renowned Chinese cure-all. But for acute life-threatening conditions such as a heart attack or appendicitis, it's best to see a Western doctor.

When reading about the theory behind Chinese medicine, the word 'holistic' appears often. Basically, this means that Chinese medicine seeks to treat the whole body rather than focusing on a particular organ or disease.

Using appendicitis as an example, a Chinese doctor may try to fight the infection using the body's whole defences, whereas a Western doctor would simply cut out the appendix. While the holistic method sounds great in theory, in practice the Western technique of attacking the problem directly often works better. In the case of appendicitis, surgery really is a more reliable treatment than taking herbs. On the other hand, in the case of migraine headaches, herbs might prove more effective than Western painkillers.

Another point to be wary of when taking herbal medicine is the tendency of some manufacturers to falsely claim that their product contains numerous potent and expensive ingredients. For example, some herbal formulas may list rhinoceros horn as an ingredient. Rhinoceros horn, widely acclaimed by herbalists as a cure for high temperature (fever, sweating and hot flashes) is so rare and extremely expensive that it is practically impossible to buy. Any formula listing rhinoceros horn may, at best, contain water buffalo horn. In any case, the rhino is a rare and endangered species, and you will not wish to hasten its extinction by demanding rhino horn products. By contrast, the Chinese demand for deer antlers now supports a whole industry of deer ranchers in New Zealand, Germany and the UK.

One benefit of Chinese medicine is that there are generally few side-effects. Compared to a drug like penicillin which can produce allergic reactions and other serious side-effects, herbal medicines are fairly safe. Nevertheless, herbs are still medicines, and not candy. There is no need to gobble herbs if you're feeling fine to begin with. Some foreigners carelessly gobbling herbal medicines have made themselves quite ill in the process.

Before shopping for herbs, keep in mind that in Western medicine, doctors talk about broad-spectrum antibiotics, such as penicillin, which are good for treating a range of infections. But for many illnesses, a specific antibiotic might be better for a specific type of infection. The same is true in Chinese medicine. A broad-spectrum remedy such as snake gall bladder may be good for treating colds, but there are many different types of colds. The best way to treat a cold with herbal medicine is to see a Chinese doctor and get a specific prescription. The pills on sale in herbal medicine shops are generally broad-spectrum, while a prescription remedy will usually require that you take home a bunch of specific herbs and cook them into a thick broth.

If you visit a Chinese doctor, you might be surprised by what he or she discovers about your body. For example, the doctor will take your pulse and then tell you that you have a slippery pulse or perhaps a thready pulse. Chinese doctors have identified more than 30 different kinds of pulses. A pulse could be empty, prison, leisurely, bowstring, irregular or even regularly irregular. The doctor may then examine your tongue to see if it is slippery, dry, pale, greasy, has a thick coating or maybe no coating at all. The doctor, having discovered that you have wet heat, as evidenced by a slippery pulse and a red greasy tongue, will prescribe the proper herbs for your condition.

Many Chinese medicines are powders that come in vials. Typically, you take one or two vials a day. Some of these powders taste OK, but others are very bitter and difficult to swallow. If you can't tolerate the taste, you may want to buy some empty gelatin capsules and fill them yourself with the powder.

A good place to purchase herbal medicines is Yue Hwa Chinese Products Emporium at the north-west corner of Nathan and Jordan Rds just above the Jordan MTR Station. Before buying anything, explain your condition to a Chinese chemist and ask for a recommendation. They consider this part of their job.

There are plenty of books available to learn more about Chinese medicine. One of the easiest to understand is *The Web That Has No Weaver: Understanding Chinese Medicine*, by Ted J Kaptchuk (Congdon & Weed, New York).

If you want a more advanced text, *The Theoretical Foundations of Chinese Medicine*, by Manfred Porkert (MIT Press, Cambridge, Mass) is good. However, the author has been criticised for introducing many Latin terms which makes the book often difficult reading.

Acupuncture Can you cure people by sticking needles into them? The Chinese think so and they've been doing it for thousands of years. Now the technique of acupuncture is gaining popularity in the West. In recent years, many Westerners have made the pilgrimage to China either to seek treatment or to study acupuncture. Guangzhou is a particularly popular place for both patients and students who want to learn more about this ancient medical technique.

Getting stuck with needles might not sound pleasant, but if done properly it doesn't hurt. Knowing just where to insert the needle is crucial. Acupuncturists have identified more than 2000 insertion points, but only about 150 are commonly used.

The exact mechanism by which acupuncture works is not fully understood. The Chinese talk of energy channels or meridians which connect the needle insertion point to the particular organ, gland or joint being treated. The acupuncture point is sometimes quite far from the area of the body being treated. Acupuncture is even used to treat impotency, but I've never wanted to ask just where the needle is inserted.

Among acupuncturists there are different schools of thought. The most common school in China is called the Eight Principles School. Another is the Five Elements School.

As with herbal medicine, the fundamental question asked by potential acupuncture patients is: 'Does it work?' The answer has to be: 'That depends'. It depends on the skill of the acupuncturist and the condition being treated. Like herbal medicine, acupuncture tends to be more useful for those who suffer from long-term conditions (like chronic headaches) rather than sudden emergencies (like an acute appendicitis).

However, there are times when acupuncture can be used for an immediate condition. For example, some major surgical operations have been performed using acupuncture as the only anaesthetic (this works best on the head). In this case, a small electric current (from batteries) is passed through the needles. This is a good example of how Western medicine and Chinese medicine can be usefully combined.

While some satisfied patients give glowing testimonials about the prowess of acupuncture, others are less impressed. The only way to really find out is to try it.

While acupuncture itself is probably harmless, one should not forget that AIDS and hepatitis B can be spread easily by contaminated needles. In Western countries, the use of disposable acupuncture needles has become routine, but this is not the case in China. If you're going to experiment with acupuncture, first find out if the doctor has disposable needles. If not, it is possible for you to buy your own needles and bring them to the doctor when you need treatment. Of course, you must find out if the doctor is willing. Also, you need to consult with the doctor to find out what size and gauge of needles you should buy. There are many varieties, and the doctor may not be willing to use whatever you just happen to purchase.

Hong Kong has a main acupuncture supply house called Mayfair Medical Supplies (☎ 7303256), 35 Austin Rd, Yaumatei. They have some acupuncture reference books. Other suppliers could be found by looking in the Yellow Pages Commercial/Industrial Guide under Medical Equipment & Supplies.

The following organisations could be worth checking: Chinese Acupuncture Association (☎ 5457640), Ground floor, 3 Aberdeen St, Central; International Acupuncture Society (☎ 7711066; fax 3888836), Room 1113A, 11th floor, Champion Building, 301-309 Nathan Rd, Yaumatei.

Public Toilets

Hong Kong suffers from a real scarcity of public toilets. There are a few but you really have to know where to look for them – perhaps my next project will be to write a guidebook entitled *Public Toilets in Hong Kong – a travel survival kit*. So far, the HKTA has not produced a brochure on the matter. Parks generally have public toilets, and there is one in the Central Market on Hong Kong Island and another hidden in a basement off Lan Kwai Fong. Past the turnstiles of the Star Ferry (lower deck only) are public toilets, but the upper deck entrance has none even though it's 1st class!

Most irritating is the fact that all the major touristy shopping malls have toilets, but keep the doors locked so only the employees with keys can use them. Perhaps what's needed is a massive protest – if all the tourists would just urinate on the floor, the shopowners might get the message. Barring that, the only recourse is to seek out the toilets in fast-food outlets (but not all have them) and in some of the large department stores.

If you find a public toilet, you won't find toilet paper so bring your own. You'd be wise to keep a stash of your own with you at all times.

Women's Health

Gynaecological Problems Poor diet, lowered resistance due to the use of antibiotics for stomach upsets, and even contraceptive pills can lead to vaginal infections when travelling in hot climates. Keeping the genital area clean, and wearing skirts or loose-fitting trousers and cotton underwear will help to prevent infections.

Yeast infections, characterised by a rash, itch and discharge, can be treated with a vinegar or even lemon-juice douche or with yoghurt. Nystatin suppositories are the usual medical prescription. Trichomonas is a more serious infection; symptoms include discharge and a burning sensation when urinating. Male sexual partners must also be treated, and if a vinegar-water douche is not effective, medical attention should be sought. Flagyl is the prescribed drug.

Pregnancy Most miscarriages occur during the first three months of pregnancy, so this is the most risky time to travel. The last three months should also be spent within reasonable distance of good medical care, as quite serious problems can develop at this time. Pregnant women should avoid all unnecessary medication, but vaccinations should still be taken where possible. Additional care should be taken to prevent illness and particular attention should be paid to diet and nutrition.

WOMEN TRAVELLERS

While Hong Kong poses no special dangers for women, unpleasant incidents can occur. And like everything else in Hong Kong, sex is a business. One woman traveller had this to report:

A young Chinese man came to the Travellers Hostel looking for an English girl who was after some modelling work. He asked me if I wanted some extra money, offering me escort/film work. I replied 'No' as I was returning home shortly and didn't need money. However, as he persisted and offered me HK$1000 for an evening solely as an escort, I agreed, with the other girl, to meet him the next evening. He turned out to be working as a pimp for Chinese 'high-class' customers. OK, I should have known better. I left as soon as possible amid threats from him and an Indian boss, and quite frankly I was really frightened. My friend who was interested in modelling stayed, but soon found out that the entire business was just to find European girls to have sex with Chinese men.

I was old enough and had money enough in Hong Kong to refuse these people who were obviously hoping to intimidate or force us into working for them, but I think some people would be too scared to say no, as they were extremely persistent!

I had gone to see this man, Mr Chan, out of idle curiosity and ended up very frightened! I'd like other women to be warned, as they tried very hard to conceal the true nature of their business and Mr Chan is extremely charming and pleasant to start with. They obviously know where to find female travellers (we were approached in the kitchen of the Travellers Hostel)!

I was really taken in, but having travelled through Asia and Central America I thought I was pretty good at spotting trouble. Please be warned!

DANGERS & ANNOYANCES
Rudeness

'Give us your money and get the hell out!', is the motto of many Hong Kong shopkeepers and hotel owners. The biggest complaint of travellers is that Hong Kong people are often appallingly rude, pushy and impatient. This impression partly results from the fact that most foreigners deal mainly with people in the tourist trade rather than the typical Hong Kong resident. However, this is a thin excuse. Sales clerks in Taiwan, Korea, Japan or the Philippines are generally cheerful and friendly, but this is seldom the case in Hong Kong.

You may encounter sales clerks who pretend you don't even exist – ask them 'where can I find the coffee' and they just pretend to have a hearing problem. The excuse that they don't speak English is also a thin one – even in countries where English is nonexistent, clerks who don't understand what you're saying just smile, laugh or shrug their shoulders. In Hong Kong, the reaction is more likely to be irritation and hostility. When they do smile, it usually means that they're Thais or Filipinos. The HKTA is aware of the problem, and has attempted to educate people to smile, say 'hello' and 'thank you'. Unfortunately, their efforts have been less than stunningly successful.

It's not just tourists who complain. Many native Hong Kongers also feel that their home town is far less friendly than it should be. Furthermore, Chinese from other parts of China feel that not only Hong Kong, but the Cantonese in general are the least hospitable people in the entire country. This doesn't mean that you will never encounter an amiable person in Hong Kong. Within this sea of frowning faces, there are smiles. You might even meet someone who will be polite, helpful, friendly and generous and not expect anything in return. Sadly, such experiences are all too rare, especially if you're only a short-term visitor.

Crime

Despite Hong Kong's obvious prosperity and low unemployment rate, there are plenty of people who live on the margin of society and will resort to crime to earn a living. This includes Western travellers, some of whom arrive in Hong Kong totally broke with no prospects for employment. There have been disturbing reports of foreigners having had their backpacks burglarised by their room-mates in the youth hostels. One fellow I know had his wallet, passport and travellers' cheques lifted during the two minutes he spent taking a shower at a hostel, and the only other people in the place were travellers. So if something of yours is stolen, don't automatically assume that the guilty party is a local Chinese.

The Triads
Much of Hong Kong's crime eminates from the notorious Triads. At one time the Triads, or secret societies, may have been a positive influence in China. It is said they opposed the corrupt and brutal Manchu (Qing) Dynasty and aided the revolution that brought down the Manchus in 1911.

Unfortunately, the Triads that exist now are the Chinese equivalent of the Mafia. Sporting such catchy names as Bamboo Union and 14K, the Triads have been increasingly successful at recruiting disaffected teenagers in Hong Kong's high-rise housing estates. Initially offering young people a bit of companionship and adventure, the 'fun' soon turns to illegal gambling, extortion, protection rackets, the smuggling of drugs and weapons, prostitution, loan sharking and sometimes outright robberies of banks and jewellery stores. Like similar organisations, once you join a Triad you cannot quit. Gwailos are not welcome to participate – even the Triad-controlled prostitution business centred in Mongkok and Shamshuipo shuns foreign clientele.

Membership in a Triad is illegal in Hong Kong – it's even illegal to claim to be a member. Yet the Triads seem to be growing, and have been trying to use their vast wealth to muscle into legitimate businesses – a recent target being Hong Kong's movie-making industry. Many fear that the growing influence of the Triads will drive out legitimate businesses and hurt Hong Kong's economy in the long term.

It was the Communists who smashed the Triad-controlled opium selling business in Shanghai after the 1949 revolution. The Triads have not forgotten, and in the countdown to 1997 many Hong Kong-based criminals are moving their operations to ethnic Chinese communities in places like Australia, Canada and the USA. Even the poverty-stricken Philippines has received some of this 'overseas investment' – Triad-arranged kidnappings of wealthy Chinese families living in the Philippines has become a new growth industry. Ironically, some Triads are expanding into China itself, establishing links with corrupt government officials and high-ranking soldiers in the People's Liberation Army (PLA). ■

If you set a bag down and don't keep an eye on it, the whole thing may disappear in seconds. A number of people have had their luggage nicked this way right in the airport when they wandered off for a minute to use the toilets or change money. You probably wouldn't leave your bags unattended in a Third World country, but tourists just assume that it's OK in wealthy Hong Kong – unfortunately, it's not OK. The same principle applies in restaurants and pubs – if your bag doesn't accompany you to the toilet, don't expect to find it when you return. Again, if your bag is pinched this way the thief could well be a foreigner.

This is not to say that the Chinese are innocent. Pickpockets (mostly Chinese) do a brisk business on buses and ferries when it's crowded. Signs posted on the ferries and MTR stations warn about this. The problem has been reduced by undercover police who specialise in catching pickpockets, but it's still a problem so keep your cash secured in a moneybelt or inside zippered pockets.

In a form of poetic justice, the colony's initial opium-based founding has rebounded and Hong Kong now has a serious dope problem. Of course, the Chinese re-inherit this mess in 1997. There are an estimated 38,000 drug addicts in Hong Kong, 90% of whom are male. While the female addicts mostly finance their habit through prostitution, the men resort to more aggressive crimes such as pickpocketing, burglary and robbery. The effect on travellers is that you have to be careful with your valuables. However, it is generally safe to walk around at night, but it's best to stick to well-lit areas. Tourist districts like Tsimshatsui are heavily patrolled by the police and there is little danger of violent crime, though theft can occur anywhere.

WORK
Visas

Stretching the cash? Legally speaking, there are only three groups of foreigners who do not need employment visas for Hong Kong: UK citizens, British passport holders or registered British subjects. Such people are granted a 12-month stay on arrival, after which extensions are merely a formality.

As for foreign nationals, including Australians, Americans and Canadians, to work in Hong Kong you must get an employment visa from the Hong Kong Immigration Department before you arrive. This is no longer easy to arrange – you need a job skill which cannot easily be performed by a local, and your employer must be willing to sponsor you.

As for under-the-table employment, that certainly exists too, but there are stiff penalties for employers who hire foreigners illegally. These rules are vigorously enforced against employers who hire labourers from China, because of the justified fear that hiring even a few undocumented workers will provoke a tidal wave of prospective illegal immigrants from across the border. Despite the rules, plenty of Westerners do find temporary illegal work in Hong Kong, but there are risks and discretion is strongly advised!

Applications for employment visas can be made to any British embassy or British consular or diplomatic office. If you arrive in Hong Kong as a visitor and get a job, you will have to leave the colony, apply for a visa and return when it is obtained. Americans are normally granted a six-month work visa. Extensions should be applied for a month before the visa expires.

Finding a Job

Many travellers drop into Hong Kong looking for short-term work to top up cash reserves before heading off to other destinations in Asia. Some wind up staying much longer than originally anticipated – the place is full of people who stopped for a few months to replenish the coffers and are still there 15 years later. Success in finding work depends largely on what skills you have. Professional people such as engineers, computer programmers and accountants will have no problem landing a job, especially now that Hong Kong's well-educated class is emigrating in droves to Canada, Australia and elsewhere. However, those who do not possess rare high-technology skills are at a distinct disadvantage.

Qualified teachers with British passports, or a British spouse, could try applying to the British Council (☎ 8795138), Ground floor, Easey Commercial Building, 255 Hennessy Rd, Wanchai, for full or part-time teaching posts (including teaching English).

If you're fluent in one or more foreign languages then you might get work as a translator. You can find such companies listed in the Yellow Pages Buying Guide under Translators & Interpreters. Some well-known ones include CIAP (☎ 8121932), Polyglot Translations (☎ 5215689) and Translanguage (☎ 8685755).

One of the ironies of the 1997 takeover is the effect that it's having on the job market. Many skilled and talented Chinese people are fleeing Hong Kong. Furthermore, as Mandarin Chinese gains in popularity in Hong Kong, the level of spoken English is declining rapidly. Those who could speak good English have already emigrated or soon will. All this is creating job opportunities for foreigners – businesses needing English-speaking staff are often unable to find local Chinese with the necessary linguistic or technical skills.

Some suggest registering with Hong Kong personnel agencies, and others suggest checking the classified sections of the local newspapers. However logical this sounds, it doesn't seem to work very well – most foreigners who have found work in Hong Kong have done so by going door-to-door and asking. A good place to start looking is at bars and Western restaurants in Lan Kwai Fong, Wanchai and Tsimshatsui. Besides finding opportunities to be a bartender or waitress, people in gwailo bars and restaurants may have tips on English-teaching opportunities, modelling jobs, secretarial work and so on. As in most other places, who you know can count for more than what you know. Finding a job really means hitting the pavement. Also, pay attention to how you look – whether you're beautiful or not, the way you dress will make a difference in fashion-conscious Hong Kong.

The legal minimum wage in Hong Kong is a meagre HK$3500 per month, which works out to approximately HK$20 per hour for full-time. These are starvation wages, so you must reach an agreement on salary before you begin any job. In general, unskilled foreign labourers (bartenders, English teachers, etc) can negotiate salaries from HK$40 to HK$70 per hour. Your nationality makes a difference – unfair as it might seem, Filipinos and Thais earn considerably less than Westerners for doing the same work.

It's fairly easy to pick up work teaching conversational English. You may find yourself doing a lot of commuting between part-time jobs. Teaching English is not always as easy as it sounds. If your students are good, it can be a pleasure, but if their English is very poor, teaching them can be both boring and frustrating. However, it does provide one opportunity to meet local people.

Modelling is another possibility for both men and women. Modelling agencies are listed in the Yellow Pages Commercial/Industrial Guide, but again, contacts are vital and the agencies are only of limited help.

For females, paid babysitting is an option. Contact Rent-a-Mum (☎ 8179799), 88B Pokfulam Rd, Hong Kong Island.

Occasionally Westerners can find work standing around as extras in Hong Kong movies (long hours and little pay). Some people even try busking, but this does not seem to be highly lucrative.

One form of employment which requires no work visa is smuggling. It's also far more risky than you might be led to believe by prospective 'employers'. Supposedly, the idea is that you cart a bagful of perfectly legal goodies – such as one watch, one cassette player, one camera, one diamond ring or some other valuable item to a place such as Vietnam or India where imports of such foreign-made goods are heavily taxed or prohibited. Westerners are employed by professional smugglers who are usually Hong Kong Chinese. The theory is that the customs people are less likely to stamp the goodies on a Western passport, thus requiring you to exit with them. Once you pass customs, you hand the goods to an accompanying Hong Kong

Chinese, who then zips off to sell them. You either get a fee for this service and go back to Hong Kong to do it again, or else you've gained yourself a free air ticket to South Korea or Nepal and saved some money. These small-time smuggling expeditions are commonly known as 'milk runs'.

It all sounds very benign, but the risks are not something that your Chinese boss will reveal to you. When I was in Hong Kong, a traveller living in Chungking Mansions was solicited to smuggle seven kg of gold into Nepal and was offered US$2000 for his trouble. He got caught and was given four years in prison. Another traveller I met got caught at Seoul Airport wearing three mink coats under his jacket – he was fined and given two months in jail before being booted out of the country. Even worse is the possibility that your employer will use you as a 'mule' to smuggle drugs hidden inside your electronic goodies. There is even a lucrative market in stolen microchips and blasting caps, and while you might not recognise these goods for what they are, trained customs agents will.

ACTIVITIES

Hong Kong may not have downhill skiing, but the city offers plenty of ways to keep fit and have fun at the same time.

Anyone who is serious about sports should contact the South China Athletic Association (☎ 5776932; fax 8909304), 88 Caroline Hill Rd, Causeway Bay, Hong Kong Island. The SCAA has numerous indoor facilities for bowling, tennis, squash, ping pong, gymnastics, fencing, yoga, judo, karate, billiards and dancing. Outdoor activities include golf, and there is also a women's activities section. Membership is very cheap and there is a discounted short-term membership available for visitors.

Another excellent place you can contact is the Hong Kong Amateur Athletic Association (☎ 5746845; fax 8384959), Room 913, Queen Elizabeth Stadium, 18 Oi Kwan Rd, Wanchai. All sorts of sports clubs have activities here or hold members meetings.

Hong Kong's largest sporting facility is the Jubilee Sports Centre (☎ 6051212), also known as the Hong Kong Sports Institute. It's near the Fo Tan KCR Station, Shatin, New Territories. This one is mainly Chinese and gwailos are a small minority, but it's a good place to meet locals who might have the same interests as you.

Billiards & Snooker

The Chinese are crazy about these games, but most facilities are rather makeshift and in places where gwailos rarely go. Probably the most accessible venues are in Tsimshatsui East, including the Peninsula Billiards Club (☎ 7390638), 3rd floor, Peninsula Centre, and the Castle Billiards Club (☎ 3679071), Houston Centre.

In Central you can check out the Olympic Billiard Association (☎ 8150456), Hollywood Commercial Centre, Hollywood Rd & Old Bailey St. In Wanchai, there are two good places, Jim Mei White Snooker (☎ 8336628), 339 Jaffe Rd, and Winsor Billiard Company (☎ 5755505), 10 Canal Rd West. In Causeway Bay there is Kent Billiard & Snooker Association (☎ 8335665), Elizabeth House, Jaffe Rd and Percival St. In Quarry Bay you can find Far East Billiards & Snooker City (☎ 5659727), 969 King's Rd.

If you make it to the Outlying Islands, you can play at the Cheung Chau Billiards Association (☎ 9813576), 95 Hoi Pong Rd, Cheung Chau.

Bowling

Some of the best facilities are at the South China Athletic Association (☎ 5776932), 88 Caroline Hill Rd, Causeway Bay. Also on Hong Kong Island is Fourseas Bowling Centre (☎ 5670703), Cityplaza Shopping Centre, Tai Koo Shing MTR Station.

In Kowloon, bowling alleys tend to be located in the backwaters. One of the most accessible is Top Bowling (☎ 3345022), Basement, Site II, Whampoa Gardens, Hunghom. You can also try the Telford Bowling Centre (☎ 7550200), Telford Garden, near Kowloon Bay MTR Station. Another obscure place is the Mei Foo Sun Chuen Bowling Centre (☎ 7425911), 1st floor, 95C Broadway St, Laichikok.

Canoeing

To find enthusiasts of this sport, contact the Canoe Union (☎ 5727008; fax 8389037), Room 1010, Queen Elizabeth Stadium, 18 Oi Kwan Rd, Wanchai. There are canoeing facilities available through the Tai Mei Tuk Water Sports Centre (☎ 6653591), Regional Council, Tai Mei Tuk, Tai Po, New Territories. You can also inquire at the Wong Shek Water Sports Centre (☎ 3282370), Wong Shek Pier, Sai Kung, New Territories. Alternatively, there is the Chong Hing Water Sports Centre (☎ 7926810), West Sea Coffer Dam, High Island Reservoir, Sai Kung, New Territories.

Computer Clubs & BBSs

Hong Kong's economic prosperity, low-priced computer equipment and the large English-speaking expatriate community all add up to this being an ideal place for computer hobbyists. You can seek the company of fellow computer freaks by joining a computer club, or plug in a modem and dial up an electronic bulletin board system (BBS).

Probably the first thing you should do is visit a bookshop and purchase a copy of *The Datafile*, Hong Kong's only locally-produced computer magazine (at least in English). In the back is a listing of all the current English-language Hong Kong BBS phone numbers. There are also Chinese BBSs around, but you need Chinese software and the ability to read it if this option is to be any use at all. Subscriptions to *The Datafile* cost HK$100 annually, but that could change so ring them up (☎ 7912446) or write (PO Box 127, Sai Kung, Kowloon). The magazine also operates the Houston BBS (☎ 7350613).

Like BBSs, computer clubs come and go, but the HKTA publication *Associations & Societies in Hong Kong* also lists a few. One of the biggest is the Computer Club of Hong Kong (☎ 3081021; fax 3081023), Room 1408, Join-In Commercial Centre, 33 Laichikok Rd, Mongkok, Kowloon. Another is the Hong Kong Computer Society (☎ 8342228; fax 8343003), Unit D, 1st floor, Luckifast Building, 1 Stone Nullah Lane, Wanchai, and with a modem you can contact BISSIG, their BBS (☎ 5723145).

The *South China Morning Post* does a small computer section every Tuesday and

HONG KONG

this can be another source of information about activities for computer buffs.

Cricket

Just north of Deepwater Bay is the Hong Kong Cricket Club (☎ 5746266), 137 Wong Nai Chung Gap Rd, Hong Kong Island. The scenery from the playing fields is stunning.

On the other side of Victoria Harbour is the Kowloon Cricket Club (☎ 3674141), 10 Cox's Rd, Yaumatei.

Additional information may be obtained by contacting the Hong Kong Cricket Association (☎ 8592414; fax 5597528), c/o School of Professional & Continuing Education, University of Hong Kong, Pokfulam Rd, Hong Kong Island.

Cycling

There are bicycle paths in the New Territories mostly around Tolo Harbour. The paths run from Shatin to Tai Po and continue up to Tai Mei Tuk. You can rent cycles in these three places, but it's very crowded on weekends. On a weekday you may have the paths to yourself.

Bicycle rentals are also available at Shek O on Hong Kong Island, and Mui Wo on Lantau Island.

The Hong Kong Cycling Association (☎ 5733861; fax 8343715) can be contacted at Room 1013, Queen Elizabeth Stadium, 18 Oi Kwan Rd, Wanchai. Or try the Hong Kong Cyclist Club (☎ 7883898; fax 7880093), Shop No 17, Fu Chak House, Chak On Estate, Shamshuipo, Kowloon.

Fishing

Sportsfishing from small-sized yachts is a popular activity for resident gwailos. To organise a trip, contact the Hong Kong Amateur Fishing Society (☎ 7300442), Lucky House, 15th floor, Flat D, 18-24 Jordan Rd, Yaumatei, Kowloon.

While there are virtually no restrictions on sea fishing, it's a different story with fishing at freshwater reservoirs. There are restrictions on the quantity and size of fish taken from reservoirs, and the fishing season is from September through March. A licence is

required, which can be obtained from the Water Authority (☎ 8245000) in Causeway Bay. Those applying for a licence must be at least aged 14.

Fitness Centres

If pumping iron, sauna, aerobics and other such activities are what you need, you can try The Gym (☎ 8778337), 18th floor, Melbourne Plaza, 33 Queen's Rd, Central.

Golf

There are four golf courses in Hong Kong. On weekends, the courses are crowded and you pay more. The Royal Hong Kong Golf Club (RHKGC) permits visitors, but you do need to pay green fees and hire equipment. The RHKGC has two venues: the less expensive one is the 9-hole course at Deepwater Bay (☎ 8127070) on the south side of Hong Kong Island. For visitors playing 18 holes, the fee is HK$350 or HK$450 for the whole day. Visitors accompanied by a member are charged HK$130 on weekdays, rising to HK$225 on weekends. Operating hours are 9.30 am to 2.30 pm from May to August, and 9.30 am to 1.30 pm from September to April.

The RHKGC operates a more expensive course at Fanling (☎ 6701211) in the New Territories. For 18 holes, green fees are HK$850 for Hong Kong residents (nonmembers), or HK$1100 for overseas visitors. However, overseas visitors accompanied by a member can play for HK$250 on weekdays, or HK$650 on weekends. The course is open from 7.30 am to 6 pm.

The Discovery Bay Golf Club (☎ 9877271) on Lantau Island offers impressive mountain and coastal scenery. The charge for 18 holes is HK$700 on weekdays (8 am until dusk) or HK$1500 on weekends (7.30 am until dusk). Visitors accompanied by a member are charged HK$280 on weekdays, HK$850 on weekends.

The Clearwater Bay Golf & Country Club (☎ 7195936) is in the Sai Kung Peninsula in the New Territories. The course is open Monday to Friday from 7.30 am to 6 pm. Overseas visitors are charged HK$1100, but those with a Hong Kong ID card pay HK$850. Guests accompanied by a member are charged HK$300 on weekdays, or HK$600 on weekends.

Handball
You can play at the Indoor Handball Court in Kowloon Park in Tsimshatsui, or at Victoria Park in Causeway Bay. Otherwise, contact the Handball Association (☎ 5746934; fax 8346937), Room 911, Queen Elizabeth Stadium, 18 Oi Kwan Rd, Wanchai.

Hiking
Although trekking in Hong Kong is less challenging than the Nepal Himalaya, some basic equipment is necessary. Most important is a full water bottle. Other useful items include food, a rainsuit, sunhat, toilet paper, maps and compass. Boots are not really necessary but running shoes are preferred over flip-flop sandals (thongs). If you're prone to getting blisters, take some plaster. Of course, just how much equipment you decide to drag along depends on how far you plan to walk.

Good maps will save you a lot of time and trouble. Check out the *Countryside* series of maps available from the Government Publications Office in the GPO near the Star Ferry Terminal on Hong Kong Island.

Serious walkers should remember that the high humidity during spring and summer is tiring. November through March are the best months for strenuous treks. At high elevations, such as the youth hostel at Ngong Ping on Lantau, it can get very cold so it's essential to bring warm clothes and even a down sleeping bag if you're staying the night.

The sun can be merciless, so a sunhat and/or UV lotion are useful. There is little shade here because there are few trees on the slopes of Hong Kong's mountains. One effect of this is that landslides still occur during heavy rainstorms, posing another hazard to hikers.

Very few hiking areas in Hong Kong are dangerous, but there have been several injuries and some deaths. The victims are mostly inexperienced walkers taking foolish risks.

It is wise to stick to the established trails and heed the signs saying 'Steep and Seasonally Overgrown' or 'Firing Range'.

Snakes are rarely encountered, and your best way of avoiding them is to stick to trails and avoid walking through dense underbrush. If you see a snake, the best thing to do is to walk away from it. Most snakes fear creatures larger than themselves, including humans, and will try to avoid you. However, most snakes will attack when cornered. Hikers get bitten when they accidentally step on a snake or attempt to beat the creature with a stick.

Mosquitoes are a nuisance, so a good mosquito repellent is essential. Autan and Off! are popular brands of repellent available from Hong Kong drugstores. Mosquito coils (incense) are also effective when you're sitting in one place, but should not be used inside a tent or any other enclosed area as they are a fire hazard and the smoke contains a poison that isn't particularly good for your lungs.

Hiking in Hong Kong has become so popular that many trails are very crowded on weekends, so try to schedule your walks during weekdays.

To contact hiking clubs, call the Federation of Hong Kong Hiking & Outdoor Activities Groups (☎ ~~7204042~~), PO Box 79435, Mongkok Post Office, Mongkok, Kowloon. More serious climbers should try the Mountaineering Association (☎ 3916892), Room 1308, Argyle Centre, Phase I, 688 Nathan Rd, Mongkok, Kowloon; or the Mountaineering Union (☎ 7477003; fax 7707115), PO Box 70837, Kowloon Central Post Office, Kowloon.

The Outward Bound School (☎ 7924333) teaches wilderness survival. It's geared towards helping young people build character and self-esteem, but the organisation is not limited to teenagers. The address is Tai Mong Tsai, New Territories.

Horseback Riding
Hong Kong's small size limits opportunities for horseback riding. The Hong Kong Riding Union (☎ 7620810), 76 Waterloo Rd,

Kowloon Tong, organises rides in the New Territories. You can also call the Hong Kong Equestrian Centre (☎ 6073131), 7½ Miles Tai Po Rd, New Territories. Some limited riding is possible at the Lantau Tea Gardens (☎ 9855718) at Ngong Ping on Lantau Island. On Hong Kong Island, riding lessons are available at the Pokfulam Riding School (☎ 5501059, 5501359), 75 Pokfulam Reservoir Rd.

The clubs and riding schools organise competitions, and if you want to participate then apply one or two months in advance. Some major events include the Mini-Hunter Trials, Lo Wu Spring Show and Lo Wu Autumn Show.

Horse Racing

Gambling is deeply ingrained in Chinese culture, though, to be fair, it was the British who introduced horse racing to Hong Kong.

Apart from mahjong games and the twice-weekly Mark Six Lottery which raises money for the government, racing is the only form of legal gambling in Hong Kong, which is why Macau is so popular with the gambling-addicted Chinese. The first horse races were held in 1846 at Happy Valley on Hong Kong Island, and became an annual event. Now there are about 65 meetings per year at two tracks and about 450 races in all. The newer and larger track is at Shatin in the New Territories, and has seats in an air-con enclosure which can accommodate 70,000 people.

The HKTA has Come Horseracing tours to Happy Valley and Shatin. See the Tours section in the Getting Around chapter for details.

The racing season is from late September to June. Normally, races at Shatin are held on Saturdays from 1 pm to 6 pm. At Happy Valley, races are normally on Wednesday evenings from about 7 pm to 11 pm. However, this schedule isn't followed religiously. Sometimes extra races are held on Sundays or holidays. Check with the HKTA in late September or early October to get the schedule for the forthcoming season. You must bring your passport to attend a race.

Betting is organised by the Royal Hong Kong Jockey Club (RHKJC). Many types of betting combinations are available. One combination is the Quinella (picking the first two horses) or Double Quinella (picking the first two horses from two specific races). There is also the Treble (picking the winner from three specific races) or the Six-Up (out of the day's six races, pick the first or second in each race).

Off-track betting is also permitted. The RHKJC maintains off-track betting centres at 39-41 Hankow Rd in Tsimshatsui, at 64 Connaught Rd in Central and elsewhere.

If you want to attend the races, a seat in the public stands cost just HK$10. A visitor's badge to sit in the members' box costs HK$50. These badges can be purchased at the gate on the day of the race, or up to two days in advance at any branch of the RHKJC.

Karting

The big event of the year for karting enthusiasts is the Hong Kong Kart Grand Prix, held in late November or early December. For more details you can contact the Hong Kong Kart Club (☎ 5747466), 18th floor, Caltex House, 258 Hennessy Rd, Wanchai.

Lawn Bowling

Victoria Park in Causeway Bay has facilities for lawn bowling. These are open on weekdays in the afternoon only, but all day on weekends. There is a Lawn Bowls Association (☎ 8915156; fax 8382416), GPO Box 1823, Central. The same phone and fax numbers are shared by the Ladies Lawn Bowls Association, but there is a different mailing address (GPO Box 7387, Central).

Parachuting

It's not a very economical sport, but you can't beat it for thrills. If you get your jollies by diving out of aircraft, contact the Hong Kong Parachute Club (☎ 8915447; fax 8915481), Flat 4, Block A, 18th floor, Grandview Towers, 126 Kennedy Rd, Hong Kong Island.

Paragliding

If floating on air appeals to you, the place to contact is the Hong Kong Paragliding

Association (☎ 8032779). The club has three sites for regular meets: Big Wave Bay on Hong Kong Island, nearby Dragon's Back at Shek O and Sunset Peak on Lantau Island. A four-day training course is required for beginners, which costs HK$1500. This course can be spread out over a long period, up to a whole year. Once the course is completed, you're qualified to use the three sites. The training spot for beginners is none of the above, but rather at Pai Mai Tuk, Taipo, in the New Territories.

Running

If you'd like a morning jog with spectacular views, nothing beats the path around Victoria Peak on Harlech and Lugard Rds. Part of this is a 'fitness trail' with various exercise machines (parallel bars and the like). Almost as spectacular is the jog along Bowen Rd, which is closed to traffic and runs in an east-west direction in the hills above Wanchai. As long as there are no races at the time, the horse racing track at Happy Valley is an excellent place to run. There is also a running track in Victoria Park in Causeway Bay.

On the Kowloon side, a popular place to run is the Promenade which runs along the waterfront in Tsimshatsui East. The problem here is that it's not a very long run, but the views are good and it's close to many of the hotels.

The Hong Kong International Marathon is held on the second day of the Chinese New Year. This has become a cross-border event, with part of the running course passing through China. The Coast of China Marathon is held in March. Contact the HKTA for more information on upcoming marathons.

If you like easy runs followed by beer and good company, consider joining Hash House Harriers (☎ 3762299; fax 8136517), 3rd floor, 74 Chung Hom Kok Rd, Stanley, Hong Kong Island. You do not need to be in particularly good shape to participate. The Hash is an international organisation geared towards young people and the young at heart.

If you're looking for folks to run with, contact the Distance Runners Club (☎ 8296254; fax 8241220), GPO Box 10368. There is a Ladies Road Runners Club (☎ 3175933; fax 3175920), PO Box 20613, Hennessy Rd Post Office, Wanchai.

There is a running clinic every Thursday morning from 7 am to 8.30 am. For information, call the Adventist Hospital (☎ 5746211 ext 777).

For those who take running really seriously, contact the Triathlon Association (☎ 6092972; fax 6092958), Room 4B, 18th floor, Block E, Wah Lok Industrial Centre, 37-41 Shan Mei St, Fotan, Shatin, New Territories.

Sauna & Massage

The art of massage has a long history in China. Sauna baths are popular in Hong Kong and many bath houses offer a good massage service. During the chilly winter season there is probably no better way to relax. The legitimate places are suitable for both men and women. The saunas tend to be crowded in the evenings. Prices typically range from around HK$100 to HK$170 per hour, but ask first. The high-priced places are mainly found in Tsimshatsui East, but you can do better than this.

Many less respectable establishments are for men only and offer additional services. The legitimate saunas are listed in the Yellow Pages Buying Guide under Baths. The questionable ones are listed under Massage or Escort. The advertisements make interesting reading even if you never make use of their services.

The most incredible sauna is Sunny Paradise Sauna (☎ 8310123), 339-347 Lockhart Rd, Wanchai. Services include saunas, jacuzzis and massage for both males and females. Over in Kowloon, another reputable establishment is Crystal Spa (☎ 7226600), Basement 2, Harbour Crystal Centre, 100 Granville Rd, Tsimshatsui. In pricey Tsimshatsui East is VIP Sauna (☎ 3112288), 13th floor, Autoplaza, 65 Mody Rd.

Scuba Diving

Diving enthusiasts should contact the Underwater Association (☎ 5723792; fax

8496499), Room 910, Queen Elizabeth Stadium, 18 Oi Kwan Rd, Wanchai. An alternative is the Sea Dragons Skin Diving Club (☎ 8912113), GPO Box 10014, Hong Kong.

Bunn's Diving Equipment (☎ 5721629), Ground floor, Shop E & G, Kwong Sang Hong Building, 188 Wanchai Rd, Wanchai, organises dives every Sunday from 9 am to 4.30 pm at a cost of HK$280. Bunn's (☎ 3805344) also has another branch on the Ground floor, 217 Sai Yee St, Mongkok.

Skating

One of the best ice-skating rinks in Hong Kong is on the first floor of Cityplaza-Two (☎ 8854697), Cityplaza Shopping Centre, 18 Tai Koo Shing Rd, Quarry Bay. The easiest way to get there is to take the MTR to the Tai Koo Station.

On the Kowloon side, the best rink is Whampoa Super Ice (☎ 7744899) in Basement Two of the Whampoa Gardens shopping complex in Hunghom. Further afield is Riviera Ice Chalet (☎ 4071100), 3rd floor, Riviera Plaza, 28 Wing Shun St, Tsuen Wan, New Territories.

If you are interested in ice dancing or ice hockey, contact the Hong Kong Ice Activities Association (☎ 8275033; fax 8272698), Room B8, 9th floor, Causeway Centre, 28 Harbour Rd, Wanchai. This is also the location of the Ice Dance Union and Ice Hockey Association.

If you prefer wheels to blades, Rollerworld at Cityplaza Shopping Centre at Quarry Bay can accommodate you. There's also a roller rink in Telford Gardens shopping mall next to the Kowloon Bay MTR Station.

The Hong Kong Amateur Roller Skating Association (☎ 8870296; fax 8879646) is at Braemar Hill Mansions, Sports Centre, 29 Braemar Hill Rd, North Point.

Soccer

Soccer has caught the imagination of the Chinese, so competition for playing fields is keen. There isn't much trouble getting a soccer pitch during working hours, but forget it on weekends, holidays or during the evening.

If you want to get serious about competing in matches, contact the Football Association (☎ 7129122; fax 7604303), 55 Fat Kwong St, Homantin, Kowloon. The association also maintains a women's division.

There are over 130 soccer pitches in Hong Kong, and you can call the Urban Services Department to locate the ones nearest you. The Urban Services Department is itself segmented into neighbourhood divisions, so look in the Business Telephone Directory to find the branch relevant to your area. Some notable soccer pitches include:

Blake Garden, Po Hing Fong, Sai Ying Pun, Hong Kong Island; King George V Park, Hospital Rd, Sai Ying Pun, Hong Kong Island; Kowloon Park, Tsimshatsui, Kowloon; Kowloon Tsai Park, La Salle Rd, Shek Kip Mei, Kowloon; MacPherson Playground, Sai Yee St, Mongkok, Kowloon; Morse Park, Fung Mo St, Wong Tai Sin, Kowloon; Southern Playground, Hennessy Rd, Wanchai; Victoria Park, Causeway Bay

Squash

There are about 600 public squash courts in Hong Kong. These are easy to find during working hours, but become totally packed-out in the evening or on holidays. The most modern facilities are to be found at the Hong Kong Squash Centre (☎ 8690611), 23 Cotton Tree Drive, Central, next to Hong Kong Park. Book in advance. This is also the home of the Hong Kong Squash Rackets Association, which has done much to promote the sport. There are also squash courts in the Queen Elizabeth Stadium, Wanchai. In the New Territories, you can play squash at the Jubilee Sports Centre (☎ 6051212), near the Fo Tan KCR Station, Shatin.

Swimming

Except for Kowloon and the north side of Hong Kong Island, there are good beaches spread throughout the colony. The most accessible beaches are on the south side of Hong Kong Island but some of these are becoming increasingly polluted. The best beaches can be found on the Outlying Islands and in the New Territories. See those chapters for details. The longest beach in Hong Kong is Cheung Sha on Lantau Island.

There is an official swimming season from 1 April to 31 October. At this time, the 42 gazetted public beaches in Hong Kong are staffed with lifeguards. When the swimming season is officially declared finished, the beaches become deserted no matter how hot the weather.

Conversely, from the first day of the official swimming season until the last, expect the beaches to be chock-a-block on weekends and holidays. On weekdays, it's not bad at all. During the official season, all beaches controlled by the Urban Council or the Urban Services Department are patrolled by lifeguards. A red flag means the water is too rough for swimming and a blue flag means it's unsafe for children and weak swimmers. At most of the beaches you will find toilets, showers, changing rooms, refreshment stalls and sometimes restaurants. The usual life-saving hours are from 9 am to 6 pm on weekdays, but extended to 7 pm on weekends during July and August only.

Hong Kong's Urban Council operates 13 public swimming pools. During school term weekdays the pools are nearly empty so this is the best time to go. There's an excellent pool in Kowloon Park, Tsimshatsui, and Victoria Park, Causeway Bay.

Waterworld, next to Ocean Park in Aberdeen, offers outdoor pools and waterslides.

You can contact the Amateur Swimming Association (☎ 5728594) at Room 1003, Queen Elizabeth Stadium, 18 Oi Kwan Rd, Wanchai. Or try the Winter Swimming Association (☎ 5118363) 10th floor, Success Commercial Building, 245 Hennessy Rd, Wanchai.

Table Tennis & Badminton

It's widely acknowledged that the Chinese are the best table tennis players in the world. It's not so widely known that they are also badminton enthusiasts. Contact the Badminton Association (☎ 8384066), Queen Elizabeth Stadium, 18 Oi Kwan Rd,

Wanchai. There are similar facilities at the South China Athletic Association (☎ 5776932), 88 Caroline Hill Rd, Causeway Bay. You can also find facilities at the Aberdeen Indoor Games Hall (☎ 5536663), 168 Wong Chuk Hang Rd, Aberdeen.

Tennis

The Hong Kong Tennis Centre (☎ 5749122) is at Wong Nai Chung Gap, a spectacular pass in the hills between Happy Valley and Deep Water Bay on Hong Kong Island. It's open from 7 am until 11 pm, but it's only easy to get a court during working hours.

There are 13 courts in Victoria Park (☎ 5706186) which can be booked and are open from 6 am until 11 pm. There are four courts open from 6 am until 7 pm at Bowen Road Sports Ground (☎ 5282983), Bowen Rd, Mid-Levels.

The South China Athletic Association (☎ 5776932), 88 Caroline Hill Rd, Causeway Bay, also operates the tennis courts at King's Park, Yaumatei, Kowloon. Other facilities in Kowloon are at Tin Kwong Rd Playground, Tin Kwong Rd, Kowloon City and at Kowloon Tsai Park, Inverness Rd, Shek Kip Mei.

In the New Territories, you can play tennis at the Jubilee Sports Centre (☎ 6051212), near the Fo Tan KCR Station, Shatin.

The Hong Kong Tennis Association (☎ 8901132) is in Victoria Park. This is the place to ask questions about available facilities and upcoming events. Spectators may be interested in the Hong Kong Open Tennis Championship, held every September. In October, there's the Hong Kong Tennis Classic in Victoria Park.

Toastmasters Club

The purpose of this organisation is to give you practice in public speaking, to practise English (if it's not your native language) and to meet people. For some, it's sort of a dating service.

Actually, Toastmasters is not one organisation – there are many informal clubs that use the same name or some variation of it. The sponsors of the clubs are often companies who want to teach speaking skills to their employees and thus build self-confidence. One is Victoria Toastmasters (☎ 8677938; fax 8100218), care of Asia Insurance Company, 16th floor, World Wide House, 19 Des Voeux Rd, Central. Another is Hong Kong Toastmasters (☎ 5256060; fax 5217990) GPO Box 9243, Central.

Waterskiing

The main venues for waterskiing are on the south side of Hong Kong Island at Deepwater Bay, Repulse Bay, Stanley and Tai Tam. The south side of Lamma Island also attracts waterskiers. The price of participating is something like HK$250 per hour unless you have your own boat and equipment.

Places to contact include the Deep Water Bay Speedboat Company (☎ 8120391), Lot 702, Island Rd and Hong Kong Waterski Association, 35 Tsing Yi Rd, Tsing Yi Island (☎ 4312290).

Windsurfing

The best months for windsurfing are September through December when a steady north-east monsoon blows. Windsurfing during a typhoon is not recommended! Equipment rentals are available in the New Territories at the Windsurfing Centre (☎ 7925605), Sha Ha (just past Sai Kung). Also check out Tai Po Sailboard Centre, Chan Uk Chuen, 77 Ting Kok Rd, Tai Po, New Territories. Ditto for the Tai Mei Tuk Water Sports Centre (☎ 6653591), Regional Council, Tai Mei Tuk, Tai Po, New Territories.

Perhaps the best spot is on Cheung Chau Island at the Outdoor Cafe (☎ 9818316), Tungwan Beach. Rentals are HK$70 for two hours, or HK$200 for a full day. Tuition (if you need it) costs HK$450 for five hours.

At Stanley Main Beach on Hong Kong Island you can try the Pro Shop (pager 1128238-287) and Wind Surf Pro Motion (☎ 8132372). Shek O is another good place on Hong Kong Island for windsurfing.

Rental fees are typically from HK$50 to HK$80 per hour. Around December, Stanley

Beach becomes the venue of the Hong Kong Open Windsurfing Championship.

The place to check for more information is the Windsurfing Association of Hong Kong (☎ 8663232; fax 8656849), Room 801, Fortune Building, 13-15 Thomson Rd, Wanchai.

Yachting & Sailing

Major yacht harbours are at Aberdeen and Causeway Bay on Hong Kong Island, at Hebe Haven in the New Territories and at Discovery Bay on Lantau Island.

This is not exactly an inexpensive activity. The Royal Hong Kong Yacht Club is the largest gwailo yachting organisation in Hong Kong, but you can contact any of the following:

Aberdeen Boat Club
    20 Shum Wan Rd, Aberdeen (☎ 5528182)
Aberdeen Marina Club
    8 Shum Wan Rd, Aberdeen (☎ 5558321)
Discovery Bay Marina Club
    Discovery Bay, Lantau Island (☎ 9879591)
Hebe Haven Yacht Club
    10½ Miles, Hirams Highway, Pak Sha Wan, Sai Kung, New Territories (☎ 7199682; fax 3581017)
Royal Hong Kong Yacht Club
    Kellett Island, Causeway Bay (☎ 8322817; fax 5725399)
Yachting Association
    Room 906, Queen Elizabeth Stadium, 18 Oi Kwan Rd, Wanchai (☎ 5742639; fax 5720701)

The Corum China Sea Race is held every other year during Easter. The yachts race from Hong Kong to Manila.

One way to make a boat trip very affordable is to get together a group and rent a junk for the day. A 16-metre junk can accommodate around 28 persons and costs HK$2500 to HK$2800 per day (eight hours), so you don't have to be independently wealthy to participate. Costs tend to be higher on weekends and holidays. This is a popular form of recreation for gwailo office parties or birthday celebrations. This is best accomplished in the Outlying Islands or at fishing harbours like Aberdeen or piers in the New Territories. A place to try is Charterboats Ltd (☎ 5558377; fax 8734014), United 6,

Ground floor, Aberdeen Marina Tower, 8 Shum Wan Rd, Aberdeen. In the same building, you can also try the Boatique (☎ 5559355), Ground floor, Shop 10-11.

Other Activities

The following is a list of some other associations and clubs which have activities that could be of interest:

Archery Association
Room 911, Queen Elizabeth Stadium, 18 Oi Kwan Rd, Wanchai (☎ 5740635)

Artists' Guild
1st floor, 5 Mui Hing St, Happy Valley (☎ 8330096; fax 5729155)

Artists' Society
PO Box 74029, Kowloon Central Post Office, Kowloon (☎ 7782557)

Arts Festival Society
13th floor, Hong Kong Arts Centre, 2 Harbour Rd, Wanchai (☎ 8243555; fax 8243798)

Astronomical Society
GPO Box 2872, Central (☎ 5474543; fax 7152345)

Backgammon Club
Room 526, Hollywood Plaza, 610 Nathan Rd, Mongkok (☎ 7822721)

Balloon & Airship Club
12B Bella Vista, 15 Silver Terrace Rd, Clearwater Bay, Kowloon (☎ 7192046; fax 7196597)

Basketball Association
Room 1101, Queen Elizabeth Stadium, 18 Oi Kwan Rd, Wanchai (☎ 5461823)

Birdwatching Society
GPO Box 12460, Central

Boxing Association
Room 1004, Queen Elizabeth Stadium, Wanchai (☎ 5722932)

Buddhist Association
1st floor, 338 Lockhart Rd, Wanchai (☎ 5749371; fax 8340789)

Fencing Association
Room 1004, Queen Elizabeth Stadium, 18 Oi Kwan Rd, Wanchai (☎ 8914448; fax 8336715)

Festival Fringe
2 Lower Albert Rd, South Block, Central (☎ 5217251; fax 8684415)

Green Power (environmental group)
Room 705, Nathan Centre, 580 Nathan Rd, Mongkok, Kowloon (☎ 7709368; fax 7823160)

Gymnastic Association
Room 905, Queen Elizabeth Stadium, 18 Oi Kwan Rd, Wanchai (☎ 5734159; fax 8389075)

Human Rights Commission
3rd floor, 52 Princess Margaret Rd, Homantin, Kowloon (☎ 7139165; fax 7613326)

International Kite Association
Ground floor, 8 Kau Yuk Rd, Yuen Long, New Territories (☎ 4779867; fax 4733934)

Mensa (for persons whose IQ is in the top 2%)
GPO Box 9858, Central (☎ 3103111; fax 8497018)

Orienteering Association
Room 910, Queen Elizabeth Stadium, 18 Oi Kwan Rd, Wanchai (☎ 8912691; fax 8935654)

Orienteering Club
PO Box 20142, Hennessy Rd Post Office, Wanchai (☎ 5552105)

Photographic Society
21st floor, Wayson Commercial House, 68-70 Lockhart Rd, Wanchai

Raja Yoga Centre
Room 16B, Hung On Building, 3 Tin Hau Temple Rd, North Point (☎ 8063008; fax 8870104)

Rugby Football Union
A1401, Seaview Estate, 2 Watson Rd, North Point (☎ 5660719; fax 8073840)

Scout Association of Hong Kong
Morse House, 9 Cox's Rd, Yaumatei, Kowloon (☎ 3673096; fax 3114701)

Weightlifting Association
Room 1005, Queen Elizabeth Stadium, 18 Oi Kwan Rd, Wanchai (☎ 8939725)

HIGHLIGHTS

The trip on the Peak Tram to Victoria Peak has been practically mandatory for visitors since it opened in 1888. A 30-minute ride on a sampan through Aberdeen Harbour is equally exciting. Lunch at a good dim sum restaurant is one of the great pleasures of the Orient, and of course, shopping is what Hong Kong is all about.

ACCOMMODATION

If you're looking for dirt-cheap accommodation, Hong Kong is no paradise. High land prices means high prices for tiny, cramped rooms. Even though new hotels are constantly being built, demand always seems to exceed supply. Still, you can usually find a room without too much hassle, although this can be difficult during peak holidays times like Chinese New Year and Easter.

The HKTA runs a hotel booking counter at the airport, and while it won't find you a rock-bottom hovel, it will do its best to get you something. This can be especially useful if you arrive at night since the cheapies are more likely to be full by then and it's no joy carting your luggage around the streets looking for elusive beds at midnight. Many won't open the door at that hour even if they have got a bed.

Camping
Camping is generally permitted next to Hong Kong Youth Hostel Association (HKYHA) hostels in remote areas, where you will be permitted to use their toilet and washroom facilities. Camping is generally prohibited on the 42 public beaches patrolled by lifeguards, but should be OK at remote beaches.

Also, several government and independent campsites on Lantau Island are listed in a HKTA camping leaflet.

Hostels
The Hong Kong Youth Hostels Association (☎ 7881638), Room 225, Block 19, Shek Kip Mei Estate, Kowloon, sells Hostelling International (HI) cards for HK$80 to Hong Kong residents (HK$150 for nonresidents). They can also give you a members handbook which shows the locations of the hostels and explains the regulations in excruciating detail, such as not bringing guns or heroin into the hostel – just in case you weren't sure. Their office is inconveniently located in a hideous housing estate near the Shek Kip Mei MTR Station.

The hostels charge HK$50 a night for a dormitory bed, which is the cheapest place to sleep in Hong Kong. The hostels close between 10 am and 4 pm, and it's lights out at 11 pm. Like hostels in other countries, you are required to own a special HI sleeping sheet (you can buy or rent these at the hostels) and you must do a few simple cleaning chores. Advance booking is required for some hostels and this can be done by either writing, telephoning or going to the head office.

In general, the comments we get from travellers staying at these hostels are highly

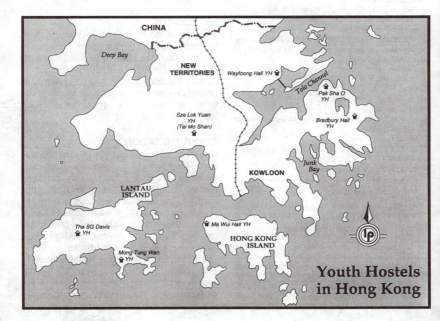

Youth Hostels in Hong Kong

negative. Extreme unfriendliness bordering on open hostility seems to be a requirement for getting a job as a hostel warden in Hong Kong.

Guesthouses

This is where most budget travellers wind up staying. The guesthouses are most numerous in dilapidated buildings in the Tsimshatsui neighbourhood or in some parts of Hong Kong Island. A few places still have dormitory beds, but these are not numerous. Expect to pay HK$70 to HK$100 for a dormitory bed if you can find one. For private rooms, prices start in the HK$150 range for doubles and can reach HK$450 for deluxe class. It definitely pays for two people to share a room as this costs little or no extra.

Warning

One thing to be cautious about are touts who hang around the airport to solicit backpackers with offers of cheap rooms. Sometimes they really do have good, cheap rooms, but you can't be sure until you actually see what you're getting. The problem is that if you go with them, see the room and decide that you don't like it, you might be faced with demands to pay HK$100 or more 'service charge' for the trouble they took to guide you from the airport. Some of them will even present the namecards of hostels and guesthouses which have been highly recommended in this book, and then they take you to some other dump.

I was approached at the airport by one man claiming to represent Man Hing Lung Guesthouse, and he showed me the namecard 'to prove it'. I asked if I could keep the namecard and go find the place by myself, but he said no, he wanted to guide me. As it turned out, I'm very familiar with Man Hing Lung so I went there by myself, and was astonished when the owner said he was all full and had not sent any touts to the airport to solicit business. I later heard the same story from Victoria Hostel, which also has a good write-up in this book. The moral of the story is that if they won't give you the

namecard and allow you to find the place by yourself, it's probably a fraud.

The same applies when you get off the airport bus. A Mr Shidric meets the A1 bus from the airport and asks travellers where they are staying. Whatever guesthouse they name, Mr Shidric says he 'works for it', then takes them to his shoddy, illegal dump of a hostel. No wonder his hostel has no sign on the door.

Hotels

Mid-range hotels start at around HK$400 and go up to around HK$800, which is hardly dirt cheap. There are plenty of hotels in this range and it shouldn't be hard to find something if you can afford the upper end of mid-range. Couples looking to save money should specify that they want one bed, since twins (two beds) are both more expensive and less romantic.

You can get as much as a 40% discount at mid-range and luxury hotels if you book through certain travel agents. One agent offering this service is Traveller Services (☎ 3752222; fax 3752233), Room 1012, Silvercord Tower 1, 30 Canton Rd, Tsimshatsui. A travel agent can also make advance bookings if you pay a deposit – ring up for details.

For the sake of definition, any hotels where rooms begin at HK$800 and up are regarded as top end. Luxury hotels are abundant in Hong Kong – apparently somebody can afford them. The HKTA's *Hotel Guide* lists all the main places. If you haven't made a reservation, you might as well use the HKTA booking office at Kai Tak Airport to make sure you have a room and don't have to drag your luggage around in a long, frustrating search.

You can be reasonably sure that any luxury hotel has whatever you need. About the only thing you need to consider is whether or not you like the location. Tsimshatsui East is the newest and most modern area and fairly close to the airport. Nearby Tsimshatsui is OK but older and a bit more tattered. On the Hong Kong Island side, there are several big hotels in the heart of Central (such as the Hilton) and a lot more further east in Wanchai and Causeway Bay.

If you stay in any proper hotels you will find a 10% service charge and a 5% government tax added to your bill, but you won't be troubled with either in the cheap places.

Rentals

For definition purposes, a long stay means a month or more. Many hotels offer big discounts for monthly rentals.

Not to be overlooked are the hotels and vacation flats on Lamma, Cheung Chau and Lantau islands – many of these are reasonably cheap if rented by the month though very expensive for short-term stays. Lamma is particularly popular, with rents around HK$5000 for a two-bedroom flat. Equivalent accommodation in Kowloon or Hong Kong Island would cost around HK$7000 or more for a smaller place. Of course, you have to tolerate a long commute if you work in the city.

The trendy gwailo housing estates all boast excellent surrounds, fine sea views, security guards and prices to match. Rents start at around the HK$9000 level for a studio flat and move up to around HK$20,000 or even HK$30,000 for three bedrooms. Many Westerners who can afford such accommodation don't pay for it – their company does. On Hong Kong Island, you can find these estates on the Peak, the Mid-Levels, Pokfulam (especially Baguio Villa), Happy Valley (Stubbs Rd), Deep Water Bay, Repulse Bay, Stanley and Shek O. In the New Territories, check out Tai Po (Hon Lok Yuen), Yuen Long (Fairview Park), Clear Water Bay and Sai Kung. In the Outlying Islands, only Discovery Bay on Lantau falls into this category.

The cheapest flats are in the ugly public housing estates and they tend to be concentrated in Kowloon. Fully half of all Hong Kongers live in these places. Pets, particularly dogs, are prohibited though people do raise them surreptitiously.

Some Westerners have moved out to the New Territories towards Tuen Mun, Shatin and Tsuen Wan. It's easier to find accommodation in the New Territories and rents are cheaper than in the centre, but the problem is commuting. Rush-hour traffic in Hong Kong grinds to a halt, though it's tolerable if you take the MTR, Kowloon-Canton Railway or a ferry. Nevertheless, expect all forms of public transport to be packed during rush hour.

An important factor in determining the cost of rent is the age of a building. Usually the younger the apartment block the higher the rents. Since even moderate Hong Kong rents are still high by international standards, most single people share flats.

Flats are generally rented exclusive of rates and unfurnished. One little trick that many gwailos have discovered is that practically all Chinese have a strong fear of anything associated with death. Consequently, apartments with views overlooking cemeteries are always cheaper and almost always rented by foreigners. If you understand the principles of fungshui (geomancy), then finding a flat with bad fungshui gives you bargaining power with the landlord in deciding what your rent should be.

If you are stuck for accommodation, 'leave' flats are worth investigating. Employees on contract are rewarded every couple of years with long holidays and usually rent their flats out while they are away. The usual duration is three months, during which time you are responsible for the rent and the wages of the *amah* (servant). Occasionally people even offer the flat rent-free with just the amah's wages to pay, in order to have someone keep an eye on the place. Nice work if you can get it. Leave flats are listed under a separate heading in the classified advertisements of the *South China Morning Post*.

The best place to look for flats is in the classified sections of the English-language newspapers. Having a Chinese person to check the Chinese-language newspapers can be a tremendous help too.

Then of course there are the real estate agents. Look in the Yellow Pages Buying Guide under Estate Agents.

If you're lucky enough to be moving to Hong Kong on contract you'll probably have your hotel room paid for you while you flat hunt. That's the custom in Hong Kong and if that isn't in your contract then you haven't negotiated very well.

Residential burglaries are a problem in Hong Kong, so keep security in mind. A steel door helps and many places have bars on the windows. Change the locks when you move in. A building with security guards is best, but this is a luxury you have to pay for.

If you're going to be doing business in Hong Kong, a number of companies are willing to rent you an instant office. You can simply rent an office with phone and fax, or you can rent secretaries and translators as well. Prices depend on how many staff persons you want, size, location, the length of the lease, etc. Most places require a three-month minimum. The HKTA can supply you with a list of companies that rent business offices.

As for buying property, realise that Hong Kong's real estate prices are amongst the highest in the world. Another question is just whether or not China will respect the property rights of foreigners after 1997. Currently, a flat in public housing estates goes for HK$1 million if you can find one. Flats often sell for a mere HK$5 million.

FOOD

The Chinese don't ask, 'Have you eaten yet?' Instead they say, 'Have you eaten rice yet?'

Rice is an inseparable part of Chinese culture – the key to survival in their long history. Among older, more conservative Chinese, wasting rice is practically a sin. If they see you've left half your rice uneaten, they may regard you with disdain.

So much for the old folks. The younger generation was brought up on waste, but one thing that hasn't changed is the quality. There are few places on earth with more gastronomic variety than Hong Kong, and the locals like to boast that their city has the best cuisine in the world.

Unfortunately, eating well in Hong Kong is no longer cheap, although with effort you can still get a good Chinese meal for a few dollars. A lot depends on the surroundings. If you're willing to eat from pushcarts and street stalls, you can save a bundle. In Hong Kong's seated restaurants you'll find that Chinese food isn't any cheaper than Western food, mainly because a high proportion of the price of a restaurant meal goes to pay for the space occupied by the customer's bottom.

Etiquette

Chinese meals are social events. Typically, four or five people eat together at the same table. The idea is to order many dishes (at least one dish per person) and then share. The Chinese think nothing of sticking their chop-

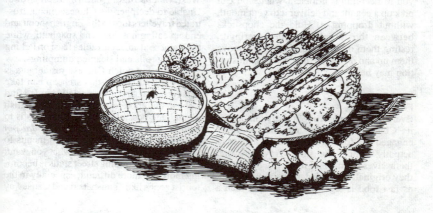

HONG KONG

sticks right into the communal dish, one reason why hepatitis is still a problem in Hong Kong (even worse in China). You may prefer to use a serving spoon.

Apart from the communal dishes, everyone gets an individual bowl of rice or small soup bowl. Proper etiquette demands that you hold the bowl near your lips and shovel the contents into your mouth with chopsticks (or a spoon for soup).

As an alternative to holding the bowl up to your mouth, place a spoon in your left hand and the chopsticks in the right, then push the food on to the spoon. Then use the spoon as you normally would. Chinese food is never eaten with a knife or fork.

If the food contains bones, spit them out on to the tablecloth or, if you want to be extra polite, into a separate bowl (most people use the tablecloth). You don't have to use a napkin to hide the spitting out of bones. As you'll discover, Chinese people generally leave a big mess when they finish eating. Restaurants know this and are prepared – they change the tablecloth after each customer leaves.

Soup is usually eaten at the end of a meal, rather than at the beginning as Westerners do.

Chopsticks
If you're planning a trip to Hong Kong or China, you'd be wise to practice with chopsticks before you leave home. You know you're becoming proficient when you can pick up a peanut and deliver it to your mouth without dropping it. Hold the chopsticks between the thumb and the forefinger, resting them on the index finger, and move them up and down like pincers. The illustration may help.

Food Locales
Even though Hong Kong is justly famous for its Chinese food, you may find yourself engaged in a frustrating search for a place to actually sample the stuff. Travellers find themselves eating a lot more Big Macs than they originally intended. Cost is one reason, as fast food is significantly cheaper than a

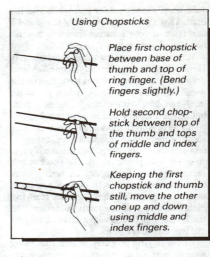

Using Chopsticks

Place first chopstick between base of thumb and top of ring finger. (Bend fingers slightly.)

Hold second chopstick between top of the thumb and tops of middle and index fingers.

Keeping the first chopstick and thumb still, move the other one up and down using middle and index fingers.

meal at many Chinese restaurants. Another reason is that after a few months in Asia many travellers find that they can't stand the sight of one more noodle.

However, the bizarre truth is that many Westerners are driven to eat fast food because of the peculiar attitude of Hong Kong restaurants. Most Chinese restaurants only list Western food in the English menu and list Chinese food in Chinese characters only – they actually seem to not want Western customers eating 'their' food. Unable to decipher the Chinese menu, frustrated travellers turn to the English menu and end up eating hot dogs and spaghetti, while the Chinese at adjacent tables feast on Peking duck, egg rolls and steamed dumplings.

Finding top-notch Chinese restaurants is easy, but finding one that's cheap can take perseverance. And it's especially hard to find a cheap but good restaurant with an English menu. One possible solution to all this is to explore the street stalls, known as *dai pai dong* in Cantonese. There are no menus to struggle with, so just point to what you want. However, even finding street stalls is becoming more and more difficult, especially in the tourist zones like Tsimshatsui and Causeway

Bay. The night markets like Temple St in Yaumatei and Apliu St in Shamshuipo are the best bet.

Several good books on eating out in Hong Kong are available at any of the English-language bookstores. The trouble with such books is that they go out-of-date quickly. Listed places go bust or are under new management (with a consequent deterioration in service or raised prices) and new places open all the time.

The HKTA's *Dining and Entertainment Guide* is updated annually, but is aimed at the well-heeled tourist rather than the budget backpacker. Nevertheless, it's hard to argue with the fact that it's free, so ask at any HKTA office for a copy.

Snacks

There are plenty of Western-style snacks, as indicated by all those Dairy Farm Creameries (ice cream shops).

The more traditional Chinese snacks are various seafood-type dishes, often served on a bamboo skewer. Squid on a stick is one such example. Fishball soup served in a styrofoam cup is a modern variation of a traditional snack. You mostly buy these Cantonese munchies from pushcarts. These tend to gather late at night in strategic locations such as off-track betting parlours or the ferry piers.

Thousand-year-old (also known as hundred-year-old) eggs are a Cantonese speciality – these are duck eggs soaked in a chemical solution for several days rather than a thousand years. This turns the white of the egg green and the yolk a greenish-black. In the old days, these eggs were made by soaking them in horse urine. Most Westerners say these eggs smell and taste like ammonia.

Main Dishes

Over many centuries the Chinese have perfected their own unique style of cooking which they regard as a fine art. Being a large country, China can be divided into many geographical areas, each with its own style of cooking, and the ingredients used tend to reflect what is available in that region.

For example, northern China is suitable for raising wheat, so noodles, dumplings and

Banquets

The Chinese love banquets and look for any opportunity to have one. Weddings are the most obvious occasions to warrant a feast, but banquets can be held almost anytime.

You might find yourself invited to a banquet if you do business in Hong Kong or if a friend gets married. Not all banquets are free – especially for weddings, as you are expected to bring a cash gift placed in a red envelope. Find out in advance if you are supposed to do this and how much you should give.

You'd be well-advised not to eat anything all day before the banquet. When the banquet begins, you may at first be disappointed – it will seem as if there isn't enough food on the table. Nevertheless, eat slowly to avoid feeling satisfied because one course will follow another. You will often be urged to eat more and more no matter how full you are. About 10 to 12 courses is considered normal at a banquet.

At banquets, eat little or no rice. Rice at banquets is considered a filler, and if you're eating a 12-course meal you'll soon become too full with seven courses yet to come.

There is plenty of toasting between courses. The host raises a glass and says *gam bei* (literally dry glass) which basically means bottoms up! You do not have to empty your glass, just take small sips, especially since Chinese liquor is powerful. Some people who can't handle strong alcohol fill their glass with tea instead. However, you definitely must go along with the toast – it would be most rude to sit and not drink something when a toast is made.

After a particularly large meal, the Chinese rarely eat dessert – fruit is preferred. When the food is all gone, the guests usually don't hang around and chat, but make a beeline for the door (usually carrying a plastic bag with some leftovers). ■

other wheat-based dishes are most common. In the south, where the climate is warm and wet, rice dominates as the basic staple. Coastal areas are where seafood is best. The Sichuan area, where spices grow well, is famous for fiery hot dishes.

However, it is not only geography that determines which ingredients are used. Tradition and culture play a part. The Cantonese, the least squeamish among the Chinese, are known for their ability to eat virtually anything. Hong Kong may be a dog-eat-dog society, but the only reason you don't find canine on the menu is because the British have prohibited it. That may well change in 1997, as just across the border in Guangzhou you'll find dogs, cats and rats on the menu. Most expats won't admit it publicly, but many Westerners who live in Hong Kong have joined the cross-border weekend dog-eating expeditions to Guangzhou.

The Chinese take the notion of 'you are what you eat' quite literally. Consequently, animals with physical and possible sexual prowess are widely sought. Eating snake, for example, is considered good for your health. The more venomous the snake, the greater its reputation as a revitaliser and cure-all. Cobras are a favourite. Little old ladies drink the blood because they think it will cure arthritis and rheumatism. Some men do the same because they believe it's an aphrodisiac. Everyone knows that tigers are strong, so tiger's meat is much in demand. Being a rare animal, tiger meat is very expensive – especially the sexual organs.

To be fair, not all Hong Kongers would eat the testicles of endangered species or what Westerners regard as pets. More mundane meat dishes are pork, duck, beef and fish. Strict Buddhists (a distinct minority in Hong Kong) have the tradition of being vegetarians, and the Chinese prepare some of the best vegetarian food around.

The Government Publications Centre in the Hong Kong GPO sell some books with colour photos and recipes for various dishes with both English names and Chinese characters. If you want to take it further, the YWCA offers Chinese cooking classes.

It's not unusual for a meal to be served with small dishes filled with various sauces. The most popular with Cantonese food is hot mustard sauce. If they don't put it on the table, you can ask for it.

I've never seen salt shakers in a Chinese restaurant unless they also served Western food, but they sometimes have pepper. Often you will find several small bottles on the table containing soy sauce, vinegar and sesame oil. Most Westerners like the soy sauce, but the vinegar and sesame oil is definitely an acquired taste. The Chinese often mix all three together. The vinegar is usually a very dark colour and is easily confused with the soy sauce, so taste some first before dumping it on your food. Actually, the Chinese don't dump sauces on their food, but prefer to pour some into a separate dish and dip the food into it.

Cooking Styles

There are many different styles of Chinese cooking, originating from the different regions of China. These regional variations are well represented in Hong Kong as a result of immigration from the mainland.

There are four major styles of Chinese cuisine: Beijing-Shandong, Cantonese-Chaozhou, Sichuan-Hunan and Shanghainese. Somewhere inbetween comes vegetarian food, and now the new innovation commonly known as 'fast food'.

Except for the last two categories, you probably won't know or care which style you're eating. For the benefit of culinary connoisseurs, a brief rundown follows.

Beijing (Peking) & Shandong Beijing and Shandong cuisine comes from the cold northland of China. Since this is China's wheat belt, steamed bread, dumplings and noodles figure prominently rather than rice.

The better Beijing restaurants put on quite a show of noodle making for the tourists. This is done by hand – the chef adroitly twirls the dough, stretches it, divides into two strands, stretches, divides into four, and so on until the noodles are thin as threads.

The most famous speciality is Beijing

Cantonese & Chaozhou This is southern Chinese cooking and the one for which Hong Kong is famous. Cooking methods include lots of steaming, boiling and stir-frying.

Specialities are abalone, shark's fin soup (very expensive), roast pig and a snake dish known as Dragon's Duel Tiger which is a combination of wild cat and snake meat. The Chinese do interesting things with edible fungi (more politely called 'truffles') of which there are numerous species with different tastes.

Pigeon is a Cantonese speciality served in various ways, often with lemon or oyster sauce, but the gourmet's delight is plain roast.

Dim sum is a snack-like variation consisting of all sorts of little delicacies. It's justifiably famous and highly addictive stuff.

One of the big rewards of coming to Hong Kong is the opportunity to indulge in a dim sum binge. Dim sum is a uniquely Cantonese dish served only for breakfast or lunch, but never dinner. The term dim sum means a snack. If the characters are translated literally, dim sum means 'to touch the heart'. The act of eating dim sum is usually referred to as *yum cha*, which literally means 'to drink tea', since this is always served with dim sum meals.

Eating dim sum is a social occasion and something you should do in a group. If you're travelling by yourself, try to round up three or four other travellers for a dim sum lunch. Of course, you can eat dim sum by yourself, but the problem is that dim sum consists of many separate dishes which are meant to be shared. You can't simply order a plate of dim sum. Having several people to share with you means you can try many different dishes.

Dim sum delicacies are normally steamed in a small bamboo basket. Typically, each basket contains four identical pieces, so four people would be an ideal number for a dim sum meal. You pay by the number of baskets you order. The baskets are stacked up on pushcarts and rolled around the dining room.

You don't need a menu, just stop the waiter or waitress and choose something from the cart, and it will be marked down on your bill. Don't try to order everything at once. Each pushcart has a different selection, so take your time and order many different dishes from different carts. It's estimated that there are about 1000 dim sum dishes. Usually dim sum is not expensive – HK$25 per person is about average for breakfast, or perhaps HK$40 for a decent lunch.

Dim sum restaurants are normally brightly lit and very large, rather like eating in an aircraft hanger.

duck, served with pancakes and plum sauce. Another northern speciality is Mongolian hotpot, composed of assorted meats and vegetables cooked in a burner right on the dining table – it's so good in Hong Kong that it's hard to believe it can be so bad in Mongolia. Hotpot is usually eaten during winter. Bird's nest soup is a speciality of Shandong cooking.

Another popular dish, beggar's chicken, is supposedly created by a beggar who stole the emperor's chicken and then had to bury it in the ground to cook it. The chicken is stuffed with mushrooms, pickled Chinese cabbage, herbs and onions, then wrapped in lotus leaves, sealed in clay and baked all day in hot ashes.

Dim sum waiter

Nevertheless, it can get very crowded, especially at lunch time.

The restaurants normally open about 7.30 am and close about 2.30 pm, with many also shutting down between 10 am to 11.30 am. Arriving after lunch is probably not a good idea as the best food will be gone. Some dim sum connoisseurs say late morning, at 10.30 am or 11 am, is the ideal time to arrive, but not all places are open at those hours. The operating hours are often extended on weekends and holidays, starting earlier and ending later. It can also be very crowded on weekends and sometimes you have to wait for a seat or join the stampede. In the evening, when dim sum is no longer served, many restaurants become dinner nightclubs and charge high prices.

Shanghainese Of all Chinese cuisines, this one is my least favourite. Shanghainese cooking is noted for its use of seafoods, but it's heavy and oily. Many Westerners say it's greasy, tasteless and disgusting, but liberal use of spices can make it almost palatable. Eels are popular, as is drunken chicken, cooked in wine. Other things to try are some of the cold-meat-and-sauce dishes, ham-and-melon soup, bean curd (tofu) and brown sauce, braised meat balls, deep-fried chicken, and pork ribs with salt and pepper.

Sichuan (Szechuan) & Hunan Sichuan food is the hottest of the four major categories – it's great stuff if you like spicy food, but keep the drinking water handy! Specialities include frogs' legs and smoked duck. Other dishes to try are shrimps with salt and garlic; dried chilli beef; bean curd with chilli; bear paws braised in brown sauce; fish in spicy bean sauce and aubergines in garlic.

Hunan food is a variation, often hot and spicy like Sichuan cuisine. Ducks, chickens and seafood are usually on the menu.

Vegetarian Chinese are masters at the art of adding variety to vegetarian cooking. Even if you are not a vegetarian it is worth giving one of the excellent vegetarian restaurants a try.

Vegetarian food is based on soybean curd – but the Chinese do some miraculous things with it. 'Fish' can be made by layering pieces of dried bean curd or can be fashioned from mashed taro root. Not only do they make it taste like any food you could think of, they make it look like it as well. *Lo lun chai* is a delicious mixed vegetable dish, a meal in itself. Try also the noodle and bean curd dishes, *congee* (rice porridge), fried spring rolls, sweet-and-sour and sweet corn soup.

Other Asian Food Many Asian people apart from Chinese live in Hong Kong and find it profitable going into the restaurant business. The cosmopolitan atmosphere assures you of plenty of ethnic food from various countries in the region. Indian restaurants are particularly abundant and you won't have trouble finding just about any Asian cuisine, from Korean *bulgogi* (barbecue) and *kimchi* to an Indonesian *satay* or *gado gado*.

Japanese food is never cheap. A Japanese meal will cost at least double what you'd spend for a similar level of service in a Chinese restaurant. It's interesting to speculate why. A lot of Japanese come to Hong Kong, and since they're used to paying exorbitant prices anyway, perhaps local restaurateurs want to make them feel at home. Bring a credit card or a suitcase full of cash.

Fast Food No matter what negative feelings you might have about fast food, after two months or more in China, the sight of rice and noodles becomes intolerable for many travellers, who find themselves dreaming of milkshakes and French fries.

Seven out of 10 of the busiest McDonald's branches in the world are in Hong Kong. If you were expecting to find these places chock full of Westerners, then you're in for a surprise. Most of the customers are Chinese. The Chinese attach no stigma to eating fast food, and in fact it actually has some snob appeal. Hanging out with an Egg McMuffin is considered chic.

The Chinese have their own versions of fast food, some not bad at all. In my opinion, the king of Chinese fast-food outlets is Fairwood. The plastic red clown face over the door puts off many foreigners, but the meals can compete with those served in mid-range Western restaurants. Some dishes disappoint though – the 'salad' is basically a bowl of mayonnaise.

Another homegrown fast-food chain is Café de Coral. It gets mixed reviews, but has gradually improved over the years. Some of the dishes are good and the Chinese are absolutely crazy about the place.

Ka Ka Lok Fast Food Shop does quick meals of rice, meat and veggies that you take away in a styrofoam box. It is fast, filling and cheap, and does a good job catering to the budget-end of the fast-food market.

Maxim's is a well-known Hong Kong chain of fast-food restaurants and cake shops. Known for its plastic enamel decor and staff who speak no English, it's not a big hit with Westerners. The Chinese food is passable and the cakes are OK, but the Western egg & sausage breakfasts look as if they've been spray-painted onto the plate. Personally, I rate this one near the bottom.

Desserts

The Cantonese have always been the best bakers amongst the Chinese by a wide margin. Part of this may be Western influence since the Cantonese have had some of the earliest contacts with the West. Nevertheless, there are certain specialties which seem to be distinctly home-grown. Things to look for include custard tarts (best when served hot), steamed buns with sweet bean-paste inside, coconut snowballs (sweet rice flour balls dressed with coconut slices) and various other sweets dressed with coconut and sesame seeds.

Incidentally, you do not find fortune cookies in Cantonese or any other real Chinese cuisine. They are a foreign invention.

Fruit

Besides mundane peaches, pears and apples, Hong Kong imports a wide variety of fruits from South-East Asia. Many of these are excellent, though some tropical varieties spoil rapidly after being picked and are definitely worse for the wear. You'll also find that prices are several times higher than you'd pay in the Philippines, Thailand or Vietnam. Some to look for include:

carambola – this is also known as starfruit, because that's what it looks like from one angle.

durian – this large fruit has tough spikey skin which looks impenetrable. After breaking it open with a big knife and peeling off the skin (not difficult), you'll encounter the next obstacle, namely a powerful odour that many can't stand. The creamy fruit is actually delicious and even used to make ice cream in South-East Asia. The season is approximately April through June. Durians spoil fairly easily and cost a bundle.

jackfruit – this large segmented fruit is fine stuff when ripe, but positively awful if it's not.

longan – the name means 'dragon eyes' in Chinese. The skin is brown, but otherwise the taste is similar to lychees. The season is later, around June through early August.

lychee – this red pulpy fruit with white flesh and a single large (inedible) seed is one of the main agriculture exports of China. It grows well in Guangdong Province, just across the border from Hong Kong. There is even a lychee-carbonated soft drink, which is fine stuff. China's lychee season is from April through June.

mangosteen – the way to eat these is to cut them in two and scoop out the delicious pulp with a spoon.

mango – these are delicious, pulpy and very messy to eat. Although the season is late spring and summer, you can easily buy dried mango at any time of year. The Chinese also eat green (unripe) mangos out of season, but pickled and sweetened – the taste is sour but not bad.

papaya – this delicious fruit is available all year round in Hong Kong. The abundant black seeds from the centre of the fruit can be dried and used as herbal medicine. The seeds have been successfully used to treat amoebic dysentery, but the taste is awful. By contrast, the fruit is delicious stuff and is even used to make milkshakes.

pomelo – it's similar to a large grapefruit but tougher.

rambutan – this fruit is very similar to lychees except for the 'hairy' skin.

Self-Catering

For true backpacker's cuisine like muesli, peanut butter and oatmeal, you've got to hit the supermarkets. Hong Kong grocery stores offer a great variety of Western foods at low prices. Even if you're not on a tight budget, after a long journey through Asia you may not be able to stand the sight of another noodle, and will appreciate the opportunity to kick back with a homemade cheese & salami sandwich on French bread with pickles & mustard.

Small convenience stores of the 7-Eleven genre feature frozen dinners (including dim sum) and a microwave oven to heat it up. These places also have the advantage of being open very late or very early, and some operate 24 hours.

Every neighbourhood has its local market. The most accessible to tourists is the Central Market on Queen's Rd, between Jubilee and Queen Victoria Sts, Central. There are three floors of meat, vegetables, fish and poultry. The daily prices are posted on a large noticeboard. In Hong Kong a foreign face is equivalent to a big sign saying 'Sucker', but in general you won't be cheated in the food markets.

Oliver's is a fast-food restaurant, but the attached grocery stores are where you can find rare items like blue cheese, melba toast, chocolate cookies from Belgium and black bread from Germany. It's a big hit with expats and definitely worth visiting. To find the addresses, see the Self-Catering heading of Places to Eat in both the Kowloon and Hong Kong Island chapters.

The supermarket in Seibu Department Store on Hong Kong Island is also worth checking out.

Dim Sum 點心

barbecued pork buns
  cha siu bau 叉燒飽
bean curd chicken roll
  gai chuk 雞紮
bean curd pork roll
  seen chuk guen 鮮竹卷
fried spring rolls
  tsun guen 春卷
fried green pepper
  yeung chen chiu 叉燒飽
fried rice flour triangle
  ham shui kok 咸水餃
fried taro puff
  woo kok 芋角
fried chicken feet
  fung jau 鳳爪
fried flour triangle
  jar fun gwor 炸粉果
minced pork dumpling
  guon tong gau 灌湯餃
pork & shrimp dumplings
  siu mai 燒賣
rice flour triangle
  fun gwor 粉果
rice wrapped in lotus leaf
  ho yip fan 荷葉飯
rice dumpling in bamboo leaf
  gwor ching chung 裹蒸粽
rice flour & shrimp roll
  har cheung fun 蝦腸粉
shark's fin dumpling
  yee chi gau 魚翅餃
spicy spare ribs
  pai gwat 排骨
steamed shrimp dumplings
  har gau 蝦餃
steamed tripe
  ngau pak yip 牛柏葉
steamed meat buns
  siu lung bau 小龍飽
steamed minced beef balls
  san juk ngau yuk 山竹牛肉

Dim Sum Desserts
coconut pudding cubes
  yeh jap go 椰汁糕
coconut snowball
  nor mai chi 糯米茲
custard tart
  daan tart 蛋撻
steamed egg pudding
  dun gai daan 炖雞蛋
steamed lotus paste bun
  lin yung bau 蓮蓉飽
sticky cake & nuts
  ma chai 馬仔
sweet red bean porridge
  hung dow sa 紅豆沙
wrapped coconut, peanut & sesame
  pun yip kok 蘋葉角

Fruits 水果
carambola
  yong tou 楊桃
durian
  laulin 榴蓮
jackfruit
  taishui boluo 大樹菠蘿
longan
  long an 龍眼
lychee
  lai chi 荔枝
mangosteen
  san juk 山竹
mango
  mong gow 芒果
papaya
  mok gwa 木瓜
pomelo
  sa tin yau 沙田柚
rambutan
  fan gwai lo lai chi 番鬼佬荔枝

DRINKS
Tea
In Chinese restaurants tea is often served free of charge, or at most you'll pay HK$1 for a big pot which can be refilled indefinitely. On the other hand, coffee is seldom available except in Western restaurants or coffee shops, and is never free.

When your teapot is empty and you would like a refill, signal this by taking the lid off the pot. To thank the waiter or waitress for pouring your tea, tap your fingers on the table. It's not necessary to say thank you. The finger-tapping is only done for tea, and not when food is brought.

There are three main types of tea: green or unfermented; *bolai* fermented, also known as black tea; and *oolong* which is semi-fermented. There are many varieties of tea. Jasmine tea *(heung ping)* is a blend of tea and flowers which is always drunk straight, without milk or sugar. Most of the tea is imported from China, but some comes from India and Sri Lanka. Hong Kong has only one tea plantation (at Ngong Ping on Lantau Island) which is basically a tourist attraction.

Fleecy
A 'fleecy' is not just what shopowners on Nathan Rd do to tourists buying cameras, but is also the name of a sweet cold drink. The distinguishing feature of a fleecy is that it contains some sort of lumpy mixture, usually red or green mung beans, but sometimes pineapple or other fruits. An interesting ingredient sometimes used is black grass jelly. Milk is usually part of the mixture, but not always. You can sample these drinks almost anywhere, even in Chinese fast-food restaurants.

Alcohol
In free-market Hong Kong, you can easily find most major brands of imported alcohol. Excellent beer is available everywhere, and San Miguel even has a brewery in Hong Kong.

What the Chinese generally call wine is not really wine at all – it's hard liquor more like whisky or rum. Many of these wines are brewed from grains like rice, sorghum and millet. To the Western palate, they resemble petrol. *Siu hing* is a rice-based wine, the fiery *go leung* is distilled from sorghum and *mao tai* is made from millet. More closely resembling wine is *ng ka pay* which has a sweet taste and is made with herbs. The Chinese seldom dilute their alcohol – they drink it just as it comes from the bottle.

You may have an opportunity to see the

finger game, a type of drinking game in which the loser is obliged to empty the glass. Women seldom play.

Happy Hour The cheapest way to get drunk is to buy a bottle of Chinese rice wine (used for cooking), preferably in a brown paper sack, and sit in Kowloon Park to finish it off. However, if you would prefer a more cheerful atmosphere, you can save considerably by taking advantage of the happy hours. During certain hours of the day, several bars, discos and nightclubs give substantial discounts on drinks. Some places give you drinks for half-price during happy hour, while others let you buy one drink and give you the second one free. Usually, happy hour is in the late afternoon or early evening, but the times vary too much for there to be any hard rule. If you enter a bar during happy hour, make note of the time when it ends. Otherwise, you may linger too long and wind up paying more than you expected.

Drinks Vocabulary
ice cold
  dong 凍
ice cubes
  bingfai 冰塊
hot
  yit 熱

Cold Drinks
water
  soi 水
mineral water
  kong chwin soi 礦泉水
fizzy drink (soda)
  hesoi 汽水
Coca-Cola
  hohau holok 可口可樂
Diet Coke
  gamfei holok 減肥可樂
Fanta Orange
  fantat changchap 芬達橙汁
Sprite
  shwe bae 雪碧
lemon tea (cold)
  dong lengmeng cha 凍檸檬茶

carrot juice
  hong lobak chap 紅蘿蔔汁
orange juice
  chang chap 橙汁
starfruit juice
  yong tou chap 楊桃汁
sugarcane juice
  gam chei chap 甘蔗汁
papaya milkshake
  mougwa aulai 木瓜牛奶
pineapple milkshake
  boluo laisek 菠蘿奶昔
watermelon milkshake
  saigwa laisek 西瓜奶昔

Fleecy
Red Bean
  hongdau bing 紅豆冰
Green Bean
  lokdau bing 綠豆冰
Black Grass Jelly
  leungfan 涼粉
Fruit Punch
  zap gou bing 雜果冰
Pineapple
  boluo bing 菠蘿冰

Tea & Coffee
tea
  cha 茶
black tea
  zai cha 齋茶
tea with milk
  lai cha 奶茶
lemon tea
  lengmeng cha 檸檬茶
green tea
  luk cha 綠茶
chrysanthemum tea
  gukfa cha 菊花茶
jasmine tea
  heung pin cha 茉莉花茶
oolong tea
  oolong cha 烏龍茶
hot chocolate
  ye jugulek 熱朱古力
Ovaltine
  ye ouwahtin 熱呵華田
Horlicks
  ye holahak 熱好立克

coffee with milk
  gafei 熱咖啡
black coffee
  zai fei 齋啡

Alcohol
beer
  beijau 啤酒
Carlsberg Beer
  gasiba 加士百
Lowenbrau Beer
  lowenbo 盧雲堡
San Miguel Beer
  sangle bei 生力啤
Tsingtao Beer
  chingdo beijau 青島啤酒
whiskey
  waisigei 威士忌
vodka
  fukte ga 伏特加
red grape wine
  hung jau 紅酒
white grape wine
  ba jau 白酒
rice wine
  mai jau 米酒
Mao Tai
  mao toi 茅台

TOBACCO
The Hong Kong government permits the advertising of tobacco products on billboards, TV and the like, but requires that the health warning be glaringly apparent. There is something perversely satisfying about seeing the photos of smiling, happy smokers, with a caption underneath warning that this activity might kill you.

Nevertheless, if you want to smoke, you'll have no trouble finding variety. All major and minor imported brands are available. Only one brand is imported from China, 'Double Happiness'.

Amongst the Chinese, smoking is largely confined to the males. Women who smoke in public may be regarded as sexually permissive and will thus lose face. Women who like to smoke usually do so in private. Conversely, men tend to smoke like chimneys and frequently ignore 'no smoking' signs in public places.

ENTERTAINMENT
In Hong Kong, you get what you pay for. This applies as much to entertainment as it does to shopping. Outside of sitting around Chungking Mansions and smashing cockroaches with a rolled up newspaper, most forms of amusement require money.

Fortunately, if your needs are simple, it doesn't have to cost a lot. You can get at least a few hours of free or almost free nightlife by exploring the street markets, the *dai pai dongs*, which are usually bustling with activity from about 8 pm to 11 pm. There are plenty of cheap snacks from pushcarts for about HK$3, and occasionally you will be entertained by a Cantonese opera performing on a makeshift stage in the street.

Harbour cruises can be taken day or night, but these are not cheap. See the Tours section in the Getting Around chapter.

The Saturday and Sunday English-language newspapers usually have a weekend entertainment insert which lists nightspots. Also have a look at the *Dining and Nightlife* pamphlet published by the HKTA. The pamphlet only gives you a vague idea of what a place is like, but it lists many with a telephone number, address and operating hours.

Cinema
Hong Kong produces many of its own films, many of which have English subtitles even though the sound track is in Cantonese or Mandarin. Hong Kong is especially famous for gongfu epics such as the Bruce Lee series. Unfortunately, Bruce Lee has died and a lot of what is produced now doesn't come up to the high standards he set. Some other stars, like Jackie Chan, have tried to take his place, but no one has yet managed (or really tried) to make their films so realistic looking.

Most of the present crop of gongfu films are essentially splatter spectaculars. The leading roles are played by super killers with supernatural abilities; they fly through the air, jump over buildings and heal dying people with 10 seconds of qigong (gongfu meditation).

Nevertheless, Hong Kong does occasionally come up with a good local film, often a drama from Chinese history, a comedy or a heartbreaking love story. Hong Kong's leading movie companies are Shaw Brothers with its huge Movietown studios on Clearwater Bay Rd in the New Territories and Golden Harvest which started the Bruce Lee series. Hong Kong films are exported to overseas Chinese communities all over the world, and many are shown in Taiwan and China too. Unfortunately, Hong Kong's criminal gangs have been trying to take over the industry, which could well destroy it as producers and stars flee to avoid both the gangsters and 1997.

Western films are very popular, particularly violent American movies featuring psychopathic killers. Most major Western films will play in Hong Kong, but it is never certain that you will see the whole movie. There is a tendency to cut movies, in part because Hong Kong does have a mild form of film censorship, but largely because cinema owners find it more profitable to shorten the films to get one or two extra showings a day (plus a few advertisements).

Young people in Hong Kong are crazy about the movies. Theatres tend to be jam-packed and it is often necessary to buy your ticket a day in advance if you want a seat. Your ticket will have an assigned seat number and you are expected to sit only there. Choose where you want to sit when you buy your ticket and remember that all the best seats sell out early. You may be approached by ticket scalpers when you arrive at the cinema, but who knows if these scalped tickets are real or fake?

To find out what's on at the cinemas, look in the *South China Morning Post* or the *Hong Kong Standard* which list the English-language movies, show times and telephone numbers. Unfortunately no addresses are listed. In fact, the papers give no clue as to what part of town the theatre is in.

Concerts & Cultural Events

Pick up the *South China Morning Post* and look in the index for the Arts page. This is where you'll find a daily section called 'What's on Today' which gives a good rundown on art exhibitions, film festivals, opera, meetings, concerts, beauty pageants, lion dances, and so on.

The Saturday edition of the *Hong Kong Standard* has a special insert called 'Buzz' which lists everything of entertainment value happening in Hong Kong, including a subsection called Special Events which mentions cultural activities.

The HKTA, the Urban Council and the Arts Centre also have programmes – information which can be obtained from the Arts Centre or HKTA offices.

The HKTA has a publication entitled *Culture* which includes a monthly schedule of events such as performances by Cantonese opera troupes, piano recitals, Fujianese puppet shows, Chinese folk singers and exhibits of Chinese watercolours.

Some of the yearly main events include a Western arts festival in February or March, the Hong Kong International Film Festival around Easter, the Hong Kong Food Festival in August or September, the Hong Kong Asian Arts Festival in October, a major tennis tournament, a rugby tournament and a Lawn Bowling Classic. The various HKTA offices around the world can be contacted for information on precise dates.

To find out more about the avant-garde cultural scene, check *Hong Kong Magazine*, the free handout available from pubs in the Lan Kwai Fong neighbourhood in Central. Keep your eyes and ears open for information on the annual Hong Kong Festival Fringe – a four-week event which includes everything from drama and dance to mime and street shows.

Discos

Hong Kong has some outstanding discos, mostly in the Wanchai district of Hong Kong Island. The disco scene still remains popular with foreigners, but surprisingly the fad has come and gone for the Chinese. Karaoke has proved to be a formidable competitor, drawing much of the Chinese clientele.

More than Just a Game

A national pastime, mahjong is a virtual way of life to the denizens of Hong Kong. Played at the office, in factories, on ad hoc tables at the beach and licenced mahjong centres, prior to marriages, anniversaries and company dinners, the game involves skill, concentration, speed of movement, prompt thinking and lots of noise.

So much noise in fact, that the unmistakeable chatter of tiles as they slam against table tops or the din and bustle of players as they announce each call is soon familiar to any visitor wandering Hong Kong's streets.

Mahjong is thought to have originated during the Sung Dynasty (960 AD-1279) but it wasn't until the Ching Dynasty (1644 AD-1912) that it gained broad appeal. Such was the games' popularity and the players' collective enthusiasm for it, that official duties were quickly forgotten as men and women succumbed to the game's addictive thrall. Alarmed, the government promptly banned mahjong on land but this proved no hindrance to the resourceful Chinese – they simply played the game at sea.

Initially, mahjong was played with some fifty paper cards. However, the cards invariably wafted away in the sea breezes and were eventually replaced by more serviceable material such as bamboo, ivory, bone tiles and, most recently, plastic. Brick-shaped and hand-engraved with Chinese characters, the tiles represent the game's nautical origins by depicting items such as boat sails, compass reading points and water buckets.

Mahjong is a frenetic game with little or no time for hesitation. And like much of the business and social activities undertaken by Hong Kongers, it aims to test the players' mettle and stamina – one game leads to another, often deep into the night. While the game's pace, clamour and duration lends an unusual amount of excitement (often mistaken by strangers as rudeness) to the proceedings, it must be remembered that mahjong, as with any game, is a form of relaxation. That is, once you've learned the rules.

It has four players and there are usually four rounds to a game: East round – the 1st round; South round – the 2nd round; West round – the 3rd round; and North round – the 4th round. Once the tiles are thoroughly shuffled, walls are stacked in a square formation. The game begins when a player throws the dice. This determines two things: who the first banker will be (each of the four players becomes banker in turn) and where the banker deals part of the wall. The banker deals four tiles and is followed, counter-clockwise beginning with north, by each player. On the fourth round, the banker takes two tiles and each player one, bringing the banker's total number of tiles to 14 and the three players 13 each. The banker then discards one tile by slamming it on the table. If north does not want the discarded tile, the player takes the next tile from the wall.

Basically, mahjong is a shirt-tail relation of rummy (a card game of collected sets and sequences), where tiles of similar values or suits are matched up. Each player attempts to prevent another winning by avoiding giving out tiles supposedly required by others. A player declares a win ('going out') by lining up four sets of three tiles, plus an additional pair which adds up to a total of 14 tiles.

And did I mention gambling? Let's just say it's simply another lure to add to what is an already heady and irresistible spell.

Stephen Townshend

Karaoke

Not many foreigners get into this, but the Chinese love it. The word *karaoke* (empty music) was borrowed from Japanese. Basically, it's sing-along video tapes. Most of the songs are in Chinese, but they have English too.

Girlie Bars

How does it feel to be legally mugged in Hong Kong? To find out, just visit one of the many sleazy-looking topless bars along Peking Rd (and adjacent streets) in Tsimshatsui.

Be wary of places where an aggressive tout, sometimes female, stands at the front door, and tries to persuade you to go inside. In the past, they would grab travellers by the arm and try to pull them inside, but the government finally banned this practice after numerous complaints. However, the rules are suspended during the Chinese New Year when you practically have to beat them off with a stick. By the way, they often solicit couples, not just males.

Very likely there will be signs on the front door promising 'Drinks Only HK$40' and naughty pictures to stimulate interest. If you go inside, expect the following:

A cocktail waitress, usually topless and often wearing nothing but knickers, will serve you a drink. She will probably be friendly and chat for a few minutes. It will be one of the most expensive conversations of your life, because after a pleasant five-minute chat you will be presented with a bill for about HK$500.

When you protest, they will undoubtedly point to the tiny sign prominently posted on the wall behind a vase which informs you of the HK$400 service charge for talking to the waitress. If you balk at paying this fee, don't be surprised if two muscular thugs suddenly happen to be standing by your elbows. Rumour has it that these heavies are connected with Hong Kong's notorious Triads. They accept travellers' cheques.

This introduction to Hong Kong's girlie bars wasn't meant to frighten you off. If you really want to be waited on by almost-naked women, that's fine, but do realise that it will cost you. In Hong Kong, you get what you pay for. Don't think that you can quietly sit in the back of the room and sip your beer and get out for HK$40. That simply doesn't happen (unless you're a card-carrying Triad member).

Illegal Gambling
There are various forms of illegal gambling. Private poker matches are popular in Hong Kong. The real hardcore gambling addicts attend dog fights and (I kid you not) cricket fights. To participate in such illegal forms of gambling you will need the help of local Chinese.

Pubs
Since British influence has been substantial in Hong Kong, it's not surprising that British-style pubs are plentiful, especially in the tourist areas. Often the owners are British or Australian, and you can expect authentic decor, meat pies, darts and sometimes Aussie bush bands. Depending on where you go, beers typically cost HK$35

a pint, which is often more expensive than the shirt you'll be wearing if you've bought any clothes in Hong Kong. Overall, Lan Kwai Fong on Hong Kong Island is best for pubs, but there are plenty on the Kowloon side as well.

Video-Game Arcades
If you have an urge to test your skills at Space Invaders or Martian Masher, check out one of the ubiquitous video arcades. These are everywhere.

Spectator Sports
The Chinese aren't real big on rugby, but many expats are. The biggest match of the year is held in late April or early March, the Cathay Pacific-Hongkong Bank Seven-A-Side Rugby Tournament.

Both Chinese and foreigners are soccer enthusiasts. Regular matches are played at Hong Kong Stadium at So Kan Po, about 300 metres due east of the horse racetrack at Happy Valley on Hong Kong Island.

Sporting events are well covered in the sports section of Hong Kong's English-language newspapers.

THINGS TO BUY
'Shop till you drop' is the motto of many visitors to Hong Kong. And while it's true that the city resembles one gigantic shopping mall, a quick look at price tags should convince you that Hong Kong is not quite the bargain it's cracked up to be. Imported goods like Japanese-made cameras and electronic gadgets can be bought for roughly the same price in many Western countries. However, what makes Hong Kong shine is the variety – if you can't find it in Hong Kong, it probably doesn't exist.

That said, there are bargains to be had on locally manufactured products. Goods which require low technology but much manual labour to produce are the best bargains, including clothing, footwear and luggage. The reason for this is the cheap labour just next door in the People's Republic.

The HKTA can give you some information to get you started, but don't accept it as gospel. They publish a handy little booklet called *Shopping* with recommended shops that are HKTA members, though I have found some of these members to be less than charitable. The HKTA publishes a number of free special interest pamphlets such as the *Shopping Guide to Consumer Electronics* and *Shopping Guide to Jewellery*, and these are worth reading.

Duty Free

'Duty free' is just a slogan. Hong Kong is a duty-free port, and the only imported goods on which duty is paid are alcohol, tobacco, perfumes, cosmetics, cars and some petroleum products. Although many shops in Hong Kong display a big sign proclaiming 'Duty-Free Goods' there is little reason to bother with them as they cater mostly to a Japanese clientele who are already accustomed to being ripped off.

The only true duty-free shops in Hong Kong are the liquor and tobacco stores in Kai Tak Airport which you find after you pass through immigration and the security check. But the other so-called duty-free shops in the check-in area of the airport aren't. Unfortunately, even the duty-free shops are ridiculously expensive in Hong Kong – you often find the same goods cheaper in the supermarkets of Kowloon.

If you want to buy some duty-free cigarettes and liquor, you might do better just buying these on the aircraft itself. The other option is to buy from the duty-free shops in Macau (at the ferry pier) or at the border crossing at Shenzhen where you enter Hong Kong from China. Or just wait until you get to another country – almost any other airport in Asia can offer cheaper deals on duty-free items than Hong Kong's Kai Tak.

Guarantees

There are too many cases of visitors being sold defective equipment, with retailers then refusing to honour warranties.

Some dealers offer a local guarantee card and occasionally an international one for better brands of goods. Every guarantee should carry a complete description of the item (including model and serial numbers) as well as the date of purchase, the name and address of the shop it was purchased from and the shop's official stamp.

Some imported items come with a warranty registration with the word 'Guarantee only valid in Hong Kong'. If it's a well-known brandname, you can often return this card to the importer in Hong Kong to get a warranty card for your home country. It's best to do this while you're still in Hong Kong, as doing it by post from abroad is dubious at best.

A common practice is to sell grey-market equipment (ie imported by somebody other than the official local agent). Such equipment may have no guarantee at all, or the guarantee might only be valid in the country of manufacture.

If you buy goods such as cameras and electronic equipment at discount prices, then make sure – if you really do need the latest model – that the model hasn't been superseded. The agent or importer can tell you this. Contacting an agent is one way of obtaining a detailed explanation of what each model actually does, though many agents aren't interested in talking to you. The HKTA *Shopping* guide has a list of sole agents and their phone numbers in the back of the pamphlet.

Always check prices in a few shops, take your time and return to a shop several times if necessary. Don't buy anything expensive in a hurry and always get a manufacturer's guarantee that is valid worldwide. When comparing prices, on cameras for example, make sure you're comparing not only the same camera body but also the same lenses and any other accessories.

Refunds & Exchanges

Many shops will exchange goods if they are defective, or in the case of clothing, if the garment simply doesn't fit. Be sure to keep receipts and go back to the store as soon as possible.

Forget about refunds. They are almost never given in Hong Kong. This applies to deposits as well as final payment. If you put a deposit on something, don't ever expect to see that money again.

Rip-Offs

Caveat emptor, or 'buyer beware', are two words which should be securely embedded in your mind while shopping in Hong Kong, especially during that crucial moment when you hand over the cash.

Rip-offs do happen. While most shops are honest, there are plenty which are not. The longer you shop in Hong Kong, the more likely it is that you'll run into a shopkeeper who is nothing but a crook. It would be wise to learn how to recognise the techniques of rip-off artists in order to avoid them.

The HKTA recommends that you only shop in stores which display the HKTA membership sign. This sounds like great advice except that the vast majority of the best stores are not HKTA members. Furthermore, many of the thieving camera and video shops in Tsimshatsui *are* HKTA members. The worst shop I've ever done business with in Hong Kong is Sunlite Computers, and it is a HKTA member! In other words, you should take the HKTA's seal of approval with a large grain of salt.

The most common way to cheat tourists is to simply overcharge. In the tourist shopping district of Tsimshatsui, you'll rarely find price tags on anything. Checking prices in several stores therefore becomes essential. However, shopkeepers know that tourists compare prices in several locations before buying, so they will often quote a reasonable or ridiculously low price on a big ticket item, only to get the money back by overcharging on small items or accessories. You may be quoted a reasonable price on a camera, only to be gouged on the lens cap, neck strap, case, batteries and flash. If you realise that you are being ripped off and casually ask why you're being charged 10 times the going rate for a set of batteries, you'll probably be told in no uncertain terms to 'get the hell out'.

Overcharging is easy to spot, so many dishonest shopowners are becoming sneakier. They sometimes remove vital components that should have been included free (like the connecting cords for the speakers on a stereo system) and demand more money when you return to the shop to get them.

You should be especially wary if they want to take the goods into the back room to 'box it up'. This provides ample opportunity to remove essential items that you have already paid for. The camera case, usually included free with most cameras, will often be sold as an accessory. Another tactic is to replace some of the good components with cheap or defective ones. Only later will you discover that the 'Nikon' lens turns out to be a cheap imitation. When it's time to put your equipment in the box, it's best if you do it yourself.

Another sneaky ploy is to knowingly sell defective merchandise. Your only safeguard is to inspect the equipment carefully before handing over the cash.

Also be alert for signs of wear and tear – the equipment could be secondhand. Whatever you do, insist on getting an itemised receipt. You should avoid handing over the cash until you have the goods in hand and they've written a receipt.

There is really no reason to put a deposit on anything unless it is being custom-made for you, like a fitted suit or a pair of eyeglasses. Some shops might ask for a deposit if you're ordering a very unusual item that they wouldn't normally stock, but this isn't a common practice.

Here are a few experiences of dissatisfied customers:

They took a deposit and demanded an extra HK$800 for the camera when I came for delivery...used abusive language and started fist fights.

I signed a receipt for a US$200 disc player. They had another receipt underneath the first one and produced a US$30 record player when they went to put the disc player in a box. So I ended up with a US$30 record player which cost US$200 – and a receipt for a record player (switched!).

Couldn't be worse. They try to provoke you! To start a fight...

Getting Help

There isn't much you can do if a shop simply overcharges. However, if you discover that the goods are defective or something is missing, return to the shop immediately taking the goods and receipt with you. Sometimes it really is an honest mistake and they will clear the problem up at once. Honest shopkeepers will give you an exchange on defective goods or replace missing components. On the other hand, if the shop intentionally cheated you, expect a bitter argument.

If you feel that you were defrauded, don't expect any help from the police. There is an unfortunate lack of consumer protection in Hong Kong. However, there are a few agencies that might be able to help you.

The first place to try is the HKTA (☎ 8017111) on the 35th floor of Jardine House, 1 Connaught Place, Central. If the shop is one of their members they can lean on them, but don't expect miracles. If not, they can at least advise you on who to contact for more help.

Another place to try is the Consumer Council (☎ 3041234) which has 16 advice centres. The Small Claims Tribunal (☎ 8254667) is the place to contact for claims less than HK$15,000. The Community Advice Bureau (☎ 5245444) can help you find a lawyer.

As a last desperate measure, you can take matters into your own hands. By this I don't mean you should punch the shopkeeper, which might make you feel better but is illegal. However, it is entirely legal to stand outside the shop and tell others about your experience. Some pickets have successfully gotten back their money after driving away other customers. However, this can be an exhausting way to spend your time in Hong Kong and results are by no means guaranteed.

Fake Goods

Watch out for counterfeit brand goods. Fake labels on clothes is the most obvious example, but there are fake Rolex watches, fake Gucci leather bags, fake jade, fake jewellery, fake herbal medicines and even fake electronics. Obviously there's more risk buying electronic goods than buying clothes, shoes or luggage, though I was nearly crippled by some fake Reebok shoes because they hurt so much. The pirated music tapes and CDs are often poor sound quality and have a tendency to rapidly deteriorate. Fortunately, Hong Kong's customs agents have been cracking down hard on the fake electronics and cameras, and this problem seems all but solved. However, counterfeit brandname watches seem to be very common. If you discover that you've been sold a fake brandname watch when you thought you were buying the genuine article, it would be worthwhile to contact the police or customs as this is definitely illegal. Also beware of factory rejects.

Shipping Goods

Goods can be sent home by post, and some stores will package and post the goods for you, but events are usually more certain when you do it yourself. You don't necessarily have to ship goods by post. United Parcel Service (UPS) offers services from Hong Kong to 40 other countries. It ships by air and accepts parcels weighing up to 30 kg. UPS (☎ 7353535) has an office in the World Finance Centre, Canton Rd, Tsimshatsui.

In Hong Kong, there are many shipping companies that transport larger items by sea freight. One of the biggest is Orient Consolidation Service (☎ 3687206), 13th floor, Albion Plaza, 2-6 Granville Rd, Tsimshatsui. Many others are listed in the Yellow Pages Commercial/Industrial Guide under Freight Forwarding or Freight Consolidating.

If you want to ship heavier goods by air, there are many air cargo companies. Most have offices at Kai Tak Airport. Among the better-known companies are DHL (☎ 7658111) and Jacky Maeder (☎ 7159611).

Shopping Hours

There are no hard and fast shopping hours in Hong Kong, but generally, shops in the four main shopping areas are open as follows: Central and Western districts from 10 am to

6 pm; Causeway Bay and Wanchai from 10 am to 10 pm; Tsimshatsui, Yaumatei and Mongkok from 10 am to 9 pm; and Tsimshatsui East from 10 am to 7.30 pm. Causeway Bay is the best part of town for late-night shopping.

Most shops are open seven days a week, but on Sundays or holidays many only open from 1 pm to 5 pm. Street markets are open every day and well into the night (with the exception of the Jade Market in Kowloon which is open from 10 am to 3.30 pm). Almost everything closes for two or three days during the Chinese New Year holiday period. However, just before the Chinese New Year is the best time to make expensive purchases – everything goes on sale at that time because the stores want to clear out old stock.

Cheapest Places to Shop
Hong Kong merchants can be divided into two general categories: those who cater to tourists only and those who sell to the general populace. Those who live entirely off the tourist trade base their marketing philosophy on a simple mathematical equation: Tourist = Sucker. The best way to counter this is to get away from touristland, which basically means get away from Tsimshatsui.

The Kowloon and Hong Kong Island chapters both give a good rundown of places to shop outside the tourist combat zone. Also, don't overlook the New Territories. One of the most impressive shopping malls in Hong Kong is the Shatin New Town Plaza in the New Territories. With a little more effort, you can visit the Tuen Mun Town Plaza in the north-west part of the New Territories which can be reached by hoverferry.

Street Markets
The reason why Hong Kong teenagers look so chic despite the fact that most have no income beyond their lunch money is that it is possible to buy just about anything in the street markets and clothing alleys. Prices are typically less than half of what you would pay in the boutiques.

They can be found at Temple St (open about 8 pm to 11 pm) in Yaumatei, Tung Choi St (noon to 10 pm) in Mongkok and Apliu St (noon to 9 pm) in Shamshuipo. These sell clothes, cassettes, watches, ballpoint pens with built-in digital clocks, radios, knives, cheap jewellery, naughty postcards, potions, lotions, false teeth and hundreds of other items.

Street markets and alleys are truly a bargain for clothing, but because of the largely Chinese clientele clothes sizes are mainly small. To complicate matters, you can't try on garments such as trousers before you buy. You're also taking a chance on quality. Most of the time you can ignore monograms as Hong Kong is monogram-mad and makes excellent reproductions of fashion luggage, handbags and clothes as well as copies of labels.

Factory Outlets
In my opinion, it's just barely worth chasing these places down. You can get bargains here on overruns, but selection is decidedly limited and there are few factory rejects amongst the occasional gems. Also, the best factory outlets tend to be in far-off neighbourhoods amongst the warehouses rather than five-star hotel districts. But since tourists often go to great lengths to search out these places, most charge only slightly less for their stylish clothing than you could buy it for in retail shops. Overall, the street markets are a better bargain. Still, if you've got the time to search, you might get a great deal on those leather trousers you've always wanted (even if the zipper is missing), or that silk shirt with one sleeve longer than the other.

Always check purchases carefully for defects as factory outlets rarely give refunds or exchanges. Many outlets post a sign saying 'All sales are final', and they mean it. Some places will accept credit cards, but most won't. If they do accept credit cards, they'll often offer a discount if you pay cash, so be sure to ask.

If you're going to spend some time hunting down factory outlets, it's essential that you get *Hong Kong Factory Bargains* by Dana Goetz, widely available from bookshops throughout Hong Kong. The book gives a thorough rundown on what's available and where to find it.

A wide range of goods is available from factory outlets, such as jewellery, carpets, camphorwood chests, leatherware, silks, shoes, handbags, ceramics and imitation antique pieces.

What to Buy

Antiques & Curios How do you tell a real Ming vase from a fake when the cracks and chips and age discolouration have been cleverly added? Hong Kong factories quite legitimately turn out antique replicas. Many dealers state when a piece is a reproduction and some even restrict their sales to these items. Unfortunately, others don't particularly feel the necessity to tell customers/suckers.

The Tang Dynasty ran from 618 AD to 906, the Song Dynasty from 960 to 1279, the Ming Dynasty from 1368 to 1644 and the Qing Dynasty from 1644 to 1911. So a Qing vase might only be less than 100 years old, which in Western terms would hardly qualify as an antique. Basically, if you don't know what to look for or who to buy from, the serious purchase of antiques is not for the tourist on a stopover!

There are still many beautiful items to buy in Hong Kong, including fine examples of Chinese art and craft – not necessarily antique, which doesn't matter as long as you don't pay antique prices.

For what it's worth, the annual International Asian Antiques Fair is held in Hong Kong.

Appliances & Electronics Remember that most electrical appliances in Hong Kong are designed to work with 220 V. Some thoughtful manufacturers now equip their computers, stereos and video machines with international power supplies that automatically sense the voltage and adapt to it – others include a little switch for 110/220 V operation. Hong Kong's standard plug design, which uses three round prongs, is not used by many other countries, but plugs are easily changed or you can buy an adaptor in Hong

Antique porcelain vase

Kong. If the shop can't supply you with the correct adaptor, ask the store to change the plug for you, which they should do free of charge.

Carpets When you talk about buying a fine Oriental carpet, you're talking serious money. Not surprisingly, the cost depends on the size, type of material and intricacy of the design. There are hand-knotted or machine-knotted carpets, and hand-woven wall hangings. Fancy decorative carpets can be made of wool or silk – these are obviously not for wiping your feet on.

It's difficult to give advice about what constitutes a fine carpet, because everyone has their own tastes. You need to do a lot of looking and cost comparison. The HKTA's *Shopping* guide gives a long list of places selling carpets. What their pamphlet doesn't say is that the further away you get from touristland, the cheaper the price.

Clothes China has a raging export-oriented textile industry, and Hong Kong is the export gateway. While you can often find this stuff more cheaply in China, quality is vastly superior in Hong Kong – China tends to dump all its cheap junk on the domestic market.

An interesting phenomena in recent years has been the proliferation of Hong Kong clothing manufacturers which have adopted Italian names. Chief amongst these are Giordano and Bossini. While the clothes are about as Italian as chopsticks, the quality is not bad at all and prices are low to moderate. There are many outlets throughout Hong Kong – prices are fixed, there's no bargaining and you can often pick up items on sale.

Hong Kong has long been famous for custom-made clothes and tailors exist in profusion. Most are ethnic Indians – the Chinese seem to be slowly abandoning this particular market niche. To find a tailor, all you need to do is walk around the shopping arcades in the tourist zones and show a passing interest – you'll practically be kidnapped. There are often pamphleteers hanging around Nathan Rd, ever eager to inform you about their custom-tailor services. There are also plenty of listings in the Yellow Pages Buying Guide and the HKTA can produce a list longer than a Chinese scroll painting. Some tailors require that you buy their material, while others will let you bring your own. The more time you give the tailor, the more fittings you will have and the better the outcome is likely to be.

Computers Hong Kong is a popular place to buy personal computers. While prices are competitive, it is also important to pay careful attention to where and what you buy. Computers are prone to breakdowns, so finding a shop with a good reputation for honesty is vital. Before leaving Hong Kong it's important to run the computer continuously for several days to make sure it is free of defects.

You may have your own ideas about what kind of computer you want to buy, but I'd recommend sticking to a brandname portable computer with an international warranty, such as Hewlett-Packard, IBM, AST, Compac or Twinhead. A portable computer is a whole lot easier to transport than a desktop machine, and if it's a brandname

computer it should have an international warranty. If it does break down, parts and service will be easier to find.

Many shops will be happy to sell you a generic (no name) desktop computer, IBM-PC compatible and custom designed to whatever configuration you desire. Buying a generic desktop machine isn't a bad idea, but only if you intend living in Hong Kong for at least a year (the typical warranty period). My first computer was one of these generic models and it had to be repaired many times. The shop was honest and did the repairs free of charge, but this wouldn't have been possible if I had taken the machine abroad. Generic desktop computers do not have international guarantees.

You may discover that your home country will hit you with a steep import tax when you return. Save your receipt because the older the machine is, the less you're likely to pay in import duty. The rules in many countries say that the machine is tax exempt if over a year old, and some shops in Hong Kong will even write you a back-dated receipt on request for just this purpose!

Some Hong Kong computer shops still sell pirated computer software, although the authorities have cracked down on this. But remember that besides being illegal, pirated programmes often contain computer viruses – there is even one called 'AIDS' and wearing a condom offers no protection whatsoever.

Ivory Ivory jewellery, chopsticks and ornaments were big sellers in Hong Kong, fuelling the demand for tusks and contributing to the slaughter of Africa's already depleted elephant population. In 1989, the Hong Kong government signed the CITES (Convention on International Trade in Endangered Species) treaty which effectively bans the import of raw ivory. The USA, Japan and Western European nations all have signatories to CITES, as are many other countries.

Since the agreement was reached, the elephants have been making a roaring comeback. Unfortunately, this hasn't been entirely welcomed in some African and Asian countries where elephants compete with humans for food and living space. Every now and then there is talk of lifting the ban and commercially herding the elephants, but so far it hasn't happened.

In the meantime, the only carved ivory products being sold in Hong Kong are those which were supposedly manufactured before the ban went into effect. Those who want to sell such ivory need to have all sorts of documentation proving where and when the goods were made. Both importing and exporting of ivory is still technically possible with a licence from Hong Kong and from the other country involved, but it's a legal mine-field and hardly worth the trouble.

Jade The Chinese attribute various magical qualities to jade, including the power to prevent aging and keep evil spirits away.

It's a pity then that jade doesn't have the magical ability to prevent lying. Fake jade exists – the deep green colour associated with some jade pieces can be achieved with a dye pot, as can the white, green, red, lavender and brown of other pieces. Green soapstone and plastic can be passed off as jade too.

Most so-called Chinese jade sold in Hong Kong comes from South Africa, New Zealand, Australia and the USA. One trick of jade merchants is to sell a supposedly solid piece of jade jewellery which is actually a thin slice of jade backed by green glue and quartz.

It is said that the test for jade is to try scratching it with a steel blade – real jade will not scratch. Another story is that water dropped on real jade will form droplets if the stone is genuine.

There are two different minerals which can be called jade: jadeite from Burma (Myanmar) and nephrite (commonly from Canada, China, New Zealand and Taiwan). Unfortunately, you would have to know your Burmese jade pretty well to avoid being fooled. While the colour green is usually associated with jade, the milk-white shade is also highly prized. Shades of pink, red, yellow, brown, mauve and turquoise come in between.

The circular disc with a central hole worn around many necks in Hong Kong represents heaven in Chinese mythology. In the old days, amulets and talismans of jade were worn by Chinese court officials to denote rank, power and wealth. One emperor was reputed to have worn jade sandals, and another gave his favourite concubine a bed of jade.

Jewellery If you have ever tried to sell a secondhand diamond ring to a jewellery shop, you no doubt already know that the price of used jewellery is a fraction of what it costs new. Yet shops which buy second-hand jewellery turn around and sell it for close to what it costs new.

The moral of the story is that buying jewellery as an investment is a non-starter. Don't buy jewellery in Hong Kong (or anywhere else) with the idea that you can sell it for more in your home country. The only way to make money from jewellery is to be well-connected with a supplier and to have your own retail outlet.

One of the great myths of the jewellery business is that the high prices in the stores reflect the rarity of the materials. While it's true that uncut diamonds sold in bulk cost far more than zircons, the high prices charged reflect the fact that people are willing to pay a lot for shiny rocks and metals. Prestige is something you pay for. A ring with US$5 worth of raw materials can sell for US$100 in the stores. If the materials are worth US$100, the retail price can be US$1000. And so on.

Part of what you pay for is the labour involved in making the rocks look good. The jewellery export business is big in Hong Kong. The reason is because gem stones are imported, cut, polished, set and re-exported using cheap Chinese labour. In theory, this should make Hong Kong a cheap place to purchase jewellery. In practice, retail prices are only marginally cheaper than elsewhere.

Your only real weapon in getting a decent price is the intense competition in Hong

Kong. Jewellery has a large markup and there is considerable latitude for bargaining. However, the jewellers have a weapon of their own, namely the inability of the common tourist to judge good quality jewellery from bad. Can you distinguish a pure diamond from a zircon? A flawed diamond from a perfect one? Most people cannot. To become an expert on jewellery requires considerable training. The law requires that jewellers stamp the content on gold and platinum products, but that isn't much help when it comes to judging gems.

If you don't know what to look for in jewellery, you should at least be careful about where you buy. If the items you want to buy do not have price tags attached to them, that's a serious danger sign and you should go elsewhere. Shops in the trendy shopping arcades of the Tsimshatsui tourist combat zone are going to be most expensive.

Opals are said to be the best value in Hong Kong because this is where they are cut. Diamonds are generally not a good deal, because the world trade is mostly controlled by a cartel. Hong Kong does not have a diamond-cutting industry and must import from Belgium, India, Israel and the USA.

There are a couple of reputable jewellers who will issue a certificate that not only states exactly what you are buying, but guarantees that the shop will buy it back at a fair market price. It's worthwhile buying from one of these places – if you later become dissatisfied with your purchase, you can at least get most of your money back on a trade-in. Two chain stores which give this guarantee are King Fook and Tse Sui Luen. Exact addresses of their branches are given in the Things to Buy sections for Kowloon and Hong Kong Island.

Finally, after you've bought something and want to find out how badly you got ripped off, you can have it appraised. This is a service you get charged for, and some stones (such as diamonds) may have to be unset for testing. You can contact the Gemmological Association of Hong Kong (☎ 3666066) for the current list of approved appraisers. Two places which do appraisals

are De Silva (☎ 522063), Two Pacific Place, Central, and Valuation Services Ltd (☎ 8106640), 11 MacDonnell Rd, Central.

Leathers & Luggage With clothing, the manufacture of luggage and leather goods is low-tech and labour intensive, which means that China is the perfect place to open a factory. Lots of what gets produced in the PRC is pure junk with zippers and straps that break instantly, and the 'leather' proves to be vinyl on closer inspection.

Fortunately, most of what gets sent to the Hong Kong market is export quality, but check carefully because there is still a lot of rubbish on sale. All the big brandnames like Gucci and Louis Vuitton are on display in Hong Kong department stores. You'll find some local vendors with odd names in the leather business, like Mandarina Duck and Companion Reptile. To be sure, you'll find a wide selection and a big spread in prices.

The best advice for buying this kind of stuff is to take your time to carefully inspect zippers, straps and stitching. Look on the inside of the luggage, as the outside may be tough leather or nylon but the inside could be cheap vinyl. Decide early on if you need an expensive label or just durability at the lowest possible price.

Video 'Video' refers to a number of commercial products you might wish to buy: a TV set, video tape player (also known as video cassette recorder or VCR), the video tapes themselves and a video camera (camcorder) to make your own movies.

In the Tsimshatsui rip-off zone, practically every video shop has a demonstration TV set in the rear of the store. You can expect a demonstration in which only the most expensive 'digital' video camera produces a crisp image. What you won't be told is that the TV is rigged so that it will only work properly with the overpriced digital model. You also won't be told that the 'digital' model is not digital at all, but an ordinary camera for which you get to pay double.

The problem of rip-offs can best be avoided by not shopping in Tsimshatsui.

However, life isn't so simple – it is also important to understand a few basics of TV broadcasting if you want to purchase a VCR, video tapes or camcorder.

In a nutshell, the problem is that no universal TV broadcasting standard exists. The most common standards are PAL (used in Australia, Hong Kong, New Zealand, UK, most of Europe), SECAM (France, Germany, Luxembourg) and NTSC (Canada, Japan, Korea, Latin America, USA). Unfortunately, there are additional complications – a PAL standard TV bought in Hong Kong may not work for you even if your home country uses PAL because the stations might be adjusted to different frequencies. A few manufacturers have started offering multi-standard TVs that can be adjusted to PAL, NTSC or SECAM with the flick of a switch, but these models cost more. Some multi-standard systems only show colour in one mode but b&w in the other two, so read the manuals carefully before purchasing.

If you're interested in purchasing a VCR, you have the same problem – a VCR must be compatible with your TV. You can't connect a PAL video player to an NTSC TV or vice versa. Also, the video player won't work if it uses a frequency different from that used by your TV set, though this problem can be adjusted by a technician (for a fee). The same is true of camcorders – they must be compatible with the VCR and TV with which they will be used. Again, there is such a thing as a multi-standard VCR which can work with PAL, NTSC and SECAM but you pay extra for this feature.

Again, you've got the same problem when purchasing video tapes. If you buy a pre-recorded video tape off the shelf in Hong Kong, it will almost certainly be PAL standard. If your home country uses NTSC or SECAM, you won't be able to view this tape unless you have a new multi-standard VCR.

If multi-standard TVs and multi-standard VCRs exist, is there also such a thing as a multi-standard camcorder? The answer is no. If you want to buy a camcorder, you must decide which standard you want, either PAL,

NTSC or SECAM. A wrong choice would be a costly mistake, so pay careful attention to the labels.

Video tapes come in two sizes: VHS and 8 mm. Virtually all pre-recorded tapes and all VCRs are VHS size. The 8 mm tapes are very small, making them ideal for use in small hand-held camcorders. If you produce a movie on 8 mm tape, many companies offer a service to transfer it to a VHS tape for home viewing. A more important complication is the new improved 'super-video' (S-video) variation. This is a high-resolution variation of the VHS and 8 mm standard, called 'Super-VHS' (S-VHS) and 'Hi-Band 8 mm' (Hi-8) respectively. You cannot play an S-video tape on a standard VCR. However, an S-VCR can play standard video tapes.

Having told you that, I have to admit that I was lying. Somebody recently introduced a more compact version of VHS, known as 'VHS-Compact' (VHS-C). It's smaller than standard VHS but larger than 8 mm. And yes, there is a high-resolution variation, 'Super-VHS-Compact' (S-VHS-C). Technology marches on.

If you've managed to digest all this discussion about video standards, you still have one more hurdle to clear – audio standards. Video tapes come with the ability to reproduce sound, and the latest rage is to have stereo sound quality. In the VHS format, there is 'VHS Hi-Fi', while 8 mm chips in with the new 'PCM' audio format. If you want to enjoy this improved sound quality, you have to buy equipment that can record it and play it back.

There is such a thing as a laser disc, more accurately called video disc. These offer a few advantages over tapes; longevity, the ability to jump from one point in the movie to another and to freeze a frame without the annoying flutter of tapes. The drawback is that you can't make your own recordings on laser discs unless you invest in expensive equipment. The real reason to buy laser discs and a laser disc player is to watch quality pre-recorded movies. For most people, this is not a wise option because the number of movies available for rental on laser discs is relatively small.

Confused? You ought to be. The problem is that what is standard today is likely to be obsolete tomorrow. There has been much talk about introducing super high-resolution 'double scan' TVs and digital TVs with pictures so clear they practically leap off the screen. Wouldn't it be nice if the various countries in the world could agree on a single standard? Don't hold your breath.

Watches About every third person you encounter on Nathan Rd in Tsimshatsui seems to be yelling 'Copy watch!' in your ear. This is not some sort of traditional Chinese greeting, but an attempt to sell you a fake Rolex or Seiko. Just why this is tolerated by the Hong Kong authorities has always mystified me – after all, it is illegal and the government is always claiming to be 'cracking down' on counterfeiters. Perhaps the purpose of letting this business go on unhindered is to teach the tourists a lesson – it seems that these fake Rolexes have a nasty habit of losing 10 to 15 minutes of time per day, and then stop working at all after a month. If by some miracle it lasts longer than

that, the 'gold' watchband starts to turn your wrist green. But at least you got a 'bargain', didn't you?

As for buying a real brandname watch, it's easily accomplished if you've got the cash. You should avoid the shops which do not put a price tag on their watches, which pretty much precludes buying anything along Nathan Rd in Tsimshatsui. The big department stores are quite alright, but compare prices.

It's worth knowing that watch cases do not have to be expensive to ensure a quality watch. The internal workings of a watch (simply known as the 'movement') is 90% of the battle. There is quite a thriving industry in Hong Kong taking top-quality Swiss movements and putting them into cheap Made-in-China cases. While you do want to find a case that isn't going to rust, you can easily solve the green wrist syndrome if you buy a leather rather than a metal watchband. A waterproof watch is another ball game – if it's made in China, let the seller dunk it into a glass of water to prove that it is indeed waterproof. If you really want a fancy gold case sporting a famous label, that's fine but it is something you will pay dearly for.

Getting There & Away

AIR

Hong Kong is the major gateway to China and much of East Asia. Consequently, international air service is excellent and competition keeps fares relatively cheap when compared to neighbouring countries. The only problem is flying during the holiday crunch – the Chinese New Year, Christmas and Easter can be difficult times to get reservations.

Air Tickets

You will have to choose between buying a ticket to Hong Kong only and then making other arrangements when you arrive, and buying a ticket allowing various stopovers around Asia. For example, such a ticket could fly you from Sydney to London with stopovers in Denpasar, Jakarta, Hong Kong, Bangkok, Calcutta, Delhi and Istanbul.

There are a host of other deals which travel agents will offer in order to sell you a cheaper ticket. Fares will vary according to your point of departure, the time of year, how direct the flight is and how flexible you can be. Whatever you do, buy air tickets from a travel agent. The airlines don't deal directly in discount tickets, only the travel agents do. However, not every travel agent offers discount tickets, and amongst those that do, there is a wide range of deals on offer. It's a good idea to call the airline first and see what their cheapest ticket costs – use that as your starting point when talking to travel agents. Thanks to intense competition, most tickets sold these days are discounted.

It's important to realise that when you buy a discounted air ticket from a travel agent, you must also go back to that agent if you want to obtain a refund – the airlines will not refund you directly unless you paid full fare. While this is no problem if you don't change your travel plans, it can be quite a hassle if you decide to change the route halfway through your trip. In that case, you'd have to return to the place where you originally purchased the ticket to refund the unused portion of the journey. Of course, if you had a reliable friend whom you could mail the ticket to, that person could possibly obtain the refund for you, but don't count on it. It's also true that some travel agents (and airlines) are extremely slow issuing refunds – I had one friend who waited a full year!

Most airlines divide the year into 'peak' (expensive), 'shoulder' (less expensive) and 'off' (cheapest) seasons. In the northern hemisphere, peak season is June through September and off season is November through February. However, holidays (Christmas and Chinese New Year) will be treated as peak season even though they come during off season. In the southern hemisphere, the seasons are reversed.

Normal Economy-Class Tickets Despite the name, these tickets are not the most economical way to go. Essentially, these are full-fare tickets. On the other hand, they do give you maximum flexibility and the tickets are valid for 12 months. Also, if you don't use them they are fully refundable by the airlines as are unused sectors of a multiple ticket.

Group Tickets Group tickets are well-worth considering. You usually do not need to travel with a group. However, once the departure date is booked it may be impossible to change – you can only depart when the 'group' departs, even if you never meet or see another group member. The good news is that the return date can usually be left open, but there could be other restrictions – you might have to complete the trip in 60 days, or fly off season or during weekdays. It's important to ask the travel agent what conditions and restrictions apply to any tickets you intend to buy.

APEX Tickets APEX (Advance Purchase Excursion) tickets are sold at a discount but will lock you into a rigid schedule. Such tickets must be purchased two or three weeks ahead of departure, do not permit stopovers and may have minimum and maximum stays as well as fixed departure and return dates. Unless you have to return at a certain time, it's best to purchase APEX tickets on a one-way basis only. There are stiff cancellation fees if you decide not to use your APEX ticket.

Round-the-World Tickets These tickets are usually offered by an airline or combination of airlines, and let you take your time (six months to a year) moving from point to point on their routes for the price of one ticket. The main restriction is that you have to keep moving in the same direction. A further drawback is that since you are usually booking individual flights as you go, and can't switch carriers, you can get caught out by flight availabilities. The result: spending more or less time in a place than you want.

Back-to-Front Tickets One thing to avoid is a back-to-front ticket. These are best explained by example – if you want to fly from Japan (where tickets are relatively expensive) to Hong Kong (where tickets are much cheaper), you can pay by cheque or credit card and have a friend or travel agent in Hong Kong mail the ticket to you. The problem is that the airlines have computers and will know that the ticket was issued in Hong Kong rather than Japan, and they will refuse to honor it. Consumer groups have filed lawsuits over this practice with mixed results, but in most countries the law protects the airlines, not consumers. In short, the ticket is only valid starting from the country where it was issued. The only exception to this rule is if you purchase a full-fare (non-discounted) ticket, but of course that robs you of the advantage you gain by purchasing a back-to-front ticket.

If the ticket is issued in a third location (such as the USA), the same rule applies. You cannot fly from Japan to Hong Kong with a ticket mailed to you from the USA – if you buy a ticket in the USA, you can fly from there to Japan and then to Hong Kong and thus enjoy a discounted price, but you can't start the journey from Japan. Again, an exception is made if you pay full fare and thus negate your savings.

Frequent Flyer Frequent-flyer plans have proliferated in recent years and are now offered by most airlines, even some budget ones. Basically, these allow you a free ticket if you chalk up so many km with the same airline. The plans aren't always as good as they sound – some airlines require you to use all your frequent-flyer credits within one year or you lose the lot. Sometimes you find yourself flying on a particular airline just to get frequent-flyer credits, but the ticket is considerably more expensive than what you might have gotten from a discount airline without a frequent-flyer bonus. Many airlines have 'blackout' periods – peak times when you cannot use the free tickets you obtained under the frequent-flyer programme. When you purchase the ticket be sure to give the ticket agent your frequent-flyer membership number, and again when you check in for your flight.

A common complaint seems to be that airlines forget to record your frequent-flyer credits when you fly with them – save all your boarding passes and ticket receipts and be prepared to push if no bonus is forthcoming. In this regard I've personally had much trouble with United Airlines, and for this reason I no longer fly with them. Taiwan's China Airlines also has a frequent-flyer programme, but it isn't the best – you must fly 160,000 km (100,000 miles) to qualify for a free ticket, which is equivalent to eight round-trip flights from Los Angeles to Taipei. Northwest Airlines has the most generous frequent-flyer programme, with a free ticket after you've flown 32,000 km (20,000 miles).

Student Discounts Some airlines offer up to 25% discount to student card holders. In some countries, an official-looking letter from the school is also needed. You also must be age 26 or younger. These discounts are generally only available on ordinary economy-class fares. You wouldn't get one, for instance, on an APEX or a round-the-world ticket since these are already discounted.

Courier Flights Courier flights can be a bargain if you're fortunate enough to find one. The way it works is that an airfreight company takes over your entire checked baggage allowance. You are permitted to bring along a carry-on bag, but that's all. In return, you get a steeply discounted ticket. These arrangements usually have to be made a month or more in advance and are only available on certain routes. Such flights are occasionally advertised in the newspapers, or contact airfreight companies listed in the phone book.

Children's Fare Airlines usually carry babies up to two years of age at 10% of the relevant adult fare – a few may carry them free of charge. Reputable international airlines usually provide nappies (diapers), tissues, talcum and all the other paraphenalia needed to keep babies clean, dry and half-happy. For children between the ages of four and 12 the fare on international flights is usually 50% of the regular fare or 67% of a discounted fare.

To/From the USA

There are some very good open tickets which remain valid for six months or one year (opt for the latter), that don't lock you into any fixed dates of departure and allow multiple stop-offs. For example, there are cheap tickets between the US west coast and Hong Kong with stopovers in Japan and Korea and continuing on to Hong Kong for very little extra money – the departure dates can be changed and you have one year to complete the journey. However, remember that it's easy to get locked out during the Chinese New Year and other peak times.

Usually, and not surprisingly, the cheapest

fare to whatever country is offered by a bucket shop owned by someone of that particular ethnic origin. San Francisco is the bucket shop capital of America, though some good deals can be found in Los Angeles, New York and other cities. Discounters can be found through the Yellow Pages or the major daily newspapers. Those listed in both Roman and Oriental scripts are invariably discounters. A more direct way is to wander around San Francisco's Chinatown where most of the shops are – especially in the Clay St and Waverly Place area. Many of these are staffed by recent arrivals from Hong Kong and Taiwan who speak little English. Inquiries are best made in person. One place popular with budget travellers is Wahlock Travel in the Bank of America Building on Stockton St.

It's not advisable to send money (even cheques) through the post unless the agent is very well established – some travellers have reported being ripped off by fly-by-night mail-order ticket agents. Nor is it wise to hand over the full amount to Shady Deal Travel Services unless they can give you the ticket straight away – most US travel agencies have computers that can spit out the ticket on the spot.

Council Travel is the largest student travel organisation and even though you don't have to be a student to use them, they do have specially discounted student tickets. Council Travel has an extensive network in all major US cities and is listed in the telephone book. There are also Student Travel Network offices which are associated with STA.

One of the cheapest and most reliable travel agents on the west coast is Overseas Tours (☎ (800) 2225292), 475 El Camino Real, Room 206, Millbrae, CA 94030. Another good agent is Gateway Travel (☎ (214) 9602000, (800) 4411183), 4201 Spring Valley Rd, Suite 104, Dallas, TX 75244. Both of these places seem to be trustworthy for mail-order tickets.

The price of flights is obviously affected by which US city you start out from. The lowest one-way/return fares to Hong Kong are as follows: Honolulu US$376/727; Los

HONG KONG

Angeles US$428/675; New York US$496/870.

To/From Canada

Getting discount tickets in Canada is much the same as in the USA – go to the travel agents and shop around until you find a good deal.

CUTS is Canada's national student bureau and has offices in a number of Canadian cities including Vancouver, Edmonton, Toronto and Ottawa – you don't necessarily have to be a student. There are a number of good agents in Vancouver for cheap tickets.

The cheapest one-way/return Vancouver-Hong Kong tickets are US$392/678.

To/From the UK

Air-ticket discounting is a long-running business in the UK and it's wide open. The various agents advertise their fares and there is nothing under-the-counter about it at all. To find out what's going, there are a number of magazines in the UK which have good information about flights and agents. These include: *Trailfinder*, free from the Trailfinders Travel Centre in Earls Court; and *Time Out* or *City Limits*, London-weekly entertainment guides widely available in the UK.

Discount tickets are mostly available in London – you won't find your friendly travel agent out in the country offering cheap deals. The danger with discounted tickets in the UK is that some of the 'bucket shops' (as British ticket-discounters are known) are unsound. Sometimes the backstairs over-the-shop travel agents fold up and disappear after you've handed over the money and before you've received the tickets. Get the tickets before you hand over the cash.

Two reliable London bucket shops are Trailfinders, in Earls Court, and STA Travel, with several offices. In Bristol, look up Regent Holidays.

Flights from London and Manchester to East Asian destinations are cheapest on THAI, Singapore Airlines, Malaysian (MAS), British Airways and Cathay Pacific. These airlines do not charge extra if passen-gers want to stopover en route, and in fact offer stopover packages which encourage it. There are also direct flights on Lufthansa and Air France – both are significantly more expensive than the aforementioned Asian-based carriers.

From London, the cheapest current one-way/return fares are approximately US$375/725.

To/From Europe

The Netherlands, Brussels and Antwerp are good places for buying discount air tickets. In Antwerp, WATS has been recommended. In Zurich, try SOF Travel and Sindbad. In Geneva, try Stohl Travel. In the Netherlands, NBBS is a reputable agency. Frankfurt is Germany's major gateway to Hong Kong, with direct flights on Lufthansa.

From most major cities in Western Europe, rock bottom one-way/return fares to Hong Kong begin at US$375/725.

To/From Australia

As an alternative to flying direct between Australia and Hong Kong, you can often get free stopovers in either Singapore or Bangkok, especially if you fly with Singapore Airlines or THAI Airways respectively.

Australia is not a cheap place to fly out of, and air fares between Australia and Asia are absurdly expensive considering the distances flown. However, there are a few ways of cutting the costs.

Among the cheapest regular tickets available in Australia are APEX tickets. The cost depends on your departure date from Australia.

It's possible to get reductions on the cost of APEX and other fares by going to the student travel offices and/or some of the travel agents in Australia that specialise in discounting.

The weekend travel sections of papers like *The Age* (Melbourne) or the *Sydney Morning Herald* are good sources of travel information. Also look at *Student Traveller*, a free newspaper published by Student Travel Australia (STA), the Australian-based student travel organisation which now has offices worldwide. STA has offices all around Australia (check your phone directory) and you definitely don't have to be a student to use them.

Also worth trying is the Flight Shop (☎ (03) 6700477), 386 Little Bourke St, Melbourne. They also have branches under the name of the Flight Centre in Sydney (☎ (02) 2332296) and Brisbane (☎ (07) 2299958).

A one-way/return Sydney-Hong Kong discounted ticket starts from US$570/825.

To/From New Zealand
Air New Zealand and Cathay Pacific fly directly from Auckland to Hong Kong. APEX fares are the cheapest way to go, but you have to pay for your ticket at least 21 days in advance and spend a minimum of six days overseas. The cheapest one-way/return tickets available on the Hong Kong-Auckland run are US$574/898.

To/From Indonesia
Garuda Airlines has direct flights from Jakarta to Hong Kong, and from Denpasar to Hong Kong via Jakarta. Cheap discount air tickets out of Indonesia can be bought from travel agents in Kuta Beach in Bali and in Jakarta. There are numerous airline ticket discounters around Kuta Beach – several on the main strip, Jalan Legian. You can also buy discount tickets in Kuta for departure from Jakarta. In Jakarta, there are a few discounters on Jalan Jaksa. Bottom-market one-way/return prices for Hong Kong-Jakarta are currently US$227/415.

To/From Japan
Japan is not a good place to buy cheap air tickets. In fact, I can't think of anything you can buy cheaply in Japan, not even rice. The cheapest way to get out of Japan is by ferry boat to either Taiwan or Korea. However, if you need a plane ticket, Council Travel (☎ (03) 35817581) does have an office in Tokyo at the Sanno Grand Building, Room 102, 14-2 Nagata-Cho, 2-Chome, Chiyoda-ku, Tokyo 100.

For tickets purchased in Hong Kong, a Hong Kong-Tokyo one-way/return flight costs as little as US$279/487.

To/From Singapore
A good place for buying cheap air tickets in Singapore is Airmaster Travel Centre. Also try STA Travel. Other agents advertise in the *Straits Times* classified columns.

One-way/return Hong Kong-Singapore tickets start at US$216/275.

To/From South Korea
The best deals are available from the Korean International Student Exchange Society (KISES) (☎ (02) 7339494), Room 505, YMCA Building, Chongno 2-ga, Seoul. The lowest one-way/return prices on the Hong Kong-Seoul route are US$201/272.

To/From Taiwan
The cheapest one-way/return fares on the Hong Kong Taipei route are US$127/214 if purchased in Hong Kong.

With an ISIC or STA youth card, discounts are available from Youth Travel International (☎ 7211978), Suite 502, 142 Chunghsiao E Rd, Section 4, Taipei. This place also issues these cards to qualified individuals.

Otherwise, look for discount travel agencies which advertise in the local English-language newspapers, the *China Post* or *China News*. A few well-known ones include:

Country Club Travel
    5th floor, 152 Chunghsiao E Rd, Section 1, Taipei
    (☎ (02) 3567003)
David's Special
    8th floor, 216 Nanking E Rd, Section 2 (at Chienkuo N Rd, Taipei (☎ (02) 5099877, 5170183)
Evergrace Travel
    11th floor, 173 Chang'an E Rd, Section 2, Taipei
    (☎ (02) 7506757)
Hawk Express
    3rd floor, 258 Nanking E Rd, Section 3, Taipei
    (☎ (02) 7416663)
Jenny Su Travel
    10th floor, 27 Chungshan N Rd, Section 3
    (☎ (02) 5947733, 5962263; fax 5920068)

To/From Guam

For Hong Kongers, Guam has emerged as a popular honeymoon and vacation spot. Guam is just four hours from Hong Kong by air. Continental Airlines Micronesia has regular flights. The price for a round-trip ticket is only US$21 more than a one-way fare, though prices tend to be higher than flights all the way to California! Current one-way/return Hong Kong-Guam fares are US$455/476.

To/From Thailand

In Bangkok, Student Travel in the Thai Hotel is helpful and efficient. Travel agents on Khao San Rd are also heavily into discounting. Discounted one-way/return fares start at US$155/220.

To/From Other Asian Countries

For one-way return tickets purchased in Hong Kong, some sample fares include: Beijing US$267/532; Guangzhou US$57/114; Ho Chi Minh City US$294/589; Kuala Lumpur US$188/314; Manila US$115/193; Phnom Penh US$272/532; Rangoon US$367/735.

Airline Offices

Listed are some of the airlines which fly into Hong Kong, along with the addresses of ticketing offices on both sides of the harbour. The reservation and reconfirmation telephone number (Res) is followed by the flight information telephone number (Info). A few airlines have only one telephone number.

Air France
  Room 2104, Alexandra House, 7 Des Voeux Rd Central (☎ Res 5248145; Info 7696662)
Air India
  10th floor, Gloucester Tower, 11 Pedder St, Central (☎ Res 5221176; Info 7696539)
Air Lanka
  Room 602, Peregrine Tower, Lippo Centre, Central (☎ 5210708)
Air Mauritius
  c/o Mercury Travel Ltd, St George's Building, Ice House St & Connaught Rd, Central (☎ 5231114)

Air New Zealand
  Suite 902, 3 Exchange Square, 8 Connaught Place, Central (☎ 5249041)
Air Niugini
  Room 705, Century Square, 1-13 D'Aguilar St, Central (☎ Res 5242151)
Air Seychelles, Hopewell Centre, Queen's Rd East, Wanchai (☎ 8213881)
Alitalia
  Room 2101, Hutchison House, 10 Harcourt Rd, Central (☎ Res 5237047; Info 7697417)
All Nippon
  Room 2512, Pacific Place Two, 88 Queensway, Admiralty (☎ Res 8107100; Info 7698606)
British Airways
  30th floor, Alexandra House, 7 Des Voeux Rd Central (☎ Res 8680303; Info 8680768)
  Room 112, Royal Garden Hotel, 69 Mody Rd, Tsimshatsui East (☎ 3689255)
CAAC (Civil Aviation Administration of China)
  Ground floor, 17 Queen's Rd, Central, Hong Kong Island (☎ 8401199)
  Ground floor, Mirador Mansion, 54-64B Nathan Rd, Tsimshatsui (☎ 7390022)
Canadian Airlines International
  Ground floor, Swire House, 9-25 Chater Rd, Central (☎ Res 8683123; Info 7697113)
Cathay Pacific
  Ground floor, Swire House, 9-25 Chater Rd, Central
  11th floor, Room 1126, Ocean Centre, Tsimshatsui
  Shop 109, 1st floor, Royal Garden Hotel, 69 Mody Rd, Tsimshatsui East (☎ Res 7471888; Info 7471234)
China Airlines (Taiwan)
  Ground floor, St George's Building, Ice House St & Connaught Rd, Central
  G5-6 Tsimshatsui Centre, Tsimshatsui East (☎ Res 8682299; Info 8439800)
Dragonair
  Room 1843, Swire House, 9 Connaught Rd, Central
  12th floor, Tower 6, China Hong Kong City, 33 Canton Rd, Tsimshatsui (☎ Res 5901188; Info 7697727)
Eupo-Air, Swire House, 9 Connaught Rd, Central (☎ 5423633)
Garuda Indonesia
  2nd floor, Sing Pao Centre, 8 Queen's Rd, Central (☎ Res 8400000; Info 7696681)
Gulf Air, Room 2508, Caroline Centre, 28 Yun Ping Rd, Causeway Bay (☎ Res 8822892; Info 7698337)
Japan Air Lines
  20th floor, Gloucester Tower, 11 Pedder St, Central
  Harbour View Holiday Inn, Mody Rd,

Tsimshatsui East (☎ Res 5230081; Info 7696524)

Japan Asia
20th floor, Gloucester Tower, 11 Pedder St, Central (☎ Res 5218102)

Jardine's
Alexandra House, 7 Des Voeux Rd Central (☎ Res 8680303; Info 8680768)

KLM Royal Dutch Airlines
Room 701-5 Jardine House, 1 Connaught Place, Central (☎ Res 8228111; Info 8228118)

Korean Air
Ground floor, St George's Building, Ice House St & Connaught Rd, Central
11th floor, South Seas Centre, Tower II, 75 Mody Rd, Tsimshatsui East
G12-15 Tsimshatsui Centre, Salisbury Rd, Tsimshatsui East (☎ 3686221)

Lauda (Austria)
M1, New Henry Housse, 10 Ice House St, Central (☎ Res 5246178; Info 7697017)

Lufthansa German Airlines
6th floor, Landmark East, 12 Ice House St, Central (☎ Res 8682313; Info 7696560)

Malaysian Airline System
Room 1306, Prince's Building, 9-25 Chater Rd, Central (☎ Res 5218181; Info 7697967)

Northwest Airlines
29th floor, Alexandra House, 7 Des Voeux Rd Central, Central (☎ 8104288)

Philippine Airlines
Room 603, West Tower, Bond Centre, Central (☎ Res 5249521)
Room 6, Ground floor, East Ocean Centre, 98 Granville Rd, Tsimshatsui East (☎ Res 3694521; Info 7696263)

Qantas
Room 1422, Swire House, 9-25 Chater Rd, Central (☎ Res 5242101; Info 5256206)

Royal Brunei Airlines
Room 1406, Central Building, 3 Pedder St, Central (☎ 8698608)

Royal Nepal Airlines
Room 704, Lippo Sun Plaza, 28 Canton Rd, Tsimshatsui (☎ 3759151)

Singapore Airlines
United Centre, Queensway, Central (☎ Res 5202233; Info 7696387)

South African Airways
30th floor, Alexandra House, Central (☎ Res 8773277; Info 8680768)

Swissair
8th floor, Tower II, Admiralty Centre, 18 Harcourt Rd, Central (☎ Res 5293670; Info 7698864)

THAI Airways
United Centre, Two Pacific Place, Queensway, Central
Shop 124, 1st floor, World Wide Plaza, Des Voeux Road & Pedder St, Central
Shop 105-6, Omni, The Hong Kong Hotel, 3 Canton Rd, Tsimshatsui (☎ Res 5295601; Info 7697421)

United Airlines
29th floor, The Landmark, Gloucester Tower, Des Voeux Rd & Pedder St, Central
Ground floor, Empire Centre, Mody Rd, Tsimshatsui East (☎ Res 8104888; Info 7697279)

LAND
To/From Europe

From Europe, you can reach Hong Kong by rail, though most travellers following this route also tour China along the way. Don't take this rail journey just to save money – a direct flight from Europe to Hong Kong works out to be about the same price and sometimes less. The idea is to get a glimpse of Russia, Mongolia and China along the way.

It's a long haul. The most commonly taken routes are from Western Europe to Moscow, then on to Beijing via the Trans-Manchurian or Trans-Mongolian Railway. From Beijing there are trains to Guangzhou, and from there express trains to Hong Kong. The minimum time needed for this rail journey (one way) is 10 days, though most travellers will spend at least a month in China before finally arriving in Hong Kong.

More details are provided in Lonely Planet's *China – a travel survival kit*, *Mongolia – a travel survival kit* and *North-East Asia on a shoestring*. For still more depth, there's the *Trans-Siberian Handbook* by Bryn Thomas (Trailblazer Publications, distributed through Roger Lascelles in the UK).

Travel Service Asia (☎ (07371) 4963; fax (07371) 4769), Kirchberg 15, 7948 Dürmentingen, Germany, is highly recommended for low prices and good service. In the UK, one of the experts in budget rail travel is Regent Holidays (UK) Ltd (☎ (0272) 211711; telex 444606; fax 254866), 15 John St, Bristol BS1 2HR. Another agency geared towards budget travellers is Progressive Tours (☎ (071) 2621676), 12 Porchester Place, Connaught Square, London W2 2BS. Several travellers have recommended Scandinavian Student Travel Service (SSTS), 117 Hauchsvej, 1825 Copenhagen V, Denmark. One agent in Germany catering to the Trans-Siberian market with Mongolia tours thrown in is Mongolia Tourist Information Service (☎ (030) 7848057), Postfach 62 05 29, D-1000 Berlin 62.

If you want to go from Beijing to Moscow, you can book the ticket in Hong Kong at Moonsky Star (☎ 7231376; fax 7236653), 4th floor, E-Block, Flat 6E, Chungking Mansions, Tsimshatsui, Kowloon. In the same building you can also book at Time Travel (☎ 3666222; fax 7395413), 16th floor, Block A, Chungking Mansions, Tsimshatsui, Kowloon.

It can be hard to book this trip during the summer peak season. Off season shouldn't be a problem, but plan as far ahead as possible.

To/From South-East Asia

The Vietnam-China border has finally opened up to rail travellers, and overland travel by bus between Cambodia and Vietnam is now reasonably safe. Things are still a little dicey on the Thai-Cambodian border, but if that gets sorted then rail and road journeys from Singapore and Bangkok to Hong Kong would be entirely feasible.

SEA

Considering the renowned beauty of Hong Kong Harbour, it's a pity so few people can arrive by ship. The days of cheap passage on a cargo ship are mostly over, though it's not impossible to get on as a paying or even working passenger on either a yacht or freighter. If you want to exit Hong Kong this way, try posting a notice on the board in the Mariners' Club (☎ 3688261), 11 Middle Rd, Tsimshatsui, Kowloon.

Of course, there are luxurious passenger ships making cruises of the Far East, but these are anything but cheap. About the only cheap ships are those coming from China, such as the popular Shanghai/Hong Kong cruise. If luxury cruises appeal to you, see a travel agent.

LEAVING HONG KONG

Adam Smith would be pleased by the free-wheeling capitalist competition which keeps ticket prices in Hong Kong among the lowest in the world.

The current slogan of the HKTA is 'Stay Another Day', but if you don't reconfirm your onward ticket you may have to stay another week or longer. The easiest place to reconfirm is right in the airport on arrival, but you can do it by telephone or drop into the airlines' downtown offices.

On all flights, carry-on hand baggage must be able to fit in a space no larger than 22½ cm x 35 cm x 55 cm (9" x 14" x 22"). This limit is strictly enforced by security guards. Putting all non-breakable items into your checked luggage makes sense, but the price for overweight baggage can be high – usually 1% of the 1st class air fare for each kg. So if you've bought a lot of clothes, the only cheap way out might be to wear them – just hope you're not flying on a hot day!

If you need a pushcart to haul luggage around the airport, these are available only on the ground floor (the arrival area). There are none in the departure area, where the carts are really needed. So go downstairs, grab a cart and take it upstairs in the lift. People have complained about this for years, but to no avail.

Cathay Pacific offers a 'CityCheck' (☎ 7477888) early check-in service on both the Hong Kong and Kowloon sides. You can check in the day before departure, or for the same day if it's at least three hours before departure. It's a useful service since you can get rid of your bags and get a first choice of seats. On Hong Kong Island, CityCheck is available on the 4th floor, Shop 403, The Mall, Pacific Place, 88 Queensway, Admiralty. In Kowloon, CityCheck is on the Lower ground floor, China Hong Kong City, Canton Rd, Tsimshatsui.

Travel Agents

Many Hong Kong travel agents hesitate to sell you the cheapest ticket available. This is not always because they want to squeeze more money out of you. Airlines have cheap special deals, but the number of such seats may be limited, and there are often severe restrictions. With the cheapest tickets, you often have to pay the travel agent first and then pick up the ticket at the airport. Nevertheless, these cheap tickets may be worth the extra trouble. If you want the cheapest flight, tell the agent, and then make sure you understand what restrictions, if any, apply.

The travel agent that I often use in Hong Kong is Traveller Services (☎ 3752222; fax 3752233), Room 1012, Silvercord Tower 1, 30 Canton Rd, Tsimshatsui.

Phoenix Services (☎ 7227378; fax 3698884) in Room B, 6th floor, Milton Mansion, 96 Nathan Rd, Tsimshatsui, is scrupulously honest and gets good reviews from travellers.

Another competitor in the budget ticket business is Victoria Travel (☎ 3760621; fax 3762609), which is connected to Victoria Hostel on the 1st floor at 33 Hankow Rd, Tsimshatsui.

Finally, you can try Shoestring Travel (☎ 7232306; fax 7212085) Flat A, 4th floor, Alpha House, 27-33 Nathan Rd, Tsimshatsui. The service is not friendly, but the prices are in the same range as the others.

Many travellers still use the Hong Kong Student Travel Bureau (☎ 7303269), Room 1021, 10th floor, Star House, Tsimshatsui. However, they are no longer cheap, though you can get a discount with an ISIC card. Still, they might be worth a try. They have several branch offices: Argyle Centre (☎ 3900421), Room 1812, 688 Nathan Rd, Mongkok; Wing On Central Building (☎ 8107272), Room 901, 26 Des Voeux Rd, Central; Circle Plaza (☎ 8339909), 11th floor, 499 Hennessy Rd, Causeway Bay.

Rip-Offs Be careful when you buy tickets – rip-offs do occur. It happens less now than it used to, but Hong Kong has long been plagued with bogus travel agents and fly-by-night operations that appear shortly before peak holiday seasons and dupe customers into buying non-existent airline seats and holiday packages. One way to tell is to see if they are listed in the telephone book, since fly-by-night operations don't stay around long enough to get listed.

The most common trick is a request for a non-refundable deposit on an air ticket. You pay a deposit for the booking, but when you go to pick up the tickets they say that the flight is no longer available, but that there is another flight at a higher price, sometimes 50% more!

It is best not to pay a deposit, but to rather pay for the ticket in full and get a receipt clearly showing that there is no balance due, and that the full amount is refundable if no ticket is issued. Tickets are normally issued the next day after booking, but for the really cheap tickets (actually group tickets) you must pick these up yourself at the airport from the 'tour leader' (who you will never see again once you've got the ticket). One caution: when you get the ticket from the tour leader, check it carefully. Occasionally there are errors, such as you're issued a ticket with the return portion valid for only 60 days when you paid for a ticket valid for one year, etc.

If you think you have been ripped off, and the agent is a member of the HKTA, the organisation can apply some pressure (and apparently has a fund to handle cases of outright fraud). Even if an agent is a member of the HKTA he does not have to comply with any set of guidelines.

Since mid-1985 all travel agencies offering outward-bound services must be licenced. A fund was also set up to compensate cheated customers. It could be worth inquiring about if you get ripped-off.

Departure Tax

A miracle has happened. Hong Kong actually lowered its airport departure tax from HK$150 to HK$50. In fact, it's even free if you can persuade the airport personnel that you're under age 12. Just how long these low rates will last are not known. Although lowering the tax is politically popular, many believe the government will soon miss the lost revenue.

Getting Around

Hong Kong is small and crowded, which makes public transport the only practical way to move people. Consequently, public transport is cheap, fast, widely used and generally efficient. It is mostly privately owned and operates at a profit.

If you want to master all the intricacies of Hong Kong's complex system of buses, minibuses, trams and ferries, pick up the book *Public Transport in Hong Kong – A Guide to Services* published by the transport department. This guide describes the routes in excruciating detail. Indeed, the worst thing about the book is that it inundates you with information, some of it confusing, and it doesn't contain maps. The guide can be purchased from the Government Publications Centre adjacent to the GPO near the Star Ferry Terminal on Hong Kong Island.

BUS

The extensive bus system offers a bewildering number of routes that will take you anywhere you want to go in Hong Kong. You are most likely to use the buses to explore the south side of Hong Kong Island and the New Territories. The north side of Hong Kong Island and most of Kowloon are well-served by the Mass Transit Railway (MTR).

In Central, the most important bus terminal is on the ground floor right under Exchange Square (just west of the GPO). In Kowloon, the Star Ferry Bus Terminal is the most crucial.

Finding the bus terminals is the easy part, but figuring out which bus you want may take some effort. One useful fact to memorise is that any bus number ending with the letter 'K' (78K, 69K, etc) means that the route connects to the Kowloon-Canton Railway. Similarly, bus numbers ending with 'M' (51M, 68M, etc) go to the MTR stations. Those ending with 'R' are recreational buses and normally run on Sunday, public holidays

or for special events like the races at Happy Valley. Buses with an 'X' are express. Air-conditioning is used without mercy even in winter – bring gloves so you don't get frost-bite. Whether you want it or not, air-con costs extra.

CMB & KMB Buses

The China Motor Bus Company (CMB) operates the blue-and-white buses on Hong Kong Island, and the Kowloon Motor Bus Company (KMB) runs the red-and-cream buses in Kowloon.

The HKTA has some useful free handouts on bus routes in Kowloon, Hong Kong Island and the New Territories.

Most buses run from about 6 am until midnight, but the 121 and 122 are 'Cross Harbour Recreation Routes' which operate through the Cross-Harbour Tunnel every 15 minutes from 12.45 to 5 am. Bus No 121 runs from Macau Ferry Pier on Hong Kong Island, through the tunnel to Chatham Rd in Tsimshatsui East before continuing on to Choi Hung on the east side of the airport. Bus No 122 runs from North Point on Hong Kong Island, through the Cross-Harbour Tunnel, Chatham Rd in Tsimshatsui East, the northern part of Nathan Rd and on to Laichikok and Mei Foo in the north-west part of Kowloon. Both of these buses cost HK$6.50. You can catch them near the tunnel entrances on either side of the harbour.

Bus fares range from HK$1.80 for the shortest routes without air-con and up to HK$12 for air-con deluxe buses on the longest route in the New Territories. Drop the exact fare into the box next to the driver as you board the bus. No change is given so keep a collection of coins with you all the time.

When you want to get off just yell out anything – the drivers usually don't speak much English. The Cantonese say *yau lok* if you want to be correct.

Citybus

These are special express buses which usually go nonstop between two points. They are air-con and generally luxurious, but cost more. For travellers, the most popular Citybus is the one going to Ocean Park which costs HK$9. However, these buses also go from Central to the various housing estates.

Minibus

This is a cream-coloured bus with a red stripe down the side and usually seats 14 people. Its final destination is written in Chinese and English on the sign at the front, but you'll have to squint to see the English squeezed in above the Chinese.

You can hail a minibus just as you do an ordinary taxi. It will stop almost anywhere to pick you up or put you down, but not at the stops for the large KMB and CMB buses or in the restricted zones where it's unsafe to stop. The fares are not much higher than the large buses and they aren't nearly as crowded. You are not allowed to stand on a minibus so they won't pick up more passengers than they have seats.

Fares range from HK$2 to HK$6, and you

Hong Kong Island

Bus	From	To	Frequency	Cost
1	Central (Rumsey St)	Happy Valley	12-20 min	HK$3.80
6	Repulse Bay/Stanley	Central	10-20 min	HK$4/6
7	Aberdeen	Central	10-15 min	HK$3.20
14	Sai Wan Ho	Stanley	20-30 min	HK$4.80
15	Central (Exchange Sq)	Victoria Peak	5-30 min	HK$5.20
15B	Causeway Bay	Victoria Peak	20 min	HK$6.00
70	Central (Exchange Sq)	Aberdeen	5-10 min	HK$3.60
73	Stanley	Aberdeen	15-30 min	HK$4.80

Kowloon

Bus	From	To	Frequency	Cost
1A	Star Ferry	Kowloon City	6-13 min	HK$3.00
2	Star Ferry	Lei Cheung Uk	5-10 min	HK$2.10
5	Star Ferry	Choi Hung	3-8 min	HK$2.10
6A	Star Ferry	Laichikok	8-15 min	HK$2.10
8A	Jordan Rd	Whampoa Gardens	12-20 min	HK$2.10
14C	Kwun Tong MTR	Lei Yue Mun	13-25 min	HK$1.80

New Territories

Bus	From	To	Via	Frequency
51	Tsuen Wan	Kam Tin	Route Twisk	10-20 min
52X	Shamshuipo	Tuen Mun	Tsuen Wan	12-20 min
54	Yuen Long	Sheung Tsuen	Kam Tin	15-25 min
60M	Tsuen Wan	Tuen Mun	Ma Wan Pier	5-10 min
60X	Jordan Rd	Tuen Mun	Tsuen Wan	5-20 min
64K	Yuen Long	Tai Po	Kam Tin	5-15 min
68M	Tsuen Wan	Yuen Long	Tuen Mun	4-14 min
68X	Jordan Rd	Yuen Long	Tuen Mun	9-16 min
75K	Tai Po	Plover Cove Res	Tai Mei Tuk	13-25 min
77K	Yuen Long	Fanling	Kam Tin	14-25 min
91	Choi Hung	Clearwater Bay	Hang Hau	12-16 min
92	Choi Hung	Sai Kung	Hebe Haven	6-15 min
94	Sai Kung	Wong Shek Pier	Pak Tam Chung	60 min
96R	Choi Hung	Wong Shek Pier	Sai Kung	holidays

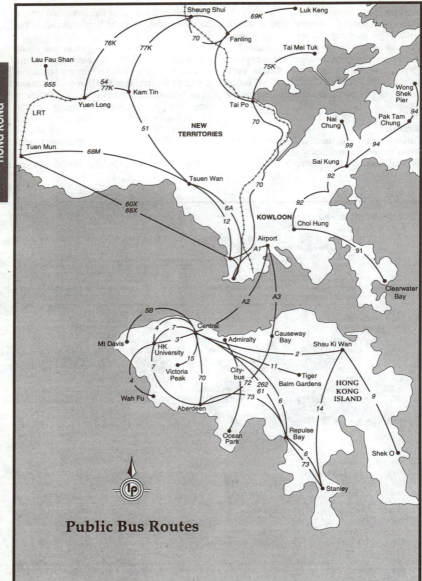

Public Bus Routes

pay when you get off, and drivers usually can give change. Minibuses to the New Territories can be picked up at the Jordan Rd Ferry Pier in Kowloon.

Maxicab

Maxicabs are like minibuses, but have a green stripe and operate on fixed routes and stop at designated places. Fares vary according to distance, running between HK$1 and HK$8. You pay when you get on and no change is given.

TRAIN
Mass Transit Railway (MTR)

One of the world's most modern metro systems, the MTR is clean, fast and safe. Trains run every two to four minutes from 6 am to 1 am daily on three lines (see map).

The cheapest fare is HK$3.50, while the most expensive is HK$9. For short hauls, the MTR is more expensive than other public transport. If you want to cross the harbour from Central to Tsimshatsui, the MTR is about five times the price of the Star Ferry with none of the view, and only marginally faster. But if you go further, such as Tsuen Wan in the New Territories, the MTR is considerably faster than a ferry or a bus and almost the same price. Also, it's air-con, which is convenient in summer.

Riding the MTR is dead easy – just follow the signs. Everything is automated, from the ticket vending machines to the turnstiles. Ticket machines take HK$5, HK$2, HK$1 and 50c pieces but do not give change, so feed in the right amount. If you put in a HK$5 coin for a HK$4 ticket the next person gets a HK$1 discount! There are change machines that accept coins only – notes must be changed at the information desks or minibanks. Once you pass through the turnstiles, you only have 90 minutes to complete the journey or the ticket becomes void.

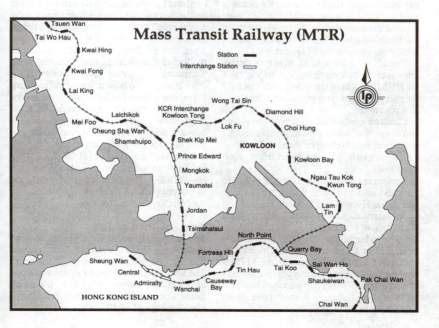

Mass Transit Railway (MTR)

Station ▬
Interchange Station ▭

Tsuen Wan
Tai Wo Hau
Kwai Hing
Kwai Fong
Lai King
Mei Foo
Laichikok
Cheung Sha Wan
Shamshuipo
KCR Interchange
Kowloon Tong
Shek Kip Mei
Prince Edward
Mongkok
Yaumatei
Jordan
Tsimshatsui
Wong Tai Sin
Lok Fu
Diamond Hill
Choi Hung
KOWLOON
Kowloon Bay
Ngau Tau Kok
Kwun Tong
Lam Tin
North Point
Fortress Hill
Quarry Bay
Sheung Wan
Central
Admiralty
Wanchai
Causeway Bay
Tin Hau
Tai Koo
Sai Wan Ho
Shaukeiwan
Pak Chai Wan
Chai Wan
HONG KONG ISLAND

The MTR uses 'smart tickets' with a magnetic coding strip on the back. When you pass through the turnstile, the card is encoded with the station identification and time. At the other end, the exit turnstile sucks in the ticket, reads where you came from, the time and how much you paid, and lets you through if you pass the test.

You can't buy return tickets, but there are 'Common Stored Value Tickets' for making multiple journeys. These are available in denominations of HK$70, HK$100 and HK$200, and are definitely worthwhile if you use the MTR frequently. They can also be used on the Kowloon-Canton Railway except for Lo Wu Station (the Chinese border station). You gain some benefit from buying the larger denominations – the encoded value of the HK$100 ticket is HK$103, and the HK$200 ticket is worth HK$212. Another benefit is the 'last ride bonus' – no matter how little the value remaining on the ticket, you don't have to pay extra for the final ride when the ticket is used up. The single-journey MTR tickets must be used the same day, so it's no good buying one to use tomorrow. You can buy these tickets at the mini banks in the MTR stations.

There's also a 'tourist ticket' – better known as the 'sucker ticket' – which is valid for HK$20 worth of travel but costs HK$25! As compensation, you get to keep the ticket as a souvenir.

Children aged two or under can travel free and there are special child/student tickets which are much cheaper than adult prices. These can only be used by children aged three to 11.

Passengers aged 12 or over can only use the child/student tickets if they are students carrying a Hong Kong Student Travel Card – an International Student Identity Card (ISIC) is not acceptable. You might be tempted to buy a child/student ticket to save money, after all, how can the machine know you aren't a student? However, the MTR is well-patrolled by plainclothes police and closed-circuit TV. If you're spotted buying a child/student ticket, you may have some explaining to do.

Smoking, eating and drinking are not permitted in the MTR stations or on the trains (makes me wonder about all those Maxim Cake Shops in the stations). The fine for eating or drinking is HK$1000, while smoking will set you back HK$2000. Busking, selling and soliciting are also prohibited activities. You are not supposed to carry large pieces of luggage, but 'large' is subject to interpretation. Apparently, backpacks and suitcases are OK, but don't try moving furniture.

There is also a passenger information hotline (☎ 7500170). There are no toilets in either the trains or the stations. If you leave something on the train and nobody steals it, you might be able to reclaim your goods at the lost property office at Admiralty Station between 11 am and 6.45 pm, Monday to Saturday.

Kowloon-Canton Railway (KCR)

This line runs from Kowloon to the China border at Lo Wu. Most trains terminate at the border but special express trains run all the way through to Guangzhou. You can change from the MTR to the KCR at the Kowloon Tong Station. The southernmost station on the line at Hunghom is easily reached from Tsimshatsui by taking green minibus No 6 from Hankow Rd (south side of Peking Rd). If you buy a stored value or tourist ticket for the MTR you can also use it on the KCR for every station but Lo Wu. You are not supposed to ride up to Lo Wu Station unless you plan to cross the border into China.

Fares are from HK$3 to HK$7.50, except for the train to the border at Lo Wu which costs HK$37. The KCR is a good way to get to various parts of the New Territories. See the New Territories chapter.

Light Rail Transit (LRT)

The latest addition to the alphabet soup of Hong Kong trains is the LRT. This is rather like a modern air-con version of the tram. The LRT runs on the road surface and stops at designated stations. However, it's much faster than the tram, at times reaching a maximum speed of 70 km/h.

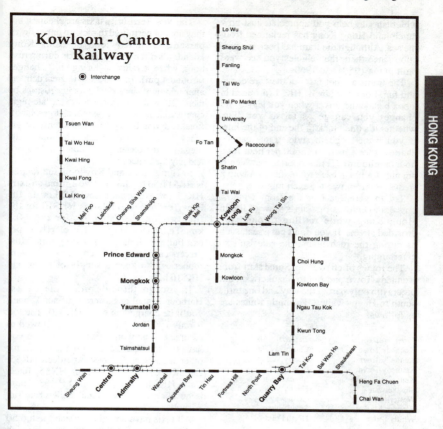

Kowloon - Canton Railway

◉ Interchange

Lo Wu
Sheung Shui
Fanling
Tai Wo
Tai Po Market
University
Racecourse
Fo Tan
Shatin
Tai Wai

Tsuen Wan
Tai Wo Hau
Kwai Hing
Kwai Fong
Lai King
Mei Foo
Lai Chi Kok
Cheung Sha Wan
Sham Shui Po
Shek Kip Mei
Kowloon Tong
Lok Fu
Wong Tai Sin

Prince Edward
Mongkok
Yaumatei
Jordan
Tsimshatsui

Mongkok
Kowloon

Diamond Hill
Choi Hung
Kowloon Bay
Ngau Tau Kok
Kwun Tong
Lam Tin

Sheung Wan
Central
Admiralty
Wanchai
Causeway Bay
Tin Hau
Fortress Hill
North Point
Quarry Bay
Tai Koo
Sai Wan Ho
Shaukeiwan
Heng Fa Chuen
Chai Wan

The LRT only runs in the New Territories, connecting the city of Tuen Mun with Yuen Long, but may be extended to connect with the MTR and KCR.

There are five LRT lines connecting the various small suburbs in the area. The system operates from 5.30 am to 12.30 am Monday to Saturday, and from 6 am to midnight on Sundays and holidays. The LRT terminus in Tuen Mun is at the hoverferry pier, where you can reach Central on Hong Kong Island in 30 minutes. Fares on the LRT are HK$3 to HK$4.30 for adults and tickets are purchased from vending machines. The system

of fare collection is unique for Hong Kong – there are no gates or turnstiles and customers are 'trusted' to pay. However, that 'trust' is enforced by occasional police spot checks with fines for those who haven't purchased a ticket.

TRAM

One of the world's great travel bargains, Hong Kong's trams are tall, narrow, double-decker streetcars that trundle along the northern side of Hong Kong Island.

The tram line was built in 1904 on what was then the shoreline of Hong Kong Island, which should help you appreciate just how much land Hong Kong has reclaimed from the sea. Although the tram has been in operation since then, the vehicles you see were built in the 1950s and 1960s.

The trams are not fast but they are cheap and fun. For a flat fare of HK$1 (dropped in a box beside the driver when you leave – no change) you can go as far as you like, whether it's one block or the end of the line. If you want to go in style, trams can be chartered for a mere HK$600 per hour (two hour minimum). Trams operate between 6 am and 1 am. On each route they run with a frequency from two to seven minutes.

Try to get a seat at the front window upstairs to enjoy a first-class view of life in Hong Kong while rattling through the crowded streets. If you don't get a seat, such as during the rush hours, the ride isn't so entertaining.

The routes often overlap. Some start from Kennedy Town and run to Shaukeiwan, but others run only part of the way and one turns south to Happy Valley. The eight routes are as follows:

From (west)	To (east)
Kennedy Town	Causeway Bay
Kennedy Town	Happy Valley
Kennedy Town	North Point
Kennedy Town	Shaukeiwan
Shaukeiwan	Happy Valley
Western Market	Causeway Bay
Western Market	Shaukeiwan
Whitty Street	North Point

TAXI

When a taxi is available, there should be a red 'For Hire' sign displayed in the windscreen and the 'Taxi' sign on the roof will be lit up at night. It's important to realise that taxis cannot stop at bus stops or where a yellow line is painted next to the kerb. A driver who ignores these rules risks a HK$300 fine, so be sure to position yourself correctly, otherwise no taxi will stop for you.

In Kowloon and Hong Kong Island, taxis are red with silver tops. In the New Territories they are green with white tops. In Lantau, the colour code is blue.

The New Territories taxis are cheapest but they are not permitted to pick up or put down passengers in Kowloon or Hong Kong Island. It's often hard to get taxis during rush hour, when it rains or during shift changes (around 4 pm). Taxis are also in great demand after midnight since public transport stops by then. Officially, there are no extra late-night charges and no extra passenger charges. Unofficially, during heavy rains and after midnight many drivers try to charge double (supposedly illegal) – just pretend you 'don't understand' and pay the meter fare.

In Hong Kong and Kowloon, the flagfall is HK$11.50 for the first two km and an extra HK$1 for every additional 0.2 km. In the New Territories, flagfall is HK$10 for the first two km, thereafter 90c for every 0.2 km. There is a luggage fee of HK$5 per bag but not all drivers insist on this. Most drivers carry very little change (to prevent robberies), so keep a supply of coins and HK$10 bills.

If you go through either the Cross-Harbour Tunnel or Eastern Harbour Tunnel, you'll be charged an extra HK$20. The toll is only HK$10, but the driver is allowed to assume that he won't get a fare back so you have to pay. You are also charged extra for other tunnels as follows: Aberdeen HK$5; Lion Rock HK$6; Shing Mun HK$5; Tate's Cairn HK$4; Tseung Kwan O HK$3. There is no charge for the tunnel under Kai Tak Airport.

All taxis have a card on which the top 50 destinations are listed in Cantonese, English and Japanese – very useful since a lot of the taxi drivers don't speak English. Even if the card doesn't list your specific destination, it will certainly have some nearby place. The card is usually kept above the driver's sun visor.

If you feel a taxi driver has ripped you off, get the licence number and call the police hotline (☎ 5277177) to lodge a complaint with the relevant details about when, where and how much. Drivers have some reason to fear the police – getting a taxi licence is extremely difficult and it can be revoked if the driver breaks the rules. The number of licences ('medallions' in taxi driver lingo) is

LRT Route Map

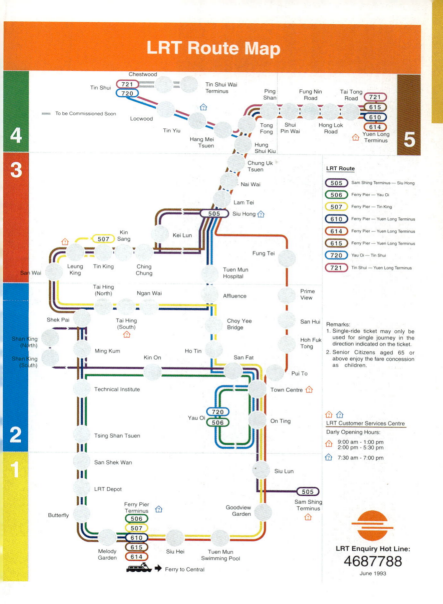

Chestwood

Tin Shui   721   Tin Shui Wai
             720   Terminus

To be Commissioned Soon

Locwood

Tin Yiu

Hang Mei
Tsuen

Hung
Shui Kiu

Chung Uk
Tsuen

Nai Wai

Lam Tei

Ping   Fung Nin   Tai Tong
Shan   Road   Road   721
                                      615
Tong   Shui   Hong Lok   610
Fong   Pin Wai   Road   614
                                 Yuen Long
                                 Terminus

505 Siu Hong

Kin
Sang

507

Kei Lun

Fung Tei

Leung   Tin King   Ching
King   Chung

San Wai

Tai Hing
(North)   Ngan Wai

Shek Pai   Tai Hing
              (South)

Shan King
(North)

Shan King   Ming Kum   Kin On   Ho Tin
(South)

Technical Institute

Tuen Mun
Hospital

Affluence

Choy Yee
Bridge

San Fat

Prime
View

San Hui

Hoh Fuk
Tong

Pui To

Yau Oi   720
          506

Town Centre

On Ting

Tsing Shan Tsuen

San Shek Wan

Siu Lun

LRT Depot

Ferry Pier
Terminus
            506
            507
Butterfly   610

505

Sam Shing
Terminus

Melody   615
Garden   614   Siu Hei   Tuen Mun
                                Swimming Pool

Goodview
Garden

Ferry to Central

LRT Route

505	Sam Shing Terminus — Siu Hong
506	Ferry Pier — Yau Oi
507	Ferry Pier — Tin King
610	Ferry Pier — Yuen Long Terminus
614	Ferry Pier — Yuen Long Terminus
615	Ferry Pier — Yuen Long Terminus
720	Yau Oi — Tin Shui
721	Tin Shui — Yuen Long Terminus

Remarks:
1. Single-ride ticket may only be used for single journey in the direction indicated on the ticket.
2. Senior Citizens aged 65 or above enjoy the fare concession as children.

LRT Customer Services Centre
Darly Opening Hours:
🏠 9:00 am - 1:00 pm
    2:00 pm - 5:30 pm
🏠 7:30 am - 7:00 pm

LRT Enquiry Hot Line:
4687788

June 1993

Light Rail Transit

Top: Whampoa Gardens, Hunghom, Kowloon (RS)
Bottom: Sculpture in Kowloon Park, Kowloon (RS)

limited and they are obtained through competitive bidding. The last time I checked the going rate was HK$1,800,000 – you can buy a house in Hong Kong for less than that!

CAR & MOTORBIKE
Road Rules
Driving is on the left side of the road, the same as Australia and Britain but the opposite to China. Seat belts must be worn by the driver and all front-seat passengers. The police are strict and there are draconian fines for traffic violations.

Driving in crowded Hong Kong has been made deliberately expensive in order to discourage it. For a local resident to get a driving licence, he or she must take an expensive driving course and wait about 18 months. The motor vehicle import tax is 100% and the petrol tax is more than 100%. Vehicle registration (based on engine size) averages about HK$8000 annually and liability insurance is compulsory.

As for foreigners, anyone over the age of 18 with a valid driving licence from their home country, or an international driving permit, can drive in Hong Kong for up to 12 months. If you're staying longer, you'll need a Hong Kong licence. Apply to the Transport Department Licensing Division (☎ 5261577), 41st floor, Wanchai Tower II, 7 Gloucester Rd, Wanchai. A driving test is not required.

Rental
The best advice that I can give about renting a car is don't! Except for touring some of the backwaters in the New Territories, a car saves no time at all. The MTR doesn't have to stop for traffic lights and taking the bus will often be faster than driving. The reason is that parking in the city is a nightmare, and it's likely that you'll have to park so far away from your destination that the time you saved will be used up walking to and from the car park. Hong Kongers who own cars mainly do so to gain face, not because they have any need for a motor vehicle. Expatriates with fragile egos also buy cars for the same reason. Another point to consider is the expense.

Several car-hire companies provide a variety of cars for self-drive or chauffeur-driven rental. Even Rolls-Royces are available. You'll find car rental agencies listed in the Yellow Pages Buying Guide under Motorcar Renting & Leasing. The following car rental agencies are HKTA members:

Ace
    Mezzanine floor, 16 Min Fat St, Happy Valley (☎ 8930541)
Avis
    Ground floor, Bonaventure House, 85 Leighton Rd, Causeway Bay (☎ 8906988)
Intercontinental
    21st floor, Lane Crawford House, 70 Queen's Rd, Central (☎ 5321388)
Windsor
    Basement 1, Bayview Mansion, 21 Moreton Terrace, Causeway Bay (☎ 5779031)

You normally get unlimited kms at no extra cost and discounts if you rent for a week or more. Many car-rental outlets and the big hotels offer a chauffeur-driven service, but using this service for one day could easily cost more than your hotel room.

Motorcycles seem impossible to rent, but can be bought if you're staying long enough. They seem unpopular in Hong Kong.

BICYCLE
Bicycling in Kowloon or Central would be suicidal, but in quiet areas of the islands or the New Territories a bike can be quite a nice way of getting around. The bike rental places tend to run out early on weekends.

Some places where you can rent bikes and ride in safety include; Shek O on Hong Kong Island; Shatin and Tai Mei Tuk (near Tai Po) in the New Territories; Mui Wo (Silvermine Bay) on Lantau Island; and on the island of Cheung Chau.

WALKING
Despite the concrete, glass and steel, Hong Kong presents plenty of good opportunities for walking.

There are many interesting city walks around Hong Kong and Kowloon, as well as

more rural walks on the Outlying Islands and in the New Territories, some of which are described in the relevant chapters.

Also useful is the HKTA free leaflet *Six Walks*. One 50 km walk twists and winds across the length of Hong Kong Island from Shek O to Victoria Peak, with the 3.5 km Peak circuit walk as the starting or finishing stretch.

Selected Walks in Hong Kong by Ronald Forrest and George Hobbins describes walks of varying lengths in all regions.

ESCALATOR

Hong Kong's latest transport scheme is attracting widespread attention. Officially dubbed the 'Hillside Escalator Link', this novel system looks like something out of a science-fiction movie. Basically, the system consists of escalators and moving walkways, called 'travelators', elevated above the street level. The present escalator-travelator is 800 metres long, the world's longest.

One of Hong Kong's long-standing problems is that many well-to-do residents live in the Mid-Levels, the lower portion of the Peak, but work in the skyscraper forest below. The roads are narrow and the distance is more vertical than horizontal, which means that walking involves a strenuous climb to get back home. The result is a rush-hour nightmare of bumper-to-bumper taxis, minibuses and private cars. The esca-lator aims to solve this problem by getting people out of their vehicles entirely. To judge from the rush-hour crowds, the project has been a smashing success.

There is talk of now expanding the system. Construction ran 500% over budget but no one is complaining, and other cities are watching with interest. Score another first for Hong Kong.

BOAT

Hong Kong's ferries are usually faster than the bus and cheaper too. There are discounts for children under 12. As long as you aren't prone to seasickness, the boats are fun and the harbour views are stunning when the weather cooperates. Though you'll find that many people break the rules, smoking is prohibited on all ferries and the fine for violating this is HK$5000.

Cross-Harbour Ferries

Star Ferry Practically every visitor takes a ride on the Star Ferry which is also an essential mode of transport for commuters. All of the ferries have names like Morning Star, Evening Star, Celestial Star, Shining Star, Twinkling Star, etc. You should also repeat the trip on a clear night.

There are three Star Ferries, but by far the most popular is the one running between Tsimshatsui (the lower tip of Kowloon) and

Central (Edinburgh Place). The trip takes seven minutes, enough time to knock off some great photos. For adults, lower and upper deck costs HK$1.20 and HK$1.50 respectively. For children under 12 the tariff is HK$1 and HK$1.20. The coin-operated turnstiles do not give change. You can get change from the ticket window if you take the upper deck, but the lower deck does not have a ticket window.

I personally find the lower deck more interesting for photography purposes, but it's worth the extra 30c to go top deck at least once. The top deck is less-crowded and gives a different perspective than bottom deck.

A special tourist ticket is available for HK$20, which allows unlimited rides on the Star Ferry and the Tramways. Seeing how cheap the normal fare is, you'd have to do at least 14 trips in four days to make this 'bargain' worthwhile.

The Star Ferry is not the only show in town. Hong Kong Ferry (HKF) Holdings Company operates a number of useful ferries and hoverferries.

Hoverferry

Hoverferries are about twice as fast as conventional boats. Inside they are luxurious with aircraft-type seats (no one stands) and air-con. They are exciting to ride in but not particularly smooth. When the water is rough, they go bouncing along the surface like a stone skipping across a pond. If you're prone to seasickness, don't get on a hovercraft after eating a big plate of greasy pork chops and lasagna. You won't have the option of getting rid of this unpleasant mess over the side as the windows on hoverferries don't open.

The following schedules are for ferries connecting Hong Kong Island to Kowloon and the New Territories.

Star Ferry

Tsimshatsui – Central (Edinburgh Place), every five to 10 minutes from 6.30 am until 11.30 pm.

Tsimshatsui – Wanchai, every 10 to 20 minutes from 7.30 to 10.50 pm.

Hunghom – Central (Edinburgh Place), every 12 to 20 minutes (every 20 minutes on Sundays & holidays) from 7 am to 7.20 pm.

Hong Kong Ferry (HKF)

Central – Yaumatei (Jordan Rd), every 12 to 15 minutes from 6.15 am to midnight.

Hunghom – North Point, every 20 minutes from 6.03 am to 10.40 pm.

Hunghom – Wanchai, Monday to Friday every 15 to 20 minutes from 6.30 am to 9.50 pm.

Kowloon City – North Point, every 20 minutes from 6.05 am to 10.25 pm.

Kwun Tong – North Point, every 15 minutes from 6 am to midnight.

HKF Hoverferry

Tsimshatsui East – Central (Queen's Pier), every 20 minutes from 8 am to 8 pm.

Tsuen Wan – Central (Government Pier), every 20 minutes from 7.20 am to 5.20 pm.

Tuen Mun – Central (Central Harbour Services Pier), every 10 to 20 minutes from 6.45 am to 7.40 pm.

Kaidos

A *kaido* is a small-to-medium sized ferry which can make short runs on the open sea. Few kaido routes operate on regular schedules, preferring to adjust supply according to demand. There is sort of a schedule on popular runs like the trip between Aberdeen and Lamma Island. Kaidos run mostly on weekends and holidays when everyone tries to 'get away from it all'.

A *sampan* is a motorised launch which can only accommodate a few people. A sampan is too small to be considered seaworthy, but can safely zip you around typhoon shelters like Aberdeen Harbour.

Bigger than a sampan, but smaller than a kaido, is a *walla walla*. These operate as water taxis on Victoria Harbour. Most of the customers are sailors living on ships anchored in the harbour.

Other Ferries

If you want to visit islands more remote than Hong Kong Island, see the chapters on the New Territories and Outlying Islands for the relevant schedules.

RICKSHAW

This was once the main means of public transport in Hong Kong. Rickshaws were invented by an American Baptist missionary in Japan in 1871 and quickly caught on in Hong Kong.

That was then and this is now – rickshaws are just for photograph-taking. Licences to operate a rickshaw have not been issued for decades and the remaining drivers are so old and frail you might have to put them in the rickshaw and do the driving yourself. You have to bargain the fare with them. For only a photograph they'll ask at least HK$30 but you can often get them down to HK$15. The fare escalates dramatically if you ask them to take you any distance, even around the block. Agree on the fare first and ignore demands for more. If the rickshaw drivers try to cheat you, threaten to call the police.

HELICOPTER

This is not exactly for the typical commuter or tourist, but if you've got cash to burn (HK$4000 for 30 minutes), you can charter a helicopter for an aerial tour. The place to contact is Heliservices (☎ 5236407, 8020200), 22nd floor, St George's Building, Ice House St & Connaught Rd, Central. The helipad is at Fenwick Pier St in Wanchai, and there is another at Shek Kong Airfield in the New Territories.

LOCAL TRANSPORT
To/From the Airport

There are three airport buses, simply known as 'Airbuses'. One goes to Kowloon and the other two go to Hong Kong Island. The buses have plenty of room for luggage and charge half fares for children under 12. No change is given on any of the buses, but there is an airport bus service centre right outside the airport exit that will give change for HK$10 notes. Departures are every 15 to 20 minutes throughout the day. Except for Airbus A5, services going to the airport begin at 7.40 am and end at midnight. From the airport into the city, buses start running at 7 am and final departures are also at midnight.

Airbus No A1 goes to Tsimshatsui on the Kowloon side and follows a circular route. It runs down Chatham Rd, then turns on Cameron Rd, then down Nathan Rd (the main artery of Tsimshatsui) and to the Star Ferry Terminal. It then runs through Tsimshatsui East and back to the airport. The fare is HK$9.

Airbus No A2 goes to Hong Kong Island via the Cross-Harbour Tunnel. It stops at all the main hotels in the Wanchai, Central and Sheung Wan districts. The bus goes down Gloucester Rd in Wanchai, and stops near the following hotels: China Harbour View, Evergreen Plaza, Furama, Victoria, Harbour, Harbour View International, Hilton, Luk Kwok, Mandarin Oriental, New Harbour and Ramada Inn. The bus turns around at the Macau Ferry Pier and follows the same route back to the airport. The fare is HK$14.

Airbus No A3 takes a circular route through Causeway Bay in Hong Kong Island. The bus stops near these hotels: Excelsior, Lee Gardens and Park Lane. The fare is HK$14.

Airbus No A4 went bankrupt some years ago, but hopefully the newly created Airbus A5 will do better. This one runs from the Airport to Quarry Bay (Tai Koo MTR Station) along a circular route and costs HK$14. It runs every 15 minutes from 9 am until 11 pm, and stops at three major hotels.

TOURS

There are so many tours available it's impossible to list them all. You can get one to just about anywhere in Hong Kong. Some popular destinations include the Sung (Song) Dynasty Village, Ocean Park,

Stanley, the Outlying Islands or the duck farms in the New Territories.

Tours can be booked through the HKTA, travel agents, large tourist hotels or directly from the tour company. There are discounts for children under age 16 and seniors aged 60 and over. Children under age six are allowed to attend free.

Watertours
There are currently 20 of these popular tours, covering such diverse places as Victoria Harbour and Cheung Chau Island. Book these trips through a travel agent or call Watertours (☎ 3671970 or 7303031). Costs vary enormously according to which tour you choose – the current price range is from HK$40 to HK$515.

Harbour Cruises
These are offered by the Star Ferry Company, and you book at the Star Ferry Pier. There are both day and evening cruises. The costs are HK$100 for adults, HK$70 for children. Options include a cocktail cruise (HK$110), lunch cruise (HK$220) and dinner cruise (HK$320).

Come Horse Racing Tour
You get to sit in the visitors' box of the Members' Enclosure of the Royal Hong Kong Jockey Club. A Western lunch or dinner is thrown in. The tours follow the racing season, and to be eligible you must be 18 or older, must be a foreign passport holder and must have been in Hong Kong less than 21 days. The cost is HK$468 and the tour is conducted by the HKTA.

Heritage Tour
This covers major historical sights, including Lei Cheng Uk, a 2000-year-old burial chamber. Trips are run on Wednesdays and Saturdays. The costs are HK$280 for a five-hour tour (HK$230 for seniors), HK$430 for eight hours (HK$380 for seniors) and the tour is conducted by the HKTA.

Family Insight Tour
You visit public housing estates and see how the people live. You also get to visit a family's apartment, a rest home and a large Taoist temple. The tour runs on Thursdays only and lasts four hours. The costs are HK$210 for adults, HK$170 for children and seniors, and special offers for families. The tour is conducted by the HKTA.

Land Between Tour
This popular six-hour tour covers the New Territories. The costs are HK$295 for adults, HK$245 for children and seniors, and special offers for families. The tour is conducted by the HKTA.

Nooks & Crannies Tours
Offered by an 'alternative' private operator, these interesting tours are limited to small groups of two to six persons. Tours can be from four to nine hours and cost from HK$270 to HK$400. Contact (☎ 5547395; pager 1168889-1810) 8H Jumbo Court, 3 Welfare Rd, Wong Chuk Hang, Aberdeen.

Kowloon 九龍

The name Kowloon is thought to have originated when the last emperor of the Song Dynasty passed through the area during his flight from the Mongols. He counted eight peaks on the peninsula and commented that therefore eight dragons must be here – but was reminded that since he himself was present there must be nine.

Kowloon means nine dragons and is derived from the Cantonese words *kau* for nine and *loong* for dragon. Now Kowloon is a mere 12 sq km of high-rise buildings extending from the Tsimshatsui waterfront at the tip of the peninsula to as far north as Boundary St.

TSIMSHATSUI 尖沙咀

Hong Kong's tourist ghetto lies at the very tip of the Kowloon Peninsula in Tsimshatsui. About one sq km of shops, restaurants, pubs, topless bars charging rip-off prices, fast-food places and camera and electronics stores are clustered on either side of Nathan Rd.

Clock Tower 鐘樓

Adjacent to the Star Ferry Terminal and the new Hong Kong Cultural Centre, the 45-metre tall clock tower is all that remains of a railway station that once existed at the tip of the Kowloon Peninsula. The railway station – the southern terminus of the present Kowloon-Canton Railway – was built in 1916 and torn down in 1978. The clock tower itself was built in 1922 and was preserved even though the railway station wasn't. The old station was a colonial-style building with columns, but was too small to handle the volume of passenger traffic. The new station, where many travellers begin their journey to China, is a huge, modern building at Hunghom to the north-east of Tsimshatsui.

Hong Kong Cultural Centre 文化中心

Adjacent to the Star Ferry Pier, the Cultural Centre (☎ 7342009) is one of Hong Kong's landmarks. The complex includes a concert hall able to seat 2100 people and a cinema that accommodates 1800, a smaller theatre with 300 seats, an arts library, two restaurants and a garden. On the south side of the building is a viewing area where you can admire Victoria Harbour, also known as Hong Kong Harbour. The Cultural Centre is open weekdays except Thursdays from 10 am to 6 pm (including Saturdays), and from 1 to 6 pm on Sundays and holidays.

Hong Kong Museum of Art 香港藝術館

The Cultural Centre complex now incorporates the Hong Kong Museum of Art (☎ 7342167). Included in the collection are paintings, calligraphy, rubbings, ceramics, bronze pieces, lacquerware, jade, cloisonné, paper-cuts and embroidery.

It's closed on Thursdays, otherwise operating hours are weekdays (including Saturdays) from 10 am to 6 pm, and Sundays and holidays from 1 to 6 pm. Admission is HK$10.

Space Museum 太空館

This is the peculiar building shaped like half a golf ball at 10 Salisbury Rd, adjoining the Cultural Centre. It's divided into three parts: the Space Theatre (planetarium), the Hall of Space Science and the Hall of Astronomy.

Exhibits include a lump of moon rock, models of rocket ships, telescopes, time lines and videos of moon walks – all very educational and worth a look. The Mercury space capsule piloted by astronaut Scott Carpenter in 1962 is displayed.

Opening times for the exhibition halls are weekdays (except Tuesdays) from 1 to 9 pm, and from 10 am to 9 pm on weekends and holidays.

The Space Theatre has about seven shows each day (except Tuesdays), some in English and some in Cantonese, but headphone translations are available for all shows. Check opening times with the museum. Admission to the Space Theatre (☎ 7342722) is HK$20 or HK$13 for students and seniors (over 60).

Star House 星光行

This building occupies a prime piece of turf right next to the Star Ferry Terminal. Astronomical rents are charged for ground floor shops, which they get back from the constant flow of tourists. There is a Watson's drugstore, the cheapest place around here to buy film, which you might need for photographing the harbour. Most of the stores inside the arcade are overpriced, but check out Chinese Arts & Crafts (owned by the People's Republic). The McDonald's here is believed to be the busiest in the world.

Ocean Terminal 海運大廈

The long building jutting out into the harbour – to the left of Star House – is the Ocean Terminal. There always seems to be one ocean liner moored here which is full of elderly millionaires. To meet their needs, the terminal and adjoining Ocean Centre are crammed with very ritzy shops in endless arcades. It's not the place for cheap souvenir hunting but interesting for a stroll. On the waterfront is a small park built on a pier, which has benches and good views of the harbour.

Peninsula Hotel 半島酒店

One of Hong Kong's most prestigious landmarks, the Peninsula used to be *the* place to stay in Hong Kong. It's on Salisbury Rd and was once right on the waterfront, but land reclamation has extended the shoreline south another block.

Before WW II it was part of a chain of prestigious hotels across Asia where everybody who was anybody stayed. The list included the rather-faded Raffles in Singapore, the Taj in Bombay and the Cathay (now called the Peace) in Shanghai.

The hotel's lobby offers high-ceilinged splendour. It is worth paying the extra for a cup of coffee or a beer here to enjoy the rarefied atmosphere and to spot people spot-ting other people. The rich and famous are said to stay here, but if so, they don't hang around the lobby.

Nathan Rd 彌敦道

The main drag of Kowloon was named after the governor of the time, Sir Matthew Nathan, around the turn of the century. It was promptly renamed Nathan's Folly since in those times Kowloon was sparsely populated and such a wide road was unnecessary. The trees that once lined the street are gone but some would say that the folly has remained.

Now the lower end of the road is known as the Golden Mile, which refers to both the price of real estate here and also its ability to suck money out of tourist pockets.

Kowloon Park 九龍公園

Shrinking Park might be a better name for this place. This was once the site of the Whitfield Barracks for British and Indian troops, but I remember a time when the park bordered Nathan Rd and was filled with trees, flowers, joggers and strolling couples. Both the troops and the natural environment are gone. Now the park is hidden behind Yue Hwa's Park Lane Store on Nathan Rd and new concrete blocks on Austin Rd. Most tourists staying in nearby hotels are not aware that the park exists.

Just as well, because the park is so artificial that it might as well be indoors. One recent creation is the Sculpture Walk, a grotesque outdoor 'art gallery' made up of metal tubes. Other highlights include the aviary, a space age Indoor Sports Hall, fountains, concrete plazas, a museum and other intrusions. The multiple swimming pools are perhaps the park's finest feature – they're even equipped with waterfalls. Of course, it's packed on summer weekends. There are still a few magnificent old trees left in the park, but just wait, they'll get those too. All that's missing are plastic talking animals, but those may be installed by the time you read this. Personally, I liked it better before it became an amusement park. Admission is free. The park is open from 6.30 am to 11.30 pm.

HONG KONG

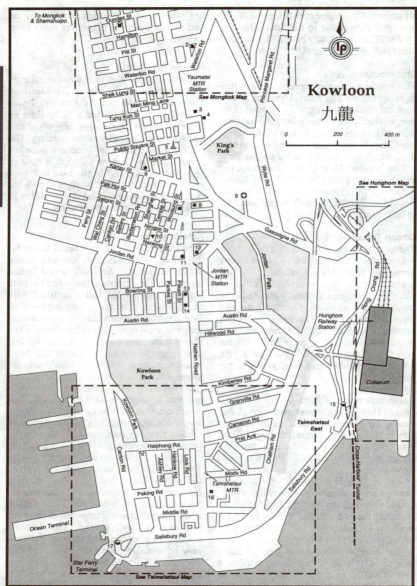

To Mongkok
& Shamshuipo

Dundas St
Hamilton
Pitt St
Waterloo Rd
Shek Lung St
Man Ming Lane
Tung Kun St
Public Square St
Market St
Kansu St
Pak Hoi St
Saigon St
Wai Ching St
Ferry St
Canton Rd
Battery St
Shanghai St
Reclamation Rd
Temple St
Nanking St
Ningpo St
Jordan Rd
Bowring St
Parkes St
Austin Rd
Kowloon Park
Kowloon Park
Canton Rd
Austin Rd
Hillwood Rd
Nathan Road
Kimberley Rd
Granville Rd
Cameron Rd
Prat Ave
Haiphong Rd
Hankow Rd
Lock Rd
Ashley Rd
Mody Rd
Peking Rd
Middle Rd
Ocean Terminal
Salisbury Rd
Star Ferry
Terminal

Waterloo Rd
Yaumatei
MTR
Station
See Mongkok Map
King's
Park
Wylie Rd
Princess Margaret Rd
Gascoigne Rd
Jordan
Jordan
Path
Jordan
MTR
Station

Kowloon
九龍

0   200   400 m

See Hunghom Map

Hunghom
Railway
Station

Hong Chong Rd

Coliseum

Tsimshatsui
East

Cross-Harbour Tunnel

Salisbury Rd

Tsimshatsui
MTR

Chatham Rd

See Tsimshatsui Map

PLACES TO STAY

1 STB Hostel
2 YMCA
3 Booth Lodge
4 Caritas Bianchi Lodge
7 Fortuna Hotel
8 Nathan Hotel
12 New Lucky Mansions
13 Shamrock Hotel
14 Bangkok Royal Hotel
16 Chungking Mansions

PLACES TO EAT

10 Night Market

OTHER

5 Tin Hau Temple
6 Jade Market
9 Queen Elizabeth Hospital
11 Yue Hwa Chinese Products
15 Cross-Harbour Bus Stop
17 Star Ferry Bus Terminal

Museum of History 香港歷史博物館

The museum (☎ 3671124) is inside Kowloon Park near the Haiphong Rd entrance. It covers all of Hong Kong's existence from prehistoric times (about 6000 years ago give or take a few) to the present and contains a large collection of 19th and early 20th-century photographs of the city.

The museum is open Monday to Thursday and Saturday from 10 am to 6 pm, and Sunday and public holidays from 1 to 6 pm. It is closed on Friday. Admission costs HK$10.

Kowloon Mosque 回教禮拜堂

Near the intersection of Nathan and Cameron Rds, the Kowloon Mosque and Islamic Centre is the largest mosque in Hong Kong. The present building was completed in 1984 and occupies the site of a previous mosque built in 1896 for Muslim Indian troops who were garrisoned in barracks at what is now Kowloon Park.

The mosque is interesting to admire from the outside, but you can't simply wander in and take photos as occurs in Buddhist or Taoist temples. If you are a Muslim, you can participate in their religious activities. Otherwise, you must obtain permission to visit the mosque. Permission isn't always granted, but you can inquire (☎ 7240095).

New World Hotel 新世界酒店

You might call this place the antithesis of the Peninsula Hotel. While the Peninsula maintains an air of old, colonial charm, the New World Hotel is a shining, glittering symbol of modernisation. Everything about it reeks of newness, even the ground it's built on, which is reclaimed from the sea.

The New World Hotel is actually part of the New World Centre, a large shopping complex complete with excellent restaurants and nightclubs. The New World Centre is at 22 Salisbury Rd. Hidden right behind it is the Regent Hotel, built on piles driven into the sea floor. It's definitely worth walking behind the Regent Hotel for the excellent harbour views.

TSIMSHATSUI EAST 尖沙咀東部

This big piece of land to the east of Chatham Rd didn't even exist until 1980. Built entirely on reclaimed land, Tsimshatsui East is a cluster of shopping malls, hotels, theatres, restaurants and nightclubs. Everything is new – there are none of the old, crumbling buildings of nearby Tsimshatsui.

Tsimshatsui East caters to Hong Kong's middle class and nouveaux riche. Oddly, foreigners are relatively few. It's interesting to speculate why this is. Perhaps the sight of all those shiny buildings makes visitors think the area is horribly expensive. Actually, prices are about the same as in Tsimshatsui, though there are no budget hotels like Chungking Mansions.

The area has one very good shopping mall, the Tsimshatsui Centre, 66 Mody Rd, between Salisbury and Mody Rds. Of course, if you're looking for real bargains you must get completely away from the tourist zone and go where the locals shop – try the malls at Shatin in the New Territories or Cityplaza (Tai Koo) on Hong Kong Island.

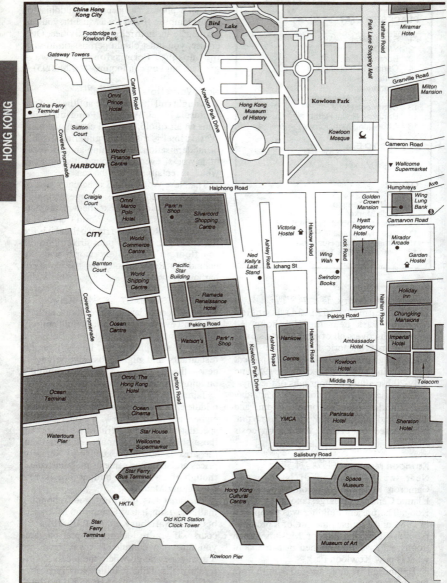

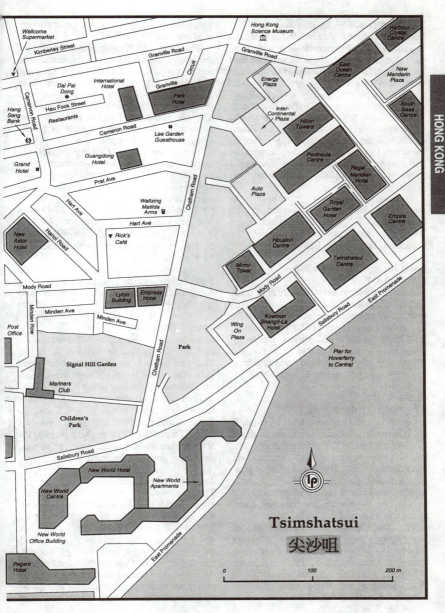

HONG KONG

Wellcome Supermarket

Kimberley Street

Granville Road

Granville Road

Hong Kong Science Museum

Harbour Crystal Centre

East Ocean Centre

New Mandarin Plaza

Circuit

Dai Pai Dong

International Hotel

Granville

Park Hotel

Energy Plaza

Inter-Continental Plaza

Hilton Towers

South Seas Centre

Cameron Road

Hang Seng Bank

Hau Fook Street

Restaurants

Cameron Road

Lee Garden Guesthouse

Peninsula Centre

Regal Meridien Hotel

Guangdong Hotel

Grand Hotel

Prat Ave

Auto Plaza

Royal Garden Hotel

Empire Centre

Chatham Road

Hart Ave

Waltzing Matilda Arms

Hart Ave

Hanoi Road

New Astor Hotel

Rick's Café

Houston Centre

Tsimshatsui Centre

Mirror Tower

Mody Road

Mody Road

East Promenade

Minden Ave

Lyton Building

Empress Hotel

Minden Ave

Minden Row

Wing On Plaza

Kowloon Shangri-La Hotel

Salisbury Road

Post Office

Park

Pier for Hoverferry to Central

Signal Hill Garden

Chatham Road

Mariners Club

Children's Park

Salisbury Road

New World Hotel

New World Apartments

New World Centre

East Promenade

Tsimshatsui

尖沙咀

New World Office Building

Regent Hotel

0   100   200 m

The Promenade 尖沙咀海濱公園

Some of the best things in life are free, and this includes the Promenade – the wide footpath along the waterfront in Tsimshatsui East on the south side of New World Centre. The views of Victoria Harbour are first-rate and it's worth repeating the trip at night. Races are held here during the Dragon Boat Festival. The area is popular with joggers and Chinese who like to fish right off the Promenade, despite the unhealthy appearance of the water. I'm not sure what they do with the fish caught, but if anyone eats it, that would partly account for Hong Kong's high incidence of hepatitis.

You can walk along the Promenade as far north as the Hong Kong Coliseum and the Hunghom KCR Station. You can also take a hoverferry from the Promenade across the harbour to Hong Kong Island.

Hong Kong Science Museum
香港科學博物館

The Science Museum (☎ 7323232) is at the corner of Chatham and Granville Rds. This multi-level complex houses over 500 exhibits. Admission costs HK$25 for adults, HK$15 for students and seniors. Operating hours are 1 to 9 pm Tuesday to Friday, and 10 am to 9 pm on weekends and holidays. The museum is closed on Mondays.

HUNGHOM 紅磡
Whampoa Gardens 黃埔花園

In the middle of a high-rise housing estate is the Whampoa, a full-sized concrete model of a luxury cruiser. While not very seaworthy, the 'ship' is impressive – 100 metres long and four decks tall. The whole thing is actually a fancy shopping mall with stores, restaurants, a cinema and a playground (top deck). The basement also harbours more shops and a car park.

The concrete ship was built by one of Hong Kong's largest companies, Hutchison Whampoa. Adjacent to the shop are other shopping areas including Bauhinia Plaza, Whampoa Plaza, Whampoa Gardens and Hong Kong Place. Hong Kong Place is notable for housing one of the three 'music fountains' in Hong Kong (the other two are at Shatin and Tsuen Wan).

The good ship Whampoa is a little bit off the beaten tourist track, but not difficult to reach. It's on the corner of Shung King and Tak Fung Sts. You can get there from Tsimshatsui by taking a green minibus No 6 from Hankow Rd (south side of Peking Rd). There is also a Star Ferry to Hunghom that lands at the waterfront a couple of blocks away from the Whampoa.

There are many factory outlets in Hunghom. If you want to track them down, consult Dana Goetz's book *Hong Kong Factory Bargains* for details. A few notable ones include High Fashion Corner (☎ 3346411), Winner Building, 32-D Man Yue St; Vica Moda Dresses (☎ 3348363, 7657333), Ground floor, Summit Building, 30 Man Yue St and Kaiser Estate Phase Two, 51 Man Yue St.

Other features of Hunghom include Hong Kong Polytechnic and the 12,500-seat Hong Kong Coliseum which hosts concerts and sporting events.

YAUMATEI 油麻地

Immediately to the north of Tsimshatsui – and indistinguishable from it – is the Yaumatei district. Its chief attraction is the Jade Market, the Temple St night market and the Chinese emporiums along Nathan Rd.

There are many interesting walks to do along the streets between Jordan Rd and Kansu St. These include Canton Rd (ivory and mahjong shops), Saigon St (a street market) and Ning Po St (paper items such as kites and paper houses, and luxury items for the dead).

Jade Market 玉器市場

The Jade Market is at the junction of Reclamation and Kansu Sts under the overpass in the Yaumatei district, just to the west of Nathan Rd. It's open daily between 10 am and 3.30 pm, but go early as you may find the sellers packing up and leaving at about 1 pm. It's more for Chinese than for tourists, but you can get some good deals here. Some sellers are reasonably honest and will quote a reasonable price – with others you may

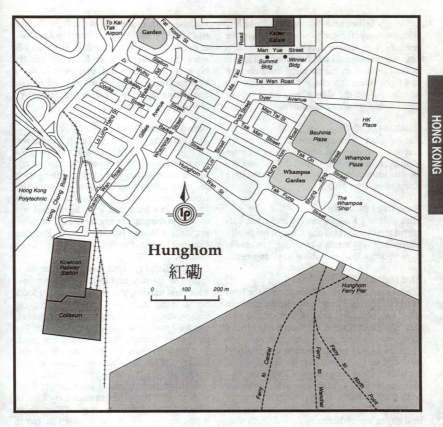

Hungham
紅磡

0   100   200 m

Hunghom Ferry Pier

Ferry to Central

Ferry to Wanchai

Ferry to North Point

have to engage in a marathon bargaining session just to get it down to shopping mall prices (so why bother?).

To get there take bus No 9 from the Kowloon Star Ferry Bus Terminal and get off at Kowloon Central Post Office and walk down to the intersection of Kowloon and Reclamation Sts. You can also take the MTR and get off at either Jordan or Yaumatei MTR stations.

Tin Hau Temple 天后廟
Between Market and Public Square Sts, a block or two to the north of the Jade Market,

is a large Tin Hau temple, dedicated to the patron goddess of seafarers. Off to the right as you face the main temple is a row of fortune tellers. The temple complex also houses an altar dedicated to Shing Wong (the City God) and To Tei (the Earth God). The temple is open daily from 8 am to 6 pm.

Temple St 廟街
The liveliest night market in the city, Temple St (and Shanghai St which runs parallel to it) is the place to go for cheap clothes, cheap food, watches, footwear, cookware and everyday items. The place used to be known

as 'Men's St' because this was a place to buy clothing only for men, but these days the vendors will relieve any tourist of excess cash without sexual discrimination. Temple St is at its best in the evening from about 8 to 11 pm when it's clogged with stalls and people. All of the side streets have lots of small shops worth looking into.

MONGKOK 旺角

The name in Cantonese means 'busy point', and it's certainly an accurate description. Mongkok is one big buy-and-sell, and it's worth a look even if you didn't come to Hong Kong to go shopping.

Tung Choi St 通菜街

This is Hong Kong's largest and most colourful street market. Tung Choi St originally featured only women's clothing, but nowadays you can find just about anything here.

Bird Market 雀鳥市場

The most exotic sight in Mongkok is the Bird Market. It's on Hong Lok St, an obscure alley on the south side of Argyle St, two blocks west of Nathan Rd. In crowded Hong Kong, few people keep dogs and cats, but birds are highly prized as pets, especially if they can sing. Aside from the hundreds of birds on display, large bags of live grasshoppers are for sale. The birds seem to live pretty well: the Chinese use chopsticks to feed the grasshoppers to their feathered friends, the bird cages are elaborately carved from teak and bamboo, and the water and food dishes are ceramic.

The Hong Kong government has plans to move the Bird Market but there has been no word yet as to where it will move too – it could, however, happen during the life span of this book. The HKTA can supply you with details on the new location once the move takes place.

NEW KOWLOON 新九龍

Beyond Kowloon proper is an area of about 30 sq km known as New Kowloon, which includes places such as Shamshuipo, Laichikok and Kwun Tong. Strictly speaking, these places are part of the New Territories but they tend to be included in Kowloon in everyday usage of the name. Boundary St marks the border between Kowloon and the New Territories, and this would have become the new border in 1997 had Britain and China failed to reach an agreement on Hong Kong's future.

Wong Tai Sin Temple 黃大仙廟

This very large and active Taoist temple was built in 1973 and is adjacent to the Wong Tai Sin housing estate. It is dedicated to the god of the same name. The image of the god in the main temple was brought to Hong Kong from China in 1915 and was originally installed in a temple in Wanchai until it was moved to the present site in 1921. For information on Wong Tai Sin see the Religion section in the Facts about Hong Kong chapter.

On a Sunday afternoon the temple is crowded with worshippers burning joss sticks and making offerings of plates of food. Some bring their own carefully prepared dishes, others buy oranges from the numerous fruit stalls that engulf the entrance. The incense is burned, the offerings are made (but not left, since the gods can't be all that hungry and no one wants good food to go to waste) and the fortune sticks are cast.

Adjacent to the temple is an arcade filled with about 150 booths operated by fortune tellers. Some of them speak good English, so if you really want to know what fate has in store for you, this is your chance to find out. Just off to one side of the arcade is a small open area where you can look up and get a magnificent view of Lion Rock, one of Hong Kong's prominent landmarks.

Getting to the temple is easy. Take the MTR to the Wong Tai Sin Station then follow the signs in the station to come out in front of the temple.

The temple is open daily from 7 am to 5 pm. The busiest times are around the Chinese New Year, on Wong Tai Sin's birthday on the 23rd day of the 8th lunar month, during the 7th lunar month (the ghost month) and most Sundays. There is no admission fee

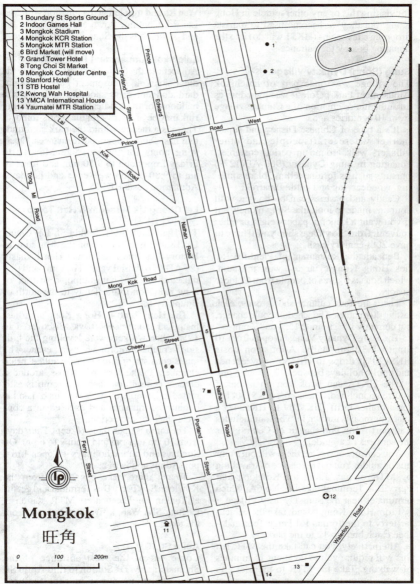

1 Boundary St Sports Ground
2 Indoor Games Hall
3 Mongkok Stadium
4 Mongkok KCR Station
5 Mongkok MTR Station
6 Bird Market (will move)
7 Grand Tower Hotel
8 Tong Choi St Market
9 Mongkok Computer Centre
10 Stanford Hotel
11 STB Hostel
12 Kwong Wah Hospital
13 YMCA International House
14 Yaumatei MTR Station

Mongkok

旺角

0   100   200m

for visiting this or any other temple in Hong Kong, but they've become used to tourists dropping a few coins (HK$1 will do) into the donation box by the entrance.

Sung (Song) Dynasty Village 宋城

The village was once part of Laichikok Amusement Park before it was hyped up as an authentic re-creation of a Chinese village from 10 centuries ago.

It's a type of Chinese Disneyland-supermarket where craftspeople and other villagers walk around in period costumes, engaging in Sung Dynasty (960 AD-1279) pursuits such as fortune telling, blacksmithing, woodcarving and getting married.

Candy and pastries can be bought with coupons made to look like Sung money, but if you want a kimono, paperweight or other souvenir from the village shop you'll have to have 20th-century cash.

Beneath the Restaurant of Plentiful Joy lies Hong Kong's largest wax museum, which houses figures of people from Chinese history.

There are four cultural shows daily, each lasting 40 minutes. The schedule could change, but currently it's 11 am, 2.15, 4 and 7 pm.

The Sung Dynasty Village is open from 10 am to 8.30 pm daily. Admission costs HK$120. It drops to HK$80 on weekends and public holidays between 12.30 and 5 pm.

The HKTA can book you on a tour if you're so inclined. These cost HK$150, but for a higher tariff (HK$209 to HK$242) a snack or meal is thrown in. The tour includes transport from Tsimshatsui or Central plus the services of a guide.

You can, of course, get there without a tour bus or guide. You have a choice of travelling by MTR or bus. From the Kowloon Star Ferry Bus Terminal take bus No 6A, which terminates near the Sung Dynasty Village.

From Hong Kong Island, take the vehicular ferry to the Jordan Rd Ferry Terminal – then catch bus No 12 to the park.

Alternatively, you can take the MTR but this will require you to do about 15 minutes of walking. Take the MTR to the Mei Foo Station. From there head north along Lai Wan Rd and turn left at the junction with Mei Lai Rd. Continue down Mei Lai Rd, at the end of which is the Sung Dynasty Village.

Laichikok Amusement Park 荔園遊樂場

Adjacent to the Sung Dynasty Village is the old Laichikok Amusement Park. It's standard dodgem cars, shooting galleries and balloons for the kiddies, but the ice-skating rink may be of interest for the sports-minded. There is a theatre within the park's grounds that has Chinese opera performances. Operating hours for the park are Monday to Friday from noon to 9.30 pm, and from 10 am to 9.30 pm on weekends and holidays. Admission costs HK$15.

Lei Cheng Uk Museum & Han Tomb 李鄭屋村古墓

The Han Tomb at 41 Tonkin St, Lei Cheng Uk Estate, is a branch of the Museum of History. The site is an actual Han Dynasty (25 AD-220) burial vault. The tomb and tiny museum are in Shamshuipo, a district of New Kowloon immediately to the north of Boundary St.

The Han Tomb is Hong Kong's earliest historical monument. It was discovered in 1955 when workers were levelling the hillside in preparation for a housing estate. The tomb consists of four barrel-vaulted brick chambers in the form of a cross, around a domed, central chamber. The tomb is estimated to be more than 1600 years old and is behind the museum and encased in a concrete shell for protection.

The tomb is open daily (except Thursday) from 10 am to 1 pm and from 2 to 6 pm. On Sundays and public holidays it's open 1 to 6 pm. Admission is free.

To get there, take bus No 2 from the Kowloon Star Ferry Bus Terminal and get off at Tonkin St. The nearest MTR station is Cheung Sha Wan, a five-minute walk from the tomb.

Apliu St 鴨寮街

Come out of the west entrance of the Shamshuipo MTR Station to find Apliu St. This enormous street market features everything from clothing to CDs at rock-bottom prices.

Descend back into the MTR and come up on the east side of the tracks to find a swarm of vendors dealing out delectable eats from pushcarts. Just next to the pushcart vendors is the Golden Shopping Centre, 146-152 Fuk Wah St, the place to see the latest in computers and other high-tech wizardry.

Lei Yue Mun 鯉魚門

To the east of the airport runway is a residential neighbourhood called Kwun Tong, and a bit further south-east is a rapidly modernising fishing village called Lei Yue Mun. *Lei yue* means 'carp' and *mun* is 'gate', and 'carp gate' refers to the channel separating eastern Kowloon from neighbouring Hong Kong Island.

While you aren't likely to find the 'village' reminiscent of ancient China, it's one of Hong Kong's prime seafood-eating venues. Locals dive into plates full of prawns and crabs, oblivious to the screech of jets overhead taking off from Kai Tak Airport. Personally, I'd rather eat seafood at the quiet restaurants in the Outlying Islands, but Hong Kongers with a passion for seafood and little love of boats prefer Lei Yue Mun.

The neighbourhood is somewhat colourful and very lively at night when the diners arrive en masse. You can get there on bus No 14C from the Kwun Tong MTR Station – take it to the end of the line (Sam Ka Tsuen Terminal).

PLACES TO STAY – BOTTOM END
Chungking Mansions

There is probably no other place in the world like *Chungking Mansions*, the bottom-end accommodation ghetto of Hong Kong. It's a huge high-rise dump at 30 Nathan Rd in the heart of Tsimshatsui.

Take a look down the lightwells off the D block stairs for a vision of hell – Chungking Mansions at its worst. They're dark, dirty, festooned with pipes and wires and covered in what looks like the debris of half a century. Why bother to put rubbish in the bin when it's so much easier to throw it out the window? Discarded plastic bags fall only halfway down before lodging on a ledge or drainpipe. Soon they're joined by old newspapers, used toilet paper, clothes fallen off lines, half-eaten apples, an expired rat (was it too dirty for the rat too?).

All manner of garbage drapes and hangs down from above. It's a horrible sight. Occasionally you're forced onto the stairs when the wait for the lift becomes too interminable. A buzzer sounds when one too many people have clambered aboard the lifts and in one of them I spotted a sign which announced, 'The Irresponsible for Accident due to Overloading'.

For years there has been much talk about tearing down Chungking Mansions because it's an eyesore and a fire trap, but the cost would be huge and the Hong Kong government tends to take a 'hands off' approach to private enterprise.

The building's electric transformer blew up in 1993, blacking out the Mansions for a whole week. The crackdown on fire-safety violations finally came at the end of 1993, and many places were shut down. Others survived by upgrading their standards to meet the now-strict building codes, and this renovation process is still continuing.

For many hostels, the cost of renovation was equal to about a year's income, and this has caused prices to rise dramatically. All this means that Chungking Mansions can't be considered dirt-cheap by international standards, but it's still the cheapest place to stay in Hong Kong. As for tearing down Chungking Mansions, that will probably only come when someone decides to put up the money to buy the place and put up a new high-rise luxury hotel.

Adding some spice to your stay in Chungking Mansions are the occasional midnight raids by the police. Mostly they are looking for illegal immigrants – if your passport is at some embassy to get visa stamps, this could create a problem. At least try to have a photocopy of your passport and some other picture ID card. Another purpose of the police raids is supposedly to round up foreign prostitutes, though the police do little more than hassle them if they haven't overstayed their visas. But the one thing travellers really have to watch out for are drugs – a few grams of hashish in your backpack could leave you with a lot of explaining to do.

The entrance to Chungking Mansions is a shopping arcade facing Nathan Rd. Wander around and you will find lifts labelled A to E. There are only two tiny overworked lifts for each 17-storey block. Long lines form in front of the lifts in A and B blocks. It's often faster to walk up the stairs if you think you can cope with up to 17 storeys.

Despite the dilapidated appearance of the building, most of the little hotels are OK – generally clean and often quite comfortable, though rooms are the size of closets. The Mansions is a good place to eat cheaply too, with several low-priced restaurants mostly run by Indians and Pakistanis. The ground floor is also filled with shops selling everything imaginable, though the mezzanine floor has better deals.

Bargaining for a bed is certainly possible when business is slack. You can often negotiate a cheaper price if you stay a long time, but never do that the first night. Stay one night and find out how you like it before handing over two weeks' rent. Once you pay, there are no refunds. Be certain to get a receipt. Paying for a room in advance so that you can have it on a certain day is *not* advised – the supposedly cheap room suddenly becomes 'not available' but a more expensive one is (threaten to call the police if necessary).

If you want to check out Mansion guesthouses other than those listed here, just stand in the lobby with your luggage. There are plenty of touts who will approach you with offers for cheap rooms.

Prices listed here are only a guide and vary with the season, peaking in summer and during certain holidays such as Easter. Furthermore, at the time of research, many places were undergoing renovation due to the fire-safety crackdown mentioned before. This renovation process is still going on as many hostels can only rebuild incrementally. As a general guideline, a single room in Chungking starts in the HK$150 to HK$180 range, reaching about HK$250 or higher for larger rooms with attached bath. A double

(two people in one bed) costs about HK$20 more, but it can be HK$50 more if you require twin beds. Dormitories generally cost HK$70 to HK$80 per bed, but you can negotiate cheaper rates for long-term rentals.

Dormitories There are now only a few places in Chungking Mansions still offering dormitories, though there are dormitories elsewhere in Tsimshatsui (see next section, Other Cheapies).

The ever-popular *Travellers' Hostel* (☎ 3687710), A Block, 16th floor, is a Chungking Mansions landmark. It has mixed dormitory accommodation for HK$60 a bed. Double rooms with/without attached bath cost HK$150/170. The management also operates a cheap beachside hostel at Ting Kau in the New Territories. See the Places to Stay section of the New Territories chapter for details.

The 12th floor of A Block is where you'll find the friendly *Super Guesthouse* where dormitory beds start at HK$60.

On the 6th floor of A Block is *New World Hostel* (☎ 7236352). Dormitories are HK$60 and double rooms go for HK$180.

Friendship Travellers' Hostel (☎ 3110797 3112523), B Block, 6th floor, has mixed dormitory accommodation. The first night costs HK$80, the second HK$70 and anything thereafter is HK$60.

A Block This and B Block have the densest concentration of guesthouses. The main drawback is the frequent long queues to get into the lifts. You may find yourself using the stairs more than you expected, which wouldn't be so terrible except that the stairwells are incredibly filthy and the cockroaches show no fear. Still, A Block is popular and you are likely to find yourself staying there.

Park Guesthouse (☎ 3681689), 15th floor, has singles from HK$150 (bath outside) to HK$180 (attached bath) with aircon. It's clean and friendly. Also on the 15th floor is *Ocean Guesthouse* (☎ 7213255). There is also the *Happy Guesthouse* where singles are HK$180 with shared bath, HK$200 with private bath.

The 14th floor offers the *New Hawaii Guesthouse* (☎ 3666127), a good deal at HK$140 for rooms with attached bath.

The 13th floor has two places, the friendly *Capital Guesthouse* which has rooms with attached bath for HK$180, and the *Rhine Guesthouse*.

Peking Guesthouse (☎ 7238320), 12th floor, has friendly management, is clean and highly recommended. All rooms have air-con and start at HK$180. Next door is the *Double Star Guesthouse*.

New International Guesthouse (☎ 369 2613), 11th floor, has doubles with attached bath for HK$200 to HK$400. Rooms have air-con, TV and a personal refrigerator, plus there is a laundry service and a friendly manager. On this floor there is also another branch of the *Rhine Guesthouse* (which is also on the 13th floor).

New Mandarin Guesthouse (☎ 3661070), 8th floor, is clean and has singles from HK$150 with a shared bath to HK$180 with an attached private bath. Next door is *Tom's Guesthouse* (☎ 7224956), where small rooms with attached bath start at HK$180. Also on this floor is the *New Asia Guesthouse* (☎ 7240426), which is clean, offers a laundry service and serves inexpensive meals and drinks.

Welcome Guesthouse (☎ 7217793), 7th floor, is run by a very friendly man. He can arrange China visas and runs a laundry service. One traveller, so taken with the place, said: 'When I got back from China and found them all full, I took a bed next to the entranceway just so I could stay there.' Next door is the *Double Seven Guesthouse* (☎ 7230148) which offers good value for money. On this floor you can also stay at the *First Guesthouse*.

London Guesthouse (☎ 7245000) 6th floor, looks very fancy. It has singles from HK$180 with TV, telephone and air-con.

Chungking House (☎ 3665362) 4th & 5th floors, while not very friendly, is the most classy place in A block with prices to match. Singles cost HK$260 to HK$276, but most

rooms are doubles which cost an extra HK$40. All rooms have a private bath. Rooms can even be booked at the HKTA office at Kai Tak Airport.

B Block This block has almost as many guesthouses as A Block, so you may still have to queue for the lifts. The stairwells support a rather large amount of wildlife, including a rare species of aggressive cockroach indigenous to this region of Chungking Mansions. Be grateful for the stray cats as they keep the rats in check.

Starting from the top, there is the *Travellers' Friendship Hostel* (☎ 3112523), 17th floor, which is also on the 6th floor. Rooms cost HK$100 to HK$150 for a double but they are little more than boxes with a bed inside.

Astor Guesthouse, 16th floor, is run by a very friendly Chinese lady who keeps the place spotlessly clean.

Carlton Guesthouse (☎ 7210720), 15th floor, has singles for HK$180. It's a very clean, tidy place with friendly people. Next door is the *Shangri-La Guesthouse*.

New Washington Guesthouse (☎ 366 5798), 13th floor, is friendly, clean and popular. Doubles start from HK$180.

Hong Kong Guesthouse (☎ 7237842), 11th floor, has singles for HK$170 and doubles for HK$220 with TV and air-con.

Kowloon Guesthouse (☎ 3699802), 10th floor, is one of the larger ones in this block. This place seems to be particularly popular with Nigerians. Singles are from HK$170.

Grand Guesthouse (☎ 3686520), 9th floor, has doubles with an attached private bath. Next door is the reception office for *Happy Guesthouse*, which also has a branch on the 8th floor.

New York Guesthouse (☎ 3395986), 7th floor, looks relatively clean and has rooms for HK$180. Next door is *Brother's Guesthouse* which was totally under renovation during my visit but it could be good when completed.

Chungking Lodge on the 5th floor reckons it's one of the more cushy places in B Block. Just next door is the deluxe

New Delhi Guesthouse (☎ 7236985) where double rooms with phone and private bath cost HK$200. This floor might be described as 'Little India', the place to be if you want to escape Chinese culture for awhile.

Down on the 3rd floor is the attractive *Dragon Inn* where single rooms with shared bath are HK$160. Just next door is another branch of the fancy *New Delhi Guesthouse* (☎ 3680738) where doubles cost HK$200.

C Block The one great advantage of staying in C Block is that there are seldom queues for the lifts. Also, the stairwells and hallways are much cleaner than elsewhere in Chungking Mansions. Just why is uncertain – perhaps C Block has its own indigenous culture.

Tom's Guesthouse (☎ 3679258) on the 16th floor is clean, quiet, friendly and has singles for HK$170. Next door is the excellent *Garden Guesthouse* (☎ 3680981) (also on the 7th floor) where singles with private bath cost HK$180.

The 15th floor has *Carlton Guesthouse*, typically clean and quiet for this block.

New Grand Guesthouse (☎ 3111702) and *Osaka Guesthouse* are both on the 13th floor and run by the same owner. All rooms have private bath and TV, with a price range from HK$150 to HK$250.

On the 11th floor you'll find *Marria Guesthouse* which is Indian-run and looks very clean. Rooms start at HK$160.

The 10th floor has *Kowloon Guesthouse*. A room with shared/private bath costs HK$150/170.

Garden Guesthouse (☎ 3687414) on the 7th floor is a branch of the place with the same name on the 16th floor. This guesthouse is clean and charges HK$180 for a room with attached bath.

New Brother's Guesthouse (☎ 7240135), 6th floor, is good but all rooms are shared bath only. Prices start at HK$150.

The 4th floor has the *Maharaja Guesthouse*. An advantage of staying here is the excellent Indian restaurant just below on the 3rd floor.

D Block This part of Chungking is almost as tattered and dirty as A and B blocks. It rates third in terms of the number of guesthouses, and you sometimes have to queue for the lifts.

Four Seas Guesthouse (☎ 3687469), 15th floor, is somewhat basic but friendly. Singles cost HK$150. Next door is the *New Chungking Mansion Guesthouse*.

Guangzhou Guesthouse (☎ 7241555), 13th floor, is not particularly friendly but has OK singles from HK$150.

China Town (☎ 7213723), 10th floor, looks like a nice place but it was under renovation at the time of this writing.

Fortuna Guesthouse (☎ 3664524), 8th floor, was also under renovation, as was its neighbour *New Shanghai Guesthouse*.

Royal Plaza Inn (☎ 3671424), 5th floor, is one of the best places in D Block. Rooms with shared bath are HK$150 to HK$250. With attached bath it's HK$150 to HK$450. The adjoining Indian restaurant is superb.

On the 4th floor is *Lai Wei Guesthouse* which is also good. The neighbouring *Head Sun Guesthouse* is decidedly so-so. *Mt Everest Guesthouse* was under heavy-duty renovation at the time of this writing but it looks like it will be fine when finished.

China Town (☎ 7213546), 3rd floor, is one of the fancier places in D Block but prices are high at HK$220 with shared bath and HK$250 with private bath.

E Block Like C Block, this area is a backwater which is relatively clean and quiet. There are very few guesthouses here, especially after the fire-safety crackdown. There are occasional queues for the lifts, especially if you hit it during rush hour.

Far East Guesthouse (☎ 3681724), 14th floor, has doubles from HK$190. Rooms are clean and have a telephone, TV and air-con.

The 13th floor is where you'll find *Chungking Mansion Mandarin Guesthouse*, which was in the middle of major renovations during the time of my visit.

Regent Guesthouse (☎ 7220833), 6th floor, seems nice enough with a phone, TV and air-con in each room. However, singles with shared bath are pricey at HK$200.

Other Cheapies

There are a few privately run hostels and guesthouses of the Chungking genre, mostly in the streets nearby. You may want to try these just to avoid the stigma of having to say: 'I'm staying in Chungking Mansions'.

Golden Crown Guesthouse (☎ 3691782) Golden Crown Mansion, 5th floor, 66-70 Nathan Rd, Tsimshatsui, has dormitory beds for HK$100, singles start from HK$250 and doubles from HK$300. Also on the 5th floor but hidden in the back, is the spotlessly clean and highly recommended *Wah Tat Guesthouse* (☎ 3666121) where singles/doubles cost HK$250/300 and more luxurious rooms go for HK$350.

Victoria Hostel (☎ 3760621), 1st floor, 33 Hankow Rd, Tsimshatsui, is one of the nicest hostels in Hong Kong. There are several dormitories at different price levels. The cheaper ones cost HK$100 for the first day and HK$80 for subsequent days. If you pay by the week, it's HK$70 per day. The more expensive dorms have only three persons per room and cost HK$150 per person. There are also double rooms for HK$250 to HK$450 per day.

The *STB Hostel* (☎ 7109199, fax 3850153), operated by the Hong Kong Student Travel Bureau, costs HK$100 in the dormitory, HK$300 to HK$350 for twins. While it's clean and quiet enough, this place has a reputation for hostel wardens who are short-tempered and drunk with power – you may feel like you're staying in prison. Travellers who value their independence would be better off staying somewhere else. The hostel is on the 2nd floor at Great Eastern Mansion, 255-261 Reclamation St, Mongkok, on the corner of Reclamation and Dundas Sts, just to the west of the Yaumatei MTR Station.

Around the corner from Chungking Mansions is the *Garden Hostel* (☎ 7218567). It's in Mirador Arcade, 58 Nathan Rd, but it's easier to find if you enter from Mody Rd. Turn right as you come out of the main entrance to Chungking and then right at the first street (Mody Rd). On the left side of the street you see an obvious sign. Enter the stairwell and go to the 3rd floor. Accommodation costs HK$80 in an air-con dormitory, but it drops to HK$65 per night if rent is paid by the week.

Mirador Arcade at 58 Nathan Rd is like a scaled-down version of Chungking Mansions, but considerably cleaner and roomier. It's on Nathan between Mody and Carnarvon Rds, one block north of Chungking. Here you'll find one of my favourite guesthouses, the *Man Hing Lung* (☎ 7220678, fax 3118807) on the 14th floor in Flat F2. All rooms come equipped with private bath, air-con and TV. Singles cost HK$260 to HK$280 and doubles are HK$320 to HK$360. If you arrive by yourself and want a roommate, the management can put you in with another traveller.

On the 13th floor of Mirador Arcade is the *Kowloon Hotel* (☎ 3112523) and *New Garden Hotel* (same phone and same owner). Dormitories are HK$60. Singles with shared bath are HK$150, rising up to HK$200 for rooms with private bath. Salubrious doubles with private bath and refrigerator cost HK$200 to HK$300. Ask about discounts if you want to rent long-term.

Down on the 12th floor of Mirador Arcade in Flat B5 is *Ajit Guesthouse* (☎ 3691201), which is very friendly and clean. Rooms are reasonable at HK$150. Down on the 7th floor in Flat F2 is *Mini Hotel* (☎ 3672551), but it was under renovation during my visit and no one could quote a price.

Star Guesthouse (☎ 7238951), 6th floor at 21 Cameron Rd, is immaculately clean. *Lee Garden Guesthouse* (☎ 3672284) is on the 8th floor, D Block, 36 Cameron Rd, close to Chatham Rd. Both guesthouses are run by the same owner, the charismatic Charlie Chan. Rooms with shared bath are HK$280 to HK$350, and with private bath it jumps to HK$370 to HK$440.

Tourists Home (☎ 3112622; fax 3688580) is on the 6th floor, G Block, Champagne Court, 16 Kimberley Rd. Doubles are from HK$280 to HK$320. All rooms have an attached private bath.

The *New Lucky Mansions*, 300 Nathan Rd (entrance on Jordan Rd), Yaumatei, is in a better neighbourhood than most of the other guesthouses. There are eight places here to choose from in various price ranges. The rundown from top floor to bottom is as follows:

Great Wall Hotel, 14th floor, has very posh doubles for HK$450 (☎ 3887645; fax 3880084).
Ocean Guesthouse, 11th floor, has singles/doubles for HK$300/350 (☎ 3850125; fax 7826441).
Nathanhouse, 10th floor, was under renovation at time of research so no price is available (☎ 7801302).
Overseas Guesthouse, 9th floor, has singles/doubles with shared bath for HK$180/190; clean and friendly.
Tung Wo Guesthouse, 9th floor, has singles for HK$150; cheap but not so nice.
Hoi Pun Uk House, 5th floor, has doubles for HK$280; good but currently no English sign. The owner speaks Mandarin (☎ 7807317).
Hitton Inn, 3rd floor, has doubles with private bath for HK$230; good value (☎ 7704880).
Hakkas Guesthouse, 3rd floor, has doubles for HK$250; nice rooms and the owner speaks good English (☎ 7701470).

The *Lyton Building*, 32-40 Mody Rd, has several good guesthouses, all with private bath, air-con and TV. There are four blocks with separate lifts, but you can walk between Blocks 1 and 2 and also between Blocks 3 and 4. *Lyton House Inn* (☎ 3673791) is on the 6th floor of Block 2, but isn't terribly cheap at HK$400 for a double. The 3rd floor of Block 1 is where you'll find *Hometown Guesthouse*, which was under renovation at the time of my visit. On the 6th floor of Block 3 is *Tourist House* (☎ 7218309), a relative bargain at HK$330 for an excellent double. *Frank's Mody House* (☎ 7244113) on the 7th floor of Block 4 is fine with doubles for HK$350 to HK$450.

The Salvation Army runs a place called *Booth Lodge* (☎ 7719266; fax 3851140), 11 Wing Sing Lane, Yaumatei, where doubles/twins are HK$380/680. Just around the corner is *Caritas Bianchi Lodge* (☎ 3881111; fax 7706669), 4 Cliff Rd, Yaumatei, where singles are HK$450 and doubles range from HK$520 to HK$640. There is another *Caritas Lodge* (☎ 3393777; fax

3382864), 134 Boundary St, Mongkok (take MTR to Prince Edward Station), where singles/doubles are HK$330/390.

Hotels
The *YMCA International House* (☎ 7719111; fax 3885926), 23 Waterloo Rd, Yaumatei, has 29 cheap rooms with shared bath for HK$150 for men only. The majority of their rooms are rented to both men and women, but these are not terribly cheap at HK$450 to HK$660. There are some suites for HK$800.

The *YWCA* (☎ 7139211; fax 7611269) is inconveniently located near Pui Ching Rd and Waterloo Rd in Mongkok. The official address is 5 Man Fuk Rd, up a hill behind a Caltex petrol station. Cheap single rooms for women only are HK$250 to HK$400, while doubles and twins are HK$500.

King's Hotel (☎ 7801281; fax 7821833), 473 Nathan Rd, Yaumatei, has 72 rooms and is one of the better deals in what looks like a mid-range hotel. Singles cost HK$340 to HK$360, doubles and twins HK$400 to HK$430.

The *Mariner's Club* (☎ 3688261), 11 Middle Rd, Tsimshatsui, is a church-affiliated hostel for sailors and members only. Doubles are HK$400.

PLACES TO STAY – MIDDLE
You can get as much as 40% off at some mid-range and luxury hotels by booking your room through a local travel agency.

By Kowloon standards, a mid-range hotel is defined as one where you can find a room costing approximately HK$400 to HK$800. Some places which fall into this category include:

Bangkok Royal, 2-12 Pilkem St, Yaumatei (Jordan MTR Station), 70 rooms, singles HK$350 to HK$450, doubles & twins HK$460 to HK$580 (☎ 7359181; fax 7302209)
Concourse, 22 Laichikok Rd, Mongkok (Prince Edward MTR Station), 359 rooms, doubles & twins HK$780 to HK$1280, suites HK$1680 (☎ 3976683; fax 3813768)

HONG KONG

Kowloon City Restaurants
九龙城餐厅

1 Heng (Sau) Thai Restaurant
2 Phuket Thai Restaurant
3 Regal Airport Hotel
4 Post Office
5 Thai Wah Restaurant
6 Ruaen Pae Thai Restaurant
7 Golden Wheat Thai Restaurant
8 Indian Curry Hut
9 Indoor Market
10 Wong Chun Chun Cantonese-Thai Restaurant
11 Taste of India Restaurant
12 Golden Harvest Thai Restaurant
13 Cambo Thai Restaurant
14 Thai Farm Restaurant
15 Golden Orchid Thai Restaurant
16 No 5 Bus Stop
17 Airbus Bus Stop

Eaton, 380 Nathan Rd, Yaumatei (Jordan MTR Station), 392 rooms, doubles & twins HK$630 to HK$1250, suites HK$1450 (☎ 7821818; fax 7825563)

Fortuna, 355 Nathan Rd, Yaumatei (Jordan MTR Station), 187 rooms, singles HK$600 to HK$1000, doubles & twins HK$900 to HK$1100 (☎ 3851011; fax 7800011)

Grand Tower, 627-641 Nathan Rd, Mongkok, 549 rooms, singles HK$760 to HK$1000, doubles & twins HK$830 to HK$1100 (☎ 7890011; fax 7890945)

Guangdong, 18 Pratt Ave, Tsimshatsui, 245 rooms, doubles & twins HK$800 to HK$990 (☎ 7393311; fax 7211137)

Imperial, 30-34 Nathan Rd, Tsimshatsui, 214 rooms, singles HK$720 to HK$920, doubles & twins HK$800 to HK$1000, suites HK$1400 to HK$1700 (☎ 3662201; fax 3112360)

International, 33 Cameron Rd, Tsimshatsui, 89 rooms, singles HK$380 to HK$680, twins HK$500 to HK$880, suites HK$1100 to HK$1400 (☎ 3663381; fax 3695381)

Metropole, 75 Waterloo Rd, Yaumatei, 487 rooms, doubles & twins HK$720 to HK$1250, suites HK$2200 to HK$4200 (☎ 7611711; fax 7610769)

Nathan, 378 Nathan Rd, Yaumatei, 186 rooms, singles HK$550, doubles & twins HK$650 to HK$700, suites HK$850 (☎ 3885141; fax 7704262)

New Astor, 11 Carnarvon Rd, Tsimshatsui, 151 rooms, doubles & twins HK$780 to HK$1080, suites HK$1500 to HK$2400 (☎ 3667261; fax 7227122)

Newton, 58-66 Boundary St, Mongkok, 176 rooms, singles HK$700 to HK$950, doubles & twins HK$750 to HK$1000 (☎ 7872338; fax 7890688)

Prudential, 222 Nathan Rd, Yaumatei (Jordan MTR Station), 434 rooms, singles HK$480 to HK$1280, twins HK$550 to HK$1350, suites HK$1680 to HK$1800 (☎ 3118222; fax 3114760)

Shamrock, 223 Nathan Rd, Yaumatei, 148 rooms, singles HK$380 to HK$650, doubles & twins HK$450 to HK$750, suites HK$800 to HK$850 (☎ 7352271; fax 7367354)

YMCA, 41 Salisbury Rd, Tsimshatsui, singles HK$590, doubles & twins HK$690 to HK$860, suites HK$1150 to HK$1350 (☎ 3692211; fax 7399315)

PLACES TO STAY – TOP END

In Kowloon, a hotel where you can't get a room for less than HK$800 is considered top end. If you can afford the ticket, luxury hotels are easy to find and usually have vacancies.

Ambassador, 26 Nathan Rd, Tsimshatsui, 313 rooms, doubles & twins HK$880 to HK$1580, suites HK$2380 to HK$3380 (☎ 3666321; fax 3690663)

Holiday Inn Crowne Plaza, 70 Mody Rd, Tsimshatsui East, 594 rooms, singles HK$1260 to HK$2260, twins HK$1360 to HK$2380, suites HK$3500 to HK$7000 (☎ 7215161; fax 3695672)

Holiday Inn Golden Mile, 46-52 Nathan Rd, Tsimshatsui, 594 rooms, singles HK$930, doubles & twins HK$1160 to HK$1830, suites HK$2500 to HK$6000 (☎ 3693111; fax 3698016)

Hyatt Regency, 67 Nathan Rd, Tsimshatsui, 723 rooms, doubles & twins HK$1900 to HK$2600, suites HK$4500 to HK$10,000 (☎ 3111234; fax 7398701)

Kimberley, 28 Kimberley Rd, Tsimshatsui, 496 rooms, doubles & twins HK$830 to HK$1300, suites HK$1500 to HK$2400 (☎ 7233888; fax 7231318)

Kowloon, 19-21 Nathan Rd, Tsimshatsui, 705 rooms, singles HK$900 to HK$1000, twins HK$930 to HK$1150, suites HK$1700 to HK$1900 (☎ 3698698)

Kowloon Shangri-La, 64 Mody Rd, Tsimshatsui East, 719 rooms, doubles & twins HK$1600 to HK$2800, suites HK$3300 to HK$15,000 (☎ 7212111; fax 7238686)

Majestic, 348 Nathan Rd, Yaumatei, 387 rooms, doubles & twins HK$900 to HK$1150, suites HK$2000 (☎ 7811333; fax 7811773)

Miramar, 130 Nathan Rd, Tsimshatsui, 500 rooms, singles HK$1000 to HK$1650, twins HK$1000 to HK$2300 (☎ 3681111; fax 3691788)

New World, 22 Salisbury Rd, Tsimshatsui, 543 rooms, singles HK$1400 to HK$2000, doubles & twins HK$1500 to HK$2000, suites HK$2200 to HK$4000 (☎ 3694111; fax 3699387)

Nikko, 72 Mody Rd, Tsimshatsui East, 461 rooms, doubles & twins HK$1550 to HK$2550, suites HK$3500 to HK$10,000 (☎ 7391111; fax 3113122)

Omni, The Hong Kong Hotel, Harbour City, 3 Canton Rd, Tsimshatsui, 709 rooms, doubles & twins HK$1450 to HK$2800, suites HK$2500 to HK$9000 (☎ 7360088; fax 7360011)

Omni Marco Polo, Harbour City, Canton Rd, Tsimshatsui, 440 rooms, doubles & twins HK$1400 to HK$1550, suites HK$2300 to HK$6000 (☎ 7360888; fax 7360022)

Omni Prince, Harbour City, Canton Rd, Tsimshatsui, 401 rooms, doubles & twins HK$1300 to HK$1450, suites HK$2100 (☎ 7361888; fax 7360066)

Park, 61-65 Chatham Rd South, Tsimshatsui, 430 rooms, singles HK$900 to HK$1100, doubles & twins HK$1000 to HK$1200, suites HK$1500 to HK$3000 (☎ 3661371; fax 7397259)

Peninsula, Salisbury Rd, Tsimshatsui, 156 rooms, twins HK$2350 to HK$3200, suites HK$7000 to HK$20,000 (☎ 3666251; fax 7224170)

Ramada, 73-75 Chatham Rd South, Tsimshatsui, 205 rooms, doubles & twins HK$880 to HK$1250, suites HK$2200 to HK$2700 (☎ 3111100; fax 3116000)

Ramada Renaissance, 8 Peking Rd, Tsimshatsui, 500 rooms, doubles & twins HK$1450 to HK$2450, suites HK$3200 to HK$12,000 (☎ 3751133; fax 3756611)

Regal Airport, Sa Po Rd, Kowloon (next to airport), 385 rooms, doubles & twins HK$750 to HK$1450, suites HK$1850 to HK$5500 (☎ 7180333; fax 7184111)

Regal Kowloon, 71 Mody Rd, Tsimshatsui East, 592 rooms, singles HK$950 to HK$2000, doubles & twins HK$1400 to HK$2000, suites HK$3000 to HK$8500 (☎ 7221818; fax 3696950)

Regent, Salisbury Rd, Tsimshatsui, 602 rooms, doubles & twins HK$1650 to HK$2600, suites HK$2800 to HK$16,000 (☎ 7211211; fax 7394546)

Royal Garden, 69 Mody Rd, Tsimshatsui East, 420 rooms, doubles & twins HK$1500 to HK$2100, suites HK$2900 to HK$6300 (☎ 7215215; fax 3699976)

Royal Pacific, China Hong Kong City, 33 Canton Rd, Tsimshatsui, 676 rooms, doubles & twins HK$880 to HK$1950, suites HK$1600 to HK$7500 (☎ 7361188; fax 7361212)

Sheraton, 20 Nathan Rd, Tsimshatsui, 791 rooms, singles HK$1430 to HK$2630, doubles & twins HK$1530 to HK$2630, suites HK$2330 to HK$6600 (☎ 3691111; fax 7398707)

Stanford, 118 Soy St, Mongkok, 194 rooms, singles HK$830, twins HK$930 to HK$1030 (☎ 7811881; fax 3883733)

Stanford Hillview, 13-17 Observatory Rd, Tsimshatsui, 163 rooms, doubles & twins HK$920 to HK$1120, suites HK$1500 (☎ 7227822; fax 7233718)

Windsor, 39-43A Kimberley Rd, Tsimshatsui, 166 rooms, doubles & twins HK$890 to HK$1090, suites HK$1800 (☎ 7395665; fax 3115101)

PLACES TO EAT
Breakfast
The window of the *Wing Wah Restaurant* (☎ 7212947) is always filled with great-looking cakes and pastries. It's at 21A Lock Rd near Swindon's Bookstore and the Hyatt Regency. Either take it away or sit down with some coffee. Prices are very reasonable and this place has kept me alive for years. Inexpensive Chinese food is also served and, a rare treat for a Hong Kong-budget Chinese cafe, there is an English menu.

A very similar cafe with cakes, coffee and other delicacies is the nearby *Kam Fat Restaurant* at 11 Ashley Rd. Prices here are slightly higher than Wing Wah but the atmosphere is also better.

Deep in the bowels of every MTR station you can find *Maxim's Cake Shops*. The cakes and pastries look irresistible, but don't sink your teeth into the creamy delights until you're back on the street as it is prohibited to eat or drink anything in the MTR stations or on the trains – HK$1000 fine if you do.

There is a chain of bakeries around Hong Kong with the name *St Honore Cake Shop*, but there's no English sign on their stores although you'll soon recognise their ideogram. You can find one at 221 Nathan Rd, Yaumatei, and a much smaller one at 8 Canton Rd, Tsimshatsui.

Uncle Russ is a take-away muffin and

coffee vendor on the north side of Peking Rd where it intersects with Canton Rd (official address is 2 Canton Rd). The muffins are possibly the best in Hong Kong and the coffee is top-flight. This is one of the few places where you can get decaffeinated coffee, and you can also buy coffee beans for home self-brewing.

If you're up early before the aforementioned places open, *7-Eleven* operates 24 hours and does good coffee, packaged breads and microwave cuisine.

Fast Food
Oliver's is on the ground floor at Ocean Centre on Canton Rd. It's a great place for breakfast – inexpensive bacon, eggs and toast. The sandwiches are equally excellent, though it gets crowded at lunchtime.

McDonald's occupies key strategic locations in Tsimshatsui. Late-night restaurants are amazingly scarce in Hong Kong, so it's useful to know that two McDonald's in Tsimshatsui operate 24 hours a day: at 21A Granville Rd, and 12 Peking Rd. There is also a McDonald's at 2 Cameron Rd, and another in Star House just opposite the Star Ferry Pier.

Domino's Pizza (☎ 7650683), Yue Sun Mansion, Hunghom, does not have a restaurant where you can sit down to eat. Rather, pizzas are delivered to your door within 30 minutes of phoning in your order. If the pizza arrives even a few minutes late, you get a HK$10 discount, and if 45 minutes late the pizza is free.

Other fast-food outlets in Kowloon include:

Café de Coral, Mezzanine floor, Albion Plaza, 2-6 Granville Rd, Tsimshatsui; 54A Canton Rd

Fairwood Fast Food, 6 Ashley Rd, Tsimshatsui; Basement Two, Silvercord Shopping Centre, Haiphong & Canton Rds

Hardee's, Arcade of Regent Hotel, south of Salisbury Rd at the very southern tip of Tsimshatsui

Jack in the Box, Cameron Plaza, 21 Cameron Rd, Tsimshatsui; Tsimshatsui Centre, Mody Rd, Tsimshatsui East

Ka Ka Lok Fast Food Shop, 55A Carnarvon Rd, Tsimshatsui; 16A Ashley Rd, but enter from Ichang St, Tsimshatsui; 79A Austin Rd,

Yaumatei; Peninsula Centre, Mody Square, Tsimshatsui East

Kentucky Fried Chicken, 2 Cameron Rd, Tsimshatsui; 241 Nathan Rd, Yaumatei

Pizza Hut, Lower basement, Silvercord Shopping Centre, Haiphong & Canton Rds, Tsimshatsui; Shop 008, Ocean Terminal, Harbour City, Canton Rd, Tsimshatsui; 1st floor, Hanford House, 221C-D Nathan Rd, Yaumatei; Port A, Basement 1, Autoplaza, 65 Mody Rd, Tsimshatsui East

Spaghetti House, 3B Cameron Rd; 1st floor, 57 Peking Rd; Basement, 6-6A Hart Ave; 1st floor, 38 Haiphong Rd, Tsimshatsui; 1st floor, Imperial Hotel, 30-34 Nathan Rd, Tsimshatsui; 001-2, Phase I, Barton Court, Harbour City, Canton Rd, Tsimshatsui

Wendy's, Basement, Albion Plaza, 2-6 Granville Rd, just off Nathan Rd, Tsimshatsui

Chinese Food

Tsimshatsui's Chinese restaurant alley is *Hau Fook St* which does not appear on the HKTA tourist map. Easy to find, it's the tiny street between Cameron and Granville Rds. Walking north on Carnarvon Rd, pass Granville Rd and it's the first alley on your right. Unfortunately, most of these places do not have English menus.

Street Stalls The cheapest place to enjoy authentic Chinese cuisine is the *Temple St Night Market* in Yaumatei. It starts at about 8 pm and begins to fade at 11 pm. There are also plenty of mainstream indoor restaurants with variable prices. Although many locals are drawn here by the seafood restaurants, any Hong Kong resident will tell you that much fresher marine cuisine is served up on the Outlying Islands.

Dim Sum This is normally served from around 11 am to 3 pm, but a few places have it available for breakfast. The following places are chosen for reasonable prices, but you can certainly get more atmosphere by spending more:

Canton Court, Guangdong Hotel, 18 Prat Ave, Tsimshatsui; dim sum served from 7 am to 4 pm (☎ 7393311).

Eastern Palace, 3rd floor, Omni, The Hong Kong Hotel, Shopping arcade, Harbour City, Canton Rd, Tsimshatsui; dim sum served from 11.30 am to 3 pm (☎ 7306011).

Harbour View Seafood, 3rd floor, Tsimshatsui Centre, 66 Mody Rd, Tsimshatsui East; dim sum served from 11 am to 5 pm and restaurant closes at midnight (☎ 7225888).

New Home, 19-20 Hanoi Rd, Tsimshatsui; dim sum served from 7 am to 4.30 pm (☎ 3665876).

North China Peking Seafood, 2nd floor, Polly Commercial Building, 21-23 Prat Ave, Tsimshatsui; dim sum served from 11 am to 3 pm (☎ 3116689).

Orchard Court, 1st & 2nd floors, Ma's Mansion, 37 Hankow Rd, Tsimshatsui; dim sum served from 11 am to 5 pm (☎ 3175111).

Tai Woo, 14-16 Hillwood Rd, Yaumatei; dim sum served from 11 am to 4.30 pm (☎ 3699773).

Beijing (Peking) One place that boasts moderate prices, good food and friendly service (a rarity in Hong Kong) is *China Garden Peking Restaurant* (☎ 3110773), 2nd floor, Mirror Tower, 61 Mody Rd, Tsimshatsui East.

Sichuan If hot spicy Sichuan cuisine is on your mind, prices are reasonable at *Fung Lum Restaurant* (☎ 3678686), 1st floor, Polly Commercial Building, 21-23 Prat Ave, Tsimshatsui.

Snake All major Cantonese restaurants serve snake, especially in the evening. Even upmarket hotel restaurants are getting into the act. The restaurant at the *Nikko Hotel*, 72 Mody Rd, Tsimshatsui East, is one such place. Prices are not cheap.

Other Asian Food

Filipino The *Mabuhay* (☎ 3673762), 11 Minden Ave, serves good Filipino and Spanish food. Many Filipino expats eat here.

Indian You won't have trouble finding restaurants dishing up Indian and similar Pakistani and Sri Lankan cuisine in Kowloon, but some places have an inexplicable 'members only' rule. In order to eat there, you must be a member, though absolutely anyone can become a member by paying about HK$20 for a membership card which is valid for one year. The card is usually sent to you by post rather than issued on the spot, and from my experience this can take weeks. I suppose that this enhances the restaurants' prestige, but it seems to me like a good way to drive away business. Fortunately, not all Indian restaurants have this requirement.

The greatest concentration of cheap Indian and Pakistani restaurants is in Chungking Mansions on Nathan Rd. Despite the grotty appearance of the entrance to the Mansions, many of the restaurants are surprisingly plush inside. A meal of curried chicken and rice, or curry with chapattis and dahl, will cost around HK$30 per person.

Start your search for Indian food on the ground floor of the arcade. The bottom of the market belongs to *Kashmir Fast Food* and *Lahore Fast Food*. These open early, so you can have curry, chapattis and heartburn for breakfast. Neither of these two offers any kind of cheery atmosphere, so it's no place to linger.

Upstairs in Chungking Mansions are many other places with better food and a more pleasant atmosphere. Prices are still low, with set meals from HK$35 or so. The following are presented in order from A – E blocks, from top floor to bottom, rather than by order of price and quality:

Nanak Mess, 11th floor, Flat A-4; decent but not one of the top spots.
Kashmir Club, 3rd floor, A Block; highly-rated and even offers free home delivery (☎ 3116308).
Centre Point Club, 6th floor, B Block; also highly recommended (☎ 3661086).
Ashok Club, 5th floor, B Block; Nepali food, atmosphere could stand some improvement.
Taj Mahal Club Mess, 3rd floor, B Block; excellent (☎ 7225454).
Sher-I-Punjab Club Mess, 3rd floor, B Block; Nepali & Indian food (☎ 3680859).

Mumtaj Mahal Club, 12th floor, C Block; good if you're staying in this block (☎ 7215591).
Delhi Club, 3rd floor; the best in C Block (☎ 3681682).
New Madras Mess, 16th floor; Muslim and vegetarian halal food, grotty atmosphere (☎ 3685021).
Royal Club Mess, 5th floor, D Block; Indian and vegetarian, offers free home delivery and is my personal favourite in Chungking Mansions (☎ 3697680).
Karachi Mess; halal food, looks like you've stepped right into Pakistan (☎ 3681678).
Khyber Pass Club Mess, 7th floor, E Block; looks decent (☎ 7212786).

Of course, you don't have to eat in Chungking Mansions, though it will cost you more to go elsewhere. *Talk of the Town* (☎ 3666591), 1st floor, 2A Humphreys Ave, Tsimshatsui, is a good place to get your briyani mutton, lamb keema sali and chicken tikka. Prices are low to moderate.

Indonesian The *Java Rijsttafel* (☎ 3671230), Han Hing Mansion, 38 Hankow Rd, Tsimshatsui, serves 'rijsttafel' – literally meaning a 'rice table'. This place packs out with Dutch expats, but I find it somewhat overrated.

There is also the *Indonesian Restaurant* (☎ 3673287) at 66 Granville Rd, Tsimshatsui.

Japanese If you want to find cheap Japanese food, make it yourself. Japanese restaurants charge Japanese prices. You can economise by looking for informal ones without the fish ponds and young Filipino women in *geisha* costumes playing ukeleles. Some places to consider include:

Ah-So, 159 Craigie Court, World Finance Centre, Harbour City, Canton Rd, Tsimshatsui (☎ 7303392)
Banka, Grand Tower Hotel, 627-641 Nathan Rd, Mongkok (☎ 7890011 ext 211)
Fukui, Hotel Fortuna, 351-361 Nathan Rd, Yaumatei (☎ 3851011)
Kotobuki, Flat A & B, 1st floor, Good Result Building, 176 Nathan Rd, Tsimshatsui (☎ 3682711)
Matsuzaka, UG23-28 South Seas Centre, 75 Mody Rd, Tsimshatsui East (☎ 7243057)
Nagoya, 1st floor, 21A Lock Rd, Tsimshatsui (☎ 7395566)

Sui Sha Ya, Ground floor, 9 Chatham Rd, Tsimshatsui
(☎ 7225001)

Korean There are several excellent and
accessible Korean restaurants. A good one is
Seoul House (☎ 3143174), 35 Hillwood Rd,
Yaumatei.

Another place is *Manna*, a chain restaurant with outlets in Tsimshatsui at 83B
Nathan Rd (☎ 7212159); Lyton Building,
32B Mody Rd (☎ 3674278); and 6A
Humphrey's Ave (☎ 3682485).

Two other centrally located Korean restaurants are *Arirang* (☎ 7352281), Ground
floor, Room 9, Sutton Court, Harbour City,
Canton Rd, Tsimshatsui, and *Korea House*
(☎ 3675674), Empire Centre, 68 Mody Rd,
Tsimshatsui East.

If you don't mind travelling a bit out of the
tourist zone, there is *Daewongak*
(☎ 3976683), 2nd floor, Hotel Concourse,
20-46 Laichikok Rd, Mongkok.

Malaysian The *Singapore Restaurant*
(☎ 3761282), 23 Ashley Rd, Tsimshatsui, is
a great bargain. It's coffee-shop style, but
forget the decor because the food is excellent
and cheap. Excellent Malaysian, Chinese
and Western food costs about HK$45 for a
set dinner. It's open from 11 am until midnight.

Thai Thai food can be devastatingly hot but
excellent. A reasonably priced and good Thai
restaurant is *Royal Pattaya* (☎ 3669919), 9
Minden Ave, Tsimshatsui. Also good is
Sawadee (☎ 3763299), 6 Ichang St,
Tsimshatsui.

The neighbourhood just opposite the passenger terminal building at Kai Tak Airport
is Kowloon City. While it wouldn't be called
one of Hong Kong's notable scenic spots, it
has an unusually high concentration of Thai
residents and therefore Thai restaurants.
There are also a few odd Indian restaurants
in the neighbourhood. The selection of
places to eat is so good and prices so reasonable (by Hong Kong standards) that it's
almost worth a trip there just for a meal.
Alternatively, if you've got a few hours to

kill while waiting for a flight, this could be
your last chance to pig out in Hong Kong.

You can get here on any of the Airbuses
(A1, A2 or A3) and cross Prince Edward
Road (follow the flyover into the Regal
Airport Hotel). However, it makes more
sense to take bus No 5 from the Kowloon
Star Ferry Pier which is cheaper and lands
you closer to the restaurants. Places to eat in
this neighbourhood include:

Cambo Thai, 15 Nga Tsin Long Rd (☎ 7167318)
Golden Harvest Thai, 19-21 Kai Tak Rd (☎ 3836131)
Golden Orchid Thai, Nos 6 & 12, Lung Kong Rd
(☎ 3833076)
Golden Wheat Thai, 34 Nam Kok Rd (☎ 7181801)
Heng (Sau) Thai, 68 Kai Tak Rd (☎ 3839159)
Indian Curry Hut, 37 Sa Po Rd (☎ 7166182)
Phuket Thai, 74 Tak Ku Ling Rd (☎ 7166616)
Ruaen Pae, 27 Nam Kok Rd (☎ 3822320)
Taste of India, 24 South Wall Rd (☎ 7165128)
Thai Farm, 21-23 Nam Kok Rd (☎ 3820992)
Thai Wah, Nos 24 & 38 Kai Tak Rd (☎ 7167877,
3827117)
Wong Chun Chun Cantonese-Thai, 70-72 Nga Tsin
Wai Rd (☎ 3834680)

Vietnamese One excellent place is *Café de
La Paix Vietnamese Cuisine* (☎ 7214665) at
25 Hillwood Rd, Yaumatei. There is another
branch (☎ 7212747) just down the street in
Hermes Commercial Centre, on the corner of
Hillwood and Nathan Rds.

Another good place is *Mekong*
(☎ 3113303), Arcade 2, Miramar Hotel, 130
Nathan Rd, Tsimshatsui. Also recommended
is *Golden Bull* (☎ 3694617), Level 1, Unit
17, New World Centre, 18 Salisbury Rd,
Tsimshatsui.

All-Asian Food An unusual place that gets
rave reviews is *The Spice Mart* (☎ 7361888),
3rd floor, Omni Prince Hotel, Harbour City,
Canton Rd, Tsimshatsui. This restaurant features spicy cuisines from various Asian
countries such as India, Indonesia, Japan,
Malaysia and Singapore. The all-you-can-
eat buffets are moderately priced, but be
careful when ordering items off the menu as
some are quite expensive. Operating hours
are from 11.30 am to 2.30 pm, and from 6.30
to 10.30 pm.

Vegetarian *Bodhi* (☎ 7392222), Ground floor, 56 Cameron Rd, Tsimshatsui, is one of Hong Kong's biggest vegetarian restaurants with several branches: 36 Jordan Rd, Yaumatei; 1st floor, 32-34 Lock Rd (entry also at 81 Nathan Rd), Tsimshatsui; and 56 Cameron Rd, Tsimshatsui. Dim sum is dished out from 11 am to 5 pm.

Also excellent is *Pak Bo Vegetarian Kitchen* (☎ 3662732), 106 Austin Rd, Tsimshatsui. Another to try is *Fat Siu Lam* (☎ 3881308), 2-3 Cheong Lok St, Yaumatei.

Western Food
Italian *Mama Italia* (☎ 7233125), 2A Hart Ave, Tsimshatsui, is mostly take-away Italian treats at very low prices. There are just a couple of stools if you want to eat the pizza and lasagna on the spot.

A great Italian restaurant is *Valentino* (☎ 7216449) at 16 Hanoi Rd. Also highly rated is *La Taverna* (☎ 3761945), Astoria Building, 36-38 Ashley Rd, Tsimshatsui.

Pizza World (☎ 3111285) Ground floor, New World Centre, 22 Salisbury Rd, is extremely popular and has the best salad bar in Hong Kong – the large size salad for HK$30 is a meal in itself.

French At 7B Hanoi Rd the *New Marseille* (☎ 3665732) is good value with French/ Chinese food and a cheap set dinner. Moderately expensive but good is *Au Trou Normand* (☎ 3668754), 6 Carnarvon Rd, Tsimshatsui. Slightly cheaper is *Napoleon Grill* (☎ 3686861), Princess Wing, Miramar Hotel, 130 Nathan Rd, Tsimshatsui.

Mexican *Someplace Else* (☎ 3691111 ext 5), Sheraton Hotel, 20 Nathan Rd, is part bar and part Mexican restaurant. The Tex-Mex luncheons are worth trying, but in the evening it becomes very busy. Operating hours are from 11 until 1 am.

American *Dan Ryan's Chicago Grill* (☎ 7356111), Shop 200, Ocean Terminal, Harbour City, Canton Rd, Tsimshatsui, is a trendy spot with prices to match.

The *San Francisco Steak House*

(☎ 7357576), 101 Barnton Court, Harbour City, Canton Rd, Tsimshatsui, serves steak and lobster, baked potatoes, jumbo onion rings and toasted garlic bread. The quality and prices are upscale, so it's not recommended for budget travellers.

Kosher The *Beverley Hills Deli* (☎ 369 8695), Level 2, Shop 55, New World Centre, Salisbury Rd, is where you'll find gefilte fish and lox. It's good, but not cheap.

Others *Woodlands* (☎ 3693718), 8 Minden Ave, Tsimshatsui, is one of the best deals in Hong Kong for Western food. A top-flight meal can be had for less than HK$50.

The Bostonian (☎ 3751133) inside the Ramada Renaissance Hotel, 8 Peking Rd, Tsimshatsui, is ostensibly a seafood restaurant. However, it has the most knock-out buffet in Kowloon, but of course not cheap.

Self-Catering
If you're looking for the best in cheese, bread and other imported delicacies, check out the delicatessen at *Oliver's* on the ground floor of Ocean Centre on Canton Rd. Another branch is on the ground floor of the Tung Ying Building, Granville Rd (at Nathan Rd).

See's Candies (☎ 3686488), 119B Ocean Terminal, Harbour City, Canton Rd, Tsimshatsui, is the place to go if you have an emergency sweet tooth to treat.

Numerous supermarkets are scattered about. A few in Tsimshatsui and Yaumatei to look for include:

Park 'n Shop, south-west corner, Peking Rd & Kowloon Park Drive; Second basement, Silvercord Shopping Centre, 30 Canton Rd
Wellcome, inside the Dairy Farm Creamery (ice-cream parlour), 74-78 Nathan Rd; north-west corner of Granville and Carnarvon Rds; Basement, Star House (next to Star Ferry Pier)
Yue Hwa Chinese Products, Basement, 301 Nathan Rd, Yaumatei (north-west corner of Nathan and Jordan Rds), both Western products and Chinese exotica (tea bricks, flattened chickens, etc)

ENTERTAINMENT
All things considered, the Hong Kong Island

side is more interesting for nightlife, particularly the Lan Kwai Fong area in Central. See the Hong Kong Island chapter for details. That said, you can certainly find ways of keeping yourself entertained on the Kowloon side, but keep in mind that Hong Kong is not a cheap city for late-night carousing.

Cinemas
The more popular English-language cinemas in Kowloon include:

Astor, Eaton Hotel, Astor Plaza, 380 Nathan Rd, Yaumatei (☎ 7811833)
Broadway, 6 Sai Yeung Choi St, Mongkok (☎ 3325731)
Chinachem, Chinachem Golden Plaza, 77 Mody Rd, Tsimshatsui East (☎ 3113000)
Harbour City I, World Shipping Centre, Canton Rd, Tsimshatsui (☎ 7356915)
Harbour City II, World Commerce Centre, Canton Rd, Tsimshatsui (☎ 7308910)
Liberty, 26A Jordan Rd, Yaumatei (☎ 7306148)
London, 219 Nathan Rd, Yaumatei (☎ 4522123)
Majestic, 348 Nathan Rd, Yaumatei (☎ 7820272)
Ocean, Omni, The Hong Kong Hotel, 3 Canton Rd, Tsimshatsui (☎ 7305444)
Rex, 242 Portland St, Mongkok (☎ 3960910)
Silvercord, 30 Canton Rd (☎ 3171083)
UA6, Whampoa Garden, Hunghom (☎ 3031040)
Washington, 92 Parkes St, Yaumatei (☎ 7710405)

The *Space Museum* (☎ 7212361) near the Star Ferry Terminal in Tsimshatsui also shows excellent quality films in the planetarium.

Night Markets
The biggest night market and the one most popular with tourists is the Temple St market in Tsimshatsui. The market gets going about 8 pm and closes around midnight.

Another big market is at Tung Choi St in Mongkok. However, this market is more geared towards selling clothing and operates mostly in the daytime.

Pubs, Bars & Discos
Rick's Cafe (☎ 3672939), Basement, 4 Hart Ave, is popular with the Tsimshatsui backpacker set.

Jouster II (☎ 7230022), Shops A & B, Hart Ave Court, 19-23 Hart Ave, Tsimshatsui, is a fun multistorey place with wild decor. Normal hours are noon to 3 am, except on Sundays when it's from 6 pm to 2 am. Happy hour is anytime before 9 pm.

Ned Kelly's Last Stand (☎ 3760562), 11A Ashley Rd, open 11 am to 2 am, became famous as a real Australian pub complete with meat pies. Now it is known mainly for its Dixieland jazz and Aussie folk music bands. It's a good party atmosphere, but the volume is set on high so it's no place for quiet conversation.

Amoeba Bar (☎ 3760389), 22 Ashley Rd, Tsimshatsui, is local new-wave live music from around 9 pm, and the place doesn't close until about 6 am.

The *Red Lion* (☎ 3760243), 15 Ashley Rd, is just down the street from the Amoeba. A feature of this pub is that customers are invited to sing along with the band.

The *Kangaroo Pub* (☎ 3120083), 1st & 2nd floors, 35 Haiphong Rd, Tsimshatsui, is an Aussie pub in the true tradition. This place does a good Sunday brunch.

Mad Dog's Pub (☎ 3012222), Basement, 32 Nathan's Rd, is a popular Aussie-style pub. From Monday through Thursday it's open from 7 until 2 am, but from Friday through Sunday it's 24-hour service.

Blacksmith's Arms (☎ 3696696), 16 Minden Ave, Tsimshatsui, is a British-style pub with darts and barstools.

Somewhere in Town, on Canton Rd opposite China Hong Kong City, has become a popular pub with budget travellers. Beer costs an incredible HK$14 a pint.

Girlie Bars & Hostess Clubs
Many of these places make a habit of cheating foreigners with hidden extra 'service charges'. See the Entertainment section in the Facts for the Visitor chapter for details.

A few girlie bars won't cheat you at all, because they are very up-front about their ridiculously high prices. The lineup of Mercedes and Rolls Royces just outside the door should suggest just what sort of clientele these places cater to. They offer live music, featuring Filipino bands. These high-class girlie bars prefer to be known as 'hostess clubs'. Most of these places are in Tsimshatsui East.

Video-Game Arcades
Blow-away bad guys and zap evil extraterrestials at the *Silver Star Amusement Centre*, 29 Lock Rd, Tsimshatsui.

Virtual Reality
In Hong Kong's quest to stay at the forefront of hedonistic pursuits, virtual reality adds yet another dimension to the pursuit of pleasure. One place offering these services is the *Virtual Reality Club* (☎ 3758891), Shop B5, Star House, 3 Salisbury Rd, Tsimshatsui. A one-year membership costs HK$200, and each four-minute experience costs HK$40 for members, or HK$50 for non members.

THINGS TO BUY
Oh yeah, shopping, I guess some people come to Hong Kong for that. In Tsimshatsui, you don't have to look for a place to shop – the shopping comes to you. People are constantly trying to stuff advertisements into your hands. Finding a place to buy a loaf of bread is almost impossible along the streets crammed with shops peddling clothes, watches, cameras, jewellery, eyeglasses and electronics. It's capitalism run amuck, and more than a few travellers who come to Hong Kong only to pick up a China visa suddenly catch the buying fever. Try to exercise some self-restraint, or attend a local meeting of Shopperholics Anonymous.

If you've decided that you really need to do some serious shopping, then Hong Kong is as good a place as any to go on a buying binge. However, if you're looking to make some expensive purchases like cameras, video and stereo equipment, please memorise the following sentence: Tsimshatsui is a rip-off. While it's quite alright to purchase clothing here, you should look elsewhere when buying hi-tech pricey items.

Tourist Shopping Malls
Exploring the malls in touristland is not a total waste of time. True, you can probably find what you need elsewhere for less money. However, sometimes the little extra you pay in Tsimshatsui might be worthwhile for the time saved that you would otherwise spend tracking down the same goods elsewhere. Also, the malls are interesting tourist attractions in themselves.

In the tourist zone of Tsimshatsui, there are three big complexes in a row on Canton Rd: Ocean Terminal near the Star Ferry, Ocean Centre and Harbour City. Across the street at 30 Canton Rd is Silvercord. The New World Centre is on Salisbury Rd, adjacent to the New World Hotel.

In Tsimshatsui East, the biggest mall is Tsimshatsui Centre at 66 Mody Rd (between Salisbury and Mody Rds). There are other malls here and you could probably spend days exploring them.

Chinese Emporiums
Yue Hwa Park Lane Shopper's Boulevard is on Nathan Rd just north of the Kowloon Mosque. It's the two-storey block that looks like the world's longest garage and is much less interesting than the main store at Jordan Rd.

The People's Republic owns Chinese Arts & Crafts, which has two branches in Tsimshatsui: Silvercord Shopping Centre, 30 Canton Rd, near the corner of Haiphong Rd; Star House, on the corner of Salisbury and Canton Rds. There is another branch in Yaumatei at 239 Nathan Rd. Everything has price tags and no bargaining is necessary.

Chung Kiu Chinese Products is also worth investigating. Branches are at 17 Hankow Rd, Tsimshatsui; 528-532 Nathan Rd, Yaumatei; and 47-51 Shantung St, Mongkok.

Department Stores
My favourite store in Hong Kong is the main branch of Yue Hwa Chinese Products Emporium at 301 Nathan Rd, Yaumatei (corner of Nathan and Jordan Rds). Unlike the touristy branch in Tsimshatsui, this store has a wide assortment of practical locally-produced and imported items (not just from China). There is also some Chinese exotica like herbal medicines and flattened chickens. However,

it's not a high-fashion store – if it's famous labels you crave, look elsewhere.

Wing On is an upmarket department store where you can find the Gucci handbags, Calvin Klein underwear, Chanel No 19 perfume and Rolex watches (real ones). There are three branches in Kowloon: 361 Nathan Rd, Yaumatei; 620 Nathan Rd, Mongkok; Wing On Plaza, Mody Rd, Tsimshatsui East. Another Hong Kong department store is Sincere, 83 Argyle St, Mongkok. Lane Crawford has a store in Manson House, 74 Nathan Rd, Tsimshatsui.

Dragon Seed operates a three-storey store at Albion Plaza, 2-6 Granville Rd, Tsimshatsui.

The major Japanese department store in Tsimshatsui is Mitsukoshi, 28 Canton Rd. If you're really interested in Japanese wares, it's better to visit the stores in Causeway Bay on Hong Kong Island.

Electronics & Appliances
Shamshuipo is a good neighbourhood to search for electrical and electronic goodies. You can even buy (and sell) secondhand appliances here. If you take any of the west exits from the MTR at the Shamshuipo Station, you'll find yourself on Apliu St. There are numerous good shops here – one I've had luck with is Success Electronics Co at No 220. Apliu St is one of the best areas in Hong Kong to go searching for the numerous permutations of plug adaptors you'll need if you're heading for China.

Mongkok is another good neighbourhood to look for electronic gadgetry. Starting from Argyle St and heading south, explore all the side streets running parallel to Nathan Rd, such as Canton Rd, Tung Choi, Sai Yeung Choi, Portland, Shanghai and Reclamation Sts. In this area you can buy just about everything imaginable.

Cameras
Tsimshatsui is perhaps the most expensive place in Asia, if not the world, to buy photographic equipment. It's amazing there aren't more homicides when you consider the way the camera shops blatantly cheat tourists.

This particularly applies to Nathan Rd. No shops here put price tags on the equipment and charging double or more is standard. In this neighbourhood, camera equipment is only 'reasonably-priced' when it's broken, secondhand or components are missing. Stanley St in Central is probably the best neighbourhood for camera equipment (see Hong Kong Island chapter), or go up to Mongkok or the shopping malls in Shatin (New Territories).

From my own experience, the best luck I've had buying cameras in Tsimshatsui was at Kimberley Camera Company (☎ 7212308), Champagne Court, 16 Kimberley Rd. There are actually price tags on the equipment, a rare find in Tsimshatsui. This place sells used equipment too, so inquire if interested.

A specialist at repairing broken cameras is Sun-Ant Camera Repair (☎ 7224966), Room 1010, 5-11 Granville Circuit, Tsimshatsui.

Computers
Star Computer City on the 2nd floor in Star House at 3 Salisbury Rd is the largest complex of computer shops in Tsimshatsui. While it's not the cheapest place in Hong Kong to find computers, it's not the worst (that honour goes to nearby Nathan Rd). Bargaining is advised. The highest markups are on small items like floppy disks and printer cartridges. From the outside of the building it's not immediately obvious how to get inside this complex; as you face Star House from the harbour side, there are two main entrances with escalators leading up to the mezzanine level. The computer shops are all cleverly concealed in there.

There are three shops in Star Computer City that I've done business with and found satisfactory, though in all three you should attempt some bargaining. These shops are: PC People (☎ 3755676), Unit A2; Reptron Computer Ltd (☎ 7302891), Unit B3; The Notebook Shop (☎ 7367260), Unit A6-7. Unfortunately, one shop here (Quasar Technologies) proved to be unsatisfactory – equipment I purchased there was defective and the shop refused to honour its warranty.

Top: A busy wharf, Kowloon (GI)
Bottom: Crowded waterways, Aberdeen, Hong Kong Island (GI)

Left: Tin Hau Temple, Repulse Bay, Hong Hong Island (RS)
Top Right: Tin Hau Temple, Repulse Bay, Hong Kong Island (RS)
Bottom Right: Trappist Haven Monastery, Outlying Islands (RS)

Mongkok Computer Centre has three floors of computer stores. It's geared more towards the local Cantonese-speaking market than foreigners, but you can generally get better deals here than in Tsimshatsui. The computer centre is at the intersection of Nelson and Fa Yuen Sts in Mongkok.

The Golden Shopping Centre, Basement and 1st floor, 146-152 Fuk Wah St, Shamshuipo, has the cheapest collection of desktop computers, accessories and components in Hong Kong. The specialty here is generic computers – machines assembled from various components by the shops themselves. Datacity Computer Ltd (☎ 3863077) is another good place for computer parts. It's at Basement Shop No 66 in the Golden Shopping Centre.

To get to the Golden Shopping Centre, take the MTR to the Shamshuipo Station. It's easy to get lost in this neighbourhood, so before you exit the station, keep your eyes open for signs in the MTR pointing to the way. If you reach the proper exit you'll be facing the shopping centre, which is on the corner of Kweilin and Fuk Wah Sts. If you can't find it, go back down into the MTR and look again for the signs.

Music & Software

A chainstore named KPS is the place to buy CDs and music tapes. Here you can find CDs for HK$90 or less, as opposed to HK$130 or more on Nathan Rd. Computer software (legal copies, that is) are also sold at substantial discounts. You can call the main office of KPS (☎ 3981234) to find the branch nearest you. There is one at Ocean Gallery, No 233-235 Harbour City on Canton Rd; another at Inter-Continental Plaza, Granville Rd, Tsimshatsui East; and one next to Whampoa Gardens in Hunghom.

You can also pick up cheap CDs in the Temple St night market and from shops in Mongkok, but selection is very limited.

Clothing

You'll find the best buys at the street markets at Tong Choi St in Mongkok and Apliu St in Shamshuipo. If you want to search around

Tsimshatsui, the best deals are generally found on the eastern end of Granville Rd. Giordano's has an outlet at Golden Crown Mansion, 66-70 Nathan Rd. Bossini has one of its many stores at Granville House, 53 Granville Rd, Tsimshatsui. Another good place is the mezzanine floor of Chungking Mansions (not the ground floor).

Fancy (read expensive) boutiques are dispersed throughout Tsimshatsui. One with a reputation is Marks & Spencer, Shops 102 & 254, Ocean Centre, Harbour City, Canton Rd.

Backpacks

Hong Kong is a good place to pick up a decent backpack, sleeping bag, tent and other gear for hiking, camping and travelling. Mongkok is by far the best neighbourhood to look for this stuff though there are a couple of odd places in nearby Yaumatei. Some places worth checking out include:

Grade IV Alpine
    13 Saigon St, Yaumatei (☎ 7820202)
Mountaineer Supermarket
    395 Portland St, Mongkok (☎ 3970585)
Rose Sporting Goods
    39 Fa Yuen St, Mongkok (☎ 7811809)
Sportsman Shop
    72 Sai Yee St, Mongkok (☎ 3956405)
Tang Fai Kee Military
    248 Reclamation St, Mongkok (☎ 3855169)
Three Military Equipment Company
    83 Sai Yee St, Mongkok (☎ 3914019, 7894326)

Opticians

Nathan Rd in Tsimshatsui is lined with opticians charging high prices for low quality, but the rude service is free. I always get my spectacles made on the 3rd floor of Yue Hwa Chinese Products, 301-309 Nathan Rd, Yaumatei (north-west corner of Nathan and Jordan Rds).

Jewellery & Gems

King Fook and Tse Sui Luen are two chain stores which guarantee to buy back any jewellery they sell to you at its current wholesale price. Of course, be sure you get the certificate and realise that you need to be in Hong Kong to take advantage of the buy-back plan. There isn't supposed to be any difference in price from one branch to another, but you might still do better to avoid Tsimshatsui. Branches are located as follows:

King Fook
> Hotel Miramar Princess Shopping Plaza, 118-130 Nathan Rd, Tsimshatsui (☎ 3132768)
> Ground floor, 644 Nathan Rd, Mongkok (☎ 7892008)
> Shop A-C, Ground floor, 26 Jordan Rd, Yaumatei (☎ 7351017)
> 611-615 Nathan Rd, Mongkok (☎ 3888108)

Tse Sui Luen
> Ground floor, 315 Nathan Rd, Yaumatei (☎ 3324618)
> Ground floor, TSL Building, 335 Nathan Rd, Yaumatei (☎ 7820110)
> Ground floor, 343 Nathan Rd, Yaumatei (☎ 3321468)
> G1 & G2, Ground floor, Nathan Centre, 580 Nathan Rd, Mongkok (☎ 7702322)
> Shop AR1005, Ground floor, Park Lane Square, 132-134 Nathan Rd, Tsimshatsui (☎ 7396673)
> Ground floor, 125-127 Ma Tau Wai Rd, Hunghom (☎ 7662613)
> Block B, Ground floor, Summit Building, 30 Man Yue St, Hunghom (☎ 3334221 ext 633)

If it's coloured rocks you're after, the following shops are HKTA members for whatever that's worth:

Chaumont
> 10th floor, Metropole Building, 57 Peking Rd, Tsimshatsui (☎ 3687331)

Opal Mine
> Burlington House Arcade, 92 Nathan Rd, Tsimshatsui (☎ 7219933)

Pharmaceuticals

Hong Kong is a good place to stock up on everyday practical items, especially if you're headed into the backwaters of China where shaving cream and deodorant are unimagin-able luxuries. Watson's is Hong Kong's biggest chainstore in the pharmaceutical arena, and there is no need to give addresses here because there seems to be one on every street corner. However, I have found prices to be somewhat better at Mannings, a much smaller chain. There is one in Tsimshatsui on the lower ground floor, Shop 37-47, Silvercord Shopping Centre, 30 Canton Rd.

Toys

These can be found everywhere, but perhaps the biggest in Hong Kong is Toys R Us (☎ 7309462), Shop 003, Basement, Ocean Terminal, Harbour City, Tsimshatsui.

Sporting Goods

Some sporting goods stores include:

Bunn's Diving Equipment
> Ground floor, 217 Sai Yee St, Mongkok (☎ 3805344)

Bunn's Sportoo (water sporting goods)
> Shop 015, Marine Deck, Ocean Terminal, Harbour City, Canton Rd, Tsimshatsui (☎ 3021379)

Flying Ball Bicycle Shop
> 201 Tung Choi St (near Prince Edward MTR Station), Mongkok (☎ 3815919)

Golf 18
> Shop 7, Hong Kong Pacific Centre, 28 Hankow Rd, Tsimshatsui (☎ 3671188)

International Elite Divers Training Centre
> Ground floor, Fulland Court, 256 Fa Yuen St, Mongkok (☎ 3812789)

Pro-Shop (windsurfing equipment)
> 1st floor, Front Unit, Ocean View Court, 31 Mody Rd, Tsimshatsui (☎ 7236816)

Wah Shing Diving Equipment
> Ground floor, 2B-2C Larch St, Mongkok (☎ 3914084)

Wind 'n Surf
> Flat 3, Block A, 1st floor, Carnarvon Mansion, 10 Carnarvon Rd, Tsimshatsui (☎ 3669293)

Windsurf Boutique
> Shop 19-23, Rise Commercial Building, 5-11 Granville Circuit, Tsimshatsui (☎ 3669911; fax 3698403)

Hong Kong Island 香港島

The commercial heart of Hong Kong pumps away on the northern side of Hong Kong Island, where banks and businesses, high-rise apartment blocks and hotels cover a good part of its 78 sq km.

From the Star Ferry Pier the island looks unbelievably crowded, and on the lower levels it certainly is, but from 400 metres up on the Peak you realise how much space is left.

As well as moving up the hill for more building space, Hong Kong keeps on moving out. Reclamation along the harbour edge continues to add the odd quarter km every so often, and buildings once on the waterfront are now several hundred metres back. At the rate things are going, some cynics have suggested that the harbour will completely disappear in another decade.

The south side of Hong Kong Island has a completely different character than the north. For one thing, there are some fine beaches here, and the water is actually clean enough to swim in. The best beaches are at Big Wave Bay, Deep Water Bay, Shek O, Stanley and Repulse Bay. Expensive villas are perched on the hillsides, and the impression is more like the French Riviera rather than crowded Hong Kong. Unfortunately, huge, multistorey apartment blocks have been going up in recent years, though it still has a long way to go before it overtakes Kowloon.

It's easy to circumnavigate the island by public transport, starting from Central and taking a bus over the hills to Stanley, then heading clockwise along the coast back to the Star Ferry Terminal.

CENTRAL 中環
Central is most people's first impression of Hong Kong Island since it's where the Star Ferry lands. As you leave the ferry terminal, immediately on your right is the GPO, in front of which is the towering Jardine House

with its distinctive port hole windows. The HKTA operates a tourist information centre in the basement arcade.

Cenotaph 紀念碑
To reach the main part of Central you have to cross Connaught Rd. Straight ahead as you leave the Star Ferry is the pedestrian underpass which surfaces at the side of the Cenotaph. This forlorn-looking monument is a memorial to Hong Kongers who died in the war.

Just to the east of the Cenotaph is the Hong Kong Club, the last bastion of the British empire.

Statue Square 皇后像廣場
The Cenotaph occupies a tiny sliver of Statue Square, but the main part of the square is across the street on the south side of Chater Rd. Statue Square is notable for its collection of fountains and places to sit, and every Sunday is transformed into the unofficial gathering place for expat Filipinos (ethnic Thais gather nearby just west of the Star Ferry Pier). A bronze statue of former chief manager of the Hong Kong & Shanghai Bank, Sir Thomas Jackson, graces the square. The ornate colonial building on the east side of the square is the former Supreme Court, now elevated to the lofty title of Legislative Council Chamber. In the front is a blindfolded statue of the Greek goddess Themis, representing justice.

Hong Kong & Shanghai Bank Building 匯豐銀行總行
At the south side of Statue Square (at Des Voeux Rd, along which the trams run) you come face to face with the bizarre-looking Hong Kong & Shanghai Banking Corporation's headquarters. Designed by architect Norman Foster, it cost over US$1 billion and was the most expensive building in the world at the time of its completion in 1985. Opinions differ on whether this place is an

HONG KONG

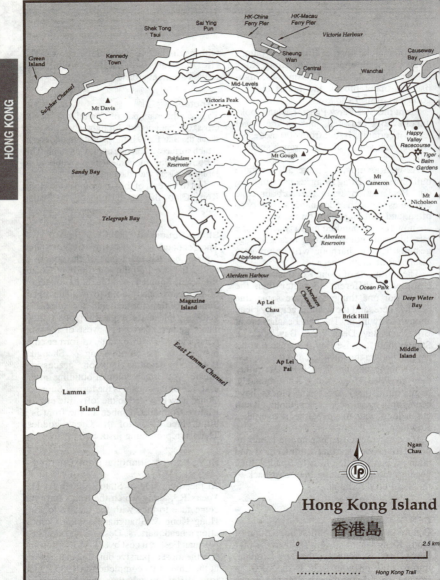

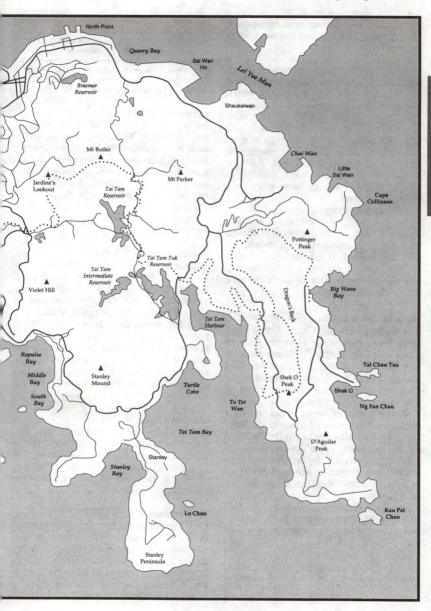

architectural masterpiece or a monstrosity, but it certainly is unique and definitely worth visiting.

Locals call this place the 'Robot Building', and it's easy to see why: it resembles one of those clear plastic models built so you can see how everything inside works. The gears, chains, motors and other moving parts of the escalators and lifts are all visible. The stairwells are also only walled in with glass, affording dizzying views to workers inside the building. Obviously, people who are afraid of heights should apply for a job elsewhere. Structurally, the building is equally radical, having been built on a 'coathanger' frame.

Definitely try to visit it during office hours when you can go inside and ride the escalator up to the bank on the 1st floor. While the bank doesn't encourage tourism, the staff are very accustomed to tourists wandering in anyway. Indeed, they're well prepared as souvenir postcards are sold inside the bank at the information desk.

Bank of China Building 中國銀行大廈

Sandwiched between Chater Garden and Hong Kong Park is the 74-storey Bank of China Building, designed by Chinese-American architect I M Pei. It used to be Hong Kong's tallest until it was surpassed by the 78-storey Central Plaza Building. It may be tall, but the Bank of China Building itself is nothing special in terms of architectural splendour. What makes it interesting to tourists is the Tsui Museum of Art (☎ 8682688) on the 11th floor. There are approximately 2000 art objects on display. Admission is HK$20, and operating hours are from 10 am to 6 pm weekdays and from 10 am to 2 pm on Saturdays.

The Bank of China is owned by the PRC, and its dominating presence in the heart of downtown has not been welcomed by everyone:

Before any building can be put up in Hong Kong a fungshui expert has to be called in to ensure the design, position and alignment don't bring bad luck, or even worse. Well, the Bank of China's fungshui is

bad news – not for the Bank of China but for the buildings around it. Reportedly, the Bank of China positively radiates bad vibes (all those sharp corners, the spikes on the roof, etc) and some neighbouring buildings have had to seal up windows or cover them over in order to keep the harmful influence out. With China, 1997, the dispute over LEGCO and the new airport, it's hardly surprising say the local cynics.

Li Yuen St 利源街

Actually this is two streets: Li Yuen St East and Li Yuen St West, which run parallel to each other between Des Voeux and Queen's Rds, opposite the Lane Crawford Department Store. Both streets are narrow alleys and are closed to motorised traffic. These two lanes are crammed with shops selling clothing, handbags, fabrics and just about everything else. Nearby Pottinger St is also worth looking into.

Central Market 中央市場

You shouldn't have any trouble finding the Central Market – just sniff the air. The smell from the fish section alone should be enough to make China think twice about taking over Hong Kong in 1997. Central Market is a large four-storey affair between Des Voeux and Queen's Rds. It's more a zoo than a market, with everything from chickens and quail to eels and crabs, alive or freshly slaughtered. Fish are cut lengthwise, but above the heart so that it continues to beat and pump blood around the body.

Lan Kwai Fong 蘭桂坊

This is Hong Kong's chief disco, pub, bar, restaurant and party neighbourhood. There is a luncheon crowd and various coffee shop afternoon hangouts, but the place really gets rocking in the evenings. See the Entertainment section for details.

Government House 督憲府

On Upper Albert Rd, opposite the Zoological & Botanic Gardens, is Government House, residence of the Governor of Hong Kong. It's closed to the public except for one day in March (always a Sunday) when the azaleas are in bloom. At this time the place is swamped with locals and tourists.

Government House

The original sections of the building date back to 1858. Other features were actually built to Japanese designs during the war, when Japan occupied the colony and the Japanese governor wanted to establish a residence and administrative centre worthy of his role.

Zoological & Botanical Gardens
動植物公園

First established in 1864, the gardens are home to statues – including an innovative sculpture of Sir Arthur Kennedy, the first governor to invite Chinese to government functions – hundreds of species of birds, exotic trees, plants and shrubs. Captive breeding of endangered species is carried out here.

If you go to the gardens at about 8 am the place will be packed with Chinese toning up with a bit of shadow-boxing on their way to work. The gardens are divided by Albany Rd, with the botanics and the aviaries in the first section, off Garden Rd, and the animals in the other. Admission is free.

The gardens are at the top end of Garden Rd, which leads up behind the Hilton Hotel – an easy walk, but you can also take bus Nos 3 or 12 to the stop in front of the Jardine House on Connaught Rd. The bus takes you along Upper Albert and Caine Rds on the northern boundary of the gardens. Get off in front of the Caritas Centre (at the junction of Upper Albert and Caine Rds) and follow the path uphill to the gardens.

Hong Kong Park 香港公園

This is one of the most unusual parks in the world – it was deliberately designed to look anything but natural. Rather, the park stresses synthetic creations such as its fountain plaza, Conservatory (greenhouse), aviary, artificial waterfall, Indoor Games Hall, Visual Arts Centre, playground, viewing tower, museum and Taichi Garden. For all that, the park is beautiful in its own weird way, and makes for dramatic photography with a wall of skyscrapers on one side and mountains on the other.

Within the park is the **Flagstaff House Museum** (☎ 8690690), the oldest Western-style building still standing in Hong Kong, dating from the mid-19th century. Enter from Cotton Tree Drive. The museum houses a Chinese teaware collection, including pieces dating from the Warring States period (475-221 BC) to the present. The museum is open daily except Wednesday, from 10 am to 5 pm and is closed on several public holidays. Admission is free. Bus Nos 3, 12, 23, 23B, 40 and 103 all go this way. Get off at the first stop on Cotton Tree Drive.

HONG KONG

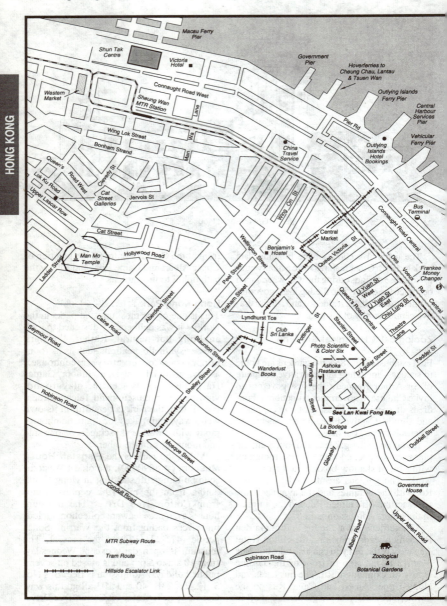

Macau Ferry Pier
Shun Tak Centre
Victoria Hotel
Government Pier
Hoverferries to Cheung Chau, Lantau & Tsuen Wan
Outlying Islands Ferry Pier
Central Harbour Services Pier
Connaught Road West
Western Market
Sheung Wan MTR Station
Lane
Pier Rd
Vehicular Ferry Pier
Wing Lok Street
Bonham Strand
China Travel Service
Outlying Islands Hotel Bookings
Queen's Road West
Cleverly St
Jervois St
Wing On St
Connaught Road Central
Bus Terminal
Lok Ku Road
Cat Street Galleries
Upper Lascar Row
Central Market
Des Voeux Rd Central
Frankee Money Changer
Cat Street
Ladder Street
Man Mo Temple
Hollywood Road
Wellington Street
Benjamin's Hostel
Queen Victoria St
Queen's Road Central
Li Yuen St West
Li Yuen St East
Chiu Lung St
Theatre Lane
Peel Street
Graham Street
Stanley Street
Caine Road
Aberdeen Street
Lyndhurst Tce
Club Sri Lanka
Pottinger St
Photo Scientific & Color Six
Pedder St
Seymour Road
Staunton Street
Shelley Street
Wanderlust Books
Ashoka Restaurant
D'Aguilar Street
Robinson Road
Wyndham Street
See Lan Kwai Fong Map
La Bodega Bar
Duddell Street
Mosque Street
Gloucester
Conduit Road
Albany Road
Government House
Upper Albert Road
Robinson Road
Zoological & Botanical Gardens

—————— MTR Subway Route
—————— Tram Route
+++++++ Hillside Escalator Link

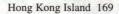

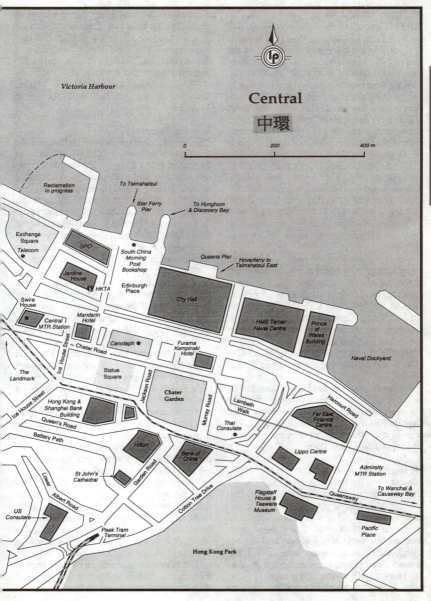

Victoria Harbour

Central
中環

0   200   400 m

HONG KONG

Reclamation in progress

To Tsimshatsui

Star Ferry Pier

To Hunghom & Discovery Bay

Exchange Square
Telecom

GPO

South China Morning Post Bookshop

Queens Pier

Hoverfarry to Tsimshatsui East

Jardine House

HKTA

Edinburgh Place

City Hall

HMS Tamar Naval Centre

Prince of Wales Building

Swire House

Central MTR Station

Mandarin Hotel

Cenotaph

Furama Kempinski Hotel

Naval Dockyard

Chater Road

Ice House Street

The Landmark

Statue Square

Jackson Road

Chater Garden

Murray Road

Lambeth Walk

Harcourt Road

Hong Kong & Shanghai Bank Building

Queen's Road

Battery Path

Hilton

Thai Consulate

Far East Finance Centre

Lippo Centre

Ice House Street

Garden Road

Bank of China

Admiralty MTR Station

St John's Cathedral

Cotton Tree Drive

Flagstaff House & Teaware Museum

Queensway

To Wanchai & Causeway Bay

Lower Albert Road

US Consulate

Peak Tram Terminal

Hong Kong Park

Pacific Place

SHEUNG WAN 上環

West of Central (on the right as you come off the Star Ferry) is Sheung Wan (the Western District), which once had something of the feel of old Shanghai about it. The comparison is a bit forced now since much of old Sheung Wan has disappeared under the jackhammers of development, and old stairway streets once cluttered with stalls and street sellers have been cleared away to make room for more new buildings or the MTR. Nevertheless the area has plenty of interest and is worth exploring.

From Queen's Rd, head south, uphill to **Hollywood Rd**. This street has several funeral shops selling everything for the best-dressed corpses, as well as wreath and coffin makers. It is also full of furniture shops with antiques of all kinds, from the genuine article to modern reproductions made before your very eyes.

Cat St (Lascar Row) used to be famous in Hong Kong for its arts & crafts, but the street has disappeared under an urban renewal project. The arts & crafts dealers are now at the **Cat St Galleries**, Casey Building, Lok Ku Rd. The galleries contain five floors of arts & crafts, antiques and souvenirs, plus an exhibition hall and auction room.

Man Wa Lane near the Sheung Wan MTR Station is the place to go to get a name chop carved.

Possession St is an obscure lane, but its name reveals that somewhere around here the flag was planted for England after Captain Elliot did his deal with Qi Shan. The area just to the west of Possession St is known as Possession Point.

Western Market 西港城

Almost directly opposite Shun Tak Centre and the Macau Ferry Pier is the Western Market. This four-storey red brick building, built in 1906, has been fully renovated and reopened in 1991. Today it's filled with modern but very trendy shops and restaurants. An unusual theme here is that the ground floor shops must present one-of-a-kind merchandise – the idea is to prevent the usual boring overlap of lookalike imitation so common in most Hong Kong shopping malls. The 1st floor is a 'cloth alley', similar to those outdoor markets which are fast disappearing. The 2nd floor is the food department. The 3rd (top) floor is a centre for performing arts and exhibits.

The restaurants in the Western Market keep late hours, generally from 11 am to 11.30 pm.

Man Mo Temple 文武廟

This temple, on the corner of Hollywood Rd and Ladder St, is one of the oldest and most famous in Hong Kong. The Man Mo – literally meaning civil and military – is dedicated to two deities. The civil deity is a Chinese statesman of the 3rd century BC and the military deity is Kuanti, a soldier born in the 2nd century AD and now worshipped as the God of War. (See the Religion section in the Facts about Hong Kong chapter.) Kuanti is also known as Kwan Tai or Kwan Kung.

Outside the entrance are four gilt plaques on poles which are carried at procession time. Two plaques describe the gods being worshipped and the others request quietness and respect, and warn menstruating women to keep away. Inside the temple are two antique chairs shaped like houses used to carry the two gods at festival time. The coils suspended from the roof are incense cones burnt by worshippers. A large bell on the right is dated 1846 and the smaller ones on the left, 1897.

The exact date of the temple's construction has never been agreed on, but it's certain it was already standing when the British arrived to claim the island as their own. The present Man Mo Temple was renovated in the middle of the last century.

The area around the Man Mo Temple was used extensively for location shots in the film *The World of Suzie Wong*. The building to the right of the temple was used as Suzie's hotel. Ironically, the real hotel in the novel (the Luk Kwok, alias the Nam Kok) was in Wanchai, several km to the east.

The extremely steep flight of steps next to the temple is Ladder St. Once it was crammed with stalls and shops selling everything, but the stall owners were cleared away. Ladder St is well over 100 years old and probably the best example of old Hong Kong remaining.

HONG KONG UNIVERSITY 香港大學
West of Sheung Wan takes you through Sai Ying Pun and Shek Tong Tsui districts to Kennedy Town, a residential and harbour district at the end of the tram line. The chief attraction of Shek Tong Tsui is Hong Kong University's Fung Ping Shan Museum.

Fung Ping Shan Museum 馮平山博物館
This museum (☎ 8592114) houses collections of ceramics and bronzes, plus a lesser number of paintings and carvings. The bronzes are in three groups: Shang and Zhou Dynasty ritual vessels; decorative mirrors from the Warring States period to the Tang, Song, Ming and Qing (Ching) dynasties; and Nestorian crosses from the Yuan Dynasty (the Nestorians were a Christian sect which arose in Syria, and at some stage found their way to China, probably during the Tang Dynasty).

A collection of ceramics includes Han Dynasty tomb pottery and recent works from the Chinese pottery centres of Jingdezhen and Shiwan in the People's Republic.

The museum is in Hong Kong University, 94 Bonham Rd. Take bus No 3 from the Edinburgh Place (adjacent to city hall), or bus Nos 23 or 103 coming from Causeway Bay, and get off at Bonham Rd, opposite St Paul's College. The museum is open Monday to Saturday, 9.30 am to 6 pm, and is closed on Sunday and several public holidays. Admission is free.

VICTORIA PEAK 太平山頂
If you haven't been to the Peak, then you haven't been to Hong Kong. Every visitor tries to make the pilgrimage, and for good reason – the view is one of the most spectacular in the world. It's also a good way to get Hong Kong into perspective. It's worth repeating the Peak trip at night – the illuminated view is something else. Bring a tripod for your camera if you wish to get some sensational night photos.

The Peak has been *the* place to live ever since the British moved in. The Taipans built their summer houses there to escape the heat and humidity (it's usually about 5°C cooler than down below), although they spent three months swathed in mist for their efforts. It's still the most fashionable place to live in Hong Kong, but the price of real estate is astronomical. Ditto for the prices charged in some of the cafes on the Peak – check the menu to avoid indigestion later.

At the top of the tram line at 400 metres elevation is the three-level Peak Galleria, a type of scenic shopping mall. The place is designed to withstand winds of over 270 km/h, hopefully more than the theoretical maximum that can be generated by typhoons. High-powered binoculars on the lower balcony cost HK$1 for a few minutes – worth every cent. Inside the tower you can find all sorts of overpriced shops peddling everything from T-shirts to dim sum.

When people refer to the Peak, this generally means the **Peak Galleria** and surrounding residential area. Victoria Peak is the actual summit, about half a km to the west and 140 metres higher. You can walk around Victoria Peak easily without exhausting yourself. Harlech and Lugard Rds encircle it. Harlech Rd is on the south side of the peak while Lugard Rd is on the north slope. Together these form a loop. For those who would rather run, not walk, this makes a spectacular jogging route.

You can walk from the restaurant to the remains of the **old governor's mountain lodge** near the summit (550 metres elevation). The lodge was burnt to the ground by the Japanese during WW II, but the gardens remain and are open to the public. The views are particularly good and there is a toposcope identifying the various geographical features you can see.

For a downhill hike you can walk about two km from the Peak to Pokfulam Reservoir Rd, which leaves Peak Rd near the car park exit. This goes past the reservoir to the main Pokfulam Rd where you can get the No 7 bus to Aberdeen or back to Central.

Another good walk is down to Hong Kong

HONG KONG

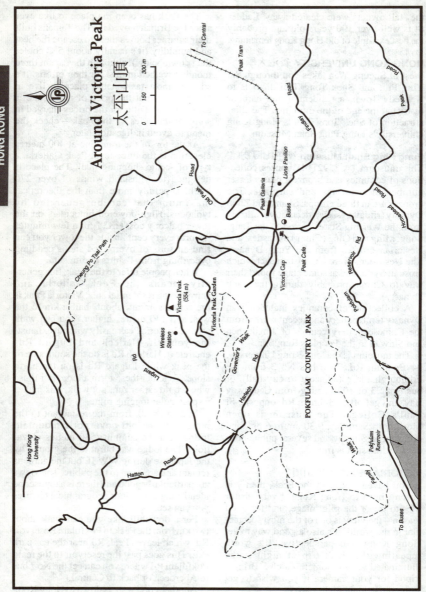

Around Victoria Peak
太平山頂

0   150   300 m

To Central

Peak Tram

Peak Road

Finlay Road

Lions Pavilion

Peak Galleria

Buses

Peak Cafe

Homestead Road

Peak Road

Old Peak Road

Cheung Po Tsai Path

Victoria Peak (554 m)

Victoria Peak Garden

Wireless Station

Lugard Rd

Governor's Walk

Victoria Gap

Harlech Rd

POKFULAM COUNTRY PARK

Pokfulam Reservoir Rd

Pokfulam Reservoir

Family Walk

Hatton Road

Hong Kong University

To Buses

University. First walk to the west side of Victoria Peak by taking either Lugard or Harlech Rds. After reaching Hatton Rd on the west side of Victoria Peak, follow it down. The descent is very steep but the path is obvious.

If you're going to the Peak, you should go by the Peak Tram – at least one way. The tram terminal is in Garden Rd, Central, behind the Hilton Hotel, 650 metres from the Star Ferry Terminal. Once every 20 minutes there is a free shuttle bus between the Star Ferry and the Peak Tram terminal from 9 am to 7 pm (8 pm on Sundays and holidays). The tram trip takes about eight minutes and costs HK$10 one way, or HK$16 round trip (discounts for children under 12). The tram operates every day from 7 am to midnight, and runs about every 10 minutes with three stops along the way. Avoid going on a Sunday when there tends to be long queues.

Running for more than a century, the tram has never had an accident – a comforting thought if you start to have doubts about the strength of the cable. In 1885 everyone thought the Honourable Phineas Kyrie and William Kerfoot Hughes were quite crazy when they announced their intentions of building a tramway to the top, but it opened three years later, wiping out the scoffers and the sedan chair trade in one go. Since then the only occurrences which stopped the tram were WW II and the violent rainstorms of 1966 which washed half the track down the hillside.

Alternatively, bus No 15 from Central Bus Terminal (the ground floor of Exchange Square) in Central will take you on a 40-minute trip around the perilous-looking road to the top. Bus No 15B runs from Causeway Bay (Yee Wo St) to the Peak. Minibus No 1 leaves from the HMS *Tamar* building, on the eastern side of City Hall.

HONG KONG TRAIL 港島徑
For those who would like a real challenge, it is possible to walk the entire length of Hong Kong Island. Start from the Peak, then go down to the hills near Aberdeen. The trail then zigzags across the ridgetops all the way to Shek O in the south-east corner of Hong Kong Island. It's not likely that you'll want

to do the entire hike in one day, though it is possible if you're very fit.

If you intend to do this hike, it would be wise to purchase the *Hong Kong Trail* map published by the Country Parks Authority (CPA). Another map worth picking up is *Countryside Series Sheet No 1: Hong Kong Island* which shows many details of the streets and topography not on the hiking map. Both maps are available from the Government Publications Centre next to the GPO on Hong Kong Island.

WANCHAI 灣仔
Heading east from Central brings you to Hong Kong's famed Wanchai district. In all the tourist-brochure hype, Wanchai is still inseparable from the name of Suzie Wong – not bad considering that the book dates back to 1957 and the movie to 1960. Although Wanchai had a reputation during the Vietnam War as a seedy red-light district, these days you can bring grandma and the kids.

Instead of brothels and girlie bars Wanchai is being taken over by high-rise office blocks spreading out from Central, but a walk down Lockhart Rd will give you a wisp of what it was like when the place was really jumping. You can still find plenty of topless bars, massage parlours and tattooists, but you don't need an appointment anymore. Further along Lockhart Rd towards Causeway Bay, the area turns into a tourist shopping district that rivals Tsimshatsui in Kowloon.

Central Plaza 中環廣場
Shaped like a giant ballpoint pen, the 78-storey Central Plaza is Hong Kong's tallest structure. Some of the tourist literature you'll read will also claim that this is Asia's tallest building, but that isn't really true. The tallest is the 105-storey Ryugyong Hotel in Pyongyang, North Korea. However, this 'hotel' is nothing but a facade, a hollow shell with no plumbing or electricity and built so North Korea could claim to have Asia's tallest building. Hong Kong's Central Plaza can rightly claim to be the tallest functioning building in Asia.

HONG KONG

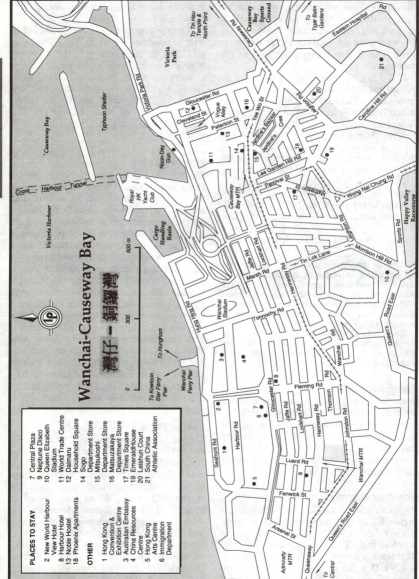

Wanchai–Causeway Bay

灣仔—銅鑼灣

PLACES TO STAY

2 New World Harbour
   View Hotel
8 Harbour Hotel
13 Noble Hostel
18 Phoenix Apartments

7 Central Plaza
9 Neptune Disco
10 Queen Elizabeth
    Stadium
11 World Trade Centre
12 Daimaru
14 Household Square
    Sogo
    Department Store
15 Mitsukoshi
    Department Store
16 Matsuzakaya
    Department Store
17 Times Square
19 EmeraldHouse
20 Leishun Court
21 South China
    Athletic Association

OTHER

1 Hong Kong
   Convention &
   Exhibition Centre
3 Australian Embassy
4 China Resources
   Centre
5 Hong Kong
   Arts Centre
6 Immigration
   Department

Hong Kong Arts Centre 香港藝術中心

Also in the Wanchai district is the Arts Centre (☎ 8230200) on Harbour Rd. The Pao Sui Loong Galleries are on the 4th and 5th floors of the centre and international and local exhibitions are held year round with the emphasis on contemporary art. Opening hours are 10 am to 8 pm daily. Admission is free. It's easy to get there on the MTR to the Wanchai Station.

Police Museum 警隊博物館

This museum (☎ 8496018) at 27 Coombe Rd places special emphasis on the history of the Royal Hong Kong Police Force, which was formed in 1844. Intriguingly, the museum also houses a Triad Societies Gallery.

Operating hours are Wednesday to Sunday, 9 am to 5 pm, and Tuesday from 2 to 5 pm. The museum is closed on Mondays and admission is free.

You can get there on bus No 15 from Central. Get off at the intersection of Peak and Stubbs Rds.

Hong Kong Convention & Exhibition Centre 香港會議展覽中心

This enormous building on the harbour boasts the world's largest 'glass curtain', a window seven storeys high – I sure wouldn't want to be the one to wash it. You can ride the escalator to the 7th floor for a superb harbour view. There are plans to build an artificial island just off the coast with yet more high-rises.

Museum of Chinese Historical Relics 文物展覽館

This museum (☎ 8274692) houses cultural treasures from China unearthed in archaeological digs. Two special exhibitions each year focus on artefacts from specific provinces.

The museum is on the 1st floor, Causeway Centre, 28 Harbour Rd, Wanchai. Enter from the China Resources Building. Operating hours are 10 am to 6 pm on weekdays and Saturdays, 1 to 6 pm on Sundays and holidays. From Central, take bus Nos 10A, 20, 21 or 104.

CAUSEWAY BAY 銅鑼灣

Catch the tram which goes through Wanchai and let it take you to Causeway Bay. The old Causeway Bay – Tung Lo Wan in Chinese, meaning Copper Gong Bay – has almost disappeared through reclamation. This area was the site of a British settlement in the 1840s and was once a *godown* (warehouse) area for merchants and a harbour for fishermen. A lot of this area has been reclaimed from swamp and the bottom of the harbour.

Causeway Bay is one of Hong Kong's top shopping and nightlife areas. Many of the big Japanese department stores are here, mostly clustered around the Hotel Excelsior and Park Lane Radisson (both famous for discos).

Typhoon Shelter 避風塘

Causeway Bay's waterfront is a mass of junks and sampans huddling in the typhoon shelter. The land jutting out is Kellett Island, which was actually an island until a causeway was built in 1956. Further land reclamation turned it into a peninsula. Now it's the headquarters of the Royal Hong Kong Yacht Club. The Cross-Harbour Tunnel comes up here too.

Noon-Day Gun 午炮

The best-known landmark in Causeway Bay is probably the noon-day gun – a recoil mounted three-pounder built by Hotchkiss in Portsmouth in 1901. It stands in a small garden in front of the Excelsior Hotel on Gloucester Rd and is fired daily at noon. Exactly how this tradition started is unknown.

One story claims that Jardine Matheson either fired it to wish bon voyage to a departing managing director or to welcome an incoming ship. The navy got so enraged that their function had been usurped (or because an ordinary person got a salute reserved for officials) that they told Jardine's to fire the gun every day as punishment.

Noel Coward made the gun famous with his satirical 1924 song *Mad Dogs and Englishmen* about colonists who braved the heat of the noon-day sun while the natives stayed indoors:

In Hong Kong they strike a gong,
and fire a noon-day gun,
To reprimand each inmate who's
in late

Jardine Matheson 怡和有限公司

Hong Kong's largest and most powerful *hong* (big company) set up shop in Causeway Bay in 1844, after moving its headquarters from Macau. Now Jardine's head office resides in the World Trade Centre next to the Hotel Excelsior.

The area is still full of company names and memorials. Percival St, which crosses Hennessy Rd, is named after Alexander Percival, a relative of Sir James Matheson who joined the firm in 1852 and ended up a partner. Matheson St leads off it. Hennessy Rd becomes Yee Wo St, Yee Wo being the name under which Jardine traded in Shanghai.

Jardine Matheson bought heavily in the first land sale in the colony in 1841. It bought a large tract of land on what was then the waterfront at Causeway Bay and hewed a whole township out of the rock. It built godowns, offices, workshops, a slipway, homes and messes for employees. All that remains of the East Point establishment is an old gateway with a couple of plaques. You'll find it up a side-street from Yee Wo St. It's still owned by Jardine Matheson but is now full of modern warehouses.

Two streets to the right behind Yee Wo St are Jardine's Bazaar and Jardine's Crescent, names which recall the old firm. A Chinese bazaar used to be held on the first street. Things haven't changed much. The area still has Chinese provision stores, herb stores and cooked-food stalls. Jardine's Crescent has a market which is very good for cheap clothes. Between Jardine's Bazaar and Crescent is the short Fuk Hing Lane, an interesting shopping alley with good, inexpensive leather handbags, silk scarves, Chinese padded jackets and well-cut jeans. ∎

Jardine's executives stand around the gun on New Year's Eve and fire it off at midnight, to the applause of a colonial gathering.

Victoria Park 維多利亞公園

Victoria Park, between Causeway Bay and Victoria Park Rd, is a large playing field built on reclaimed land. Football matches are played on weekends and the Urban Services League puts on music and acrobatic shows. Early in the morning it's a good place to see the slow-motion choreography of taijiquan practitioners.

Victoria Park becomes a flower market a few days before the Chinese New Year. Other New Year goods on display include peach and kumquat trees (symbols of good luck). The park is also worth a visit during the evening of the Mid-Autumn (Moon) Festival when people turn out en masse carrying lanterns. Other events in the park include the Hong Kong Tennis Classic and the Hong Kong International Kart Grand Prix.

Causeway Bay Sports Ground 銅鑼灣運動場

This is the most popular sports ground in Hong Kong and home of the Chinese Recreation Club. The sports ground is on the south side of Causeway Rd, just south of Victoria Park. Among the public facilities are areas to play football, volleyball, badminton and tennis.

Tin Hau Temple 天后廟

One more thing worth a look in Causeway Bay is a tiny Tin Hau temple on Tin Hau Temple Rd (at the junction with Dragon Rd), on the east side of Victoria Park (near the Tin Hau MTR Station). Before reclamation, the temple to the seafarers' goddess stood on the waterfront. An old bell inside dates back to the 15th century. The temple itself is about 200 years old.

Tiger Balm Gardens 虎豹別墅

Not actually in Causeway Bay but in the adjacent Tai Hang District are the famous (infamous?) Tiger Balm Gardens, officially known as the Aw Boon Haw Gardens. A pale relative of the better-known park of the same name in Singapore, Hong Kong's Tiger Balm Gardens are three hectares of grotesque statuary in appallingly bad taste. These concrete gardens were built at a cost of HK\$16 million (and that was in 1935!) by Aw Boon Haw, who made his fortune from the Tiger Balm cure-everything medication.

Aw is widely described as having been a philanthropist, though perhaps his millions could have been put to a more philanthropic use.

The gardens are just off Tai Hang Rd, within walking distance of Causeway Bay, or take bus No 11 from the Admiralty MTR Station or Exchange Square in Central. The gardens are open daily from 9.30 am to 4 pm and admission is free.

HAPPY VALLEY 跑馬地

There are two neighbourhoods on the north side of Hong Kong Island that have been colonised by gwailos with expense accounts. One is the Mid-Levels and the other is Happy Valley.

However, gwailo-watching is not the main reason for coming here. There are two horse-racing tracks in Hong Kong – one at Shatin in the New Territories and the other at Happy Valley. The racing season is from late September to May. For details, see the Activities section in the Facts for the Visitor chapter of this book.

Besides losing your money at the track, the other main activity in Happy Valley is taking advantage of some fine restaurants which have sprouted in the neighbourhood. See Places to Eat for details.

Getting to Happy Valley is easy. A tram, marked Happy Valley, runs from Central.

QUARRY BAY 鰂魚涌

The main attraction of Quarry Bay is the Cityplaza Shopping Centre, one of Hong Kong's finest. Although not normally considered a tourist attraction, it has much to recommend it. For one thing, shopping is much more pleasant once you get out of the tourist zones. Shops have price tags on merchandise and there is no bargaining, yet prices are generally lower than you could bargain for in Tsimshatsui.

Even if you don't want to buy anything, Cityplaza has other amenities: it's the only shopping mall in Hong Kong with an ice skating rink; its Tivoli Terrace cafe is one of the nicest in town; and it has a good dim sum place, the Cityplaza Palace Restaurant.

To get to Cityplaza, take the MTR to Tai Koo Station from where there is an exit which leads directly into the shopping mall.

SHEK O 石澳

Shek O, on the south-east coast, has one of the best beaches on Hong Kong Island. All around Shek O are homes that belong to Hong Kong's wealthy entrepreneurial class, but many of the best homes are protected by walls which are cleverly hidden by landscape gardening. Shek O is a prestigious place to live, though the Peak still ranks as number one in terms of snob appeal.

To get to Shek O, take the MTR or tram to Shaukeiwan, and from Shaukeiwan take bus No 9 to the last stop.

Big Wave Bay, another excellent beach, is two km to the north of Shek O, but there is no public transportation. It does make a nice walk, passing the Shek O Country Club and Golf Course along the way.

Shek O is one of the few places in Hong Kong where you can hire a bicycle to explore the coast.

STANLEY 赤柱

This is the trendy, out-of-town gwailo place to live. It's on the south-east side of the island just 15 km as the crow flies from Central. Once the village was indeed a village. About 2000 people lived here when the British took over in 1841, making it one of the largest settlements on the island at the time. The British built a prison near the village in 1937 – just in time to be used by the Japanese to intern the expatriates.

Now it's used as a maximum-security prison. Hong Kong's contingent of British troops is housed in Stanley Fort at the southern end of the peninsula, which is off-limits to the public.

There is an OK beach (not as crowded as the one at Repulse Bay) at Stanley Village. It's also possible to rent windsurfers here. The **Stanley Market** dominates the town and on weekends it's wall-to-wall tourists. The market is open from 10 am to 7 pm, sells clothes, furniture, household goods, hardware, foodstuffs and imitation designer jeans.

HONG KONG

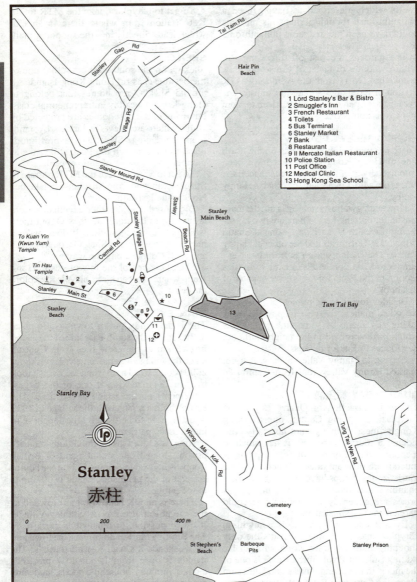

Tai Tam Rd

Stanley Gap Rd

Hair Pin
Beach

Village Rd

Stanley

Stanley Mound Rd

Stanley

1 Lord Stanley's Bar & Bistro
2 Smuggler's Inn
3 French Restaurant
4 Toilets
5 Bus Terminal
6 Stanley Market
7 Bank
8 Restaurant
9 Il Mercato Italian Restaurant
10 Police Station
11 Post Office
12 Medical Clinic
13 Hong Kong Sea School

Stanley
Main Beach

Beach Rd

To Kuan Yin
(Kwun Yum)
Temple

Carmel Rd

Stanley Village Rd

Tin Hau
Temple

4

1 2 3   5
Stanley   Main St
6

10

7
8 9
11
12

Tam Tai Bay

13

Stanley
Beach

Stanley Bay

Stanley
赤柱

Wong Ma Kok Rd

Tung Tau Wan Rd

0   200   400 m

Cemetery

St Stephen's
Beach

Barbeque
Pits

Stanley Prison

Stanley has a **Tin Hau temple** which dates back to 1767. On one of the walls hangs the skin of a tiger killed by Japanese soldiers outside the temple. The temple is on the corner of Stanley Main St, approaching Ma Hang Village.

Further up from the Tin Hau temple is **the Kuanyin (Kwun Yum) Temple** in Ma Hang Village. Kuanyin is the Goddess of Mercy and the temple contains a six-metre statue of her. The statue is sheltered by a pavilion specially built in 1977 following a claim by a woman and her daughter that they'd seen the statue move and a bright light shine from its forehead. Maybe Stanley isn't such a dull place?

From Stanley you can take bus No 73A to **St Stephen's Beach** a bit further down the coast. Both Stanley and St Stephen's beaches have all the usual facilities. The cemetery at St Stephen's Beach is for military personnel who have died since the British occupation of Hong Kong and during WW II. The oldest graves date from 1843.

Getting There & Away

To get to Stanley from Central take bus No 6 or express bus No 260 from the Central Bus Terminal under Exchange Square in Central. Fares are HK$3 for the ordinary bus and HK$4.80 for the express bus. The bus to Stanley takes a very scenic trip down Tai Tam Rd to the reservoir, then along the coast at Tai Tam Bay. Along the way you pass Turtle Cove, a small but pretty beach. If you're coming from Shaukeiwan (eastern terminus of the tram), take bus No 14 down to Stanley. Bus No 73 connects Stanley with Repulse Bay.

REPULSE BAY 淺水灣

The prime attraction is the beach and, on weekends and holidays, the **Flea Market** on Beach Rd. Also, the posh **Repulse Bay Shopping Arcade** at 109 Repulse Bay Rd is a good place to get out of the heat, enjoy the air-con and burn up some cash.

Along the beachfront is an unusual Tin Hau temple popularly known as the Life Saver's Club. In front of the temple is Lon-

gevity Bridge – crossing it is supposed to add three days to your life.

When the temperature sizzles, the beach attracts so many people on hot weekends you're just about swimming in suntan lotion. To find even a niche in the sand you have to get there early. Otherwise the place looks OK from the road and makes a scenic drive. You could also walk down the coast a bit to Middle Bay and South Bay, about 10-minute and 30-minute walks respectively.

To reach Repulse Bay from Central, take bus No 6 or bus No 61 from the Central Bus Terminal just to the west of the Star Ferry. The No 6 bus carries on to Stanley. Bus No 73 connects Repulse Bay with Stanley and Aberdeen.

OCEAN PARK 海洋公園

Next around the coast is Deep Water Bay, now famous for Ocean Park, which opened in 1976. Although generally advertised as an oceanarium or a marine world, the emphasis is on the fun fair with its roller coaster, space wheel, octopus, swinging ship and other astronaut-training machines. There's also a sensurround cinema housed in a 20-metre-high dome. Ocean Park has to rate as one of the best theme parks in the world.

The complex is built on two levels connected by a seven-minute cable car ride, and looks down on Deep Water Bay below. At the park entrance are landscaped gardens with a touch-and-feed section where kids can pet tame llamas, goats, calves and kangaroos. I never saw such cooperative kangaroos in Australia, not even in a zoo, and I wonder how the Chinese managed this. Perhaps the kangaroos were given prefrontal lobotomies.

Chinese arts like gongfu, opera and so on are often staged in the gardens. There's an exotic bird section too. There are several theatres where penguins, whales, sea lions, monkeys and other animals perform. Bring a pen and paper to write down the various showtimes – these are displayed on a noticeboard at the entrance but there is no hand-out available.

At the rear entrance to Ocean Park is the

Middle Kingdom, a sort of Chinese cultural village representing 13 dynasties. The village has temples, pagodas, traditional street scenes and Middle Kingdom employees dressed in the fashionable outerwear of ancient China.

Entrance fees are HK$130 for adults, or HK$65 for kids aged three to 11. Opening hours are 10 am to 6 pm daily. Get there early because there's much to see. It's best to go on weekdays since weekends are very crowded.

Getting There & Away

The cheapest way to get to Ocean Park from Central is to take bus No 70 (HK$2.80) from the Central Bus Terminal (under Exchange Square, near Star Ferry) and get off at the first stop after the tunnel. From there it's a 10-minute walk. Slightly more expensive is minibus No 6 from the Central Bus Terminal (HK$6), but it does not run on Sundays and holidays. Most expensive is the air-con Ocean Park Citybus which leaves from both the ground floor of Exchange Square and from underneath Bond Centre (Admiralty MTR Station) every half-hour from 8.45 am (HK$9). You can also buy your admission tickets for Ocean Park from the Citybus kiosks.

Bus No 73 connects Ocean Park with Aberdeen to the west and Repulse Bay and Stanley to the east.

WATER WORLD 水上樂園

Adjacent to the front entrance of Ocean Park is Water World, a collection of swimming pools, water slides and diving platforms. Water World is open from June to October. During July and August, operating hours are from 9 am to 9 pm. During June, September and October it is open from 10 am to 6 pm. Admission for adults/children costs HK$60/30 during the daytime, but in evenings falls to HK$40/20.

From the Central Bus Terminal in Exchange Square (Central), take bus No 70 and get off at the first stop after the tunnel, then follow the signs to Ocean Park. Alternatively, take minibus No 6 from the Central

Bus Terminal (HK$6), but it does not run on Sundays and holidays. You can also take the Ocean Park Citybus from Bond Centre, Admiralty, but it's very important that you get off at the first stop, which is the front entrance of Ocean Park. The second stop is the rear entrance of Ocean Park, which is far away from Water World.

ABERDEEN 香港仔

Hong Kong's top tourist attraction outside of the Peak is Aberdeen, where nearly 6000 people live or work on junks anchored in the harbour. Also moored in the harbour are three palace-like floating restaurants, sightseeing attractions in themselves.

Sampan tours of Aberdeen Harbour are inexpensive and definitely worth it. The price should run at about HK$35 per person and they will usually wait until they have four persons before going. A little bit of bargaining is in order. Watertours does a 20-minute trip around the harbour for HK$40 per person, but it's more fun to charter a sampan. If you're with a group, you can charter a sampan for about HK$100 for 30 minutes. The price goes down the further away from the bus stop you get. If you are by yourself, just hang out by the harbour as the old women who operate the boats will leap on you and try to get you to join a tour. Some travellers take a free harbour tour by riding the boat out to the Jumbo Floating Restaurant and then riding back.

On one side of the harbour is the island of Ap Lei Chau. The island used to be nothing more than a junk-building centre, but now it's covered with housing estates. The walk across the bridge to Ap Lei Chau affords good views of the harbour.

At the junction of Aberdeen Main and Aberdeen Reservoir Rds is a Tin Hau temple built in 1851.

Getting There & Away

A tunnel linking Aberdeen with the northern side of Hong Kong Island provides rapid access to the town. From the Central Bus Terminal in Exchange Square, take bus Nos 7 or 70 to Aberdeen. No 7 goes via Hong

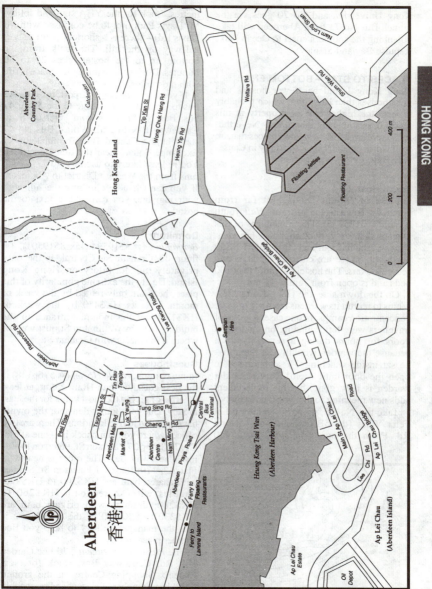

Aberdeen
香港仔

Aberdeen Country Park

Catchwater

Hong Kong Island

Yip Kan St
Wong Chuk Hang Rd
Heung Yip Rd
Welfare Rd

Nam Long Shan

Shum Wan Rd

Floating Jetties

Floating Restaurant

400 m
200
0

Ap Lei Chau Bridge

Aberdeen Reservoir Rd

Yue Kwong Road

Sampan Hire

Peel Rise

Tsung Man St
Tin Hau Temple
Lok Yeung
Aberdeen Main Rd
Market
Tung Sing Rd
Cheng Tu Rd
Aberdeen Centre
Nam Ning
Central Bus Terminal

Aberdeen Praya Road

Ferry to Floating Restaurants

Ferry to Lamma Island

Heung Kong Tsai Wan
(Aberdeen Harbour)

Main St Ap Lei Chau

Road

Ap Lei Chau
(Aberdeen Island)

Lee Chi Rd
Ap Lei Chau Bridge

Ap Lei Chau Estate

Oil Depot

Kong University, and No 70 goes via the tunnel. Bus No 73 from Aberdeen will take you along the southern coast to Ocean Park, Repulse Bay and Stanley.

PLACES TO STAY – BOTTOM END

Hong Kong Island has fewer hostels and guesthouses than Kowloon, which probably reflects the higher cost of property in this more desirable neighbourhood. Nevertheless, there are a few very good places that are well worth considering, especially in Causeway Bay.

Youth Hostel

On top of Mount Davis, not far from Kennedy Town is the *Ma Wui Hall* youth hostel (☎ 8175715). The advantages of this place is that it's very clean, quiet, has great views of the harbour and costs only HK$50 per night. There are cooking facilities and secure lockers. The hostel has more than 100 beds and is open from 7am to 11 pm.

On the down side, the Hong Kong YHA seems to recruit its wardens from prisons and concentration camps. In one case, a group of travellers were left pounding on the locked doors for hours during a severe typhoon because the warden wouldn't let them in – he sat inside watching TV and refused to open the door until 4 pm! That particular warden is now gone, but his replacement adds new meaning to the word 'unfriendly'.

Take bus No 5B, 47 or 77 and get off at Felix Villas (the 5B terminus) on Victoria Rd. From the bus stop, walk back 100

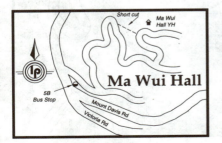

metres. Look for the YHA sign and follow Mt Davis Path (not to be confused with Mt Davis Rd) – there is a shortcut (with a sign) halfway up the hill. The walk from the bottom up to the hostel takes 20 to 30 minutes. During the summer, the place is rife with mosquitos.

If you come from the airport, take the A2 bus to Central, then change to the 5B or 47 bus. Bus No 5B runs from Paterson St in Causeway Bay to Felix Villas. Bus No 47 starts at the Central Bus Terminal, under Exchange Square near the Star Ferry Pier. You're least likely to use bus No 77, which runs from the Western District to Aberdeen. If you can't handle climbing the hill with your luggage, you can take a taxi to the hostel.

Dormitory

Benjamin's (☎ 8519594; fax 8519501), 1st floor, 13 Graham St, Central, is the only privately-run dormitory on Hong Kong Island. Due to the extreme popularity of this place, beds are only rented by the week or month. It costs HK$450 by the week or HK$1750 by the month. Entrance to the building is from Wellington St, just west of where it intersects with Graham St.

Guesthouses

In my opinion, *Noble Hostel* (☎ 5766148) is the best guesthouse in Hong Kong, at least in terms of giving the most value for the least money. Due to popular demand, the owner has expanded to five locations. There are two offices where you can check in – one at Flat C1, 7th floor, 37 Paterson St, Paterson Building, Causeway Bay. The other is nearby at Flat A3, 17th floor, 27 Paterson St. Singles with shared bath are HK$200 to HK$220; doubles with shared bath HK$260 to HK$280; doubles with private bath are HK$330 to HK$350. If the guesthouse is full, the manager will try to help you find another place to stay.

The *Phoenix Apartments*, 70 Lee Garden Hill Rd, Causeway Bay, (look for New Phoenix Shopping Centre on the ground floor) has a number of elegant and reasonably priced guesthouses. The catch here is that most are short-time hotels where rooms are rented by the hour. One hotel proudly advertises 'Avoidance of Publicity & Reasonable Rates'. Nevertheless, rooms are available for overnighters, and as long as management have changed the sheets recently it's not a bad place to stay. The *Sunrise Inn* (☎ 5762419) on the 1st floor advertises rooms for HK$128 if you stay overnight, or HK$58 for two hours. Another cheapie is *Garden House* (☎ 5777391), 2nd floor, which has rooms for HK$160. The *Hoi Wan Guesthouse* (☎ 5777970), 1st floor, Flat C, has plush rooms starting at HK$250. The 1st floor also has the *Baguio Motel* (☎ 5761533) where very fancy rooms go for HK$400. The *Fulai Hotel* on the 5th floor also charges HK$400. There are numerous other guesthouses in Phoenix Apartments where you might be able to negotiate a cheaper rate for a longer term (or shorter term).

Nearby is *Emerald House* (☎ 5772368), 1st floor, 44 Leighton Rd, where clean doubles with private bath and round beds (no kidding) are HK$350. Enter the building from Leighton Lane just around the corner. Guesthouses are plentiful in this section of Leighton Rd, but some are pretty grotty.

Leishun Court at 116 Leighton Rd, Causeway Bay, is another cheap option. The building houses a number of low-priced guesthouses, mostly on the lower floors. *Fuji House* (☎ 5779406), 1st floor, is excellent at HK$250 for a room with private bath. On the same floor is the *Villa Lisboa Hotel* (☎ 5765421). On the 3rd floor is *Sam Yu Apartment*.

PLACES TO STAY – MIDDLE

Wanchai is now pretty tame and you're unlikely to accidentally find yourself checking into a brothel as did the lead character in Richard Mason's novel *The World of Suzie Wong*. The hotel mentioned in that novel, the *Nam Kok*, was in fact the *Luk Kwok*, a real hotel at 67 Gloucester Rd, Wanchai. The original *Luk Kwok* has long since been demolished, but there is now a modern highrise hotel by the same name.

For definition purposes, mid-range hotels are those where single or double rooms cost over HK$400 but no more than HK$800 for the cheapest rooms.

China Merchants, 160-161 Connaught Rd West, Sheung Wan, 285 rooms, doubles & twins HK$650 to HK$950, suites HK$1800 (☎ 5596888; fax 5590038)

Emerald, 152 Connaught Rd West, Sheung Wan, 316 rooms, singles HK$500, doubles & twins HK$600 to HK$800, suites HK$850 to HK$1200 (☎ 5468111; fax 5590255)

Harbour, 116-122 Gloucester Rd, Wanchai, 200 rooms, singles HK$500 to HK$800, doubles & twins HK$680 to HK$950, suites HK$1400 (☎ 5118211; fax 5072185)

Harbour View International, 4 Harbour Rd, Wanchai, 320 rooms, doubles & twins HK$620 to HK$850, suites HK$950 to HK$1050 (☎ 8021111; fax 8029063)

New Cathay, 17 Tung Lo Wan Rd, Causeway Bay, 223 rooms, singles HK$550 to HK$800, doubles & twins HK$690 to HK$850, suites HK$1300 to HK$1500 (☎ 5778211; fax 5769365)

New Harbour, 41-49 Hennessy Rd, Wanchai, 173 rooms, doubles & twins HK$680 to HK$1050, suites HK$1100 to HK$1400 (☎ 8611166; fax 8656111)

Newton, 218 Electric Rd, North Point (Fortress Hill MTR Station), 362 rooms, singles HK$700 to HK$1050, doubles & twins HK$750 to HK$1100, suites HK$1750 to HK$1800 (☎ 8072333; fax 8071221)

Wesley, 22 Hennessy Rd, Wanchai, 251 rooms, doubles & twins HK$650 to HK$950 (☎ 8666688; fax 8666633)

YWCA – Garden View International, 1 MacDonnell Rd, Central, 131 rooms, doubles & twins HK$480 to HK$580, suites HK$780 (☎ 8773737; fax 8456263)

PLACES TO STAY – TOP END

Hotels in this category have price tags that start from HK$800 and rise rapidly towards the moon. Obviously, all of these places have excellent facilities. Hotels in this category include:

Century Hong Kong, 238 Jaffe Rd, Wanchai, 506 rooms, twins HK$1150 to HK$1750, suites HK$2400 to HK$8500 (☎ 5988888; fax 5988866)

Charterhouse, 209-219 Wanchai Rd, Wanchai, 241 rooms, doubles & twins HK$1000 to HK$1200, suites HK$1500 to HK$2000 (☎ 8335566; fax 8335888)

China Harbour View, 189-193 Gloucester Rd, Wanchai, 316 rooms, doubles & twins HK$750 to HK$1350, (☎ 8382222; fax 8380136)

City Garden, 231 Electric Rd, North Point (Fortress Hill MTR Station), 615 rooms, singles HK$950 to HK$1300, doubles & twins HK$1050 to HK$1400, suites HK$2400 (☎ 8872888; fax 8871111)

Conrad, Pacific Place, 88 Queensway, Central (Admiralty MTR Station), 513 rooms, doubles & twins HK$1650 to HK$2600, suites HK$3500 to HK$16,000 (☎ 5213888; fax 5213888)

Evergreen Plaza, 33 Hennessy Rd, Wanchai, 332 rooms, doubles & twins HK$850 to HK$1150, suites HK$1500 to HK$3500 (☎ 8669111; fax 8613121)

Excelsior, 281 Gloucester Rd, Causeway Bay, 910 rooms, doubles & twins HK$1150 to HK$1970, suites HK$2500 to HK$6500 (☎ 8948888; fax 8956459)

Furama Kempinski, 1 Connaught Rd, Central, 517 rooms, doubles & twins HK$1680 to HK$2280, suites HK$2380 to HK$7380 (☎ 5255111; fax 8459339)

Grand Hyatt, 1 Harbour Rd, Wanchai, 573 rooms, doubles & twins HK$1800 to HK$2800, suites HK$4300 to HK$20,000 (☎ 5881234; fax 8020677)

Grand Plaza, 2 Kornhill Rd, Quarry Bay (Tai Koo MTR Station), 248 rooms, doubles & twins HK$860 to HK$1580, suites HK$1780 to HK$2600 (☎ 8860011; fax 8861738)

Hilton, 2 Queen's Rd, Central, 750 rooms, singles HK$1800 to HK$2300, twins HK$1950 to HK$2450, suites HK$3000 to HK$8000 (☎ 5233111; fax 8452590)

Island Shangri-La, Pacific Place, Supreme Court Rd, Central (Admiralty MTR Station), 565 rooms, doubles & twins HK$1800 to HK$2700, suites HK$4500 to HK$21,000 (☎ 8773838, 5218742)

JW Marriott, Pacific Place, 88 Queensway, Central (Admiralty MTR Station), 605 rooms, doubles & twins HK$1750 to HK$2350, suites HK$3000 to HK$13,500 (☎ 8108366; fax 8450737)

Lee Gardens, Hysan Rd, Causeway Bay, 660 rooms, doubles & twins HK$1100 to HK$2400, suites HK$2200 to HK$3300 (☎ 8953311; fax 5769775)

Luk Kwok, 72 Gloucester Rd, Wanchai, 198 rooms, singles HK$1000 to HK$1200, twins HK$1100 to HK$1300, suites HK$2300 (☎ 8662166; fax 8662622)

Mandarin Oriental, 5 Connaught Rd, Central, 542 rooms, doubles & twins HK$1750 to HK$2750, suites HK$3500 to HK$22,000 (☎ 5220111; fax 8106190)

New World Harbour View, 1 Harbour Rd, Wanchai, 862 rooms, singles HK$1480 to HK$2600, twins HK$1630 to HK$2600, suites HK$3300 to HK$9500 (☎ 8028888; fax 8028833)

Park Lane, 310 Gloucester Rd, Causeway Bay, 815 rooms, doubles & twins HK$1350 to HK$1950 (☎ 8903355; fax 5767853)

Richmond, 1A Wang Tak St, Happy Valley, 111 rooms, doubles & twins HK$1300 to HK$1600, suites HK$2800 to HK$3800

South Pacific, 23 Morrison Hill Rd, Wanchai, 293 rooms, singles HK$880 to HK$1200, doubles & twins HK$800 to HK$1550, suites HK$2400 to HK$3880 (☎ 5723838; fax 8937773)

Victoria, Shun Tak Centre, 200 Connaught Rd, Sheung Wan, 536 rooms, doubles & twins HK$1500 to HK$1800, suites HK$2500 to HK$8000 (☎ 5407228; fax 8583398)

Wharney, 57-33 Lockhart Rd, Wanchai, 335 rooms, doubles & twins HK$1050 to HK$1300, suites HK$2500 (☎ 8611000; fax 8656023)

PLACES TO EAT

Besides what is listed here, please refer to the Entertainment section in this chapter to find pub grub and other assorted late-night munchies. All the places to eat in Lan Kwai Fong are also listed in the Entertainment section.

Central

Breakfast To save time and money, there are food windows adjacent to the Star Ferry that open shortly after 6 am. It's standard commuter breakfasts consisting of bread, rolls and coffee with no place to sit except on the ferry itself. As you face the ferry entrance, off to the right is a *Maxim's* fast-food outlet, also with no seats.

If you'd prefer something better, *Jim's Eurodiner* (☎ 8686886), Paks Building, 5-11 Stanley St, does outstanding morning meals between 8 am and 10.30 am for around HK$20 to HK$30. From noon until 10 pm it's standard Western fare.

If you absolutely want to pig out, there is a breakfast buffet Mondays through Fridays from 8 am to 10 am at *Galley* (☎ 5263061), Basement, Jardine House, Connaught Rd (opposite the GPO).

Fast Food *Domino's Pizza* (☎ 8109729), 9 Glenealy, Central, has no restaurant facilities but delivers to any address within a two-km radius. Delivery is supposedly guaranteed within 30 minutes even in Hong Kong's horrendous traffic.

Famous fast-food chains have the following outlets in Central:

Café de Coral, 10 Stanley St; 18 Jubilee St; 88 Queen's Rd
Fairwood, Ananda Tower, 57-59 Connaught Rd
Hardee's, Grand Building, 15 Des Voeux Rd
Kentucky Fried Chicken, 6 D'Aguilar St; Pacific Place
Maxim's, Sun House, 90 Connaught Rd
McDonald's, Hang Cheong Building, 5 Queen's Rd; Basement, Yu To Sang Building, 37 Queen's Rd; Sanwa Building, 30-32 Connaught Rd; Shop 124, Level 1, The Mall, Pacific Place, 88 Queensway
Pizza Hut, B38, Basement 1, Edinburgh Tower, The Landmark, 17 Queen's Rd
Spaghetti House, Lower ground floor, 10 Stanley St

Chinese Dim sum is relatively cheap, but it's served for lunch only though a few restaurants have breakfast dim sum. In the evening, they roll out more expensive Cantonese fare such as pigeon, snake and shark's fin soup. You can easily find expensive Cantonese restaurants in big tourist hotels, but all of the following places are in the middle to lower price range:

Tai Woo, 15-19 Wellington St, Central; dim sum served from 10 am to 5 pm (☎ 5245618).
Luk Yu Tea House, 26 Stanley St, Central; dim sum served from 7 am to 6 pm (☎ 5235464).
Zen Chinese Cuisine, LG 1, The Mall, Pacific Place Phase I, 88 Queensway, Central; dim sum served from 11.30 am to 3 pm (☎ 8454555).

Indian Indian food is plentiful and popular, but like the Kowloon side there are some restaurants that maintain this idiotic 'members only' rule. One which does not is the ever-popular *Ashoka* (☎ 5249623), 57 Wyndham St.

Just next door to Ashoka in the basement at 57 Wyndham St is *Gunga Din's Club* (☎ 5231439). It's a fine place except that it's 'members only'. At the same address but

lower down into the basement is the excellent *Village Indian Restaurant* (☎ 5257410).

Greenlands (☎ 5226098), 64 Wellington St, is another superb Indian restaurant offering all-you-can-eat buffets for HK$68.

Club Sri Lanka (☎ 5266559) in the basement of 17 Hollywood Rd (almost at the Wyndham St end) has great Sri Lankan curries. Their fixed price all-you-can-eat deal is a wonderful bargain – HK$66 for lunch and HK$75 for dinner.

Japanese Eating Japanese cuisine can quickly lead to bankruptcy, so if you don't have deep pockets, eat elsewhere.

Equally excellent and expensive is *Ichizen* (☎ 5236031), Seibu Food Court, Level LG1, Pacific Place, 88 Queensway (near Admiralty MTR Station). Teppanyaki beef dinners go for HK$200 and an Asahi beer is HK$60.

Malaysian If you like Malaysian food, try the *Malaya* (☎ 5251675), 15B Wellington St, Central. It has Western food too, but it's considerably more expensive.

Vegetarian If you crave curry dishes of the Indian and Sri Lankan variety, check out the *Club Lanka II* (☎ 5451675) in the basement at 11 Lyndhurst Terrace, Central. The all-you-can-eat luncheon buffet costs HK$65 (all drinks free), and dinner is HK$70 (includes one drink).

Other If you've got cash to burn, one of the two revolving restaurants in Hong Kong is *La Ronda* on the roof of the Furama Kempinski Hotel, 1 Connaught Rd.

French Wine, cheese, the best French bread and bouillabaisse can be found at *Papillon* (☎ 5265965), 8-13 Wo On Lane. This narrow lane intersects with D'Aguilar St (around No 17) and runs parallel to Wellington St.

Kosher The *Shalom Grill* (☎ 8516300), 2nd floor, Fortune House, 61 Connaught Rd, serves up kosher and Moroccan cuisine. If you're in the mood for a Jerusalem *falafel* or a Casablanca *couscous*, this is the place.

HONG KONG

American *Dan Ryan's Chicago Grill*
(☎ 8454600), Unit 114, The Mall, Pacific
Place, 88 Queensway, is an international
chain with outstanding food. This place features a big screen video showing sports
shows, and it packs out during the American
World Series baseball games. Operating
hours are from 8.30 am until midnight and
it's not terribly cheap.

Other Western Food At the top end of the
price scale is *Jimmy's Kitchen* (☎ 5265293),
Ground floor, South China Building, 1
Wyndham St. Expect to pay up to HK$700
for steak dinners for two persons, though you
can rest assured that it's the best steak in
town. It opens at noon, and latest dinner
orders are at 11 pm.

Self-Catering A health-food store with great
bread and sandwiches is *Eden's Natural
Synergy* (☎ 5263062), 2nd floor, 226-227
Prince's Building, 10 Chater Rd, Central.

For imported delicacies, check out
Oliver's Super Sandwiches with three loca-
tions: Shop 104, Exchange Square II, 8
Connaught Place; Shop 233-236, Prince's
Building, 10 Chater Rd (at Ice House St);
Shop 8, Lower ground floor, The Mall,
Pacific Place, 88 Queensway.

The delicacies at *USA & Company*
includes everything from tortilla chips to
Cheese Whiz. One branch (☎ 8683083) is in
Ruttonjee House, 11 Duddell St and also
right across the street in Printing House, 18
Ice House St. Another branch (☎ 5286640)
is at Queensway Plaza, Tamar St, right next
to the Admiralty MTR Station.

The largest stock of imported foods is
found at the Seibu Department Store, Level
LG1, Pacific Place, 88 Queensway (near
Admiralty MTR Station). Besides the
imported cheeses, breads and chocolates,
tucked into one corner is the Pacific Wine
Cellar. This is *the* place to get wine, and there
are frequent sales on wine by the case. It's
open from 11 am until 8 pm.

Of special interest to chocolate addicts is
See's Candies with two stores in Central:
B66 Gloucester Tower, The Landmark, 11

Pedder St; and Shop 245, Pacific Place,
Phase II, Queensway (near Admiralty MTR
Station).

Sheung Wan

Chinese There are a few good places to try
for dim sum, including the following:

Diamond, 267-275 Des Voeux Rd, Sheung Wan; dim
  sum is served from 6.30 am to 5 pm and the
  restaurant closes at 11 pm (☎ 5444708).
Dragon Court Seafood, China Merchants Hotel, 160
  Connaught Rd West; dim sum hours are 10 am to
  2.30 pm and the restaurant closes at 11 pm
  (☎ 5496168).
Fortune Court, 1st floor, Emerald Hotel, 152 Connaught Rd West, Sheung Wan; dim sum hours
  are 11 am to 5 pm (☎ 5468111).

Wanchai

Fast Food Wanchai's contribution to fast-
food cuisine can be found at the following
location:

Café de Coral, 76 Johnston Rd; 13 Fleming Rd; 151
  Lockhart Rd
Domino's Pizza, Canal Rd East, is not a sit-down
  restaurant but delivers to any address within two
  km (☎ 8336803)
Ka Ka Lok, 10E Canal Rd West
Fairwood Fast Food, 165 Wanchai Rd
Oliver's Super Sandwiches, Shop A, Ground floor,
  Fleet House, 38 Gloucester Rd
McDonald's, CC Wu Building, 302-308 Hennessy
  Rd
Spaghetti House, 1st floor, 68 Hennessy Rd; Ground
  floor, Hay Wah Building, 85B Hennessy Rd; 1st
  floor, 290 Hennessy Rd

Chinese Restaurants doing Chinese cuisine
tend to be expensive in Wanchai. A few dim
sum places charging reasonable prices
include:

Broadway Seafood, Hay Wah Building, 73-85B
  Hennessy Rd, Wanchai; dim sum is served from
  11 am to 5 pm, other food and delectables to 11
  pm (☎ 5299233).
Dat Yat Chuen, 25-28 Hennessy Rd (corner of Luard);
  open for breakfast.
Pepper Garden, 6th & 7th floors, Hong Kong Arts
  Centre, 2 Harbour Rd, Wanchai; dim sum available from 11 am to 2 pm, other food from 5.30
  until 11 pm (☎ 8020006).

Filipino The best Filipino food on Hong Kong Island is from *Cinta* (☎ 5299752), 41 Hennessy Rd. There is also a newer branch, *Cinta-J* (☎ 5294183), Malaysia Building, 50 Gloucester Rd. Unfortunately, both are very expensive – around HK$300.

Indian *Jo Jo Mess Club* (☎ 5273776) 86 Johnston Rd, has great Indian food, including vegetarian dishes. There are also numerous vegetarian places nearby.

Ashoka (☎ 8918981) is on the ground floor, Shop 1, Connaught Commercial Building, 185 Wanchai Rd, Wanchai. Prices are reasonable for big luncheon and dinner buffets. Also reasonably priced is the *Maharaja* (☎ 5749838), 222 Wanchai Rd.

Vietnamese A very nice Vietnamese restaurant is *Saigon Beach* (☎ 5297823), at 66 Lockhart Rd, Wanchai.

Italian You can try the pleasantly relaxed *Rigoletto's* (☎ 5277144) at 16 Fenwick St in Wanchai. Pizza and lasagna is tantalising at *La Bella Donna* (☎ 5279907), 1st floor, Shui On Centre, 6-8 Harbour Rd, Wanchai.

Greek *Bacchus* (☎ 5299032), Hop Hing Centre, 8-12 Hennessy Rd, has the best Greek food in Wanchai.

American *USA Deli & Restaurant* (☎ 8653278), Hop Hing Centre, 8-12 Hennessy, boasts a massive menu. There is a lot of veggie food here, but the meat sandwiches are exquisite.

Aussie & British While the cuisines of Oz and the UK have not taken the world by storm, Hong Kong has a dedicated following of expat fish & chips lovers. *Brett's Seafood* (☎ 8666608), 72-86B Lockhart Rd, is the Aussie fast-food hangout that gets rave reviews.

Most of the Brits congregate at *Harry Ramsden's* (☎ 8329626), Wu Chung House, Queen's Rd East (near Spring Garden Lane) in Wanchai. A very full meal in this place will set you back around HK$70.

Other There are two revolving restaurants in Hong Kong, and one is *Revolving 66* which is atop the concrete cylinder known as Hopewell Centre, Queen's Rd East. The restaurant is reached by an outside lift which gives you a dizzying view as you contemplate how much this adventure is going to cost you.

Causeway Bay

Fast Food The line-up of popular fast-food chains is as follows:

Café de Coral, Basement, Matsuzakaya Department Store, 6 Paterson St; 50 Leighton Rd; 483 Jaffe Rd; 19 Jardine's Bazaar
Fairwood Fast Food, 9 Cannon St
Jack in the Box, 53 Paterson St, Causeway Bay
Kentucky Fried Chicken, 40 Yee Wo St
McDonald's, 46 Yee Wo St; Basement 2, Mitsukoshi Department Store, 500 Hennessy Rd
Oliver's Super Sandwiches, Shop G, 1st floor, Windsor House, 311 Gloucester Rd, Causeway Bay
Pizza Hut, 482 Hennessy Rd, upstairs above Dahsing Bank with entrance on Percival St
Spaghetti House, 5 Sharp St East; Shop 50-54, PJ Plaza, Paterson St; 1st floor, 483 Jaffe Rd
Wendy's, 42 Yee Wo St

Chinese Some places that do dim sum and other Chinese delights include:

Andy's Kitchen, 25 Tunglowan Rd, Causeway Bay; specialising in Shanghainese food (☎ 8908137).
Dim Sum Burger, Ground floor, Miami Mansion, 13-15 Cleveland St; Shanghainese dim sum served from 7.30 am to 6pm (☎ 5777199).
Maxim's Chinese, 1st & 2nd floors, Hong Kong Mansion, 1 Yee Wo St, Causeway Bay; dim sum served from 8 am to 5 pm (☎ 8949933).

Indonesian Most popular is the *Indonesia Padang Restaurant* (☎ 5761828), 85 Percival St, Causeway Bay. There is also the *Indonesian Restaurant* (☎ 5779981) at 28 Leighton Rd, Causeway Bay.

Japanese Causeway Bay caters to a large number of Japanese tourists and is perhaps the best area in Hong Kong to look for this type of food. Japanese food is never cheap, but you can save a bit by looking in the basements of Japanese department stores.

HONG KONG

Daimaru Household Square on Kingston St and Gloucester Rd has take-away Japanese food but no place to sit.

Tomokazu (☎ 8912989) is on the ground floor, 17-19 Percival St. Less than a block away is another branch (☎ 8336339) at Shop B, Lockhart House, 441 Lockhart Rd. For Japanese food, consider it a bargain. The set lunches for two persons cost HK$200 and the amount of food is more than most people can finish.

Sui Sha Ya (☎ 8381808), 1st floor, Lockhart House, 440 Jaffe Rd, Causeway Bay, is good and somewhat cheaper than hotel restaurants.

Korean *Koreana* (☎ 5775145), Vienna Mansion, 55 Paterson St, is one of Causeway Bay's two prime spots for Korean cuisine. The other is *Myong Dong Chong* (☎ 8363877), 1st floor, 500 Jaffe Rd.

Thai The *Chilli Club* (☎ 5272872), 88 Lockhart Rd, does outstanding Thai food. There is another branch (☎ 5202318) at Hennessy Rd. *Baan Thai* (☎ 8319155) is on the 4th floor at Causeway Bay Plaza I, 489 Hennessy Rd.

Burmese Hong Kong has only one place to sample Burmese food, *Rangoon Restaurant* (☎ 8921182), Ground floor, 265 Gloucester Rd, Causeway Bay.

Vietnamese Also excellent is the reasonably priced *Yin Ping* (☎ 8329038), 24 Cannon St, Causeway Bay.

Vegetarian If you want a non-meat option, one of the best-known vegetarian restaurants in town is the *Wishful Cottage* (☎ 5735645), Ground floor, 336 Lockhart Rd, Causeway Bay. They serve delicious vegetarian dim sum at lunchtime.

Vegi Food Kitchen (☎ 8906660), Ground floor, Highland Mansions, 8 Cleveland St, Causeway Bay, has a sign warning you not to bring meat or alcohol onto the premises. If you're carrying meatloaf and bottle of Johnny Walker in your backpack, you'd better check it at the door.

One of Hong Kong's biggest Chinese vegetarian restaurants is the somewhat pricey *Bodhi* (☎ 5732155), Ground floor, 388 Lockhart Rd, Causeway Bay. There is another branch (☎ 8905565) at 60 Leighton Rd, Causeway Bay. A competitor is *Vegi Good Kitchen* (☎ 8906660) which does vegetarian dim sum from 11 am to 5 pm, and regular meals until midnight.

French *Barcelona* (☎ 5778076) doesn't sound very French, but the *bouillabaisse* definitely is. It's at Prospect Mansion, Ground floor, 68 Paterson St, Causeway Bay.

American *Division Eighteen* (☎ 8822844), Shop D, Ground floor, Eton Tower, 8 Hysan Ave, is notable for healthy American food (check out the salmon steak and veggies). A set lunch costs HK$68. A big screen video helps draw in the crowds.

Happy Valley
Chinese *Dim Sum* (☎ 8348893), 63 Sing Woo Rd, boasts incredible decor and good food. Only open from Monday to Friday, 11 am to 11 pm.

Golden Era (☎ 5749922), Basement, Richmond Hotel, 1A Wang Tak St, does its dim sum from 11 am to 3 pm and becomes a regular Cantonese restaurant from 6 to 11 pm.

Korean You'll have no trouble remembering the name which is simply *Korean Restaurant* (☎ 5736662), 1st floor, 8 King Kwong St. Prices are mid-range.

Malaysian Malaysian restaurant have a reputation for good food at cheap prices, and *Motor Restaurant* (☎ 5749537), 19 Wong Nai Chung Rd, is no exception. The menu is enormous and it's open from 9 am until midnight.

Vegetarian Perhaps someone will suggest I get my head examined, but one of the biggest bargains in Hong Kong is the vegetarian cafeteria on the 6th floor of the *Adventist*

Hospital at 40 Stubbs Rd. Opening hours are short: breakfast 6 am to 7.30 am, lunch noon to 1.30 pm and dinner 5 pm to 6.30 pm.

Italian *Numero Uno* (☎ 8388118), 1 Village Rd, thoroughly deserves its name. The pizzas are especially recommended.

North Point
Chinese Some places doing dim sum include:

Fortune Court, City Garden Hotel, 231 Electric Rd, North Point; dim sum hours are 11 am to 3 pm (☎ 8872888).
Fung Shing, 62-68 Java Rd, North Point; dim sum hours are 11.30 am to 2.30 pm (☎ 5784898).

Thai Buried inside the Garden City housing estate is *Thai Food* (☎ 8071962), Ground floor, Shop 26, Block 8-9, City Garden Plaza, Electric Rd.

Vegetarian *Vegetarian House* (☎ 5786696), 102 Hing Fat St, is at the north end of Victoria Park. Most dishes cost less than HK$40. This place is near the Tin Hau MTR Station.

Mexican *Casa Mexicana* (☎ 5665560) is probably the real reason to trek out to this neighbourhood. It's considered Hong Kong's finest Mexican restaurant, but it's pricey. Don't eat anything all morning so you can pig out for HK$170 during the Sunday buffet. The restaurant is in Units 1-4, 20-30 & 32-48, Ground floor, Victoria Centre, 15 Watson Rd, North Point. Take the MTR to the Fortress Hill Station.

Quarry Bay
Fast Food *Pizza Hut* and *McDonald's* are to be found inside Taikoo Shing's Cityplaza Shopping Centre.

Chinese The line-up of dim sum and other Chinese restaurants includes:

Cityplaza Palace Restaurant Unit 310 Cityplaza, Taikoo Shing; dim sum is served from 7 am to 4.30 pm (☎ 5670330).

Cityplaza Harbour Restaurant (more upmarket than the preceding), Unit 255, Cityplaza, Taikoo Shing; dim sum is served from 11 am to 3.30 pm (☎ 8844188).

Stanley
Il Mercato (☎ 8139090) is an Italian restaurant near the Stanley post office at 126 Stanley Main St. Also excellent but somewhat upmarket is *Stanley's Oriental Restaurant* (☎ 8139988), 90B Stanley Main St. Definitely upmarket is *Stanley's French Restaurant* (☎ 8138873), 86 Stanley Main St. Ditto for *Tables 88* (☎ 8136262), 88 Stanley Village Rd, which serves Western food in what was once the old Stanley police station.

Repulse Bay
While there aren't any affordable restaurants of special interest in Repulse Bay, travellers are often pleased to find two of Hong Kong's best delicatessens. *Oliver's* (☎ 8127739) and *USA & Company* (☎ 8121958) are adjacent to each other in the Dairy Farm Shopping Centre, which is right on the beach at 35 Beach Rd.

Aberdeen
Dim Sum Try the *Blue Ocean* (☎ 5559415), 9th floor, Aberdeen Marina Tower, 8 Shum Wan Rd. Dim sum hours are from noon to 5.30 pm and the restaurant closes at 11.30 pm.

Floating Restaurants There are three floating restaurants moored in Aberdeen Harbour, all specialising in seafood. Dinner in such a place will cost about HK$150 and up depending on what you order. My own opinion is that the food is average, prices are high – you're paying for the atmosphere.

Top of the line is the *Jumbo Floating Restaurant* (☎ 5539111), which also serves relatively cheap dim sum from 7.30 am to 5 pm. The adjacent *Floating Palace Restaurant* (☎ 5540513) also does dim sum but is more expensive. Nearby is the *Tai Pak Floating Restaurant* (☎ 5525953) which has no dim sum but plenty of seafood. Another alternative is to take an evening kaido from Aberdeen to Sok Kwu Wan on Lamma Island (see Outlying Islands chapter) where seafood is somewhat cheaper.

ENTERTAINMENT
Central
Cinema There are only a couple of cinemas in Central geared towards English-language films. One is *Queen's* (☎ 5227036), Luk Hoi Tung Building (rear entrance), 31 Queen's Rd. The other is *UA Queensway* (☎ 8690372) which is the plushest cinema in Hong Kong. It also has the best sound system. It's at Pacific Place One, Central, near the Admiralty MTR Station.

Lan Kwai Fong Running off of D'Aguilar St is a narrow L-shaped alley closed to cars. This is Lan Kwai Fong, and along with neighbouring streets and alleys is Hong Kong's No 1 eating, drinking, dancing and partying venue. The crowd here is very mixed – refugees from Chungking Mansions looking for a cheap meal and cheap beer; businessmen in suits walking hand-in-hand with Filipino bar girls; fashionably-dressed Western women in slit gowns and high heels; backpackers in sandals and T-shirts; African traders, Russian sailors and Chinese yuppies (invariably called 'chuppies').

There is no place quite like it in the world – beer costs HK$25 or HK$100 depending on where you go; buy a dinner of Vietnamese spring rolls for HK$15 or spend HK$500 for a New York steak; disco music thumps in the

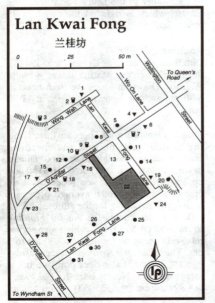

Lan Kwai Fong
兰桂坊

1	Bon Appetit
2	Club 64
3	Le Jardin Club
4	Kiyotaki
5	Acropolis
6	Top Dog
7	D'Aguilar 26 Bar
8	Beirut
9	Schnurrbart
10	Bit Point Bar
11	Flower Stalls
12	Japanese Dining Bar
13	California Entertainment Building - Cafe de Paris, Cafe Flipp, California, Tony Roma's
14	Oscar's
15	Hardy's Folk Club
16	McDonald's
17	Al's Diner
18	Yelt's Inn
19	Midnight Express
20	Public Toilets
21	Graffiti
22	California Entertainment Building - American Pie, Hanagushi, Il Mercato, Jazz Club, Koh-I-Noor
23	Supatra's Thai Restaurant
24	Yorohachi Japanese Restaurant
25	Mecca 97
26	Berlin Disco-Karaoke
27	Post 97
28	Yakitori Japanese Restaurant
29	HK Baguette Pizza
30	Cactus Club
31	F-Stop

background everywhere; the streets are packed with people and everybody is there to see and be seen. Just how Lan Kwai Fong ever got started is a mystery. Equally uncertain is how it will end – high rents have already driven out many fine pubs and everybody's eyes are focused on 1997.

Lan Kwai Fong almost did come to a sudden end on New Years' Eve, 31 December 1992. The street was so thoroughly mobbed with drunken revelers that 21 people were trampled to death and many others were injured. Since then, the authorities have instituted 'crowd control' – the number of customers permitted inside a business establishment is supposedly limited, sidewalk cafes have theoretically been banned (some continue to resist), the authorities are getting very tough with liquor licences and so on. Some places were judged unsafe and closed, and business is definitely down compared to what it used to be. Nevertheless, the reports of Lan Kwai Fong's demise are greatly exaggerated.

Pubs, Bars & Discos One place which continues to play a cat and mouse game with the authorities is *Club 64* (☎ 5232801), 12-14 Wing Wah Lane, D'Aguilar St. The bureaucrats' complaint is also the pub's greatest asset – it's one of the few places in Hong Kong where you can sit outside while eating, drinking and chatting. For the backpacker set, this is *the* place to be in Lan Kwai Fong. On warm summer evenings practically the entire alley is filled with foreigners on a drinking spree.

As you face the entrance of Club 64, off to your left are some stairs (outside the building, not inside). Follow the stairs up to a terrace to find *Le Jardin Club* (☎ 5262717), 10 Wing Wah Lane. This is an excellent place to drink, relax and socialise, but it's certainly more upmarket than Club 64.

Facing Club 64 again, look to your right to find *Bon Appetit* (☎ 5253553), a Vietnamese restaurant serving up cheap but scrumptious meals.

Top Dog (☎ 8689195, 8689196), 1 Lan Kwai Fong, produces every kind of hot dog imaginable. Opening hours are late and the management's policy is to stay open 'until nobody is left in the street'.

As the name implies, late-night hours are kept at *Midnight Express* (☎ 5255010, 5234041), 3 Lan Kwai Fong. This place has a combination menu of Greek, Indian and Italian food, with deliveries available from Monday to Saturday. The kebabs are outstanding and cost around HK$35 to HK$45. Opening hours are 11.30 am to 3 am the next day, except on Sundays when it opens at 6 pm.

While *glasnost* is already becoming yesterday's buzzword, you can still find it at *Yelt's Inn* (☎ 5247796), 42 D'Aguilar St. This place boasts Russian vodka, a bubbly party atmosphere and extremely loud music.

If it's fine Lebanese food, beer and rock music you crave, what better place to find it than in *Beirut* (☎ 8046611)? It's at 27 D'Aguilar St.

If you prefer Europe to the Middle East, visit *Berlin* (☎ 8778233), 19 Lan Kwai Fong. This place features loud disco music with members of the audience invited to sing along – think of it as disco karaoke. The food here is also good.

Post 97 (☎ 8109333), 9 Lan Kwai Fong, is a very comfortable eating and drinking spot. During the daytime it's more of a coffee shop, and you can sit for hours to take advantage of the excellent rack of Western magazines and newspapers. It can pack out at night, and the lights are dimmed to discourage reading at that time, but it's a fine place to take a date.

Next door in the same building and under the same management is *1997* (☎ 8109333), known for really fine Mediterranean food. Prices are mid-range.

Graffiti (☎ 5212202), 17 Lan Kwai Fong, is a very posh and trendy restaurant and bar, but high drink prices don't seem to have hurt business.

It's raging revelry at *Acropolis* (☎ 8773668), situated in the Corner II Tower, Ground floor, 21 D'Aguilar St. Shoulder-to-shoulder crowds, loud music and reasonably cheap drinks contribute to the party atmosphere.

The California Entertainment Building is on the corner of Lan Kwai Fong and D'Aguilar St. There are numerous places to eat here at varying price levels, but it tends to be upmarket. Note that the building has two blocks with four separate entrances. The entrance adjacent to McDonald's is 34-36 D'Aguilar St while the one at the corner of Lan Kwai Fong is Nos 30-32. This creates some confusion, so if you don't find a place mentioned in this book be sure to check out the other block.

Top-flight food at high prices can be found at *Koh-I-Noor* (☎ 8779706), an Indian restaurant. *Il Mercato* (☎ 8683068), steals the show for Italian food. It's in the California Entertainment Building. Prices are mid-range. The *California* (☎ 5211345), California Entertainment Building, is perhaps the most expensive bar mentioned in this book. Open from noon to 1 am, it's a restaurant by day, but there's disco dancing and a cover charge Wednesday through Sunday nights from 5 pm onwards. A friend of mine from California was once refused admission because he 'was dressed like a Californian'.

The American Pie (☎ 5213381) is *the* locale for desserts in Hong Kong. Not only pies, but all sorts of killer desserts like cakes, tarts, puddings and everything else containing sinful amounts of sugar, not to mention superb coffee and tea. If you're on a diet, don't even go near the place. Despite it's very upmarket appearance, prices are reasonable. This shop is on the 4th floor of the California Entertainment Building.

The *Jazz Club* (☎ 8458477), 2nd floor, California Entertainment Building, has a great atmosphere. Bands playing blues and reggae are a feature here, as well as friendly management and customers. Beer is reasonable at HK$40 a pint, but a cover charge is tacked on for special performances, sometimes up to HK$250 (half-price for members).

DD II (☎ 5235863) is short for 'disco disco'. This trendy place is in the California Entertainment Building. It's open from 9.30 pm until 3.30 am.

The *Cactus Club* (☎ 5256732), 13 Lan Kwai Fong, does passable Mexican food. It seems like more of a pub than a restaurant, with top-grade beer and tequila imported from Mexico. Their Mescal, brewed from the peyote cactus, is pretty strong stuff – tastes like it still has the needles in it.

Supatra's (☎ 5225073), 50 D'Aguilar St, is Lan Kwai Fong's top venue for Thai food.

Al's Diner (☎ 5218714), 39 D'Aguilar St, Lan Kwai Fong, is a Hong Kong institution. The place looks like it was lifted lock, stock, burgers and French fries from a New York diner of the 1930s. Other delectables on the menu include eggs with hash brown potatoes, chilli and toast, but none of this comes cheaply.

A Japanese restaurant popular with Westerners is *Yorohachi* (☎ 5241251), 5-6 Lan Kwai Fong. Not far away *Kiyotaki* (☎ 8771772), 19 D'Aguilar St, which does a mean teppanyaki. In the fancy California Entertainment Building is *Hanagushi* (☎ 5210868).

Schnurrbart (☎ 5234700) in the Winner Building on D'Aguilar St, Lan Kwai Fong, is a Bavarian-style pub. There are a couple of other German pubs on either side.

Oscar's (☎ 8046561), 2 Lan Kwai Fong, is a very posh cafe and bar combination. Specialties include pizza, pasta and sandwiches on pita bread. Food is available from noon until 11 pm and the place stays open until 2 am. Bring lots of money.

Food by Phone (☎ 8686969) brings home the bacon if you live in Central or Mid-Levels. There is no service charge – you pay the same price you get it for in the restaurant. The catch is that they only deliver food from the most expensive restaurants in Lan Kwai Fong. This delivery service operates daily, but hours are short – 6.30 to 10.30 pm.

Other Central Pubs & Grub The *Fringe Club* (☎ 5217251), 2 Lower Albert Rd, is an excellent pub known for cheap beer and an avant-garde atmosphere. Live music is provided nightly by various local folk and rock musicians.

The *Mad Dogs Pub* (☎ 5252383), 33 Wyndham St, Central, is just off the trendy Lan Kwai Fong. It's a big two-floor Australian-style pub serving pub grub and drinks.

LA Cafe (☎ 5266863), Ground floor, Shop 2, Lippo Centre, 89 Queensway (near Admiralty MTR Station) has a large loyal following of late-night revelers. The mostly-Mexican luncheons are not to be discounted either – great guacamole, burritos and other Tex-Mex delights, but it isn't cheap.

La Bodega (☎ 8775472), 31 Wyndham St, is an unusual place. It's a comfortable bar with a Mediterranean flavour. Although moderately-expensive, drinks are half-price on Friday until somebody goes to the toilet! A Spanish-style band (with Filipino musicians) provide the entertainment.

The *Bull & Bear* (☎ 5257436), Ground floor, Hutchison House, 10 Harcourt Rd, Central, is a British-style pub and gets pretty lively in the evenings. It opens from 8 to 10.30 am, and again from 11 am to midnight.

Portico (☎ 5238893), Lower ground floor, Citibank Plaza, 3 Garden Rd, has fine live music every Saturday night from around 10 pm.

Just above Lan Kwai Fong where Lower Albert Rd joins Wyndham St you will find the *African* (☎ 8689299), on 7 Glenealy St. This cafe and wine bar is open from noon until midnight.

Wanchai

Cinema For real movie fanatics, some cultural organisations show films occasionally. *Alliance Française* (French Institute) (☎ 5277825; fax 8653478) at 123 Hennessy Rd, is one place to try. Also contact the *Goethe Institute* (German Cultural Centre) (☎ 8020088; fax 8024363), 14th floor, Hong Kong Arts Centre, 2 Harbour Rd.

Wanchai has three other cinemas specialising in English-language features, as follows:

Cine-Art, Sun Hung Kai Centre, 30 Harbour Rd (☎ 8384820)
Columbia Classics, Great Eagle Centre, 23 Harbour Rd (☎ 5738291)
Imperial, 29 Burrows St (☎ 5737374)

Pubs, Bars & Discos The name 'Wanchai' has so long been associated with The World of Suzie Wong, sailors, bar girls and brothels that the neighbourhood has an unseemly reputation. The image of sleazy bars crowded

with drunken sailors and nearly-naked Filipino and Thai women dancing on the tables is part of the Wanchai legend, but this form of entertainment has declined sharply. Just what will happen to the naughty shows and pick-up joints after 1997 remains to be seen, but Wanchai has already evolved into a very upmarket neighbourhood with fashionable pubs, deluxe restaurants, five-star hotels, raging discos, quiet folk-music lounges and trendy coffee shops. Of course, prices have also moved upmarket as well – there are few bargains around. However, if there is a place in Hong Kong that can give Lan Kwai Fong formidable competition in the nightlife arena, Wanchai is it. Most of the action concentrates around the intersection of Luard and Jaffe Rds.

Joe Bananas (☎ 5291811), 23 Luard Rd, Wanchai, has become a trendy disco nightspot and has no admission charge, but you may have to queue to get in. Happy hour is from 11 am until 9 pm (except Sundays) and the place stays open until around 5 am.

Neptune Disco (☎ 5283808), basement of Hong Kong Computer Centre, 54-62 Lockhard Rd, is pure disco and heavy metal from 4 pm until 5 am. To say this place is popular is an understatement. To survive the night, spend the previous week doing aerobic exercises, bring your dancing shoes and earplugs.

To accommodate the spillover crowds, there is now *Neptune Disco II* (☎ 8652238), 98-108 Jaffe Rd. This place has live bands and a weekend cover charge of HK$70.

West World (☎ 8241066), also known as *The Manhattan*, is known for its fine late-night dancing music. Admission is free except on Fridays and Saturdays when it costs HK$140 (one drink included). It's on the 4th floor of the New World Harbour View Hotel – ask at the front desk where to find the lift.

JJ's (☎ 5881234 ext 7323), Grand Hyatt Hotel, 1 Harbour Rd, Wanchai, is known for its rhythm & blues bands. There is a cover charge after 9 pm.

The Big Apple Pub & Disco (☎ 5293461), 20 Luard Rd, is thumping disco. There is a weekend cover charge of HK$60 for men, HK$40 for women. From Monday to Friday it operates from noon until 5 am, and on weekends and holidays it's open from 2 pm until 6 am.

Old Hat (☎ 8612300), 1st floor, 20 Luard Rd, keeps some of the latest hours around – it's open 24 hours on Friday and Saturday nights, so you can stay up all evening and have breakfast there. There are daily set lunches Monday to Friday from noon until 2.30 pm, happy hours, crazy hours, satellite TV and take-away burgers, French fries, pizza and satay.

Crossroads (☎ 5272347), 42 Lockhart Rd, Wanchai, is a loud disco that attracts a young crowd. Dancing is from 9 pm to 4 am. There is a cover charge, but one drink is included.

At 54 Jaffe Rd just west of Fenwick Rd is the *Wanchai Folk Club* (☎ 5590058), better known as *The Wanch*. It stands in sharp contrast to the more usual Wanchai scene of hard rock and disco. This is a very pleasant little folk-music pub with beer and wine at low prices, but it can pack out.

If you've got an ID card or other proof that you are a member of the journalistic community, you should drop into the *Hong Kong Press Club* (☎ 5112626), 3rd floor, 175 Lockhart Rd, Wanchai. Besides the good food and congenial company, it's one of the few places in Hong Kong where you can play pool.

Causeway Bay
Compared to the raging atmosphere of Lan Kwai Fong and Wanchai, Causeway Bay is relatively tame at night. However, it's an up and coming neighbourhood – expect big changes here in the near future.

Cinema The line-up of English-language cinemas in Causeway Bay include the following:

Isis, 7 Moreton Terrace (☎ 5773496)
Jade, Paterson & Great George Sts (☎ 5771011)
New York, 475 Lockhart Rd (☎ 8387380)
Palace, 280 Gloucester Rd (☎ 8951500)

Pearl, Paterson St between Kingston & Great George Sts (☎ 5776352)
President, 517 Jaffe Rd (☎ 8331937)
Windsor, Windsor House, Gloucester Rd & Great George St (☎ 8822621)

Pubs, Bars & Cafes One place to enjoy a rendezvous in subdued settings is the very pleasant *Martino Coffee Shop* (☎ 5767666), Ground floor, 66 Paterson St. This place can boast the fanciest namecards I've seen in Hong Kong, shaped like a coffee pot.

The atmosphere is a little more raucous at *Hot Shot* (☎ 8057001), 1st floor, 2-4 Kingston St.

A reliable expat hangout in this neighbourhood is *China Jump* (☎ 8329007), Causeway Bay Plaza, on the corner of Percival St and Lockhart Rd. It's basically a bar and restaurant that's great for a late-night rendezvous, but tends towards the expensive side.

North Point
While this neighbourhood is a bit out of the way, it's just starting to be explored by gwailos. The English-language cinemas in the neighbourhood include:

Park, 180 Tunglowan Rd (☎ 5704646)
State, 291 King's Rd (☎ 5706241)
Sunbeam, 423 King's Rd (☎ 5632959)

Stanley
There are a number of gwailo pubs that get raging around late afternoon and continue until after midnight. A large share of this market belongs to *The Smugglers' Inn* (☎ 8138852), 90-A Main St.

Lord Stanley's Bar & Bistro (☎ 8131876), 92A Main St, offers a similar atmosphere of loud music and good food. The same management owns the adjacent *Beaches* (☎ 8137313) at No 92B.

Repulse Bay
Sun Of A Beach (☎ 8031765) is also known as the *Water Front Bar & Disco*, though the former name is certainly more memorable. It's right near the surf at 26 Beach Rd, a few

doors west of McDonald's and Kentucky Fried Chicken.

Deep Water Bay

The drinking and food scene is supplied by a single restaurant right on the beach called *Sampan East* (☎ 8121618). It's open from noon until 10.30 pm.

THINGS TO BUY

Central is the big tourist shopping district on Hong Kong Island, closely followed by Wanchai and Causeway Bay, but prices are slightly lower in the non-touristy neighbourhoods. The most glitzy tourist shopping mall in Hong Kong is at Pacific Place, 88 Queensway, by the Admiralty MTR Station, which is also the venue of the Seibu Department Store. You might do better to go out to Cityplaza, a big shopping mall in Quarry Bay at the Tai Koo MTR Station.

Chinese Emporiums

Chinese Arts & Crafts is owned by the PRC and offers a wide selection. The locations are as follows:

Shell House
    24-28 Queen's Rd, Central (☎ 5223621)
Ground & 1st floors
    Lower Block, China Resources Building, 26 Harbour Rd, Wanchai (☎ 8276667)
Unit 230
    The Mall, Pacific Place, 88 Queensway, Central (☎ 5233933)
Ground floor
    Prince's Building, 3 Des Voeux Rd, Central (☎ 8450092)

China Products gives a 15% discount to foreign-passport holders. This is not to say that their goods are really cheap, but any discount is better than none. There are two branches: Lok Sing Centre, 31 Yee Wo St, Causeway Bay; and 488-500 Hennessy Rd, Causeway Bay.

Department Stores

These are not very cheap, so if you're looking for bargains, look elsewhere. Hong Kong's original Western-style department store is Lane Crawford which has branches as follows: Lane Crawford House, 70 Queen's Rd, Central; The Mall, One Pacific Place, 88 Queensway, Central; Windsor House, 311 Gloucester Rd, Causeway Bay; Times Square, Matheson and Russel Sts, Causeway Bay.

Hong Kong Chinese department stores in the Central district include Wing On with branches at 26 and 211 Des Voeux Rd; Sincere at 173 Des Voeux Rd; and Dragon Seed, 39 Queen's Rd.

Japanese department stores are heavily concentrated in Causeway Bay. The main branch of Daimaru is on the corner of Paterson and Great George Sts. Personally, I find the smaller Daimaru Household Square (Kingston & Gloucester Rds) to be more interesting – amongst other things it houses the Asahiya Japanese Bookstore. Matsuzakaya is at 6 Paterson St and Sogo is at 545 Hennessy Rd. Another good one is Mitsukoshi at 500 Hennessy Rd.

Cameras & Photoprocessing

Stanley St in Central is one of the best spots in Hong Kong for buying photographic equipment – there are seven camera shops in a row and competition is keen. Everything carries price tags, though some low-level bargaining might be possible.

Photo Scientific (☎ 5221903), 6 Stanley St, is the favourite of Hong Kong's resident professional photographers. You might find equipment elsewhere for less, but Photo Scientific has a rock-solid reputation – labelled prices, no bargaining, no arguing and no cheating.

Almost next door is Color Six (☎ 5260123), 18A Stanley St, which has the best photoprocessing in town. Colour slides can be professionally processed in just three hours. Many special types of film are on sale here which can be bought nowhere else in Hong Kong, and all the film is kept refrigerated.

Stanley St also has about six other camera shops in close proximity and competition is keen. Most are reputable, but if you don't find labelled prices on all the equipment then it's a shop to avoid.

Union Photo Supplies (☎ 5266281), 13 Queen Victoria St (next to Central Market) is excellent for colour slide processing. However, I have found camera prices to be higher here than on Stanley St so do some comparisons before buying anything expensive.

Computers

Most people buy computers on the Kowloon side where there is more variety and lower prices. Nevertheless, Hong Kong Island does have one reasonable computer arcade called Computer 88, Windsor House (also known as 'In Square'), 311 Gloucester Rd, Causeway Bay.

CDs & Tapes

Tower Records (☎ 5060811), 7th floor, Shop 701, Times Square, Matheson St, Causeway Bay, offers the widest selection of recorded music in Hong Kong.

KPS is another place to go for discounted CDs and music tapes. It's also a good place to buy (legal) computer software. You can ring up the main office KPS (☎ 3981234) to find the store location. In Central, there is one in the Prince's Building, 9-25 Chater Rd. There is another in the Far East Finance Centre, Central, which is just next to the Admiralty MTR Station.

Clothing

In Central the clothing alleys run between Queen's and Des Voeux Rds. One alley sells only buttons and zips. Li Yuen St sells costume jewellery, belts, scarves and shoes. Another street is devoted almost exclusively to handbags and luggage, and yet another to sweaters, tights, underwear and denims. However, high rents are starting to push out these shops and the cloth vendors have already moved to the Western Market in Sheung Wan.

Johnston Rd in Wanchai is perhaps the best place on Hong Kong Island to search for cheap clothes. If you like the relatively low-priced stuff at Giordano's, you can find branches at 541 Lockhart Rd and 22 Paterson St, both in Causeway Bay.

You can spend cash quickly in upmarket boutiques. One well-known place is Vogue Alley in Causeway Bay. Within a one-block area there are over 30 shops plugging the latest fashions. The area was once known as Food St, but the restaurants are gradually being pushed out by the pricey boutiques. Vogue Alley is at the intersection of Paterson and Kingston Sts.

Marks & Spencer also caters to the trendy with travellers' cheques. Branches can be found at Shops 120 & 229, The Mall, Pacific Place Two, Central; Ground floor to 2nd floor, Excelsior Plaza, East Point Rd, Causeway Bay; Basement, The Landmark, Pedder St, Central; and shops 100 & 217, Cityplaza I, Quarry Bay.

For silk clothing, you might do better in the shopping malls. However, one specialty place to try is The Silkwear House (☎ 8772373), Shop 207, Pedder Building, 12 Pedder St, Central. There is another branch (☎ 5769228) at Shop 29E, Paterson Plaza, Paterson St, Causeway Bay.

Another special interest clothing shop is Festival & Party Accessories (☎ 5292956), Shop 73, 1st floor, Admiralty Centre Tower II, 18 Harcourt Rd, Central.

Jewellery

King Fook and Tse Sui Luen are two chain stores which guarantee to buy back any jewellery they sell to you at fair market value. Branches are located as follows:

King Fook
King Fook Building, 30-32 Des Voeux Rd, Central (☎ 5235111)
Shop 216-217, The Mall, Pacific Place, 88 Queensway, Central (☎ 8486766)
Ground floor, Hong Kong Mansion, 1 Yee Wo St, Causeway Bay (☎ 5761032)
Ground floor, 458-568 Hennessy Rd, Wanchai (☎ 8920068)

Tse Sui Luen
Ground floor, Commercial House, 35 Queen's Rd, Central (☎ 5240094)
Factory outlet, Ground floor, Wah Ming Building, 34 Wong Chuk Hang Rd, Aberdeen (☎ 8782618)

Shop B, Ground floor, Kin Tak Fung Commercial Building, 467-473 Hennessy Rd, Causeway Bay (☎ 8386737)

Ground floor, Hong Chiang Building, 141-143 Johnston Rd, Wanchai (☎ 8932981)

Shop G10 & A7, Tai On Building, 57-87 Shau Kei Wan Rd, Shaukeiwan (☎ 5697760)

Pharmaceuticals

Watson's is all over the place, but a slightly more economical chainstore is Mannings. There is one in Shop B, 22-23, 1st Basement, The Landmark, 12-16A Des Voeux Rd, Central; and Shop J1-J8, Queensway Plaza, Queensway, Central.

Toys

Toys R Us is the big American-owned chain with a shop on the 3rd floor, Windsor House, on the corner of Great George St and Gloucester Rd, Causeway Bay. Another large toy store on Hong Kong Island is Wise Kids (☎ 8680133), Shop 134, Phase II, Pacific Place, 88 Queensway, Central.

Sporting Goods

The largest selection of sporting goods shops is found in Mongkok on the Kowloon side. Nevertheless, Hong Kong Island chips in with the following:

Bike Boutique (bicycles)
    Ground floor, 3 Wood Rd, Wanchai (☎ 8360547)
Bunn's Diving Equipment
    Ground floor, Shop E & G, Kwong Sang Hong Building, 188 Wanchai Rd, Wanchai (☎ 5721629)
Mountain Services International (mountaineering equipment)
    Shop 106, Vicwood Plaza, 199 Des Voeux Rd, Central
Po Kee Fishing Tackle Co
    6 Hillier St, Central (☎ 5437541)

Auctions

Serious antique buyers should check out the auction houses. Three good ones are: Christie's Swire (☎ 5215396), Room 2806, 28th floor, Alexandra House, 16-20 Chater Rd, Central; Lammert Brothers (☎ 5223208), 9th floor, Malahon Centre, 10 Stanley St, Central; Sotheby's Hong Kong Ltd (☎ 5248121), Room 502, Tower Two, Exchange Square, Central.

The New Territories 新界

The New Territories is Hong Kong's bedroom. About one-third of Hong Kong's population lives in the New Territories, mostly in appropriately named new towns which have been constructed since 1972.

Everything north of Boundary St on the Kowloon Peninsula up to the China border is the New Territories. This land was leased from China in 1898 for 99 years. The lease covers all of the Outlying Islands except tiny Stonecutters Island off the west coast of Kowloon, which is now no longer an island due to land reclamation.

Excluding the Outlying Islands, the New Territories make up 70% of Hong Kong's total land area. With the expiration of the lease in 1997, China could have legally taken all this back, plus the Outlying Islands. Instead, they're getting back all of Hong Kong.

Since its inception, the New Towns Programme has consumed more than half of the government's budget, with a lot of that money spent on land reclamation, sewage, roads and other infrastructure projects. About 60% of the new housing units have been built by the government.

The population of the New Territories has mushroomed from less than half a million in 1970 to the present two million, and is expected to reach 3.5 million by the year 2000.

The biggest impediment to growth in the New Territories used to be the lack of good transportation. This changed dramatically in 1982 with the opening of the MTR Tsuen Wan Line.

In the same year, the KCR underwent a major expansion when the system was electrified and double-tracked.

The LRT system opened in 1988 and hoverferries now connect Tuen Mun to Central, reducing commuting time to just 30 minutes.

However, fewer people in the New Territories need to commute to Kowloon and Hong Kong Island because many industries are moving into the New Territories to take advantage of the cheaper land.

Only a small percentage of visitors to Hong Kong take the time to visit the New Territories. This is a shame since it has a character very different from the bustling commercial districts of Kowloon and Hong Kong Island. The New Territories is large – larger than Hong Kong Island, Kowloon and Lantau Island combined. You can see a lot of the New Territories in one day, but not all of it. Still, any effort you make to see this part of Hong Kong will be very rewarding.

The area in the very northern part of the New Territories, within one km of the China border, is a closed area which is fenced and

198

New Territories farmer

well-marked with signs. Sometimes the fence has large holes in it, usually created by would-be immigrants from China. Holes or not, don't be tempted to walk inside the closed area just to have a look, even briefly. You probably won't see any police around, but the area is well-staked out with the latest in high-technology motion detectors. There is a heavy fine for entering this forbidden zone.

If you don't want to hassle with public transport, take a tour to the New Territories. The HKTA can book you on the 'Land Between Tour' which takes six hours and costs HK$295. You can do it yourself by public transport for about HK$50.

The Getting Around chapter at the start of this book has a map and a table of bus routes which includes the New Territories – you'd do well to study it before venturing out. The HKTA has a useful information sheet with a map of New Territories' bus routes.

Do yourself a favour and pick up the map called *Countryside Series Sheet No 2: New Territories – West*, which covers most of the important places you're likely to want to see in the New Territories.

If you plan to visit the Sai Kung Peninsula, Map No 4 *Sai Kung & Clearwater Bay* is helpful. Few foreigners visit Plover Cove Reservoir, but if you'd like to see it, Map No 5 *North-East New Territories* covers this area. Each of these maps is available from the Government Publications Office next to the GPO in Central.

TSUEN WAN 荃灣
The easiest place to reach in the New Territories, Tsuen Wan is an industrial and residential area just to the north-west of Kowloon. Simply take the MTR to the Tsuen Wan Station, the last stop on the line. There is also a hoverferry from Government Pier in Central to Tsuen Wan.

Tsuen Wan is a major government-backed development scheme with a population of 900,000, half of whom are employed in Tsuen Wan itself.

Yuen Yuen Institute & Western Monastery 圓玄學院
The main attraction in Tsuen Wan is the Yuen Yuen Institute, a Taoist temple complex, and the adjacent Buddhist Western Monastery.

The monastery is very quiet, but the Yuen Yuen Institute is extremely active during festivals.

I was fortunate to visit during the ghost month when people were praying and burning ghost money, and when cymbals were crashing and worshippers were chanting.

This place also sells filling vegetarian meals at the monastery's cafeteria. To reach the monastery and temple complex, take Minibus No 81 from Shiu Wo St which is two blocks south of the MTR station. Alternatively, take a taxi, which is not expensive. The monastery is about 1.5 km to the north-east of the MTR station. It would be possible to walk except that there seems to be no way for a pedestrian to get across Cheung Pei Shan Rd, which is basically a super highway.

Chuk Lam Sim Yuen 竹林禪院
This temple complex in the hills north of

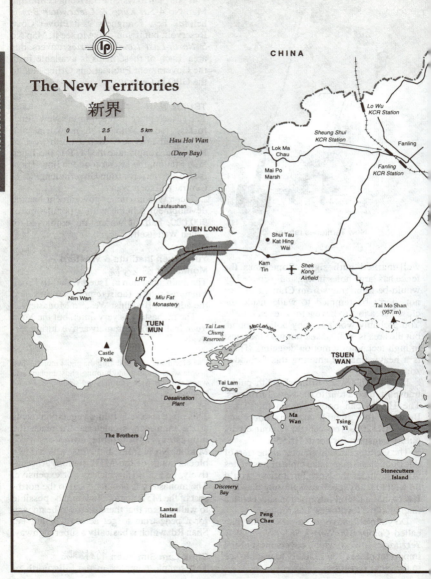

The New Territories

新界

CHINA

Hau Hoi Wan
(Deep Bay)

Lo Wu
KCR Station

Sheung Shui
KCR Station

Fanling

Fanling
KCR Station

Lok Ma
Chau

Mai Po
Marsh

Laufaushan

YUEN LONG

Shui Tau
Kat Hing
Wai

Kam
Tin

Shek
Kong
Airfield

LRT

Miu Fat
Monastery

Nim Wan

Tai Mo Shan
(957 m)

TUEN
MUN

Tai Lam
Chung
Reservoir

MacLehose Trail

TSUEN
WAN

Castle
Peak

Tai Lam
Chung

Desalination
Plant

Ma
Wan

Tsing
Yi

The Brothers

Stonecutters
Island

Discovery
Bay

Lantau
Island

Peng
Chau

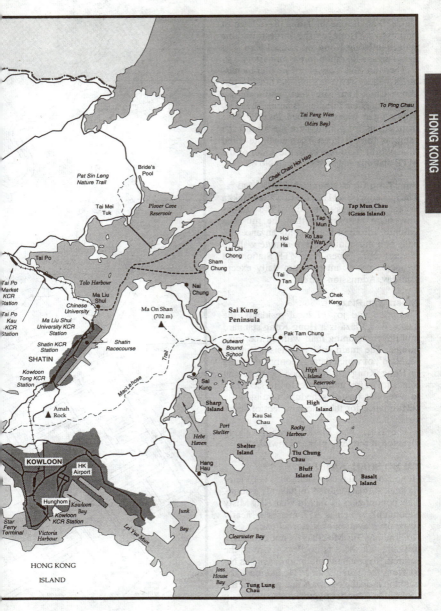

Tsuen Wan is one of Hong Kong's most impressive. Three of the largest Buddha statues in Hong Kong are housed here. The name means 'bamboo forest monastery'.

There are also a couple of smaller monasteries nearby. Two are on the hillside just above Chuk Lam Sim Yuen, and a third – Tung Lam Nien Temple – is across the road. This temple was established in 1927. The instructions for getting here are almost the same as for the Yuen Yuen Institute. Find Shiu Wo St (two blocks to the south of the MTR station) and take maxicab No 85.

Sam Tung Uk Museum 三棟屋博物館
The museum (☎ 4112001) is a walled Hakka village which was founded in 1786 and has now been restored. Within the museum grounds are eight houses plus an ancestral hall. The museum is a five-minute walk to the east of the Tsuen Wan MTR Station and is open from 9 am to 4 pm daily except Tuesday. Admission is free.

Tsuen Wan Plaza 荃灣廣場
The pride and joy of local residents, the Tsuen Wan Plaza is a Hong Kong standard multilevel shopping mall with all the trimmings. The main lobby boasts a 'music fountain', of which there are only two others in Hong Kong (at Whampoa Gardens and Shatin). The fountain comes to life according to a regular posted schedule, putting on a performance for the entertainment of shoppers.

The Tsuen Wan Plaza is within walking distance of the ferry pier and town hall.

TAI MO SHAN 大帽山
Hong Kong's highest mountain is not Victoria Peak as many tourists mistakenly assume. That honour goes to Tai Mo Shan (Big Misty Mountain), which at 957 metres is nearly twice the elevation of Victoria Peak.

Climbing Tai Mo Shan is not extremely difficult, but there is no Peak Tram to the summit. To reach the mountain, take bus No 51 from the Tsuen Wan MTR Station – the bus stop is on the overpass that goes over the roof of the station, or you can also pick it up

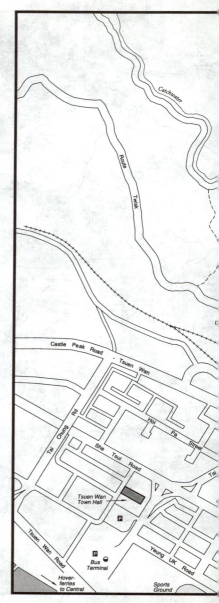

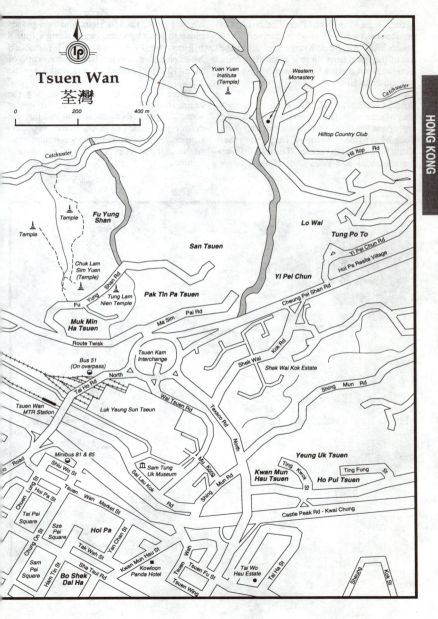

Tsuen Wan
荃灣

0   200   400 m

Catchwater

Yuen Yuen Institute (Temple)

Western Monastery

Catchwater

Hilltop Country Club

Hilltop Rd

Temple

Fu Yung Shan

Lo Wai

Tung Po To

Temple

San Tsuen

Yi Pei Chun Rd

Hoi Pa Resite Village

Chuk Lam Sim Yuen (Temple)

Shan Rd

Yi Pei Chun

Fu Yung

Tung Lam Nien Temple

Pak Tin Pa Tsuen

Cheung Pei Shan Rd

Muk Min Ha Tsuen

Ma Sim Pai Rd

Kok Rd

Route Twisk

Shek Wai

Shek Wai Kok Estate

Bus 51 (On overpass)

Tsuen Kam Interchange

Shing Mun Rd

North

Tai Ho Rd

Wai Tsuen Rd

Texaco Rd

Tsuen Wan MTR Station

Luk Yeung Sun Tsuen

Minibus 81 & 85

Mu Kong

North

Yeung Uk Tsuen

Shiu Wo St

Sam Tung Uk Museum

Ting Kwok St

Ting Fung St

Chuen Lung St

Hoi Pa St

Sai Lau Kok

Shing Mun Rd

Kwan Mun Hau Tsuen

Ho Pui Tsuen

Road

Tsuen Wan Market St

Tai Pei Square

Sze Pei Square

Rd

Castle Peak Rd - Kwai Chung

Chung On St

Hoi Pa

Tak Wah St

Yan Chau St

Sam Pei Square

Ham Tin St

Sha Tsui Rd

Kwan Mun Hau St

Tsuen Fu St

Tai Wo Hau Estate

Tai Ha St

Bo Shek Dai Ha

Kowloon Panda Hotel

Tsuen Wing

Sheung

Kok St

at the Tsuen Wan Ferry Pier. The bus heads up Route Twisk (Twisk is derived from Tsuen Wan Into Shek Kong). Get off at the top of the pass, from there it's uphill on foot. You walk on a road but it's unlikely you'll encounter traffic.

MACLEHOSE TRAIL 麥理浩徑

The MacLehose Trail is about 100 km long and spans the New Territories, running from Tuen Mun in the west to Pak Tam Chung (Sai Kung Peninsula) in the east. The trail follows the ridgetops and goes over Hong Kong's highest peak, Tai Mo Shan, and also passes close to Ma On Shan, Hong Kong's fourth highest peak. It was named for Lord MacLehose, a former British governor of Hong Kong whose hobby was walking in the hills.

There are breathtaking views along the entire route. If you want to hike anywhere along this trail, it's essential that you buy the countryside series of maps on the New Territories. Map No 2 covers the western portion of the trail and Map No 4 covers the eastern section.

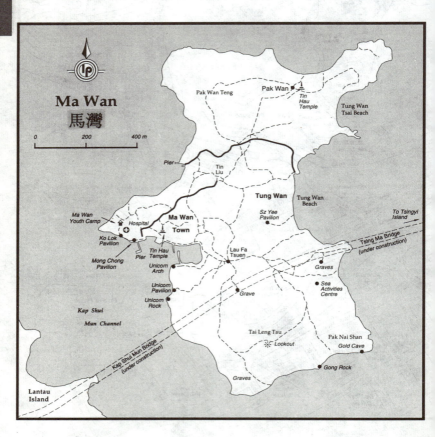

The easiest access is from Tsuen Wan. Take bus No 51 to the top of Route Twisk. From here you have the choice of heading off to the east (towards Tai Mo Shan) or west along the MacLehose Trail to Tai Lam Country Park, the Tai Lam Reservoir and eventually all the way to Tuen Mun, the western terminus of the trail. From Tuen Mun, you can catch a bus to Kowloon or a hoverferry to Central.

MA WAN 馬灣

Ma Wan is a flat and forested island off the north-eastern tip of the much larger Lantau Island. It was once famous as the Gate to Kowloon, where foreign ships would collect before entering Chinese waters.

The island was once a charming place to visit but these days it's hardly worth bothering. The two beaches where swimming is possible – Tung Wan and Tung Wan Tsai – have become polluted. However, swimming is still allowed and a lifeguard is present. The view on the eastern side of Ma Wan has been hopelessly marred by the construction of oil storage tanks on nearby Tsingyi Island.

The view on the western side of the island, looking towards Lantau, is OK but it's no place for swimming. This is the notorious Kap Shui Mun (rapid water gate) where dangerous currents have been known to push back unmotorised junks. Legend has it that a treasure junk, belonging to the pirate Cheung Po Tsai, sank in this channel as it had become impossible to recover in the deadly current. About the only thing you can do is sit on the pier and watch the hoverferries rush by on their way to Tuen Mun (New Territories) and China.

The Chinese like to come to Ma Wan on weekends to eat seafood. There are several seafood restaurants on the islands and prices are reasonable. During weekdays, the restaurant owners have little to do and pass the time playing mahjong.

The island is going to be strongly affected by the new airport development project, assuming that the airport ever gets completed. The Lantau Fixed Crossing (a bridge) will connect Ma Wan to both Lantau and the New Territories. Having already been colonised by the British, the island is destined to be 'Kowloonised' by the bridge.

Adding injury to insult, Ma Wan has many unleashed dogs who have a special antipathy to peculiar-looking foreigners. Keep in mind the advice of former American president Theodore Roosevelt: 'Speak softly and carry a big stick.'

Getting There & Away
If you really want to visit Ma Wan, the only boat is a kaido from the Ma Wan Pier (Ma Wan Matou) just to the north of the island in the New Territories. Any bus running between Tsuen Wan and Tuen Mun can let you off there. This includes bus Nos 52X, 60M, 60X, 68M and 68X. Ask the bus driver where to get off. The kaido runs every hour. It's entirely possible that the kaidos will be cancelled once the new bridge is completed.

TUEN MUN 屯門
This is the main new town in the north-west of the New Territories. There are no slums here, just endless rows of high-rise housing estates. Nevertheless, there are interesting things to see.

If you have the slightest interest in shopping, be sure to visit the Tuen Mun Town Plaza, easily reached by taking the LRT line to the Town Centre Station. This gigantic shopping mall is Hong Kong's largest. It's dominated by the Yaohan Department Store, a Japanese-owned chain.

The Ching Chung Koon (Green Pine) Temple is just to the north of Tuen Mun. It's a huge Taoist temple which is very active during festivals. From Tuen Mun, you can easily get to the temple by taking the LRT to the Ching Chung Station.

Bus Nos 60M and 68M start from Tsuen Wan and follow the coast from Tsuen Wan to Tuen Mun. Or you can take bus Nos 60X or 68X, both of which start from Jordan Rd Ferry Pier in Kowloon. Sit upstairs on the left side for spectacular views. En route you pass another Hong Kong high-tech wonder, the world's largest seawater desalination plant at Lok An Pai.

HONG KONG

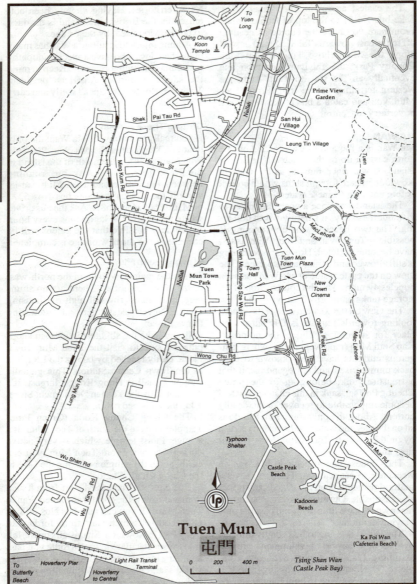

To Yuen Long

Ching Chung
Koon Temple

Prime View
Garden

Shek Pai Tau Rd

San Hui
Village

Leung Tin Village

Ho Tin St

Ming Kum Rd

Pui To Rd

Tuen Mun Trail

MacLehose Trail

Catchwater

Nullah

Tuen Mun Town
Park

Tuen Mun Heung Sze Wui Rd

Town
Hall

Tuen Mun
Town Plaza

New
Town
Cinema

MacLehose Trail

Nullah

Castle Peak Rd

Wong Chu Rd

Tuen Mun Rd

Lung Mun Rd

Typhoon
Shelter

Castle Peak
Beach

Wu Shan Rd

Kadoorie
Beach

Wu King Rd

Ka Foi Wan
(Cafeteria Beach)

Tuen Mun
屯門

0   200   400 m

Tsing Shan Wan
(Castle Peak Bay)

To
Butterfly
Beach

Hoverferry Pier

Light Rail Transit
Terminal

Hoverferry
to Central

The fastest and most enjoyable way to get to Tuen Mun is by hoverferry. These depart from the Central Harbour Services Pier in Central, Hong Kong Island. The ride takes 30 minutes and lets you off at the LRT Terminal.

MIU FAT MONASTERY 妙法寺
Head a few km to the north from Tuen Mun to Lam Tei to find the Miu Fat Buddhist Monastery. The top floor has three large golden statues of Buddha plus thousands of little images clinging to the walls. Often there are monks inside the temple chanting. Try not to disturb them by taking photographs with a flash.

The temple is easily reached by taking the LRT to Lam Tei. The monastery is on Castle Peak Rd, between Tuen Mun and Yuen Long, a five-minute walk along Castle Peak Rd from the Lam Tei LRT Station.

YUEN LONG 元朗
There isn't anything special here, but it's the last stop on the LRT line so you have to get off. It's not a bad place to eat lunch. Other than that, there isn't any reason to linger.

LAUFAUSHAN 流浮山
If you're interested in oyster beds and oyster restaurants, Laufaushan is the place to go. Most of the shellfish are turned into oyster sauce, a basic ingredient in Chinese cooking. A large portion of the oysters are also dried and exported. Take the LRT to Yuen Long and get off at Ping Shan Station. From the station, it's a return trip to Laufaushan on bus No 655.

Just how long Laufaushan retains its rural charm remains to be seen. Right next to Laufaushan is the oyster-raising community of Tin Shui Wai, the site of a soon-to-be-built town with 35-storey housing estates. Enjoy the oysters while you can.

MAI PO MARSH 米埔
If you're a bird-watching aficionado, the 300-hectare Mai Po Marsh in the north-west part of the New Territories is one of the few places in Hong Kong where you can see your feathered friends (besides on the dinner plate at the Temple St night market). The majority of the birds are migratory, which means the marsh is at its best in the spring and autumn. Winter is also not too bad, but the birds are fewest during summer. Over 250 species have been identified.

The good news is that this is a protected area. The bad news is that you must have an authorised guide to be allowed in. There is nothing wrong with that, except it means you must go with a group and pay HK$50 per person (transport *not* included) and you can only go when there are sufficient numbers to make the tour economically feasible. Individual tours may be possible for a much higher fee, so inquire if interested. The place to contact for bookings is World Wide Fund for Nature (☎ 5264473), 1 Tramway Path, Central (adjacent to the Peak Tram entrance). This is also a good place to pick up the *Birds of Hong Kong* guide and other useful publications.

Visitors are advised to bring their own binoculars, cameras, walking shoes or boots, and not to wear bright clothing.

KAM TIN 錦田
The small town of Kam Tin contains two walled villages – Kat Hing Wai and Shui Tau. Most tourists go to Kat Hing Wai. Shui Tau is larger and less touristy, but don't expect to find ancient China here either.

Other walled villages in the colony have mostly vanished under the jackhammers of development. The walled villages are one of the last reminders that Hong Kongers were once faced with marauding pirates, bandits and soldiers. Of course, they might be again in 1997.

Kam Tin was, and still is, the home of the Tang clan who have lived there for centuries. They were high-ranking public servants in the imperial court of China in the 19th century.

Kat Hing Wai 吉慶圍
Just off the main road is this tiny 500-year-old village, walled sometime during the Ming Dynasty (1368 AD-1644). It's really

one small street with a maze of dark alley-ways leading off it. The high street is packed with souvenir sellers. Just to remind you that this is indeed Hong Kong, you are expected to give a 'donation' of HK$5 when you enter the village. Put the money into the coin slot by the entrance.

You can take photographs of the Hakka women in their black traditional dress, but first agree on a fee. Most of them are anxious to model as long as you pay. Agree on a price beforehand – between HK$5 and HK$10 is usually sufficient.

Shui Tau 水頭

This place might not even exist by the time you read this as there are rumours that it will be 'renovated' with more high-rise housing estates. To reach Shui Tau get off the bus on the outskirts of Kam Tin and walk down the road leading north. The 17th-century village is famous for its carved roofs, ship-prow shaped with stone fish and dragons. Tiny traditional-style Chinese houses huddle inside Shui Tau's walls.

The ancestral hall in the middle of the village is used as a school in the mornings but was originally built for the clan to worship its forebears.

Their ancestors' names are listed on the altar in the inner hall and on the long boards down the side. The stone fishes on the roof of the entrance hall represent husband and wife and are there for good luck. Soldiers painted on the doors guard the entrance.

The Tin Hau temple on the outskirts of the town was built in 1722. Its enormous bell weighs 106 kg.

Getting There & Away

To reach Kam Tin, take bus No 64K which runs from Yuen Long to Tai Po, passing Kam Tin along the way. Another option is bus No 77K between Yuen Long and Sheung Shui. Bus 54 also goes from Yuen Long to Kam Tim. You can reach Kam Tin from Tsuen Wan by taking bus No 51 over scenic Route Twisk.

SHEK KONG AIRFIELD 石崗跑道

No, this isn't an insider's tip on how to fly to Hong Kong while bypassing the crowds at Kai Tak Airport. This small airfield has been used for military training, but it's also the venue for aerial sports such as parachuting and flying private helicopters. Obviously, these are not activities for backpackers trying to stretch the budget. Information about parachuting can be found in the Activities section in the Facts for the Visitor chapter. To rent a helicopter, see the Getting Around chapter.

SHEUNG SHUI 上水

This is where you can get on the KCR. From Yuen Long or Kam Tin, take bus No 77K. Buy a ticket and take the train just one station south to Fanling. A stored value ticket or tourist ticket from the MTR can be used on the KCR.

FANLING 粉嶺

The main attraction in this town is the **Fung Ying Sin Kwun Temple**, a Taoist temple for the dead. The ashes of the departed are deposited here in what might be described as miniature tombs with a photograph on each one. It's an interesting place to look around, but be respectful of worshippers.

Easy to find, the temple is across from the Fanling KCR Station.

TAI PO 大埔

Another of the residential and industrial new towns, Tai Po is home to many of Hong Kong's high-tech industries. There isn't much which is special about the town, but one worthwhile activity is to hire a bicycle and ride to Plover Cove Reservoir and/or the Chinese University in Ma Liu Shui. Although there is an inland route, follow the coastal route along Tolo Harbour for the best views.

Bicycle rentals are easy to find around the Tai Po Market KCR Station. Definitely do this trip on a weekday, as on weekends and holidays thousands of Chinese descend on the place with the same idea. At these times,

Top: Repulse Bay, Hong Hong Island (RS)
Left: Repulse Bay, Hong Kong Island (RS)
Right: Tung Wan, Cheung Chau, Outlying Islands (RS)

Top: Typhoon Shelter, Cheung Chau, Outlying Islands (RS)
Left: Typhoon Shelter, Cheung Chau, Outlying Islands (RS)
Right: Festival at Cheung Chau, Outlying Islands (RS)

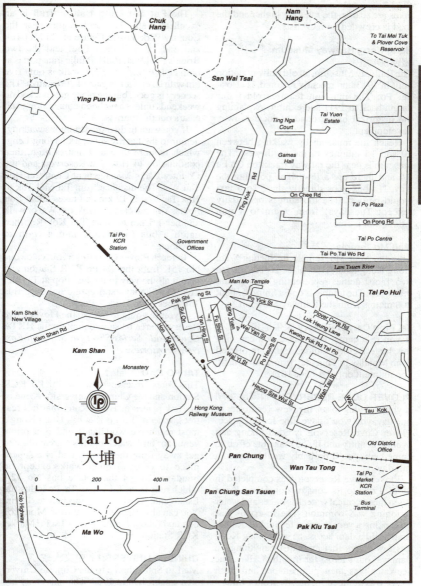

Tai Po
大埔

0   200   400 m

bikes are scarce, the rates are higher and the road is crowded with cyclists.

Hong Kong Railway Museum
鐵路博物館

The Railway Museum, an old railway station built in 1913 and recently restored, is also at Tai Po. The museum features old trains dating back to 1911 and exhibits explaining the historical background of local railway development.

Reach the museum by walking between 10 and 15 minutes to the north-west. The museum is near the railway tracks on On Fu Rd and there are a few signs pointing the way. No bus goes directly there so a taxi would be best. The museum is open daily (except Tuesdays) from 9 am to 4 pm. Admission is free.

Man Mo Temple 文武廟

Like the Man Mo Temple in Sheung Wan, Hong Kong Island, this place is dedicated to two Taoist deities representing the pen and the sword. The temple is on Fu Shin St, about 200 metres from the Railway Museum.

Tai Ping Carpet Factory 太平地毯

If you're a carpet enthusiast, you can visit this large factory. Guided tours are offered from Monday to Thursday from 2 to 4 pm by appointment only (☎ 6565161).

PLOVER COVE RESERVOIR 船灣淡水湖

If you're trying to see the New Territories in one day, you won't have time for this place. Plover Cove Reservoir is good hiking and cycling country and if you make the effort to come here, you'll probably want to spend a full day.

Plover Cove Reservoir was completed in 1968. Prior to its construction Hong Kong often faced critical water shortages and water rationing was common. The reservoir was built using a very unusual technique. Rather than build a dam across a river (Hong Kong has few rivers that amount to anything), a dam was built across the mouth of a bay. The seawater was then pumped out and fresh water was pumped in, mostly from China.

The **Pat Sin Leng Nature Trail** is an excellent walk. The trail begins near the Country Park Visitor Centre at Tai Mei Tuk and ends near Bride's Pool and the two Bride's Pool Waterfalls. Public transport is at both ends of the trail. The walk is only five km with an elevation gain of 300 metres. The scenery is good, but the place gets packed on weekends unless a typhoon comes along and clears out the tourists.

If you want to do more strenuous walking, detour to the nearby summit of Wong Leng, which is more than 600 metres high, then continue on to Hok Tau Reservoir and the Country Parks Management Centre at Hok Tau Wai. The distance from Tai Mei Tuk to Hok Tau Wai is 12 km and takes about four hours. You can camp at Hok Tau Wai or walk another 1.5 km to Shau Tau Kok Rd, then catch a bus to Fanling and a train to Kowloon.

To reach Plover Cove Reservoir, catch bus No 75K from the Tai Po KCR Station and take it all the way to the last stop at Tai Mei Tuk. On Sundays and public holidays Bus 75R goes on to Bride's Pool.

If you're going to hike in the Plover Cove Reservoir area be sure to pick up the HKTA *Countryside Series Sheet No 5: North-East New Territories*.

TAI PO KAU 大埔滘

This forest reserve between Tai Po KCR Station and the Chinese University is one of the few places in Hong Kong that has real trees. Indeed, Tai Po Kau has Hong Kong's most extensive woodlands and is a prime venue for bird-watching. It's a great place to get away from the crowds and is a superb place to enjoy a quiet walk, except on Sundays. To get there, take bus No 72A which runs from Tai Wai to Tai Po Industrial Estate and get off at the stop before Shatin. You can also take bus No 72 from Mongkok or a taxi (about HK$20) from Tai Po Market KCR Station.

CHINESE UNIVERSITY 中文大學

Ma Liu Shu is home to the Chinese University, established in 1963. The university has a beautiful campus and is certainly worth a visit.

Inside the campus, the Institute of Chinese Studies has an interesting Art Gallery (☎ 6952218) which houses local collections as well as those from museums in China. There's an enormous exhibit of paintings and calligraphy by Guangdong artists from the Ming period to modern times, as well as a collection of 2000-year-old bronze seals and a large collection of jade flower carvings.

The gallery is open weekdays and Saturday from 10 am to 4.30 pm, and on Sundays and public holidays from 12.30 to 4.30 pm (closed on some public holidays). Admission is free.

You can easily reach the Chinese University by taking the KCR to the University Station. A free bus outside the station runs through the campus to the top of the hill. It's easiest to take the bus uphill and then walk back down to the station. Near the top of the hill is a student cafeteria – a good, cheap place for lunch.

SHATIN 沙田
In a long, narrow valley, Shatin is a new town built mostly on reclaimed land that was a big mudflat just a few years ago. Unlike some of the other new towns, Shatin is both a desirable place to live and an attractive town for tourists to visit.

Shatin is easy to get to by taking the KCR to the Shatin Station.

Ten Thousand Buddha Monastery 萬佛寺
There are in fact 12,800 miniature Buddha statues inside the monastery's main temple. Built in the 1950s, it sits on a hillside about 500 metres to the west of the Shatin New Town Plaza. You can get there only by walking because transport can't negotiate the 400-odd steps up to the temple. The trail starts from the Shatin KCR Station – just ask anyone to point the way. The temple complex is open from 8 am to 6.30 pm.

From the main monastery area, walk up more steps to find a smaller temple housing a gold-plated monk who died in 1965 at the age of 87. He was the founder of the monas-tery. His body was encased in gold leaf and is now on display behind a glass case. It is considered polite to put a donation in the box next to the display case to help pay for the temple's upkeep.

Che Kung Miu 車公廟
This is a small, active Taoist temple about 1.5 km to the south-west of the Shatin KCR Station. It's dedicated to Che Kung, a Sung dynasty general. The temple is interesting, but not nearly so impressive as some of the larger Taoist temples (Wong Tai Sin in Kowloon, for example) so don't be afraid to give it a miss. However, it is very popular with the Chinese, especially on holidays.

As you enter the temple grounds, be prepared to be mugged by little old ladies who excitedly stuff red pieces of paper with Chinese characters into your hands and then demand money for them. With the help of a Chinese friend, I was able to discern that the papers are a type of blessing. The old women will insist that 'the more money you give, the more blessing you will receive'. Unfortunately, they prove to be insatiable, as 'the more you give, the more they want'. The best bet is to keep your hands in your pockets and run past them quickly, as they won't follow you inside the temple.

From the Tai Wai KCR Station, you can walk to the temple. Bus 80K from the Shatin KCR Station stops near Che Kung Miu. A taxi ride from the station would also be inexpensive.

Shatin Racecourse 沙田馬場
Shatin is the site of Hong Kong's second racecourse, opened in 1980 after seven years in the making at a cost of HK$500 million. It was financed by the introduction of night racing at Hong Kong Island's Happy Valley racecourse.

In the centre of the racetrack is the interesting eight-hectare Penfold Park, open to the public most days except on race days, Mondays and the day following public holidays. It can pack out on weekends, an indication of just how desperate Hong

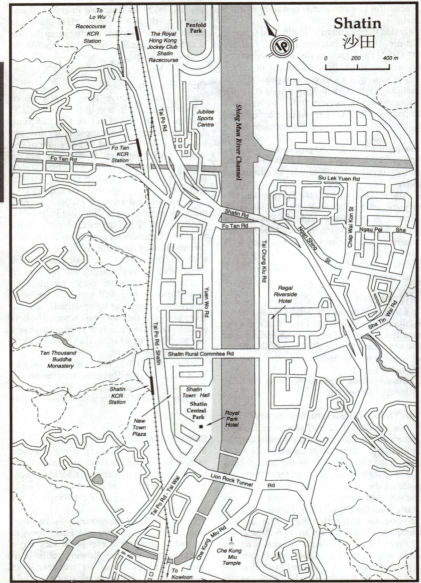

Shatin
沙田

To
Lo Wu

Racecourse
KCR
Station

The Royal
Hong Kong
Jockey Club
Shatin
Racecourse

Penfold
Park

0   200   400 m

Shing Mun River Channel

Jubilee
Sports
Centre

Tai Po Rd

Fo Tan Rd

Fo Tan
KCR
Station

Shatin Rd

Fo Tan Rd

Siu Lek Yuen Rd

Nam Shing St

Chap Wai Kon St

Ngau Pei   Sha

Sha Tin Wai Rd

Tai Chung Kiu Rd

Regal
Riverside
Hotel

Yuen Wo Rd

Shatin Rural Commitee Rd

Ten Thousand
Buddha
Monastery

Tai Po Rd · Shatin

Shatin
KCR
Station

Shatin Town Hall

Shatin
Central Park

Royal
Park
Hotel

New
Town
Plaza

Lion Rock Tunnel   Rd

Tai Po Rd · Tai Wai

Che Kung Miu Rd

Che Kung
Miu
Temple

To
Kowloon

HONG KONG

Kongers are to find a bit of greenery amongst the concrete housing estates.

You can get to the racecourse by taking the KCR to either Fo Tan or Racecourse stations.

Amah Rock 望夫石

It may just be a rock, but like many Chinese landmarks, a local legend has grown up around it.

The story goes that for many years a fisherman's wife, with her baby on her back, climbed to this vantage point to watch for her husband's return. The husband never came back and the gods took pity on her and transported her to heaven with a lightning bolt which left a rock in her place.

As you take the train south towards Kowloon, you can spot Amah Rock to the left on the hillside after passing the Tai Wai KCR Station before the train enters the tunnel.

Shatin New Town Plaza 新城市廣場

Many Hong Kongers flock to Shatin on weekends to shop at one of the biggest shopping malls in Hong Kong. In addition to the plethora of shops and restaurants, there is a huge indoor swimming pool, roller rink and bowling alley. The 'music fountain' in the lobby is one of three such devices in Hong Kong, the other two being in Whampoa Gardens and Tsuen Wan Plaza.

Adjacent to the New Town Plaza is a well-stocked public library, the largest in the New Territories. Many cultural events are held in the adjoining Shatin Town Hall. There is also Bun's Amusement Centre which offers bowling and roller skating. The whole complex is adjacent to the Shatin KCR Station.

CLEARWATER BAY 清水灣

Clearwater Bay is in the extreme southeastern corner of the New Territories and, as the name implies, has brilliant, cerulean water. It certainly stands in sharp contrast to nearby Junk Bay which, as the name implies, has plenty of junk floating in it.

Clearwater Bay is beautiful and has one of the best beaches in Hong Kong. It's very popular, in fact too popular, as on a hot summer weekend it's standing room only. If someone were to faint, they would never hit the ground, but would just be pushed around by the crowd until the beach closed.

Naturally the beauty of Clearwater Bay has not gone unnoticed by Hong Kong's monied class. Mediterranean-style villas have sprouted on the hillsides and there is now a Clearwater Bay Country Club, complete with golf course, squash and tennis courts, jacuzzi, badminton, etc.

Junk Bay, just a stone's throw from Clearwater Bay, is to be the site of another huge new town housing project built on reclaimed land. A new tunnel is to be built across Junk Bay, making Clearwater Bay much more accessible. Development pressure is sure to follow, though perhaps sanity will prevail and Clearwater Bay will be at least partially preserved, like Stanley on Hong Kong Island.

There are some country parks on the peninsula and some decent trails, but serious hikers desiring a strenuous walk should look elsewhere in the New Territories.

One of Hong Kong's leading movie companies is Shaw Brothers which has its huge Movietown studios on Clearwater Bay Rd. To visit the studios, phone the company's public relations office (☎ 7191551).

Clearwater Bay is easily accessible. Take the MTR to the Choi Hung Station. From there, walk to the nearby bus terminus and catch bus No 91 which goes all the way to Clearwater Bay.

SAI KUNG PENINSULA 西貢半島

This is the garden spot of the New Territories. The Sai Kung Peninsula is the last chunk of Hong Kong besides the Outlying Islands that remains a haven for hikers, campers, swimmers and boating enthusiasts. Hikers sometimes encounter unpleasant dogs – carry a stick, dog repellent, cattle prod or whatever you deem necessary.

Some of Hong Kong's best swimming beaches are on the Sai Kung Peninsula, where windsurfing equipment can also be hired.

The peninsula is largely undeveloped, and those who care about Hong Kong's environment would like to keep it that way. Meanwhile, real estate agents look at all those virgin beaches devoid of villas and lick their chops.

Sai Kung Town 西貢

The only town of any significant size in the area, Sai Kung Town was mainly a marketplace for farmers and fishers in the area. Now it's beginning to be infected with that dreaded disease – creeping condominiums – but the town still retains much of its charm.

To get there, take the MTR to the Choi Hung Station. Exit the station where the sign says 'Clearwater Bay Road North'. Here you can catch bus No 92 to Sai Kung Town, or alternatively the No 1 maxicab which is more frequent. The ride from Choi Hung to Sai Kung Town takes about 30 minutes.

Hebe Haven 白沙灣

Bus No 92 (or maxicab No 1) from Choi Hung MTR Station to Sai Kung Town passes the small bay of Hebe Haven (*Pak Sha Wan*), the yachting centre of the New Territories. The Hebe Haven Yacht Club is here.

If you're not a yachting buff, catch a sampan to the tiny peninsula across the bay to swim off the sandy beach. The beach is excellent and the sampan trip should only be a couple of dollars. Alternatively, walk out to the peninsula from Sai Kung Town, a distance of about 2.5 km each way.

Ma On Shan 馬鞍山

At 702 metres, Ma On Shan is the fourth highest peak in Hong Kong, only surpassed by Tai Mo Shan in the New Territories and two peaks on Lantau Island (Lantau Peak and Sunset Peak).

Ma On Shan (the mountain) is not to be confused with Ma On Shan (the village). Ma On Shan Village is to become yet another new town, complete with a row of high-rise housing estates and shopping malls.

Access to Ma On Shan is by the MacLehose Trail. The trail does not actually go over the summit, but comes very close and the spur route to the peak is obvious. This is a steep, strenuous climb. You can walk from Ma On Shan (mountain) down to Ma On Shan (the new town) and get a bus to Shatin, then back to Kowloon by train.

Get to the MacLehose Trail by walking from Sai Kung Town or get closer to the peak by taking bus No 99 from Sai Kung Town. The bus runs along Sai Sha Rd. To find the right bus stop, let the driver know you want to climb Ma On Shan.

Pak Tam Chung 北潭涌

This is the easternmost point you can reach by bus in the Sai Kung Peninsula. It's also the eastern terminus of the MacLehose Trail. You can get to Pak Tam Chung on bus No 94 from Sai Kung Town, but this bus runs only once an hour. On Sundays and holidays only there is the additional bus No 96R from Choi Hung which runs every 20 to 30 minutes.

Along the way, the bus passes **Tai Mong Tsai** where there is an Outward Bound school, an international organisation that teaches wilderness survival.

From Pak Tam Chung you can walk to **High Island Reservoir**. The reservoir, opened in 1978, used to be a sea channel. Both ends were blocked with dams and the seawater was pumped out, then fresh water pumped in.

While in Pak Tam Chung, visit the **Sai Kung Country Parks Visitor Centre** which has excellent maps, photographs and displays of the area's geology, and flora & fauna. The centre is open everyday from 9 am to 5 pm.

From Pak Tam Chung, it's a 25-minute walk south along a trail to find the **Sheung Yiu Folk Museum**, a restored Hakka village typical of those found in Hong Kong in the 19th century. The museum is open daily, except Tuesday, from 9 am to 4 pm. Admission is free.

If you want to explore the north shore of the Sai Kung Peninsula, bus No 94 continues from Pak Tam Chung to Wong Shek Pier in Tai Tan.

TOLO HARBOUR & TAP MUN CHAU
大埔海/塔門洲

From Ma Liu Shui, ferries cruise through Tolo Harbour to Tap Mun Chau (Grass Island) and back again, calling in at various villages on the way.

Tap Mun Chau is in the north-east of the New Territories where Tolo Harbour empties into Mirs Bay. The island has an old-world fishing village atmosphere and is noted for its Tin Hau temple where whistling sounds occur at the altar when easterly winds roar. The Tin Hau Festival is very big here.

Other main attractions are the Tap Mun Cave on the eastern side of the island and the beautiful beaches.

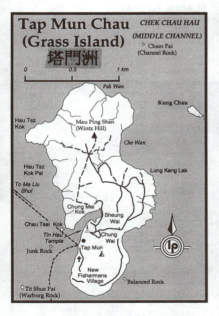

Many visitors claim that Tap Mun Chau is the most interesting island of all those around Hong Kong. Unfortunately, the beach is carpeted with beer cans, plastic bags

and other detritus, plus getting there is a bit of a hassle and few foreigners bother. For the Chinese, the big attraction is the seafood. There is no accommodation on the island.

The Tolo Harbour ferry is operated by the Polly Ferry Co (☎ 7711630). Ferries begin the journey at Ma Liu Shui, which is about a 15-minute walk from the University Station of the KCR. The HKTA can supply you with the current ferry schedule, but at the time of writing it was as follows:

Monday – Saturday

	1st class	2nd class
Ma Liu Shui	8.30 am	3.15 pm
Sham Chung	9.00	3.45
Lai Chi Chong	9.15	4.00
Tap Mun Chau	9.45	4.30
Ko Lau Wan	9.50	4.35
Tai Tan	10.05	5.00*
Chek Keng	10.20	4.45*
Tap Mun Chau	10.40	5.20
Lai Chi Chong	11.10	5.50
Sham Chung	11.15	6.05
Ma Liu Shui	11.55	6.35

Sunday & Holidays

	1st class	2nd class
Ma Liu Shui	8.30 am	3.15 pm
Sham Chung	9.00	3.45
Lai Chi Chong	9.15	4.00
Tap Mun Chau	9.45	4.30
Ko Lau Wan	9.50	4.35
Tai Tan	10.05	5.00*
Chek Keng	10.20	4.45*
Tap Mun Chau	10.40 arr	5.20
	1.45 pm depart	
Lai Chi Chong	2.15	5.50
Sham Chung	2.30	6.05
Ma Liu Shui	6.35	6.35

* Second boat arrives at Chek Keng before sailing to Tai Tan, which is in the opposite order of the first boat.

As an alternative to the Tolo Harbour ferry, an easy way to reach Tap Mun Chau is to take a kaido from Tai Tan (Wong Shek Pier), which is the last stop of bus No 94. The kaidos run once hourly.

PING CHAU 平洲

This small island is in Mirs Bay in the far north-east of the New Territories. It's very close to the coast of China and it used to be one of the most popular destinations for people who wanted to leave China by swimming – braving the sharks and Mao's patrol boats.

At one time the island supported a population of 3000, but now it is uninhabited. The mass exodus started in the 1960s when everyone suddenly decided that life in a Hong Kong factory was preferable to life on a peaceful fishing isle. There are several abandoned buildings on the island, but visitors are advised to bring camping equipment.

The island's highest point is only about 30 metres, but it has unusual rock layers in its cliffs, which glitter after a night of rain. There are beautiful white-sand beaches, especially Lai Tau Wan. The island is also good for swimming, though some of the beaches are slate.

Getting to Ping Chau is practically an expedition. Unless you have your own yacht, you must take the ferry from Ma Liu Shui (near the Chinese University) in the New Territories. The ferry only runs on weekends, departing on Saturday and returning on Sunday, so a visit to Ping Chau involves a mandatory camping trip.

Depart from Ma Liu Shui on Saturday at 11.15 am and return on Sunday from Ping Chau at 1.10 pm. Check these times since the schedule can change and you certainly don't want to miss the boat back to Hong Kong. Only round-trip tickets are sold.

Tickets for this ferry can be bought at the head office of the Hong Kong & Yaumatei Ferry Company (☎ 5423081), 1st floor, Central Harbour Services Pier, Pier Rd, Central, or at the pier in Ma Liu Shui on the day of travel. They only sail if the weather is good.

PLACES TO STAY
Private Hostels
Travellers' Hostel (☎ 3687710), Chungking Mansions, 16th floor, A Block, Tsimshatsui,

also operates a *Beachside Hostel* (☎ 4919179) at Ting Kau near Tsuen Wan, opposite Tsing Yi Island. Dorm beds at the hostel cost HK$80 a night. A private room with private bath costs HK$150/170. You get there by taking the MTR to Tsuen Wan, then minibus No 96 or 96M. It's hard to find this place if you've never been there, so ring them up first and they'll send someone to meet you.

YHA Hostels

Sze Lok Yuen (☎ 4888188) is on Tai Mo Shan Rd. Beds cost HK$40 and tent camping is permitted. A YHA card is needed to stay there and advanced booking is essential. Take the No 51 bus (Tsuen Wan Ferry Pier – Kam Tin) at Tsuen Wan MTR Station and alight at Tai Mo Shan Rd. Follow Tai Mo Shan Rd for about 45 minutes, then turn on to a small concrete path on the right-hand side which leads directly to the hostel. This is a good place from which to climb Tai Mo Shan, Hong Kong's highest peak. Because of the high elevation, it can get amazingly cold at night, so be prepared.

Bradbury Hall is another YHA hostel. The hostel is at the base of Plover Cove Reservoir on Ting Kok Rd, just a few hundred metres south of Tai Mei Tuk. Take the KCR train to Tai Po Station, then take bus No 75K to Tai Mei Tuk and follow the access road with the sea on your right side.

Pak Sha O Hostel (☎ 3282327) charges HK$40 a bed and also permits tent camping. A YHA card is needed. Take bus No 92 from the Choi Hung Estate bus terminus and get off at the Sai Kung terminus. From Sai Kung, take Bus No 94 towards Wong Shek Pier, but get off at Ko Tong Village. From there, find Hoi Ha Rd and a road sign 30 metres ahead showing the way to Pak Sha O.

Also on the Sai Kung Peninsula is *Bradbury Hall* (☎ 3282458), in Chek Keng. From Choi Hung Estate bus terminus, take bus No 92 to the Sai Kung terminus. From Sai Kung, take bus No 94 to Yellow Stone Pier, but get off at Pak Tam Au. There's a footpath at the side of the road leading to Chek Keng Village. Open seven days, the hostel is right on the harbour just facing the Chek Keng Ferry Pier. An alternative route is to take the ferry from Ma Liu Shui (adjacent to the Chinese University KCR Station) to Chek Keng Pier.

Hotels

Shatin has some high-standard pricey hotels. The *Regal Riverside* (☎ 6497878; fax 6374748), Tai Chung Kiu Rd, is huge with 828 rooms and has doubles from HK$900 to HK$1200. The *Royal Park* (☎ 6012111; fax 6013666), 8 Pak Hok Ting St, Shatin, has doubles for HK$950 to HK$1200.

One of the newest hotels in Hong Kong is the *Kowloon Panda Hotel* (☎ 4091111; fax 4091818), 3 Tsuen Wah St, Tsuen Wan, where double rooms go for HK$800 to HK$1300. There are a total of 1026 rooms in this huge place. The upmarket suites cost HK$1600 to HK$4500.

PLACES TO EAT

You can find all the usual noodle shops and fast-food outlets, but there are a couple of places that are especially notable. Probably most interesting is the *Treasure Floating Restaurant* (☎ 6377222), moored in the river at 55 Tai Chung Kiu Rd in Shatin. Dim sum hours are from 8 am to 5 pm, and the restaurant dishes up pricier seafood until 11.30 pm.

Also of special interest is *Yucca De Lac Restaurant* (☎ 6921835) in Ma Liu Shui, which provides outdoor tables affording a view of Tolo Harbour. No dim sum here, but standard Chinese dishes are served.

If you're looking for dim sum in Yuen Long, it's served from 7 am to 3 pm at the *Kar Shing Restaurant* (☎ 4763228) in Room 333, 3rd floor, Yuen Long Plaza, 249 Castle Peak Rd.

Outlying Islands 離島

Take away Hong Kong Island itself and you've still got 234 other islands. Together the Outlying Islands make up about 20% of the total land area of Hong Kong. Officially, they are part of the New Territories, except for tiny Stonecutters Island which is in Kowloon (and soon will be attached to the Kowloon Peninsula by reclamation).

The tiny islands of Ma Wan, Tap Mun Chau and Ping Chau are covered in the New Territories chapter because they are only accessible as a trip from the New Territories. The islands in this chapter are all accessible from Hong Kong Island.

While many of the islands are little more than uninhabited rocks, occasionally seen above sea level, Lantau Island is actually larger and higher than Hong Kong Island. Nevertheless, in all the Outlying Islands put together there are still less than 100,000 people, which is under 2% of Hong Kong's total.

Just a few decades ago, almost all of the habitable islands had permanent settlements supported mostly by the fishing industry. Now many of these villages have become ghost towns, the inhabitants lured away by the promise of wealth in the nearby glittering metropolis.

Ironically, while Chinese fishing families have been lured off the islands by high-paying jobs in the city, foreigners have been moving in the opposite direction. Perhaps unsurprisingly, the foreigners have become some of the staunchest defenders of the traditional island way of life, fiercely opposing proposals to build high-rises and introduce cars to the islands. By contrast, the Chinese embrace continued development but most of them do not care for island life (they say it's 'boring').

Another twist of irony is that the foreigners have become the major threat to the islands' environment. Since few Chinese move to the islands while foreigners continue to flood in, it's the gwailos who are driving up the rents and spurring new housing developments that make the rural atmosphere a little less rural every year. Developments such as Lantau's Discovery Bay – where matchbox high-rises now compete for a view of the sea – could be an indication of the way the islands are heading. Foreigners talk about instituting a building moratorium, but it seems unlikely. The problem is that every new resident wants to be the last.

The one factor that has kept these islands unspoilt has been inconvenient transport. Discovery Bay only developed into suburbia thanks to the introduction of jet-powered high-speed ferries which cut commuting time to 20 minutes. Elsewhere, it takes nearly an hour each way. Unfortunately for preservationists, plans are afoot to introduce high-speed ferries to *all* the major islands. When that happens, Cheung Chau, Lamma and Lantau could all be headed the same way as Kowloon. But at least for the moment, the Outlying Islands remain tranquil backwaters free of motor vehicles, noise, crowds and pollution.

Cars are prohibited on all of the Outlying Islands except Lantau, where a special vehicle permit is required and not easily obtained. Consequently, the number of motor vehicles on Lantau is very small.

A minor but real hazard on all the islands are dogs. Although it's illegal to have an unleashed and unmuzzled dog in Hong Kong, the rules are largely ignored here. While the Chinese are happy to ignore the leash laws, gwailos are some of the biggest offenders. The dogs are mostly friendly but some are fond of taking a bite out of tourism. If you are bitten, take a good look at the dog and then call the police. They may be able to track down the dog and the owner, who will have to pay your medical expenses plus a fine.

Unfortunately, many dogs have no owner. The strays (which often starve to death) are largely a result of thoughtless foreigners who come to Hong Kong for a brief time to work, often taking dogs as pets. When they depart Hong Kong, they give the dog to a friend who soon abandons it. In 1993, one irate resident of Lamma Island decided to wipe out the ever-growing population of stray dogs by poisoning them.

Only those islands which are accessible by public ferry are included in this chapter. You probably won't get to visit the numerous other islands unless you can afford to charter a boat. Many of the remote islands are popular destinations for Hong Kong's fleet of yachts, where boat owners often participate in such prohibited pastimes as nude swimming and sunbathing.

ORIENTATION & INFORMATION
If you intend to do a major hike, it would be wise to equip yourself with the excellent *Countryside* series of maps produced by the Crown Lands & Surveys Office. The essential map for the Outlying Islands is *Countryside Series Map No 3: Lantau & Islands*. Another useful map is *Lantau Trail*. The maps are cheap and can be bought at the Government Publications Centre in the GPO block near the Star Ferry Terminal on Hong Kong Island.

ACCOMMODATION
Individual places to stay are listed in the relevant sections in this chapter. However, you can book rooms in the city before your arrival at the islands. In Central, located at the ferry pier for departures to Lamma Island, there is the Outlying Islands Holiday Flats Booking Office (☎ 5413357). Actually, the 'office' is just a small booth between the two newsstands. The signs identifying this booth are in Chinese only, but photographs of bedrooms prominently displayed make it obvious. If you book a room through this office, you'd better get the staff to write down the address and directions to your hotel or flat in Chinese so you can actually find the place.

GETTING THERE & AWAY
The main Outlying Islands are linked to Hong Kong by regular ferry services – not primarily for tourists but for locals who work in the city and live on the islands. The ferries are comfortable and cheap, though many have an air-con top deck which costs extra. They all have a basic bar serving drinks and snacks.

An important thing to know – fares double on weekends and holidays but island-residents get a concession fare. If you're staying on the islands and want to make a day-trip into the city, definitely buy a round-trip ticket (holidays only). The ticket is only good on the day you bought it, but comes with a 50% discount. However, no such discount is allowed on weekdays and it is not available on tickets sold in the city.

Hoverferries also connect the islands but cost over twice as much as the conventional ferries and go twice as fast. They're also fun, but not for those prone to seasickness! Eat lightly or bring a plastic bag.

The timetables are pretty stable but subject to slight changes over time. You can pick up the latest timetables from the HKTA.

If you want to catch breakfast on Hong Kong Island while waiting for the ferry, the *Seaview Restaurant*, upstairs in the Outlying Islands Ferry Pier, does a mean dim sum.

The islands are popular holiday destinations for Hong Kongers – in fact too popular! On weekends the ferries become so crowded that it's a wonder the boats don't sink. As soon as business offices close on Saturday afternoon there is a mad rush for the boats. The fares are also higher on weekends and the more accessible beaches are practically standing room only. Most of the hotels charge double rates during weekends, and that's if you can find a room!

Try to keep at least HK$20 worth of change with you and a small wad of HK$10 notes. You can buy the ticket from a booth, but you'll save time by putting exact change into a turnstile as you enter the pier. On some of the smaller ferries, they run out of change so it helps to have small coins. In no circumstances will the ticket offices change bills larger than HK$100. You can also buy return tickets.

If your time is limited, Watertours (☎ 5254808) runs trips to the islands.

Cheung Chau 長洲

Only 2.5 sq km in size, Cheung Chau is 10 km west of Hong Kong, off the south-east tip of Lantau. Despite the small size, it's the most populous of the Outlying Islands with 20,000 residents. Cheung Chau means 'long island' in Cantonese.

Archaeological digs have shown that Cheung Chau, like Lamma and Lantau, was inhabited in prehistoric times. The island had a thriving fishing community 2500 years ago and a reputation for piracy from the year dot – probably started by the earliest Cantonese and Hakka settlers who supplemented their incomes with piracy and smuggling.

When Guangzhou and Macau opened up to the West in the 16th century the island was a perfect spot from which to prey on passing ships stacked with goodies. The infamous and powerful pirate Cheung Po Tsai is said to have had his base here during the 18th century.

The piracy and smuggling have gone, but fishing is still an important industry for a large number of the island's inhabitants. About 40,000 people now live on the island – about 10% on junks and sampans anchored offshore.

There are several interesting temples on the island, the most important being the Pak Tai Temple which is the focus of the annual Cheung Chau Bun Festival.

There are a couple of OK beaches on the island. Overlooking the largest beach is Cheung Chau's tallest building, the six-storey Warwick Hotel, which may be a portent of abominations to come. The island is getting crowded, but there are still a few unspoilt headlands where you can get away from the claustrophobia of Hong Kong Island. Because of the crowded situation, the island can no longer supply its own drinking water, so it's brought in by an undersea pipeline from Lantau.

While Cheung Chau is not for serious walkers, it's ideal if you like concrete paths through lush vegetation and butterflies to spot along the way. The island is packed with missionary schools, churches, retreats and youth centres of every denomination and has built up a fair-sized community of gwailos who have escaped from the rat-race and high rents on Hong Kong Island.

There is no traffic noise on the island. In fact, there is no motorised transport other than a few tiny cargo tractors powered by lawn-mower engines. Cheung Chau is extremely popular with the locals who come to pig-out on seafood, but on weekends and holidays it tends to become a circus.

CHEUNG CHAU VILLAGE 長洲村
No longer a village but a small town, the main built-up area on the island is along the narrow strip at the centre of the two headlands that make up the dumb-bell-shaped island. The waterfront is a bustling place any time of day and late into the night.

Cheung Chau Typhoon Shelter 避風塘
This is the second largest typhoon shelter in Hong Kong, only surpassed by Aberdeen. As in Aberdeen, touring the typhoon shelter by boat is a must. Chartering a sampan for 20 minutes costs around HK$40 (subject to negotiation). Virtually any small boat you see in the harbour is a water taxi and can be hired for a tour. Simply wave to the boats and two or three of them will usually stop to offer a ride, but agree on the fare first.

PAK TAI TEMPLE 北帝廟
There are several temples on the island, two of the most interesting being on the waterfront. To find them, turn left as you get off the ferry and walk up Kwok Man Rd. You will come to the Pak Tai Temple dedicated to the god Pak Tai – see the Religion section in the Facts about Hong Kong chapter. The temple is the oldest on the island and the focus of the famous Bun Festival held annually.

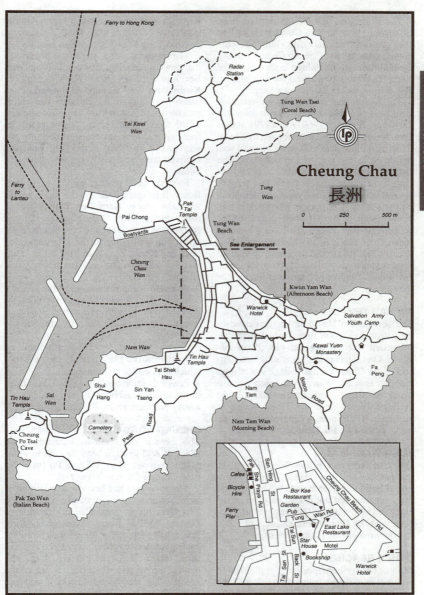

Ferry to Hong Kong

Radar Station

Tung Wan Tsai
(Coral Beach)

Tai Kwai Wan

Tung Wan

Ferry
to
Lantau

Pak Tai Temple

Pai Chong

Tung Wan Beach

Boatyards

Cheung Chau
長洲

0   250   500 m

Cheung Chau Wan

See Enlargement

Kwun Yam Wan
(Afternoon Beach)

Warwick Hotel

Salvation Army
Youth Camp

Nam Wan

Tin Hau Temple

Kawai Yuen Monastery

Fa Peng

Tai Shek Hau

Shui Hang

Sin Yan Tseng

Nam Tam

Don Bosco Road

Tin Hau Temple

Sai Wan

Peak Road

Cemetery

Nam Tam Wan
(Morning Beach)

Cheung Po Tsai Cave

Pak Tso Wan
(Italian Beach)

Cafes

Bicycle Hire

Ferry Pier

San Hing St

Pak She Praya Rd

Tung Wan Rd

Cheung Chau Beach Rd

Bor Kee Restaurant

Garden Pub

Tai Sun St

San Hing Tai

Back St

Star House

Bookshop

East Lake Restaurant

Motel

Warwick Hotel

The story goes that the first settlers from Guangdong Province in China brought Pak Tai, protector of fisherfolk (among other things) with them to Cheung Chau. Carrying the god through the village in the year 1777 is supposed to have scared away a plague. The temple was built six years later.

The temple has several historic relics. A large iron sword said to have been forged in the Sung Dynasty (960 AD-1279) stands here. It was recovered from the sea by a local fisherman more than 100 years ago and was presented to the god by the islanders. The sword is regarded as a symbol of good luck and its disappearance from the temple several years ago caused great consternation on the island. The person who took it was kind enough to return it when he realised the concern he had caused. There is a wooden sedan chair, made in 1894, which was used to carry Pak Tai around the island on festival days, and also two pillars depicting dragons, hewn out of hunks of granite at the turn of the century.

TIN HAU TEMPLES 天后廟
The several Tin Hau temples, dedicated to the patron goddess of fishermen, indicate the important role fishing has played on this island. One Tin Hau temple is at the southern end of the Cheung Chau village waterfront. Another is at Sai Wan on the south-western tip of the island – walk here or take a kaido (village ferry) near the Hong Kong & Yaumatei (HYF) pier. A third temple is to the north of the Pak Tai Temple.

TUNG WAN 東灣
From the ferry pier, follow Tung Wan Rd to the east side of the island. This is where you'll find Tung Wan Beach, the biggest and most popular, but not necessarily the prettiest beach on the island. The best part of Tung Wan is at the far southern end. It's possible to hire windsurfing equipment here.

OTHER BEACHES
Most of the northern headland is uninhabited with not much more than a reservoir on it. At the north-west corner of the island is **Tai Kwai Wan** which has a sandy beach. On the north-east corner of the island is the more isolated Tung Wan Tsai, another beach.

The southern part of the island is perhaps the most interesting. South of Tung Wan Beach past the six-storey Warwick Hotel is **Kwun Yum Wan Beach**. At the end of the beach is a footpath which takes you uphill past the small Kwun Yum Temple dedicated to the Goddess of Mercy. Continue up the footpath and look for the sign pointing the way to the **Fa Peng Knoll**. The concrete footpath takes you past quiet, tree-shrouded villas.

From the knoll you can walk down to Don Bosco Rd (again look for the sign) which will take you to **Nam Tam Wan** which is rocky but swimming is possible. If you ignore Don Bosco Rd and continue straight down you will come to the intersection of Peak and Kwun Yum Wan Rds. Kwun Yum Wan Rd will take you back to Cheung Chau village.

Peak Rd is the main route to the island's cemetery. You'll pass several pavilions on the road, built for coffin bearers who have to sweat their way along the hilly climb to the cemetery.

Once at the cemetery it's worth dropping down to **Pak Tso Wan**, a sandy, isolated spot which is good for swimming.

Peak Rd continues to Sai Wan (West Bay) on the south-west bulge of the island. There's a ferry pier here and a Tin Hau temple.

CHEUNG PO TSAI CAVE 張保仔洞
This cave in the south-west corner of the island is said to have been the hiding place of the infamous pirate, Cheung Po Tsai, who used Cheung Chau as a base.

The cave area has become a local tourist attraction and there is a nearby Cheung Po Tsai Cave picnic area. The glorification of Cheung Po Tsai seems ironic, considering that he had a reputation for extreme brutality, having ruthlessly robbed, murdered and tortured many innocent people. Near the maniac's cave and picnic area is one of the island's Tin Hau temples, which you can easily visit at the same time.

Reach the cave by walking almost two km from Cheung Chau village, or take a kaido to the pier at Sai Wan. From Sai Wan the walk is less than 200 metres.

BUN FESTIVAL 飽山節

The festival takes its name from the bun towers – bamboo scaffolding covered with edible buns. The towers can be up to 20 metres high.

If you go to Cheung Chau a week or so before the festival you'll see these huge bamboo towers being built in the courtyard of the Pak Tai Temple.

In previous times, at an appointed hour, hundreds of people would scramble up the bun towers to fetch one of the holy buns for good luck. It was believed that the buns higher up would bring better luck, so naturally it got to be something of a riot as everyone headed for the top. This sounds like a recipe for disaster and indeed, a serious accident occurred in 1978. Now the buns are handed out and no one is allowed to climb up to fetch their own.

The third day of the festival (a Sunday) is the most interesting due to a procession with floats, stilt walkers and people dressed as legendary characters. Children in amazingly colourful costumes are one of the prime attractions.

Most fascinating are the 'floating children' who are carried through the streets on poles, as if floating over the crowd. In fact, they are cleverly strapped into metal supports hidden under their clothes. The supports include built-in footrests and a padded seat for the child. On Pak She St, a few doors down from the Pak Tai Temple, there is a photo exhibition of the floating children. One of the supports for carrying the floating children is displayed.

During the celebrations several deities are worshipped, including Tin Hau, Pak Tai and Hung Hsing (the God of the South) – all significant to people who make their living from the sea. Homage is also paid to Tou Tei, the God of the Earth, and to Kuanyin, the Goddess of Mercy.

Offerings are made to the spirits of all the fish and animals whose lives have been sac- rificed to provide food, and during the four days of worship no meat is eaten. A priest reads a decree calling on the villagers to abstain from meat-eating so that no animal will be killed on the island during festival time.

The festival is unique to Cheung Chau and its origins are not really known. One popular theory is that the ceremony is to appease the ghosts who were killed by pirates, otherwise they would bring disasters such as typhoons to the island.

The bun festival is held over four days in May. Accommodation in Cheung Chau is heavily booked at this time. The stacks of extra ferries laid on for the festival are always packed. Still, it's worth making the journey if you can.

PLACES TO STAY

There are several good places to stay, but prices escalate dramatically on weekends unless you book for a long term, like a month.

As you exit the ferry pier, in front of you and to the left are numerous tables and booths displaying photographs of various rooms for rent. Practically none of the people who operate these booths speak English, but if you can make yourself understood, it's possible to find a cheap room. Some of these people are renting out rooms in their own flat, while others will rent you a whole flat or villa for yourself. Prices vary wildly, but you can negotiate cheaper rates for a longer term.

The best cheap place to stay is the *Star House Motel* (☎ 9812186) at 149 Tai Sun Bak St. Double rooms start at HK$200 on weekdays and run between HK$600 and HK$700 a night on weekends.

The *Warwick Hotel* (☎ 9810081; fax 9819174) is a luxury resort, a six-storey eyesore on the beach with 70 rooms. Doubles cost HK$920 on a weekday and HK$1050 on a weekend, plus a 10% service charge and 5% tax. The hotel has a good Cantonese and Western restaurant.

PLACES TO EAT

Like most islands around Hong Kong, seafood is the local specialty but you won't have any trouble finding other types of Chinese food. In the morning many restaurants along the waterfront serve dim sum.

As you get off the ferry, turn to your left and head about 200 metres up the street. Here you'll find numerous sidewalk cafes. Prices are low, and you can sit here by the waterfront and watch the world go by as you eat.

Two restaurants offering good food and low prices are *Bor Kee* and *East Lake*, on Tung Wan Rd just east of the Garden Pub. Both are popular with local expatriates. During summer evenings, they set up outdoor tables and the place takes on the atmosphere of an open-air party.

There are a couple of restaurants on the eastern waterfront overlooking Tung Wan Beach.

From the cargo pier, you can take a free sampan (the one with the flag) to the *Floating Restaurant*. Fishing families hold their wedding parties there.

ENTERTAINMENT

There is only one real nightlife spot, the *Garden Cafe/Pub* (☎ 9814610), 84 Tung Wan Rd, just to the west of the Bor Kee Restaurant. It's a friendly place and always packed with gwailos. This is the only place on the island which serves European food, but it's rather expensive.

There's a bar at the Warwick Hotel, but it's high-priced and doesn't attract much following among the expatriate community.

GETTING THERE & AWAY

See the ferry schedules for Central to Cheung Chau and Kowloon to Cheung Chau which are listed below.

Central - Cheung Chau

Monday - Saturday		Sunday & Holidays	
From Central	From Cheung Chau	From Central	From Cheung Chau
6.25 am	5.35 am*	6.25 am	5.35 am*
7.30	6.00	7.30	6.00
8.00	6.40	8.40	6.40
9.00	7.25	9.15!	7.30
10.00	7.45	10.00	8.45
11.00	8.00	10.45!	10.00
noon	8.40	11.15	11.15
1.00 pm	9.15	noon!	12.10 pm!
2.00	10.15	12.30 pm	12.30
3.00	11.15	1.20!	1.20!
4.15	12.15 pm	2.00	1.45
5.15	1.15	3.00	2.45!
5.45	2.15	4.30	3.15
6.20	3.15	5.45	4.00!
6.45	4.15	6.25!	4.30
7.30	5.20	7.05	5.15!
8.15	6.20	8.20	5.40
9.30	7.00	9.30	6.50
10.30	7.45	10.30	8.00!
11.30	8.30	11.30	8.20
12.30 am	9.30	12.30 am	9.30
-	10.30	-	10.30
-	11.30	-	11.30
* Via Peng Chau & Mui Wo	! Optional		

Inter-Island Ferry Schedule

Monday to Saturday

From Peng Chau	From Mui Wo	From Chi Ma Wun	From Cheung Chau
6.10 am	5.35 am	-	-
-	5.40 am	6.05 am	6.25 am
7.55 am	7.30 am	7.00 am	-
-	8.20 am	8.40 am	9.00 am
10.20 am	10.00 am	9.30 am	-
-	10.45	11.10 am	11.30 am
12.50 pm	12.30 pm	noon	-
-	1.20 pm	1.40 pm	2.00 pm
3.05 pm	2.30 pm	-	-
-	3.25 pm	3.45 pm	4.05 pm
5.20 pm	5.00 pm	4.30 pm	-
-	5.45 pm	-	6.05 pm
7.25 pm	7.05 pm	6.40 pm	-
-	7.50 pm	8.10 pm	8.30 pm
9.00 pm	-	-	-
-	-	-	9.35 pm
10.50 pm	10.35 pm	10.10 pm	-

Sundays & Public Holidays

From Peng Chau	From Mui Wo	From Chi Ma Wun	From Cheung Chau
6.10 am	5.35 am	-	-
-	6.00 am	6.25 am	6.45 am
7.55 am	7.35 am	7.10 am	-
-	8.20 am	8.45 am	9.05 am
10.10 am	9.55 am	9.30 am	-
-	10.45 am	11.10 am	11.30 am
12.50 pm	12.20 pm	noon	-
-	1.20 pm	1.40 pm	2.00 pm
3.10 pm	2.50 pm	2.30 pm	-
-	3.40 pm	4.10 pm	4.30 pm
5.50 pm	5.25 pm	5.00 pm	-
-	6.20 pm	6.40 pm	7.00 pm
7.45 pm	-	7.25 pm	-
-	-	8.10 pm	8.30 pm
9.20 pm	-	9.00 pm	-
-	-	-	9.40 pm
10.55 pm	10.35 pm	10.15 pm	-

Hoverferries

Monday - Friday except Holidays

From Central	From Cheung Chau
9.00 am	9.40 am
10.15	10.50
12.15 pm	12.50 pm
2.15	2.50
4.05	4.50

Kowloon - Cheung Chau

Saturday Only	Sunday & Holidays	
From Kowloon	From Kowloon	From Cheung Chau
4.00 pm	8.00 am	12.45 pm
-	10.00 am	-

GETTING AROUND

Apart from walking you can hire bikes on the island, though you'll have a few big hills to tackle outside the built-up areas. Bicycles can be hired from the shop right on the western waterfront near the north end of Praya St.

Lamma 南丫島

Also known as Pok Liu Chau, Lamma is the large island (13 sq km) clearly visible from

Victoria Peak as you look to the south-west. Lamma is believed to have been settled before Hong Kong Island, yet it's now the least developed of the large islands.

There is a devoted Western community on Lamma which has fled Hong Kong's sky-high rents and urban congestion. Lamma officially supports a population of about 3000 – unofficially, it's three times that largely due to the resident expats who don't have Hong Kong ID cards.

Plans to build an oil refinery on Lamma were dropped in 1973 after a lot of heated opposition. Instead, Hongkong Electric con-

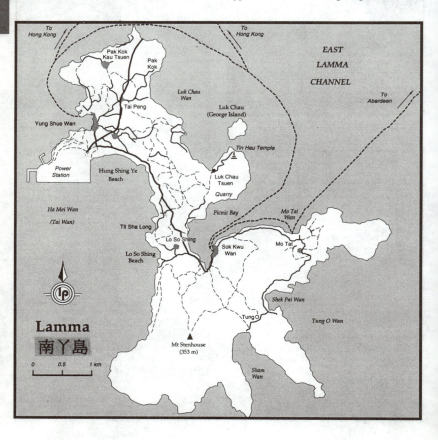

structed a huge coal-fired power station on the north-west coast of the island. The two enormous smoke stacks are clearly visible from Hong Kong Island. Meanwhile, on the south-east side of the island, the hillsides around Sok Kwu Wan are slowly being quarried away. Patrons at the bayside seafood restaurants can admire the quarry and adjacent cement plant while dining on crabs and prawns.

Vigorous objections were raised by local residents at the time these schemes were proposed, but 'progress' won out over environmental concerns. Given the fact that there are more than 200 uninhabited islands around Hong Kong which could have been reduced to rubble without anyone complaining, just why Lamma was singled out for such development is a mystery to many.

Despite all this seemingly bleak news, enough of Lamma is still unspoilt to make it well-worth visiting. The island is good for walking and swimming and a favourite weekend mooring spot for gwailo junks. It's also a fishing port and you can get good seafood on both ends of the island.

YUNG SHUE WAN 榕樹灣

The larger of the two townships on Lamma, Yung Shue Wan (Banyan Tree Bay) is still a pretty small place. Plastic used to be the big industry here – a few decades ago people in almost every house sprayed a vast assortment of plastic parts for toys and other goods. The plastics sweatshops have vanished and now restaurants and other tourist-related businesses are the main employers. There is a small Tin Hau temple here.

Places to Stay

There are several places to stay in and around Yung Shue Wan. The cheapest hotel in Yung Shue Wan is the *Lamma Vacation House* (☎ 9820427) at 29 Main St. The smallest rooms are Chungking Mansions-style coffins renting for HK$120, but reasonably cushy flats with private bath go for HK$200. Prices double on weekends.

Man Lai Wah Hotel (☎ 9820220) is adjacent to the ferry pier. Singles and doubles cost HK$300 on weekdays, rising to HK$500 to HK$600 on weekends. All rooms have air-con and an attached bath. The management speaks English.

The *Hoi Yee Holiday Resort* is inside the Man Kee Restaurant in Yung Shue Wan, and rents expensive holiday flats.

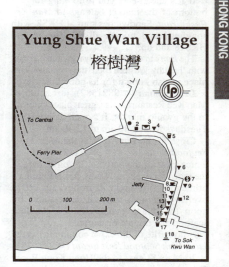

Yung Shue Wan Village
榕樹灣

To Central
Ferry Pier
Jetty
0   100   200 m
To Sok Kwu Wan

1	Public Library
2	Man Lai Wah Hotel
3	Post Office
4	Man Fung Seafood Restaurant
5	The Island Bar
6	Sampan Seafood Restaurant
7	Hong Kong & Shanghai Bank
8	Banyan Cafe
9	Lung Wah Seafood Restaurant
10	Capital Restaurant
11	Man Kee Restaurant
12	Lamma Vacation House
13	Sau Kee Restaurant
14	Lamcombe Restaurant
15	Tai Hing Restaurant
16	Nam Wah Yuen Cafe
17	The Waterfront Bar
18	Tin Hau Temple

Places to Eat

Yung Shue Wan has a string of good restaurants along Main St, and though most of them have signs advertising seafood, there's plenty of meat and vegetable dishes. Most of these places have English menus if you ask for them. Because of the large expat community, Western food is readily available.

If it's cheap eats you're looking for, the bottom of the market belongs to the *Man Kee Restaurant*. Sandwiches start at HK$8, with spaghetti and noodle dishes for around HK$18 and up.

The *Banyan Cafe* is strictly a gwailo hangout with 'healthy Western food' the specialty. This place is also known for its good breakfasts.

Deli Lamma (☎ 9821582), just south of Man Kee Restaurant, is a great place catering to the gwailo market. It's open daily except Tuesdays from 8.30 am to 12.30 am.

Close to the ferry pier is the *Man Fung Seafood Restaurant* (☎ 9821112) which has a nice view of the harbour. If you're here in the morning (6 am to 11 am), this is Lamma's prime dim sum shop with trolleys stacked to overflowing with trays of delectables. By noon this place evolves into a standard seafood and noodle restaurant.

A favourite of the expat community is the *Lung Wah Seafood Restaurant* (☎ 9820791) at 20 Main St next to the Hong Kong Bank. This place also does a fine morning dim sum from 6 am to 11 am (until afternoon on weekends), though it's not immediately obvious – no trolleys and the dim sum is kept in covered steaming baskets.

Lamcombe Restaurant is the best in the mid-range. Outstanding specialties include fried squid, sweet & sour pork and scallop broccoli garlic.

Sampan Seafood Restaurant (☎ 9822388), 16 Main St, is the fanciest and most expensive in Yung Shue Wan.

Further down Main St are the *Capital*, *Lee Garden*, *Sau Kee* and *Tai Hing* restaurants.

Down at the south end of main street is the *Nam Wah Yuen Cafe*, which does fine Chinese meals and features low prices but the atmosphere is dingy. The clientele is mostly Cantonese.

Entertainment

The large number of expats in Yung Shue Wan supports two pubs which become quite busy from about 6 pm until midnight. The *Island Bar* is where the real old-timers hang out.

The *Waterfront Bar* is the 'yuppie pub' – it certainly looks flashy and attracts Lamma's trendy professionals. Beer is pricey at HK$35. By way of compensation, this place has the best Western food on the island – check out the pizza. Another specialty is Indian food.

The *Man Loon*, a 10-minute walk from Yung Shue Wan on the path to Hung Shing Ye beach, is a store rather than a pub with picnic tables set up outside. On Sundays it becomes an impromptu all-day drinking party.

HUNG SHING YE 洪聖爺海灘

The most interesting way to see Lamma Island is to walk between Yung Shue Wan and Sok Kwu Wan which takes a little more than an hour. At the southern end of Yung Shue Wan is a sign pointing to the Lamma Youth Hostel. Follow the signs and you will soon find yourself in the countryside on a paved track.

The first developed place you reach is Hung Shing Ye Beach which is very nice although the view of the nearby power station takes some getting used to. The beach has lifeguards, a small restaurant and a few hotels. It would be a pleasant place to stay on weekdays, though on weekends the crowds multiply rapidly.

Continuing south from Hung Shing Ye, the path climbs steeply until it reaches a Chinese-style pavilion near the top of the hill. This is a nice place to relax with fine views of the power station. From this vantage point, it becomes obvious that the island is mostly hilly grassland and large boulders with very few trees.

Continuing south from the pavilion, you soon come to a ridge where you can look down at Sok Kwu Wan. It's a beautiful sight until you notice the quarry and adjacent cement works. The trail forks here with one branch going to the Lamma Youth Hostel. The hostel isn't a place where you'll stay – it's for school kids only and is mainly used as a summer weekend camp.

Places to Stay
Also at Hung Shing Ye is the classy and expensive *Concerto Inn* (☎ 8363388). Rooms in the bachelor/deluxe suites cost HK$680/928 on weekends, with a 30% discount on weekdays.

Another place at Hung Shing Ye is *Han Lok Yuen* (☎ 9820608) where double rooms start at HK$350. There are also several beachside hotels at Hung Shing Ye.

SOK KWU WAN 索罟灣
Although only a small settlement, Sok Kwu Wan (Picnic Bay) supports about a dozen or more excellent waterfront seafood restaurants.

There's a Tin Hau temple as you enter the township from Lo So Shing. From Sok Kwu Wan you can head back to Hong Kong on the ferry or do some more walking.

The small harbour at Sok Kwu Wan is filled with floating fish farms which are rafts from which cages are suspended. Some people live on the rafts or on boats anchored in the harbour, but others work on the rafts and commute by rowboat to their homes in the village.

LO SO SHING BEACH 蘆鬚城海灘
Just to the north of Sok Kwu Wan, the path diverges west and crosses the island's narrow saddle to Lo So Shing Beach. Like Hung Shing Ye, this is a developed beach with lifeguards and other modern amenities.

Places to Eat
An evening meal at Sok Kwu Wan is the most fun, and a good way to end a trip to the island. The restaurants are in a row along the waterfront. Some have interesting names like the *Lamma Hilton* and *Lamma Regent*. A few years ago these buildings were little more than shacks, but now they are modern buildings, an indication of the money that the island has since come by.

If you haven't noticed by now, Hong Kong people like to eat, and they are particularly fond of seafood. A steady convoy of kaidos brings customers to Sok Kwu Wan every evening from Hong Kong Island.

MO TAT WAN 模達灣
If you'd like a clean and uncrowded beach (on weekdays), it's worthwhile to make the 20-minute walk from Sok Kwu Wan to Mo Tat Wan along a path that runs by the coast. Mo Tat Wan is good for swimming but has no lifeguards. You can also get there on a kaido, but these are infrequent – they start at Sok Kwu Wan, stop at Mo Tat Wan and then continue on to Aberdeen.

Places to Eat
Mo Tat Wan has a superb by-the-water dining spot, *Coral Seafood Restaurant* (☎ 9828328). While the food is similar to what you get at Sok Kwu Wan, the prices are lower and the surroundings better.

SHEK PAI WAN & SHAM WAN
石排灣/深灣
There are a couple of good remote beaches down in the south-east – Shek Pai Wan and Sham Wan. These are relatively isolated and do not have lifeguards or other modern facilities. Get to them by the path which leads south from Mo Tat Wan.

MT STENHOUSE 山地塘
Most of the southern part of the island consists of the 353-metre Mt Stenhouse which you can walk to the top of. The climb up and back takes no more than two hours, but the paths are rough and not well-defined, so be prepared for a climb. The coastline around here is rocky and it's hard to find somewhere good to swim.

GETTING THERE & AWAY
Ferries run from Central to Lamma's two main villages, Yung Shue Wan and Sok Kwu Wan. One-way ordinary/deluxe class tickets for adults cost HK$6.50/12 on weekdays, and HK$8.50/23 on weekends and holidays. For children, ordinary/deluxe tickets are

Central - Yung Shue Wan

Monday - Saturday		Sunday & Holidays	
From Central	*From Yung Shue Wan*	*From Central*	*From Yung Shue Wan*
6.50 am	6.25 am	8.15 am	6.50 am
8.35	7.45	8.45	7.50
10.30	9.30	9.45	9.00
noon	11.30	10.45	10.30
12.50 pm	12.50 pm	11.15	noon
2.00	1.40	12.45 pm	1.30 pm
3.50	3.00	2.15	3.00
4.30*	4.40	3.45	4.30
5.30	5.20*	5.15	5.30
6.40	6.20	6.20	6.00
8.20	7.30	7.10	7.30
9.50	9.05	9.30	8.00
11.20	10.35	11.20	10.35
12.30 am	-	12.30 am!	-

* Monday - Friday only   ! Saturday only

Central - Sok Kwu Wan

Monday - Saturday		Sunday & Public Holidays	
From Central	*From Sok Kwu Wan*	*From Central*	*From Sok Kwu Wan*
8.00 am	6.50 am	7.30 am	8.20 am
10.00	9.00	9.15	10.05
2.30 pm	11.00	11.00	noon
4.15	3.30 pm	1.00 pm	2.00 pm
7.10	5.20	3.00	4.00
9.00	8.05	4.50	5.45
11.00	10.00	6.35	7.30
-	-	9.00	10.00
-	-	11.00	-

Journey Time: Central - Yung Shue Wan, 40 minutes; Central - Sok Kwu Wan, 50 minutes

Aberdeen - Mo Tat Wan - Sok Kwu Wan

Monday - Saturday		Sunday & Holidays	
From Aberdeen	*From Sok Kwu Wan*	*From Aberdeen*	*From Sok Kwu Wan*
6.45 am	6.05 am	8.00 am	6.15 am
8.00	7.25@	8.45	7.30
9.30	8.45	9.30	8.45
11.15	10.15	10.15	9.30
2.00 pm	12.45 pm	11.00	10.15
4.00	3.00	11.45	11.00
6.00	5.00	12.30 pm	11.45
7.25	6.45	2.00	12.30 pm
-	-	2.45	2.00
-	-	3.30	2.45

From Aberdeen	From Sok Kwu Wan		From Aberdeen	From Sok Kwu Wan
-	-		4.15	3.30
-	-		5.00	4.15
-	-		5.45	5.00
-	-		6.30	5.45
-	-		7.15	6.30
-	-		7.55	7.15

@ Doesn't stop at Mo Tat Wan

HONG KONG

HK$3.20/12 on weekdays and HK$4.50/13 on weekends and holidays. For definition purposes, a weekend includes all-day Saturday. The journey between Central and Yung Shue Wan takes 40 minutes, and between Central and Sok Kwu Wan it's 50 minutes.

There is also a smaller ferry running between Sok Kwu Wan and Aberdeen on the south side of Hong Kong Island. The kaido also makes a brief stop at Mo Tat Wan along the way. Journey times between Sok Kwu Wan and Mo Tat Wan is 10 minutes; from Mo Tat Wan to Aberdeen is 25 minutes.

Gwailos attending late-night parties in the city often miss the last ferry back to the island. The solution in that case is to charter a sampan or kaido from Aberdeen. Depending on how late it is, the boat crew may want HK$200 or more for the service. Fortunately, it's often not difficult to round up 10 other inebriated late-night revelers at the pier to split the cost!

A proposal to add a new high-speed ferry to Lamma might throw the following schedule completely out of whack, but for the moment please check tables.

GETTING AROUND

Like Cheung Chau, the island has no motorised traffic except for some carts used to haul seafood to the restaurants. Lamma's only road was built to service the power station, but you could spend a whole day here and not see a single vehicle go by. A concrete path links the two main villages, Yung Shue Wan in the north and Sok Kwu Wan in the south, but elsewhere there are mostly over-grown dirt trails. You can walk from Yung Shue Wan to Sok Kwu Wan and there is a kaido service between Sok Kwu Wan and Mo Tat Wan (see Getting There & Away earlier).

Lantau 大嶼山

Lantau means 'broken head' in Cantonese, but it also has a more appropriate name, Tai Yue Shan (Big Island Mountain). And big it is – 142 sq km, almost twice the size of Hong Kong Island. Amazingly, only abut 30,000 people live here, compared to Hong Kong's population of over a million. Most of those 30,000 are concentrated in just a couple of centres along the coast, mainly because the interior is so mountainous.

Lantau is believed to have been inhabited by primitive tribes before being settled by the Han Chinese. The last Sung Dynasty emperor passed through here in the 13th century during his flight from the Mongol invaders. He is believed to have held court in the Tung Chung Valley, which takes its name from a hero said to have given his life for the emperor. He's still worshipped on the island by the Hakka people who believe he can predict the future.

Over the years Lantau acquired a reputation as a base for pirates, and is said to have been one of the favourite haunts of the famous 18th-century pirate Cheung Po Tsai. The island was also important to the British

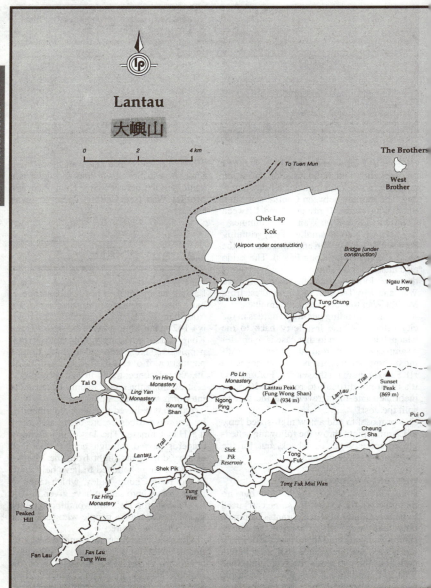

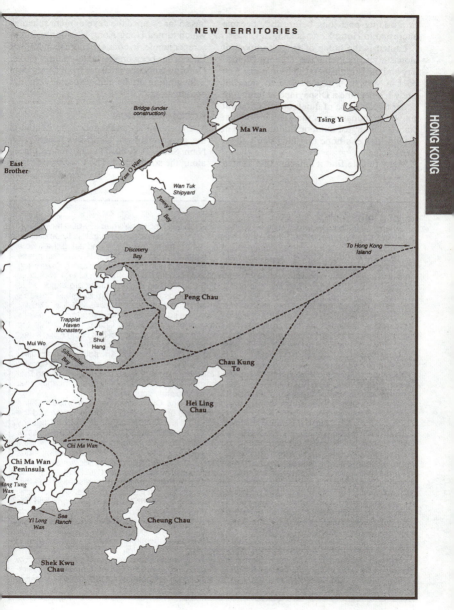

as a trading post long before they became interested in Hong Kong Island.

Lantau is the home of several important monasteries, including the Trappist Monastery and the Buddhist Po Lin Monastery. The Po Lin was rebuilt several years ago but lately it's become a Disneyland in miniature rather than a place of quiet retreat. On a hill above the monastery is the Tiantan Buddha Statue, the largest outdoor Buddha statue in the world. Let's hope that they don't add a ferris wheel.

Many people find it amazing that Lantau has so far escaped the development schemes which turned Hong Kong Island into a skyscraper jungle. In contrast, more than 50% of Lantau has been preserved as country parks. Unfortunately, the pressure from developers is beginning to be felt, especially in the coastal areas.

ACCOMMODATION

The cheapest accommodation on Lantau is the government-run campsites near Pui O, Nam Shan, Pak Fu Tin and many places along the south coast. The *Countryside* map

Flying into Trouble

Perhaps the first major casualty of the 1997 takeover will be Hong Kong's partially-built new airport on Chek Lap Kok Island, just off the north coast of Lantau. The proposed airport is to be built on reclaimed land, which requires chopping off the tops of nearby mountains and using the rubble to fill in the sea. Much of the reclamation work has already been completed. The second phase of construction calls for linking Lantau to the New Territories with bridges, a six-lane highway and a high-speed train which will reach Hong Kong Island via a third cross-harbour tunnel. Needless to say, with that much infrastructure in place, high-rise housing developments are expected to follow. There is no question that the airport scheme holds all the potential to cause Lantau's economy to boom and turn it into another Hong Kong Island.

Given its negative impact on Lantau's largely unspoilt surroundings, the airport project has its opponents. Ironically, environmentalists have found an unusual ally: China. It's not that the leadership of the PRC has suddenly become fond of green politics, it's just that Hong Kong's new landlords only want an airport if they don't have to pay for it. The airport's estimated price tag is HK$60 billion (US$7.7 billion) and still rising due to construction delays. Any public works project of this size requires the issuing of government bonds which must be paid off gradually – a decade or two would be a reasonable payback period for this amount of debt. China has insisted that when Britain quits Hong Kong, there must be a surplus in the coffers and no debts, meaning that the airport project must be paid off before 1997. This is clearly impossible.

In 1991, talks on the airport issue between Britain and China became acrimonious. China accused Britain of trying to strip Hong Kong of its funds prior to 1997, while the British told the Chinese they didn't understand even the basics of public finance. China then announced that any government debts extending beyond 1997 will be repudiated by the PRC. Thus, no sane investor will buy bonds with a payback period beyond 1997, and the airport project seemed doomed as a result. Nevertheless, the Hong Kong government is pushing ahead with construction using funds from its budget surplus and sales of reclaimed land that the project is creating. However, the lack of immediately available borrowed funds has slowed down construction and raised the total cost, and China might well inherit an airport 75% finished in 1997. Most Hong Kongers then hope that China will then relent and allow the project to be completed, but it's still a gamble.

Meanwhile, Hong Kong's Kai Tak Airport has become the fourth busiest in the world and has reached saturation point. With no room for expansion, this infrastructure bottleneck could do serious damage to Hong Kong's economy in the next decade. Ultimately, damage to Hong Kong means damage to the rest of China, so it would be myopic indeed if Beijing calls a halt to construction in 1997. Many point to China's recalcitrance on the airport issue as the most glaring example yet of the PRC's interference in Hong Kong's internal affairs.

China's motive for doing this seems to be nothing more than a tit-for-tat gesture to show displeasure with Governor Chris Patten's democratic reforms, which China vehemently opposes. But no matter what China's motive, the row over the airport has done much to destroy confidence in the post-1997 future. ∎

or the HKTA *Hostels, Campsites & Other Accommodation in Hong Kong* leaflet will tell you where they are. There is no camping charge at most of these sites.

MUI WO (SILVERMINE BAY) 梅窩
Mui Wo (Five Petal Flower) is often called Silvermine Bay by Westerners because of the old silver mines which were once on the outskirts of the settlement.

This is where the ferries from Hong Kong land and where you can catch buses to other parts of the island. There's a swimming beach, but the water tends to be murky and frequently choked with floating plastic bags. However, the views are fine, there are opportunities for walking and the township is not a bad place for seafood restaurants. About a third of Lantau's population lives in Mui Wo and surrounding hamlets.

Places to Stay
At Mui Wo, turn to your right as you exit the ferry pier – the beach and all places to stay are down in this direction along Tungwan Tau Rd. One of the best deals around is the *Mui Wo Inn* (☎ 9841916) with doubles from HK$243 to HK$435 on weekdays, and HK$435 to HK$565 on weekends.

There's a place with no English sign at No 23 Tungwan Tau Rd which offers beachside accommodation starting from HK$250 for a double. *Sea House* (☎ 9847757) has rather dumpy-looking rooms starting from HK$200 on weekdays, HK$400 on weekends. Top of the line is the *Silvermine Beach Hotel* (☎ 9848295; fax 9841907) which has doubles from HK$680 to HK$980 plus a 15% surcharge.

If you arrive at Mui Wo during the summer months, even on weekdays, you'll find a swarm of people at the pier renting holiday flats. Not much English is spoken, but these places are readily identified by the photos of the rooms on display. Not all the places being rented here are in Mui Wo – many of the flats are at Cheung Sha Beach and Pui O Beach.

Places to Eat
As you exit the ferry, just to your right is the *Mui Wo Cooked Food Market* which harbours a large number of food stalls and relatively cheap restaurants. Further down the beach, there's the *Seaview Restaurant*.

Cheapest for self-catering is the *Wellcome Supermarket* and *Park 'n Shop*. To find both places as you exit the ferry, walk one block straight ahead and then to your left.

Getting Around
Bicycles can be hired from Lantau Friends Bicycle Shop, opposite the Park 'n Shop in the centre of town. During summer, bikes can be hired on weekends from stalls in front of the Silvermine Bay Beach Hotel.

TRAPPIST HAVEN MONASTERY
熙篤會神學院
To the north-east of Mui Wo is the Trappist Monastery. The Trappist order was established by a French clergyman, Armand de Rance, in 1644 and gained a reputation as one of the most austere orders of the Roman Catholic church. The Lantau order was established in Beijing. The Lantau monks run a dairy farm and sell the milk locally – Trappist Haven Milk can be bought in Hong Kong.

The monastery is not for those who like wild nightlife as the monks have all taken a vow of silence and there are signs asking visitors to keep their radios and cassette players turned off and to speak in low tones. If it's a carnival you're after then try the Po Lin Monastery on a weekend.

You can get to the monastery by taking a ferry to Peng Chau and then crossing over to the monastery on a kaido for HK$3. The kaidos leave from a small pier just to the south of the main ferry pier on Peng Chau and head for Discovery Bay, stopping at the monastery en route but *only if you ask them to*. There is no extra charge, but if you don't say anything the kaidos probably will go directly to Discovery Bay. From the monastery you can easily walk along the coast for one hour to Discovery Bay. You can also walk between the monastery and Mui Wo, but the eroded trail is steep, slippery and

HONG KONG

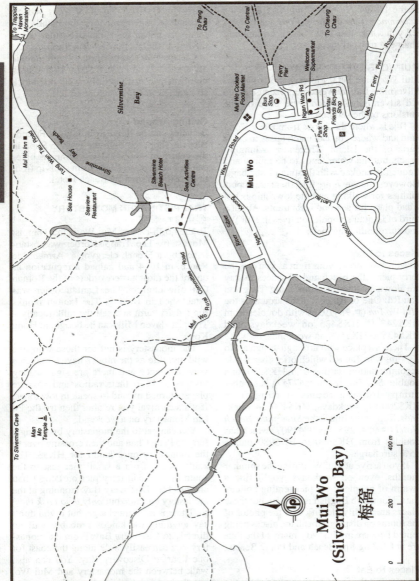

Mui Wo
(Silvermine Bay)
梅窩

0   200   400 m

poorly marked so ask local advice before heading out.

Places to Stay

You stay at the monastery, but applications have to be made in advance in writing or by phone. Apply to the Grand Master (☎ 9876286), Trappist Haven, Lantau Island, PO Box 5, Peng Chau, Hong Kong. Men and women must sleep in segregated dorms.

NGONG PING 昂坪

Perched 500 metres up in the western hills of Lantau is the Ngong Ping region, the major drawcard for Hong Kong day-trippers and foreign tourists.

Po Lin Monastery 寶蓮寺

The original temple was built in 1921, but the place has undergone considerable renovation since then. Today, the Po Lin (Precious Lotus) Monastery is a Buddhist retreat-cum-fairground. It's a large temple complex of mostly new buildings with the simpler, older buildings tucked away behind

them. From here the warm hand of friendship is offered not just to tourists but also to local film and tv companies who frequently use it as a set.

On a hill above the monastery is the largest outdoor **Buddha statue** in the world, which is 40 metres high and financed by Hong Kong Buddhists. The bronze statue was forged in China. There has been at least one concession to good taste – the statue is not the fat, jolly Buddha often portrayed in tacky souvenir shops. The Birthday of Buddha, around May, is a good time to be here.

Whatever you do, don't visit on a weekend. The place is flooded with day-trippers with their radios and families, so you're more likely to trip over a dinky toy than a meditating monk.

Since this is a monastery, visitors are requested to observe some decorum in dress and behaviour – getting too intimate with your boyfriend or girlfriend in public is not on. Also, it is prohibited to bring meat on the grounds – hard-core carnivores who smuggle chicken wings in their pockets should take note.

Po Lin Monastery

Lantau Tea Gardens 昂坪茶場

Beside the Po Lin Monastery are the Lantau Tea Gardens (☎ 9855718), the only tea gardens in Hong Kong. The tea bushes are in sad shape, but that hardly matters – the emphasis is on commercial tourism. There are horses for hire, and sitting on one for 10 minutes to get your photo taken costs HK$50; 30 minutes of riding is HK$150; one hour is HK$250, and you are supposed to ride with a minimum group of three persons. The tea plantation also operates an outdoor skating rink which is in incredibly bad condition and is deserted on weekdays, but can be noisy with screaming kids on weekends. Skate rentals cost HK$25 per hour. You can also spend the night here.

Lantau Peak 鳳凰山

Also known as Fung Wong Shan, this mountain, at 934 metres, is the second highest peak in Hong Kong. Only Tai Mo Shan in the New Territories is higher. The views from the summit of Lantau Peak are stunning and on a clear day it is possible to see Macau. Unfortunately, a number of moral cretins have trashed the summit with plastic wrappers, styrofoam lunch boxes and drink cans.

The easiest way to make the climb is to spend the night at the Po Lin Monastery, tea gardens or the S G Davis Youth Hostel. Get up at the crack of dawn and head for the summit. Many climbers get up earlier and try to reach the summit to see the sunrise, which appears to be a big deal for the Chinese. Personally, I think climbing this peak in the dark is a good way to get yourself killed – it is very steep in parts. The trail begins just to the east of the tea plantation and there is an information board there.

Places to Stay

People who stay at Ngong Ping normally do so to climb nearby Lantau Peak in time to catch the sunrise.

A 10-minute walk to the east of the Lantau Tea Gardens is the YHA's *S G Davis Youth Hostel* (☎ 9855610), which has dormitory beds, a campsite and is open all week. It costs HK$40 a night and you have to be a YHA member to stay here. The hostel is open on weekends and public holidays only. To get there, take a ferry from the Outlying Islands Ferry Pier to Mui Wo, then catch a bus to Ngong Ping.

The *Po Lin Monastery* (☎ 9855113) at Ngong Ping has separate dormitories for men and women. A bed costs HK$200 a night, which includes three vegetarian meals. To make a booking, call the monastery. Despite the holy surroundings, this place has a reputation for indifference bordering on rudeness.

Also at Ngong Ping are the *Lantau Tea Gardens* (☎ 9855161). Accommodation for two people on weekdays/weekends costs HK$200/300.

Places to Eat

The *Po Lin Monastery* has a good reputation for its vegetarian food. Some people find it bland, but apparently you get what the monks eat. In the monastery's large canteen HK$35 gets you a big plate of spring rolls, mushrooms, vegetables and rice.

LANTAU TRAIL 鳳凰徑

This footpath, 70 km long, runs the whole length of the island along the mountain tops and then doubles back along the coast. At a normal pace, the estimated walking time for the entire trail (not allowing for rests) is 23½ hours. Unless you're a marathon runner you probably won't cover it in one day, though no doubt someone will try.

A more realistic approach is to do the middle section of the trail (the highest and most scenic part) which goes over Lantau Peak and is easily accessible from the Po Lin Monastery at Ngong Ping. From Ngong Ping to Mui Wo via Lantau and Sunset peaks, is 17½ km and is estimated to take at least seven hours by foot.

The western part of the trail – along the south-western coast of Lantau – is also very scenic.

Equip yourself with food, water, rain gear and UV (sunblock) lotion. Start out early, allowing yourself plenty of time to reach civilisation or a campsite.

If you're going to walk on this route, it would be wise to pick up the *Lantau Trail* map published by the Country Parks Authority and available from the Government Publications Centre next to the GPO in Central, Hong Kong Island.

TAI O 大澳

For many years this village was the largest single settlement on the island, though it has recently been surpassed by Discovery Bay. A hundred years ago, along with Tung Chung village, Tai O was an important trading and fishing port, exporting salt and fish to China. The salt pans are still there but are almost unused. The locals make a living from duck farming, fishing, rice growing, making shrimp paste and processing salt fish. Processing tourists has in recent years become a major contributor to the economy.

Tai O is built partly on Lantau and partly on a tiny island a few metres from the shore – two women pull a rope-drawn boat across the creek. This ferry service could easily be replaced with a modern bridge but no one wants to as the ferry is one of the most photographed spots in town. The cost for the ferry is 50c.

A few of the old-style village houses still stand, but most are being replaced by modern concrete block houses. There are still many stilt houses on the waterfront as well as other shanties, including houseboats that haven't set sail for years and have been extended in such a way that they never could again. It's an interesting place but there are some pretty powerful odours from the fish-processing industry. The local temple is dedicated to the God of War, Kuanti.

Places to Eat

The village is famous for its seafood, and has several seafood restaurants, mostly unnamed. There is a decent Chinese restaurant with no English sign, but to get there, cross the creek on the hand-pulled boat, then go to the end of the road. The restaurant will be directly in front of you at the T-intersection.

Getting There & Away

Take bus No 1 from Mui Wo to Tai O. The ride takes 45 minutes. Getting from Ngong Ping to Tai O can be a hassle – the No 2 bus from Ngong Ping will drop you off at the intersection of Mountain Rd and the main highway, from where you must get bus No 1. Unfortunately, this latter bus is often full and won't stop. The alternative is to walk, which takes about one hour, but at least it's downhill all the way.

On Saturday afternoons, Sundays and holidays, there is a ferry from Central to Tuen Mun in the New Territories, which then continues on to Sha Lo Wan on the north side of Lantau and finally terminates at Tai O before heading back. There are also ferries running between Discovery Bay and Mui Wo.

FAN LAU 分流

Fan Lau on the south-west tip of Lantau has a couple of very good beaches and another old fort, very overgrown but with a good view. From Tai O village, it's a couple of hours clamber along the coastal section of the Lantau Trail.

CHEUNG SHA BEACH & TONG FUK
長沙海灘/塘福

Buses head to the Po Lin Monastery from Mui Wo along the road that hugs the southern coast. There are long stretches of good beaches (with occasional good surf) from Cheung Sha to Tong Fuk on the south coast of Lantau. Both are major tourist-beach centres. There is also a medium-security prison in Tong Fuk – at least it's a scenic prison.

SHEK PIK RESERVOIR 石壁水塘

At Tong Fuk the bus starts to go inland along the Shek Pik Reservoir (completed in 1963) which provides Lantau with its drinking water. Underwater pipes also supply Cheung Chau and parts of Hong Kong Island with fresh water from this reservoir. It's considered a pretty place with forest plantations and picnic spots, but a notorious maximum-security prison spoils the view. If you're feeling fit, you can walk down from Ngong Ping.

CHI MA WAN 芝麻灣

Chi Ma Wan, the peninsula in the south-east, takes its name from the large prison there. You can walk down through the Chi Ma Wan Peninsula to the beaches at Yi Long and Tai Long, but arm yourself with a map. You can also get there by kaido from Cheung Chau, though it stops at the prison and you may be asked what you're doing around there.

At the southern end of the peninsula is Sea Ranch, an upmarket residential area which might be described as a 'weekend Discovery Bay'. It's not really geared towards tourism, but more towards well-to-do Hong Kongers who own villas here which mostly get used on weekends. A ferry runs from Central twice daily on weekdays but much more frequently on weekends. The ferry costs HK$25 on weekdays, HK$30 on weekends, and special bookings (☎ 9892128) can be made by ringing up the office between 9.30 am and 9 pm daily.

Places to Stay

The HKYHA operates a beach-side hostel in the south-east corner of Chi Ma Wan called *Mong Tung Wan* (☎ 9841389). Beds cost HK$40 and camping is permitted. It's advisable to phone the hostel first as it's sometimes shut for a day so the warden can take time off. From Mui Wo, take the bus to Pui O, then walk along the road to Ham Tin. At the junction of Chi Ma Wan Rd and the temple, take the footpath to Mong Tung Wan, about a 45-minute walk. An alternative route is to take a ferry to Cheung Chau Island, and hire a sampan to the jetty at Mong Tung Wan – a sampan carries about 10 people. There are also campsites in the area.

TUNG CHUNG 東涌

This relatively flat farming region is centred around the village of Tung Chung on the northern shore of Lantau. There are several Buddhist establishments in the upper reaches of the valley, but the main attraction is the 19th-century Tung Chung Fort which still has its old cannon pointing out to sea. The fort dates back to 1817 when Chinese troops were garrisoned on Lantau. The area was used as a base by the infamous pirate Cheung Po Tsai, and the Japanese briefly occupied it during WW II but found little military use for it and soon abandoned the neighbourhood. The fort was completely restored in 1988.

About one km to the north is the much smaller Tung Chung Battery, another fort built around the same town. All that remains is a wall, the rest of it having fallen down. Currently, there are no plans for restoration. These ruins were only discovered in 1980, having been hidden for about a century by vegetation which has now been cleared.

Relatively few tourists come here because of the poor transport. This will change if the new airport is ever completed and Tung Chung becomes another Kowloon-style housing estate. In the meantime, it's a peaceful place. You can walk from the Ngong Ping tea gardens down to Tung Chung (five km) in two hours and then take the bus back. Otherwise hike from Mui Wo to Tung Chung – this takes about 4½ hours and wanders through old Hakka villages before reaching the coast and the farming settlement. Hiking from Tai O to Tung Chung takes about five hours.

DISCOVERY BAY 愉景灣

Discovery Bay was discovered by real estate developers around 1975. Nearly everyone thought they were crazy trying to build luxury condominiums in a remote corner of Lantau. To make the long commute tolerable, high-speed ferries were introduced. A massive advertising campaign had to be launched to draw in buyers and renters for the condos – 'Discover Discovery Bay' was the slogan. The cynics laughed and predicted early bankruptcy for the whole project.

Now it's the developers who are laughing all the way to the bank. The massive building boom is continuing at a feverish pace and rents are just as high as Mid-Levels on Hong Kong Island.

It's every inch a gwailo community, and the gwailos live high. The Chinese minority that live here is also in the upper income bracket. The golf course and yacht club make it pretty clear that Discovery Bay is no place

Top: Silvermine Bay, Lantau Island, Outlying Islands (RS)
Bottom: Discovery Bay, Lantau Island, Outlying Islands (RS)

Top: Aberdeen Harbour, Hong Kong Island (PS)
Left: Junk under construction, Cheung Chau, Outlying Islands (TW)
Right: Near Po Lin Monastery, Lantau, Outlying Islands (TW)

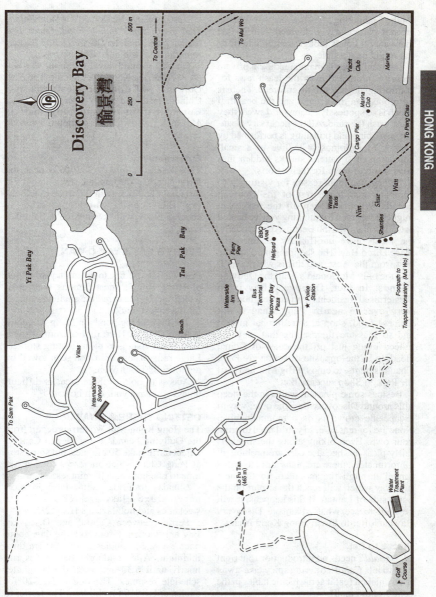

Discovery Bay
愉景灣

500 m
250
0

To Central
To Mui Wo
To Sam Pak
To Peng Chau

Yi Pak Bay

Tai Pak Bay

Beach

Villas

International School

Waterside Inn

Bus Terminal

Ferry Pier

BBQ Area

Helipad

Discovery Bay Plaza

★ Police Station

Yacht Club

Marina

Marina Club

Cargo Pier

Water Taxis

Nim Shue Wan

Shanties

Footpath to Trappist Monastery (Mui Wo)

Lo Fu Tan (465 m)

Water Treatment Plant

Golf Course

for the Chungking Mansions crowd. Tourists are not particularly welcomed, and in fact there are no hotels though renting a holiday flat might be possible.

Law and order is maintained by a private security force, and even the leash laws for controlling dogs is strictly enforced. There is no rubbish on the ground and the beautiful beach is so spotlessly clean you'd swear they must wash the sand. All the necessary cleaning, sweeping and polishing is performed by a crew of Filipinos, who live in a small collection of squatters' shacks hidden in a cove south of town for their efforts.

Perhaps the main reason for visiting is to compare it with the rest of the Outlying Islands. When you step off the ferry, you might be forgiven for thinking you've landed at California's Malibu Beach. Appropriately, the locals have unofficially renamed the place Disco Bay. The shopping mall has the best from the West, and this is where you'll find the only McDonald's in all the Outlying Islands. In fact, Discovery Bay is so Westernised residents sometimes hop the ferry over to nearby Peng Chau to eat Chinese food, shop at a traditional market and to reassure themselves that they are indeed living just off the coast of China. Heading in the opposite direction are Peng Chau residents, to enjoy a Big Mac and visit the Park 'n Shop supermarket.

Besides some pleasant walks in the steep hills around Discovery Bay, the other way to escape the crowd is on a mountain bike. None are for rent here, so you'll need to bring your own. Even biking along the streets is fairly pleasant, because cars are prohibited. Unfortunately, there are plans afoot to drill a tunnel through the mountain to the new highway which will reach the airport on the north side of Lantau. If this happens, it will be hard to see what advantage Discovery Bay can offer to life in Hong Kong Island.

Places to Eat
McDonald's needs no introduction, but right next to it is *Cajun's* offering spicy take-away fried chicken (eat it at the picnic tables in the centre of the mall).

Upstairs above McDonald's is *Siam Palace Thai Food*, *Jojo's Indian Food*, *Lunch Box* (Italian pizza) and the *Discovery Bay Restaurant* (dim sum and other Chinese food).

On the ground level is *Seoul Garden* (☎ 9870073), a Korean restaurant. The *New Garden Food Court* does cafeteria-style Chinese fast food and Western breakfasts. Buried within the shopping mall is *Mövenpick*, known for its premium Swiss ice cream.

Entertainment
The *Waterside Inn* (☎ 9870063) near the ferry pier has the market sewn up. It's a restaurant and pub with a terrace overlooking the scenic waterfront and is chock-a-block with gwailos on a Saturday night.

PENNY'S BAY & YAM O WAN
竹篙灣/陰澳灣
Penny's Bay is home to the main yard of one of Hong Kong's most famous boatyards, which specialises in building sailing cruisers for the export market.

The biggest log ponds in Hong Kong are at Yam O Wan. Here timber from all over South-East Asia is kept in floating storage. Large rafts of logs are often seen towed by tug towards Tsuen Wan.

Access to both of these areas is difficult unless you have your own boat.

GETTING THERE & AWAY
The Hong Kong-Mui Wo ferries depart from the Outlying Islands Ferry Pier in Central. Direct ferries take 50 minutes, but some stop at Peng Chau which increases total travel time to one hour and 10 minutes.

Monday to Friday adult fares in ordinary/deluxe class are HK$7/12. On weekends and holidays it's HK$12/23.

Ferries between Central and Discovery Bay are frequent throughout the day, about once every 20 minutes from 6.30 am until midnight. After midnight the ferries run hourly until 6.30 am when the commuter schedule resumes. The fare is HK$20 for adults, or HK$10 for children. The ferries to

Discovery Bay depart from Star Ferry East Pier in Central.

You can also take ferries from Peng Chau to Mui Wo. See the Inter-Island ferry schedule for details. There is also a ferry between Mui Wo and Discovery Bay.

There are boats sailing daily on Saturdays, Sundays and holidays to Tai O on the west end of the island. The boats run from either Tuen Mun or Tsuen Wan in the New Territories to Tai O via Sha Lo Wan on the northern side of Lantau. One of the boats begins at Central (see the following timetables for details).

Central - Mui Wo

Monday to Saturday		Sunday & Holidays	
From Central	From Mui Wo	From Central	From Mui Wo
7.00 am*	6.10 am*	7.00 am*	6.10 am*
8.30	7.00	8.00!	7.00*
9.30	7.15*	8.30	8.15*
10.30	8.30	9.00!	9.30
11.30	9.30	9.30	10.30
12.30 pm	10.30	10.00!	11.30
1.30	11.30	10.30	12.30 pm
2.00!	12.30 pm	11.00!	1.30
2.30	1.30	11.30	2.30
3.00!	2.30	12.30 pm	3.00!
3.30	3.30	1.30	3.30
4.30	4.30	2.30	4.00!
5.30	5.30	3.30	4.30
6.30	6.30	4.30	5.00!
7.30	7.30	5.30	5.30
8.30	9.00*	6.30	6.00!
9.00*	10.00*	7.45*	6.30
10.00*	11.10*	8.50*	7.30
11.15*	-	10.00*	9.00*
12.20 am	-	11.15*	10.00*

* Via Peng Chau   ! Optional Sailing on Weekends & Holidays

Mui Wo Hoverferries

Monday - Friday, except Holidays

From Central	From Mui Wo
9.40 am	10.20 am
11.20	12.10 pm
2.25 pm	3.10
4.25	5.10

Saturday

From Central	From Tuen Muen	From Sha Lo Wan	From Tai O
9.15 am	10.40	11.20	11.50
3.00 pm	4.25	5.05	5.35

Saturday

From Tai O	From Sha Lo Wan	From Tuen Muen
11.50 am	12.20 pm	1.00
5.45 pm	6.15	6.55

Sunday & Holidays

From Central	From Tuen Muen	From Sha Lo Wan	From Tai O
8.15 am	9.40	10.20	10.50
-	4.15 pm	4.55	5.25

Sunday & Holidays

From Tai O	From Sha Lo Wan	From Tuen Muen	From Central
3.00 pm	3.30	4.10	-
5.30 pm	6.00	6.40	8.20

Sunday & Holidays

From Tsuen Wan	From Tuen Mun	From Sha Lo Wan	From Tai O
8 am	8.45	9.15	9.45

Sunday & Holidays

From Tai O	From Sha Lo Wan	From Tuen Mun	From Tsuen Wan
4.45 pm	5.15	5.45	6.30

Central - Sea Ranch

Monday to Friday		Saturday		Sunday & Holidays	
From Central	From Sea Ranch	From Central	From Sea Ranch	From Central	From Sea Ranch
8.15 am	7.30 am	8.15 am	7.30 am	10 am	9 am
6.30 pm	5.15 pm	12.30 pm	11.45	2.45 pm	noon
-	-	2.00	1.15 pm	2.15	1.30 pm
-	-	5.45	5.00	5.45	5.00
-	-	7.15	6.30	8.15	7.30

Discovery Bay - Mui Wo

Monday to Friday		Saturday		Sunday & Holidays	
From Discovery Bay	From Mui Wo	From Discovery Bay	From Mui Wo	From Discovery Bay	From Mui Wo
7.25 am	7.45 am	7.25 am	7.45 am	8.40 am	9 am
11.00	11.20	10.50	11.10	10.50	11.10
3.00 pm	3.20 pm	1.20 pm	1.40 pm	1.20 pm	1.40 pm
4.20	4.40	4.20	4.40	4.20	4.40
6.20	6.40	6.20	6.40	6.20	6.40
-	-	7.50	8.20	7.50	8.20

GETTING AROUND
Bus
Services run by the New Lantau Bus Company all leave from the car park by the ferry pier in Mui Wo. Bus Nos 1, 2 and 3 are the most frequent – the others are occasional. During weekends, bus service is often inadequate to meet the crushing demand – they may fill up and you could find yourself waiting for hours. The seven bus routes are as follows:

Bus No	Bus Route
No 1	Mui Wo to Tai O
No 2	Mui Wo to Ngong Ping
No 3	Mui Wo to Tung Chung
No 4	Mui Wo to Tong Fuk
No 5	Mui Wo to Shek Pik
No 6	Student Bus
No 7	Mui Wo to Pui O

Taxi
If you think the bus service is rotten, just wait until you try Lantau taxis. In supposedly free-market Hong Kong, Lantau taxi drivers are a protected lot. The number of taxis is inadequate, they will not pick you up along country roads where you desperately need them and the drivers are often hostile to customers. It's easiest to find taxis in Mui Wo and occasionally in Tong Fuk – elsewhere, they are a rare item indeed.

Taxis are prohibited from taking you all the way to Ngong Ping – they will drop you off at the bottom of the access road, from where you have a steep climb up the mountain.

Hitching
Forget it. I tried, accompanied by a Chinese girl who certainly looked harmless – but we didn't even have a crumb of success.

Peng Chau 坪洲

Shaped like a horseshoe, tiny Peng Chau is just under a sq km in area. It is inhabited by around 8000 souls, making it far more crowded than nearby Lantau.

Of all the islands mentioned in this chapter, Peng Chau is perhaps the most traditionally Chinese – narrow alleys, crowded housing, a good outdoor market (near the ferry pier) and heaps of closet-sized restaurants and shops. There are a couple of small temples. The main reminder that you are still in Hong Kong is the 7-Eleven store.

There's been a drift of middle-class Hong Kong Chinese towards this island, much as there has been a drift of Westerners to Cheung Chau and Lamma. Besides Hong Kong commuters, the economy is supported by some tiny cottage industries, notably the manufacture of furniture, porcelain and metal tubes. Weekend tourists also contribute significantly to Peng Chau's coffers – arriving Hong Kongers head straight for the seafood restaurants and spend a small fortune on banquet-sized meals.

There are no cars on Peng Chau and you can walk around it with ease in an hour. Climbing up to the island's highest point at Finger Hill (95 metres) will give you some light exercise and excellent views when the weather is clear. Unfortunately, most of Peng Chau's sewage, plastic bags and styrofoam end up in the sea, making the otherwise pleasant beach on the east side of the island too dirty for swimming.

PLACES TO EAT
There are two popular pub/restaurant combinations that are a big hit with the gwailos. The larger of the two is the *Sea Breeze Club* (☎ 9838785), 38 Wing Hing St, known for its fine T-bone steak dinners. The food is so good and so reasonably priced that residents from nearby Discovery Bay take the ferry across just to eat there. It packs out on Sundays, especially in the afternoon.

The *Forest Pub* (☎ 9838837) is next door at No 38C. It's a small but cosy place with good pub grub. It owes much of its ambience to the friendly owner, an expat New Zealander.

GETTING THERE & AWAY
The regular ferry from Central takes 50 minutes. For the regular ferry, ordinary

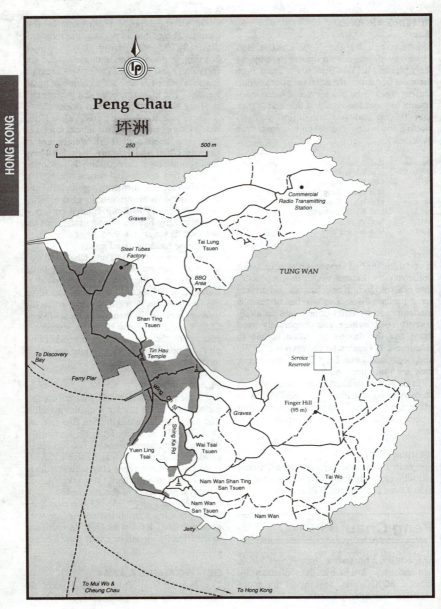

/deluxe fares on Monday to Friday cost HK$6.50/12, and on weekends and holidays it's HK$11/23.

There are four hoverferries daily (Monday to Friday) from Central to Mui Wo, and all stop in Peng Chau along the way. From Central to Peng Chau by hoverferry takes 25 minutes and costs HK$16.

The ferry from Peng Chau to Mui Wo on Lantau Island costs HK$4.50 for adults, HK$2.30 for children.

Peng Chau is also the place to depart for the Trappist Monastery on Lantau. The monastery's kaido takes passengers over the short stretch of water to Lantau.

Central - Peng Chau

Monday - Saturday		Sunday & Holidays	
From Central	From Peng Chau	From Central	From Peng Chau
7.00 am	6.30 am	7.00 am	6.30 am
8.15	7.15	8.15	7.20
9.15	7.40	9.15	8.35
10.15	8.15	10.15	9.15
11.15	9.15	11.15	10.15
12.15 pm	10.15	12.15 pm	11.15
1.15	11.15	1.15	12.15 pm
2.15	12.15 pm	2.15	1.15
3.15	1.15	3.15	2.15
4.15	2.15	4.15	3.15
5.15	3.15	5.15	4.15
6.15	4.15	6.15	5.15
7.15	5.15	7.15	6.15
8.15	6.15	7.45	7.15
9.00	7.15	8.50	8.15
10.00	8.15	10.00	9.20
11.15	9.20	11.15	10.20
12.20	10.20	12.20 am	11.30
-	11.30	-	-

Peng Chau - Discovery Bay

Monday - Saturday except Holidays

From Peng Chau	From Discovery Bay	From Trappist Haven
5.30 am	5.45 am	-
6.30	6.55	-
7.10	7.20	-
7.45*	8.00*	8.10 am
8.30	8.45	-
9.05*	9.15*	9.30
11.15*	11.40	11.30
12.15 pm*	12.40 pm	12.30 pm
1.15!	1.30!	-
2.20*	2.35*	2.45
4.20*	4.40	4.30

From Peng Chau	From Discovery Bay	From Trappist Haven
5.25	5.45	-
6.15	6.30	-
6.45	7.00	-
7.30#	7.45#	-
7.45!	8.00!	-
8.45!	9.00	-
9.45	10.00	-

* via Trappist Haven Monastery   ! Saturday only   # Monday - Friday only

Peng Chau - Discovery Bay
Sundays & Holidays

From Peng Chau	From Disco Bay	From Trappist Haven
5.30 am	5.45 am	-
6.30	6.55	-
7.10	7.20	-
7.45*	8.00*	8.10 am
9.20	9.30	-
10.00*	10.30	10.15
11.00	11.15	-
noon*	12.30 pm	12.15 pm
1.30 pm	1.40	-
2.30*	2.45*	3.00
4.30*	5.00	4.45
5.15	5.40	-
6.15	6.30	-
6.45	7.00	-
7.45	8.00	-
8.45	9.00	-
9.45	10.00	-

* via Trappist Haven Monastery

Central - Peng Chau
Monday - Friday except Holidays

From Central	From Peng Chau
9.40 am	10.30 am
11.20	12.20 pm
2.25 pm	3.20
4.25	5.20

Peng Chau - Mui Wo

From Peng Chau	From Mui Wo
10.05 am	10.20 am
11.45	12.10 pm
2.50 pm	3.10
4.50 pm	5.10

Tung Lung Chau 東龍洲

Guarding the eastern entrance to Victoria Harbour is remote Tung Lung Chau, meaning 'east dragon island'. The island's position was at one time considered strategic to protect the harbour, but in this age of jet aircraft and Stinger missiles, it hardly matters. Tung Lung Fort on the north-east corner of the island was eventually abandoned but is now preserved as a historical site. Pirates no doubt used the island as a staging post, but there is little remaining evidence of their presence.

Humans have apparently been on Tung Lung Chau for a long time. The north-west corner of the island has some ancient rock carvings, the largest ever found in Hong Kong. No one knows who the original artists were and the carvings are simply classified as dating from the 'bronze age'. The carvings are believed to represent a dragon, which may be another way of saying nobody really knows what kind of animal it is. Whoever the artists were, they and their descendants have fled the

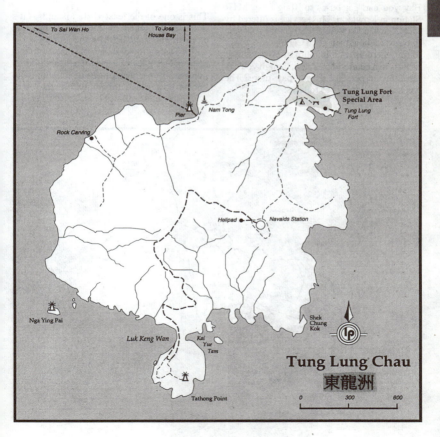

Tung Lung Chau
東龍洲

scene. Except for nomadic bands of weekend tourists, the island is now uninhabited.

GETTING THERE & AWAY

Unless you have your own boat or charter one, the only time you can visit Tung Lung Chau is on weekends. The one-way fare is HK$10. Kaidos depart from Sai Wan Ho just east of Quarry Bay on Hong Kong Island, stop at Tung Lung Chau and then continue on to Joss House Bay in the New Territories. The ride to Joss House Bay is significantly shorter than the trip from Sai Wan Ho, and you could go by one route and return by the other. From Joss House Bay you can get buses to Tong Choi MTR Station in Kowloon. This service is offered by Lam Kee Kaido (☎ 5609929), and if you want to charter a boat then get a Cantonese speaker to ring them up. A minimum of 30 persons is usual when chartering a kaido, though you can have fewer persons if you pay more. The weekend schedule is as follows:

Sai Wan Ho – Tung Lung Chau

Saturday

From Sai Wan Ho	*From Tung Lung*
8.30 am	4 pm
3.30 pm	9.40 am

Sunday & Holidays

From Sai Wan Ho	*From Tung Lung*
8.15 am	2 pm
3 pm	4 pm

Poi Toi 蒲台

This is one of the least visited islands – it's not even crowded on Sundays! That fact alone might make it worth the journey.

Poi Toi is a rocky island off the south-east coast of Hong Kong Island. There are a small number of permanent residents, but who knows how much longer before they will

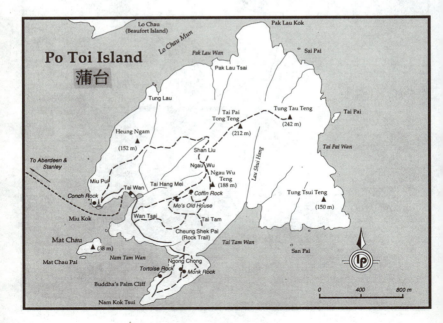

finally give up their peaceful outpost and migrate to the sin and glitter of the city just beyond their shores?

GETTING THERE & AWAY
Ferries to Poi Toi depart from Aberdeen on Tuesdays, Thursdays and Saturdays at 9 am. They return from Poi Toi at 10.30 am, which means that if you want to explore the island, you must stay overnight. However, on Sundays, there are three boats, so you can go and return the same day. The earliest Sunday boat departs from Aberdeen at 8 am. There are two Sunday boats departing from Stanley at 10 and 11.30 am. Going the other way, there are Sunday departures from Poi Toi at 9.15 and 10.45 am, and 3, 4.30 and 6 pm.

A reservation is needed for all these boats. This can be booked by phone (☎ 5544059), but they don't speak English. Locals pay HK$15 for a one-way journey, but nonresidents of Poi Toi pay HK$30 for the round-trip if returning the same day. If staying overnight, the fare jumps to HK$50 for the round-trip. The Aberdeen-Poi Toi trip takes 70 minutes, but only 35 minutes from Stanley.

HONG KONG

MACAU 澳門

Facts about Macau

Only 65 km from Hong Kong but predating it by 300 years, Macau is the oldest surviving European settlement in Asia, and is Portugal's last colony. It is a city of cobbled side streets, baroque churches, Portuguese fortresses and unpronounceable Portuguese street names. Macau's culture, cooking and people are a hybrid of Portuguese and Chinese.

There are several Chinese temples and restored colonial villas, and it is the final resting place of many European seafarers and soldiers. You will also find casinos, discos, high-rises and five-star hotels.

Tourism has had a shot in the arm in recent years, with several large luxury hotels being built on the mainland and on the islands. Yet apart from the Chinese gamblers, most tourists who go to Macau spend just a few whistle-stop hours there. Many who visit Hong Kong don't bother going to Macau at all – a misfortune because it is one of those curious places where something new can be found on every visit.

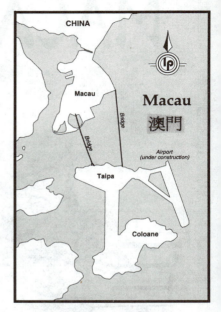

HISTORY

Macau means the 'City of God' and takes its name from A-Ma-Gau, the Bay of A-Ma. At Barra Point stands the A-Ma Temple which dates back to the early 16th century.

According to legend, A-Ma, a poor girl looking for a passage to Guangzhou, was turned away by the wealthy junk owners, so a fisherman took her on board. A storm blew up and wrecked all the junks except the boat carrying the girl. When it landed in Macau the girl disappeared, only to reappear later as a goddess on the spot where the fisherman built her temple.

Portuguese Exploration & Colonisation

Macau is an oddity which has managed to cling to the Chinese coast since the mid-16th century, despite attempts by the Chinese, the Spanish and the Dutch to brush it off. For more than a hundred years previously the Portuguese had been pushing down the west

African coast in their search for a sea route to the Far East. But they were delayed by the attractions of slaves and gold from Guinea which brought immediate material rewards, and by their ambition to find the mysterious Christian king Prester John who would join them in a crusade against the Muslims.

When, in 1498, Vasco da Gama's ships rounded the southern cape of Africa and arrived in Calicut (Calcutta) in India, the Portuguese suddenly got a whiff of the enormous profits to be made from the Asian trade. Also, because the trade was almost exclusively in the hands of Muslims, they had the added satisfaction (and excuse) that any blow against their commercial rivals was a blow against the infidels.

There had never been any real intention to

conquer large tracts of territory, colonise foreign lands or convert the native populations to Christianity en masse. Trade was always first and foremost in Portuguese minds. To this end, a vague plan was devised to bring all the important Indian Ocean trading ports under Portuguese control and to establish the necessary fortifications to protect their trade.

Thus, the Portuguese captured Goa on the west coast of India in 1510, and then Malacca on the Malay Peninsula in 1511 (their first ships having arrived there in 1509). They then attempted to subdue the Spice Islands of the Moluccas, in what is now Indonesia, and thus control the lucrative spice trade.

The Portuguese never did manage to monopolise the trade. As the years rolled by their determination and ability to do so declined. By the end of the 16th century their efforts were brought to a close by the arrival in Indonesia of powerful Dutch fleets also bent on wresting control of the spice trade.

More encouraging for the Portuguese was the trade with China and Japan. On their earliest voyages to India the Portuguese had heard of a strange, light-skinned people called the Chin, whose huge ships had once visited India but whose voyages had suddenly ceased. (From 1405-1433, the second Ming Emperor Yong Le had dispatched several enormous maritime expeditions which had made contact with many parts of Asia and Africa.)

When the Portuguese arrived in Malacca in 1511 they came upon several junks with Chinese captains. Realising that the Chins were not a mythical people and concluding that they had come from the 'Cathay' of Marco Polo's travels, a small party of Portuguese were sent northwards to find out what they could do to possibly open trade with the Chinese.

The first Portuguese set foot on Chinese soil in 1513 at the mouth of the Pearl River, near what is now Macau and Hong Kong. They reached Japan by accident in 1542, their ship having been blown off course.

By and large, initial Portuguese contact with China did not go well, and for years their attempts to gain a permanent trading base on the Chinese coast met with little success. But in the early 1550s they reached some sort of agreement with Cantonese officials to settle on Sanchuang, a small island about 80 km to the south-west of the mouth of the Pearl River. Sanchuang's exposed anchorage led the Portuguese to abandon the island in 1553, moving to another island closer to the Pearl River.

To the north-east was a peninsula of land where the Portuguese also frequently anchored. It had two natural harbours – an inner harbour on the West River and an outer harbour in a bay facing the Pearl River – and to its south were some sheltering islands. In 1556 or 1557 the Portuguese and some Guangzhou officials made an agreement which allowed the Portuguese to rent this peninsula of land – known variously as Amagao, Amacon, Aomen and Macau – apparently in return for ridding the area of marauding pirates who plagued this stretch of the coast. However, the peninsula was never formally ceded to the Portuguese.

Macau grew rapidly as a trading centre, largely because the Chinese wanted to trade with foreign countries but were forbidden to go abroad on penalty of death. The most lucrative trade route for the Portuguese was the long circuit from the west of India to Japan and back, with Macau as the essential link. Acting as agents for Chinese merchants, they took Chinese goods to the west coast of India, exchanging them for cotton and textiles which they took to Malacca and sold to local merchants in exchange for spices and aromatic woods. The Portuguese then continued to Japan where they sold their Malacca cargo for Japanese silver, swords, lacquerware and fans, returning to Macau to exchange them for more Chinese goods.

The Japanese were forbidden to enter Chinese ports and the trade of other Asian nationals with China was largely insignificant. The Portuguese displaced the Arabs and, with no other Europeans yet on the scene, they became the carriers of all large-scale international commerce with China and Japan.

MACAU

MACAU

17th-Century Macau

By the start of the 17th century Macau supported several thousand permanent residents, including about a thousand Portuguese. The rest were Chinese Christian converts, mixed-race Christians from Malacca, Japanese Christians and a large number of African, Indian and Malay slaves. Large numbers of Chinese citizens worked in the town as hawkers, labourers and servants. There were many Chinese traders too.

Trade was the most important activity of the new town, but Macau was also fast becoming a centre of Christianity in the Far East. Priests and missionaries accompanied Portuguese ships, though the attack was not jointly planned and the interests of traders and missionaries frequently conflicted. Among the earliest missionaries was Francis Xavier (later canonised) of the Jesuit order. He had spent two years in Japan (1549-1551) attempting to convert heathens, before turning his attention to China. Xavier was stalled by Portuguese who feared the consequences of his meddling in Chinese affairs, but he made it as far as Sanchuang, where he died in December 1552. In the years to follow it was Jesuit missionaries, not traders, who were able to penetrate China beyond Macau and Guangzhou.

The Portuguese who stayed in Macau, along with their Macanese (mixed-blood) descendants, succeeded in creating a home away from home with luxurious rococo houses and splendid baroque churches, paid for with the wealth generated by their monopoly on trade with China and Japan. These structures included the Basilica of St Paul, hailed as the greatest monument to Christianity in the East.

Apart from traders and priests, this odd little colony attracted some colourful adventurers, eccentrics, artists and poets. Among them was the 16th-century poet Luis de Camoes, who was banished from Portugal to Goa and then to Macau, although some say he was never in the colony. He is said to have written in Macau at least part of his epic poem Os Lusiadas, which recounts the voyage of Vasco da Gama to India. British artist George Chinnery spent a quarter of a century in Macau, from 1825 until his death in 1852, and is remembered for his paintings of the place and its people.

Portuguese Decline

The Portuguese decline was as rapid as its success. In 1580 Spanish armies occupied Portugal, then in the early years of the 17th century, the Dutch began making their presence felt in the Far East. In response, the Portuguese at Macau began building fortresses in anticipation of Dutch attacks. The Dutch made several forays on Macau, including major but unsuccessful attacks in 1607 and 1627.

Next the Japanese became suspicious of Portuguese (and also Spanish) intentions, and began persecuting Japanese Christians, eventually closing the country to foreign trade in 1637. In 1640 the Dutch took Malacca by force. Although Portugal regained its independence in 1640, all trade connections with China and Japan were cut off. The Portuguese could no longer provide the Chinese with the Japanese silver they wanted in exchange for their silk and porcelain, nor with spices since the spice trade was now in the hands of the Dutch. Macau was no longer of any use to the Chinese and by 1640 they had closed the port of Guangzhou to the Portuguese, leaving Macau to deteriorate rapidly into an impoverished settlement in danger of extinction.

But Macau managed to survive by other means. From the mid-18th century – as the French, Dutch, Danes, Swedes, Americans and Spanish all profited from trading with China via Guangzhou – restrictions and regulations concerning non-Portuguese residing in Macau were lifted. In effect the colony became an outpost for all of Europe in China, a position which it held until the British took possession of Hong Kong in 1841 and other Chinese ports were forced open to foreign trade in the years following.

Until the middle of the 19th century the history of Macau was a long series of incidents – stand-offs, threats, disputes and attacks, involving the Portuguese, Chinese and British – as the Portuguese attempted to maintain their grasp. The Portuguese even made plans around 1850 to attack Guangzhou as the British had done during the Opium Wars, in order to dictate a Chinese-Portuguese treaty. A series of disasters, including the intended flagship of the fleet blowing up off Taipa Island, meant that this plan never came to fruition. The Portuguese were once again forced to settle their differences with China through negotiation, though it was not until 1887 that a treaty was signed in which China effectively recognised Portuguese sovereignty over Macau. As for the problem of keeping Macau financially afloat, that had been more or less solved by Governor Isidoro Francisco Guimaraes (1851-1863), who introduced what has become the best-known feature of the colony – licensed gambling.

20th-Century Macau

Macau had turned into something of a decaying backwater by the late 19th century, though it continued to serve as a place of refuge for Chinese who were fleeing war and famine in the north.

When the Sino-Japanese War erupted in the 1930s, the population swelled to a formidable 500,000. Europeans also took refuge in Macau during WW II because the Japanese honoured Portuguese neutrality and did not take Macau as they did Hong Kong. More people came in 1949 when the Communists took power in China, and from 1978 until about 1980 Macau was a destination for Vietnamese boat people. Somehow the tiny place managed to contain them all.

Macau's last great convulsion occurred in 1966 when China's Cultural Revolution spilled over into the colony. Macau was stormed by Red Guards and there were violent riots in which a few Red Guards were shot dead by Portuguese troops. The then governor reportedly proposed that the troubles could be ended if Portugal simply left Macau forever, but fearing the loss of foreign trade through Macau and Hong Kong, the Chinese backed off.

In 1974 a military coup in Portugal brought a left-wing government to power which proceeded to divest Portugal of the last remnants of its empire (including Mozambique, Angola and East Timor), yet the Chinese told the Portuguese that they preferred to leave Macau as it was.

Until 1975, Portugal maintained a 'touch-base' policy regarding Chinese immigrants. That is, any Chinese reaching Macau could obtain residency, even if they reached it by swimming. From 1975, the policy was changed and all Chinese sneaking into Macau are now regarded as illegal immigrants.

Macau Today

Once the Joint Declaration over Hong Kong was signed by Britain and China, it was inevitable that China would also seek a similar agreement with Portugal on Macau's future. That agreement was finally inked in March 1987.

Under the Sino-Portuguese pact, Macau will become a Special Administrative Region (SAR) of China for 50 years after 20 December 1999. Like Hong Kong, Macau is to enjoy a 'high degree of autonomy' in all matters except defence and foreign affairs.

An important change occurred in 1982 regarding the status of Macau's Chinese majority. Prior to 1982, any person born in Macau could have full Portuguese citizenship. Partly due to pressure from China, and partly due to a scandal involving the selling of Portuguese passports to Hong Kongers, the rules were changed. Now, one parent must be a Portuguese citizen, though he or she need not be of Portuguese descent. Less than one-fifth of Macau's ethnic Chinese population holds Portuguese passports.

Nevertheless, China continues to raise objections, claiming that anyone of Chinese descent is a Chinese citizen. In other words, race should be the deciding factor, not place of birth. China has threatened to revoke the Portuguese citizenship of Macau's ethnic Chinese, which has caused much anxiety. However, so far there has not been a massive flight of people and capital as there has been in Hong Kong. The reason may have more

MACAU

"Cidade do Santo Nome de Deus" - MACAU

to do with the fact that few Chinese have the financial resources to flee Macau.

The pro-democracy demonstrations in 1989 that swept through China before being brutally suppressed, also caught on in Macau. Shortly before the tanks started rolling over students in Beijing, a huge pro-democracy rally was held in Macau and attracted over 100,000 participants, more than one-fifth of the population.

All in all, 1990 was not a good year for Macau. Tourism was already down because of the Beijing massacre, but China's wheelchair leadership shook everyone's confidence even further by interfering in Macau's internal affairs. Deputy Director Lu Ping of China's Hong Kong & Macau Affairs Office, launched a verbal barrage against the Macau government. Lu insisted that the Macau government should tear down the statue of former governor Joao Ferreira do Amaral because it was 'too colonial'. He then went on to condemn the opening of a Taipei Trade & Tourism Office in Macau, and insisted that the government should move faster to make Chinese (Putonghua) the official language of Macau, and that all Portuguese laws should be translated into Chinese. He also wanted Macau's civil service to be controlled by local Chinese, rather than Portuguese and Macanese as is presently the case.

Macau's governor Carlos Melancia launched a verbal counterattack, but he soon had serious problems of his own. He was forced to resign as the result of a scandal involving kickbacks for construction contracts on Macau's new airport. The evidence against him was weak and many believe the accusations were politically motivated.

Between the entrance of the Hotel Lisboa and the Macau-Taipa Bridge was a statue to Joao Ferreira do Amaral, a governor of Macau in the mid-19th century. He was responsible for the expulsion of the Chinese customs officials from Macau, the declaration of the colony as a free port and the annexation of Taipa Island. The statue was erected in 1940 and quickly became one of the most photographed monuments in Macau.

Amaral, who had lost his right arm in a battle several years before, was set upon by Chinese assassins one day near the border and was beheaded. The statue showed him on horseback with a whip in his left hand fighting off the attackers.

It wasn't his last battle. The Chinese government has apparently decided to assert its control over Macau long before 1999 – the Portuguese administration was told that the statue had to go because it was 'too colonial'. In 1992, Joao Ferreira do Amaral was packed up in crates and shipped back to Portugal. Many now believe that China – the new colonial power – will dismantle other Portuguese monuments, and perhaps a statue of Mao will appear where Joao Ferreira de Amaral once rode his horse.

The aftershock of the 1989 Beijing massacre has gradually worn off. Tourism and foreign investment are both picking up again, but Macau enters its final decade under Portuguese rule with a bad case of the jitters. Nervousness about China's intentions has already hurt the economy, but many also believe that China wouldn't dare harm Macau. As for the illegal immigrants, they have no doubts – despite the official policy of returning them to China, they continue to swim to what they hope will be a better life.

GEOGRAPHY

Macau is divided into three main sections – the Macau Peninsula which is attached to China at the northern tip, and the two islands of Taipa and Coloane. Taipa is to the south of Macau and is attached by two bridges. Coloane is south of Taipa and connected by a causeway.

Macau is a tiny place. It has a total land area of 16 sq km, only 1.6% of Hong Kong's land total. The Macau Peninsula is just 5.5 sq km, while the islands of Taipa and Coloane occupy 3.3 sq km and 7.2 sq km respectively. However, due to land reclamation, the place is gradually getting bigger.

The northern tip of the Macau Peninsula, near the China border, is the newer part of town where many high-rise apartments have been built, mostly on reclaimed land.

Most of the interesting historical buildings are in the central and southern parts of the peninsula. The southern part (near the Penha Church) is the high-class area of town, with expensive homes perched on the hillsides with views of the sea.

CLIMATE

Macau's climate is almost the same as Hong Kong, but with one nice difference – the cool sea breeze is delightful on summer nights and acts as natural air-conditioning.

GOVERNMENT

Officially, Macau is not considered a colony. Instead, the Portuguese government regards Macau as a piece of Chinese territory under Portuguese administration. The difference is largely a matter of semantics.

The colony/Chinese territory has a governor who is appointed by the president of Portugal. The governor appoints five under

secretaries, each with a specific field of administration. There is also a legislative assembly with 23 members. Eight of them are directly elected, another eight are elected by various 'economic interest groups', and seven are appointed by the governor. The assembly then elects its own president. There are three mayors: one for the Macau Peninsula and one each for the two islands, Taipa and Coloane.

ECONOMY

For many years, gambling was Macau's *raison d'etre*, and although that's no longer true, it's still Macau's No 1 cash cow. The 'gaming industry' (as it prefers to be called) is monopolised by a small but wealthy Chinese business syndicate which trades under the name of STDM – Sociedade de Turismo e Diversoes de Macau (Macao Travel and Amusement Co). It was STDM that introduced the hydrofoils (later replaced with jetfoils) to Macau and built the Hotel Lisboa. This group won monopoly rights on all licensed gambling in Macau in 1962.

Although Macau has had a reputation for centuries as a gambling centre, casino gambling only got under way in 1934 when a Chinese syndicate called the Tai Hing obtained monopoly rights from the colonial government. Monopoly rights were renewed

MACAU

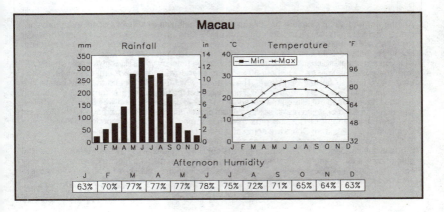

every five years and the monopoly went to whichever company would pay the most tax. The story goes that the original owners of the Tai Hing were able to pay a puny tax sum, but held on to the monopoly by paying off competitors. It wasn't until after the death of the two founders of the Tai Hing that the STDM gained a monopoly on the gambling industry.

About one-third of government revenue comes from gambling, another third from direct and indirect taxes and the rest from land rents and service charges.

Macau entertains almost six million tourists a year, or more than 12 times the local population. Over 80% of the tourists come from Hong Kong, with most of the remainder from Japan, the UK, Taiwan, the USA, Thailand and South Korea. Gambling and tourism provide about 25% of gross domestic product. The colony has various light industries, such as fireworks, textile and garment production, and wages are much lower than in Hong Kong.

The main reason why wages have remained low despite a labour shortage is that Macau has an agreement with China which allows a large number of Chinese workers to cross the border daily from Zhuhai. The agreement is controversial since it weakens the position of Macau's workers so they cannot demand better wages, but it also greatly benefits workers living in Zhuhai. The cheap supply of labour is attracting foreign investment. Taiwan, which suffers from its own labour shortage, is reportedly keen to invest heavily in Macau.

Macau closely follows the economic success formula employed in Hong Kong. It is a duty-free port and the maximum rate of taxation is 15%, as in Hong Kong.

The biggest news for Macau's economy is the construction of an international airport on the east side of Taipa Island at an estimated cost of US$625 million. This requires reclaiming land from the sea, and so far the project has moved slowly because of a dispute with the neighbouring city of Zhuhai in China.

Officially, Zhuhai's complaint is that the airport will create considerable noise pollution. For its part, Macau denies the problem, but a quick look at the map indicates that Zhuhai might find itself right under the flight path of approaching aircraft. But the real reason for the dispute is that Zhuhai is building its own airport and doesn't appreciate competition from Macau. Zhuhai officials successfully delayed the project by over six months by refusing to supply sand which

Prostitution

Another form of sinful pleasure besides gambling contributes to Macau's economic prosperity, though many tourists remain blissfully unaware of it. Efforts are made to keep the sex trade low-key to preserve Macau's family image. You probably won't encounter prostitutes in Macau – assuming, of course, that you look like the family type (accompanied by a spouse and kids) or if you're female.

If you are male and check into a mid to upper-range hotel by yourself, that 'friendly phone call' from the porter usually comes about 30 seconds after arriving at your room. Last time, I didn't even have time to put my bag down. The saunas, which are also found in many hotels, are well-known for this sort of entertainment. The majority of the hostesses are from Thailand, though Filipinos have staked out a large market share. In the old days when Asia was poor and the West was rich, it used to be white males seeking Asian prostitutes. The economic boom in the Far East and the recent import of Russian prostitutes has turned the tables – reportedly, high-ranking Communist officials from China are some of the most enthusiastic customers.

The prostitution business is not a happy profession, but the plight of the Thai hostesses is probably the saddest. As in Thailand, many are sold into virtual slavery by their parents. The Thai girls (they are too young to be called women) are rarely over 16. The Macau government is very concerned about AIDS spreading into the local population – that is why foreign women are imported for this business. ■

was necessary to construct the runway. Macau finally broke the impasse by appealing directly to Beijing, which overruled Zhuhai officials and resumed shipments of landfill material. To appease Zhuhai, Macau says it will share the airport with China. This will be accomplished by setting up a separate customs terminal so passengers heading to or from China will not have to pass through Macau customs.

The airport isn't the only big news for Macau's economy. A project is also under way to build a deep-water port on the northeast side of Coloane Island. In order to develop export-oriented industries like electronics, some way must be found to accommodate container ships. At present, Macau does not have a container terminal and all freight is handled inefficiently in crates. Ironically, while Macau's shallow harbour is constantly choked with mud flowing down from China's Pearl River, nearby Hong Kong has one of the finest natural deep-water harbours in the world.

The third major project is the construction of Taipa City, a large high-rise housing development on Taipa Island. In order to handle an expected increase in motor vehicle traffic, a second bridge was built between Taipa and the Macau Peninsula. And on the Chinese side of the border, a new freeway is being built between Zhuhai and Guangzhou, which will connect with the freeway being built from Hong Kong to Guangzhou. There is even talk of extending the railway from Guangzhou down to Zhuhai and maybe into Macau as well.

Another scheme now underway is a massive land reclamation project right on the Praia Grande, Macau's historical waterfront. Known as the Nam Van Lakes project because it will create two artificial freshwater lakes, the project has stirred considerable controversy. However, economics usually win out over aesthetics and construction is proceeding apace.

In view of all the preceding, you'd be right to conclude that Macau's former image as a peaceful, colonial backwater is rapidly changing. Already, old-timers are appalled at the traffic and new high-rise buildings. Nevertheless, there is no denying that these projects will benefit the economy. With Hong Kong's crowded airport close to saturation point, foreign airlines are already falling over themselves trying to secure landing rights in Macau.

POPULATION

A census conducted in 1992 found that Macau's population was 354,000. This shocked almost everyone, since the previous official figure had been 453,000 plus an estimated 40,000 illegal immigrants. The new figures have been met with widespread disbelief – perhaps the 99,000 missing souls just want to keep a low profile.

About 98% of the people live on the Macau Peninsula, making it one of the most crowded areas in the world. Ironically, the two islands have remained essentially rural, but this is due to change soon with the construction of Taipa City, a new high-rise development on Taipa Island.

PEOPLE

The population consists of about 95% Chinese and about 3% Portuguese and Macanese (Macau-born Portuguese and Eurasians). Nearly 1% of the population is from Thailand, mostly female, and employed in what is loosely called the entertainment industry.

EDUCATION

Macau University on Taipa Island is the main institute of higher learning. The school was once the small, privately-owned University of East Asia, but has been renamed, taken over by the government and now has a student body of 5000. The school is still rapidly expanding and even attracts students from Hong Kong and overseas.

The only other tertiary schools in Macau are a hotel catering academy and an industrial training centre.

ARTS

Chinese art is covered well in the Hong Kong section of this book. As for the Portuguese, their art is most apparent in the old churches and cathedrals which grace Macau's skyline. It's here that you'll see some fine examples of painting, stained-glass windows and sculpture.

CULTURE
About 95% of the population is Chinese and is culturally indistinguishable from Hong Kong. See the Hong Kong chapter of this book for details.

Of course, the Portuguese minority has a vastly different culture, which they have kept largely intact. Although mixed marriages are not uncommon in Macau, there has been surprisingly little assimilation between the two ethnic groups – most Portuguese cannot speak Chinese and vice versa.

RELIGION
For the Chinese majority, Taoism and Buddhism are the dominant religions. However, nearly 500 years of Portuguese influence has definitely left an imprint, and the Catholic church is very strong in Macau. Many Chinese have been converted and you are likely to see Chinese nuns.

LANGUAGE
Portuguese is the official language, though Cantonese is the language of choice for about 95% of the population. English is regarded as a third language, even though it's more commonly spoken than Portuguese. Mandarin Chinese or *Putonghua*, as it's officially called, is understood by more than half the Chinese population.

Within the Macau educational system, English is now the main language of instruction and starts at elementary school. So, if you're having trouble communicating, your best bet is to ask a young person.

Although there is no compelling reason for you to learn Portuguese while in Macau, there are a few words which are fun to know for reading street signs and maps. The most useful ones are:

admiral
  almirante
alley
  beco
avenue
  avenida
bay
  baía
beach
  praia
big
  grande
bridge
  ponte
building
  edifício
bus stop
  paragem
cathedral
  sé
church
  igreja
courtyard
  pátio
district
  bairro
fortress
  fortaleza
friendship
  amizade
garden
  jardim
guesthouse
  hospedaria or *villa*
guide
  guia
hill
  alto or *monte*
hotel
  pousada
island
  ilha
lane
  travessa
library
  biblioteca
lighthouse
  farol
lookout point
  miradouro
market
  mercado

moneychanger
  casa de cambio
museum
  museu
of
  da, do
path
  caminho
pawn shop
  casa de penhores
pier
  ponte-cais
police station
  esquadra da polícia
post office
  correio
restaurant (small)
  casa de pasto

road
  estrada
rock, crag
  penha
school
  escola
small hill
  colina
square
  praça
square (small)
  largo
steep street
  calçada
street
  rua
teahouse
  casa de chá

MACAU

Facts for the Visitor

VISAS & EMBASSIES

For most visitors, all that's needed to enter Macau is a passport. Everyone gets a 20-day stay on arrival. Visas are not required for the following nationalities: Australia, Austria, Belgium, Brazil, Canada, Denmark, Finland, France, Germany, Greece, Hong Kong, India, Ireland, Italy, Japan, Luxembourg, Malaysia, Netherlands, New Zealand, Norway, Philippines, Singapore, South Africa, South Korea, Spain, Sweden, Switzerland, Thailand, the UK and USA.

All other nationalities must have a visa, which can be obtained on arrival in Macau. Visas cost M$175 for individuals, M$350 for married couples and families and M$88 per person in a bona fide tour group (usually 10 people minimum). Visitors from countries which do not have diplomatic relations with Portugal must obtain visas from an overseas Portuguese consulate before entering Macau. An exception is made for Taiwanese, who can get visas on arrival despite their lack of diplomatic relations. The Portuguese Consulate (☎ 5225488) in Hong Kong is on the 10th floor, Tower Two, Exchange Square, Central.

Visa Extensions

After your 20 days are up, you can obtain a one-month extension from the Immigration Office. A second extension is not possible, though it's easy enough to go across the border to China and then come back again. The Immigration Office (☎ 577338) is on the 9th floor, Macau Chamber of Commerce Building, 175 Rua de Xangai, which is one block to the north-east of the Hotel Beverly Plaza.

Foreign Embassies in Macau

There are no foreign embassies in Macau, but North Korea has a visa office and Taiwan has a trade and tourism office which does not issue visas. The North Koreans are in Macau apparently because they weren't permitted to open a visa office in Hong Kong. In the case of Taiwan, opening this office appears to have been an 'in-your-face' gesture to Beijing, though it might be axed in 1999 when the PRC takes over. The addresses of these two representative offices are as follows:

DPR Korea-Macau International Tourism Company, 23rd floor, Nam Van Commercial Centre, 57-59 Rua da Praia Grande (☎ 333355)

Taipei Trade & Tourism Office, Edificio Commercial Central, 150 Andar, Avenida Infante D Henrique No 60-64 (☎ 306282)

CUSTOMS

Customs formalities are few and it's unlikely you'll be bothered by them. You're allowed to bring in a reasonable quantity of tobacco, alcohol and perfumes. Like Hong Kong, Macau customs takes a very dim view of drugs. Weapons aren't allowed, so leave your AK-47 behind. There are no export duties on anything bought in Macau. You aren't supposed to bring fireworks bought in Macau back to Hong Kong – many Hong Kongers do just that which is why they get searched.

When heading back to Hong Kong, you are supposedly only permitted to bring one litre of alcohol and a miserly 50 cigarettes.

MONEY

There are no moneychanging facilities at the Jetfoil Pier, so make sure you have some Hong Kong dollars or you'll have difficulty getting from the pier to town!

The casino moneychangers are more convenient than the banks as they operate 24 hours a day, but banks give a better exchange rate. The best place to change money is the Taifung Bank. The Bank of China also gives a very good exchange rate. Both of these banks have branches all over Macau, including the arcade of the Hotel Lisboa. The

Taifung Bank in the Lisboa Arcade stays open late into the evening. The Jetco auto-teller machines at the Bank of China also works with American Express cards and some foreign ATM cards. There are also Jetco-based auto-teller machines in some of the casinos.

The worst place to change money is the Hongkong Bank, which not only gives a poor exchange rate, but also hits you with a M$30 service charge for each transaction involving travellers' cheques.

There are also private moneychangers. Like the casinos, they keep longer hours but give poorer exchange rates. To find a moneychanger, look for a sign that says 'casa de cambio'. Big hotels offer moneychanging services if you are staying there, but banks are still your best bet.

If you have a Hong Kong Electronic Teller Card (ETC), it will work in Macau's ETC machines. You can find an ETC machine at the Hongkong Bank branch at Rua da Praia Grande and Rua Palha. However, if you merely have a bankbook from Hongkong Bank, you cannot make withdrawals at their Macau branch.

Currency

Macau's currency is called the *pataca*, normally written as M$, and one pataca is divided into 100 *avos*. Coins come as 10, 20 and 50 avos and one and five patacas. Notes are M$10, M$50, M$100, M$500 and M$1000 patacas. Commemorative gold M$1000 and silver M$100 coins have been issued, though it's hardly likely you'll see them used as currency. There are no exchange control regulations and money can be freely transferred into and out of Macau. All major credit cards are accepted in big hotels, car-rental agencies, etc.

Exchange Rates

You'll find that Hong Kong dollars, including coins, are readily accepted everywhere in Macau just as if they were patacas. However, patacas are worth 4% less than Hong Kong dollars, so by converting into patacas you get a 4% discount on everything you buy in Macau.

Unfortunately, patacas are not so well-received in Hong Kong. Moneychangers in Hong Kong will not accept patacas. Even worse, most Hong Kong banks won't take your patacas either! The only place that will change patacas for Hong Kong dollars is the Hang Seng Bank at their main branch at 18 Carnarvon Rd, Tsimshatsui. You lose a little bit by changing them in Hong Kong rather than in Macau, and even Hang Seng Bank doesn't want the coins. You would be wise to use all your patacas before departing Macau.

Australia	A$1	=	M$5.83
Canada	C$1	=	M$5.84
China	Y1	=	M$0.94
France	Ffr1	=	M$1.52
Germany	DM1	=	M$5.19
Japan	¥100	=	M$8.15
New Zealand	NZ$1	=	M$4.80
Singapore	S$1	=	M$5.31
Switzerland	Sfr1	=	M$6.08
Taiwan	NT$1	=	M$0.30
Thailand	B1	=	M$0.32
UK	UK£1	=	M$12.54
USA	US$1	=	M$8.02

Costs

As long as you don't go crazy at the roulette wheel or slot machines, Macau is cheaper than Hong Kong. To help keep costs down, avoid weekends.

Tipping

Classy hotels and restaurants will automatically hit you with a 10% service charge, which is supposedly a mandatory tip. Just how much of this money actually goes to the employees is another matter for speculation.

You can follow your own conscience, but tipping is not customary among the Chinese. Of course, porters at expensive hotels have become accustomed to hand-outs from well-heeled tourists.

Bargaining

Most stores have fixed prices, but if you buy clothing, trinkets and other tourist junk from

MACAU

the street markets, there is some scope for bargaining.

Macau is noticeably friendlier than Hong Kong, and therefore you should be too. Bargain politely – the rough manners of Hong Kong don't go down well in Macau, and if you're nasty you'll get nowhere in a bargaining session. Smile, tell them you don't have much money and would like a discount, then see what they say.

It's a different story at the pawn shops. Bargain ruthlessly! See the section on Things to Buy later for more detail.

Consumer Taxes

There is a Macau government 5% tourist tax which affects the price of hotel rooms and upmarket restaurant meals. However, this tax isn't applied to the real cheapie hotels and hole-in-the-wall restaurants.

WHEN TO GO

While most times of the year are OK as far as weather is concerned, there are certain times you should definitely avoid. Weekends and holidays will always create accommodation and transport problems. The Macau Grand Prix (3rd week of November) is a real crunch time.

WHAT TO BRING

Macau is a perfectly modern place and you'll be able to buy whatever you need.

TOURIST OFFICES
Local Tourist Offices

The Macau Government Tourist Office (☎ 315566), or MGTO, is well organised and very helpful. It's at Largo do Senado, Edificio Ritz No 9, next to the Leal Senado building in the square in the centre of Macau. This office is open Monday to Friday from 9 am to 1 pm, and 2 to 5.30 pm. It's also open on Saturday from 9 am to 12.30 pm.

There is a small but very helpful tourist information counter right at the Jetfoil Pier. They can answer questions and issue maps and other brochures.

Overseas Reps

On Hong Kong Island there's a useful branch of the Macau Government Tourist Office (☎ 5408180) at Room 3704, Shun Tak Centre, 200 Connaught Rd, next to the Macau Ferry Pier. If you're taking the jetfoil or ferry to Macau, you can collect all the MGTO literature and read it while you're on the boat. The MGTO is closed for lunch from 1 to 2 pm. Macau also maintains overseas tourist representative offices as follows:

Australia
　Macau Tourist Information Bureau, 449 Darling St, Balmain, Sydney, NSW 2041 (☎ (02) 5557548; fax 5557559)
Canada
　Macau Tourist Information Bureau, Suite 157, 10551 Shellbridge Way, Richmond, BC V6X 2W9 (☎ (604) 2319040; fax 2319031)
　13 Mountalan Ave, Toronto, Ontario M4J 1H3 (☎ (416) 4666552)
France
　Portuguese National Tourist Office, 7 Rue Scribe, 75009 Paris (☎ 7425557)
Germany
　Portuguese National Tourist Office, Kaiserstrasse 66-IV, 6000 Frankfurt am Main (☎ (0611) 234097; fax 231433)
Japan
　Macau Tourist Information Bureau, 4th floor, Toho Twin Tower Building, 5-2 Yurakucho 1-chome, Chiyoda-ku, Tokyo 100 (☎ (03) 35015022; fax 35021248)
Malaysia
　Macau Tourist Information Bureau, c/o Discover the World Marketing Sdn Bhd, 10.03 Amoda, 22 Jalan Imbi, 55100, Kuala Lumpur (☎ 2451418; fax 2486851)
Portugal
　Macau Tourist Representative, Avenida 5 de Outubro 115, 5th floor, 1000 Lisbon (☎ 769964)
Singapore
　Macau Tourist Information Bureau, 11-01A PIL Building, 140 Cecil St, Singapore 0106 (☎ 2250022; fax 2238585)
Thailand
　Macau Tourist Information Bureau, 150/5 Sukhumvit 20, Bangkok 10110, or GPO Box 1534, Bangkok 10501 (☎ 2581975)
UK
　Macau Tourist Information Bureau, 6 Sherlock Mews, Paddington St, London W1M 3RH (☎ (071) 2243390; fax 2240601)
USA
　Macau Tourist Information Bureau, 3133 Lake Hollywood Drive, Los Angeles, CA, or PO Box

1860, Los Angeles, CA 90078 (☎ (213) 8513402, (800) 3317150; fax 8513684)

Suite 2R, 77 Seventh Ave, New York, NY 10011 (☎ (212) 2066828; fax 9240882)

630 Green Bay Rd, PO Box 350, Kenilworth, IL 60043-0350 (☎ (708) 2516421; fax 2565601)

PO Box 2218, Honolulu, HI 96922 (☎ (808) 5387613)

BUSINESS HOURS & HOLIDAYS

The operating hours for most government offices in Macau are weekdays from 8.40 am to 1 pm and 3 to 5 pm, and Saturday from 8.40 am to 1 pm. Private businesses keep longer hours and some casinos are open 24 hours a day.

Banks are normally open on weekdays from 9 am to 4 pm, and on Saturdays from 9 am until noon.

Chinese in Macau celebrate the same religious festivals as their counterparts in Hong Kong, but there are several Catholic festivals and some Portuguese national holidays too. The tourist newspaper *Macau Travel Talk*, available from the Macau Government Tourist Office, has a regular listing of events and festivals. Here are some of the more important holidays in Macau. See the Hong Kong section for details about Chinese holidays.

New Year's Day – the first day of the year is a public holiday.

Chinese Lunar New Year – as in Hong Kong, this is a three-day public holiday in late January or early February.

Lantern Festival – not a public holiday, but a lot of fun, this festival occurs two weeks after the Chinese New Year. See the Facts about Hong Kong chapter.

Procession of Our Lord of Passion – not a public holiday, but interesting to watch. The procession begins in the evening from St Augustine's Church and goes to the Macau Cathedral. The statue is kept in the cathedral overnight and the procession returns to St Augustine's the following day.

Feast of the Earth God Tou Tei – a minor holiday for the Chinese community in March or April.

Ching Ming Festival – a major public holiday in April. See the Facts about Hong Kong chapter.

Easter – a four-day public holiday starting on Good Friday and lasting through Monday.

Anniversary of the 1974 Portuguese Revolution – this public holiday on 25 April commemorates the overthrow of the Michael Caetano regime in Portugal in 1974 by a left-wing military coup.

Procession of Our Lady of Fatima – celebrated on 13 May, this commemorates a miracle that took place at Fatima, Portugal in 1917. It is not a public holiday. The procession begins from Santa Domingo Church and ends at Penha Church.

A-Ma Festival – this is the same as the Tin Hau Festival in Hong Kong and occurs in May. It's not a public holiday.

Festival of Tam Kong – a relatively minor holiday usually celebrated in May.

Camoes & Portuguese Communities Day – held on 10 June, this public holiday commemorates 16th-century poet Luis de Camoes.

Dragon Boat Festival – as in Hong Kong, this is a major public holiday held in June.

Procession of St John the Baptist – the procession for the patron saint of Macau is held on 10 June.

Feast of St Anthony of Lisbon – this June event celebrates the birthday of the patron saint of Lisbon. A military captain, St Anthony receives his wages on this day from a delegation of city officials, and a small parade is held from St Anthony's Church. This is not a public holiday.

Battle of 13 July – celebrated only on the islands of Taipa and Coloane, this holiday commemorates the final defeat of pirates in 1910.

Ghost Month – this festival, in August or September, is an excellent time to visit temples in Macau. See the Hong Kong Facts for the Visitor chapter.

Mid-Autumn Festival – a major public holiday in September. See the Hong Kong Facts for the Visitor chapter.

Portuguese Republic Day – a public holiday on 5 October.

Cheung Yeung Festival – a public holiday in October. See the Hong Kong Facts for the Visitor chapter.

All Saints' Day – held on 1 November. Both All Saints' Day and the following day, *All Souls' Day*, are public holidays.

Portuguese Independence Day – celebrated on 1 December, it is a public holiday.

Winter Solstice – not a public holiday, but an interesting time to visit Macau. Many Macau Chinese consider the winter solstice more important than the Chinese New Year. There is plenty of feasting and temples are crammed with worshippers.

Christmas – both the 24th and 25th of December are public holidays.

CULTURAL EVENTS

Find out about cultural events, concerts, art exhibitions and other such activities from the tourist newspaper *Macau Travel Talk*. Free copies are available from the tourist office.

MACAU

The Dragon Boat Festival is a Chinese holiday well known for its exciting dragon boat races. Macau's dragon boat races are usually held at the tip of the Macau Peninsula (Barra Fortress), but check with the MGTO to be certain. Similar races are held in Hong Kong and Taiwan. The Dragon Boat Festival is scheduled according to the lunar calendar, but usually falls sometime during June.

The Miss Macau Contest is held every August. Whether this event is cultural or otherwise depends on one's point of view.

The International Music Festival is held during the third week of October.

POST & TELECOMMUNICATIONS

The postal service is efficient and the clerks can speak English. Besides a few main post offices, there are also numerous mini-post offices throughout Macau. These are little red booths that sell stamps from vending machines.

Postal Rates

Domestic letters cost M$1 for up to 20 grams. As for international mail, Macau divides the world into zones. Zone 1 is East Asia, including Korea, Taiwan, etc. Zone 2 is everything else. There are special rates for China and Portugal. The rates for airmail letters, postcards and aerogrammes are as follows:

Grams	China	Portugal	Zone 1	Zone 2
10	2.00	3.00	3.50	4.50
20	3.00	4.50	4.50	6.00
30	4.00	6.00	5.50	7.50
40	5.00	7.50	6.50	9.00
50	6.00	9.00	7.50	10.50

Printed matter receives a discount of about 30% off the preceding rates. Registration costs an extra M$12.

Sending Mail

The GPO on Leal Senado is open from 9 am to 8 pm, Monday to Saturday. Large hotels like the Lisboa also sell stamps and postcards and can post letters for you.

Express courier service is also available. Right in the GPO is Macau Express (☎ 596688) (look for the sign saying 'ENS'). Alternatively, contact DHL (☎ 569916).

Receiving Mail

The GPO is in Leal Senado Square on Avenida de Almeida Ribeiro. The GPO has an efficient poste restante service and English-speaking postal clerks.

Telephone

Macau's telephone monopoly is Companhia de Telecomunicacoes (CTM). For the most part, service is good, but public pay phones can be hard to find, being mostly concentrated around the Leal Senado. Most large hotels have one in the lobby, but this is often insufficient and you may have to stand in line to use it. However, once you find a phone, it generally works OK.

Local calls are free from a private or hotel telephone. At a public pay phone, local calls cost M$1 for five minutes. All pay phones permit international direct dialling (IDD). The procedure for dialling to Hong Kong is totally different than for all other countries. You first dial 01 and then the number you want to call – you must *not* dial the country code.

The international access code for every country *except* Hong Kong is 00, after which you must dial the country code, the area code and finally the number you wish to reach. If the area code begins with a zero, omit the first zero (see this section in the HK Facts for the Vistor chapter on the change of area codes in the UK). To call Macau from abroad, the country code is 853.

You can call home collect or use a credit card by using the 'home direct' system. This method only works for a few countries. You need to dial an access code, and then an operator from your home country will come on the line and ask which number you want to reach and how you want to charge the call. The access codes are as follows:

Country	Code
Australia	☎ (0800) 610
Canada	☎ (0800) 100
Holland	☎ (0800) 310
Hong Kong	☎ (0800) 852
Japan	☎ (0800) 810
Malaysia	☎ (0800) 600
Portugal	☎ (0800) 351
Singapore	☎ (0800) 650
South Korea	☎ (0800) 820
Taiwan	☎ (0800) 886
UK	☎ (0800) 440
USA (AT&T)	☎ (0800) 111
USA (MCI)	☎ (0800) 131
USA (Sprint)	☎ (0800) 121

You'll need a big pocket full of change to make an IDD call unless you buy a telephone card from CTM. These are sold in denominations of M$50, M$100 and M$200. Phones which accept these cards are numerous around Leal Senado, the Jetfoil Pier and at a few large hotels.

Yet another way is to make a call from the telephone office at Leal Senado, next to the GPO. The way to do it is to leave a deposit with a clerk and they will dial your number. When your call is completed the clerk deducts the cost from the deposit and refunds the balance. The clerks speak English and the office is open from 8 am until midnight, Monday to Saturday, and from 9 am until midnight on Sundays. There is another telephone office north of the Hotel Lisboa on Avenida do Dr Rodrigo Rodriques, but this one is open only from 9 am to 8 pm, Monday through Saturday.

Useful Phone Numbers

Directory Assistance (Hong Kong)	☎ 101
Directory Assistance (Macau)	☎ 181
Emergency	☎ 999
Police	☎ 573333
Time	☎ 140

Fax, Telex & Telegraph

Unless you're staying at a hotel that has its own fax, the easiest way to send and receive faxes is at the GPO (not the telephone office) on Leal Senado. The number for receiving faxes at this office is ☎ (853) 550117, but check because the number can change. The person sending the fax must put your name and hotel telephone on top of the message so the postal workers can find you. The cost for receiving a fax is M$7.50 irregardless of the number of pages.

Telex messages are sent from the telephone office next to the GPO. The telephone office also handles cables (telegrams).

TIME

Like Hong Kong, Macau is eight hours ahead of GMT and does not observe daylight savings time.

When it is noon in Macau it is also noon in Singapore, Hong Kong and Perth; 2 pm in Sydney; 8 pm the previous day in Los Angeles; 11 pm the previous day in New York; and 4 am in London.

ELECTRICITY

Macau's electricity system is the same as in Hong Kong and China – 220 V AC, 50 Hz. The electric outlets are the same as Hong Kong's older design, that is, they accept three round pins. There are still a few old buildings wired for 110 V, but as long as you

MACAU

see three round holes on the outlets you can be assured it's 220 V.

Macau supplies 90% of its own power while the rest comes from China.

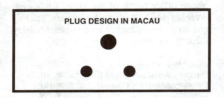

PLUG DESIGN IN MACAU

WEIGHTS & MEASURES

Macau subscribes to the international metric system. As in Hong Kong, street markets and medicine shops sell things by the *leung* (37.5 grams) and the *catty* (600 grams).

BOOKS & MAPS

Books about Macau are scarce. Much of what's been published is in Portuguese, but there are a few good books in English.

People & Society

There are several pictorial coffee-table books about Macau. One such book, simply called *Macau*, is by Jean-Yves Defay. Another, also called *Macau*, is by Leong Ka Tai and Shann Davies and is part of the Times Editions series. It's an excellent hardback pictorial and history of the colony.

A good coffee-table sketchbook of the colony is *Old Macau* by Tom Briggs and Colin Crisswell, published by South China Morning Post.

A Macao Narrative (Oxford University Press) is by Austin Coates, a well-known Hong Kong magistrate, who also wrote *City of Broken Promises*.

Another good book with the title of *Macau* is by Cesar Guillen-Nuñez (Oxford University Press).

Novels set in Macau are rare, but there is one, also entitled *Macau* (Corgi Books) by Daniel Carney.

History

Historic Macao (Oxford University Press, Hong Kong, 1984) by C A Montalto de Jesus was first published in 1902 as a history of the colony. In 1926 the author added extra chapters in which he suggested that the Portuguese government cared so little about the colony and did so little to meet its needs that it would be better if Macau was administered by the League of Nations. The Portuguese government was outraged and copies of the book were seized and destroyed. The book can be bought at the Luis de Camoes Museum in Macau.

Travel Guides

Absolutely essential for anyone who is considering gambling at Macau's casinos is the *Macau AOA Gambling Handbook*. This comes as part of a set which includes the *Macau Pictorial Guide* and an excellent map of Macau. The whole package only costs HK$20 and is available from most of the main bookstores in Hong Kong. If not, you could try the MGTO in Hong Kong or go directly to the publisher, AOA Ltd (☎ 3890352), 10th floor, 174 Wai Yip St, Kwun Tong, Hong Kong.

Behind the service counter at the MGTO on Leal Senado, there is a small collection of books and other goods for sale. Check their list to see what is currently available.

Bookshops

There are few shops in Macau that carry English-language books, and those few only have a limited selection. The easiest to find is Livraria Sao Paulo (☎ 323957) on Rua do Campo (near McDonald's). Many of the books are in Portuguese and oriented towards the Catholic Church, but they have some general interest English books and good maps of Macau. They also stock Lonely Planet guides.

For Portuguese-language publications, check out Livraria Portuguesa (☎ 566442), 18-20 Rua Sao Domingos.

Maps

The best map of Macau I've seen is the *Map*

of Macau & Zhuhai published by Universal Publications Ltd. These are easily obtained in Hong Kong as well as Macau for about HK$15. The map has a complete street index on the back, shows the bus routes and has streets labelled in both Chinese characters and Portuguese.

You can get a free *Mapa Turistico* from the MGTO. It includes all the major tourist sights in both Portuguese and Chinese characters – useful for navigating by taxi when the driver doesn't speak English.

MEDIA
Newspapers & Magazines
Other than the free monthly tourist newspaper, *Macau Travel Talk*, there is no English-language newspaper published in Macau. However, both the *South China Morning Post* and *Hong Kong Standard* are readily available from big hotels and some bookshops. It's also easy to buy major foreign news magazines.

Radio & TV
Macau has three radio stations, two of which broadcast in Cantonese and one in Portuguese. There are no local English-language radio stations, but you should be able to pick up Hong Kong stations.

Teledifusao de Macau (TdM) is a government-run TV station which broadcasts on two channels. Shows are mainly in English and Portuguese, with some Cantonese programmes. It's easy to pick up Hong Kong stations in Macau (but not vice versa) and you can also receive stations from China. Hong Kong newspapers list Macau TV programmes.

Hong Kong's famous satellite TV system, STAR TV, is readily available in Macau at any hotel with a cable or satellite dish hook-up.

FILM & PHOTOGRAPHY
You can find most types of film, cameras and accessories in Macau, and photo processing is of a high standard. The best store in town for all photographic services is Foto Princesa (☎ 555959), 55-59 Avenida Infante D

Henrique, one block east of Rua da Praia Grande. This is also the best place to get quick visa photos.

HEALTH
Vaccinations and inoculation certificates are not normally required unless cholera has been detected in Hong Kong or Macau or if you're arriving from an infected area.

About 90% of Macau's water supply is pumped from a reservoir 13 km away in China. The water is purified and chlorinated and is probably OK to drink. Nevertheless, the Chinese always boil it (more out of custom than necessity). Hotel rooms are always supplied with a thermos filled with hot water, so you might as well take advantage of it just to be on the safe side. Distilled water is widely available from grocery stores.

EMERGENCY
The emergency telephone number for fire, police and ambulance is ☎ 999.

There are two government-run hospitals. English is mainly spoken at the Government Hospital (☎ 514499, 313731), just on Estrada Sao Francisco, north of the Hotel Lisboa. Chinese-speaking people are usually treated at the Kiang Vu Hospital (☎ 371333) on Estrada do Repouso and Rua Coelho do Amaral.

WOMEN TRAVELLERS
Wearing a skimpy bikini at the beach will elicit some stares, but travel in Macau is as safe for women as in any Western country.

DANGERS & ANNOYANCES
In terms of violent crime, Macau is pretty safe, but residential burglaries and pickpocketing are problems. Most hotels are well-guarded, and reasonable care with your valuables should be sufficient to avoid trouble.

Traffic is heavy and quite a few tourists have been hit while jaywalking. Macau police have been cracking down on this, and though they go light with foreigners, you can still get fined. Be especially careful at rush

MACAU

hour when the traffic (and the police) come out in force.

Cheating at gambling is a serious criminal offence, so don't even think about it.

WORK

Unless you hold a Portuguese passport, you can pretty much forget it. Most Portuguese speak excellent English, so there is little need to import foreign English teachers. Most of the foreigners employed in Macau are Thai prostitutes and Filipino musicians. Unskilled labour is supplied by Chinese workers from nearby Zhuhai, who are paid a pittance.

ACTIVITIES

Future Ice Skating Rink (☎ 9892310) is on Praca Luis de Camoes, just on the south side of Camoes Grotto & Gardens.

Up around the Guia Lighthouse is the best track for jogging. It's also the venue for early morning taiji exercises.

There are two good swimming beaches on Coloane, Hac Sa and Cheoc Van. Cheoc Van Beach has a yacht club and Hac Sa has a horse-riding stable. Hac Sa Beach also has a number of sea toys for rent, including windsurfers and water scooters. In the hills of Coloane is a hiking trail over eight km in length. Bicycles are available for hire on both islands, but not on the Macau Peninsula. Coloane also boasts a golf course.

HIGHLIGHTS

Although gambling is what draws most people to Macau, the fine colonial architecture is what makes this place unique. Highlights include the Ruins of St Paul, Monte Fortress, Guia Fortress, Leal Senado and the Penha Church. St Michael Cemetery is a fascinating place to walk through, and many visitors are impressed by A-Ma Temple (Ma Kok Min). Taipa Village on Taipa Island is unique, and there is no better way to round off a trip to Macau than a fine meal at a Portuguese restaurant.

ACCOMMODATION

There's good and bad news. The bad news is that hotel prices in Macau continue to rise –

the old dumps are being torn down and replaced with comfortable hotels, which usually charge uncomfortable prices. Nor are there dormitories catering to the budget backpacker market.

But don't close the book yet, there is good news. Macau hotels are cheaper than those in Hong Kong. For the same price that you'd pay in Hong Kong for a dormitory bed, you'll be able to find a private room (though without private bath). For about the same you'd pay for a dumpy room in Hong Kong's Chungking Mansions, you can get a comfortable room in Macau with air-con, private bath, TV and fancy carpeting. In other words, staying in Macau will probably wind up costing you the same as Hong Kong – you won't live cheaply, but you'll live better.

The all-important factor is that you must avoid weekends and holidays. At such times, room prices double and accommodation of any kind is difficult to get. For definition purposes, 'weekend' means both Saturday and Sunday nights. Friday night is usually not a problem unless it's also a holiday. Also, during special events like the Macau Grand Prix rooms can be impossible to obtain.

Another way to save money is to avoid the peak season (summer). Peak-season prices are quoted in this book because that's when most travellers visit, but be aware that you can get substantial discounts in winter (except during Chinese New Year). For example, one fancy hotel quoted M$550 for a double when I visited in August but was asking only M$250 for weekdays in January.

Camping

It seems hard to believe that in tiny, crowded Macau, there could be a camping area. But there is a small one in Coloane Park, which is on Coloane Island south of the city. Whether or not you think it's worth the trouble to go this far to save some money on a night's accommodation is something you'll have to decide. See the section on Coloane Island for more details on how to reach this park by bus.

Top, Left & Right: At the Po Lin Monastery, Lantau, Outlying Islands (TW)

Top: Pedicabs in Central Macau (TW)
Bottom: Cannon in Forteleza do Monte, Macau Peninsula (RH)

Hostels

There is only one hostel in Macau, and like the campground it's also on Coloane Island. The hostel is small and almost always booked out by groups, so your chances of getting in are just about nil – except during off-season (winter). You should not consider this a serious option in summer.

Guesthouses

By government edict, all guesthouses must have signs in both Chinese and Portuguese. Guesthouses usually call themselves *vila*, but sometimes they are called *hospedaria* or *pensao*.

There are a few old classic (dumpy) guesthouses still remaining in Macau – cheap prices and plenty of dirt, not to mention cockroaches and other things that crawl in the night. However, these are becoming difficult to find – the dumps are being torn down (sometimes burned down). Many old guesthouses being renovated are moving upmarket. These remodelled guesthouses now offer luxurious rooms with air-con, shag carpeting, etc, but the prices are about the same as those charged for the mid-range hotels. Prices at the old dumps can be as cheap as M$50, but the usual bottom-end at guesthouses is now about M$120 and many want M$200 or more. While this compares favourably to Hong Kong, it's not exactly budget travellers' heaven.

Hotels

Macau has an incredible variety of hotels. Some are architectural museum pieces which have been fully renovated while others are the modern high-rise glass-and-concrete cylinders you see in Hong Kong. The old renovated hotels are definitely cheaper, and often more interesting – prices start at around M$220. The new shiny glass towers come with price tags of M$500 or so. Then there are the really luxurious resorts – the type with swimming pools, saunas, tennis courts and carpeting around the toilet (glad I don't have to clean it). Elegance like this doesn't come cheaply – starting prices of M$1000 or more are usual.

Most hotels in the mid-range and above charge a 5% government room tax plus a 10% service charge.

FOOD

For some travellers, eating is the most rewarding part of a trip to Macau. Given its cosmopolitan past, it's not surprising that the food is an exotic mixture of Portuguese and Chinese cooking. There is also a little influence from other European countries and Africa. The English-speaking waitresses are invariably from the Philippines.

The most famous local specialty is African chicken baked with peppers and chillis. Other specialties include *bacalhau*, which is cod, served baked, grilled, stewed or boiled. The cod is imported and rather salty. Sole, a tongue-shaped flatfish, is another Macanese delicacy. There's also ox tail and ox breast, rabbit prepared in various ways, and soups like *caldo verde* and *sopa a alentejana* made with vegetables, meat and olive oil. The Brazilian contribution is *feijoadas*, a stew made of beans, pork, potatoes, cabbage and spicy sausages. The contribution from the former Portuguese enclave of Goa on the west coast of India is spicy prawns.

Apart from cod, there's other seafood aplenty – shrimp, prawns, crab, squid and white fish. You won't find Macau's baked crab or huge grilled and stuffed king prawns anywhere else. There are lots of little seafood restaurants where you can pick your meal from the tank at the front of the shop.

If you're going out for a meal, it's worth remembering that people eat early in Macau – in many places the dining room is clear and the chef has gone home by 9 pm.

DRINKS

The Portuguese influence is most visible in the many fine imported Portuguese red and white wines, port and brandy. Wines are cheap. Mateus Rose is the most famous but even cheaper are bottles of red or white wine. Most are drinkable for those not heavily into chateaux wines.

Spirits and beer are cheaper in Macau than in Hong Kong – even cheaper than at duty-free stores. Wine prices vary in the restaurants but are usually not too expensive. Many people leave the place with a bottle of Mateus tucked under their arm.

ENTERTAINMENT
Gambling

I once worked in a Las Vegas casino as a slot machine mechanic and later as a slot machine attendant. During that time I saw humanity at its worst.

Although the games in Macau are somewhat different from Las Vegas, the same basic principles apply. The most important principle to remember is this – if you want to win at gambling, own a casino. In every game, the casino enjoys a built-in mathematical advantage. The casinos don't cheat the players because they don't have to. In the short-term, anyone can hit a winning streak and get ahead, but the longer you play, the more certain it is that the odds will catch up with you. There is no system that can help you win. I know of one Las Vegas casino that caught a woman with a portable computer in her handbag, but they let her go because, the manager said, 'a computer won't help'.

Your best bet is to gamble for fun only. Don't bet more than you can afford to lose and don't think you can 'make up your losses' by gambling more. If you win, consider yourself lucky – this time.

The most popular form of gambling in Macau is mahjong, played not in the casinos but in private homes. You can hear the rattle of mahjong pieces late into the night if you walk through any side street.

The legal gambling age in Macau is 18 for foreigners and 21 for Macau residents. Photography is absolutely prohibited inside the casinos.

If you want to play casino games which are more sophisticated than the slot machines, it's essential that you track down a copy of the *Macau AOA Gambling Handbook*.

Slot Machines These are the classic sucker games in any casino. Maybe the reason why slot machines are so popular is because it takes no brains to play – just put the coin in the slot and pull the handle. Some machines allow you to put in up to five coins at a time, which increases your chance of winning by five times (but costs you five times as much, so you're no better off). Contrary to popular belief, how hard or gently you pull the handle has no influence on the outcome. There are many small payoffs to encourage you to keep playing, but the goal of every slot player is to hit the grand jackpot (or megabucks as it is called in Macau).

The odds for winning on a slot machine are terrible. Usually machines are designed to give the casino a 25% advantage over the player. It's easy to win small payoffs, but the odds of hitting the grand jackpot are very small indeed. It's like spinning five roulette wheels at once and expecting them to all land on number seven. The more reels on the machine, the more unlikely they will line up for the ultimate payoff. Three-reel machines give you one chance in 8000 of hitting the jackpot. You have one chance in 160,000 of lining up four reels. If you play a five-reel machine, your chances of lining up all five winning numbers is one in 3.2 million.

Contrary to popular belief, slot machines are not controlled by computers, magnets or any other sophisticated device. The machines are as dumb as a pair of dice. Another popular myth is that the machines will eventually fill up with money and therefore pay out. Quite simply, this is untrue. When the machine is full, coins overflow down a tube into a bucket placed under the machine. The buckets are inside the cabinets that the machines rest on. The cabinets are unlocked and the buckets are emptied at about 4 am when the casino is nearly deserted.

Buckets filled with coins are heavy – one was dropped on my foot and broke my big toe. To this day, the toenail has not grown back.

If you do hit a jackpot, don't move away from the machine. Bells will ring, lights will flash, and a slot machine attendant will come running over to pay you in bills because the machine cannot possibly hold enough coins to pay a large jackpot.

People have tried all sorts of methods to cheat slot machines, but the machines have been designed to counter these efforts. Attempts to influence the spinning reels with magnets doesn't work because they are made from antimagnetic materials. More professional thieves try to pick the lock on the machine's door to gain access to the cash box – the machines are equipped with alarms and various antitheft devices to thwart this. Less professional thieves attempt to cheat the machines by inserting metal wires or pouring Coca-Cola into the coin slot hoping that the machine will malfunction and pay out. This doesn't work but it creates employment for slot machine mechanics. Back in the early days of Las Vegas when the casinos were owned by the Mafia (some say they still are), cheating at gambling could earn the cheater a pair of 'cement shoes'. These days, the penalty is more likely to be a free holiday behind bars. As with all other casino games, the slots are carefully watched by the famed 'eye-in-the-sky' – video cameras constantly monitored by security personnel.

Blackjack Also known as 21, this card game is easy to play, although it requires a little skill. The dealer takes a card and also gives one to the player. Each card counts for a particular number of points. The goal is to get enough cards to add up as close as possible to 21 without going over. If you go over 21, then you 'bust' which means you lose. If both you and the dealer go bust at the same time, the dealer still wins and this is what gives the casino the edge over the player. If the dealer and player both get 21, it's a tie and the bet is cancelled. If the player gets 21 (blackjack) then he or she gets even money plus a 50% bonus.

Dealers must draw until they reach 16 and stand on 17 or higher. The player is free to decide when to stand or when to draw.

You may occasionally see a book or newspaper article describing a system for beating the casinos at blackjack. Such a system does exist and is called card counting. To do it you need a good memory and a quick mind. Basically, if you can remember which cards have been dealt from the deck you will know which cards still remain. As the dealer nears the end of the deck, you can make very good guesses about which cards remain and therefore estimate your chances of going bust and know when to stand and when to draw. When you're sure that you can beat the dealer's hand, you bet heavily.

It sounds great. The problem is it no longer works because to defeat card counters the casino dealers play with multiple decks and reshuffle the cards frequently.

Roulette This is a very easy game to play and I don't know why it isn't more popular in Macau. At the moment, the only roulette wheel remaining in all of Macau is at the Hotel Lisboa, and who knows how long before it gets retired?

The dealer simply spins the roulette wheel in one direction and spins a ball in the opposite direction. Roulette wheels have 36 numbers plus a zero, so your chance of hitting any given number is one in 37. The pay-off is 35 to one which is what gives the casino its advantage.

Rather than betting a single number, it's much easier to win if you bet odd or even, or red versus black numbers. If the ball lands on zero, everyone loses to the house (unless you also bet the zero). If you bet red or black, odd or even, the casino's advantage is only 2.7%.

Very similar to roulette is boule. In fact it's identical except that it's played with a large ball about the size of a billiard ball. There are fewer numbers too. Boule has 24 numbers plus a star. The payoff is 23 to one on numbers. On all bets (numbers, red or black, odd or even) the casino has a 4% advantage over the players.

Craps This game is extremely popular in the West and I don't know why it's rare in Macau. In fact, on my last trip to Macau I didn't see a single craps table and I wonder if they've been done away with. Maybe the casinos prefer not to have this game because the house has such a small advantage – only about 1.4%.

Craps is played with a pair of dice which are tossed down a long and narrow table. The dice are thrown by the players, not the dealers, so there is more of a feeling of participation. The person tossing the dice, the shooter, is permitted to shoot until he or she loses, then the dice are passed to the next player at the table in a counter-clockwise direction.

This game is more complicated than most. On the first roll (the 'come-out' roll) the shooter automatically wins if he or she throws a seven or 11. If a two, three or 12 is thrown on the first roll, it's an automatic loss. Any other number results in a point. The shooter must continue to toss the dice until the point is thrown again. However, if a seven is rolled before the point is made, then it's a loss. This method of betting is called betting the 'come' or 'front line'.

There are other ways to play. You can also bet that the shooter will lose (don't come) or that a pair of fours (a hard eight) will be thrown before other combinations adding up to eight (a soft eight). The complexity of the game is one of its attractions. If a shooter gets

hot (wins several rolls in succession) the game gets exciting with lots of players jumping up and down and yelling. The exhilaration probably explains why craps is a favourite with compulsive gamblers.

Baccarat Also known as chemin de fer, this has become the card game of choice for the upper crust. Baccarat rooms are always the most classy part of any casino and the minimum wager is high, at least M$50 and up to M$1000 in some casinos.

Two card hands are dealt at the same time – the player hand and the bank hand. The hand which scores closest to nine is the winner. Players can bet on either their own hand or the bank hand. Neither is actually the house hand. The casino deducts a percentage if the bank hand wins, which is how the house makes its profit.

If the player understands the game properly, the house only enjoys slightly better than a 1% advantage over the player.

Fan Tan This is an ancient Chinese game practically unknown in the West. The dealer takes an inverted silver cup and plunges it into a pile of porcelain buttons, then moves the cup to one side. After all bets have been placed, the buttons are counted out in groups of four. You have to bet on how many will remain after the last set of four has been taken out. You can bet on numbers one, two, three or four, as well as odd or even.

Dai Siu This is Cantonese for 'big-small'. The game is also known as *sik po* (dice treasure) or *cu sik* (guessing dice). It's extremely popular in Macau.

The game is played with three dice which are placed in a covered glass container. The container is then shaken. You then bet that the total of the toss will be from three to nine (small) or from 10 to 18 (big). However, you lose on combinations where all three dice come up the same, like 2-2-2, 3-3-3, etc, unless you bet directly on three of a kind.

For betting 'big-small' the house advantage is 2.78%. Betting on a specific three of a kind gives the house a 30% advantage – a sucker bet.

Pai Kao This is Chinese dominoes and reminds me a lot of mahjong. One player is designated the role of banker and the other players individually compare their hands against the banker. The casino doesn't play, but deducts a 3% commission from the winnings for providing the gambling facilities.

Keno Although keno is played in Las Vegas and other Western casinos, it's believed to have originated in China more than 2000 years ago. Keno was introduced to the USA by Chinese railway workers in the 19th century.

Keno is basically a lottery. There are 80 numbers of which 20 are drawn in each game. You are given a keno ticket and the object is to list as many numbers as you think will be drawn. You can bet on four numbers and if all four are among those drawn in the game, you're a winner. You can play five numbers, six, seven and so on. You have about one chance in nine million of guessing all 20 winning numbers. With only about two drawings per hour, it's a slow way to lose your money. I consider keno to be the most boring game in the casino.

Dog Racing Macau has a Canidrome – yes, that's what they call it – for dog racing. It's off Avenida General Castelo Branco not far from the Barrier Gate. Greyhound races are held three times a week on Tuesday, Thursday and either Saturday or Sunday starting at 8 pm. You can call (☎ 574413) to check the schedule. There are 14 races per night with six to eight dogs per race. Admission to the Canidrome costs M$2, or M$5 in the members stand, or there are boxes for six persons costing M$80 for the whole group and a VIP room for M$25.

Off-Course Betting Centres will accept bets starting from 5 pm. The centres are in the Hotel Lisboa, Floating Casino and Jai-Alai Casino.

Once a year (usually at the end of summer) the Macau Derby is held at the Canidrome.

This is the year's biggest race and the winner's purse is currently M$80,000.

Horse Racing Horse racing has a long history in Macau. In the early 1800s horse races were held outside the city walls on an impromptu course. You may notice on the Macau map that there is a street called Estrada Marginal do Hipodromo in the extreme north-east corner of town near the Barrier Gate. This was a popular race course in the 1930s, but the area has now been taken over by flats and factories.

A trotting track was opened on Taipa Island, but closed in 1989. This has given way to the fancy Macau Jockey Club where regular horse races are held. See the section on Taipa Island in the Macau Islands chapter for details.

Want to visit Macau for free? All you've got to do is buy HK$5000 worth of gambling chips and the Hotel Lisboa will provide you with a free jetfoil ticket. Buy HK$30,000 worth of chips and they'll give you a free night's accommodation as well. It doesn't stipulate that you actually have to lose the chips although I guess they'd like it if you did. The proliferation of pawn shops around the casinos would seem to indicate that some people do lose the lot.

Grand Prix

The biggest event of the year is no doubt the Macau Grand Prix. As in Monaco, the streets of the town make up the racetrack. The six-km circuit starts near the Hotel Lisboa and follows the shoreline along Avenida da Amizade, going around the reservoir and back through the city.

The Grand Prix consists of two major races – one for cars and one for motorcycles. Both races attract many international contestants. Pedicab races are included as a novelty event.

The race is a two-day event held on the third weekend in November. More than 50,000 people flock to see this event and accommodation, a problem on normal weekends, becomes as rare as a three-humped camel. Be sure to book a return ticket on the jetfoil if you have to return to Hong Kong. If you don't book, you may still be able to squeeze on board one of the ferries. Otherwise, if you have a China visa, you might consider making your exit through the People's Republic and staying at a hotel in Zhuhai. Ferries connect Zhuhai to Shenzhen and Hong Kong.

Certain areas in Macau are designated as viewing areas for the races. Streets and alleyways along the track are blocked off, so it's unlikely you'll be able to get a good view without paying. Prices for seats in the Reservoir stand are M$175 for adults, M$88 for children; Lisboa stand, M$520; Mandarin Oriental stand, M$520; Grandstand, M$575.

If, one week after the Grand Prix, you still haven't managed to get out of Macau (a possibility), you can join the Macau Marathon. Like the Grand Prix, this race is attracting a lot of international attention. It's held in the first week of December.

THINGS TO BUY

Pawnshops are ubiquitous in Macau, and it is possible to get good deals on cameras, watches and jewellery, but you must be prepared to bargain without mercy.

In Macau pawnshops, it's no holds barred. These guys would sell their own mother to a glue factory. I saw a nice camera – a Ricoh KR-5 – in a pawnshop window with a M$850 price tag. That's about how much it cost new, and this camera was eight years old! After examining it, I found the automatic timer was broken. After an exhaustive bargaining session, I got the price down to M$600. I bought the camera and the next day had it appraised at a camera shop. They told me I shouldn't have paid more than M$200. Just for fun, I took it over to another pawnshop and asked how much they would give me for it. They said it was worth M$50.

The MGTO has T-shirts for sale at bargain prices. Ditto for posters, postcards, umbrellas and raincoats.

If you've got the habit, Macau is a bargain for booze and tobacco (including cigars and pipe tobacco).

The largest department store in Macau is the well-known Japanese retailer Yaohan. The store is near the Jetfoil Pier.

Getting There & Away

Macau has a very small land border with China and most arrivals are by sea from Hong Kong. You won't see any huge cruise ships in Macau simply because the harbour isn't deep enough to accommodate them. However, a wide variety of small craft use Macau's harbour. Some business consortiums have been talking about creating a deep-water port on the east side of Coloane Island. This would involve an expensive dredging project, but so far it's just talk.

AIR
To/From Hong Kong

Helicopter For people in a hurry to lose their money, East Asia Airlines runs a helicopter service between Hong Kong and Macau. Flying time from Hong Kong is 20 minutes at a cost of HK$1086 on weekdays, M$1189 on weekends – quite an expense just to save the extra 30 minutes required by boat. There are at least 12 flights daily in each direction, and departures are from the ferry piers in both Hong Kong and Macau. You can get the tickets in Hong Kong (☎ 8593359) at Shun Tak Centre, 200 Connaught Rd, Sheung Wan, Hong Kong Island. In Macau, you can book at the Jetfoil Pier (☎ 572983, 550777).

Macau's new airport is planned for completion in 1995. When it finally opens, expect major changes – not only to transport, but to Macau's character.

LAND
To/From China

From Gongbei in the Zhuhai Special Economic Zone, simply walk across the border, which is open from 7 am until 9 pm.

There is a bus from Macau to Guangzhou, but it's more hassle than it's worth. The bus stops at the border for over an hour while all the passengers go through immigration and customs formalities. It would be easier to take a bus to the border, walk across, and catch a minibus to Guangzhou from the other side. However, if you prefer the 'direct' bus, tickets are sold at Kee Kwan Motors (☎ 572264), across the street from the Floating Casino. Buses leave daily at 7 am and noon, taking about six hours.

SEA
To/From Hong Kong

Although Macau is separated from Hong Kong by 65 km of water, the journey can be made in as little as one hour. There are frequent departures throughout the day from 7 am to 9.30 pm.

You have a wide selection of boats to choose from. There are jetfoils, hoverferries, jetcats (jet-powered catamaran), jumbocats (large jetcat) and high-speed ferries. The fastest, smoothest and most popular boats are the jetfoils and jumbocats. The high-speed ferry has the most room and is comfortable for walking around. Least popular is the hoverferry because it gives a choppy ride – a definite downer to seasick-prone Hong Kongers.

The leading lights of marketing management have decided to rename the jumbocats the 'super-shuttle'. The jumbocats are roomier and therefore marginally more comfortable than the jetfoils, but neither this nor the catchy 'super-shuttle' slogan has been able to increase market share. The jetfoils remain far more popular with the Hong Kongers apparently because of the big 10 minutes they save. Perhaps the management of the super-shuttle should try another marketing gimmick, like a karaoke lounge or on-board casino.

Smoking is prohibited on the jetfoils and super-shuttle. All jetfoils, high-speed ferries and most (but not all) jumbocats depart from the pier at Shun Tak Centre, 200 Connaught Rd, Sheung Wan, Hong Kong Island. This is easily reached by MTR to the Sheung Wan Station.

All hoverferries depart from the China

Hong Kong City Ferry Pier in Tsimshatsui, Kowloon. Some jumbocats also depart from this pier, but most leave from Shun Tak Centre. If you buy a jumbocat ticket in advance, be certain you know which pier it departs from.

Luggage space on the jetfoils is limited – there is no room under the seat and no overhead racks, so you have to sit on your bag or it sits on your lap. On the jetfoils you can check one bag up to 30 x 22 x 9 cm and 40 kg. On the super-shuttle and high-speed ferries, there is a little more luggage space. In Macau, there is a left-luggage room at the Jetfoil Pier.

If you have to return to Hong Kong the same day as departure, you'd be wise to book your return ticket in advance because the boats are often full, especially on weekends and holidays. Even Monday mornings can be difficult for getting seats back to Hong Kong. If you can't get on the jetfoil or super-shuttle, you might have a chance with the hi-speed ferries which have a lot more room. You need to arrive at the pier at least 15 minutes before departure, but from my experience you'd be wise to allow 30 minutes because of occasional long queues at the immigration checkpoint, especially on the Hong Kong side (immigration works faster in Macau).

Jetfoil tickets can be purchased up to 28 days in advance in Hong Kong at the pier (Shun Tak Centre) or booked by phone (☎ 8596596) if you have a credit card (American Express, MasterCard or Visa). The MTR Travel Services Centre in the following MTR stations also sells these tickets: Admiralty, Causeway Bay, Central, Kwun Tong, Mongkok, Taikoo, Tsimshatsui and Tsuen Wan.

Super-shuttle bookings can be made 28 days in advance, but no phone bookings are available. You can buy these at Shun Tak Centre, or at China Hong Kong City in Kowloon.

High-speed ferries can be booked 28 days in advance at Shun Tak Centre or any Ticketmate outlet.

There are three different classes on the hi-speed ferries (economy, tourist and first) – in 1st class you can go out on the deck to take photos. The jetfoils have two classes (economy and first). All other boats have only one class. The Hong Kong government charges HK$26 departure tax which is included in the price of your ticket. Macau charges M$20, also included in the ticket price. Boats departing at 5.30 pm or later are surcharged as night services. The following prices are what you pay in $HK:

Travel Time	Weekday	Weekend	Night
Hi-Speed Ferry			
95 minutes	$59/78/93	$81/101/116	-
Super-Shuttle			
65 minutes	$11	$129	-
Hoverferry			
80 minutes	$9	$11	$125
Jetfoil			
55 minutes	$111/126	$119/134	$138/158

In Macau, you can book tickets on all boats at the Jetfoil Pier. You can also book tickets for all boats except the hoverferry right in the lobby of the Hotel Lisboa.

To/From China

From Zhoutouzui Wharf in Guangzhou you can take an overnight ferry directly to Macau. Buy tickets at the wharf or from the large hotels such as the White Swan.

Going the other way, pick up the ferry to Guangzhou at the wharf near the Floating Casino in Macau. Departures are at 8 pm, arriving in Guangzhou at 7.15 am the next day. Fares are M$93 in 2nd class (six to 22 beds per room); M$124 in 1st class (four beds per room); and M$176 in special class (two beds plus private shower and TV).

There is also a once-daily ferry at 2.30 pm from Macau to Shekou in the Shenzhen Special Economic Zone (north of Hong Kong). The fare is M$97.

Getting Around

It's possible and very pleasant to tour most of the Macau Peninsula on foot. If you want to explore the islands of Taipa and Coloane, you'll have to deal with public transport.

BUS

There are minibuses and large buses, and both offer air-con and frequent services. They operate from 7 am until midnight.

You'll find it easier to deal with the bus system if you buy a good map of Macau showing all the routes. For most tourists, the No 3A bus is the most important since it connects the Jetfoil Pier to the downtown area and Floating Casino.

Listed here are all the bus routes within the Macau Peninsula. For buses to Taipa and Coloane, see the Macau Islands chapter. The fare on all these buses is M$1.80 and no change is given.

No 3
Jetfoil Pier, Beverly Plaza Hotel, Hotel Lisboa, San Francisco Garden, Avenida Almeida Ribeiro, GPO, Hotel Grand, Avenida do Almirante Lacerda, Lotus Temple, Barrier Gate

No 3A
Jetfoil Pier, Beverly Plaza Hotel, Hotel Lisboa, San Francisco Garden, Avenida Almeida Ribeiro, GPO, Floating Casino, Praca Ponte e Horta

No 9
(loop route) Barra Fortress, A-Ma Temple, Floating Casino, GPO, Rua do Campo, Lou Lim Ieoc Garden, Avenida Horta e Costa, Barrier Gate, Lotus Temple, Canidrome, Avenida do Almirante Lacerda, Avenida do Ouvidor Arriaga, Flora Garden, Sun Yatsen Memorial Home, St Dominic's Church, GPO, Avenida Almeida Ribeiro, Rua da Praia Grande, Government House, Avenida da Republica, Barra Fortress

No 10
Barra Fortress, Floating Casino, Hotel Grand, Avenida Almeida Ribeiro, GPO, Metropole Hotel, Sintra Hotel, Hotel Lisboa, Presidente Hotel, Macau Forum, Outer Harbour, Barrier Gate

No 12
Jetfoil Pier, Beverly Plaza Hotel, Hotel Lisboa, Rua do Campo, Lou Lim Ieoc Garden, Mondial Hotel, Avenida Horta e Costa, Avenida Coronel Mesquita, Kun Iam Temple, Bairro da Areia Preta

No 18
Barra Fortress, Floating Casino, Avenida Almeida Ribeiro, Camoes Gardens, Rua da Barca, Rua Francisco Xavier Pereira, Avenida Coronel Mesquita, Montanha Russa Garden, Areia Preta, Avenida Coronel Mesquita, Jun Iam Temple, Lou Lim Ieoc Garden, Avenida Sidonio Pais, Rua do Campo, Government House, St Lazarus Church, Barra Fortress

No 28C
Jetfoil Pier, Beverly Plaza Hotel, Hotel Lisboa, Estrada de Sao Francisco, Hotel Matsuya, Guia Hotel, Royal Hotel, Lou Lim Ieoc Gardens, Mondial Hotel, Avenida Horta e Costa, Avenida Coronel Mesquita, Kun Iam Temple, Bairro da Areia Preta, Barrier Gate

TAXI

Macau's metered taxis are black with cream roofs. Flagfall is M$6.50 for the first 1.5 km, thereafter it's 80 avos every 250 metres. There is a M$5 surcharge to go to Taipa, and M$10 to go to Coloane, but there is no surcharge if you're heading the other way back to Macau. There is also an additional M$1 service charge for each piece of luggage carried in the boot (trunk). Not many taxi drivers speak English, so it would be helpful to have a map with both Chinese and English or Portuguese.

It can be difficult to get a taxi during rush hour, but otherwise it shouldn't be a problem. Taxis can be dispatched by radio if you ring ☎ 519519.

You can hire a taxi and driver for a whole day or half a day. The price as well as the itinerary should be agreed on in advance. Large hotels can usually help you to arrange this.

CAR & MOTORBIKE

For exploring the islands of Taipa and Coloane, renting a car (or moke) is a convenient way to get around if you can afford it. As for driving on the Macau Peninsula, I think it's an insane idea. Taking a bus tour of the peninsula would be cheaper, faster and less aggravating than driving.

Apart from the bumper to bumper traffic, there is really no place to park a car in Macau. To stop to look at something, it's entirely possible that you'll spend more than 30 minutes searching for a parking place and wind up parking several hundred metres from your destination.

While driving on the Macau Peninsula is not recommended, a rented car (or moke) can be a convenient, though expensive, way to explore the islands. Dividing the cost amongst several travellers makes it more reasonable.

It appears that motorcycles are impossible to rent unless you have a Macau driver's licence.

Road Rules

Drivers must be at least 21 years of age and must have held a driving licence recognised in Portugal for not less than two years. Portugal recognises the licences of most countries in the world, but not all. Licences which Portugal does not recognise includes those issued by Canada, Japan, Hong Kong, India and Singapore. If you fall into this category, you'll need an international driving licence.

As in Hong Kong, driving is on the left side of the road. Another local driving rule is that motor vehicles must always stop for pedestrians at a crosswalk if there is no traffic light. It's illegal to beep the horn – if only Hong Kong had this rule!

Police in Macau are strict and there are stiff fines for traffic violators, so obey the rules unless you want to contribute even more to Macau's economy.

Rental

Macau's rent-a-car pioneer is Macau Mokes Group Ltd (☎ 378851), Avenida Marciano Baptist, just across from the Jetfoil Terminal in Macau. They also have a Hong Kong office (☎ 5434190) at 806 Kai Tak Commercial Building, 317-321 Des Voeux Rd, Sheung Wan, near the Macau Ferry Pier on Hong Kong Island. You can rent an Austin moke for M$280 on weekdays and M$310 on weekends and holidays. You can also rent a fancier car such as a Subaru van (M$380), Honda Civic (M$480) or a Mercedes-Benz 230E (M$2500).

You can also rent mokes from Avis Rent-A-Car (☎ 336789, 567888 ext 3004) which is located at the Mandarin Oriental Hotel. It's probably not necessary on weekdays, but you can book in advance at the Avis Hong Kong office (☎ 5412011).

BICYCLE

Bicycle rentals are no longer available on the Macau Peninsula. You can still rent bikes on the islands of Taipa and Coloane. Forget about renting a bike on the islands and riding it back into the city – riding a bike on the Macau-Taipa Bridge is illegal, and it would be suicidal to attempt it.

WALKING

Macau is certainly small enough that most areas of interest can be reached on foot. However, it's going to be a long and exhausting day if you don't take to motorised transport, so at least start early if you're going to rely on foot power alone.

PEDICABS

These are three-wheeled bicycles, known as *triciclos* in Portuguese. In many Third World countries, pedicabs are used as cheap taxis. In Macau, which is hardly the Third World, pedicabs are a tourist novelty which are actually more expensive than taxis. As pedicabs don't have meters, agree on the fare before getting in. A short ride will cost M$15 or from M$50 to M$60 for an hour of sightseeing. As pedicabs cannot negotiate hills, you'll be limited to touring the waterfront.

It's easiest to find the pedicabs near the Hotel Lisboa. You won't have to solicit the drivers. If you so much as look their way they'll come chasing after you.

TOUR MACHINE

If you want to do something really touristy, you can ride the 'Tour Machine', a replica of a 1920s English bus equipped with leather upholstery. The machine is painted fire engine-red and has bright yellow letters spelling out 'Tour Machine' – if you want to be conspicuous, this is the way to do it. The machine seats nine people and runs on a few fixed routes – you need to get the little brochure to figure out the routes and times. The machine can be chartered for M$200 per hour in Macau, or M$300 for trips across the border into China.

If this interests you, contact Vacations International Travel Service (☎ 555686) in the Mandarin Oriental Hotel.

TOURS

Tours offer a fast way to see everything with minimum hassle and can easily be booked in Hong Kong, or in Macau after arrival. Tours booked in Macau are generally much better value as those booked in Hong Kong usually cost considerably more (yet include transportation to and from Macau and a side-trip across the border to Zhuhai in China). These are usually one-day whirlwind tours departing for Macau in the morning and returning to Hong Kong the same evening, and cost about HK$500.

A typical city tour (booked in Macau) of the peninsula takes three to four hours and costs about M$70 per person, often including lunch. Bus tours out to the islands run from about M$20 per person. You can also book a one-day bus tour across the border into Zhuhai in China, which usually includes a trip to the former home of Dr Sun Yatsen in Zhongshan County.

There is an exhausting one-day tour that departs Hong Kong at 7 am, takes you to Shekou (in the Shenzhen Special Economic Zone north of Hong Kong), then by boat to Zhuhai Special Economic Zone north of Macau, then to the home of Dr Sun Yatsen in Zhongshan County, then by bus to Macau, then by jetfoil back to Hong Kong by 7.30 pm. This trip costs HK$760, not including the medical treatment you might need for seasickness or cardiac arrest.

If you'd like a slower pace, a three or four day tour from Hong Kong to Macau, Zhuhai,

Cuiheng (home of Dr Sun Yatsen), Zhongshan, Foshan, Guangzhou and then back to Hong Kong by train, costs about HK$1500.

Finding these tours is not difficult. In Hong Kong, the ubiquitous moneychangers often have a collection of free pamphlets offering tours to Macau. The Macau Tourist Office at Shun Tak Centre (Macau Ferry Pier) has piles of information on tours and this is probably the best place to go. Most Hong Kong travel agencies also book tours.

In Macau, contact the tourist office or go directly to one of these tour agencies:

Able Tours
    5-9 Travessa do Padre Narciso (☎ 89798, HK 5459993)
Asia
    23-B Rua da Praia Grande (☎ 593844, HK 5488806)
China Travel Service
    Xinhua Building, Rua de Nagasaki (☎ 700888, HK 5406333)
Estoril Tours
    Mezzanine floor, New Wing, Hotel Lisboa, Avenida da Amizade (☎ 710361; fax 567193, HK 5810022)
F Rodrigues
    71 Rua da Praia Grande (☎ 581777)
Guangdong Macau Tours
    37-E Rua da Praia Grande (☎ 588807; fax 512153, HK 8329118)
Hi-No-De Caravela
    6A-4C Rua de Sacadura Cabral (☎ 338338; fax 566622, HK 3686181)
H Nolasco, Lda
    20 Avenida Almeida Ribeiro (☎ 76464)
International Tourism
    9 Travessa do Padre Narciso, Loja B (☎ 975183, HK 5412011)
Lotus
    Edificio Fong Meng, Rua de Sao Lourenco (☎ 81765)
Macau Mondial
    74-A Avenida do Conselheiro Ferreira de Almeida (☎ 566866; fax 574531)
Macau Star Tours
    Room 511, Tai Fung Bank Building, 34 Avenida Almeida Ribeiro (☎ 558855, HK 3662262)
Macau Tours Ltd
    35 Avenida Dr Mario Soares (☎ 385555; fax 700050, HK 5422338)
MBC Tours
    7-9 Rua Santa Clara, Edificio Ribeiro, Loja D (☎ 88462)

Sintra Tours
Room 207, Hotel Sintra, Avenida Dom Joao IV
(☎ 710111; fax 510527, HK 5408028)
South China
1st floor, 15 Avenida Dr Rodrigo Rodrigues, Apt
1-B (☎ 781811, HK 8150208)

TKW
4th floor, 27-31 Rua Formosa, Apt 408
(☎ 591122, HK 7237771)
Vacations International
Shopping arcade, Mandarin Oriental Hotel,
Avenida da Amizade, (☎ 555686 ext 3004; fax
314112)

Macau Peninsula 澳門半島

CENTRAL MACAU 中環澳門

Avenida de Almeida Ribeiro is the main street of Macau and is as good a place to start your tour as any. It crosses Rua da Praia Grande just up from the waterfront and effectively divides the narrow southern peninsula from the rest of Macau. It continues down to the Hotel Lisboa under the name of Avenida do Infante D Henrique (Macau's streets may not be very big but their names certainly are). A good place to start is the Hotel Lisboa, that grotesquely distinctive building which dominates the waterfront of Macau.

Jorge Alvares Statue 歐維士石像

The monument is on the corner of Rua da Praia Grande and Avenida da Amizade. Alvares is credited with being the first Portuguese to set foot on Chinese soil when he and his party landed on the island of Lin Tin, halfway between Macau and Hong Kong.

Leal Senado 市政廳

Across the street from the GPO on Avenida de Almeida Ribeiro is the Leal Senado which houses the municipal government offices.

The Leal Senado (Loyal Senate) is the main administrative body for municipal affairs, but it once had much greater power and dealt on equal terms with Chinese officials in the last century. It's called the Loyal Senate because it refused to recognise Spanish sovereignty over Portugal when the Spanish marched into Portugal in the 17th century and occupied it for 60 years. When Portuguese control was re-established, the city of Macau was granted the official name of Cidade do Nome de Deus de Macau, Nao ha Outra Mais Leal or 'City of the Name of God, Macau. There is None more Loyal'.

Above the wrought-iron gates leading to the garden, inside the main building, is an interesting bas-relief, the subject of some dispute. Some say the woman depicted is the Virgin Mary sheltering all those in need of mercy. Others hold that it represents the Portuguese Queen Leonor of the 16th century.

Also inside the Leal Senado is the **public library**, open on weekdays from 9 am to noon and from 2 to 5.30 pm, and on Saturdays from 9 am to 12.30 pm. In front of the Leal Senado is the **Largo do Senado**, the Senate Square.

St Dominic's Church 玫瑰堂

The most beautiful of Macau's baroque churches is St Dominic's (Sao Domingo) Church. The huge 17th-century building has an impressive tiered altar with images of the Virgin and Child and of Our Lady of Fatima, which is carried in procession during the Fatima Festival. There is a small museum at the back full of church regalia, images and paintings. The church is only open in the afternoon. To get in, ring the bell by the iron gates at the side. It is on Rua do Sao Domingos, at the northern end of Largo do Senado.

Luis de Camoes Museum 賈梅士博物館

A few blocks to the north of St Dominic's Church is the modern **Church of St Anthony**. The church is memorable for having been burnt to the ground three times.

To the left is the entrance to the Luis de Camoes Museum, a historically interesting building and once the headquarters of the British East India Company in Macau. The museum has an extensive collection that includes early Chinese terracotta, enamel ware and pottery, paintings, old weapons, religious objects and a collection of sketches and paintings of old Macau and Guangzhou. However, the building itself (which dates back to the 18th century) is of great interest. It's open from 11 am to 5 pm daily, except Wednesdays and public holidays. Admission is M$1.

Camoes Grotto & Gardens
白鴿巢賈梅士花園

Behind the museum in the Camoes Grotto &

MACAU

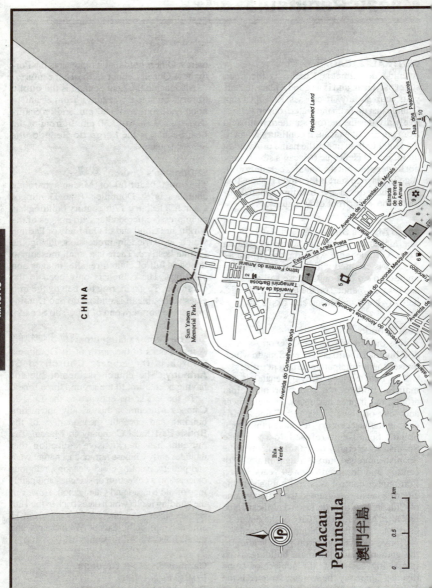

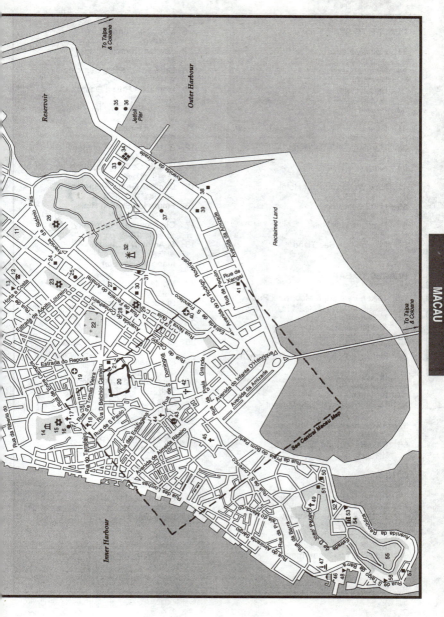

MACAU

To Taipa
& Coloane

Outer Harbour

Reclaimed Land

Reservoir

Jetfoil
Pier

Inner Harbour

See Central Macau Map

To Taipa
& Coloane

PLACES TO STAY

21 Holiday Hotel
假期酒店
24 Mondial Hotel
環球酒店
27 Estoril Hotel
愛都酒店
30 Royal Hotel
皇都酒店
31 Guia Hotel
東望洋酒店
38 Mandarin Oriental Hotel
文華東方酒店
39 Kingsway Hotel
金域酒店
41 New World Emperor Hotel
新世界帝濠酒店
50 Hotel Bela Vista
峰京酒店
51 Pousada Ritz Hotel
豪璟酒店
57 Pousada de Sao Tiago
聖地牙哥酒店

PLACES TO EAT

6 Talker, Pyretu's & Moonwalk Pubs
高地烏街104號 (觀音堂對面)
13 McDonald's III
麥當勞
28 Restaurante Violeta
紫晶閣餐廳
34 McDonald's II & Yaohan Department
Store
麥當勞/八佰伴
48 A Lorcha Restaurant
船屋餐廳
52 Henri's Galley & Café Marisol
美心餐廳/咖喱屋
53 Ali Curry House
咖喱屋
56 Pele Restaurant
比利餐廳

OTHER

1 Barrier Gate
關閘
2 CTM Telephone Company
澳門電訊有限公司
3 Canidrome
跑狗場
4 Lin Fong Miu Lotus Temple
蓮峰廟

5 Mong-Ha Fortress
望廈古堡
7 Kun Iam Temple
觀音堂
8 Our Lady of Piety Cemetery
新西洋境場
9 Montanha Russa Garden
螺絲山公園
10 Macau-Seac Tin Hau Temple
馬交石天后廟
11 Pak Vai Plaza
柏蕙廣場
12 CTM Telephone Company
澳門電訊有限公司
14 Luis de Camoes Museum
賈梅士博物館
15 Camoes Grotto & Garden
白鴿巢賈梅士花園
16 Future Ice Skating Rink
佳景樂園 (白鴿巢賈梅士花園對面)
17 Old Protestant Cemetery
舊基督教墳場
18 St Anthony's Church
聖安多尼堂
19 Kiang Vu Hospital
鏡湖醫院
20 Monte Fort
中央大炮台
22 St Michael's Cemetery
聖美基西洋境場
23 Lou Lim Ioc Garden
盧廉若花園
25 Sun Yatsen Memorial House
孫中山紀念館
26 Flora Garden
二龍喉花園
29 Vasco da Gama Garden
華士占達嘉馬花園
32 Guía Lighthouse
松山燈塔
33 Jai-Alai Casino
回力球娛樂場
35 HK-Macau Ferry Pier
澳港碼頭
36 Heliport
直昇機停機坪
37 Macau Forum
綜藝館
40 Government Hospital
山頂醫院
42 Cathedral
大堂
43 Tourist Office
旅遊司
44 St Dominic's Church
玫瑰堂

MACAU

45	St Augustine's Church 聖奧斯定堂
46	Maritime Museum 海事博物館
47	A-Ma Temple 媽閣廟
49	Penha Church 西望洋堂
54	Governor's Residence 總督私邸
55	Barra Hill 媽閣山

Gardens is another memorial to Luis de Camoes, the 16th-century Portuguese poet who has become something of a local hero, though his claim is not all that strong. He is said to have written his epic *Os Lusiadas* by the rocks here, but there is no firm evidence that he was ever in Macau. A bust of him is in the gardens, looking rather better than the man, so it is said. A pleasant, cool and shady place, the gardens are popular with the local Chinese and you may find old men sitting here playing checkers. They don't mind an audience. There are good views from the top of the hill.

Old Protestant Cemetery 舊基督教墳場

Beside the Camoes Museum is the Old Protestant Cemetery – the resting place of numerous non-Portuguese who made their way to Macau.

The cemetery was needed because ecclesiastical law forbade the burial of Protestants on Catholic soil – which meant the whole of Macau, at least inside the city walls. Beyond the walls was Chinese soil, and the Chinese didn't approve of foreigners desecrating their pitch either. The unhappy result was that Protestants had to bury their dead either in the nearby hills and hope the Chinese wouldn't notice, or else beneath the neutral territory of the city walls.

Finally the governor allowed a local merchant to sell some of his land to the British East India Company – despite a law forbidding foreign ownership of land – and the cemetery was established in 1921. A number of old graves were then transferred there, which explains the earlier dates on some of the

tombstones. The gate shows the date 1814, which was when the cemetery committee was set up.

Among the better known people buried here is artist George Chinnery, noted for his portrayals of Macau and its people in the first half of the 19th century. Also buried here is Robert Morrison, the first Protestant missionary to China, who, as his tombstone records, 'for several years laboured alone on a Chinese version of the Holy Scriptures which he was spared to see completed'. Morrison is buried beside his wife Mary who became one of the cemetery's first burials after dying in childbirth – 'erewhile anticipating a living mother's joy suddenly, but with a pious resignation, departed this life after a short illness of 14 hours, bearing with her to the grave her hoped-for child'. Also buried here is Lord John Spencer Churchill, an ancestor of Sir Winston Churchill.

Other inscriptions on the tombstones indicate that ships' officers and crew are well represented. Some died from accidents aboard, such as falling off the rigging, while others died more heroically, like Lieutenant Fitzgerald 'from the effects of a wound received while gallantly storming the enemy's battery at Canton'. Captain Sir Humphrey Le Fleming Senhouse died 'from the effects of fever contracted during the zealous performance of his arduous duties at the capture of the Heights of Canton in May 1841'.

Fortune tellers have set up shop just outside the cemetery.

St Paul's Ruins 大三巴牌坊

Some say the ruins (Ruinas de Sao Paulo) of St Paul's Cathedral are the greatest monument to Christianity in the east. The cathedral was finished in the first decade of the 17th century, and the crowned heads of Europe competed to present it with its most prestigious gift.

Built on one of Macau's seven hills, it was designed by an Italian Jesuit and built by early Japanese Christian exiles. All that remains is the facade, the magnificent mosaic floor and the impressive stone steps

St Paul's Ruins

keg on one of the invader's ships, which exploded, blowing the Dutch out of the water. It's the only time these cannons were ever fired in combat. Since this event occurred on St John the Baptist's Day, 24 June, he was promptly proclaimed the city's patron saint, perhaps adding new meaning to the term 'canonised'.

Now the old building is used as an observatory and a museum. From it there are sweeping views across Macau. Enter the fort from a narrow cobbled street leading off Estrada do Repouso near Estrada do Cemiterio. There is also a path from the fortress down to the ruins of St Paul.

St Michael Cemetery 聖美基西洋境場

This beautiful Catholic cemetery is in the centre of the Macau Peninsula on Estrada do Cemiterio. Although a few of the tombs are plain to look at, most are stunning works of art. The whole cemetery is adorned with statues of angels. This is the largest cemetery on the peninsula, though there is an even bigger Chinese cemetery on Taipa Island.

Lou Lim Loc Gardens 盧廉若花園

The restful Lou Lim Loc Gardens are on Ferreira de Almeida. The gardens and the ornate mansion with its columns and arches, now the Pui Ching School, once belonged to the wealthy Chinese Lou family. The gardens are a mixture of European and Chinese plantings, with huge shady trees, lotus ponds, pavilions, bamboo groves, grottoes and strangely shaped doorways. The twisting pathways and ornamental mountains are built to represent a Chinese painting and are said to be modelled on those in the famous gardens of Suzhou in eastern China.

Sun Yatsen Memorial Home
孫中山紀念館

Around the corner from the Lou Lim Loc Gardens, at the junction of Avenida da Sidonio Pais and Rua de Silva Mendes, is a memorial house dedicated to Dr Sun Yatsen. Sun practised medicine in Macau for some years before turning to revolution and seeking to overthrow the Qing Dynasty. A

leading up to it. The church caught fire during a disastrous typhoon in 1835. For awhile it seemed like the whole thing might eventually fall apart, but renovation work was undertaken and finally completed in 1991.

The facade has been described as a sermon in stone, recording some of the main events of Christianity in the various carvings. At the top is the dove, representing the Holy Spirit, surrounded by stone carvings of the sun, moon and stars. Beneath the dove is a statue of the infant Jesus surrounded by stone carvings of the implements of the crucifixion. In the centre of the third tier stands the Virgin Mary, with angels and two types of flowers – the peony representing China and the chrysanthemum representing Japan. The fourth tier has statues of four Jesuit saints.

Monte Fort 大炮台

The fort (Fortaleza do Monte) is on a hill overlooking the St Paul ruins and was built by the Jesuits around the same time. The first Portuguese settlers in Macau built their homes in the centre of the peninsula, and the fort once formed the strong central point of the old city wall of Macau. The cannons on the fort are the very ones that dissuaded the Dutch from further attempts to take over Macau. In 1622 a cannon ball hit a powder rundown on Sun's involvement with the anti-Qing forces and later with the Kuomintang and Communist parties is in the Facts about Guangzhou Chapter.

The memorial house in Macau was built as a monument to Sun and contains a collection of flags, photos and other relics. It replaced the original house which blew up when used as an explosives store. The house is open every day except Tuesday. Hours are Mondays, Wednesdays, Thursdays and Fridays from 10 am to 1 pm and Saturdays and Sundays from 10 am to 1 pm and 3 to 5 pm.

Guia Lighthouse 松山燈塔
This was once a fortress occupying the highest point on the Macau Peninsula. The 17th-century **chapel** here is the old hermitage of Our Lady of Guia. The Guia Lighthouse (*guia* means guide in Portuguese) is the oldest on the China coast, first lit in 1865.

Around the lighthouse are the only two hiking trails on the peninsula, which are also excellent for jogging. One trail circumnavigates the mountain, a total distance of 1.7 km, and is called the Walk of 33 Curves. Inside this loop trail is a shorter loop, the Fitness Circuit Walk, which has 20 gymnastic-type exercise stations along the route.

Vasco da Gama Garden 華士占達嘉馬花園
This monument in a small garden is on the corner of Rua Ferreira do Amaral and Calcada do Gaio, just to the west of the Parsee Cemetery and Guia Lighthouse. Da Gama's was the first Portuguese fleet to round the southern cape of Africa and make its way to India.

Military Museum 軍事博物館
The Military Museum (one block north of Hotel Lisboa) is the former Military Club and was built in 1872. It's one of the oldest examples of Portuguese architecture still standing in Macau. Behind it are the **Sao Francisco Barracks**, now part of the museum. The museum is open to the public daily from 2 to 5 pm.

THE SOUTH
There are a number of interesting sights on the peninsula – once known to the Chinese as the Water Lily Peninsula – south of Avenida de Almeida Ribeiro. A good way to start exploring this region is to walk up the steep Rua Central near the Leal Senado.

St Augustine Church 聖奧斯定堂
Around the corner from the Leal Senado in the Largo de Santo Agostinho is St Augustine (Sao Agostinho) Church, which has foundations dating from 1586 although the present church was built in 1814. Among the people buried here is Maria de Moura, who in 1710 married Captain Antonio Albuquerque Coelho after he had lost an arm through an attack by one of Maria's unsuccessful suitors. Unfortunately Maria died in childbirth and is buried with her baby and Antonio's arm.

St Lazarus Church 聖老愣佐堂
Heading back down to and continuing along Rua Central, you'll find yourself on Rua de Sao Lourenco. On the right is the St Lazarus (Sao Lourenco) Church with its twin square towers. Stone steps lead up to the ornamental gates, but if you want to go in, use the side entrance. The original church is thought to have been built on this site at the time the Portuguese first settled in Macau, but the present church only dates from 1846.

A-Ma Temple (Ma Kok Miu) 媽閣廟
At the end of Calcada da Barra is the A-Ma Temple at the base of Penha Hill. It is otherwise known as the A-Ma Temple and is dedicated to the goddess A-Ma (or Mother). A-Ma is more commonly known by her Hong Kong pseudonym Tin Hau, which means Queen of Heaven.

The original temple on this site was probably already standing when the Portuguese arrived, although the present building may only date back to the 17th century.

A-Ma became A-Ma-Gao to the Portuguese and they named their colony after it. The temple consists of several shrines dating from the Ming Dynasty. The boat people of

MACAU

Rua Colonos
C Botelho
Rua dos Faitloes
Rua de Cinco Outubro
Rua do Teatro
Rua Nova do Comercio
Rua Visconde Paco de Arcos

† 1
L da Companhia
Rua D Belchior Carneiro
Calcada de S Paulo
2
3
Rua Santo Antonio   Rua S Paulo
R Nossa Senhora do Amparo
T Armazem Velho
Rua das Estalagens
Rua Palha
Rua de S Domingos
25
Largo da Se
† 26
Rua do Pagode
Rua Camilo Passanha
T do Soriano
Rua Mercadores
Travessa Pagode
Rua da Madeira
36
37
35
38
39
42
43
Largo do Senado
27
28
29
30
Avenida de Almeida Ribeiro
34
40
41
Rua Caldeira
Travessa Caldeira
31
Travessa Auto Novo
32
T da Felicidade
33
Rua Felicidade
T Aterro Novo
Rua Cules
Calcada Tronco Velho
Macau-Guangzhou
Ferry Wharf
71
70
72
69
73
Rua das Lorchas
Rua do Bocage
74
Rua Gamboa
68
75
67
66
Rua Alfandega
† 65
Santo
Praca Ponte
e Horta
76
Patio Francisco Antonio
Rua do Seminario
Rua de S Lourenco
Travessa
Travessa Chan Loc
Rua do Barao
Rua Prata
77 †
Travessa
Rua Central

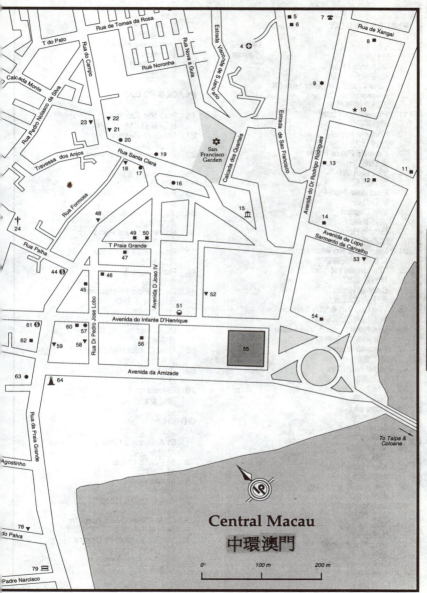

Central Macau
中環澳門

0   100 m   200 m

PLACES TO STAY

5 Vila Tak Lei
德利別墅
6 Matsuya Hotel
松屋酒店
8 New World Emperor Hotel &
Immigration Office
人民入境事務處
11 Presidente Hotel
總統酒店
12 Fortuna Hotel
財神酒店
13 Beverly Plaza Hotel
富豪酒店
14 Vila San Vu
珊瑚別墅
27 East Asia Hotel
東亞酒店
28 Vila Capital
京華賓館
29 Grand Hotel
國際酒店
31 Man Va & Ko Wah Hotel
文華酒店/高華酒店
32 Vila Universal
世界迎賓館
38 Central Hotel
新中央大酒店
45 Vila Loc Tin & Vila Sam Sui
樂天別墅/山水別墅
46 Vila Nam Loon & Vila Meng Meng
南龍別墅/明明別墅
47 Pensao Nam In
南苑賓館
49 Hotel Nam Tin
南天酒店
50 Vila Nam Pan
南濱小築
54 Hotel Lisboa
葡京酒店
56 Sintra Hotel
新麗酒店
60 Vila Kimbo
金賓別墅
62 Metropole Hotel
京都酒店
66 Pensao Kuan Heng
群興賓館群
67 London Hotel
英京酒店
68 Vila Tai Loy
大來賓館
69 Hou Kong Hotel
濠江酒店
71 Peninsula Hotel
半島酒店

73 Masters Macau Hotel
萬事發酒店
74 Ung Ieong Hotel
五洋酒店
75 Hospedaria Vong Hong
皇宮旅館

PLACES TO EAT

18 Pizzeria Toscana
比薩餐廳
21 Maxim's Bakery
美心西餅
22 Portugués Restaurant
葡國餐廳
23 McDonald's I
麥當勞
33 Fat Siu Lau Restaurant
佛笑樓
34 Yoghurt Shop
義順牛奶公司
36 Fairwood Fast Food
大快活餐廳
39 Restaurant Long Kei
龍記餐廳
40 Restaurant Safari
金池餐廳
48 Ze do Pipo Restaurant
八比龍葡國餐廳
52 Foodstalls
大排檔
53 Pizza Hut
必勝客
58 New Ocean Restaurant
新海洋大酒樓
59 Solmar Restaurant
沙利文餐廳
78 Estrela do Mar
海星餐廳

OTHER

1 St Anthony's Church
聖安多尼堂
2 St Paul's Ruins
大三巴牌坊
3 Monte Fort
大炮台
4 Government Hospital
山頂醫院
7 CTM Telephone Company
澳門電訊有限公司
9 Macau Exhibition Centre
澳門展覽中心
10 Main Police Station
總警署

15 Military Museum
    軍事博物館
16 Chinese Library
    八角亭
17 Livraria Sao Paulo (bookshop)
    聖保祿書局
19 Cineteatro Macau
    澳門大會堂
20 Watson's Drugstore
    屈臣氏
23 Capitol Theatre
    京華戲院
24 Cathedral
    大堂
25 Livraria Portuguesa (Portuguese
    Bookshop)
    葡文書局
26 St Dominic's Church
    玫瑰堂
30 Casino Kam Pek
    金碧娛樂場
35 St Dominic's Market
    營地街市場
37 Tourist Office
    旅遊司
41 Leal Senado
    市政廳
42 GPO
    郵政局
43 CTM Telephone Office
    澳門電訊有限公司
44 Hongkong Bank
    匯豐銀行
51 Bus Stop to Taipa & Coloane
    往路環車站
55 Bank of China
    中國銀行
57 Foto Princesa
    照相館
61 Bank of China
    中國銀行
63 Days & Days Supermarket
    大利時超級市場
64 Jorge Alvares Statue
    歐維士石像
65 St Augustine Church
    聖奧斯定堂
70 Kee Kwan Motors (Buses to
    Guangzhou)
    往廣州公共汽車
72 Floating Casino (Macau Palace)
    皇宮娛樂場
76 Park 'n Shop
    百佳超級市場
77 St Lazarus Church
    聖老愣佐堂
79 Government House
    澳督府

Macau come here on pilgrimage each year in April or May. The temple is actually a complex of temples, some dedicated to A-Ma and others to Kun Iam.

There are several stories about A-Ma, one of which is related in the Hong Kong Religion section, but in Macau the tale goes that she was a beautiful young woman whose presence on a Guangzhou-bound ship saved it from disaster. All the other ships in the fleet, whose rich owners had refused to give her a passage, were destroyed in a storm.

The A-Ma Temple is one of the venues in Macau where fortune tellers ply their trade.

Maritime Museum 海事博物館
This museum, opposite the A-Ma Temple, is really world class and not to be missed. It has a collection of boats and other artefacts related to Macau's seafaring past. There is also a dragon boat which is used in races held during the Dragon Boat Festival, plus a flower boat, a tugboat and a Chinese fishing vessel.

A motorised junk moored next to the museum offers 30-minute rides around the harbour on Saturdays, Sundays and Monday. Departures are at 10.30 and 11.30 am, 3.30 and 4.30 pm. The fare is M$15, which includes the admission fee (M$5) for the museum.

The Maritime Museum is open from 10 am until 5.30 pm, Wednesday through Monday. It's closed on Tuesdays.

Barra Hill 媽閣山
From the A-Ma Temple you can follow Rua de Sao Tiago da Barra around to the Barra Hill at the end of Avenida da Republica. At one time the hill was topped by a fortress which had great strategic importance when it was built in 1629, as ships entering the harbour had to come very close to the shore. The **Pousada de Sao Tiago Hotel** has been built within the walls of the fortress and is worth seeing even if you can't afford to stay there. The hilltop is now a park, and you can circumnavigate it and enjoy the views by walking along Calcada da Penha which is closed to motorised traffic.

MACAU

Governor's Residence 總督私邸

On the east side of the tip of the Macau Peninsula is Rua da Praia Grande, one of the most scenic streets in the city. Here you find the pink Governor's Residence, built in the 19th century as a residence for a Macanese aristocratic family. The building is not open to tourists, but you can admire the architecture from outside. Slightly further to the north is the **Bela Vista Hotel**, Macau's equivalent to Singapore's Raffles, built at the end of the 19th century.

Penha Church 西望洋聖堂

On a hill above the Bela Vista is the Bishop's Residence and Penha Church. From here you get an excellent view of the central area of Macau. You can also see across the Pearl River into China. In front of the church is a **replica of the Grotto of Lourdes**.

Government House 澳督府

The Government House on Rua da Praia Grande is pink like the Governor's Residence. Originally built for a Portuguese noble in 1849, it was acquired by the government at the end of the 19th century.

THE NORTH

The northern part of the peninsula has been recently developed at the expense of the southern and central areas. Nevertheless, there are a few interesting historical sites in this region of Macau. The best way to see them is with a bicycle, since this area is far too spread out to do much walking.

Kun Iam Temple 觀音堂

The Kun Iam Temple on Avenida do Coronel Mesquita is really a clutch of temples, the most interesting in Macau, and is dedicated to the goddess Kun Iam (Guanyin), the Queen of Heaven and the Goddess of Mercy. The temple dates back about 400 years, though the original temple on the site was probably built more than 600 years ago.

This was also the place where the first treaty of trade and friendship between the USA and China was signed in 1844. These days it's a place for fortune-telling rather than treaties and gets quite a lot of visitors.

Lotus Temple (Lin Fong Miu) 蓮峰廟

Near the Canidrome is Estrada do Arco where you'll find the Lotus Temple. The main hall of this temple is dedicated to Kun Iam. Another shrine is for A-Ma, the Goddess of Seafarers, and another is for Kuanti, the God of War, Riches, Literature & Pawnshops. The temple complex probably predates the arrival of the Portuguese in Macau.

Barrier Gate 關閘

Once a popular tourist spot, the Barrier Gate (Portas do Cerco) is the gate between Macau and China. In Portuguese, Portas do Cerco literally means Gate of Siege. Before 1980, when 'China-watching' was meant literally, Macau's Barrier Gate and Hong Kong's Lok

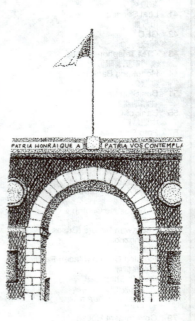

Barrier Gate

Ma Chau attracted many curious visitors simply because it was the border, and that was as close as any foreigner ever got to the People's Republic. These days the Barrier Gate is just a busy border crossing, but if you want to see it, head straight up Istmo Ferreira do Amaral from the Lotus Temple.

Macau-Seac Tin Hau Temple
馬交石天后廟
From the Barrier Gate you can loop back down to the Hotel Lisboa along the eastern perimeter of the city. Head east along Avenida de Venceslau de Morris. At its extremity by the sea and the Macau Reservoir is the tiny Macau-Seac Tin Hau Temple. From here you can walk to the Jai-Alai Casino and the Jetfoil Pier, and from there catch bus No 3 to the Hotel Lisboa.

PLACES TO STAY
Hotels on the Macau Peninsula are concentrated in two areas – near the Floating Casino or near the waterfront by the Rua da Praia Grande and Jetfoil Pier. The ones near the Floating Casino tend to be slightly cheaper, though not by much.

For definition purposes, 'budget' in Macau is anything costing up to M$200. Over M$200 but under M$500 is 'mid-range' and over M$500 is the top-end. Realise though that there is some room for bargaining, especially during the winter season, so you might be able to do somewhat better than the prices quoted here.

Places to Stay – bottom end
The key to finding a good, cheap room is patience. If one place charges too much, then try another. As long as you haven't arrived on a weekend, you should find something acceptable in half an hour or so after you begin your search.

The street in front of the Floating Casino is Rua das Lorchas, at one time a happy hunting ground for cheap guesthouses but most have now been torn down. There are two numbering systems on this street, which causes some confusion. One place still remaining is *Hospedaria Vong Hong*.

Depending on which numbering scheme you believe, it's either No 45 or 253 – the street has been renumbered, and both numbers are clearly visible on the building! This place is truly depressing, but if you can tolerate it, rooms are just M$50. Communicating with the very elderly Cantonese woman who runs the place can be tricky – last time I went to see her, I thought she was dead (only slumped over the table sleeping).

Just around the back is an alley called Rua do Bocage. At No 17 you'll find *Hotel Ung Ieong* (☎ 573814), though a sign on the door says 'Restaurante Ung Ieong'. The rooms are so huge you could fit an army in there! Auditorium-sized doubles go for M$52 and some have attached bath. Before you pay, go upstairs and take a look – it's quite run down.

Two blocks to the south of the Floating Casino, on Rua das Lorchas, is a large square called Praca Ponte e Horta. It looks like it might once have been a park, but now it's mainly a car park (most of Macau's open space is buried under cars these days). There are several villas around the square. On the east end of the square, I recommend *Pensao Kuan Heng* (☎ 573629, 937624), 2nd floor, Block C, Rua Ponte e Horta. Singles/doubles are M$150/250 and it's very clean and well-managed.

The *Vila Tai Loy* (☎ 937811) is on the corner of Travessa das Virtudes and Travessa Auto Novo. At M$200, it's barely in the budget class, but the rooms are attractive and the manager is friendly.

Moving to the east side of the peninsula, the area between the Hotel Lisboa and Rua da Praia Grande has some budget accommodation. Intersecting with Rua da Praia Grande is a small street called Rua Dr Pedro Jose Lobo where there's a dense cluster of guesthouses, including *Vila Meng Meng* (☎ 710064) on the 3rd floor at No 24. If you don't mind a shared bathroom, this is one of the best deals in town – air-con rooms are M$130. Next door is the *Vila Nam Loon* – possibly a cheapie but it was being renovated at the time of writing and the new prices are unknown.

Just above Foto Princesa (the camera shop) at Avenida Infante D Henrique 55-59 is *Vila Kimbo* (☎ 710010) where singles go for M$130 and up.

On Rua Dr Pedro Jose Lobo, the *Vila Sam Sui* (☎ 572256) seems very nice and just barely qualifies as budget with rooms for M$200. Its neighbour, *Vila Loc Tin* has moved upmarket – rooms are M$250.

Running off Avenida D Joao IV is an alley called Travessa da Praia Grande. At No 3 you'll find *Pensao Nam In* (☎ 710024), where singles with shared bath are M$110, or M$230 for a pleasant double with private bath. On the opposite side of the alley is the *Vila Nam Tin* (☎ 711212), which looks cheap but isn't – singles are M$330! *Vila Nam Pan* (☎ 572289) on the corner has also become too pricey with singles for M$250, but try polite bargaining.

Behind the Hotel Lisboa on Avenida de Lopo Sarmento de Carvalho is a row of pawnshops and a couple of guesthouses. The *Vila San Vu* is friendly and has good rooms for M$200.

Places to Stay – middle

An excellent place to stay in Macau is the *East Asia Hotel* (☎ 922433), Rua da Madeira 1-A. This is one of the city's classic colonial buildings – the outside maintains its traditional facade, but it's been fully-remodelled on the inside. Spotlessly clean singles are M$230 with private bath and fierce air-con. The dim sum restaurant on the 2nd floor has outstanding breakfasts for only about M$20 or so. But this hotel is definitely geared towards a Chinese clientele – foreigners are few.

Almost next door to the East Asia Hotel is the *Vila Capital* (☎ 920154) at Rua Constantino Brito 3. Singles/doubles are M$230/280.

True to its name, the *Hotel Central* (☎ 373838) is centrally located at Avenida Almeida Ribeiro 26-28, a short hop west of the GPO. The hotel looks better on the outside than it does on the inside – go upstairs and look at the rooms before you decide to stay. Singles/doubles with private bath cost from M$207/238.

The *Hotel London* (☎ 937761) on Praca Ponte e Horta (two blocks south of the Floating Casino) has singles for M$230. Rooms are comfortable and clean.

A few doors to the south of the Floating Casino, on the left as you enter Travessa das Virtudes, is the *Hotel Hou Kong* (☎ 937555) which has singles/doubles for M$230/322. The official address is Rua das Lorchas 1.

Just a block to the north of the Floating Casino, at Avenida Almeida Ribeiro 146, is the *Hotel Grand* (☎ 922418) where singles/doubles cost M$262/386.

One block to the east of the Floating Casino is a street called Travessa Caldeira where you'll find the *Hotel Man Va* (☎ 388655), Rua da Caldeira 32, with doubles at M$340. Nearby at Rua de Felicidade 71, close to Travessa Auto Novo, is *Hotel Ko Wah* (☎ 375599) which has doubles for M$250.

Right in the same neighbourhood is the very clean and friendly *Vila Universal* (☎ 573247) at Rua Felicidade 73. The manager speaks good English and singles/doubles cost M$200/240. The problem with this place is that it seems to be perpetually full – I've never been able to get a room there!

Just on the north side of the Floating Casino on Rua das Lorchas is the *Peninsula Hotel* (☎ 318899). Singles/twins cost M$300/350. This hotel is large, clean and popular.

One more place to look around is the area north of the Hotel Lisboa on a street called Estrada Sao Francisco. You have to climb a steep hill to get up this street, but the advantage is that the hotels have a little sea breeze and it's quiet. Up here you'll find the fancy *Hotel Matsuya* (☎ 577000; fax 568080) where doubles/twins cost M$330/390 and suites are M$650.

Next to the Hotel Matsuya at Estrada Sao Francisco 2A is *Vila Tak Lei* (☎ 577484), where doubles go for M$300. However, bargaining is entirely possible – as I was walking out the price dropped to M$250.

Stretching the definition of 'mid-range' is the *Macau Masters Hotel* (☎ 937572; fax 937565), Rua das Lorchas 162 (next to the

Floating Casino). This new and fancy place has singles/doubles starting at M$440/550, and cushier rooms for M$1000.

Also at the top-end of the middle is *Guia Hotel* (☎ 513888; fax 559822; 89 rooms) at Estrada do Eng Trigo 1-5. It's a relatively small hotel with twins from M$470 to M$570, while triples cost M$650.

The *Metropole* (☎ 388166; fax 330890; 112 rooms) has a prime location at Rua da Praia Grande 63. Doubles are M$460, twins M$600 and suites M$1050 to M$1150.

The *Mondial Hotel* (☎ 566866; fax 514083; 141 rooms) is on a side street called Rua de Antonio Basto, on the east side of Lou Lim Ieoc Gardens. It's rather far from the centre but still not cheap. Doubles go for M$360 to M$580, twins M$480 to M$630 and suites M$1050 to M$2300.

Places to Stay – top end

Macau's booming tourist industry has given rise to many new four and five-star hotels, and more are planned. Rooms, however, are not always easy to get. During the summer travel season, many of these places are solidly booked, even during weekdays. I don't know just where all these rich high-rollers come from, but there seem to be plenty of them.

The *Lisboa* (☎ 377666; fax 567193; 750 rooms) is Macau's most famous landmark. It's difficult to find the right adjective to describe the unique architecture (orange background with white circles), but it certainly is memorable. Regardless of what you think of the external design, the interior is first rate. The Lisboa has the best arcade in Macau, which is filled with shops, restaurants, banks, a billiard room and bowling alley. Even if you don't stay here, it's worth a look. Rooms cost M$600 to M$3500.

If I could afford it, the place I'd choose to live it up at in Macau would be the *Pousada de Sao Tiago* (☎ 378111; fax 552170; 23 rooms), Rua da Boa Vista 2. The location at the very southern tip of the peninsula is dramatic enough, but the architecture has to be seen to be appreciated. The hotel blends into the hillside overlooking the harbour. It's

MACAU

Hotel Lisboa

worth coming here to have a drink at the bar and take a look. Originally the hotel was a fortress, the Fortaleza da Barra, which was built in 1629. Doubles are M$1080 to M$1380 and suites cost M$3000. Despite the high prices, this place is frequently booked solid.

The *Hotel Bela Vista* (☎ 965333; fax 965588) is one of Macau's most famous hotels. This grand colonial building is more than 100 years old and overlooks the waterfront on the south-east corner of the peninsula on Rua Comendador Kou Ho Neng. This is Macau's answer to Hong Kong's *Peninsula* or Singapore's *Raffles*. Prices at the Bela Vista are now M$1500 to M$4000.

There are many other hotels that fall into the top-end category, including some on Taipa and Coloane (see Macau Islands chapter for details).

The following is a brief rundown of the upmarket hotel battlefield:

Beverly Plaza, Avenida do Dr Rodrigues, has twins for M$740 to M$900, suites M$1600 to M$1800; 300 rooms (☎ 337755; fax 308878)

Fortuna, Rua da Cantao, has twins for M$780 to M$980, suites M$1800; 368 rooms (☎ 786333; fax 786363)

Grandeur, Rua Pequim, has twins for M$800 to M$1000, suites M$1300 to M$7000; 350 rooms (☎ 781233; fax 785896)

Holiday Inn, Rua Pequim, has twins for M$700 to M$1200, suites M$2400 to M$9600; 451 rooms (☎ 783333; fax 782321)

Kingsway, Rua de Luis Gonzaga Gomes, has twins for M$680 to M$880, suites M$1080 to M$3380; 410 rooms (☎ 702888; fax 702828)

Mandarin Oriental, has doubles for M$1080 to M$1680, suites for M$3500 to M$17,500; 347 rooms (☎ 567888; fax 594589)

New World Emperor, Rua de Xangai, has twins for M$780 to M$980, suites for M$1380 to M$4380; 405 rooms (☎ 781888; fax 782287)

Pousada Ritz, Rua da Boa Vista 2, has twins for M$1180 to M$1280, suites M$1680 to M$8880; 31 rooms (☎ 339955; fax 3178326)

Presidente, Avenida da Amizade, doubles M$620 to M$740, has twins for M$690 to M$850, suites M$1800 to M$3800; 340 rooms (☎ 553888; fax 552735)

Royal, Estrada da Vitoria 2-4 (across from the Vasco da Gama Monument), has doubles for M$750,

twins M$870, suites M$1850 to M$2980; 380 rooms (☎ 552222; fax 563008)

Sintra, Avenida Dom Joao IV, has twins for M$560 to M$820, suites M$1180; 236 rooms (☎ 710111; fax 510527)

PLACES TO EAT
Portuguese & Macanese

Henri's Galley (☎ 556251) is right on the waterfront at Avenida da Republica 4 G-H, the southern end of Macau Peninsula. Also known as *Maxims* (not the Hong Kong fast-food chain), Henri's Galley is known for its African chicken, spicy prawns and prawn fondue. It also serves Chinese food. Don't forget to check out its neighbour, *Cafe Marisol*.

Just a stone's throw south of Henri's is *Ali Curry House* (☎ 555865), Avenida da Republica 4 K. This place also features outdoor tables and fine curry dishes.

For relatively cheap Portuguese and Macanese food, the *Estrela do Mar* (☎ 322074) at 11 Travessa do Paiva off Rua da Praia Grande is the place to go.

Solmar (☎ 74391) at 11 Rua da Praia Grande is famous for its African chicken and seafood.

Fat Siu Lau (☎ 573580) – or 'House of the Smiling Buddha' – serves Portuguese and Chinese food. It's at 64 Rua da Felicidade, once the old red-light Street of Happiness. Turn left opposite the Central Hotel in Avenida de Almeida Ribeiro. It's supposed to be the oldest restaurant in Macau or at least the oldest Macanese restaurant in the colony, dating back to 1903. The specialty is roast pigeon.

Another place known for good Portuguese food is *Portugues* (☎ 375445) at 16 Rua do Campo.

An excellent place to eat is *Restaurante Safari* (☎ 574313) at 14 Patio do Cotovelo near the Leal Senado. It has good coffee-shop dishes as well as spicy chicken, steak and fried noodles. This is a good place for breakfast.

A Lorcha (☎ 313193), a Portuguese restaurant near the A-Ma Temple at the south-west tip of the Macau Peninsula, is reputed to have some of the best food in Macau. Just next door is another fine Portuguese restaurant, *Barra Nova* (☎ 512287). Just a bit to the south is *Pele* (☎ 965624), Rua de Sao Tiago da Barra 25.

Ze do Pipo (☎ 374047), 95A Rua da Praia Grande (near Rua do Campo) is a two-storey splashy Portuguese restaurant with all the trimmings. Once you get past the mirrors and the marble, it's not a bad place to eat, but check the menu prices first.

Café a Bica (☎ 3910168), 223-225 Avenida do Dr Rodrigo Rodrigues, is a new place with a quaint atmosphere. It's actually inside the Macau Exhibition Centre – take the escalator up to the 1st floor. This place is open for breakfast.

Near Vasco da Gama Garden is *Restaurante Violeta* (☎ 522500), Rua Joao de Almeida 7, which features fine European food.

If you can afford the ticket, outstanding Portuguese food is served at the restaurant balcony of the *Bela Vista Hotel* (☎ 965333), Rua Comendador Kou Ho Neng. Opening hours are long, from 7 am until 11 pm.

Chinese

All hotel Chinese restaurants do a breakfast and lunch dim sum, which can be amazingly cheap in the mid-range hotels. Except for the five-star hotels, a decent dim-sum breakfast in a Chinese restaurant will set you back about M$25. A dim-sum lunch should cost no more than M$40.

The *Restaurant Long Kei* (☎ 573970) on Leal Senado Square is a straightforward Cantonese place with bright overhead lights and sparse surroundings, but it also has top notch Cantonese food and amiable waiters.

Restaurante New Ocean (☎ 371533), 4th floor, 11 Avenida da Amizade and Rua Dr Pedro Jose Lobo, is another standard dim sum and Cantonese restaurant.

Street Stalls

As in other Chinese cities, the evening street markets are about as cheap as cooking for yourself.

Seafood is the local specialty. Eating the sea snails takes a little practice. The idea is to use two toothpicks to roll the organism out of its shell, then dip it in sauce and devour.

Foodstalls are conveniently located in Rua da Escola Commercial, a tiny lane one block west of the Hotel Lisboa, just next to a sports field. There are also many cheap Chinese restaurants setting up chairs outdoors at night near the Floating Casino on Rua das Lorchas.

In the somewhat unlikely event that you find yourself near the Barrier Gate at night, there is a good dai pai dong on Estrada do Arco, a small street in front of the Lotus Temple.

Other Places to Eat

Snacks For economy snacks, try the *Yoghurt Shop* at 65 Avenida Almeida Ribeiro – yoghurt is served Chinese-style in a rice bowl. There is a similar shop next door to the Restaurant Long Kei, close to the Macau Government Tourist Office. You can put together a decent breakfast here too.

Fast Food *Pizzeria Toscana* (☎ 592267), Rua Formosa 28B (opposite Watson's and near McDonald's) is a nice little place that is good for coffee and pizzas.

At M$9.20, Macau's Big Macs are the cheapest in the world. You can find it at *McDonald's*, Rua do Campo 17-19. A second McDonald's (informally called McDonald's II) is upstairs in the Yaohan Department Store near the Jetfoil Pier. And a third (McDonald's III?) is at Praca de Luis de Camoes 6-8.

On the opposite side of the street is a *Maxim's Cake Shop*, a good place to grab a quick take-away breakfast.

Pizza Hut plys its pies on Avenida de Lopo Sarmento de Carvalho, just behind the Hotel Lisboa. You can enter through the Hotel Lisboa shopping arcade – it's in the basement.

Just to the north side of the tourist office in the plaza fronting Leal Senado is the *Food Plaza*, which among other restaurants features *Fairwood Fast Food*.

Japanese If you can afford the ticket, there are Japanese restaurants in the Hotel Royal *(Ginza)* and Hotel Lisboa *(Furusato)*.

Korean If you have a craving for *bulgogi* (marinated strips of beef) and *kimchi* (the Korean national dish, made up of cabbage, garlic and chilli), good food can be found at *Hoi Fu Garden* (☎ 566402) at 25 Estrada de Cacilhas (the street running along the east side of the Guia Lighthouse). The Hotel Presidente on Avenida da Amizade (just east of Hotel Lisboa) also has a Korean restaurant.

Thai *Restaurante Thai* (☎ 573288) has the usual fiery-hot dishes. It's at 27E Rua Abreu Nunes, a narrow street one block west of the Vasco da Gama Monument. At the intersection of Calcado do Gaio and Rua do Campo is *Restaurant Ban Thai* (☎ 552255).

Vietnamese *Kam Ngau Un* (☎ 309883) at 57-67 Avenida da Amizade offers good Vietnamese meals.

Buffets Many hotels offer all-you-can-eat luncheon specials, though these aren't really all that cheap. By way of example, the *Royal Hotel* offers one from noon to 2 pm for HK$105. Dinner buffets are offered on Saturday evenings.

ENTERTAINMENT
Cinemas
The Cineteatro Macau is on Rua Santa Clara, down the street from Watson's drugstore. The main theatre often has good quality films in English, as well as some Hong Kong movies.

To the left of the main theatre is the Centro Cultural Shalom, a mini theatre seating about 30 people, which often shows excellent foreign films. Admission is M$35.

Pubs
There are three pubs in a row that can claim to be the centre of Macau's nightlife. All are near the Kun Iam Temple on the same street, Rua de Pedro Coutinho. At No 104 is *Talker Pub* (☎ 550153, 528975). Just next door at

No 106 is *Pyretu's Bar* (☎ 581063). And at No 114 is *Moonwalk Pub* (☎ 529201). All of these places open around 8 pm but don't get moving until after 9 pm. Portuguese and other Westerners make up the majority of the customers here.

Billiards & Pinball
The shopping arcade at the Hotel Lisboa also includes a video games centre to keep the kids busy, and a billiards room for grown-up kids.

Discos
The most popular with the locals is the *Mondial Disco* at the Hotel Mondial, Rua da Antonio Basto. There is no cover charge, but you are obligated to buy two drinks for M$70.

The Hotel Presidente is home to the *Skylight Disco*. There is no cover charge here, but you must buy one drink for M$80.

Other hotels have their discos, with cover charges of M$60 to M$150 with one or two free drinks thrown in.

Karaoke
These are everywhere and the music is mostly Cantonese. Every hotel of any size has a karaoke bar. To find one, just look for the sign saying 'OK'.

Nightclubs
These places tend to appeal more to the Hong Kongers than the Westerners. The *Mikado Nightclub* in the Hotel Lisboa is a huge place. They have no trouble keeping the place packed in spite of the M$200 cover charge (which includes two drinks). The club features a Filipino band and floor show.

The *Crazy Paris Show* is performed nightly in the Mona Lisa Hall of the Hotel Lisboa and is very similar to the revue-style shows in Las Vegas. Basically, you get to watch several dozen European women dance on stage wearing nothing but a bunch of feathers. There's lots of bright lights and music. Some people find it glamorous, while others are somewhat less impressed. One visitor who saw the show concluded that the performers are transsexuals. Shows scheduled from Sunday to Friday are at 8.30 and 10 pm. On Saturday, shows are at 8.30, 10 and 11 pm. Admission is M$90 on weekdays or M$100 on weekends. There is no admittance for anyone under 18.

The *China City Nightclub* is at the Jai-Alai Casino near the Jetfoil Terminal. This is basically a male-oriented girlie club, with hostesses who circulate and keep the clientele smiling. There is even a scantily-clad hostess in the men's washroom who opens the water tap and hands paper towels to the customers. Admission is M$200 and there may be additional charges for time simply talking with the hostesses.

Casinos

None of the casinos in Macau offer the atmosphere or level of service considered minimal in Las Vegas. There are no seats for slot-machine players and no cocktail waitresses offering free drinks to gamblers. Incredibly, they don't even have 'change girls' who walk the casino floor giving change to slot players so they can keep playing. The most obnoxious custom is that the dealers will tip themselves 10% of your winnings without asking! Any dealer doing this in Las Vegas would be immediately fired, and possibly subject to criminal prosecution. The casinos have no windows, the dealers don't talk to the customers and no one smiles. Perhaps smiling is against the rules?

Nevertheless, the casinos have no trouble attracting customers. Indeed, they are jam-packed. One thing they do have in common with Las Vegas is that there are no clocks in the casinos – no sense letting people know how late it is, lest they be tempted to stop playing and go to bed. With the exception of the tiny Casino Victoria on Taipa Island, all casinos in Macau stay open 24 hours, unless a major typhoon blows in. Here is a rundown of the casino battlefield:

Lisboa Casino Although it's by no means the newest casino in town, the Lisboa is still the largest and liveliest. When typhoon signal eight is hoisted and all the other casinos shut down, only this one stays open.

There are four storeys of gambling halls. The Lisboa has a more comfortable feel about it than the other casinos – maybe this is because it's just so much more spacious. The adjacent hotel offers the comforts of a good but overpriced shopping arcade, fine restaurants and a video arcade to keep the kids busy while mum and dad lose their life savings at the blackjack tables. There is a big meter in the casino which shows how much will be paid if you hit the grand jackpot on the five-reel slot machines. The total shown on the meter increases until someone hits 'megabucks', then the meter is reset to zero and starts again. Of all the gambling halls in Macau, this one comes closest to matching the grandeur of a Las Vegas casino, though it still falls short despite frequent remodelling.

Floating Casino Officially, the name is Macau Palace, but everyone calls it the Floating Casino. Built in an old, converted ferry anchored on the west side of Macau, the concept sounds appealing. The name 'Floating Casino' conjures up romantic images of riverboat gambling, but the reality is somewhat different. Apart from being earthquake-proof, the casino has little to recommend it. Inside, it's a crowded, windowless, smoke-filled box where players climb over each other to get at the tables. It's one of Macau's oldest casinos and looks it. The players look very serious and oblivious to all else but the next roll of the dice.

Kam Pek Casino The original Kam Pek Casino used to look like a Salvation Army soup kitchen, but the new one near the Floating Casino has been considerably improved. However, it still leaves me cold – the casino hardly looks like a place to enjoy a holiday. The Kam Pek is known as a 'neighbourhood casino' – it appeals mainly to the locals and foreign tourists are made to feel unwelcome. When I tried to enter, the stern-faced security guys first searched me and then wanted to take my moneybelt – did it look

MACAU

like a dangerous weapon? Like the Floating Casino, the Kam Pek is usually full. Perhaps the one positive footnote is that the Kam Pek is the only casino in Macau that allows players to bet with Macau patacas – the others insist that you play with Hong Kong dollars.

Mandarin Oriental Hotel Casino This place appeals to the upper crust and is located to the south of the Jetfoil Pier.

The first time I visited I wasn't allowed in because I was wearing shorts. On the other hand, women are permitted to wear shorts inside the casino, so I guess my legs just weren't beautiful enough. I changed clothes, but when I finally did get in I was still the worst dressed person in the casino (not intentionally). Even the hotel lobby looks like a museum. I could swear the toilet paper was perfumed.

Jai-Alai Casino Known as the *Palacio de Pelota Basca* in Portuguese, this casino once distinguished itself as the venue for *jai-alai* (pronounced hi-a-lie) games. Jai-alai is reputed to be the world's fastest ball game and is popular in many Latin American countries, particularly Cuba and Mexico. The game is similar to handball, racquetball or squash. The ball is three-quarters the size of a baseball and harder than a golf ball. Each

player alternatively catches it and throws it with his pletora – an elongated wicker basket with an attached leather glove that is strapped to his wrist. As with horse racing and dog racing, jai-alai is something else for gamblers to wager on.

Sadly, the jai-alai games are no more. The game just never caught on with Hong Kongers, and the present-day Jai-Alai Casino just has the standard table games and slots. Nevertheless, this casino remains popular, partially because it's close to the Jetfoil Pier, thus giving arriving visitors their first chance to gamble (or departing visitors their last chance).

Kingsway Hotel Casino Close to the Jai-Alai Casino is the Kingsway. This is Macau's newest casino and aspires to be the best with fancy decor. Games are the same as elsewhere, but the minimum bets at some tables are too high for many players.

THINGS TO BUY
The St Dominic Market is in the alley just behind the Hotel Central and next to the MGTO. It's a good place to pick up cheap clothing.

Top: View of the Pearl River, Guangzhou (China) (RS)
Left: Sentry on duty, Nanhu Amusement Park, Guangzhou (China) (RS)
Right: Space shuttle, Nanhu Amusement Park, Guangzhou (China) (RS)

Top: Lotus Mountain, Guangzhou (China) (RS)
Bottom: Town near Lotus Mountain, Guangzhou (China) (RS)

Macau Islands 澳門島

The islands of Taipa and Coloane have a completely different character from the crowded Macau Peninsula. The relatively quiet environment and sandy beaches stand in sharp contrast to Macau's glittering casinos and busy streets. The islands were once a haven for pirates – the last raid took place in 1910.

Once known as a peaceful paradise, the islands are coming under intense development pressure. Taipa now has two major hotels, a university, horse racing track, high-rise apartments and an almost-finished airport. A golf course and deepwater port on Coloane heralds the new era of change at any cost. A massive land reclamation project to connect Taipa and Coloane could be the final nail in the coffin. Still, these islands have a way to go before reaching the level of intense development seen on the peninsula.

GETTING THERE & AWAY

Bus Nos 21 and 21A go to Coloane. All the others only run as far as Taipa Island. Most buses to Taipa typically cost M$2.30, while buses to Coloane are M$3.50. The complete bus routes to the islands are:

No 11
Barra Fortress, Floating Casino, Avenida Almeida Ribeiro, GPO, Hotel Lisboa, Macau-Taipa Bridge, Hotel Hyatt Regency (Taipa), University of Macau, Taipa Village, Macau Jockey Club

No 14
Taipa Village, Causeway, Coloane Park, Coloane Village, Pousada de Coloane, Hac Sa Beach

No 15
Coloane Village, Kau-O

No 21
Barra Fortress, Praca Ponte E Horta, Floating Casino, Avenida Almeida Ribeiro, GPO, Hotel Lisboa, Macau-Taipa Bridge, Hotel Hyatt Regency (Taipa), Coloane Park, Coloane Village

No 21A
Barra Fortress, Praca Ponte E Horta, Floating Casino, Avenida Almeida Ribeiro, GPO, Hotel Lisboa, Macau-Taipa Bridge, Hotel Hyatt Regency (Taipa), Taipa Village, Coloane Park, Coloane Village, Cheoc Van Beach, Hac Sa Beach

No 28A
Jetfoil Pier, Beverly Plaza Hotel, Hotel Lisboa, Macau-Taipa Bridge, Hotel Hyatt Regency (Taipa), Macau University, Taipa Village

No 33
Fai Chi Kei, Lotus Temple, Avenida Almeida Ribeiro, Hotel Lisboa, Hotel Hyatt Regency (Taipa), Macau University, Taipa Village, Macau Jockey Club

No 38
Special bus running from the city centre to the Macau Jockey Club one hour before the races

GETTING AROUND
Bicycle

Bicycle rentals are available in both Taipa and Coloane villages. There are good 10-speed bikes as well as the heavyweight clunkers.

Walking is permitted on the Macau-Taipa Bridge, but bicycles are prohibited. However, bikes are allowed on the Taipa-Coloane Causeway, but it's not very safe as the causeway is narrow and traffic can be heavy. One false move and you may wind up staying in Macau a lot longer than you intended. It would make a lot more sense to rent a bicycle on each island. Otherwise you may find, as I did, that the buses and walking are perfectly adequate.

TAIPA ISLAND 氹仔

When the Portuguese first saw Taipa (*Tamzai* in Chinese) it was actually two islands, but during the past few hundred years the east and west halves have joined – one of the more dramatic demonstrations of the power of siltation. Tiny Macau is one part of the huge Pearl River delta. The siltation process continues and, if the mudflats to the south of Taipa Village are any indication, Taipa and Coloane are destined to become one island unless the greenhouse effect submerges everything but the high-rises.

MACAU

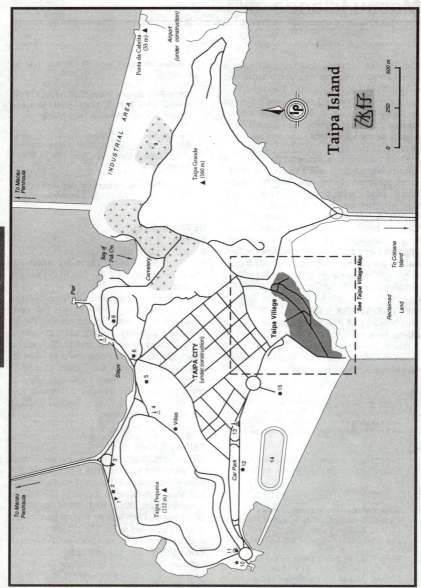

To Macau Peninsula

Ponta da Cabrita (33 m) ▲

Airport (under construction)

INDUSTRIAL AREA

9

Taipa Grande ▲ (160 m)

Taipa Island

冰仔

0   250   500 m

To Coloane Island

See Taipa Village Map

Reclaimed Land

Bay of Pak On

Cemetery

Pier

8

Steps

7

6

5

Taipa Village

TAIPA CITY (under construction)

15

To Macau Peninsula

Villas

4

3

2

1

Taipa Pequena ▲ (112 m)

Car Park

13

12

14

11

10

1	Rasa Sayang Restaurant 莎洋餐廳
2	Ocean Garden Luxury Flats 海洋花園
3	Restaurant Bee Vee 葡國餐廳
4	Pou Tai Un Temple 菩提園
5	Hotel Hyatt Regency 凱悅酒店
6	New Century Hotel 新世紀酒店
7	Kun Iam Temple 觀音岩
8	Macau University 澳門大學
9	United Chinese Cemetery 孝思墳場
10	Police Station 警察局
11	Petrol Station 加油站
12	Macau Jockey Club 澳門賽馬會
13	Four-Faced Buddha 四面佛
14	Horse Racetrack 賽馬場
15	Kartodrome 小型賽車場

Casinos 賭博場

Hyatt Regency When you come over the bridge, the first large building you encounter is the Hyatt Regency. Aside from being the only hotel on the island, it has one of Macau's upper-crust casinos. Apparently the out-of-the-way location has not hurt business.

Casino Victoria It's hard to take this casino seriously. It's basically just a gaming room at the Macau Jockey Club on Taipa Island. It's only open on race days from 11 am to 3 pm.

Macau University 澳門大學
Just a few hundred metres to the east of the Hyatt is a set of large modern buildings on a hill overlooking the sea. This is Macau University, the only university in this tiny enclave. It's worth dropping in for a quick look around and the cafeteria is a cheap place to eat. The vast majority of the students are from Macau and Hong Kong, but making conversation with them should be no problem since the language of instruction is English. The university is open seven days a week throughout the year, except for public holidays.

Kun Iam Temple 觀音岩
Walking downhill from the university (back towards the Hyatt Regency) you should find some stone steps off to your right going down towards the sea. Follow these a short distance and you'll soon reach the Kun Iam Temple. The temple is very small, and it's by the sea as Kun Iam is a goddess who protects sailors.

Pou Tai Un Temple 菩提園
Less than 200 metres to the west of the Hyatt Regency is the Pou Tai Un Temple, the largest temple on the island. It overlooks the tennis courts of the Hyatt. If you're around during lunch time, the temple operates a vegetarian restaurant – the vegetables are said to be grown in the temple's own garden.

From the temple you can walk back to the Hyatt and catch a bus to Taipa Village at the south end of the island, or you could walk the 1.5 km to Taipa Village.

Taipa Village 氹仔市區
This is the only settlement on the island large enough to be called a village. The chief attraction is a street at the south-east corner of town called **Avenida da Praia**. This means Avenue of the Beach, but as you'll see, siltation has overwhelmed the beach and it has become a mudflat extending almost all the way to Coloane at low tide. Nevertheless, this is an attractive area with a tree-lined promenade, wrought-iron benches and several old houses.

One of the houses has been preserved as the **Taipa House Museum** which is open to the public. Not much is known about the former residents of the house, but it's a good example of the architecture of the time (early

MACAU

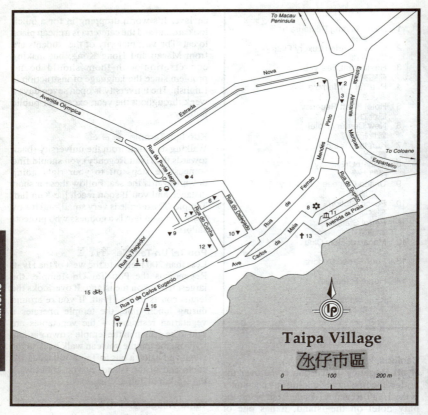

Taipa Village

冰仔市區

0   100   200 m

20th century). It's open everyday except Monday from 9.30 am to 1 pm and from 3 to 5.30 pm.

From the Taipa House Museum, walk west and up a few steps to find **Our Lady of Carmel Church**.

The rest of the village is much more Chinese in its appearance. At the south-west corner of the village is a divided street called Largo Governador Tamagnini Barbosa where there is a small **Tin Hau temple**. It's very close to the main bus stop and bicycle-rental shops.

Just around the corner on Rua do Regedor

is the **Pak Tai Temple**. The only other sight-seeing spot in town is a narrow alley called **Rua do Cunha** which has many tiny shops, though there isn't much that foreigners would want to buy.

Macau Jockey Club 澳門賽馬會

If you know your quinellas from your trifec-tas and six-ups, this is the place to go. The Macau Jockey Club opened on Taipa Island in 1991. Also known as the Hippodrome, it's Macau's venue for horse racing. The five-storey grandstands can accommodate 18,000 spectators and are air-con. Unlike the race-

1   Tee Jei Tandoori Restaurant
    印度餐廳
2   Restaurante Mediterraneo
    葡國餐廳
3   Restaurante O'Manel
    葡國餐廳
4   Fire Station
    消防站
5   Bus Stop
    公共汽車站
6   Pinocchio's Restaurant
    木偶餐廳
7   Restaurant Leong Un
    餐廳
8   Carmel Garden
    十字公園
9   A Petisqueira
    葡國美食天地
10 Panda Restaurant
    熊貓餐廳
11 Taipa House Museum
    屋宇博物館
12 Galo Restaurant
    公雞餐廳
13 Our Lady of Carmel Church
    教堂
14 Pak Tai Temple
    北帝廟
15 Bicycle Hire
    自行車出租
16 Tin Hau Temple
    天后廟
17 Main Bus Stop
    總公共汽車站

Bangkok and another in (brace yourself) Las Vegas. Praying to the Buddha is supposed to bring good fortune, which is what one undoubtedly needs in Macau's casinos.

Kartodrome   小型賽車場
You've heard of the Canidrome and Hippodrome, and now there's the Kartodrome. This is a venue for go-cart racing. Officially, it's called the Karting School (Escola de Karting), but locals prefer to call it the Kartodromo. Just why anyone would need to go to school to learn how to operate a go-cart is something I haven't determined. The Karting School is open from 10 am to 6 pm.

United Chinese Cemetery   孝思墳場
The cemetery on the north-east corner of the island is worth a look. Amongst the graves is a 30-metre-high statue of Tou Tei, the Earth God. Some say that Tou Tei is a bit perturbed by the presence of the nearby newly-constructed Macau Airport. No telling what kind of bad fungshui is being stirred up by all those aircraft.

Places to Stay
There's nothing here for budget travellers. The *Hyatt Regency* (☎ 831234; fax 830195; 346 rooms) offers everything you'd expect in a five-star hotel with prices to match. Twins range from M$990 to M$1190, suites M$2500 to M$9000. The hotel operates its own shuttle bus to the Macau Peninsula.

The *New Century Hotel* (☎ 831111; fax 832222; 600 rooms), is just across the street from the Hyatt Regency. Twins are M$950 to M$1800 and suites cost M$2800 to M$18,000. However, this place does offer one 'bargain' – apartments available for rent by the month. These cost M$18,000 per month for two bedrooms, or M$23,000 for three bedrooms.

Places to Eat
Taipa Village has several good medium-priced restaurants. The best known for excellent Portuguese food is *Restaurante Panda* (☎ 827338) at No 4-8 Rua Direita Carlos Eugenio. At 47 Rua do Cunha is *Galo*

tracks at Hong Kong's Happy Valley and Shatin, the Macau Jockey Club operates throughout the summer. Now Hong Kongers can lose their money any season of the year. Races are held twice-weekly on differing days, and race times can be at 2, 3.30 or 7.30 pm. The entrance fee is M$20 for visitors and the minimum bet is M$10. You can ring ☎ 321888 for the schedule. There is also an information office in Hong Kong (☎ 5170872).

Outside the Macau Jockey Club is a Four-Faced Buddha Shrine. There are several similar statues located worldwide – one in

(☎ 827318), easily recognised by the picture of a rooster above the door. Also nearby is *Pinocchio* (☎ 827128) at 4 Rua do Sol, an obscure alley near the fire station. Also in an obscure alley is the excellent *A Petisqueira* (☎ 825354), 15 Rua de Sao Joao. An exquisite but reasonably-priced little place is *Restaurante Mediterraneo* (☎ 825069) on Rua de Fernao Mendes Pinto. Just next door at No 90 is *O'Manel* (☎ 321071), and across the street is one of Macau's few Indian restaurants, *Tee Jei Tandoori Restaurant* (☎ 320203).

For those on a budget, the best deal is the student cafeteria at Macau University.

Near the north-west part of the island is a fine Malaysian-Singaporean restaurant called *Rasa Sayang* (☎ 810187, 810189). It's buried in a forest of luxury apartments called Ocean Gardens – official address is Plum Court, Estrade Noroeste da Taipa.

Entertainment

Taipa has one of Macau's best nightclubs, the *Lok Ün*. It's popular with the local Portuguese, but tourists are few. Beer costs M$25 a glass and there is no cover charge. It's a bit hard to find (see map) because it's down an obscure alley called Caminho das Hortas, but at night there is a large, brightly lit sign which you can see from the main highway.

As you might imagine, the *Hyatt Regency* has an upmarket casino. It's also fairly small and doesn't radiate that atmosphere of chaos that many gamblers enjoy. On the other hand, if you're attracted by the glitter of high-stakes gambling, this is the place to see it.

1	Power Plant 發電所
2	Macau Cement Plant 水泥場
3	Catholic School Centre 天主教堂
4	Golf Course 高爾夫球俱樂部
5	Coloane Park 路環郊野公園
6	Balichao Restaurant 金龍餐廳
7	Aviary 鳥舍
8	Westin Hotel 威斯登酒店
9	Waterscooter & Windsurfer Rentals 水上電單車出租
10	Fernando's Restaurant 法蘭度餐廳
11	Bus Stop 黑沙車站
12	Swimming Pool & Tennis Courts 游泳池/網球場
13	Horseback Riding Ranch 騎術訓練中心
14	Pousada de Coloane 竹灣酒店
15	Satellite Station 天線
16	La Torre Italian Restaurant 斜塔餐廳
17	Snack Bar & Changing Rooms 小吃部
18	Yacht Club 帆船俱樂部
19	Villas 別墅
20	Swimming Pool 竹灣游泳池
21	Youth Hostel 青年會

COLOANE ISLAND 路環

Of the two islands, Coloane (*Luhuan* in Chinese) is larger and better known for its beautiful beaches, one attraction Taipa is lacking. Coloane still lacks the high-rises which have invaded Taipa, but new hotels, villas and even a golf course have sprouted near the previously pristine beaches. The deep-water port now under construction has the potential to turn north-east Coloane into a jumble of factories, wharfs and warehouses. Still, at the moment the island is largely unspoiled and will probably remain that way for a few years longer.

Coloane Park 路環郊野公園

About one km south of the causeway, Coloane Park covers 20 hectares. There is a fountain and well-tended gardens, but the most notable feature is the aviary behind Balichao Restaurant.

The park is open from 9 am to 7 pm daily,

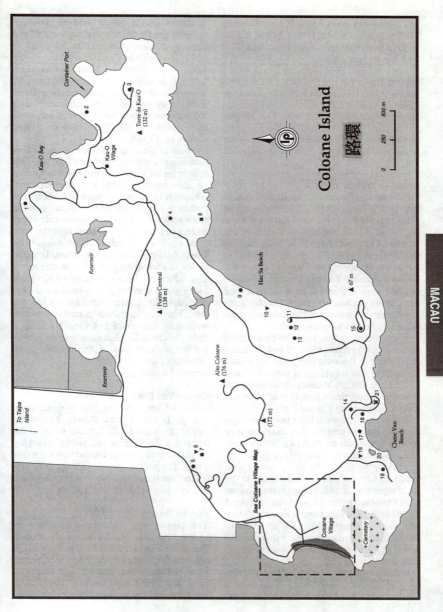

MACAU

Coloane Island 路環

Container Port

Kau-O Bay

Torre de Kau-O
(132 m)

Kau-O
Village

Reservoir

Reservoir

To Taipa
Island

Ponto Central
(138 m)

Hac Sa Beach

67 m

Alto Coloane
(176 m)

(172 m)

See Coloane Village Map

Cheoc Van
Beach

Coloane
Village

+ Cemetery

0   250   500 m

and admission costs M$5. It costs another M$5 to visit the aviary, and M$20 if you want to rent a table in the picnic area. The park has a camping area.

Hiking Trails Behind Coloane Park are two hiking trails. The longest is simply called the Coloane Trail *(Trilho de Coloane)* and the entire loop walk is 8.6 km. The shorter North-East Coloane Trail *(Trilho Nordeste de Coloane)* is on the north-east corner of the island near Kau-O, and the total length is 6.2 km.

Coloane Village 路環市

The only real town on the island, this is largely a fishing village although in recent years tourism has given the local economy a big boost. At the northern end of town are numerous junk building sheds. Just how long this business can last is debatable – siltation threatens to make the harbour a mudflat within a decade. You can walk to the sheds and see how the junks are built, but take along a big stick as several of the sheds are guarded by vicious xenophobic dogs that are definitely hostile to foreigners!

If you arrive by bus, you'll be dropped off near the village roundabout. If you walk one short block to the west you'll see the waterfront. Here you'll get a good view of China. It's so close one could easily swim across the channel. In fact, many people used to do just that to escape from China.

A sign near the waterfront points towards the **Sam Seng Temple**. This temple is very small – not much more than a family altar. Just past the temple is the village pier.

Walking to the south along Avenida de Cinco de Outubro, you'll soon come to the main attraction in this village – the **Chapel of St Francis Xavier**. This interesting chapel was built in 1928 to honour St Francis Xavier who died on nearby Shang Ch'an Island in 1552. He had been a missionary in Japan and to this day Japanese come to Coloane to pay their respects.

Inside the chapel is a piece of the right arm bone of Xavier (other pieces of St Francis can be found in southern India). The bone

fragment stands beside several boxes of bones of the Portuguese and Japanese Christians who were martyred in Nagasaki in 1597, Vietnamese Christians killed in the early 17th century and Japanese Christians killed in a rebellion in Japan in the 17th century. Near the chapel is a monument surrounded by cannon balls to commemorate the successful final battle against pirates in these islands in 1910. The battle is celebrated locally on 13 July.

South of the chapel is a library and a sign pointing towards the **Kun Iam Temple**. This temple is also very tiny – not much more than an altar inside a little walled compound. Although there are no signs to indicate the path, if you walk just a little further past the stone wall you'll find the considerably larger and more interesting **Tin Hau Temple**.

At the very southern end of Avenida de Cinco de Outubro is the **Tam Kong Temple**. Inside is a whalebone, more than one metre long which has been carved into a model of a ship with a wooden dragon head and a crew of painted little men with Chinese pointed hats. The temple custodian enthusiastically welcomes foreigners and then holds up a little placard in English soliciting donations for the maintenance of the temple. Such donations are voluntary so let your conscience be your guide.

Cheoc Van Beach 竹灣海灘

About 1.5 km down the road from Coloane Village is Cheoc Van Beach. The name means 'Bamboo Bay'. You can swim in the ocean for free (there are public changing rooms) or at the pool in **Cheoc Van Park** (for a fee). The pool is open from 9 am to 10 pm. Cheoc Van Beach also has a yacht club where you can inquire about boat rentals.

Hac Sa Beach 黑沙海灘

The largest and most popular beach in Macau, the name Hac Sa means black sand. The sand does indeed have a grey to black colour and this makes the water look somewhat polluted, but actually it's perfectly clean and fine for swimming. The area is beautiful and on a clear day you get good

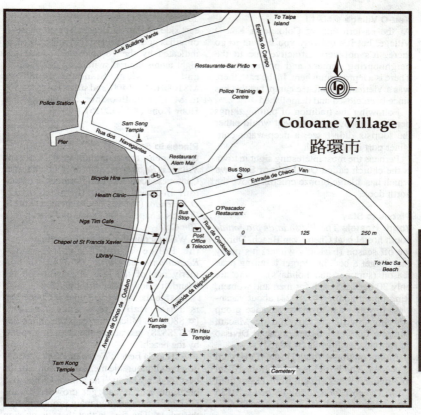

Coloane Village
路環市

views of the islands south of Hong Kong. Though you can't see Hong Kong's skyscrapers from here, on a clear day you can see the mountains on Hong Kong's Lantau Island.

Just near the bus stop is **Hac Sa Sports & Recreation Park**. Within the park is a large swimming pool, roller-skating rink, playground and miniature golf course. It's open 9 am to 9 pm daily and admission costs M$5. Use of the pool costs an additional M$15.

Behind Fernando's Restaurant is the Macau Horse Riding Centre (☎ 328303). It costs M$250 per hour with a two-hour

minimum and two-person minimum. The horses are retired runners from the Macau Jockey Club on Taipa Island.

At the far end of Hac Sa Beach is a place to rent windsurfers and – if you can stand the noise – water scooters.

The golf course at the Westin Hotel is open to non-guests as well, but you have to pay. Green fees for 18 holes are M$600 on weekdays and M$800 on weekends, topped off by a 5% tax.

Bus No 21A provides frequent service to Hac Sa. On weekends the buses are even more frequent.

Kau-O Village 九澳村

At the eastern end of Coloane is Kau-O Village, but it's unlikely you'll want to go there. It's not very attractive due to the neighbouring cement and power plants. There is a leprosarium here. In the past, there was a Vietnamese refugee camp, but this has since been closed and demolished.

Following the tradition of putting things here that Macau's government would rather the tourists didn't see, a deep-water container port is being built.

Perhaps the most interesting sight in town is the church called **Our Lady of Sorrows** which has a large bronze crucifix above the north door.

Places to Stay

Youth Hostels The *Pousada de Juventude* youth hostel is at Cheoc Van Beach. During the off season (basically winter) it's pretty easy to get a bed, but forget it during peak season (summer and holidays). There are only 30 beds, 15 each for men and women. Ring up to inquire (☎ 28024) about vacancies. If you want to make advance group bookings, write to Governo de Macau, Direccao dos Servicos de Educacao, Divisao de Actividades Juvenis (☎ 88151).

An International Youth Hostel (IYH) card is needed. The hostel is closed from 10 am to 3 pm and lights are out from 11 pm until 7 am. The cost for a dormitory bed is M$35 for foreigners and M$20 for Macau residents.

Hotels Very close to the beach at Cheoc Van Beach is a luxury hotel, the *Pousada de Coloane* (☎ 328143, fax 328251; 22 rooms). Without a doubt it has the most relaxing atmosphere of any hotel in Macau. Twins range from M$550 to M$580. The hotel has its own sauna and swimming pool and is well known for its excellent Sunday lunch buffet.

The *Westin Hotel* (☎ 871111; fax 871122;

208 rooms) is a luxury resort complex on the east side of Hac Sa Beach. The emphasis is on villas and a country club atmosphere, as indicated by the 18-hole golf course and eight tennis courts, swimming pools, sauna and gymnasium. Standard rooms are M$1080 to M$1400, and suites cost M$3500 to M$15,000. Bookings can be made in Hong Kong (☎ 8032015).

Places to Eat

Right near the roundabout at Coloane Village is *Restaurant Alem Mar* which serves Cantonese food. The best Portuguese restaurant in town is near the post office, *O'Pescador* (☎ 880197). Right next to the St Francis Chapel is the small and cheap *Nga Tim Café*.

Walking out of town to the north, just past the Police Training Centre, is the *Restaurante-Bar Pirao* (☎ 328215). Formerly one of the best restaurants on the island, it's now rather shabby.

Next to the swimming pool at Cheoc Van is a fine Italian restaurant, *La Torre* (☎ 880156). Much cheaper is the *Snack Bar* (☎ 328528) just above the changing rooms by the beach.

At Hac Sa Beach, *Fernando's* (☎ 328264) deserves honourable mention for some of the best food in Macau. The atmosphere is also pleasant, and it can get crowded in the evening. There are two main problems with this place. The first is that there is no sign above the door and it's possible to wander around for quite a while looking for it. The restaurant is at the far end of the car park, close to the bus stop. The other problem is that the menu is in Portuguese and Chinese only. Fernando himself (the manager) will gladly translate for you, and he recommends the clams.

Balichao (☎ 870098) is in Coloane Park and serves fine Portuguese food.

CANTON

广州

Facts about Guangzhou (Canton)

Step across the border from either Hong Kong or Macau and you're in Guangdong Province. 'Canton' is the traditional Western name for both the Chinese province of Guangdong, and also its capital city, Guangzhou. In recent years, the Chinese have been most insistent that the official pinyin romanisation system be applied to geographical names. Thus, 'Peking' is now known as 'Beijing', 'Nanking' became 'Nanjing', and so on. Nevertheless, English speakers are happier with the adjective 'Cantonese' when describing the food, the people and the language.

Guangzhou has burned its image into the Western consciousness. The image of 'Chinatown' that most Westerners now have is based on the Cantonese. In Chinatowns from Melbourne to Toronto to London, Cantonese food is eaten and the Cantonese dialect predominates.

HISTORY

China is a sleeping giant. Let her sleep, for when she awakes, she will astonish the world.

Napoleon

It was the people of Guangdong who first made contact (often unhappily) with both the merchants and the armies of the modern European states, and it was these people who spearheaded the Chinese emigration to America, Australia and South Africa in the mid-19th century. The move was spurred by gold rushes in those countries, but it was mainly the wars and growing poverty of the century which induced the Chinese to leave in droves.

The history of Guangdong Province over the past 2000 years is known to us in outline. While the Chinese were carving out a civilisation centred on the Yellow River region in the north, the south remained a semi-independent enclave peopled by native tribes, the last survivors of which are now minority groups.

It was not until the Qin Dynasty (221 BC-207 BC), when the Chinese states of the north were for the first time united under a single ruler, that the Chinese finally conquered the southern regions. However, revolts and uprisings were frequent and the Chinese settlements remained small and dispersed among a predominantly aboriginal population.

Chinese emigration to the region began in earnest around the 12th century AD. The original native tribes were killed by Chinese armies, isolated in small pockets or pushed further south – like the Li and Miao peoples who now inhabit the mountainous areas of Hainan Island off the southern coast of China.

By the 17th century the Chinese had outgrown Guangdong. The pressure of population forced them to move into adjoining Guangxi Province and into Sichuan, which had been ravaged and depopulated after rebellions in the mid-17th century.

As a result of these multiple migrations, the people of Guangdong are not a homogeneous group. The term Cantonese is sometimes applied to all people living in Guangdong Province, but there are significant minorities such as the Hakka people who started moving southward from the northern plains around the 13th or 14th centuries.

What the migrants from the north found beyond the mountainous areas of northern and western Guangdong was the Pearl River delta, cutting through a region which is richer than any in China, except around the Yangtze and Yellow rivers. Because of their fertility, the delta and river valleys could support a very large population. The abundant waterways, heavy rainfall and warm climate allowed wet-rice cultivation of two crops a year.

The first town to be established on the site of present-day Guangzhou dates back to the

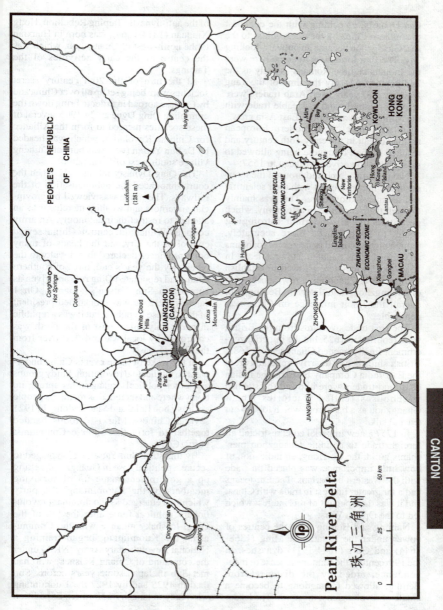

CANTON

Pearl River Delta
珠江三角洲

Qin Dynasty, coinciding with the conquest of southern China by the north. Close to the sea, Guangzhou became an outward-looking city. The first foreigners to come here were the Indians and the Romans as early as the 2nd century AD. By the time of the Tang Dynasty 500 years later, Arab traders were arriving regularly and a sizeable trade with the Middle East and South-East Asia grew.

Initial contact with modern European nations began in the early 16th century and resulted in the Portuguese being allowed to set up base downriver at Macau in 1557.

Next, Jesuits came and aroused the interest of the imperial court with their scientific and technical knowledge. This was mainly through their expertise in astronomy, which permitted the all-important astrological charts to be produced more accurately, though others worked as makers of fountains and curios or as painters and architects. In 1582 the Jesuits were allowed to establish themselves at Zhaoqing, a town north-west of Guangzhou, and later in Beijing, but overall the Jesuit influence on China was negligible.

The first trade overtures from the British were rebuffed in 1625, but the imperial government finally opened Guangzhou in 1685. British ships began to arrive regularly from the East India Company bases on the Indian coast and traders were allowed to establish warehouses (called 'factories') near Guangzhou as a base from which to ship out tea and silk.

In 1757 a new imperial edict restricted all foreign trade to a single Guangzhou merchants guild, the Co Hong, an indication of how little importance was placed on trade with the Western barbarians. The Europeans had a far greater interest in trade with China, and it was their pursuit of this interest which led to the Opium Wars.

Nanjing and Beijing were the centres of power under the isolationist Ming (1368-1644) and Qing (1644-1911) dynasties. In the 19th century the Cantonese sense of independence, aided by the distance from Beijing, allowed Guangdong to become a cradle of revolt against the north. The leader

of the anti-dynastic Taiping Rebellion, Hong Xiuquan (1814-1864), was born in Huaxian to the north-west of Guangzhou, which was the centre of the early activities of the Taipings.

At the turn of the 20th century secret societies were being set up all over China and by Chinese abroad in order to bring down the crumbling Qing Dynasty. In 1905 several of these societies merged to form the Alliance for Chinese Revolution which was headed by Dr Sun Yatsen (who was born at Cuiheng village south-west of Guangzhou).

The Qing Dynasty fell in 1911 when the court announced the nationalisation of the railways. The move was viewed by provincial governors and wealthy merchants as an attempt to restrict their autonomy. An army coup in Wuhan in central China seized control of the city and the heads of many other provinces declared their loyalty to the rebels. By the year's end, most of southern China had repudiated Qing rule and given its support to Sun Yatsen's alliance. On 1 January 1912 he was proclaimed president of the Chinese Republic, but it was a republic in name only since most of the north was controlled by local warlords left over from the Qing Dynasty.

In the wake of these events China underwent an intellectual revolution. Study groups and other political organisations sprang up everywhere and included as members people such as Zhou Enlai and Mao Zedong. In 1921 several Chinese Marxist groups banded together to form the Chinese Communist Party (CCP).

By this stage Sun Yatsen had managed to secure a political base in Guangzhou, setting up a government made up of surviving members of the Kuomintang, the party which had emerged as the dominant revolutionary political force after the fall of the Qing. In shaky alliance with the Communists, the Kuomintang began training a National Revolutionary Army (NRA) under the command of Chiang Kaishek, who had met Sun in Japan some years before. Sun died in 1925 and by 1927 the Kuomintang was ready to launch its Northern Expedition

– a military venture under the command of Chiang designed to subdue the northern warlords.

However, Chiang was also engaged in a power struggle within the Kuomintang. As the NRA moved in on Shanghai (then under the control of a local warlord whose strength had been undermined by a powerful industrial movement organised in the city by the Communists), Chiang took the opportunity to massacre both the Communists and his enemies in the Kuomintang.

By mid-1928 the Northern Expedition had reached Beijing and a national government was established with Chiang holding the highest political and military positions. Those Communists who survived the massacres made their famous Long March to the Jinggang Mountains on the Hunan-Jiangxi border and other mountainous areas of China, from where they began a war against the Kuomintang which lasted just over 20 years and ended in victory for the Communists in 1949.

The assimilation of southern China was a slow process, reflected in the fact that the southerners referred to themselves as men of Tang (of the Tang Dynasty of 618-907 AD), while the northerners referred to themselves as men of Han (of the Han Dynasty of 206 BC-220 AD). The northerners regarded their southern compatriots with disdain, or as one 19th-century northern account put it:

The Cantonese...are a coarse set of people...Before the times of Han and Tang, this country was quite wild and waste, and these people have sprung forth from unconnected, unsettled vagabonds that wandered here from the north.

Despite the nasty rhetoric, the Cantonese are admired for their entrepreneurial skills. Of all the Chinese, the Cantonese have probably been the most influenced by the outside world. Almost everyone in southern Guangdong has relatives in Hong Kong who for years have been storming across the border loaded down with the latest fashions and gifts of electronic appliances, music tapes (legal), smuggled video tapes (illegal) and even motorcycles.

Free enterprise, private business and individualism – things which are still anathema to the hardline Communists – is the path that Guangdong is attempting to take. In spite of constant interference from Beijing bureaucrats, Guangdong continues to drag China – kicking and screaming – into the capitalist era.

GEOGRAPHY

Guangdong Province lies on the south-east coast of China and occupies just 2.2% of China's total land area. The dominant feature is the Pearl River delta, a fertile plain which supports a huge population and provides a natural harbour. The river provides a natural transport system and is a chief reason for Guangzhou's existence as a major economic hub. Not surprisingly, the Cantonese have a much closer affection for Hong Kong than Beijing – Guangzhou is a mere 120 km from Hong Kong and 2300 km from the national capital.

CLIMATE

Most of Guangdong Province has a subtropical climate, but temperatures tend to be extreme as one moves inland. Average monthly temperatures and rainfall for Guangzhou are on next page.

GOVERNMENT

Every revolution evaporates, leaving behind only the slime of a new bureaucracy.
Franz Kafka

Precious little is known about the inner workings of the Chinese government, but Westerners can make educated guesses.

The highest authority rests with the Standing Committee of the Communist Party Politburo. Below is the 210-member Central Committee, made up of younger Party members and provincial Party leaders. At grassroots level, the Party forms a parallel system to the administrations in the Army, universities, government and industries. Real authority is exercised by the Party representatives at each level in these organisations. They, in turn, are responsible

CANTON

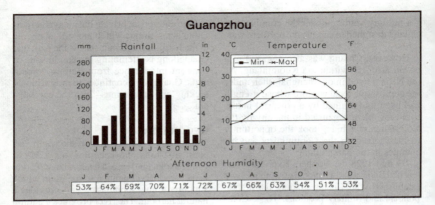

to the Party officials in the hierarchy above them, thus ensuring strict central control. Democracy in the Western sense simply does not exist.

Throughout the system, there exists various antagonistic factions. Governing the country seems to be a delicate balance between these rivals, and as a result the government is often too paralysed to make any significant policy decisions.

Things are somewhat different in Guangdong Province, of which Guangzhou is the capital. While paying lip service to the official line taken by geriatric socialists in Beijing, Guangdong officials from the governor on down have continued to push their own programme of economic liberalisation. Although political liberalisation is not presently possible, officials have a relaxed attitude and are much less interested in controlling people's lives than making money.

At grassroots level, the basic unit of government organisation is the work unit (*dānwèi*). Every Chinese is a member of one. Many Westerners may admire the cooperative spirit this system is supposed to engender, but they would cringe if their own lives were so intricately controlled. Nothing can proceed without the work unit. It decides if a couple may marry or divorce and when they can have a child. It assigns housing, sets salaries, handles mail, recruits Party members, keeps files on each unit member, arranges transfers to other jobs or other parts of the country, and gives permission to travel abroad. Work unit members are also compelled to attend endless, fruitless propaganda meetings which the government calls 'political education'.

ECONOMY

China's economic policies have undergone a radical change since the death of Mao Zedong. Under Mao, China had largely isolated itself from the economies of the rest of the world, apprehensive that economic links with other countries would make China dependent on them.

The Cultural Revolution, launched by Mao in the 1960s, put an end to even the most basic forms of private enterprise – free markets, simple food stalls and privately owned restaurants were regarded as bourgeois capitalism. All aspects of the economy, from restaurants to steel mills to paddy fields, came under state ownership and rigid state control. Schools were closed and intellectuals were sent to labour in the countryside, depriving China of properly trained economists, managers and people with high-technology skills.

As the state tightened its grip, the economy reeled. Farmers were told to plant unprofitable crops and were paid a pittance for their labour, so production fell. As food shortages developed, peasants spent hours every day standing in long queues with ration coupons to buy their basic staples and factories produced shoddy goods which nobody wanted.

The Red Guards, who produced nothing, roamed the countryside terrorising the populace, burning schools and libraries and destroying temples. Many innocent people were denounced as 'capitalist roaders' and were killed, tortured or persecuted. Deng Xiaoping's son, Deng Pufang, was crippled for life when Red Guards threw him out a 4th-floor window. Red Guard factions even battled each other and the country seemed to be moving towards civil war and financial collapse.

Mao died in 1976. Soon after, members of the so-called Gang of Four led by Mao's wife, Jiang Qing, were arrested. Jiang Qing remained imprisoned until 1991, when she committed suicide.

Under the leadership of Deng Xiaoping, China turned away from the narrow path of centralised planning, state ownership and control of all facets of the economy. The Maoist policies of isolation were reversed and China opened up to the West.

In 1989, the Tiananmen massacre and subsequent brutal suppression of the pro-democracy movement in Beijing had a major impact on China's economy. Tourism, foreign aid and investment fell sharply. Many feared China would revert to its xenophobic past and withdraw from the outside world. This, at least, has not happened, and China's economy has been booming since 1991. Despite disillusionment and cynicism with the Communist system, Guangzhou remains the least likely place in China to close itself off to the outside world.

But concerns about human rights remains a sore spot, and when it was revealed that prison labour was used to produce cheap manufactured goods, some of China's trading partners suggested an economic embargo. Certainly, recent revelations of a grisly and lucrative business – Chinese prisoners in Guangzhou have reportedly been executed after being tissue-matched to Hong Kongers in need of organ transplants – has not helped China's international image.

The USA has been harshly critical of China's human rights record, and relations between the two powers have soured. In 1991, the US congress almost revoked China's status as a Most Favoured Nation (MFN). Having MFN status is crucial to China's export industries which have greatly depended on US markets. Loss of MFN status would be a crippling blow to Guangdong's economy, as well as Hong Kong. Although MFN status has been renewed every year, some US representatives have vowed to revoke it in the future if China's human rights record does not improve. However, China has shown little willingness to make any concessions at all. The Chinese leadership has gambled – so far correctly – that the USA, while creating plenty of noise about sanctions, will value its trade with China above all else.

One of the oddest things about China's booming economy is that it could become a victim of its own success. Economic growth

Mao Zedong

causes people to consume more. New roads, railways, power stations, telephone lines and container ports are being built, but demand continues to outstrip supply. Developing industries require capital, which in capitalist countries is supplied by the stock market. But China's fledgling stock exchanges in Shanghai and Shenzhen are little more than gambling casinos. Shortages of capital has led to all sorts of interim 'solutions' such as paying peasants for their crops with IOUs rather than cash. Unfortunately, this has led to anti-government riots in the countryside which have been systematically quashed. The printing press is another source of funds, causing inflation to race ahead at rates not seen since the 1940s. The lack of an independent central bank has made it easy for officials to use the state-run banking system as their personal slush fund – state money has drifted into speculative real estate deals and losses are being hidden with creative accounting. The surging money supply and double-digit inflation has caused virtually all economists to agree that China's booming economy is overheating at a dangerous rate. However, attempts by Beijing to slow growth have been stubbornly resisted by the provinces. China is starting to resemble what economists call a 'bubble economy,' and when the bubble bursts the country could be in for a hard landing.

POPULATION

Nationwide there are nearly 1.2 billion people. Guangdong Province has about 72 million people, or 6% of the nation's total.

Although overpopulation is a problem that predates the Communist takeover, Mao Zedong must share a lot of the blame for the present mess. Mao believed that birth control was a capitalist plot to weaken China. Like Marx, he was not impressed by arguments that overpopulation could outstrip agricultural and natural resources. Rather, he felt that more people meant more production. Accordingly, up until 1973 the Chinese were urged to have as many children as possible for the good of the nation.

These policies have been reversed and

China now has the world's most stringent birth-control policies. The legal marriageable age for men is 22 and for women it's 20. If a woman delays marriage until after the age of 25 she is entitled to extra maternity leave. Couples are urged to have one child only and those who violate this policy are subject to stiff fines and loss of privileges. The one-child family is fairly common in the large cities, but in rural areas many have continued to have two or more children, despite fines and threats of demotions, loss of employment and housing benefits. Many women have been known to hide until they've given birth to a second or third child, and then, to avoid sanctions, not registering the child's birth. Such women are known as 'birth guerillas'.

Furthermore, government officials, anxious to meet quotas set by Beijing, have been known to falsify figures and sometimes force women to have abortions. Although the forced abortions have made big headlines in the West, it does not seem to be a common practice.

More disturbing are cases of female infanticide. Again, it is not an official policy and indeed, is highly illegal. Nevertheless, China is definitely a male-oriented society and female children are considered worthless. Female infanticide has had a long history in China and did not start with the one-child per family policy, but the new restrictions on family size have no doubt aggravated the problem.

All methods of birth control are free. The most commonly used are IUDs, abortion and sterilisation, although condoms and birth control pills are also available. Posters urging the masses to practise family planning are ubiquitous in China.

Although the growth rate has slowed as a result of the one-child policy, the average population is still very young, and China's population will continue to grow for the next two decades before declining. It is projected to reach 1.28 billion by the year 2000.

PEOPLE

More than 98% of inhabitants of Guangdong are Han Chinese while the rest belong to small minority groups such as the Miao and Li.

ARTS

Basically, it's the same as Hong Kong, but there are a few differences. Communist poster art has experienced a revival since the Tiananmen massacre – or rather, it should be said that the leadership is trying to ram it down everyone's throats. You can see these posters in Guangzhou: bright, flaming red hammers and sickles with Chinese slogans in the background saying things like 'The socialist road leads to happiness'. Most people pay no attention.

Disco music is big with the hip young urban Chinese. Love songs and soft rock from Taiwan and Hong Kong are in vogue in Guangzhou while in Beijing, tastes run more towards heavy metal and punk. There are dance halls in all the major cities to cater for the craze – sometimes with taped music, often with live bands featuring batteries of horns and electric violins.

Attempts to tailor Chinese classical music, song and dance to Western tastes have resulted in an unholy hybrid of spectacular schmaltz and sweeping film score. Chinese rock star Cui Jian released 'Rock for the New Long March' which became a big hit and, in an attempt to show that the geriatric leadership is also hip, government officials authorised a disco version of 'The East is Red'. There are also orchestras organised on Western lines which substitute Chinese for Western instruments. Exactly where all this is leading no one knows.

RELIGION

The situation is similar to Hong Kong and Macau, the basic difference being that all forms of religion were harshly suppressed during the Cultural Revolution. Priests, nuns and monks were imprisoned, executed or sent to labour in the countryside while temples and churches were ransacked and converted into factories and warehouses. Since the early 1980s, temples have been restored, at least for the sake of tourism. There has been a religious revival of sorts,

but the main feature you will note about temples in China is that they are usually devoid of worshippers. However, Communist Party members are not permitted to belong to any religious organisation.

Catholics have a particularly hard time – loyalty to the Pope is regarded as treason and priests are still rotting in prison for refusing to denounce the Holy See. The government has set up an alternative Catholic church which does not recognise the Vatican.

LANGUAGE

What a difference a border can make. Cantonese is still the most popular dialect in Guangzhou and the surrounding area, but the official language of the People's Republic is the Beijing dialect, usually referred to in the West as 'Mandarin'. In China it's referred to as *pǔtōnghuà* or 'common speech' and the Chinese government set about popularising it in the 1950s. A large percentage of foreigners living and working in China manage to gain a reasonable level of fluency in the spoken language, but the written form is another story. Most would agree that foreigners are more successful at learning Mandarin than Cantonese.

Pinyin

In 1958 the Chinese officially adopted a system known as *pīnyīn* as a method of writing their language using the Roman alphabet. Since the official language of China is the Beijing dialect, this pronunciation is used. The original idea was to eventually do away with characters completely and just use pinyin. However, tradition dies hard and the idea has gradually been abandoned.

Pinyin is often used on shop fronts, street signs and advertising billboards. The popularisation of this spelling is still at an early stage, so don't expect Chinese to be able to use pinyin. In the countryside and the smaller towns you may not see a single pinyin sign anywhere, so unless you speak Chinese you'll need a phrasebook with Chinese characters if you're travelling in these areas. Though pinyin is helpful, it's not an instant

CANTON

key to communication since Westerners usually don't get the pronunciation and intonation of the romanised words correct.

Since 1979 all translated texts of Chinese diplomatic documents and Chinese magazines published in foreign languages have used the pinyin system of spelling names and places. The system replaces the old Wade-Giles and Lessing systems of romanising Chinese script. Thus, under pinyin, 'Mao Tse-tung' becomes *Mao Zedong*; 'Chou En-lai' becomes *Zhou Enlai*; and 'Peking' becomes *Beijing*. The name of the country remains as it has been generally written: 'China' in English and German, and 'Chine' in French – in pinyin it's *Zhongguo*.

Tones

Mastering tones is tricky for the untrained Western ear, but with practice it can be done. There are four basic tones used in Mandarin, which makes it easier for foreigners to learn than Cantonese. As in Cantonese, changing the tone changes the meaning. For example, in Mandarin Chinese the word *ma* can have four distinct meanings depending on which tone is used:

high tone	*mā*	mother
rising tone	*má*	hemp or numb
falling-rising tone	*mǎ*	horse
falling tone	*mà*	to scold or swear

Technically, there is a fifth tone, the so-called 'neutral' tone. It can be indicated by a dot over the vowel, such as *mà* but in practice it is usually not indicated at all. A neutral tone does not need to be pronounced and does not affect the meaning.

The following is a description of the sounds produced in spoken Mandarin Chinese. The letter **v** is not used in Chinese. For beginners, the trickiest sounds in pinyin are **c, q** and **x** because their enunciation isn't remotely close to English. Most letters are pronounced as in English, except for the following:

Vowels

a	like the 'a' in 'father'
ai	like the 'i' in 'I'
ao	like the 'ow' in 'cow'
e	like the 'u' in 'blur'
ei	like the 'ei' in 'weigh'
i	like the 'ee' in 'meet' or the 'oo' in 'book'*
ian	as in 'yen'
ie	like the English word 'yeah'
o	like the 'o' in 'or'
ou	like the 'oa' in 'boat'
u	like the 'u' in 'flute'
ui	like 'way'
uo	like 'w' followed by an 'o' like in 'or'
yu	like German umlaut 'ü' or French 'u' in 'union'
ü	like German umlaut 'ü'

Consonants

c	like the 'ts' in 'bits'
ch	like in English, but with the tongue curled back
h	like in English, but articulated from the throat
q	like the 'ch' in 'chicken'
r	like the 's' in 'pleasure'
sh	as in English, but with the tongue curled back
x	like the 'sh' in 'shine'
z	like the 'ds' in 'suds'
zh	like the 'j' in 'judge' but with the tongue curled back

*The letter **i** is pronounced like the 'oo' in 'book' when it occurs after c, ch, r, s, sh, z, zh.

Consonants can never appear at the end of a syllable except for **n, ng,** and **r**.

In pinyin, apostrophes are occasionally used to separate syllables. So, you can write *ping'an* to prevent the word being pronounced as *pin'gan*.

Body Language

Hand signs are often used in China. The 'thumbs-up' sign has a long tradition as an indication of excellence or, in Chinese, *guā guā jiào*.

The Chinese have a system for counting on their hands. If you can't speak the language, it would be worth your while to at

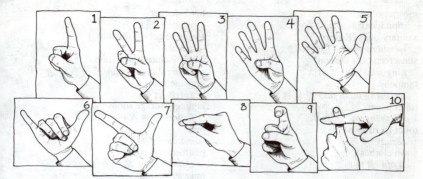

least learn Chinese finger counting. The symbol for number 10 is to form a cross with the index fingers, but in many locations the Chinese just show a fist.

Useful Phrases
Lonely Planet's *Mandarin Chinese Phrasebook* includes common words, useful phrases and word lists in English, simplified Chinese characters and pinyin. Here are some survival phrases to get you started:

Pronouns
I
  wǒ 我
you
  nǐ 你
he, she, it
  tā 他
we, us
  wǒmen 我们
you (plural)
  nǐmen 你们
they, them
  tāmen 他们

Greetings & Civilities
hello
  nǐ hǎo 你好
goodbye
  zàijiàn 再见
thank you
  xièxie 谢谢

you're welcome
  búkèqì 不客气
I'm sorry/excuse me
  duìbùqǐ 对不起
name card
  míngpiàn 名片

Negotiation
I want...
  wǒ yào... 我要
I want to buy...
  wǒ yào mǎi... 我要买..
No, I don't want it
  búyào 不要
yes, have
  yǒu 有
no, don't have
  méiyǒu 没有
How much does it cost?
  duōshǎo qián? 多少钱
too expensive
  tài guì 太贵
Do you understand?
  dǒng bùdǒng? 懂不懂
I don't understand
  wǒ tīng bùdǒng 我听不懂
I do understand
  wǒ tīngde dǒng 我听得懂

Necessities
bathroom (washroom)
  xǐshǒujiān 洗手间
mosquito incense coils
  wénxiāng 蚊香

mosquito mats
diàn wénxiāng 电蚊香
sanitary pads (Kotex)
wèishēng mián 卫生棉
sunscreen (UV) lotion
fáng shài yóu 防晒油
tampons
wèishēng mián tiáo 卫生棉条
toilet paper
wèishēng zhǐ 卫生纸
toilet (restroom)
cèsuǒy 厕所
wash clothes
xǐyīfú 洗衣服

Air Transport
airport
fēijīchǎng 飞机场
boarding pass
dēngjì kǎ 登记卡
CAAC
zhōngguó mínháng 中国民航
cancel
qǔxiāo 取消
reserve a seat
dìng wèizǐ 定位子
ticket
piào 票
buy a ticket
mǎi piào 买票
one-way ticket
dānchéng piào 单程票
reconfirm air ticket
quèrèn 确认
refund a ticket
tuìpiào 退票
round-trip ticket
láihuì piào 来回票
ticket office
shòu piào chù 售票处

Getting Around
bicycle hire
zìxíngchē chūzū 自行车出租
bus
gōnggòng qìchē 公共汽车
1st-class waiting room
tóuděng hòuchē lóu 头等候车楼
hard-seat
yìngxí, yìngzuò 硬席/硬座

hard-sleeper
yìngwò 硬卧
I want to get off (bus/taxi)
xià chē 下车
long-distance bus station
chángtú qìchē zhàn 长途汽车站
luggage
xínglǐ 行李
luggage storage room
jìcúnchù 寄存处
pier
mǎtóu 码头
platform ticket
zhàntái piào 站台票
railway station
huǒchē zhàn 火车站
soft-seat
ruǎnxí, ruǎnzuò 软席/软座
soft-sleeper
ruǎnwò 软卧
taxi
chūzū chē 出租车
train
huǒchē 火车
upgrade ticket (on train)
bǔ piào 补票
Which platform?
dìjǐ hào zhàntái 第几号站台

Directions
alley
nòng 弄
boulevard
dàdào 大道
Go straight
yìzhí zǒu 一直走
I'm lost
wǒ mí lù 我迷路
lane
xiàng 巷
No 21
21 hào 21号
road
lù 路
section
duàn 段
street
jiē, dàjiē 街/大街
Turn around
xiàng huí zǒu 向回走

Turn left
 zuǒ zhuǎn 左转
Turn right
 yòu zhuǎn 右转
Where is the...?
 ...zài nǎlǐ? ...在那里

Accommodation
bed
 chuángwèi 床位
big hotel
 jiǔdiàn, bīnguǎn 酒店/宾馆
book the whole room
 bāofáng 包房
check-in (register)
 dēngjì 登记
deposit
 yājīn 押金
dormitory
 duōrénfáng 多人房
double room (2 beds)
 shuāngrénfáng 双人房
economy room
 jīngjì fáng 经济房
economy room with bath
 jīngjì tàofáng 经济套房
hostel
 zhāodàisuǒ 招待所
hotel (all kinds)
 lüguǎn 旅馆
luxury room with bath
 háohuá tàofáng 豪华套房
reserve a room
 dìng fángjiān 定房间
room
 fángjiān 房间
single room (1 bed)
 dānrénfáng 单人房
standard room with bath
 biāozhǔn tàofáng 标准套房

Post
aerogramme
 hángkōng yóujiǎn 航空邮简
airmail
 hángkōng xìn 航空信
envelope
 xìnfēng 信封
GPO
 zǒng yóujú 总邮局

international express mail (EMS)
 kuàijié 快捷
package
 bāoguǒ 包裹
post office
 yóujú 邮局
postcard
 míngxìn piàn 明信片
poste restante
 cún jú hòu lǐng lán 存局候领栏
registered mail
 guà hào 挂号
stamp
 yóupiào 邮票
surface mail
 píngyóu 平邮
telegram
 diànbào 电报

Telecommunications
collect call
 duìfāng fùqián 对方付钱
direct dial
 zhí bō diànhuà 直拨电话
fax
 chuánzhēn 传真
international call
 guójì diànhuà 国际电话
telephone card
 diànhuà kǎ 电话卡
telephone office
 diànxùn dàlóu 电讯大楼
telephone
 diànhuà 电话
telex
 diànchuán 电传

Visas & Documents
Foreign Affairs Branch
 wàishìkē 外事科
passport
 hùzhào 护照
Public Security Bureau
 gōng ān jú 公安局
visa extension
 yáncháng qiānzhèng 延长签证
visa
 qiānzhèng 签证

CANTON

Emergencies

antibiotics
  kàngjūnsù 抗菌素
Fire!
  huǒ zāi! 火灾
Help!
  jiùmìng a! 救命啊
hospital
  yīyuàn 医院
I'm a diabetic
  wǒ yǒu tángniào bìng 我有糖尿病
I'm allergic to...
  wǒ duì...hěn guòmǐn 我对..很过敏
I'm injured
  wǒ shòushāng 我受伤
I'm sick
  wǒ shēng bìng 我生病
penicillin
  qīngméisù 青霉素
pickpocket
  páshǒu 勒贰
rapist
  qiángjiānfàn 强奸犯
Thief!
  xiǎo tōu! 小偷

Time

What is the time?
  jǐ diǎn? 几点
hour
  diǎn 点
minute
  fēn 分
now
  xiànzài 现在

today
  jīntiān 今天
tomorrow
  míngtiān 明天
yesterday
  zuótiān 昨天
Wait a moment
  děng yī xià 等一下

Numbers

0	*líng*	零
1	*yī*	一
2	*èr, liǎng*	二, 两
3	*sān*	叁
4	*sì*	四
5	*wǔ*	五
6	*liù*	六
7	*qī*	七
8	*bā*	八
9	*jiǔ*	九
10	*shí*	十
11	*shíyī*	十一
12	*shí'èr*	十二
20	*èrshí*	二十
21	*èrshíyī*	二十一
100	*yìbǎi*	一百
200	*liǎngbǎi*	两百
1,000	*yìqiān*	一千
2,000	*liǎngqiān*	两千
10,000	*yíwàn*	一万
20,000	*liǎngwàn*	两万
100,000	*shíwàn*	十万
200,000	*èrshíwàn*	二十万

CANTON

Facts for the Visitor

VISAS & EMBASSIES

Visas for individual travel in China are easy to get and readily available in Hong Kong and Macau. China will even issue visas to individuals from countries which do not have diplomatic relations with the People's Republic of China (PRC). So don't worry if you have a Taiwanese visa in your passport – plenty of Taiwanese now visit the PRC.

Chinese residents of Hong Kong and Macau can apply for a *huí xiāng zhèng* which entitles them to multiple visa-free entry to the PRC.

You'll normally be issued a one-month single-entry visa for US$12. The visa is only good for one month from the date of entry you specify on your application. It is possible to get visas valid for three months, but only if you apply through a travel agent (which costs extra).

You can also obtain a dual-entry visa for US$32, or a multiple-entry visa for US$90. The multiple-entry visa allows unlimited entries and is valid for six months from the date of issue, but you are only permitted to stay for 30 days at a time and this cannot be extended inside China. It is usually easy to obtain the multiple-entry visa if you've been in China previously and have stamps in your passport to prove it.

It normally takes two days to process a visa application, but if you're in a hurry, you can obtain an express visa in one day for US$32.

Visa applications require one photo. The application asks you to specify where you plan to go, but once inside China no one knows or cares what you wrote on your visa application. You're advised to have one entire blank page in your passport. You'll have to part with your passport while your visa application is processed, so be sure you have enough money since you need the passport for cashing travellers' cheques.

Any travel agency in Hong Kong can easily get the visa for you, but will charge for this service. If you don't mind queuing, the cheapest visas can be obtained from the Visa Office of the Ministry of Foreign Affairs of the PRC (☎ 8939812), 5th floor, Low block, China Resources Building, 26 Harbour Rd, Wanchai, Hong Kong Island. It's open Monday to Friday, 9 am to 12.30 pm and 2 to 5 pm, Saturdays 9 am to 12.30 pm.

Chinese Embassies

Australia
247 Federal Highway, Watson, Canberra, 2600 ACT

Austria
Metterrichgasse 4, A-1030 Vienna

Belgium
21 Blvd Général Jacques, 1051 Brussels

Canada
411-415 Andrews St, Ottawa, Ontario KIN 5H3

Denmark
25 Oeregaardsalle, DK 2900 Hellerup, Copenhagen 2900

France
11 Ave George V, Paris 75008

Germany
5307 Wachtbergeriederbachen, Konrad-Adenauer Str, 104 Bonn

Italy
56 Via Bruxelles, Roma 00198

Japan
15-30 Minami-Azabu, 4-chome, Minato-ku, Tokyo

Netherlands
Adriaan Goehooplaan 7, Den Haag

New Zealand
2-6 Glenmore St, Kelburn, Wellington

Spain
Trafalgar 11, Madrid

Sweden
Bragevagen 4, Stockholm

Switzerland
Kalecheggweg 10, Berne

UK
31 Portland Place, London WIN 3AG

USA
2300 Connecticut Ave NW, Washington, DC 20088. Consulates: 3417 Montrose Blvd, Houston, Texas 77006; 104 South Michigan Ave, Suite 1200, Chicago, Illinois 60603; 1450

Laguna St, San Francisco, CA 94115; 520 12th
Ave, New York, NY 10036

Visa Extensions

Visa extensions are handled by the Foreign
Affairs section of the local Public Security
Bureau (PSB, China's police force). Extensions cost US$3 for most nationalities, but
others pay US$6 and others get it free. The
general rule is that you can get one extension
of one month's duration. At an agreeable
PSB you may be able to wangle more, especially with cogent reasons like illness
(except AIDS), transport delays or a pack of
Marlboros, but second extensions are
usually only granted for one week with the
understanding that you are on your way out
of China.

Re-Entry Visas

Most foreign residents of China have multiple-entry visas and don't need a re-entry
visa. However, there might be other requirements (tax clearance, vaccinations, etc) – if
in doubt, check with the PSB before departing.

DOCUMENTS

Given the Chinese preoccupation with
impressive bits of paper, it's worth carrying
around a few business cards, student cards
and anything else that's printed and lami-
nated in plastic.

These additional IDs are useful for leaving
with bicycle-renters who often want a
deposit or other security for their bikes –
sometimes they ask you to leave your passport, but you should insist on leaving another
piece of ID or a deposit. Some hotels also
require you to hand over your passport as
security, even if you've paid in advance – an
old expired passport is useful for these situ-
ations.

Chinese Documents

Foreigners who live, work or study in China
will be issued a number of documents, and
some of these can be used to obtain substantial discounts on trains, flights, hotels,
museums and tourist sites.

Most common and least useful is the so-
called 'white card', a simple student ID card
with pasted-on photo and usually kept in a
red plastic holder (some call it a 'red card'
for this reason). Having one of these supposedly allows you to pay Chinese prices for
railway tickets – it works about 50% of the
time. A white card is easily forged – you
could reproduce one with a photocopy
machine – and the red plastic holders are on
sale everywhere. For this reason, you might
be approached by touts wanting to sell you a
fake one. The fact is that outside of major
cities like Guangzhou and Shenzhen,
railway clerks really have no idea what a
white card is supposed to look like – fake
ones sometimes work when real ones don't!

One French student had a knockdown drag-out battle
in a railway station with a smug booking clerk who
threw her absolutely genuine white card into the
rubbish bin and told her it was a fake.

The so-called 'yellow card' (really orange)
is not so much a card as a small booklet. The
cover is orange and the pages are white.
Except for the cover, the book can be easily
forged with a photocopier, but there don't
seem to be too many fakes around – yet. The
value of the yellow card is that it seems to
work better than white cards.

The 'green card' is a residence permit,
issued to English teachers, foreign experts
and students who live in the PRC. It's such
a valuable document that you'd better not
lose it if you have one, or the PSB will be all
over you. Foreigners living in China say that
if you lose your green card, you might face
to leave the country rather than face the
music. A green card will permit you to pay
Chinese prices in hotels, on flights, trains
and elsewhere. In addition, many hotels offer
major discounts to green-card holders (even
five-star hotels!). The green card is not really
a card but resembles a small passport – it
would be very difficult to forge without
modern printing equipment and special
paper. Green cards are issued for one year
and must be renewed annually.

CANTON

CUSTOMS

Chinese border crossings have gone from the traumatic to exceedingly easy. While there seems to be lots of uniformed police around, the third degree at customs seems to be reserved for pornography-smuggling Hong Kongers rather than the stray backpacker.

You'll note that there are clearly marked 'green channels' and 'red channels', the latter reserved for those with such everyday travel items like refrigerators, motorcycles and colour TV sets.

You're allowed to import 600 cigarettes or the equivalent in tobacco products, two litres of alcohol and one *pint* of perfume. You're also allowed 915 metres of movie film and a maximum of 72 rolls of still film. Importation of fresh fruit is prohibited.

It's illegal to import any printed material, film, tapes, etc 'detrimental to China's politics, economy, culture and ethics'. But don't be too concerned about what you take to read. As you leave China, any tapes, manuscripts, books, etc 'which contain state secrets or are otherwise prohibited for export' can be seized. Cultural relics, handicrafts, gold and silver ornaments, and jewellery purchased in China have to be shown to customs on leaving. You'll also have to show your receipts, otherwise the stuff may be confiscated. Don't get paranoid – they seldom search foreigners.

MONEY
Currency

The basic unit of Chinese currency is the *yuan* – (Y). In spoken Chinese, the word *kuai* is often substituted for yuan. Ten *jiao* make up one yuan – in spoken Chinese, it's pronounced *mao*. Ten *fen* make up one jiao, but these days fen are becoming rare because they are worth so little – some people will not accept them.

Renminbi (RMB) Renminbi or 'People's Money' is issued by the Bank of China. Paper notes are issued in denominations of one, two, five, 10, 50 and 100 yuan; one, two and five jiao; and one, two and five fen. Coins are in denominations of one yuan; five

jiao; and one, two and five fen. The one-fen note is small and yellow, the two-fen note is blue, and the five-fen note is small and green – all are next to worthless.

Exchange Rates

Australia	A$1	=	Y6.20
Canada	C$1	=	Y6.21
France	Ffr1	=	Y1.61
Germany	DM1	=	Y5.52
Hong Kong	HK$1	=	Y1.10
Japan	¥100	=	Y8.67
New Zealand	NZ$1	=	Y5.10
Singapore	S$1	=	Y5.65
Switzerland	Sfr1	=	Y6.47
Taiwan	NT$1	=	Y0.32
Thailand	B1	=	Y0.34
UK	UK£1	=	Y13.33
USA	US$1	=	Y8.53

Changing Money Foreign currency and travellers' cheques can be changed at the main centres of the Bank of China, the tourist hotels, some Friendship Stores, and some of the big department stores. Hotels usually give the official rate, but some will charge a small commission. A bigger problem is that a few five-star hotels only change money for their own guests – you can always lie and make up a false room number, but this may not work if you're dressed like a slob. The rates charged at various ports of entry (airports, wharves, Hong Kong border, etc) are usually the official rate, so don't be afraid to change as much as you need on arrival.

Always be sure to keep enough money on you to last for at least a few days. Public holidays can pose a big problem because even hotel money-exchange counters don't want to transact business since they can't call up the bank to get the latest official rates.

Australian, Canadian, US, UK, Hong Kong, Japanese and most West European currencies are acceptable in China. In some of the backwaters, it may be hard to change lesser known currencies – US$ are still the easiest to change.

Whenever you change foreign currency into Chinese currency you'll be given a money-exchange voucher recording the

CANTON

transaction. If you've got any leftover yuan when you leave the country and want to reconvert it to hard currency you *must* have those vouchers – not all of them, but at least equal to *double* the amount of yuan you want to re-exchange. In other words, only 50% of what you originally exchanged can be re-exchanged on departure – the government is saying that you must spend the rest while in China.

Black Market The words 'Hello, change money' have become as popular as spitting in China. And, unfortunately, black-market moneychangers in China are almost universally thieves.

The best advice is to avoid the black market totally unless you enjoy the thrill of getting robbed. For the few cents on the dollar that you could possibly gain from black market dealings, you run the risk of losing it all. You might think that you're good at changing money on the street, but we assure you that the rip-off artists are also very good at what they do.

There are different techniques. If you are so foolish as to hand over your money first, you're finished – you will be short-changed and nothing short of outright violence will get your money back. But even if you demand that they hand over their cash first, you can still get cheated. In this case, the amount they give you will be slightly less than what was agreed upon. When you protest, they ask you to hand it back so they can recount it. When they recount it in front of your very eyes, they discover the 'mistake' and add a Y50 bill to the top of the pile just as they are removing a Y100 from the bottom. They are skilled magicians! They hand you the money back and expect you to hand over yours straight away. If you hand yours over, then the transaction is over and now you've lost Y100. If you don't, and decide to recount the lot and discover that you've been short-changed again by an even larger amount, they may claim that you cheated them! In the ensuing very ugly scene (often created with the help of accomplices) you may be threatened with violence and many foreigners at that point are intimidated enough to hand over their Hong Kong dollars and accept the loss.

Another crude but effective technique is simply for the moneychangers to grab the cash out of your hands and run off, and in a few cases they've thrown mace or some other chemical into a foreigner's eyes to prevent resistance.

It seems to be the experience of most travellers that female moneychangers are less likely to use threats, intimidation, violence or grab the cash out of your hands. However, female moneychangers have been known to often short-change customers, and may resort to the 'sobbing technique' to gain sympathy if a confrontation ensues. The worst thing to do is change with a group of young men on the street – if there's just one of you versus three young men, you might as well just hang a sign around your neck saying 'Rob me'.

If you wind up with excess yuan, you can unload it in Hong Kong. Not all Hong Kong moneychangers deal in Chinese money, but one that does is Frankee Money Changer, just opposite Exchange Square on Des Voeux, Central.

As for bringing things into China to sell, you'll probably find that the Chinese strike too much of a hard bargain to make it worth the trouble.

Travellers' Cheques Besides the advantage of safety, travellers' cheques are useful to carry in China because the exchange rate is actually more favourable than what you get for cash. Cheques from most of the world's leading banks and issuing agencies are now acceptable in China – stick to the major companies such as Thomas Cook, American Express and Bank of America, and you'll be OK.

Credit Cards It wouldn't be worthwhile to get a credit card especially for your trip to China, but if you already have one you might find it useful. Plastic is gaining more acceptance in China for use by foreign visitors in major tourist cities. Useful cards include Visa, MasterCard, American Express, JCB and Diners Club. It's even possible to get a cash advance against your card.

Telegraphic Transfers Getting money sent to you while you're in China is a real drag – try to avoid it. On the average, it takes about five weeks for your money to arrive. If you have high-placed connections in the banking system it can take considerably less time, but most travellers are not so fortunate.

Bank Accounts Foreigners can indeed open bank accounts in China – both Chinese yuan and US dollar accounts (the latter only at special foreign-exchange banks). You do not need to have resident status – a tourist visa is sufficient. Automatic-teller machines have been introduced at the Bank of China.

Warning There is no bank or moneychanger at Lo Wu on the Hong Kong side of the border with Shenzhen. Many travellers have crossed the border here and got stuck with no money to pay for the train into the city. If you need Hong Kong dollars, get them on the Shenzhen side of the border!

Costs

China is experiencing rapid inflation, and for that reason most of the prices quoted hereafter are in US$. China devaluates its currency periodically, but prices in US$ terms have remained relatively stable.

Although China is cheaper than Hong Kong or Macau, it's not nearly as cheap as you would expect given the low wage levels earned by most Chinese. The main reason is a deliberate government policy of squeezing as much money as possible out of foreign tourists. Foreigners must pay triple for train fares and about 30% more than locals for airfares. Accommodation is usually the biggest expense. If you get into a dormitory, then China is cheap – otherwise, your daily living expense could be higher than in Hong Kong.

Hotel restaurants in Guangzhou have grown accustomed to charging high prices for food, but you can get around this by eating at hole-in-the-wall restaurants. If you manage your money properly, you can still live in Guangzhou on US$15 per day but it will take effort.

Tipping

Tipping is not normally a custom. Bribery is another matter. Don't be blatant about it, but if you need some special service, it's customary to offer someone a cigarette and just tell him/her: 'Go ahead and keep the pack – I'm trying to quit'. In China, a 'tip' is given before you receive the service, not after.

Bargaining

Since foreigners are so frequently overcharged in China, bargaining becomes essential. You can bargain in shops, hotels, with taxi drivers, with most people – but not everywhere. In large stores where prices are clearly marked, there is usually no latitude for bargaining. In small shops and street stalls, bargaining is expected, but there is one important rule to follow – be polite. There is nothing wrong with asking for a discount, if you do so with a smile. Some foreigners seem to think that bargaining should be a screaming and threatening contest. This is not only unpleasant for all concerned, it seldom results in you getting a lower price – indeed, in 'face-conscious' China, intimidation is likely to make the vendor more recalcitrant and you'll be overcharged.

You should keep in mind that entrepreneurs are in business to make money – they aren't going to sell anything to you at a loss. Your goal should be to pay the Chinese price, as opposed to the foreigners' price – if you can do that, you've done well.

Consumer Taxes

Although big hotels and fancy restaurants may add a tax or 'service charge' of 10% or more, all other consumer taxes are included in the price tag.

WHEN TO GO

Since the weather is tolerable almost any time of year, the main consideration will be avoiding the crowds. One rule to remember is to avoid travelling on weekends and (even more so) at holiday times such as Easter and Chinese New Year. At those times everything is booked out and the herds stampede across the border from Hong Kong, leaving trampled backpackers in their wake.

Accommodation in Guangzhou is impossible to find during the Guangzhou Fair, held twice annually in April and October. However, it is quite alright to visit other places in Guangdong Province as long as you don't need to spend the night in Guangzhou itself.

WHAT TO BRING

If you acquired a heap of heavy junk in Hong Kong, put it in storage. Some travel agents

CANTON

and hotels in Hong Kong store luggage. Another option is the bonded baggage room at Kai Tak Airport.

Pharmaceuticals

All of the following pharmaceutical items can be purchased in any Watson's drugstore in Hong Kong:

Anti-diarrhoeal drugs (Lomotil, Imodium), birth-control pills & condoms, contact lens & cleaning solution, dental floss, deodorant, mosquito repellent, pain killer (Panadol), etc), shaving cream & razor blades, sunblock (UV) lotion, tampons, thermometer and vitamins.

Reading Material

To preserve your sanity, bring some reading material. Good books in English are scarce in China, though occasionally you may find a real collector's item.

Clothing

After Hong Kong, which resembles one big fashion show, you may actually find China a relief. Most people in China dress casually. Foreigners can get away with wearing almost anything as long as it isn't overly revealing.

In summer, shorts are OK. Many Chinese men walk around outdoors bare-chested at this time. However, Western men with a lot of body hair should not try this, as displaying a hairy chest in public will attract a large crowd of enthusiastic onlookers. Children may actually pull your body hair to test if it's real!

Beachwear should be conservative. Men with hairy chests should wear a T-shirt when swimming and women should wear one-piece swimsuits. Bikinis will attract spectators and public nudity will get you arrested.

You can wear flip-flop sandals (thongs) inside your hotel room or in a youth hostel, but if you set foot outside with them on you can expect stares and rude remarks. You may see some Chinese wear thongs outdoors, but don't think that means it's OK – it's considered an extremely low-class thing to do, like begging. As in Hong Kong, sandals are OK

if they have a strap across the back of the ankle.

Chinese rain gear is cheap, but foreign-made stuff is far better quality.

Gifts

Foreign cigarettes and beer are especially popular. A bag of M&M candy-covered chocolates or other foreign chocolates will go down well.

For Chinese who speak English, foreign books, magazines and newspapers are greatly appreciated, but try to take care that you don't give your friends reading material which is way beyond their level of comprehension.

The duty-free shop at the Hong Kong-Shenzhen border is a good place to buy cigarettes.

Don't go overboard with gift giving. There's a thin line between being nice and corrupting someone. On the other hand, don't do the opposite – giving away your old jacket as a gift will be taken as an insult. Foreign-made T-shirts of exotic design are much in demand, but make sure it's new (or looks new). A second-hand rag is not a suitable gift.

A Chinese with good manners is supposed to refuse (at least once, maybe twice) the gift you want to offer. You are supposed to insist. They will then 'reluctantly' accept it. To accept a gift too readily is considered greedy. If you receive a present that is gift-wrapped, it is customary not to open it in front of the giver. If you open it immediately, it makes you look greedy.

TOURIST OFFICES
Local Tourist Offices

Most mid-range and top-end hotels have a desk in the lobby supplying tour information, a service you can use without being a hotel guest. Often hotel information desks have timetables for planes and trains and staff can sometimes book tickets for public transport. If you want to sign up for a city tour, the information desk can usually arrange that too, and often has pamphlets explaining which tours are available. Sometimes the staff at these information desks can speak good English, but don't count on it. The only way to find out is to ask.

CITS China International Travel Service (CITS) deals with China's foreign tourist hordes, and mainly concerns itself with organising and making travel arrangements for group tours. CITS existed as far back as 1954 when there were few customers. Now they're inundated with a couple of hundred thousand big-noses a year. Unfortunately, after 40 years of being in business, CITS has still not gotten its act together.

CITS can buy rail and plane tickets for you (and some boat tickets), reserve hotel rooms, organise city tours, and even get you tickets for the cinema, opera, acrobatics and other entertainment, as well as organise trips to communes and farms, and provide vehicles (taxis, minibuses) for sightseeing or transport.

All rail tickets bought through CITS will be tourist-priced (an extra 200% on top of the Chinese price) and there will usually be a small service charge added on to the price of rail, boat or plane tickets. They can get you into places that are normally closed to foreigners but you will have to pay heavily for the privilege.

Generally speaking, solo travellers will rarely have to deal with them. One thing about CITS is fairly consistent – their tours tend to be expensive. Furthermore, CITS has been known to cheat travellers outright – selling 10-day tours but just giving eight, charging for services not rendered, booking tourists onto a bus that breaks down but no refund given, and so on.

Service varies. Some CITS people are friendly and full of useful information about the places they're stationed in – a few may even invite you out to dinner! There are others who are downright rude and only interested in squeezing money out of foreigners – Beijing CITS stands out as a glaring example of the latter. Golmud CITS (in Qinghai Province) is even worse. They may lie to you – claiming that a certain area is closed to foreigners (except via an expensive CITS tour) when in fact it's open. You may find CITS offices staffed by people who speak sparse or zero English and who got their jobs through the back door. But everything depends on who you're dealing with – some CITS offices deserve eternal praise while others deserve all the abuse you can heap on them.

CITS offices and desks are usually in the major tourist hotels in each town or city open to foreigners. If they aren't you can get the hotel reception desk to phone them.

Getting information out of CITS is potluck. In years past, a CITS office was at least an office – you could walk in, sit down at a desk and talk to someone in a casual and friendly manner. That's still possible in the backwaters, but these days the trend is to make all CITS offices into a row of ticket counters – you fill out a form, stand in line, pay your money and leave. Especially in large cities like Beijing and Guangzhou, a 'modern' CITS office looks just like an airport check-in counter.

CTS China Travel Service (CTS) was originally set up to handle tourists from Hong Kong, Macau and Taiwan, and with foreign nationals of Chinese descent (Overseas Chinese). The reason why CITS and CTS were set up as separate organisations supposedly had to do with language. CTS staff were not required to learn English – instead, Mandarin Chinese and Cantonese were the main languages. However, this couldn't explain why Overseas Chinese (many of whom cannot speak Chinese at all) were required to go with CTS tours rather than CITS. Many foreigners couldn't help but get the nagging feeling that race was the real reason – keep the foreign devils away from the Chinese.

These days it makes little difference – CTS has now become a keen competitor with CITS. CITS is trying to cash in on the lucrative Taiwan and Hong Kong markets, while CTS is targeting the Western market which was previously the exclusive domain of CITS. And this competition is healthy as both CITS and CTS have had long records of dismal service. It still could stand plenty of improvement, but things have improved. Nevertheless, we periodically get complaints – as one disillusioned traveller wrote:

CANTON

Although we are seasoned independent travellers, we decided we were better off on a tour in China and contacted CTS via a Hong Kong travel agent. We were extremely disappointed with our trip for a number of reasons. The principle one was that the restaurants were extremely dirty and unhygienic. We were paying more than US$350 a day for two and were taken to eat in restaurants that cost US$2.50 (for foreigners!). The hotel restaurants (where group price was US$5 at the White Swan as an example) were 'too expensive'.

We signed up for a group tour, and when we turned up at the Hong Kong meeting point, we found there were only the two of us. At that point, it was impossible to cancel the trip without forfeiting the entire cost. Being only the two of us increased the costs considerably because we had to support the entire cost of the guide, driver and car, which meant that the value to the two of us was drastically reduced...had we known there would have been only the two of us, we would have gone on our own, stayed at good hotels, skipped some of the uninteresting spots on the itinerary, eaten at *clean* restaurants and probably saved 50% of the overall cost!

Lee S Hubert

Many foreigners make use of the CTS offices in Hong Kong and Macau to obtain visas and book trains, planes, hovercraft and other transport to China. CTS can sometimes get you a better deal on hotels booked through their office than you could obtain on your own (of course, this doesn't apply to backpackers' dormitories). CTS has 19 branch offices in Hong Kong, and the Kowloon, Mongkok and Wanchai offices are open on Sundays and public holidays. These offices can be crowded – avoid this by arriving at 9 am when the doors open.

Overseas Reps

CITS The main office of CITS in Hong Kong (Tsimshatsui East) can book air tickets to China and has a good collection of English-language pamphlets. The main office and Central branch office are open Monday to Friday 9 am to 5 pm and from 9 am to 1 pm on Saturday. The Mongkok branch office keeps longer hours (9 am to 6.30 pm on Saturday and a half-day on Sunday).

Outside of China and Hong Kong, CITS is usually known as China National Tourist Office. Some of the offices overseas are:

Australia
  China National Tourist Office, 11th floor, 55 Clarence St, Sydney NSW 2000 (☎ (02) 294057; fax 2901958)
France
  China National Tourist Office, 51 Rue Saint-Anne, 75002, Paris (☎ 42969548; fax 42615468)
Germany
  China National Tourist Office, Eschenheimer Anlage 28, D-6000 Frankfurt am Main-1 (☎ (069) 555292; fax 5973412)
Hong Kong
  Main Office, 6th floor, Tower Two, South Seas Centre, 75 Mody Rd, Tsimshatsui East, Kowloon (☎ 7325888; fax 7217154)
  Central Branch, Room 1018, Swire House, 11 Chater Rd, Central (☎ 8104282; fax 8681657)
  Mongkok Branch, Room 1102-1104, Bank Centre, 636 Nathan Rd, Mongkok, Kowloon (☎ 3881619; fax 3856157)
  Causeway Bay Branch, Room 1104, Causeway Bay Plaza, 489 Hennessy Rd, Causeway Bay (☎ 8363485; fax 5910849)
Japan
  China National Tourist Office, 6F Hachidal Hamamatsu-cho Building, 1-27-13 Hamamatsu-cho Minato-ku, Tokyo (☎ (03) 34331461; fax 34338653)
UK
  China National Tourist Office, 4 Glentworth St, London NW1 (☎ (071) 9359427; fax 4875842)
USA
  China National Tourist Office, Los Angeles Branch, 333 West Broadway, Suite 201, Glendale CA 91204 (☎ (818) 5457505; fax 5457506)
  New York Branch, Lincoln Building, 60E, 42nd St, Suite 3126, New York, NY 10165 (☎ (212) 8670271; fax 5992892)

CTS Overseas representatives include the following:

Australia
  Ground floor, 757-759 George St, Sydney, NSW 2000 (☎ (02) 2112633; fax 2813595)
Canada
  556 West Broadway, Vancouver, BC V5Z 1E9 (☎ (604) 8728787; fax 8732823)
France
  10 Rue de Rome, 75008, Paris (☎ (1) 45229272; fax 45229279)
Germany
  Düsseldorfer Strasse 14 6000, Frankfurt am Main-1 (☎ (69) 250515; fax 232324)
Hong Kong
  Central Branch, 2nd floor, China Travel Building, 77 Queen's Road, Central (☎ 5217163; fax 5255525)

CANTON

Kowloon Branch, 1st floor, Alpha House, 27-33 Nathan Rd, Tsimshatsui (☎ 7214481; fax 7216251)

Mongkok Branch, 62-72 Sai Yee St, Mongkok (☎ 7895970; fax 3905001)

Wanchai Branch, Ground floor, Southern Centre, 138 Hennessy Rd, Wanchai (☎ 8323888)

China Hong Kong City Branch, 10-12 China Hong Kong City, 33 Canton Rd, Tsimshatsui (☎ 7361863)

Indonesia
PT Cempaka Travelindo, Jalan Hayam Wuruk 97, Jakarta-Barat (☎ (21) 6294256; fax 6294836)

Japan
Nihombashi-Settsu Building, 2-2-4, Nihombashi, Chuo-Ku, Tokyo (☎ (03) 3273-5512; fax 3273-2667)

Macau
Hotel Beverly Plaza, Avenida do Dr Rodrigo Rodrigues (☎ 388922)

Malaysia
Yuyi Travel Sdn Bhd, 1st floor, Sun Complex, Jalan Bukit Bintang 55100, Kuala Lumpur (☎ (03) 2427077; fax 2412478)

Philippines
489 San Fernando St, Binondo, Manila (☎ 474187; fax 407834)

Singapore
Ground floor, SIA Building, 77 Robinson Rd, Singapore, 0106 (☎ 2240550; fax 2245009)

Thailand
559 Yaowaraj Rd, Bangkok 10500 (☎ (2) 2260041; fax 2264712)

UK
24 Cambridge Circus, London WC2H 8HD (☎ (071) 8369911; fax 8363121)

USA
2nd floor, 212 Sutter St, San Francisco, CA 94108 (☎ (800) 3322831, (415) 3986627; fax 3986669)

Los Angeles Branch, Suite 138, 223 East Garvey Ave, Monterey Park, CA 91754 (☎ (818) 2888222; fax 2883464)

USEFUL ORGANISATIONS
Public Security Bureau (PSB)

The Public Security Bureau (*gōng'ān jú*) is the name given to China's police, both uniformed and plain clothes. Its responsibilities include suppression of political dissidence, crime detection, preventing foreigners and Chinese from having sex with each other (no joke), mediating family quarrels and directing traffic. The Foreign Affairs Branch (*wài shì kē*) of the PSB deals with

foreigners. This branch is responsible for issuing visa extensions.

The PSB is responsible for introducing and enforcing regulations concerning foreigners. For example, they make decisions concerning the exclusion of foreigners from certain hotels. If this means you get stuck for a place to stay, they can offer advice. Don't pester them with trivia or try to 'use' them to bully a point with a local street vendor. Do turn to them for mediation in serious disputes with hotels, restaurants, taxi drivers, etc. This often works since the PSB wields omnipotent power.

There are several ways of inadvertently attracting the attention of the PSB. The most common way is to overstay your visa. Another risky proposition is to ride your bicycle between cities – in some places, a foreigner riding a bicycle still seems to be a crime. Foreign males who are suspected of being 'too friendly' with Chinese women could have trouble with the PSB.

If you do have a run-in with the PSB, you may have to write a confession of your guilt and pay a fine. In more serious cases, you can be expelled from China (at your own expense). But in general, if you aren't doing anything particularly nasty like smuggling suitcases of dope through customs, the PSB will probably not throw you in prison.

BUSINESS HOURS & HOLIDAYS

Banks, offices, government departments and the PSB are open Monday to Saturday. As a rough guide only, they open around 8 to 9 am, close for two hours in the middle of the day, and then reopen until 5 or 6 pm. Sunday is a public holiday, but some businesses are open Sunday morning but make up for this by closing on Wednesday afternoons. CITS offices, Friendship Stores and the foreign-exchange counters in the tourist hotels and some of the local branches of the Bank of China have similar opening hours, and are generally open on Sundays as well, at least in the morning.

Many parks, zoos and monuments have similar opening hours, and are also open on

CANTON

Sundays and often at night. Shows at cinemas and theatres finish around 10 pm.

Government restaurants are open for early morning breakfast (sometimes as early as 5.30 am) until about 7.30 am, then open for lunch and again for dinner around 5 to 8 or 9 pm. Chinese eat early and go home early – by 9 pm you'll probably find the chairs stacked and the cooks gone home. Privately-run restaurants are usually open all day, and often late into the night especially around railway stations.

Long-distance bus stations and railway stations open their ticket offices around 5 or 5.30 am before the first trains and buses pull out. Apart from a one or two-hour break in the middle of the day, they often stay open until about 11 or 11.30 pm.

The Chinese work six days a week and rest on Sunday. The nine national holidays during the year are as follows:

New Year's Day – 1 January
Chinese New Year – the first day of the first lunar month, this holiday usually falls in the first half of February but sometimes occurs during the last week of January. Also known as the Spring Festival, the actual holiday lasts three days but many people take a week off. It's a bad time to travel as all accommodation and transport is full. Most businesses are closed as this is a family holiday. If you have to be in China at this time, settle down in a nice quiet place with some books and try not to go anywhere until the chaos ends.
International Working Women's Day – 8 March
International Labour Day – 1 May
Youth Day – 4 May, commemorates the Beijing student demonstrations of 4 May 1919 when the Versailles Conference gave German 'rights' in the city of Tianjin to Japan.
Children's Day – 1 June
Anniversary of the founding of the Communist Party of China – 1 July
Anniversary of the founding of the Chinese People's Liberation Army – 1 August
National Day – 1 October celebrates the founding of the PRC in 1949.

POST & TELECOMMUNICATIONS
Postal Rates
International letters cost US$0.21 to send (0-20 grams), with a discount for printed matter. International postcards cost US$0.13 by surface mail and US$0.18 by air mail to anywhere in the world. Aerogrammes are US$0.21 to anywhere in the world. The registration fee for letters, printed matter and packets costs US$0.12.

Parcel rates vary depending on the country of destination. Charge for a one-kg parcel sent surface mail from China to the UK is US$6, to the USA it is US$3.50, and to Germany US$3.50. Charge for a one-kg parcel sent by air mail to the UK is US$9.40,

to the USA US$8.85, and to Germany US$8.10.

Post offices are very picky about how you pack things. Don't finalise your packing until the thing has got its last customs clearance. Most countries impose a maximum weight limitation (10 kg is typical) on packages received – this rate varies from country to country but the Chinese post office should be able to tell you what the limitation is. If you have a receipt for the goods, then put it in the box when you're mailing it, since it may be opened again by customs further down the line.

EMS International express mail service (EMS) charges vary according to country, and whether you are sending documents or parcels. For documents, EMS to Hong Kong and Macau costs US$5.75; to Japan, Korea and South-East Asia, US$8; South Asia, US$9.20; Europe, Canada and the USA, US$10.90; Middle East and Africa, US$12; and to South America, US$13.20. It's worth noting that EMS is not available to every country.

Sending Mail

The international postal service seems efficient, and air-mailed letters and postcards will probably take around five to 10 days to reach their destinations. If possible, write the country of destination in Chinese, as this should speed up the delivery. Domestic post is amazingly fast, perhaps one or two days from Guangzhou to Beijing. Within a city it may be delivered the same day that it's sent.

As well as the local post offices there are branch post offices in just about all the major tourist hotels where you can send letters, packets and parcels (the contents of packets and parcels are checked by the post office staff before mailing). Even at cheap hotels you can usually post letters from the front desk – reliability varies but in general it's OK. In some places, you may only be able to post printed matter from these branch offices. Other parcels may require a customs form attached at the town's main post office, where their contents will be checked.

Large envelopes are a bit hard to come by so try the department stores. If you expect to send quite a few packets, stock up when you come across such envelopes. A roll of strong, sticky tape is a useful item to bring along and serves many purposes. String, glue and sometimes cloth bags are supplied at the post offices, but don't count on it. The Friendship Stores will sometimes package and mail purchases for you, but only goods actually bought at the store.

Private Carriers In a joint-venture with China's Sinotrans, fast airfreight is offered by two foreign carriers, DHL and UPS. Express document and parcel service is offered by two other foreign carriers, Federal Express and TNT Skypak. Such service is only offered in major cities and doesn't come cheap – costs start at around US$50.

Receiving Mail

There are poste-restante services in just about every city and town, and they seem to work. Unfortunately, since Chinese does not use an alphabet, most post offices haven't discovered alphabetical order. In some cities, the GPO will assign numbers to letters as they are received and post the numbers and names on a noticeboard. You have to find your name and write down the number(s) of your letters, then tell the clerk at the counter. We've seen some strange names on the noticeboards – 'Par Avion, General Delivery', and 'Hold Until Arrival'.

Some major tourist hotels will hold mail for their guests, but this doesn't always work. Try writing instructions on the envelope.

It's worth noting that some foreigners living in China have had their mail opened or parcels pilfered before receipt – and some have their outgoing mail opened and read. This seems to affect tourists less, although letters with enclosures will almost certainly be opened. Your mail is less likely to be opened if it's sent to cities that handle high volumes of mail, like Guangzhou.

Officially, the PRC forbids several items from being mailed to it – the regulations specifically prohibit 'reactionary books, magazines and propaganda materials, obscene or immoral articles'. You also cannot mail Chinese currency abroad, or receive it by post. As elsewhere, mail-order hashish and other recreational chemicals will not amuse the authorities.

Telephone

China's creaky phone system is being over-hauled, at least in major cities. Whereas just a few years ago calling from Guangzhou to Shanghai could be an all-day project, now you can just pick up a phone and dial direct. International calls have also become much easier.

Many hotel rooms are equipped with phones where local calls are free. Local calls can be made from public pay phones (there are some around but not many). China's budding entrepreneurs try to fill the gap – people with private phones run a long cord out the window and stand on street corners, allowing you to use their phone to place local calls for around US$0.05 each – long-distance domestic and international calls are not always possible on these phones, but ask. In the lobbies of many hotels, the reception desks have a similar system – free calls for guests, US$0.05 for non-guests, and long-distance calls are charged by the minute.

You can place both domestic and international long-distance phone calls from main telecommunications offices. However, dealing with these offices can be a nuisance – you have to fill out forms in Chinese, pay for the call in advance, wait for perhaps 30 minutes and finally someone gestures to you indicating that you've been connected so pick up the phone and start talking.

Domestic long-distance rates in China vary according to distance, but are almost ridiculously cheap. International calls are relatively expensive, though not outrageous by world standards. Rates for station-to-station calls to most countries in the world are US$2.07 per minute, but Hong Kong is slightly cheaper at US$1.40 per minute. Some hotels might bill you at a higher rate than this, so ask first. There is no discount for calling late at night, and there is a

minimum charge of three minutes. Reverse-charge calls are sometimes cheaper than calls paid for in China. Time the call yourself – the operator will not break in to tell you that your minimum period of three minutes is approaching. After you hang up, the operator will ring back to tell you how much it cost. There is no call cancellation fee.

If you are expecting a call – either international or domestic – try to advise the caller beforehand of your hotel room number. The operators frequently have difficulty understanding Western names, and the hotel receptionist may not be able to locate you. If this can't be done, try to inform the operator that you are expecting the call and write down your name and room number – this increases your chances of success.

Direct Dialling Domestic direct dialling (DDD) and international direct dialling (IDD) calls are cheapest if you can find a phone which accepts magnetic cards. These phones are usually available in the lobbies of major hotels, at least in big cities, and the hotel's front desk should also sell the phone cards. These cards come in two denominations, Y20 and Y100 – for an international call, you'll need the latter.

If card phones aren't available, you can usually dial direct from the phones in the business centres found in most luxury hotels. You do not have to be a guest at these hotels to use these facilities.

If your hotel lacks card phones or a business centres, you should be able to dial direct from your hotel room. You'll have to ask the staff at your hotel what's the dial-out code for a direct line (usually a '7' on most switchboards, or sometimes a combination like '78'). Once you have the outside line, dial ☎ 00 (the international access code – always the same throughout China) followed by the country code, area code and the number you want to reach. If the area code begins with zero (like '03' for Melbourne, Australia) omit the first zero. On changes to UK area codes see the HK Facts for the Visitor chapter.

There are a few things to be careful about. The equipment used on most hotel switchboards is not very sophisticated – it's often a simple timer and it begins charging you starting from 30 seconds after you dial '7' (or '78' or whatever) – the timer does not know if your call succeeds or not so you get charged if you stay on the line over 30 seconds, even if you just let the phone ring repeatedly or get a busy signal! On the other hand, if you complete your conversation within 30 seconds and hang up, you don't get charged at all. The hotel switchboard timer keeps running until you hang up, not when the other party hangs up, so replace the receiver immediately when the conversation ends.

The usual procedure is to make the call and someone comes to your room five or 10 minutes later to collect the cash. If the hotel does not have IDD, you can usually book calls from your room through the switchboard and the operator calls you back, but this procedure will be more expensive.

With domestic direct dialling, it's useful to know the area codes of China's cities. These all begin with zero, but if you're dialling into China from abroad, omit the first zero from each code. China's country code is 86. Some important area codes in Guangdong Province include:

Foshan 0757; Guangzhou 020; Shenzhen 0755; Zhaoqing 0758; Zhongshan 07654; Zhuhai 0756

Essential Numbers There are several telephone numbers which are the same for all major cities. The problem is that the person answering the phone will likely be Chinese-speaking only – if you're looking to practice your Chinese, this is one way to do it.

Fire Hot Line	☎ 119
HK & Macau Directory Assistance	☎ 115
Local Directory Assistance	☎ 114
Long-Distance Directory Assistance	☎ 113, 173
Phone Repair	☎ 112
Police Hot Line	☎ 110

Telecommunication for Expats Short-term visitors need not read this, but those planning to do business, work or study in the PRC have several telecommunication options not available to tourists.

Getting a private telephone installed in your hotel room or apartment is possible in large cities like Guangzhou or Shanghai, but there are long waiting lists and costs are high. Foreigners are sometimes charged extra (and therefore get priority over locals) but installation can still take months and costs approximately US$2000. To get your own phone line, a residence permit is required.

Though considered a luxury in the West, pagers are far more common in China than telephones – even street vendors have them! This is due to the fact that the number of telephone lines available is inadequate to meet demand, but no such problem exists with pagers. Those with a residence permit can obtain a pager in just a couple of weeks, and the cost is low at around US$3 per month.

Those living on a budget, such as foreign students, may well find pagers a more realistic option than having a phone installed.

Cellular telephones are all the rage with status-conscious urban Chinese with money to burn. Despite initial costs of over US$2000 and monthly fees of around US$200, demand easily outstrips the supply of available channels and year-long waiting lists are common in many cities. On the other hand, those who already have a cellular line can sell it to others at a profit, because buying a secondhand line allows one to jump the queue. Indeed, applying for a cellular phone line only to resell it later has become a lucrative business.

Fax, Telex & Telegram

Major hotels usually operate a business centre complete with telephone, fax and telex service, not to mention photocopying and perhaps the use of typewriters and word processors. As a rule, you do not have to be a guest at the hotel to use these services, but you certainly must pay. Prices seem to be pretty uniform regardless of how fancy the hotel is, but it's still not a bad idea to ask the rates first.

International faxes and telexes (other than those to Hong Kong or Macau) cost US$2.65 per minute with a three-minute minimum charge – absurdly expensive to send a one-page fax! International telegram rates are usually around US$0.40 per word, and more for the express service. Rates to Hong Kong and Macau are less.

TIME

Time throughout China is set the same as Hong Kong: eight hours ahead of GMT. China experimented with daylight savings time but has now dropped it.

ELECTRICITY

As in Hong Kong, China uses AC 220 V, 50 Hz. The only difference is in the design of the electrical outlets. There are at least four permutations of electric outlet designs (see illustration).

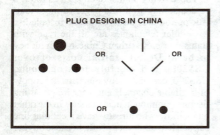

PLUG DESIGNS IN CHINA

Conversion plugs are easily purchased in Hong Kong but are almost impossible to find in China. Battery chargers are widely available, but these are generally unwieldy and not suitable for travelling – buy a small one in Hong Kong. Chinese cities have increasingly experienced power cuts in recent years as the demand for power grows. This is a serious problem in summertime because of the increasing use of air-conditioning.

Given the situation with power failures, a torch (flashlight) is essential survival gear. Chinese flashlights are awful – 50% of the time they don't work and the bulbs seldom last as long as the batteries. Bring a small but good-quality torch from abroad.

LAUNDRY

Most hotels have a laundry service, but check the prices first – some places charge so much you could buy new clothes cheaper. Many travellers wind up washing their own clothes. If you plan on doing this, dark clothes are better since the dirt doesn't show up so clearly.

WEIGHTS & MEASURES

The international metric system is in use. Local Chinese units of weight are still used in markets: the *liang* (37.5 grams) and the *jin* (16 *liang*).

BOOKS & MAPS

There are numerous books about China but rather few dealing specifically with Guangzhou or the Guangdong Province. One of the few is *Kwangtung or Five Years in South China* (Oxford University Press, London, 1982) by the English Wesleyan minister Reverend John Arthur Turner, who worked as a missionary in China from 1886 to 1891. His book was originally published in 1894.

Another early account of Western contact with China comes from the Jesuit priest and missionary Matteo Ricci, who was permitted to take up residence at Zhaoqing near Guangzhou in the late 16th century and in Beijing in 1601. An English translation of his diaries has been published under the title *China in the 16th Century – the Journals of Matteo Ricci 1583-1610*. This book is not easy to find.

Other rare books about Guangzhou include *Canton in Revolution – The Collected papers of Earl Swisher, 1925-1928* (Westview Press, USA, 1977). Also, Ezra F Vogel's *Canton Under Communism* (Harvard University Press, 1969) covers the history of the city from 1949 to 1968.

More general books about China are easier to find and usually more interesting.

People & Society

Classics & Fiction The best-known English fiction about China is *The Good Earth* by Pearl S Buck.

If you want to read a weighty Chinese classic, you could try *Journey to the West*, available in English in a four-volume set in China and some Hong Kong bookstores. Since much of the action takes place along the Silk Road, it's recommended for travellers following that route.

The Dream of the Red Chamber (also known as *The Story of the Stone*) by Cao Xueqin, is a Chinese classic written in the late 18th century. Published in five volumes by Penguin, it's not an easy read. Fortunately, an abridged edition is available from some of the Friendship Stores and foreign language bookshops in China, and perhaps from some shops in Hong Kong and abroad.

The third great Chinese classic is *Outlaws of the Marsh* which is also available in abridged form.

George Orwell's *1984* was ahead of its time in predicting the political trends in the Communist world. *Animal Farm* is perhaps a closer approximation to post-1949 China and its bloated cadres.

Franz Kafka's *The Trial* wasn't written with China in mind, yet his book is a potent reminder of the helplessness of individuals against the all-powerful state bureaucracy.

Recent Accounts *The Search for Modern China* by Jonathan D Spence is the definitive work, often used as a textbook in college courses. If you want to understand the PRC, this is the book to read.

Fox Butterfield's *China – Alive in the Bitter Sea* (Coronet, 1983) is one of the biggest sellers. A harshly critical account, it tells you everything from the location of Chinese labour camps to how women cope with menstruation.

To Get Rich is Glorious (Pantheon Books, 1984) by American scholar and many-times China traveller Orville Schell is a concise and easy-to-read overview of the major changes in China's economic policies and political thinking over the last few years.

An abrasive view of China under Deng Xiaoping is Italian journalist Tiziano Terzani's *Behind the Forbidden Door* (Allen & Unwin, 1986). Terzani, once an avid socialist, became disillusioned after living in China from 1980 to 1984, when he was finally booted out for his critical reporting.

An intriguing and popular book is *The New Emperors* by Harrison E Salisbury. The 'emperors' he refers to are Mao Zedong and Deng Xiaoping.

A moving and now popular book is *Wild Swans* by Jung Chang. The author traces the lives of three Chinese women – the author's grandmother (an escaped concubine with bound feet), her mother and herself.

Seeds of Fire: Chinese Voices of Conscience (Far Eastern Economic Review Ltd, 1986) is an anthology of blistering eloquence from authors such as Wei Jingsheng, Liu Qing, Wang Xizhe and Xu Wenli (imprisoned for their roles in the Democracy Movement) and the poet Sun Jingxuan. Wei Jingsheng's description of Q1, China's top prison for political detainees, is utterly horrific.

The issue of human rights is covered in Amnesty International's *China: Violations of Human Rights* – a grim aspect of the country that should not be ignored.

And a new book by Anchee Min titled *Red Azalea* candidly approaches illicit love in China during the Cultural Revolution. Fiercely critical of the social upheavals under Mao, the book has garnered favourable reviews in the West but been banned in China.

Cultural Revolution The best seller seems to be *Life & Death in Shanghai* by Nien Cheng (Grafton). The author was imprisoned for 6½ years, and this is her gripping story of how she survived.

Other stories from this period include *Born Red* by Gao Yuan (Stanford University Press) and *Son of the Revolution* by Liang Heng and Judith Shapiro (Fontana Paperbacks).

History

The classic on the Chinese Revolution is *Red Star Over China* (Pelican, 1972; first published in 1937) by Edgar Snow. Snow managed to get through the Kuomintang blockade of the Communists and spent four months with them in Yan'an in 1936. His book has been criticised as naive in that it glosses over some of the worst aspects of the Communist movement, but it conveys the hope and idealism of the time.

Chinese Shadows by Simon Leys is one of the most critical books on Mao and the Cultural Revolution. It was published in 1974, based on Leys' visits to China in 1972 and 1973. It's interesting to draw comparisons between the China of the post-Mao era and the one that Leys visited.

Roger Garside's *Coming Alive – China After Mao* describes the events which led to the downfall of the 'Gang of Four' and the rise of Deng Xiaoping. Garside served at the British Embassy in Beijing from 1968 to 1970, and was first secretary from 1976 to 1979.

The Dragon Wakes by Christopher Hibbert (Penguin) is a good history from 1793 to 1911.

The Chinese People Stand Up by Elizabeth Wright (BBC) examines China's turbulent history from 1949 up to the brutal suppression of pro-democracy demonstrators in 1989.

The Soong Dynasty by Sterling Seagrave (Sidgwick & Jackson) is one of the most popular books on the corrupt Kuomintang period. Unfortunately, the author severely damaged his credibility when he later published *The Marcos Dynasty* which contains more rumour than fact.

Random House is due to release *My Life with Chairman Mao*. The author, Dr Li Zhisui, was the personal physician of Mao Zedong. Despite the Communist Party's attempts to depict Mao as a paragon of virtue, Dr Li asserts that the old chairman in his later years spent nearly all his free time in bed with young teenage girls. If true, it could be argued that Mao differed little from the emperors he replaced, who were notorious for keeping legions of concubines.

Guides & Coffee-Table Books

The classic coffee-table book is *A Day in the Life of China* (Merehurst Press). It's very expensive but you get what you pay for.

Just in case you didn't know, Lonely Planet has a few other titles concerning the Chinese world; the *Beijing City Guide* and travel survival kits for *Taiwan* and the big blockbuster *China*.

Maps

Finding maps of Guangzhou and other Chinese cities is easy enough if you don't mind one printed in Chinese characters only. To find one in English, look in the gift shops of the major hotels. Especially recommended are the maps of Guangzhou and Shenzhen by Universal Publications of Hong Kong, which show both Chinese and English. You cannot buy these in China, but they are readily available from most Hong Kong bookstores.

MEDIA

Newspapers & Magazines

News Agencies China has two news agencies, the Xinhua News Agency and the China News Service. The Xinhua (New China) Agency is a national agency with its headquarters in Beijing and branches in each province as well as in the army and many foreign countries. It provides news for the national, provincial and local papers and radio stations, transmits radio broadcasts abroad in foreign languages, and is responsible for making contact with and exchanging news with foreign news agencies. In Hong Kong, Xinhua acts as the unofficial embassy.

The main function of the China News Service is to supply news to Overseas Chinese newspapers and journals, including those in Hong Kong and Macau. It also distributes Chinese documentary films abroad.

Chinese-Language Publications There are nearly 2000 national and provincial newspapers in China. The main one is *Renmin Ribao* (the People's Daily), with nationwide circulation. It was founded in 1946 as the official publication of the Central Committee of the Communist Party. Most of these tend to be exceedingly boring though they do provide a brief rundown of world events.

At the other end of the scale there is China's version of the gutter press – several hundred 'unhealthy papers' and magazines hawked on street corners and bus stations in major cities with nude or violent photos and stories about sex, crime, witchcraft, miracle cures and UFOs. These have been severely criticised by the government for their obscene and racy content – they are also extremely popular. There are also about 40 newspapers for the minority nationalities.

Almost 2200 periodicals were published at the last count, of which about half were technical or scientific. The rest were concerned with social sciences, literature, culture and education, or were general periodicals, pictorials or children's publications. One of the better-known periodicals is the monthly *Hongqi* (Red Flag), the main Communist philosophical and theoretical journal.

In China the newspapers, radio and TV are the last places to carry the news. Westerners tend to be numbed by endless accounts of heroic factory workers and stalwart peasants, and dismiss China's media as a huge propaganda machine. Flipping through journals like *China Today, Women of China* and *China Pictorial* only serves to confirm this view.

Nevertheless, the Chinese press does warrant serious attention since it provides clues to what is happening in China. When Deng Xiaoping returned to public view after being disposed of in the Cultural Revolution, the first mention was simply the inclusion of his name in a guest list at a reception for Prince Sihanouk of Kampuchea, printed in the *People's Daily* without elaboration or comment. Political struggles between factions are described in articles in the Chinese newspapers as a means of warning off any supporters of the opposing side and undermining its position rather than resorting to an all-out, dangerous conflict. The 'Letters to the Editor' section in the *People's Daily* provides something of a measure of public opinion, and complaints are sometimes followed up by reporters.

Newspapers and journals are useful for following the 'official line' of the Chinese government – though in times of political struggle they tend to follow the line of whoever has control over the media.

Foreign-Language Publications China publishes various newspapers, books and magazines in a number of European and Asian languages. The only English-language newspaper (and one which you are most likely to come across during your travels) is *China Daily*, first published in June 1981 which now has two overseas editions (Hong Kong and the USA). Overseas subscriptions can be obtained from the following sources:

Hong Kong
Wen Wei Po, 197 Wanchai Rd (☎ 5722211; fax 5720441)
USA
China Daily Distribution Corporation, Suite 401, 15 Mercer St, New York, NY 10013 (☎ (212) 2190130; fax 2100108)

Although you might stumble across some of the English-language magazines in luxury hotels and Friendship Stores, they are readily available by subscription. These can be posted to you overseas. The place to subscribe is not in China itself, but Hong Kong. If interested, contact Peace Book Company (☎ 8967382; fax 8976251), 17th floor, Paramount Building, 12 Ka Yip St, Chai Wan, Hong Kong. You can write, fax or drop by the office for their catalogue. A rundown of what's available in English and other foreign languages follows, in alphabetical order:

Beijing Review – a weekly magazine on political and current affairs. Valuable for learning about China's latest half-baked political policies. The magazine is published in English, French, Spanish, German and Japanese.
China Medical Abstracts – a special-interest quarterly magazine in English.
China Philately – a bimonthly magazine in English for stamp collectors.
China Pictorial – a monthly large-format glossy magazine with neat photos, cultural and historical stuff. It's available in English, French, Spanish, German and Japanese.
China Screen – a quarterly magazine in English or Chinese with a focus on the Chinese motion picture industry.
China Sports – an English-language monthly which helps demonstrate the superiority of Chinese athletes over foreigners.

China Today – a monthly magazine. The magazine was founded in 1952 by Song Qingling (the wife of Sun Yatsen) and used to be called *China Reconstructs*. The name was changed in 1989 because – as one official said – '37 years is a hell of a long time to be reconstructing your country'.

China's Foreign Trade – a monthly publication in English, French, Spanish or Chinese, with a self-explanatory title.

China's Patents & Trademarks – a quarterly magazines in Chinese and English. The title is self-explanatory.

China's Tibet – a quarterly magazine in Chinese or English. Its chief purpose is to convince overseas readers that China's historical claim to Tibet is more than just hot air. Some of the articles about Tibetan culture and religion might prove interesting.

Chinese Literature – a quarterly magazine in English or French. Topics include poetry, fiction, profiles of Chinese writers and so on.

El Popola Cinio – a monthly magazine in Esperanto – good if you want to familiarise yourself with this language.

Kexue Tongbao – a semi-monthly publication in English with a focus on the sciences.

Nexus – a quarterly magazine in English. It is claimed that this is China's first non-government funded magazine in English (who knows?). Articles cover various aspects of Chinese culture and society.

Shanghai Pictorial – a bimonthly magazine available in Chinese or English. Photos of fashionable women dressed in the latest, as well as container ships, cellular telephones and other symbols of Shanghai's developing economy.

Social Sciences in China – a quarterly publication in English. The magazine covers topics like archaeology, economics, philosophy, literature and a whole range of academic pursuits by Chinese scholars.

Women of China – a monthly magazine in English designed to show foreigners that Chinese women are not treated as badly as they really are.

The government also publishes impressive glossy magazines in minority languages such as Tibetan. These appear to be strictly for foreign consumption – they are not available in China.

Imported Publications In large cities like Beijing, Shanghai and Guangzhou, it's fairly easy to score copies of popular imported English-language magazines like *Time*, *Newsweek*, *Far Eastern Economic Review* and *The Economist*. Occasionally you might find European magazines in French or German. Foreign newspapers like the *Asian Wall Street Journal*, *International Herald-Tribune* and Hong Kong's *South China Morning Post* are also available. Imported periodicals are available from the big tourist hotels.

To China's credit, foreign-language magazines and newspapers are seldom, if ever, censored, even when they contain stories critical of the PRC. Of course, a different set of rules apply to Chinese-language publications from Hong Kong and Taiwan – essentially, these cannot be brought into China without special permission.

There seems to be no import duty on foreign magazines and newspapers, and prices are not out of line with what you'd pay in Hong Kong.

Radio & TV
After years attempting to tear down their TV antennas and jam foreign broadcasting, many Cantonese now own satellite dishes and receive Hong Kong's transmission of the latest bourgeois and subversive episodes of Western programmes which the authorities believe have ruinous influences on their moral and ideological purity.

In the border areas of Shenzhen and Zhuhai it is easy to pick up English-language broadcasts from Hong Kong. In Guangzhou, some hotels have good enough antennas to pick up Hong Kong TV stations.

Chinese TV is broadcast in either Cantonese or Mandarin. The only English-language programmes are occasional old foreign movies or educational shows that attempt to teach English. Most foreigners find Chinese TV dull, but it has at least one redeeming feature – there are very few advertisements.

Noticeboards
Apart from the mass media, the public noticeboard retains its place as an important means of educating the people or influencing public opinion. Other people who want to get a message across glue up big wallposters in public places. This is a traditional form of communicating ideas in China and if the

content catches the attention of even a few people then word-of-mouth can spread it very quickly. Deng Xiaoping personally stripped from China's constitution the right to put up wallposters.

Public noticeboards abound in China. Two of the most common subjects are crime and accidents. In China it's often graphic – before-and-after photos of executed criminals are plugged up on boards along with descriptions of their heinous offences. Some memorable photos include any number of people squashed by trucks, blown-up by fireworks or fried after smoking cigarettes near open petrol tanks. Other popular themes include industrial safety and family planning. Inspiring slogans such as 'The PLA Protects the People' or 'Follow the Socialist Road to Happiness' are also common.

FILM & PHOTOGRAPHY

In China you'll get a fantastic run for your money – for starters there are 1.2 billion portraits to work your way through. Religious reasons for avoiding photographs are absent among the Han Chinese – some guy isn't going to stick a spear through you for taking a picture of his wife and stealing part of her soul – though you probably won't be allowed to take photos of statues in many Buddhist temples.

Some Chinese shy away from having their photo taken, and even duck for cover. Others are proud to pose and will ham it up for the camera – and they're especially proud if you're taking a shot of their kid. Nobody expects any payment for photos – so don't give any or you'll set a precedent. What the Chinese would go for, though, is a copy of a colour photo, which you could mail to them. People also tend to think that the negative belongs to the subject as well, and they'll ask for both the negative and the print – but through the post there's no argument.

There are three basic approaches to photographing people. One is the polite 'ask-for-permission-and-pose-it' shot, which is sometimes rejected. Another is the 'no-holds barred and upset everyone' approach. The third is surreptitious, standing

half a km away with a metre-long telephoto lens. Many Chinese will disagree with you on what constitutes good subject matter. Somehow, they don't really see why anyone would want to take a street scene, a picture of a beggar or a shot of butchered dogs on display in the market.

Another objection often brought up is that the subject is not 'dignified' – be it a labourer straining down the street with a massive load on his handcart, or a barrel of excrement on wheels. The official line is that peasants and workers are the glorious heroes of China, but you'll have a tough time convincing your photo subject of this.

A lot of Chinese still cannot afford a camera and resort to photographers at tourist places. The photographers supply dress-up clothing for that extra touch. The subjects change from street clothing into spiffy gear and sometimes even bizarre costumes and make-up for the shot. Others use cardboard props such as opera stars or boats.

The standard shot is one or more Chinese standing in front of something significant. A temple, waterfall, heroic statue or important vintages of calligraphy are considered suitable backgrounds. At amusement parks, Mickey Mouse and Donald Duck get into nearly every photo – Ronald McDonald and the Colonel of Kentucky Fried fame are favourite photo companions at these prestigious restaurants. If you hang around these places you can sometimes clip off a few portrait photos for yourself, but don't be surprised if your photo subjects suddenly drag you into the picture as an exotic prop!

Film

Imported film is relatively expensive, but major Japanese companies like Fuji and Konica now have factories in China – this has brought prices of colour print film down to what you'd pay in the West, sometimes less. While colour print film is available almost anywhere, it's often 100 ASA (21 DIN).

Genuine Chinese brands of film are a big unknown – some are good and some are trash, so you'll just have to experiment if you want to use the stuff. Another big unknown is whether or not these films will work with fully-automatic cameras which need to sense the film speed. The letters 'DX' printed on a box of film indicates that it is suitable for automatic cameras, but I have yet to see a Chinese brand carrying this designation. However, most automatic cameras default to 100 ASA when the film isn't DX, which should eliminate the problem.

Black & white film can be found in Guangzhou's larger department stores, but in general it's hard to buy in China – colour photos are now all the rage.

In general, colour slide film is hard to find – check out major hotels, department stores and Friendship Stores if you get caught short. When you do find slide film, it's usually expensive and sometimes out-of-date, though last year's slide film is still better than none. Ektachrome and Fujichrome can be found in Guangzhou – Kodachrome and Agfachrome are practically unknown in China. Polaroid film is rumoured to exist, but if you need the stuff, you'd better bring your own supply.

Finding the special lithium batteries used by many cameras is also hit or miss and you'd be wise to bring a spare. Some cameras have a manual mode which allows you to continue shooting with a dead battery, though the light meter won't work. Fully-automatic cameras totally drop dead when the battery goes.

Video cameras were once subject to shaky regulations but there seems to be no problem now. The biggest problem is recharging your batteries off the strange mutations of plugs in China – bring all the adaptors you can, and remember that it's 220 V.

You're allowed to bring in 8 mm movie cameras but 16 mm or professional equipment may raise eyebrows with customs. Motion picture film is hard enough to find in the West these days, and next to impossible in China.

Processing
Major cities like Guangzhou and Shenzhen are equipped with the latest Japanese photoprocessing machines. Quality colour prints

can be turned out in one or two hours at reasonable cost.

It's a different situation with colour slides. Ektachrome and Fujichrome can be processed in Guangzhou but this can be expensive and quality is not assured. If you don't want your slides scratched, covered with fingerprints or over-developed, save the processing until you get home. Kodachrome film cannot be processed in China.

Undeveloped film can be sent out of China and, going by personal experience only, the dreaded X-ray machines do not appear to be a problem.

Prohibited Subjects
Photography from planes and photographs of airports, military installations, harbour facilities and railroad terminals are prohibited. Bridges may also be a touchy subject. These rules invariably get enforced if the enforcers happen to be around.

One traveller, bored at the airport, started photographing the X-ray procedure in clearance. PLA men promptly pounced on her and ripped the film out.

In an age where satellites can zoom down on a number plate it all seems a bit absurd, but many countries have similarly ridiculous restrictions on photography.

Taking photos is not permitted in most museums, at archaeological sites and in many temples, mainly to protect the postcard and colour slide industry.

Be aware that these rules are generally enforced. If you want to snap a few photos in prohibited spots then start with a new roll of film – if that's ripped out of your camera at least you don't lose 20 other photos as well. Monks can be vigorous enforcers of this rule in temples. They can rip film out of cameras faster than you can cock the shutter – must be some special martial arts training.

HEALTH
China presents few health problems for the short-term visitor. The following discussion is a somewhat paranoid worse-case scenario of what could happen to you. Still, it's worth

reading to understand what nasty diseases are about and how to best prevent them.

Predeparture Preparations

Vaccinations Very few people are required to have vaccinations but there are several that are certainly recommended. If you're arriving within six days after leaving or transiting a yellow fever infected area then a vaccination is required.

Vaccinations which have been recommended by various health authorities include: cholera, meningitis, rabies, hepatitis A, hepatitis B, BCG (tuberculosis), polio, and TABT (protects against typhoid, paratyphoid A and B, and tetanus) and diphtheria. Most travellers from Western countries will have been immunised against various diseases during childhood but your doctor may still recommend booster shots against measles or polio. Always be aware that the period of protection offered by vaccinations differs widely and some are contraindicated if you are pregnant.

You should have your vaccinations recorded in an International Health Certificate. If you are travelling with children, it's especially important to be sure that they've had all necessary vaccinations.

Health Insurance This is covered in the Hong Kong section. If you don't have health insurance, Hong Kong is not a bad place to pick up a policy.

Basic Rules

Food & Water Water is chlorinated in large cities like Guangzhou, but it's still advisable to boil it. Virtually all hotels provide flasks with boiled water. Bottled water is widely available from kiosks and stores.

Shellfish and seafood of any kind pose the greatest risks of all, from spoilage (due to lack of refrigeration) and water pollution. Some of the rivers and bays in China are positively toxic, yet you often see people fishing in them. Better restaurants only buy fish which are raised in commercial ponds, and the fish are kept alive in aquariums until just before cooking – unfortunately, not all restaurants are so scrupulous.

Medical Problems & Treatment

Diarrhoea See the Hong Kong section for details.

The 'China Syndrome' The Chinese call it *ganmao* and it's usually the most common and serious ailment to afflict visitors in China. In most countries it's known as influenza or even the common cold, but it's uncommonly bad in China. Few probably remember the notorious 'Hong Kong flu' of 1968, but you may have heard of the 'Shanghai flu' which in 1989 killed over 26,000 people in the UK alone. There have been various other influenza strains named after Chinese cities. The fact is that China is the world's prime reservoir of influenza viruses.

What distinguishes Chinese viruses from the Western variety is the ubiquitousness of the infections – practically the entire population of 1.2 billion is stricken during the winter. Many wonder why this is so. Medical experts give several reasons: respiratory infections are aggravated by cold weather, poor nutrition and China's notorious air pollution. Smoking definitely makes it worse, and practically everyone in China smokes. Overcrowded conditions increase the opportunity for infection. But the main reason is that Chinese people spit a lot, thereby spreading the disease. It's a vicious circle: they're sick because they spit and they spit because they're sick.

The law of natural selection (only the fit survive) guarantees that the average Chinese person has a fairly high level of immunity to influenza. However, visiting foreigners are easy prey for these diseases. Now that so many people visit previously-closed China, the viruses are easily spread worldwide.

Like any bad case of the flu, it starts with a fever, chills, weakness, sore throat and a feeling of malaise normally lasting a few days. After that, a prolonged case of coughing sets in, characterised by coughing up large quantities of thick green phlegm, occasionally with little red streaks (blood). This

CANTON

condition is known as bronchitis and it makes sleep almost impossible. This exhausting state of affairs can continue for as long as you stay in China, and many foreigners find that they can only get well by leaving the country.

During the initial phase of influenza, bed rest, drinking warm liquids and keeping warm are helpful. The Chinese treat bronchitis with a powder made from the gall bladder of snakes – of questionable value but probably no harm in trying it. If you continue to cough up green phlegm, run a fever and can't seem to get well, it's time to roll out the heavy artillery – you can nuke it with antibiotics. Tetracycline (250 mg) taken orally four times daily for a minimum of five days is usually effective. Once you start on a course of antibiotics, it's important to continue until the pills are all gone, not just for three days until you feel better. Otherwise, a complete relapse is likely.

Antibiotics are not always available in China. While they are sometimes obtained in hospitals, it wouldn't be a bad idea to bring some with you for emergency use. They can often be bought cheaply across the counter in many countries in South-East Asia (Taiwan and Thailand are good places to stock up). Antibiotics can have unpleasant side effects, especially on women since it makes them prone to yeast infections. In both sexes, antibiotics can upset the balance of intestinal flora. Therefore, this should be a measure of last resort.

Finally, if you can't get well in China, leave the country and take a nice holiday on a warm beach in Thailand.

Malaria Malaria exists in China, but it's hardly a problem in the Guangzhou area. If you intend visiting the cities only briefly, you shouldn't worry much about it. However, long-term visitors heading for remote rural areas could encounter the disease, especially during summer.

Malaria is spread by mosquitoes which transmit the parasite that causes the disease. Symptoms include headaches, fever, chills and sweating which may subside and recur.

Without treatment malaria can develop more serious, potentially fatal effects.

Protection is simple – a daily or weekly tablet which kill the parasites if they enter your bloodstream. The most common anti-malarials are chloroquine, maloprim and proguqanil. Chloroquine is available over the counter from pharmacies in Hong Kong. You have to start taking it about two weeks before entering the malarial zone and must continue taking them for several weeks after you've left. Some strains of malaria are now chloroquine-resistant. In any event, you should not take this drug (or any other) over the long-term without medical supervision.

Doxycycline is a good preventative for the short term (under one month) traveller. It's definitely not recommended for long-term use. Doxycycline is a long-acting tetracycline (antibiotic). It is not recommended during pregnancy, breastfeeding or for children under age 10 years. Side effects include nausea, photosensitivity (severe sunburn) and vaginal yeast infections in women. It should not be taken with milk products. The preventative dose is 100 mg (one pill) daily. You should start taking doxycycline the day you enter the malarial area, and stop taking it the day you leave. Doxycycline is available in Hong Kong by prescription only and is often taken in combination with chloroquine.

Qing Haosu (Artemesinine) is a herbal medicine from China which has been used successfully to treat and prevent malaria. It's important to note that just because this is a 'herbal medicine' it does not mean it's harmless. Preliminary testing in animals suggest it is toxic to the foetus and not recommended in pregnancy.

Whether or not you decide to take anti-malarial drugs, you should at least try to avoid getting bitten in the first place. Take some rub-on mosquito repellent – OFF! and Autan are two popular brands widely available in Hong Kong. Some Chinese hotels have mosquito nets (wénzhàang). Mosquito repellent is available but you may have trouble finding it, so bring your own. Mosquito coils (wénxiāng) are readily available, but a more modern innovation are the 'electric mosquito mats' *(diàn wénxiāng)* on sale at Chinese department stores.

Tuberculosis *(jiéhé bìng)* The tuberculosis (TB) bacteria is transmitted by inhalation. Coughing spreads infectious droplets into the air. In closed, crowded spaces with poor ventilation (like a train compartment) the air can remain contaminated for some time. In overcrowded China, where the custom is to cough and spit in every direction, it's not hard to see why infection rates remain high.

Many carriers of TB experience no symptoms, but the disease stays with them for life. The infection is opportunistic – the patient feels fine, but the disease suddenly becomes active when the body is weakened by other factors such as injury, poor nutrition, surgery or old age. People in good health are less likely to catch it. TB strikes the lungs and the fatality rate is about 10%.

There are good drugs to treat TB, but prevention is the best cure. If you're only going to be in China for a short time there is no need to be overly worried. TB is usually contracted after repeated exposures. Budget travellers – those who often spend a long time staying in cramped dormitories and travelling on crowded buses and trains – are at greater risk than tourists who remain relatively isolated in big hotels and tour buses.

The effective vaccine for TB is called BCG and is most often given to school children (a high-risk group). The disadvantage of the vaccine is that, once given, the recipient will always test positive with the TB skin test.

Sexually Transmitted Diseases The Chinese government for decades pretended that prostitution, premarital and extramarital sex simply didn't exist in the PRC, and that sexually transmitted diseases (STDs) were a foreign problem.

The Cultural Revolution may be over, but the sexual revolution is booming in China and STDs are spreading rapidly. Refer to the Hong Kong section on Health for further details.

Hepatitis A *(A gān yán)* Hepatitis is a disease which affects the liver. There are several varieties, but the most common are hepatitis A and B. Hepatitis A occurs in countries with poor sanitation – this would have to include the more remote parts of China. It's spread from person to person via infected food or water, or contaminated cooking and eating utensils.

Hepatitis is often spread in China due to the Chinese custom of everybody eating from a single dish rather than using separate plates and a serving spoon. It is a wise decision to use the disposable chopsticks now freely available in most restaurants in China, or else buy your own chopsticks and spoon.

Symptoms appear 15 to 50 days after infection (generally around 25 days) and consist of fever, loss of appetite, nausea, depression, complete lack of energy, and pains around the bottom of your rib cage (the location of the liver). Your skin turns progressively yellow and the whites of your eyes change from white to yellow to orange.

The best way to detect hepatitis is to watch the colour of your urine, which will turn a deep orange no matter how much liquid you drink. If you haven't drunk much liquid and/or you're sweating a lot, don't jump to conclusions since you may only be dehydrated.

The severity of hepatitis A varies. It may last less than two weeks and give you only a few bad days, or it may last for several months and give you a few bad weeks. You could feel depleted of energy for several months afterwards. If you get hepatitis, rest and good food is the only cure. Don't use alcohol or tobacco since that only gives your liver more work to do. It's important to keep up your food intake to assist recovery.

A vaccine for hepatitis A came on the market in 1992. It's not widely available yet, but it should be possible to get it. Check with your doctor.

Hepatitis B *(B gān yán)* Hepatitis B is transmitted the same three ways the AIDS virus spreads: by sexual intercourse; contaminated needles; or inherited by an infant from an

CANTON

infected mother. Some Chinese 'health clinics' re-use needles without proper sterilisation – no one knows how many people have been infected this way. Acupuncture can also spread the disease.

There is a vaccine for hepatitis B, but it must be given before you've been exposed. Once you've got the virus, you're a carrier for life and the vaccine is useless. Therefore, you need a blood test before the vaccine is administered to determine if you're a carrier. The vaccine requires three injections each given a month apart, and it's wise to get a booster every few years thereafter. Unfortunately, the vaccine is expensive.

Hepatitis C & Others Recent research has found other varieties of hepatitis of which little is yet known. Hepatitis C, which is similar to B but less common, and other strains are considered serious. Hepatitis D is also similar to B and always occurs in concert with it; its occurrence is currently limited to IV drug users. Hepatitis E, however, is similar to A and is spread in the same manner – by water or food contamination.

Travellers shouldn't be too paranoid about this apparent proliferation of hepatitis strains; they are fairly rare (so far) and following the same precautions as for A and B should be all that's necessary to avoid them.

Bedbugs & Lice (*chòuchóng, shī*) Bedbugs live in various places, particularly in dirty mattresses and bedding. Spots of blood on bedclothes or on the wall around the bed can be read as a suggestion to find another hotel. Bedbugs leave itchy bites in neat rows that swell up, but they generally heal quickly if you don't scratch.

All lice cause itching and discomfort. They make themselves at home in your hair (head lice), your clothing (body lice) or in your pubic hair (crabs). You catch lice through direct contact with infected people or by sharing combs, clothing and the like. Powder or shampoo treatment will kill the lice and infected clothing should then be washed in very hot water.

Women's Health

Women may need to take special precautions with their health. For example, if you're prone to yeast infections, bring your own medication (Nystatin suppositories). Tampons are not available and Chinese sanitary pads are big and bulky. Contraceptives are widely available but not always reliable.

Public Toilets

Toilet paper is never provided in the toilets at bus and railway stations or other public buildings (mainly because people steal it), so you'd be wise to keep a stash of your own with you at all times. Only in big modern hotels can you hope to find toilet paper.

In hotels, the toilets are clearly labelled in English, but in most public buildings only Chinese is used. To avoid embarrassment, try to remember:

Men   Women

In China, as in most Asian countries, you can expect to encounter squat toilets. For the uninitiated who don't know what I'm talking about, a squat toilet has no seat for you to sit on while reading the morning newspaper. In other words, it's a hole in the floor but it flushes (usually).

At other times, instead of finding a hole you might encounter a ditch with water running through it. Both the hole and the ditch take some getting used to. It takes skill to balance yourself over this device, all the while taking care that your comb, passport and other valuables in your pockets don't fall into the abyss. It's not made any easier by the fact that most public toilets don't have doors, so all the world can watch as you try to deal with this particular aspect of culture shock.

If it's any consolation, you may be pleased

to know that the squat position is considered more natural and better for your body's digestive system. Also, many Westerners consider it more sanitary since no part of the body touches the toilet.

Apparently, many Chinese do not care for the sit-down toilets used in the West. In China's big hotels where Western-style toilets are available, you'll often find big black footprints and urine on the seats, as it seems that many Chinese stand on the toilet seat and then squat – they really do make a mess out of it.

In many places, the plumbing system cannot adequately handle toilet paper. In that case, you should toss the paper into a waste basket provided for that purpose.

WOMEN TRAVELLERS
Western women report relatively little sexual harassment in China. The biggest complaints come from women with Asian features – indeed, some have been raped. All women visitors should take the precaution of dressing conservatively. Shorts are acceptable for women, though it's better to wear the longish variety rather than the fashionable 'hot pants' favoured by young Hong Kong women.

DANGERS & ANNOYANCES
Visiting any country involves hassles and some culture shock. China is not the worst for this, but there are certain aspects of the culture that set Westerners on edge. Remember not to get overly upset and lose your temper. The best advice is to learn to laugh it off. Among the things you will have to learn to live with are:

Staring Squads
You'd better get used to it. Getting stared at is a common feature of travel in Asia, but in China it's a national sport. Pity the poor travellers who came to China 10 years ago when very few Chinese had ever seen a foreigner. At that time, it wasn't unusual for a visitor to quickly be encircled by a congregation of gaping onlookers. Walk down the street and the crowd would follow. Stop

awhile and the crowd would wait, never growing tired and never making any attempt to communicate with the extraterrestrial being. Staring back never seemed to help. Indeed, the crowd would love it. Some people would run and get their children so they could enjoy the show too.

The good news is that things have improved, especially in Guangzhou where foreigners are plentiful. The audience is beginning to show signs of staring fatigue, but it depends partly on how foreign you look. Tall, blond-haired blue-eyed travellers can still attract a larger crowd than the monkeys at the Guangzhou Zoo. Black people seem to get it worst – some black travellers have said they would never go back to China for just this reason.

The best way to avoid being stared at is to keep moving. Stopping on the street to read a map or to write something is particularly inviting. People will come to stare over your shoulder to see what you're reading.

Spitting
Clearing your throat and discharging the phlegm on the floor or out the window (to the peril of those below) is perfectly acceptable in China. Everyone does it – any time, any place. It's not as bad in summer, but in winter – when many people are afflicted by the notorious 'China Syndrome' – you'll have a hard time keeping out of the crossfire!

Littering
The environmental movement has not reached China. Rather than carry the trash down the stairs once a day to the rubbish bins, many Chinese find it more convenient to dump it out the window. (You get a hint of this in Hong Kong at Chungking Mansions – just look in the light-wells in the centre of the building.) Sewer grates are also convenient garbage dumps. Restaurants and street vendors usually dump all uneaten food down the sewer, much to the joy of the rats who inhabit the underworld.

I once took a boat cruise on the Pearl River in Guangzhou, and while sitting on the lower deck, I watched in astonishment as it literally rained garbage from the upper deck. Unable to bring myself to toss trash in the river, I deposited my garbage in a rubbish bin near the ship's snack bar. About an hour later, I saw an employee take the rubbish bin and dump the contents overboard.

Nevertheless, the streets in China are reasonably clean, but not because civic-minded citizens are careful with their rubbish. The government employs a small army of people who do nothing all day but sweep up the continual mess. Otherwise the country would be buried in it.

Push & Shove

When Mao was alive, leftists in Western countries pointed to the PRC as a model of harmony and happiness, where smiling peasants joined hands and worked together in a cooperative effort to build a better society.

Undoubtedly, many of them were dismayed when they finally did get to visit the PRC and saw what the Chinese go through to get on a bus. No cooperative effort, just panicked mobs frantically pushing, shoving and clawing to be first. Those who want to get off the bus are shoved right back inside by those who want to get on. In a few notorious incidents (mostly involving overcrowded ferries), people have been trampled to death.

When it comes to buying railway tickets, the same situation exists – mobs of people battle for a limited number of seats. Only the fit survive. Foreign tourists can be spared this. CITS will buy railway and aeroplane tickets for you, or you can get them from special ticket offices in the railway stations which only serve foreigners and high-ranking cadres.

Crime

Until recently, China was safer than most Western countries and the police did not even carry guns. Unfortunately, the situation is deteriorating quickly and Guangzhou is easily the worst city in China when it comes to crime. Pickpockets are common and foreigners, who are always assumed to be rich,

are prime targets. Some pickpockets have become quite professional, working in groups in which one person diverts your attention while another slits open your bag or pocket with a razor blade and empties the contents. There is no foolproof defence, but keeping your passport and travellers' cheques deeply buried under your clothes in a moneybelt is wise. Be especially careful on buses and other crowded places.

Violent crime is also increasing. Knife-wielding gangs attack passengers on trains and jump off as the train approaches a station. So far, the criminals have shown a preference for robbing Chinese and leaving foreigners alone, but this is starting to change too. Although there are periodic roundups and executions of criminals, the police often show a stunning lack of interest in getting involved when someone reports a crime.

Beware of getting robbed in the Qingping Market in Guangzhou. First some young man kept following us and asked if we wanted to buy all sorts of things. Then some old man asked if we were interested in buying a Ming vase. We started to follow him 'to his shop' and he tried to lead us into a narrow dark alley full of waiting unemployed 'street people'.

Price Gouging

Overall, Hong Kong is worse when it comes to price gouging, but Guangzhou is hardly a hotbed of honesty. It probably wouldn't matter if they only charged us double, but I've seen attempts to charge foreigners 10 times the going price for services such as doing laundry or a simple shoe repair.

It's a good idea to agree on a price before using a service. Barring that, if you're absolutely sure that somebody is trying to rip you off, the best defence is to start making a lot of noise. A crowd will immediately gather, and this tends to intimidate the person who is trying to cheat you. Furthermore, many Chinese are likely to intervene on your behalf if they see that someone is trying to cheat you. Cheating is not, as some foreigners believe, culturally acceptable in China.

WORK

There are opportunities to teach English and

other foreign languages, or even other technical skills if you're qualified. Teaching in China is not a way to get rich – pay is roughly US$180 a month, payable in Chinese yuan rather than foreign currency. While this is roughly four times what the average urban Chinese worker earns, it won't get you far after you've left China. There are usually some fringe benefits like free or low-cost housing and special ID cards that get you discounts on trains and flights. As a worker in China, you will be assigned to a 'work unit', but unlike the locals you'll be excused from political meetings and the all-encompassing controls over your life that the typical Chinese has to endure.

It's become fairly typical for universities to pressure foreigners into working excessive hours. A maximum teaching load should be 20 hours per week, and even this is a lot – you can insist on no more than 15. Chinese professors teach far fewer hours than this – some hardly show up for class at all since they often have outside business interests.

Two topics which cannot be discussed in the classroom are politics and religion. Foreigners teaching in China have reported spies being placed in their classrooms. Other teachers have found microphones hidden in their dormitory rooms (one fellow we know took revenge by attaching his stereo to the microphone wires and blasting the snoops with punk music!).

People with technical skills and the ability to speak Chinese can sometimes land lucrative jobs with large foreign companies, but this is not accomplished easily. Such jobs are often advertised in the *China Daily*.

Doing Business

At one time, China was the world's most advanced nation. The Chinese invented gunpowder, rockets, the printing press and paper currency. How did such an advanced nation fall so far behind? Probably because the Chinese also invented bureaucracy.

In bureaucratic China, even simple things can be made difficult – renting property,

---

Setting Up Business in China

Buying is simple, selling more difficult, but setting up business in China is a whole different can of worms.

If yours is a high-technology company, you can go into certain economic zones and register as a wholly foreign-owned enterprise. In that case you can hire people yourself without going through the government, enjoy a three-year tax holiday, obtain long-term income tax advantages, import duty-free personal items for corporate and expat use (including a car!). The alternative is listing your company as a representative office, which does not allow you to sign any contracts in China – these must be signed by the mother company. The Foreign Service Company (FESCO) is where you hire employees. FESCO currently demands around US$325 per month per employee, 75% of which goes to the government.

It's easier to register as a representative office. First find out where you want to set up (a city or Special Economic Zone), then go through local authorities (there are no national authorities for this). Go to the local Commerce Office, Economic Ministry, Foreign Ministry, or any ministry that deals with foreign economic trade promotion. Setting up in a 'high-technology zone' is recommended if you can qualify, but where you register depends on what type of business you're doing. Contact your embassy first – they can advise you.

The most important thing to remember when you go to register a company is not to turn away when you run into a bureaucratic barrier. Bureaucrats will tell you that everything is 'impossible'. In fact, anything is possible – it all depends on your *guanxi* (relationships). Whatever you have in mind is negotiable – all the rules are not necessarily rules at all.

Tax rates vary from zone to zone, authority to authority – it seems to be negotiable but 15% is fairly standard in economic zones. Every economic zone has a fairly complete investment guide in English and Chinese – your embassy's economic council might have these, and these investment guides are becoming very clear (but even all these printed 'rules' are negotiable!). ■

getting a telephone installed, hiring employees, paying taxes, etc, all generate mind-boggling quantities of red tape. Many foreign business people who have worked in China say that success is usually the result of dogged persistence and finding cooperative officials.

If you have any intention of doing business in China, be it buying, selling or investing, it's worth knowing that most towns and – in large cities – many neighbourhoods, have a Commerce Office (*shāngyè jú*). If you approach one of these offices for assistance, the reaction you get varies from enthusiastic welcome to bureaucratic inertia. In case of a dispute (the goods you ordered are not what was delivered, etc), the Commerce Office could assist you, provided that they are willing.

ACTIVITIES
Taijiquan
If you don't mind getting up at the crack of dawn, you can join the Chinese in any park for an early morning taiji session.

Fitness Clubs
Swimming pools, gymnasiums, weightlifting rooms, etc, are popular ways to keep fit and enjoy yourself. While swimming pools and gymnasiums exist for the Chinese public, they are generally overcrowded and in poor condition. You'll find better facilities at the tourist hotels, but of course it won't be free (unless you're a guest at the hotel). Most hotels in big cities like Guangzhou permit non-guests to use the workout rooms, pools, saunas, tennis courts, etc, on a fee basis. This is not a bad idea if you're staying for a month or more – monthly fees typically start at around US$50.

Sauna & Massage
Sauna and massage have really caught on, but tend to be expensive, though still cheaper than Hong Kong. You can find these at the large hotels, though there are now some small, privately run spas. Unlike Macau, saunas in China are not generally connected with prostitution (but that too might be changing).

Courses
As China continues to experiment with capitalism, universities have found it increasingly necessary to raise their own funds and not depend so much on State largesse. For this reason, most universities welcome fee-paying foreign students. Most of the courses offered are Chinese language study, but other possibilities include Chinese medicine, acupuncture, brush painting, music, etc. If you've got the cash, almost anything is possible.

There is considerable variation in the quality of instruction and the prices charged. Tuition alone typically runs from US$1000 to US$3000 per year, sometimes double that, and it may depend on your nationality. The university is supposed to arrange your accommodation (no, it's not free) – living conditions vary from reasonably comfortable to horrific.

It's worth knowing that you'll probably have to pay some additional fees and service charges you weren't told about when you first enrolled. Examples include extra fees for a 'health certificate' or a 'study licence', etc. Sometimes these fees are imposed by the PSB which wants its share of the cash, but often the university itself is keeping the money – the fees vary from reasonable to ridiculous.

If possible, don't pay anything in advance – show up at the school to assess the situation yourself, and talk to other foreign students to see if they're satisfied. Once you've handed over the cash, don't expect a refund.

The Chinese Language Centre of Zhongshan University in Guangzhou, at 135 Xingang Xilu, offers a language course in Chinese.

HIGHLIGHTS
Guangzhou is an interesting city and a worthwhile place to visit, but it would be dishonest to describe it as beautiful. The main attraction is the feeling of being in China – the street markets, temples, the food, the chaos, surprising prosperity amidst

crushing poverty, etc. The same could be said for most of the area around Guangzhou known as the Pearl River delta. While just over a decade ago the area was primarily farmland, the delta is now covered by factories, dishevelled worker flats and shanties. Many tourists take one look and conclude that this area is extremely poor. In fact, it's much the opposite. The Pearl River delta is the wealthiest region in China. The wrecked environment is the price paid for rapid economic growth unencumbered by planning or organisation.

However, there are some major attractions in and around Guangzhou. Within the city itself are a few charming spots like Yuexiu Park, the Pearl River Cruise and Shamian Island. The Qingping Market is morbidly fascinating but not for animal lovers. The Southern Yue Tomb Museum and Chen Clan Academy get good reviews from travellers.

Real scenic beauty can be found outside the cities. Highlights include Zhaoqing, Dinghushan, Luofushan, Xiqiao Hills, Lotus Mountain and the White Cloud Hills.

ACCOMMODATION

The PSB prohibits foreigners from staying in the dirt-cheap Chinese hotels. Privately run guesthouses, such as Hong Kong's Chungking Mansions, are also forbidden. As a result, travellers are forced into more upmarket accommodation.

This is a real problem for budget travellers, who would prefer a cheap dormitory to luxurious accommodation. At the present time, there is only one real budget hotel remaining in Guangzhou – the Guangzhou Youth Hostel on Shamian Island, and this place often fills up.

Fortunately, there are a few tricks in keeping the hotel bill down. The simplest way is to share a room – double rooms usually cost the same as singles in China. Triple rooms are only slightly more, and most hotels will even install a fourth bed in your room for a small extra fee. With four travellers sharing a room, a mid-range hotel should cost no more than a dormitory. If you hang out near the door of the Guangzhou Youth Hostel when it's all full, you can probably solicit some other travellers to be your roommates.

A mid-range hotel in China costs about US$25 and up for a double room. If this is in your price range, then China is a real bargain. Most mid-range hotels are quite luxurious for the price, with large rooms, twin beds, air-con, private bath, colour TV and telephone.

Accommodation in Shenzhen is somewhat more expensive than Guangzhou, while Zhuhai is slightly cheaper.

Discounts

If you're a foreign student in the PRC you can get a discount on room prices. Students usually have to show their government-issued 'green card', though sometimes a fake 'white card' will do the trick. Foreign experts working in China usually qualify for the same discounts as students.

If you are really stuck for a place to stay, it sometimes helps to phone or visit the local PSB and explain your problem. Just as the PSB makes the rules, the PSB can break them – a hotel not approved for foreigners can be granted a temporary reprieve by the PSB and all it takes is a phone call from the right official. Unfortunately, getting such an exemption is not a usual practice.

Hotel Etiquette

Most hotels have an attendant on every floor. The attendant keeps an eye on the hotel guests. This is partly to prevent theft and partly to stop you from bringing locals back for the night (this is no joke).

To conserve energy, in many cheaper hotels hot water for bathing in only available in the evening – sometimes only for a few hours a night or once every three days! It's worth asking when/if the hot water will be turned on.

The policy at every hotel in China is that you check out by noon to avoid being charged extra. If you check out between noon and 6 pm there is a charge of 50% of the room price – after 6 pm you have to pay for another full night.

Almost every hotel has a left-luggage room (*jìcún chù* or *xínglǐ bǎoguān*), and in many hotels there is such a room on every floor. If you are a guest in the hotel, use of the left-luggage room might be free (but not always).

The trend in China over the last few years has been to equip every room – even in the cheap hotels – with TV sets permanently turned to maximum volume. The Hong Kong-style ultra-violent movies are noisy enough, but the introduction of Nintendo-style video games and karaoke microphones (which can be attached to TV sets) has added a new dimension to the cacophony. The combination of screams, screeches, shootings, songs, rings, gongs, beeps and buzzers which reverberate through the vast concrete corridors could force a statue to run away.

The Chinese method of designating floors is the same as used in the USA, but different from that used in Hong Kong, Australia or the UK. What would be the 'ground floor' in Hong Kong is the '1st floor' in China, the 1st is the 2nd, and so on. However, there is some inconsistency – a few Hong Kong-owned hotels in southern China use the British system!

Rental

Most Chinese people live in government-subsidised housing – the price is almost always dirt cheap. For foreigners, the situation is totally different.

If you're going to be working for the Chinese government as a teacher or other type of foreign expert, then you'll likely be provided with cheap or low-cost housing. Conditions probably won't be luxurious, but it should be inexpensive.

The news is not good for those coming to China to do business or work for a foreign company. The cheap apartments available to the Chinese are off-limits to foreigners, which leaves you with two choices – living in a hotel, or renting a luxury flat in a compound specifically designated for foreigners.

If you live in a hotel, you might be able to negotiate a discount for a long-term stay, but that's not guaranteed. As for luxury flats and villas, prices start at around US$2000 and reach US$5000 or more. Even at these prices, there is a shortage of flats available for foreigners.

Considering the sky-high rents, buying a flat or villa might seem like a good idea for companies with the cash. It's actually possible, but the rules vary from city to city. In some cities, only Overseas Chinese are permitted to buy luxury villas – real estate speculators from Taiwan do a roaring trade. Shenzhen has long been in the business of selling flats to Hong Kongers, who in turn rent them out to others. Foreigners can buy flats in some cities (at astronomical prices), and doing this can actually gain you a residence permit.

As for simply moving in with a Chinese family and paying them rent, forget it – the PSB will swoop down on you (and the hapless Chinese family) faster than ants at a picnic.

FOOD

The food is similar to what you'll find in Hong Kong, except that there's a good deal of wildlife on the menu. Snake, monkey, pangolin (an armadillo-like creature), bear, giant salamander and racoon are among the tastes that can be catered for, not to mention more mundane dog, cat and rat dishes.

One look at the people fishing in the sewage canals around Guangzhou might dull your appetite for Pearl River trout.

Western food is a rarity, and is mostly limited to fast-food cuisine of the Big Mac variety. Hong Kong's fast-food chains like Fairwood have entered the Chinese market.

Useful Expressions

bill (cheque)
   zhàngdān 帐单
chopsticks
   kuàizi 筷子
fork
   chāzi 叉子
I can't eat spicy food
   wǒ bùnéng chī là 我不能吃辣
I'm a vegetarian
   wǒ shì chīsùde 我是吃素的

knife
　dāozi 刀子

menu
　càidān 菜单

restaurant
　cāntīng 餐厅

spoon
　tiáogēng 调羹

Rice 饭

plain white rice
　mǐfàn 米饭

rice noodles
　mǐfěn 米粉

watery rice porridge
　xīfàn 稀饭

Bread, Buns & Dumplings 麦类

boiled dumplings
　jiǎozi 饺子

fried bread stick
　yóutiáo 油条

fried roll
　yínsī juǎn 馒头

prawn cracker
　lóngxiā piàn 龙虾片

steamed buns
　mántóu 银丝卷

steamed meat buns
　bāozi 包子

Vegetable Dishes 菜类

assorted hors d'oeuvre
　shíjǐn pīnpán 什锦拼盘

assorted vegetarian food
　sù shíjǐn 素什锦

bean curd & mushrooms
　mógū dòufǔ 磨菇豆腐

bean curd casserole
　shāguō dòufǔ 沙锅豆腐

black fungus & mushroom
　mù'ěr huákǒu mó 木耳滑口磨

broiled mushroom
　sù chǎo xiānme 素炒鲜麼

Chinese salad
　jiācháng liángcài 家常凉菜

fried bean curd in oyster sauce
　háoyóu dòufǔ 蚝油豆腐

fried beansprouts
　sù chǎo dòuyá 素炒豆芽

fried cauliflower & tomato
　fānqié càihuā 炒蕃茄菜花

fried eggplant
　sùshāo qiézi 素烧茄子

fried garlic
　sù chǎo dàsuàn 素炒大蒜

fried rape in oyster sauce
　háoyóu pácài dǎn 蚝油扒菜胆

fried rape with mushrooms
　dōnggū pácài dǎn 冬菇扒菜胆

fried green beans
　sù chǎo biǎndòu 素炒扁豆

fried green vegetables
　sù chǎo qīngcài 素炒青菜

fried noodles with vegetables
　shūcài chǎomiàn 蔬菜炒面

fried peanuts
　yóuzhà huāshēng mǐ 油炸花生米

fried rice with vegetables
　shūcài chǎofàn 蔬菜炒饭

fried white radish patty
　luóbo gāo 萝卜糕

garlic & morning glory
　dàsuàn kōngxīn cài 大蒜空心菜

spiced cold vegetables
　liángbàn shíjǐn 凉拌什锦

spicy hot bean curd
　mápó dòufǔ 麻婆豆腐

spicy peanuts
　wǔxiāng huāshēng mǐ 五香花生米

Egg Dishes

egg & flour omelette
　jiān bǐng 煎饼

fried rice with egg
　jīdàn chǎofàn 鸡蛋炒饭

fried tomatoes & eggs
　xīhóngshì chǎo jīdàn 西红柿炒鸡蛋

preserved egg
　sōnghuā dàn 松花蛋

Beef Dishes

beef braised in soy sauce
　hóngshāo niúròu 红烧牛肉

beef curry & noodles
　gālí jīròu miàn 咖哩牛肉面

beef curry & rice
　gālí jīròu fàn 咖哩牛肉饭

beef platter
　niúròu tiěbǎn 牛肉铁板

CANTON

beef with green peppers
  qīngjiāo niúròu piàn 青椒牛肉片
beef with oyster sauce
  háoyóu niúròu 蚝油牛肉
beef with tomatoes
  fānqié niúròu piàn 蕃茄牛肉片
beef with white rice
  niúròu fàn 牛肉饭
fried noodles with beef
  niúròu chǎomiàn 牛肉炒面
fried rice with beef
  niúròusī chǎofàn 牛肉丝炒饭
noodles with beef (soupy)
  niúròu tāng miàn 牛肉汤面
spiced noodles with beef
  niúròu gān miàn 牛肉干面

Chicken Dishes
chicken braised in soy sauce
  hóngshāo jīkuài 红烧鸡块
chicken curry & noodles
  gālǐ jīròu miàn 咖喱鸡肉面
chicken curry & rice
  gālǐ jīròu fàn 咖哩鸡肉饭
chicken curry
  gālǐ jīròu 咖哩鸡肉
chicken leg with white rice
  jītuǐ fàn 鸡腿饭
chicken pieces in oyster sauce
  háoyóu jīdīng 蚝油鸡丁
chicken slices & tomato sauce
  fānqié jīdīng 蕃茄鸡丁
fried noodles with chicken
  jīsī chǎomiàn 鸡丝炒面
fried rice with chicken
  jīsī chǎofàn 鸡丝炒饭
fruit kernel with chicken
  guǒwèi jīdīng 果味鸡丁
mushrooms & chicken
  cǎomó jīdīng 草蘑鸡丁
noodles with chicken (soupy)
  jīsī tāng miàn 鸡丝汤面
sauteed chicken with green peppers
  jiàngbào jīdīng 酱爆鸡丁
sauteed chicken with water chestnuts
  nánjiè jīpiàn 南芥鸡片
sauteed spicy chicken pieces
  làzi jīdīng 辣子鸡丁
sliced chicken with crispy rice
  jīpiàn guōbā 鸡片锅巴

spicy hot chicken & peanuts
  gōngbào jīdīng 宫爆鸡丁
sweet & sour chicken
  tángcù jīdīng 糖醋鸡丁

Duck Dishes
Beijing Duck
  běijīng kǎoyā 北京烤鸭
duck with fried noodles
  yāròu chǎomiàn 鸭肉炒面
duck with noodles
  yāròu miàn 鸭肉面
duck with white rice
  yāròu fàn 鸭肉饭

Pork Dishes
boiled pork slices
  shuǐzhǔ ròupiàn 水煮肉片
Cantonese fried rice
  guǎngzhōu chǎofàn 广州炒饭
fried black pork pieces
  yuánbào lǐjī 芜爆里肌
fried noodles with pork
  ròusī chǎomiàn 肉丝炒面
fried rice (assorted)
  shíjǐn chǎofàn 什锦炒饭
fried rice with pork
  ròusī chǎofàn 肉丝炒饭
golden pork slices
  jīnyín ròusī 金银肉丝
noodles, pork & mustard greens
  zhàcài ròusī miàn 榨菜肉丝面
pork & fried onions
  yángcōng chǎo ròupiàn 洋葱炒肉片
pork & mustard greens
  zhàcài ròusī 榨菜肉丝
pork chop with white rice
  páigǔ fàn 排骨饭
pork cubes & cucumber
  huángguā ròudīng 黄瓜肉丁
pork fillet with white sauce
  huáliū lǐjī 滑溜里肌
pork with crispy rice
  ròupiàn guōbā 肉片锅巴
pork with oyster sauce
  háoyóu ròusī 蚝油肉丝
pork, eggs & black fungus
  mùxū ròu 木须肉
sauteed diced pork & soy sauce
  jiàngbào ròudīng 酱爆肉丁

sauteed shredded pork
qīngchǎo ròusī 清炒肉丝
shredded pork & bamboo shoots
dōngsǔn ròusī 冬笋肉丝
shredded pork & green beans
biǎndòu ròusī 扁豆肉丝
shredded pork & green peppers
qīngjiāo ròusī 青椒肉丝
shredded pork & hot sauce
yúxiāng ròusī 鱼香肉丝
shredded pork fillet
chǎo lǐjī sī 炒里肌丝
soft pork fillet
ruǎnzhá lǐjī 软炸里肌
spicy hot pork pieces
gōngbào ròudīng 宫爆肉丁
spicy pork cubes
làzi ròudīng 辣子肉丁
sweet & sour pork fillet
tángcù lǐjī 糖醋里肌
sweet & sour pork fillet
tángcù zhūròu piàn 糖醋猪肉片

Seafood Dishes
braised sea cucumber
hóngshāo hǎishēn 红烧海参
clams
gé 蛤
crab
pángxiè 螃蟹
deep-fried shrimp
zhà xiārén 炸虾仁
diced shrimp with peanuts
gōngbào xiārén 宫爆虾仁
fish braised in soy sauce
hóngshāo yú 红烧鱼
fried noodles with shrimp
xiārén chǎomiàn 虾仁炒面
fried rice with shrimp
xiārén chǎofàn 虾仁炒饭
fried shrimp with mushroom
xiānmó xiārén 鲜蘑虾仁
lobster
lóngxiā 龙虾
sauteed shrimp
qīngchǎo xiārén 清炒虾仁
squid with crispy rice
yóuyú guōbā 鱿鱼锅巴
sweet & sour squid roll
suānlà yóuyú juàn 酸辣鱿鱼卷

Soup
bean curd & vegetable soup
dòufǔ cài tāng 豆腐菜汤
clear soup
qīng tāng 清汤
corn & egg thick soup
fènghuáng lìmǐ gēng 凤凰栗米羹
cream of mushroom soup
nǎiyóu xiānmó tāng 奶油鲜蘑汤
cream of tomato soup
nǎiyóu fānqié tāng 奶油蕃茄汤
egg & vegetable soup
dànhuā tāng 蛋花汤
fresh fish soup
shēng yú tāng 生鱼汤
mushroom & egg soup
mógu dànhuā tāng 蘑菇蛋花汤
pickled mustard green soup
zhàcài tāng 榨菜汤
squid soup
yóuyú tāng 鱿鱼汤
sweet & sour soup
suānlà tāng 酸辣汤
three kinds seafood soup
sān xiān tāng 三鲜汤
tomato & egg soup
xīhóngshì dàn tāng 西红柿蛋汤
vegetable soup
shūcài tāng 蔬菜汤
wanton soup
húndùn tāng 馄饨汤

Miscellanea & Exotica
deermeat (venison)
lùròu 鹿肉
dogmeat
gǒu ròu 狗肉
eel
shàn yú 鳝鱼
frog
qīngwā 青蛙
goat, mutton
yáng ròu 羊肉
kebab
ròu chuàn 肉串
Mongolian hotpot
huǒguō 火锅
pangolin
chuānshānjiǎ 穿山甲

CANTON

ratmeat
   lǎoshǔ ròu 老鼠肉
snake
   shé ròu 蛇肉
turtle
   hǎiguī 海龟

Condiments
black pepper
   hújiāo 胡椒
butter
   huáng yóu 黄油
garlic
   dàsuàn 大蒜
honey
   fēngmì 蜂蜜
hot pepper
   làjiāo 辣椒
hot sauce
   làjiāo jiàng 辣椒酱
jam
   guǒ jiàng 果酱
ketchup
   fānqié jiàng 蕃茄酱
MSG
   wèijīng 味精
salt
   yán 盐
sesame seed oil
   zhīmá yóu 芝麻油
soy sauce
   jiàng yóu 酱油
sugar
   táng 糖
vinegar
   cù 醋

Desserts & Snacks
biscuits
   bǐnggān 饼干
cake
   dàngāo 蛋糕
ice cream
   bīngqílín 冰淇淋
yoghurt
   suānnǎi 酸奶

DRINKS
Besides tea, China is also well known for beer. The brands made in China are excel-lent, the most popular being *Tsingtao*, now a major export. It's actually a German beer – the town where it is made, Tsingtao (Qingdao) was once a German concession. The Chinese inherited the brewery when the Germans were kicked out.

Drinks Vocabulary
hot
   rè 热
ice cold
   bīngde 冰的
ice cubes
   bīngkuài 冰块

Alcoholic Drinks
beer
   píjiǔ 啤酒
San Miguel Beer
   shēnglì pí 生力啤
Tsingtao Beer
   qīngdǎo píjiǔ 青岛啤酒
Zhujiang Beer
   zhūjiāng píjiǔ 珠江啤酒
vodka
   fútèjiā jiǔ 伏特加酒
whiskey
   wēishìjì jiǔ 威士忌酒

Non-Alcoholic Drinks
Coca-Cola
   kěkǒu kělè 可口可乐
Sprite
   xuěbì 雪碧
coffee
   kāfēi 咖啡
fizzy drink (soda)
   qìshuǐ 汽水
mineral water
   kuàng quán shuǐ 矿泉水
red grape wine
   hóng pútáo jiǔ 红葡萄酒
rice wine
   mǐ jiǔ 米酒
tea
   chá 茶
black tea
   hóng chá 红茶
jasmine tea
   mòlìhuā chá 茉莉花茶

CANTON

oolong tea
 wūlóng chá 乌龙茶
tea with milk
 nǎichá 奶茶
water
 kāi shuǐ 开水
white grape wine
 bái pútáo jiǔ 白葡萄酒

TOBACCO

A typical Chinese smoker puffs away three packs or more of cigarettes daily, but only one match – after lighting the first cigarette, they can then light the remaining three packs by using one butt to light the next.

Some Westerners speculate that cigarette smoking is a more effective means of reducing China's population than the one-child family policy. Although the government has made some grumblings about starting an anti-smoking campaign, there is little indication that this is being taken seriously. Nor is it likely to be taken seriously since tax revenues from tobacco sales is a major source of income for the government. It also seems that few are taking seriously the warnings to be careful with lit cigarettes – in hotel rooms note the burns in the carpets, bedsheets and furniture. Perhaps it's a good thing that Chinese hotels are made from bricks and concrete rather than wood.

If you're the sort of person who gets all upset by people smoking in crowded public places like buses and restaurants, either change your attitude, leave the country or buy a gas mask – the Chinese will be positively offended if you tell them not to smoke. As with drinking hard liquor, smoking in public is largely a male activity – a woman who smokes in public may be regarded as a prostitute.

The Chinese place considerable prestige value on smoking foreign cigarettes. Famous brand names such as Marlboro, Dunhill and 555 are high-priced and widely available – the ultimate status symbol for aspiring Chinese yuppies. Not surprisingly, the counterfeiting of foreign cigarettes has become a profitable cottage industry. As for rolling your own, you occasionally see the older

Chinese doing this, but young people sneer at this proletarian activity – much better to spend a full day's pay for a pack of imported pre-rolled cigarettes which will elevate one's social status.

Many foreigners consider Chinese tobacco to have the gentle aroma of old socks, but some good-quality stuff is grown, mostly in Yunnan Province. Chinese-made Red Pagoda Mountain (*hóng tǎ shān*) smokes cost more than Marlboros. Many foreigners are familiar with Double Happiness (*shuāngxǐ*) cigarettes, the only brand so far which has been developed for export.

ENTERTAINMENT

Overall, China is not known for its nightlife. Karaoke bars at the big hotels dominate the scene, while discos are on the decline. There are some fledgling Western-style pubs in Guangzhou, but nothing to compete with the raging nightlife in Hong Kong. China's English-language newspaper, the *China Daily*, has a reasonably good entertainment section which covers only the major cities favoured by tourists. Video-game arcades keep the kids entertained.

Warning

Besides any mental damage you may suffer from listening to karaoke, these places can be ruinous to your budget.

There have been disturbing reports that the 'Tokyo Nightclub Syndrome' has hit China. Basically, foreigners (chiefly male) sitting in a karaoke bar are suddenly joined by an attractive young woman (or maybe several women) who 'just want to talk'. A few drinks are ordered – maybe just Coke or orange juice – and at the end of an hour's conversation a bill of perhaps US$500 or so is presented to the hapless foreigner. The drinks might only cost US$10, while the other US$490 is a 'service charge' for talking to the women, who are in fact bar hostesses.

Even more sinister is that these women often approach foreigners on the street, ostensibly just to 'practice their English'. Somewhere in the conversation they suggest going to a 'nice place', which happens to be a karaoke bar. What they fail to mention is that they

CANTON

work for the bar and get a percentage of the profits for every sucker they bring in.

It needs to be mentioned that the victims of these schemes are not only foreigners. Overseas Chinese, Hong Kongers, Taiwanese and even mainland Chinese who appear to have money are also targeted. It's a system that seems to be spreading.

THINGS TO BUY

The Chinese do produce some interesting items for export – tea, clothing, silkworm missiles – the latter not generally for sale to tourists.

Gone are the ration cards and the need for connections to buy TV sets and refrigerators – the consumer boom has arrived. Chinese department stores are like Aladdin's Cave, all stocked to the rafters with goodies – tourist attractions in themselves.

Unfortunately, quality has not kept pace with quantity. There is an awful lot of junk on sale – zippers which break the first time you use them, music cassette players which last a week, electric appliances that go up in smoke the first time they're plugged in, etc. Given this state of affairs, you might wonder how China manages to successfully export so much – the simple fact is that export items are made to a much higher standard while junk is dumped on the local markets. Always test zippers, examine stitching, and in the case of electrical appliances, plug it in and make sure it won't electrocute you before handing over the cash. Chinese sales clerks expect you to do this – they'll consider you a fool if you don't.

More than Meets the Eye...

Once upon a time in China you got what you paid for. A mixed blessing: if the sales clerk said it was top-quality jade then it was top-quality jade and you'd pay through the nose for it. Times have changed – now there are all sorts of cheap forgeries and imitations about, from Tibetan jewellery to Qing coins, phoney Marlboro cigarettes, fake Sony Walkmans (complete with fake Maxell cassette tapes), imitation Rolex watches, even fake Garden biscuits (Garden Bakeries is Hong Kong's biggest seller of bread, cakes and biscuits).

While eating counterfeit brandname biscuits probably won't kill you, phoney jewellery is disappointing at best and fake electronic goodies have a life expectancy of a few weeks.

Nor are fakes limited to consumer items – as high-technology filters down to the masses, the manufacture of fake railway tickets, fake lottery tickets and fake Y100 notes have become new cottage industries. Cadres now pad their expense accounts with fake receipts – one reason why State-run

Selling It

Advertising for the foreign market is one area the Chinese are still stumbling around in. A TV advertisement in Paris for Chinese furs treated viewers to the bloody business of skinning and cadavers in the refrigerator rooms before the usual parade of fur-clad models strutting down the catwalk. It would be fun to handle the advertising campaigns for their more charming brandnames. There's Pansy underwear (for men) or you can pamper your stud with Horse Head facial tissues. Wake up in the morning with a Golden Cock alarm clock (since renamed Golden Rooster). You can start your breakfast with a glass of 'Billion Strong Pulpy C Orange Drink', or finish your meal with a cup of 'Imperial Concubine Tea'. For your trusty portable radio it may be best to stay away from White Elephant batteries, but you might try the space-age Moon Rabbit variety. Long March car tyres should prove durable, but we aren't too sure about the ginseng product with the fatal name of Gensenocide. Out of the psychedelic sixties comes White Rabbit candy. Flying Baby toilet paper seems to have ceased, but you might still be able to find a pack of Puke cigarettes. The characters for Coca-Cola translate as 'tastes good, tastes happy' but the Chinese must have thought they were really on to something good when the 'Coke Adds Life' slogan got mistranslated and claimed to be able to resurrect the dead. And, as a sign of the times, one enterprising food vendor has started a chain store named 'Capitalist Road'. ■

companies are losing money. While counterfeiting brandname goods is supposedly illegal, enforcement has been slack. China's foreign trading partners are none too happy about the fake Rolexes and pirated cassette tapes, and have threatened retaliation if China doesn't crack down. Meanwhile, the government is having a hard enough time plugging the leak of State funds caused by the fake tickets and receipts.

What to do? It's not easy to say, but if you want to buy things like genuine antiques, try to get an official certificate of verification – just make sure the ink is dry.

Getting There & Away

For specific details for getting to Guangzhou, Shenzhen and Zhuhai from Hong Kong or Macau, see the relevant Getting There & Away sections for each of those cities. What follows is general information about travel to China.

One rule to remember is to avoid travelling on weekends and (even more so) at holiday times such as Easter and Chinese New Year. At those times everything is full and the crowds pour across the border from Hong Kong, leaving trampled backpackers in their wake.

In most cities, there are left-luggage rooms at the long-distance bus stations and railway stations.

AIR
To/From Hong Kong

CAAC There are international flights from Hong Kong, and infrequently, from other countries. Civil Aviation Administration of China (CAAC) is China's domestic and international carrier and flights can be booked at either of the CAAC offices. Both tend to be crowded so go early (9 am) when they first open. Hong Kong travel agents can book some CAAC flights via telephone or computer, but this doesn't always work. Trying to book a flight on CAAC is often a frustrating experience – you can stand in a queue for an hour just to find all flights are full. Calling on the telephone to get information seems to be impossible. The two CAAC offices in Hong Kong are at Central, Ground floor, 17 Queen's Rd (☎ 8401199) and Kowloon, Ground floor, Mirador Mansion, 54-64B Nathan Rd, Tsimshatsui (☎ 7390022).

On domestic and international flights the free baggage allowance for an adult passenger is 20 kg in economy class and 30 kg in 1st class. You are also allowed five kg of hand luggage, though this is rarely weighed.

CAAC publishes a combined international and domestic timetable in both English and Chinese in April and November each year. These can be obtained for free in Hong Kong, but are sold in China if you can find them at all. It's important to realise that many of CAAC's flights are technically charters, even if they do run according to a regular schedule. If you purchase one of these 'charter' tickets, there will be no refund for cancellations and no changes are permitted. Don't count on the CAAC staff to tell you this. The following are the one-way fares between China and Hong Kong on CAAC, and flights marked with an asterisk are 'charters':

Beijing	US$292	Changsha*	US$182
Chengdu*	US$272	Chongqing*	US$272
Dalian	US$309	Fuzhou	US$197
Guangzhou	US$85	Guilin*	US$164
Guiyang*	US$210	Haikou*	US$151
Hangzhou	US$197	Harbin*	US$342
Hefei*	US$194	Ji'nan*	US$269
Kunming	US$203	Meixian*	US$148
Nanchang*	US$184	Nanjing*	US$216
Nanning*	US$158	Ningbo	US$205
Qingdao*	US$285	Shanghai	US$215
Shantou	US$145	Shenyang	US$343
Tianjin	US$293	Wuhan*	US$185
Xi'an	US$254	Xiamen	US$166
Zhanjiang*	US$152	Zhengzhou*	US$246

Dragonair Dragonair is a joint-venture between CAAC and Hong Kong's Cathay Pacific. It has flights from Hong Kong to 14 cities in China: Beijing, Changsha, Chengdu, Dalian, Guilin, Haikou, Hangzhou, Kunming, Nanjing, Ningbo, Shanghai, Tianjin, Xiamen and Xi'an. Within China, Dragonair tickets can be bought from CITS.

In Hong Kong, any travel agent with a computer can book you onto a Dragonair flight but you can directly contact the ticketing offices of Dragonair (☎ 7360202), Room 1843, Swire House, 9 Connaught Rd, Central; and 12th floor, Tower 6, China Hong Kong City, 33 Canton Rd, Tsimshatsui.

There is virtually no discounting on flights into China. Dragonair's prices are slightly cheaper than CAAC's and service is better. Not surprisingly, Dragonair's flights tend to fill up fast, leaving you with no alternative but CAAC.

LAND
To/From Hong Kong
Bus A consortium of Hong Kong companies and the Chinese government is constructing a six-lane 240-km super highway from Hong Kong to Guangzhou to Zhuhai. Bus service will improve, and it will also be possible to bring your own vehicle – obviously trade, tourism and commerce will benefit. Just when all this is going to happen is uncertain – construction has been proceeding slowly for over a decade.

Train There is one international railway line from Hong Kong to Guangzhou. For details, see the Getting There & Away section in the Guangzhou chapter.

SEA
To/From Hong Kong
Travel to China by boat is usually less stressful than either trains or buses. There are both fast jet-powered catamarans and slow overnight ferries to major destinations in the Pearl River delta region. The overnight boats have beds and are generally preferred to fast boats since you sleep through most of the trip and save one night's accommodation in a hotel.

The most popular boat is the overnight ferry to Guangzhou, but another one to consider is the overnight ferry to Zhaoqing. Some travellers make use of the fast catamarans plying the route from Hong Kong to Shenzhen, Huangtian Airport (also in Shenzhen), Zhuhai and Zhongshan. For details, see the Getting There & Away sections for these individual cities.

CTS is the main booking agent for boats and charges US$3 for the service. You can get tickets cheaper at the pier in Hong Kong China City on Canton Rd in Kowloon, but the level of spoken English there is abysmally low. The ferry company also has a booking office (☎ 8853876) at 24 Connaught Rd West, but the language of business there is Cantonese.

TOURS
If time is more important than money, then the brief tours to China from Hong Kong are worth considering. Although expensive, you'll never complain about not being shown enough on a tour. Itineraries are invariably jam-packed, with as much activity as possible in a day. The Chinese expect stamina from their guests.

Nor could you complain about the quantity of food – you may complain about the quality or style of cooking, but there is no way the Chinese will let you starve.

There are innumerable tours you can make from Hong Kong or Macau. The best information on tours is available from Hong Kong travel agents, CITS or CTS. They all keep a good stock of leaflets and information on a range of tours to China. You usually have to book tours one or two days in advance.

There is an endless variety of China tours, from one-day trips across the border to Shenzhen to a Long March across the country. The trips to Shenzhen are popular. These are usually daily, except on Sundays and public holidays, and cost from US$72. The cost of the visa is usually *not* included, but everything else is – transport, lunch and admission fees. Inquire about discounts for children. Some of these tours visit Shenzhen Reservoir (from which Hong Kong gets most of its water), the Shenzhen art gallery, a kindergarten, a souvenir shop and Shenzhen's prime tourist traps, 'Splendid China' and 'China Folk Culture Villages' (see Shenzhen section for details). Some trips include the Shekou port district from where you can return to Hong Kong by hovercraft.

Day trips from Hong Kong also go to Zhuhai, north of Macau. The cost is about US$104 and you're taken by jetfoil to Macau and then by bus to Zhuhai. These tours include a visit to Cuiheng Village, the birthplace and former residence of Sun Yatsen, and the industrial sewer-city of Zhongshan.

Day tours to Guangzhou and Shenzhen are available for about US$142 – travelling by hovercraft or jetcat (jet-powered catamaran) to Guangzhou in the morning and returning by train in the evening with a stop-off at Shenzhen. More popular is the two-day tour of the preceding which costs US$259.

There are also three-day tours which visit Guangzhou, Zhongshan, Zhuhai, Zhaoqing and Foshan for about US$360. There are combined Hong Kong, New Territories and Guangzhou tours, and combined Macau and Guangzhou tours and so on.

Essentially the same tours can be booked in Macau at CTS.

Warning
Judging by the mail we receive at Lonely Planet, many people who have booked extended tours through CTS and CITS have been less than fully satisfied. Although the one-day tours seem to be OK, tours further afield frequently go awry. The biggest complaints are ridiculous overcharging for substandard accommodation and tours being cut short to make up for transport delays. Some people have booked a tour only to find that they were the only person on the tour. No refunds are given if you cancel – you forfeit the full amount. Other travellers report additional charges being tacked on which were not mentioned in the original agreement.

CITS drivers have been known to show up with all their relatives who want to tag along for free. One traveller reported booking a week-long tour – the female driver showed up with her boyfriend and asked if he could come along. The traveller foolishly agreed. At the first lunch stop, the driver and her boyfriend took off and left the foreigner behind – the couple then apparently spent the rest of the week enjoying a lovers tryst at the traveller's prepaid hotel rooms!

LEAVING CHINA
Departure Tax
Airport departure tax is US$10 and rising. Many airports in China are even charging departure tax on *domestic* flights. There is no departure tax if you leave by boat.

Money
It's important to remember that you have to change money before entering the immigration and customs area. This applies to the airport, wharf, railway station (for international trains) or the land border crossings at Shenzhen and Zhuhai. At Zhoutouzui Wharf, the Bank of China opens two hours before departure.

Getting Around

AIR
Local Air Services
CAAC's flights cover about 80 cities and towns throughout the country. Foreigners pay a surcharge at least 20% higher than the Chinese. There are occasionally people outside the CAAC office peddling black-market air tickets, but I don't recommend you buy these. The airlines can tell a Chinese-priced ticket from a foreign one, and if you have a Chinese ticket you will not be permitted to board the aircraft.

It is possible to buy all of your domestic CAAC tickets from the CITS in Hong Kong, and even from some non-Chinese airlines that have reciprocal arrangements with CAAC. However, this is generally not a good idea. First of all, it saves you no money whatsoever. Secondly, the tickets issued outside of China need to be exchanged for a proper stamped ticket at the appropriate CAAC offices in China – a few of these offices get their wires crossed and refuse to honour 'foreign' tickets. Furthermore, CAAC flights often cancel, but you'll have to return the ticket to the seller in order to get a refund.

Stand-by tickets do exist on CAAC flights. Some seats are always reserved in case a high-ranking cadre turns up at the last moment. If no one shows up it should be possible to get on board.

CAAC has been 'broken up' into new 'competing airlines', including Air China, China Eastern Airlines and China Southern Airlines. This was supposed to stimulate competition and improve service. For the most part, this has made little difference. All these airlines are listed in the CAAC timetable, sell tickets through CAAC offices and even have the CAAC logo on the tickets. It's a start and perhaps one day there will be real competition. But for now the 'new' airlines are simply old and disreputable medicine in new, shiny bottles.

BUS
Classes
There are two kinds of buses. The east side of the Guangzhou Bus Station (closest to the Liuhua Hotel) is where the big government-run buses are. These are cheaper but definitely more crowded, slower and less comfortable. You can get minibuses on the west side of the station. These are privately run and have luxuries such as air-con, much appreciated during the sweatbox conditions of June through to October. Unlike the train – there is no additional charge for foreigners.

The company that runs the minibuses employs a big guy with a bamboo pole to make sure nobody jumps the queue.

When I was there, everyone lined up as they were supposed to. Then someone pulled the usual trick of shoving their way to the front. The big guy yelled *Pai dui*! (stand in line). The other guy continued to shove, and was promptly knocked halfway across the car park! I like this bus company.

TRAIN
Trains in China are reasonably fast, frequent and convenient. Trains also have the great advantage of being safer than buses. See the Getting There & Away sections of the Guangzhou and Shenzhen chapters for details.

TAXI
Taxis cruise the streets and are easily found at hotels. Drivers meet incoming flights and try to charge foreigners about three times the going rate and will often ask for payment in US dollars. Don't accept any of this nonsense – either bargain a decent rate or insist they use the meter.

MOTORCYCLE TAXIS
A fine example of China's nascent free enterprise reforms, people who own motorcycles hang around railway stations and bus stops to solicit passengers. It is required that pas-

sengers wear a safety helmet, and the drivers will supply one. There are no meters on motorcycles, so get the fare established in advance. In general, a ride on a motorcycle will be at least 30% cheaper than a regular taxi.

Guangzhou 广州

Guangzhou is the sixth largest city in China and the capital of Guangdong Province. It's an honour that wasn't bestowed upon Guangzhou by accident – it occurred because Guangzhou occupies a key position on the Pearl River delta, 120 km north-west of Hong Kong.

Guangzhou was originally three cities. The inner city was enclosed behind sturdy walls and was divided into the new and old cities. The outer city was everything outside these walls. The building of the walls began during the 11th century and was completed in the 16th century. The walls were eight metres high, between five and eight metres thick and 15 km in circumference.

ORIENTATION

The main thoroughfares, now called Jiefang Lu (Liberation Rd) and Zhongshan Lu, run north-south and east-west respectively. They divided the old walled city and met the walls at the main gates.

Outside the former city walls to the west lies Xiguan, the western quarter. Wealthy Chinese merchants built their residences the same distance from the centre of the city as the foreign enclave of Shamian Island. The thoroughfare, still known as Shibapu, became the street of millionaires in the 19th century and remained the exclusive residential district of the well-to-do class. It was these people who patronised the famous old restaurants of the area.

In the north-east of the city is the Xiaobei (Little North) area. During dynastic times it was inhabited mainly by out-of-town officials because it was close to the offices of the bureaucracy. It was later developed into a residential area for civil servants, which it remains.

At the eastern end of Zhongshan Lu is a residential district built in the 1930s using modern town planning. It's known as Dongshan (East Mountain). Part of the Dongshan residential area is called Meihuacun (Plum Blossom Village) – a model village laid out in the 1930s with beautiful residences constructed for high-ranking officials. Dongshan is rapidly developing into Guangzhou's upmarket neighbourhood.

Guangzhou is now a large, sprawling city with traffic that hardly moves. The streets are usually split into sectors, each with a number or, more usually, labelled according to their position relative to the other sectors. For example, Zhongshan Lu (Zhongshan Road) might be split into an east and a west sector – the east sector designated Zhongshan Donglu and the west sector called Zhongshan Xilu.

INFORMATION
Tourist Office

There is an enormous CITS office (☎ 6677151) at 179 Huanshi Lu next to the main railway station, but they have little information. It's one big ticket office and the only thing the overworked clerks are likely to say to you is 'next please'. You can buy tickets here for trains, planes, hovercraft and ships. The office is open from 8.30 to 11.30 am and 2 to 5 pm.

Public Security

The Public Security Bureau (PSB) (☎ 3331060) is at 863 Jiefang Beilu, opposite the road which leads up to the Zhenhai Tower – a 15-minute walk from the Dongfang Hotel.

Money

You can change money at branches of the Bank of China in most of the large tourist hotels. The White Swan Hotel has a bank – the staff asks your room number and scowls if you're not a guest in their hotel, but they will change money even for backpackers at the nearby youth hostel.

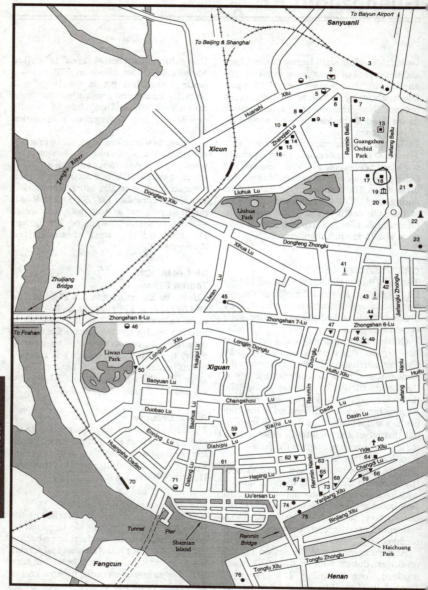

CANTON

a Hotel
流花宾馆

Zhanqian Hotel
站前酒店

9　New Mainland Hotel
新大地宾馆

10　Jinhuan & Maoming Shihua Hotels
金环酒店/茂名石化宾馆

11　Hotel Equatorial
贵都酒店

12　Friendship Hotel
友谊宾馆

14　Overseas Chinese Hotel
华侨酒店

15　Leizhou Hotel
雷州酒店

16　Sinochem Hotel
中化大酒店

17　Dongfang Hotel
东方宾馆

18　China Hotel
中国大酒店

26　Gitic Plaza Hotel & McDonald's
广东国际大厦/麦当劳

27　Baiyun Hotel
白云宾馆

29　Garden Hotel
花园酒店

30　Cathay Hotel
国泰宾馆

31　Holiday Inn
文化假日酒店

32　Ocean Hotel
远洋宾馆

34　Hakkas & Hua Shan Hotels
嘉应宾馆/华山宾馆

35　Guangdong Jinye Hotel
广东金叶大厦

36　Yuehai Hotel
粤海大厦

42　Guangdong Guesthouse
广东迎宾馆

57　Hotel Landmark Canton
华厦大酒店

58　Guangzhou Hotel
广州宾馆

63　New Asia Hotel
新亚酒店

64　Furama and GD Hotels
富丽华大酒店/广东大酒店

67　Bai Gong Hotel
白宫酒店

69　Aiqun Hotel
爱群大厦

PLACES TO EAT

25　North Garden Restaurant
北园酒家

44　Xiyuan Restaurant
西园饭店

47　Muslim Restaurant
回民饭店

48　Caigenxiang (Veg) Restaurant
菜根香素菜馆

50　Panxi Restaurant
泮溪酒家

59　Guangzhou Restaurant
广州酒家

62　Snake Restaurant
蛇餐馆

65　Yan Yan Restaurant
人人菜馆

66　Kentucky Fried Chicken
肯德基家乡鸡

68　Timmy's Fast Food Restaurant
添美食

73　Xinhua Hotel & Datong Restaurant
新华酒店/大同饭店

OTHER

1　Long-Distance Bus Station
广东省汽车客运站

2　GPO
邮政总局 (流花邮局)

3　Guangzhou Railway Station
广州火车站

4　CAAC/CITS
中国民航/国际旅行社

5　Minibus Station
小公共汽车站

7　Telecommunications Office
国际电话大楼

13　Mohammedan Tomb
穆罕默德墓

19　Southern Yue Tomb Museum
南越王汉墓

20　PSB
公安局外事科

21　Sculpture of the Five Rams
五羊石像

22　Sun Yatsen Monument
孙中山纪念碑

23　Sun Yatsen Memorial Hall
孙中山纪念堂

24　Zhenhai Tower
镇海楼

28　Friendship Store
友谊商店

33 Mausoleum of the 72 Martyrs
黄花岗七十二烈士墓

37 Zhongshan Medical College
中山医科大学

38 Memorial Garden to the Martyrs
烈士陵园

39 Peasant Movement Institute
农民运动讲习所

40 Buses to White Cloud Hills
开往白云山的汽车站

41 Bright Filial Piety Temple
光孝寺

43 Temple of the Six Banyan Trees *yes!*
六榕寺花塔

45 Chen Clan Academy
陈氏书院/陈家词

46 Buses to Foshan & Xiqiao Hills
广佛车站

49 Huaisheng Mosque
怀圣寺光塔

51 Down jacket & sleeping bag store
工农服装场

52 Guangzhou Department Store
广州百货大楼

53 Foreign Language Bookstore
外文书店

54 Dongshan Department Store
东山百货大楼

55 Dashatou Wharf
大沙头码头

56 Tianzi Pier
天字码头

60 Sacred Heart Church
石室教堂

61 Qingping Market
清平市场

70 South Station (cargo only)
南站(货运站)

71 Huangsha Bus Station
黄沙车站

72 Cultural Park
文化公园

74 Nanfang Department Store
南方大厦

75 No 1 Pier
一号码头

76 Zhoutouzui Wharf
洲头嘴码头

On Shamian Island, the black-market moneychanging industry is controlled by a large gang. Almost without exception, every foreigner who changes money on the streets of Shamian Island gets ripped off.

Post & Telecommunications

All the major tourist hotels have post offices where you can send letters and packets containing printed matter.

If you're posting parcels overseas you have to go to the post office at 43 Yanjiang Xilu near the riverfront. You have to get the parcel contents checked and fill out a customs form.

Adjacent to the railway station is the GPO, locally known as the Liuhua Post Office (☎ 6662735) (liúhuā yóu jú). You can collect poste-restante letters here, despite there being no poste-restante window. Names are written on a noticeboard and you are supposed to see if your name is there and then find someone (but who?) to get the letter for you.

The telecommunications office is across from the railway station on the east side of Renmin Beilu. Most hotels have direct-dial service to Hong Kong which is quite cheap. All main tourist hotels have 'business centres' offering domestic and international telephone, fax and telex facilities.

Foreign Consulates

There are several consulates which can issue visas and replace stolen passports. In late 1992, the Chinese government forced the French Consulate to close in retaliation as France had agreed to sell 60 Mirage fighter jets to Taiwan over Beijing's protests. Just weeks earlier the Americans signed contracts to sell 150 F-16 jet fighters to Taiwan, but Beijing – with an eye on its annual US$22 billion trade surplus with the USA – dared only throw a tantrum.

Depending on what passport you hold, the Polish Consulate can be useful if you want to do the Trans-Siberian. These days most Western nationalities do not require a visa for Poland.

The US Consulate might better be called the 'Emigration Information Centre'. If you go there with some other intention besides emigrating to the USA, the staff will be so happy to see you they might throw a party.

CANTON

Japan
    Garden Hotel Tower, 368 Huanshi Donglu
    (☎ 3338999)
Poland
    Shamian Island near the White Swan Hotel
Thailand
    Rooms 309-310 and 303-316, White Swan Hotel,
    Shamian Island (☎ 8886968)
USA
    1 Shamian Nanjie, Shamian Island (☎ 8882222)

Emergency

If you get sick you can go to one of the hospitals or to the medical clinic for foreigners – Guangzhou No 1 People's Hospital (☎ 3333090) *(dìyī rénmín yīyuàn)*, 602 Renmin Beilu.

If you're staying on Shamian Island or the riverfront, a nearby hospital is the Sun Yatsen Memorial Hospital (☎ 8882012) *(sūn yìxiān jìniàn yīyuàn)*, 107 Yanjiang Xilu next to the Aiqun Hotel. Not much English is spoken here but medical facilities are pretty good and prices low.

Just next to Shamian Island and the Qingping Market is the Traditional Chinese Medicine Hospital *(zhōngyī yīyuàn)* on Zhuji Lu. If you want to try acupuncture and herbs, this is the place to go. Many foreigners come here to study Chinese medicine instead of being patients.

Dangers & Annoyances

Guangzhou is easily the most dangerous city in China. Because Guangzhou is widely perceived as the richest place in China, a large number of immigrants from the countryside have poured into the city in search of instant wealth. Needless to say, most become disillusioned when they find that money doesn't grow on trees, and many turn to begging and theft. Guangzhou taxis have knife-proof plastic shields or wire screens separating the driver from the passengers. Before these became mandatory, many drivers were attacked and some were killed.

For foreigners, there is little physical danger walking the streets, but pickpocketing is a problem, especially on crowded buses. You should also be cautious of bag snatchers, especially around the railway station. Some thieves

use bicycles as their getaway vehicle – they grab the bag right out of your hand and are gone before you know what's happened. Another tactic is to slit your bag or pocket open with a razor blade and remove the contents. The police are not always helpful.

Peasant Movement Institute

(nóngmín yùndòng jiǎngxí suǒ)
农民运动讲习所
Guangzhou's Peasant Movement Institute was built on the site of a Ming Dynasty Confucian temple in 1924. In the early days of the Communist party, its members (from all over China) were trained at the Institute. It was set up by Peng Pai, a high-ranking Communist leader who believed that if a Communist revolution was to succeed in China then the peasants must be its main force. Mao Zedong – of the same opinion – took over as director of the institute in 1925 or 1926. Zhou Enlai lectured here and one of his students was Mao's brother, Mao Zemin. Peng was executed by the Kuomintang in 1929, and Mao Zemin was executed by a warlord in Xinjiang Province in 1942.

The buildings were restored in 1953 and they're now used as a revolutionary museum. There's not a great deal to see: a replica of Mao's room, the soldiers' barracks and rifles, and old photographs. The institute is at 42 Zhongshan 4-Lu.

Memorial Garden to the Martyrs

(lièshì língyuán) 烈士陵园
This memorial is within walking distance of the Peasant Movement Institute, east along Zhongshan 4-Lu to Zhongshan 3-Lu. It was officially opened in 1957 on the 30th anniversary of the December 1927 Guangzhou uprising.

In April 1927, Chiang Kaishek ordered his troops to massacre Communists in Shanghai and Nanjing. On 21 May the Communists led an uprising of peasants on the Hunan-Jiangxi border, and on 1 August they staged another in Nanchang. Both uprisings were defeated by Kuomintang troops.

On 11 December 1927 the Communists

staged another uprising in Guangzhou, but this was also bloodily suppressed by the Kuomintang. The Communists claim that over 5700 people were killed during or after the uprising. The memorial garden is laid out on Red Flower Hill (Honghuagang), which was one of the execution grounds.

There's nothing of particular interest here, though the gardens themselves are attractive. You'll also see the Pavilion of Blood-Cemented Friendship of the Sino-Soviet Peoples and the Pavilion of Blood-Cemented Friendship of the Sino-Korean Peoples.

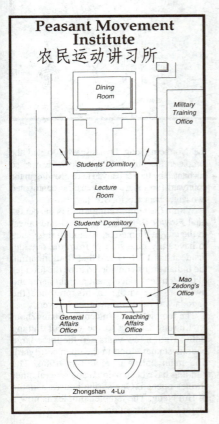

Peasant Movement Institute
农民运动讲习所

Dining Room

Military Training Office

Students' Dormitory

Lecture Room

Students' Dormitory

Mao Zedong's Office

General Affairs Office

Teaching Affairs Office

Zhongshan 4-Lu

Mausoleum of the 72 Martyrs & Memorial of Yellow Flowers
(huánghuā gāng qīshí'èr lièshì mù)
黄花岗七十二烈士墓

This memorial was built in memory of the victims of the unsuccessful Guangzhou insurrection of 27 April 1911. (It was not until October 1911 that the Qing Dynasty collapsed and a Republic of China was declared in the south of the country.) The uprising had been planned by a group of Chinese organisations which opposed the Qing and had formally united at a meeting of representatives in Tokyo in August 1905, with Sun Yatsen as leader.

The memorial was built in 1918 with funds provided by Chinese from all over the world, and was the most famous revolutionary monument of pre-Communist China. It's a conglomeration of architectural symbols of freedom and democracy used worldwide, since the outstanding periods of history in the rest of the world were going to be used as guidelines for the new Republic of China.

What that really means is that it's an exercise in architectural bad taste. In front, a small Egyptian obelisk carved with the words 'Tomb of the 72 Martyrs' stands under a stone pavilion. Atop the pavilion is a replica of the Liberty Bell in stone. Behind stands a miniature imitation of the Trianon at Versailles, with the cross-section of a huge pyramid of stone on its roof. Topping things off is a miniature replica of the Statue of Liberty. The Chinese influence can be seen in the bronze urns and lions on each side.

The monument stands on Yellow Flower Hill (Huanghuagang) on Xianli Zhonglu, east of the Baiyun and New Garden hotels.

Sun Yatsen Memorial Hall
(sūn zhōngshān jìniàn táng) 孙中山纪念堂
This hall on Dongfeng Lu was built in honour of Sun Yatsen, with donations from Overseas Chinese and from Guangzhou citizens. Construction began in January 1929 and finished in November 1931. It stands on

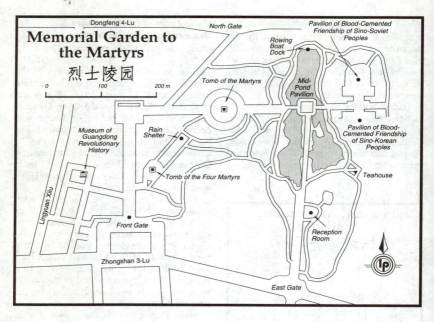

the site of the residence of the governor of Guangdong and Guangxi during the Qing Dynasty, later used by Sun Yatsen when he became president of the Republic of China. The Memorial Hall is an octagonal Chinese monolith some 47 metres high and 71 metres wide. The seating capacity is about 4000.

Temple of the Six Banyan Trees
(liù róng sì huā tǎ) 六榕寺花塔
The temple's history is vague, but it seems the first structure on this site, called the Precious Solemnity Temple, was built during the 6th century AD, and was ruined by fire in the 10th century. The temple was rebuilt at the end of the 10th century and renamed the Purificatory Wisdom Temple since the monks worshipped Hui Neng, the sixth patriarch of the Zen Buddhist sect. Today it serves as the headquarters of the Guangzhou Buddhist Association.

The temple was given its name by Su Dongpo, a celebrated poet and calligrapher of

the Northern Song Dynasty who visited the temple in the 11th or 12th century. He was so enchanted by the six banyan trees growing in the courtyard (no longer there) that he contributed two large characters for Six Banyans.

Within the temple compound is the octagonal **Flower Pagoda**, the oldest and tallest in the city at 55 metres. Although it appears to have only nine storeys from the outside, inside it has 17. It is said that Bodhidharma, the Indian monk considered to be the founder of the Zen sect, once spent a night here, and owing to the virtue of his presence the pagoda was rid of mosquitoes forever.

The temple stands in central Guangzhou, on Liurong Lu just to the west of Jiefang Beilu. Until a few years ago the three large buddha statues stood in the open courtyard. The main hall was rebuilt in 1984. The buddhas have been painted and several other shrines opened. One shrine houses a statue of Hui Neng. The temple complex is now a major tourist attraction.

I would like to suggest that you make a point of reminding readers that many of the temples listed are 'working', they're not there for tourists. At Liu Rong Si...some Americans and French were happily snapping shots of the kneeling worshippers; some even snuck up in front of the altar to do so. My Chinese friend said her blood was close to boiling...she did indeed seem awfully close to losing her temper.

Bright Filial Piety Temple
(guāngxiào sì) 光孝寺

This temple is one of the oldest in Guangzhou. The earliest Buddhist temple on this site possibly dates as far back as the 4th century AD. The place has particular significance for Buddhists because Hui Neng was a novice monk here in the 7th century. The temple buildings are of recent construction, the original buildings having been destroyed by fire in the mid-17th century. The temple is on Hongshu Lu, just west of the Temple of Six Banyan Trees. A section of the complex now houses the Guangdong Antique Store.

Five Genies Temple
(wǔ xiān guān) 五仙观

This Taoist temple is held to be the site of the appearance of the five rams and celestial beings in the myth of Guangzhou's foundation – see the section on Yuexiu Park below for the story.

The stone tablets flanking the forecourt commemorate the various restorations that the temple has undergone. The present buildings are comparatively recent, as the earlier Ming Dynasty buildings were destroyed by fire in 1864.

The large hollow in the rock in the temple courtyard is said to be the impression of a celestial being's foot which the Chinese refer to as Rice-Ear Rock of Unique Beauty. The great bell weighs five tonnes and was cast during the Ming Dynasty – it's three metres high, two metres in diameter and about 10 cm thick, probably the largest in Guangdong Province. It's known as the 'calamity bell', since the sound of the bell, which has no clapper, is a portent of calamity for the city.

At the rear of the main tower stand life-size statues with Greek smiles. These appear to represent four of the five genies. In the temple forecourt

are four stat...
temple walls...

The temple...
with an entran...
runs westwards...
are daily from 8...
5.30 pm. Next d...
equipment dates b...

Sacred Heart Chur...
(shí shì jiàotáng) 石...教堂

This impressive edifice is known to the Chinese as the House of Stone, as it is built entirely of granite. Designed by the French architect Guillemin, the church is an imitation of a European Gothic cathedral. Four bronze bells suspended in the building to the east of the church were cast in France as was the original coloured glass, but almost all of it is gone.

The site was originally the location of the office of the governor of Guangdong and Guangxi provinces during the Qing Dynasty, but the building was destroyed by British and French troops at the end of the second Opium War in the 19th century. The area was leased to the French following the signing of the Sino-French Tianjin Treaty. Construction of the church began in 1863 and was completed in 1888. It's on Yide Lu, not far from the riverfront, and is normally closed except on Sundays when mass is said. All are welcome.

Another church you may find interesting is the **Zion Christian Church** at 392 Renmin Zhonglu. The building is a hybrid of Gothic outlines and Chinese eaves. It's an active place of worship.

Huaisheng Mosque
(huáishèng sì guāng tǎ) 怀圣寺光塔

The original mosque on this site is said to have been established in 627 AD by the first Muslim missionary to China, possibly an uncle of Mohammed. The present buildings are of recent construction. The name of the mosque means 'remember the sage', in memory of the prophet. Inside the grounds of the mosque is a minaret because of its flat, even appearance and is known as the Guangta (Smooth Tower). The mosque

...Lu, which runs eastwards
...onglu.

...hmedan Tomb & Burial Ground
(...hàn mò dé mù) 穆罕默德墓

Situated in the Orchid Garden at the top of
Jiefang Beilu, this is thought to be the tomb
of the Muslim missionary who built the original Huaisheng Mosque. There are two other
Muslim tombs outside the town of Quanzhou
on the south-east coast of China, thought to
be the tombs of missionaries sent by
Mohammed with the one who is now buried
in Guangzhou.

The Guangzhou tomb is in a secluded
bamboo grove behind the Orchid Garden.
Continue past the entrance to the garden,
walk through the narrow gateway ahead and
take the narrow stone path on the right.
Behind the tomb compound are Muslim
graves and a monumental stone arch. The
tomb came to be known as the Tomb of the
Echo or the Resounding Tomb because of the
noises that reverberate in the inner chamber.

Pearl River (zhūjiāng) 珠江

The northern bank of the Pearl River is one
of the most interesting areas of Guangzhou.
Filled with people, markets and dilapidated
buildings. Before the Communists came to
power, the waterfront on the south side of the
Pearl River was notorious for its gambling
houses and opium dens. It's fair to say that
things have changed a bit.

One of the best ways to see the river is to
take the Pearl River Cruise (hǎishàng
lèyuán) which is actually a restaurant ship.
There is a lunch cruise from 11 am to 2 pm
and a dinner cruise from 5 to 8 pm. The trip
is popular with both Chinese and foreigners.
Departures are from Pier No 2 which is about
200 metres east of the Renmin Bridge and
just south of the Nanfang Department Store.

Liu'ersan Lu (liù'èrsān lù) 六二三路

Just before you reach the south end of
Renmin Lu, Liu'ersan Lu heads west. 'Liu
er san' means '6 2 3', referring to 23 June
1925, when British and French troops fired
on striking Chinese workers during the Hong
Kong-Guangzhou Strike.

Qingping Market
(qīngpíng shìchǎng) 清平市场

A short walk east on Liu'ersan Lu takes you to
the second bridge which connects the city to
the north side of Shamian Island. Directly opposite the bridge, on the city side, is the entrance to
Qingping Market on Qingping Lu –
Guangzhou's largest and most interesting market.

The market came into existence in 1979.
Although such private (capitalist) markets
are a feature of all Chinese cities today, it was
one of Deng Xiaoping's more radical economic experiments at that time. Deng
probably did not realise that he was also
creating one of Guangzhou's more extreme
tourist attractions – if you want to buy, kill
or cook it yourself, this is the place to come
since the market is more like a takeaway zoo.
Near the entrance you'll find the usual selection of medicinal herbs and spices, dried
starfish, snakes, lizards, deer antlers, dried
scorpions, leopard and tiger skins, bear
paws, semi-toxic mushrooms, tree bark and
unidentifiable herbs and plants.

Further up you'll find the live ones
waiting to be butchered. Sad-eyed monkeys
rattle at the bars of their wooden cages; tortoises crawl over each other in shallow tin
trays; owls sit perched on boxes full of
pigeons; fish paddle around in tubs aerated
with jets of water. You can also get bundles
of frogs, giant salamanders, pangolins, dogs
and raccoons, alive or contorted by recent
violent death – which may just swear you off
meat for the next few weeks.

The market spills out into Tiyun Lu, which
cuts east-west across Qingping Lu. Further
north is another area supplying vegetables,
flowers, potted plants and goldfish. There
are small food stalls in the streets on the
perimeter of the market – very cheap.

Shamian Island (shāmiàn) 沙面

Liu'ersan Lu runs parallel to the north bank
of Shamian Island. The island is separated
from the rest of Guangzhou by a narrow

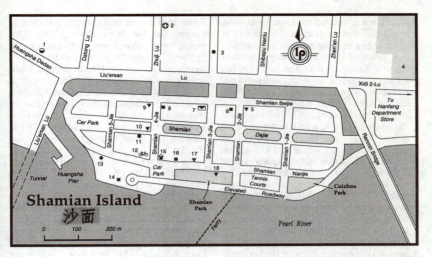

1	Huangsha Bus Station 黄沙车站	10	Li Qin Restaurant 利群饮食店
2	Hospital of Traditional Chinese Medicine 中医医院	11	Polish Consulate 波兰领事馆
3	Qingping Market 清平市场	12	Happy Bike Rental Station 租自行车店
4	Cultural Park 文化公园	13	US Consulate 美国领事馆
5	Sea Dragon Restaurant 海龙渔港	14	White Swan Hotel 白天鹅宾馆
6	Victory Hotel (new annex) 胜利宾馆 (新楼)	15	Guangzhou Youth Hostel 广州青年招待所
7	Post Office 邮局	16	Shamian Hotel 沙面宾馆
8	Victory Hotel 胜利宾馆	17	Pearl Inn 披明珠酒店
9	Victory Bakery 胜利饼屋	18	Lucy's Bar & Cafe 露丝咖啡室

canal to the north and east, and by the Pearl River to the south and west. Bridges connect the island to the city.

'Shamian' means 'sand surface', which is all the island was until foreign traders were permitted to set up their warehouses (factories) here in the middle of the 18th century. Land reclamation has increased its area to its present size: 900 metres from east to west, and 300 metres from north to south. The island became a British and French concession after they defeated the Chinese in the Opium Wars, and is covered with decaying colonial buildings which housed trading offices and residences.

The French Catholic church has been

restored and stands on the main boulevard. The old British church at the western end of the island has been turned into a workshop, but is betrayed by bricked-up gothic-style windows. Today most of the buildings are used as offices or apartment blocks and the area retains a quiet residential atmosphere detached from the bustle across the canals.

Another 30,000 sq metres of land was added to the south bank of the island for the site of the 35-storey White Swan Hotel, which was built in the early 1980s. It's worth a walk along the north bank of Shamian Island to get a view of the houses on Liu'ersan across the canal – seedy three and four-storey terrace houses probably dating to the 1920s and 1930s, but a pretty sight in the morning or evening sun. A few buildings of much the same design survive in the back streets of Hong Kong Island.

Just near the island, by the riverbank on Yanjiang Lu near the Renmin Bridge overpass, stands the **Monument to the Martyrs of the Shaji Massacre** (as the 1925 massacre was known).

Cultural Park (wénhuà gōngyuán)
文化公园

The Cultural Park – just east of Shamian Island – was opened in 1956. Inside are merry-go-rounds, a roller-skating rink, an aquarium with exhibits from Guangdong Province, nightly dance classes, acrobatic shows, films and live performances of Cantonese opera (sometimes in full costume).

One of the most breathtaking motorcycle stunt shows you'll ever see is held here in the evenings. Just as interesting is to watch the deadpan audience – no applause, no reaction. A foreigner walks down the street and all of China turns to stare, but a motorcycle stuntman performs a 360-degree mid-air flip and people act like it's nothing.

The Cultural Park is usually open until 10 pm – worth dropping into.

Haichuang Park
(hǎichuáng gōngyuán) 海幢公园

Renmin Bridge stands just east of Shamian Island and connects the north bank of the Pearl River to the area of Guangzhou known as Henan, the site of Haichuang Park. This would be a nondescript park but for the remains of what was once Guangzhou's largest monastery, the **Ocean Banner Monastery**. It was founded by a Buddhist monk in 1662, and in its heyday the monastery grounds covered 2½ hectares. After 1911 the monastery was used as a school and soldier's barracks. It was opened to the public as a park in the 1930s. Though the three colossal images of the Buddha have gone, the main hall remains and is now used at night as a dance hall (live band). During the day the grounds are full of old men chatting, playing cards and chequers (draughts), and airing their pet birds.

The large stone which decorates the fish pond at the entrance on Tongfu Zhonglu is considered by the Chinese to be a tiger struggling to turn around. The stone came from Lake Tai in Jiangsu Province. During the Qing Dynasty the wealthy used these rare, strangely shaped stones to decorate their gardens. Many are found in the gardens of the Forbidden City in Beijing. This particular stone was brought back by a wealthy Cantonese merchant in the last century. The Japanese took Guangzhou in 1938 and plans were made to ship the stone back to Japan, though this did not happen. After the war the stone was sold to a private collector and disappeared from public view. It was finally returned to the park in 1951.

Yuexiu Park 越秀公园
(yuèxiù gōngyuán)

This is the biggest park in Guangzhou, covering 93 hectares, and includes the **Zhenhai Tower**, the **Sun Yatsen Monument** and the large **Sculpture of the Five Rams**.

The Sculpture of the Five Rams, erected in 1959, is the symbol of Guangzhou.

It is said that long ago five celestial beings wearing robes of five colours came to Guangzhou riding through the air on rams. Each carried a stem of rice, which they presented to the people as an auspicious sign from heaven that the area would be free from famine forever. Guangzhou means Broad Region, but from this myth it takes its other name, City of Rams or just Goat City.

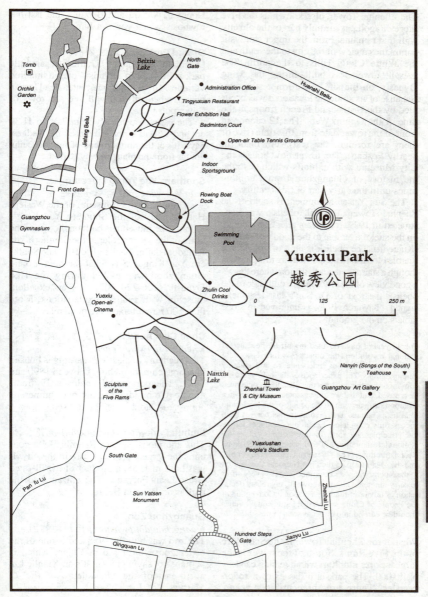

Tomb

Orchid Garden

Beixiu Lake

North Gate

Administration Office

Tingyuxuan Restaurant

Flower Exhibition Hall

Badminton Court

Open-air Table Tennis Ground

Indoor Sportsground

Jiefang Beilu

Huanshi Beilu

Front Gate

Guangzhou Gymnasium

Rowing Boat Dock

Swimming Pool

Yuexiu Park

越秀公园

Zhulin Cool Drinks

0   125   250 m

Yuexiu Open-air Cinema

Nanxiu Lake

Nanyin (Songs of the South) Teahouse

Zhenhai Tower & City Museum

Guangzhou Art Gallery

Sculpture of the Five Rams

South Gate

Yuexiushan People's Stadium

Zhenhai Lu

Sun Yatsen Monument

Pan fu Lu

Hundred Steps Gate

Jiaoyu Lu

Qingquan Lu

CANTON

The Zhenhai Tower, also known as the Five Storey Pagoda, is the only part of the old city wall that remains. From the upper storeys it commands a view of the city to the south and the White Cloud Hills to the north. The present tower was built during the Ming Dynasty, on the site of a former structure. Because of its strategic location it was occupied by the British and French troops at the time of the Opium Wars. The 12 cannon in front of the tower date from this time (five of them are foreign, the rest were made in nearby Foshan). The tower now houses the City Museum with exhibits which describe the history of Guangzhou from Neolithic times until the early part of this century.

The Sun Yatsen Monument is south of the Zhenhai Tower. This tall obelisk was constructed in 1929, four years after Sun's death, on the site of a temple to the goddess Guanyin (Kuanyin). The obelisk is built of granite and marble blocks and there's nothing to see inside, though a staircase leads to the top where there's a good view of the city. On the south side of the obelisk the text of Dr Sun's last testament, signed 11 March 1925, is engraved in stone tablets on the ground:

For 40 years I have devoted myself to the cause of national revolution, the object of which is to raise China to a position of independence and equality among nations. The experience of these 40 years has convinced me that to attain this goal, the people must be aroused, and that we must associate ourselves in a common struggle with all the people of the world who treat us as equals. The revolution has not yet been successfully completed. Let all our comrades follow the principles set forth in my writings 'Plans for National Renovation', 'Fundamentals of National Reconstruction', 'The Three Principles of the People' and the 'Manifesto of the First National Convention of the Kuomintang' and continue to make every effort to carry them into effect. Above all, my recent declaration in favour of holding a National Convention of the People of China and abolishing unequal treaties should be carried into effect as soon as possible.

West of the Zhenhai Tower is the Sculpture of the Five Rams. South of the tower is the large **sports stadium** with a seating capacity of 40,000. The park also has its own **rollercoaster**. There are three **artificial lakes**:

Dongxiu, Nanxiu and Beixiu – the last has rowboats which you can hire.

Orchid Park (lánpǔ) 兰圃
Originally laid out in 1957, this pleasant little park is devoted to orchids – over a hundred varieties. Great in summer, but a dead loss in winter when all you will see are rows of flowerpots.

The park is open daily from 7.30 to 11.30 am and 1.30 to 5 pm and closed on Wednesdays. It's at the northern end of Jiefang Beilu, not far from the main railway station.

Southern Yue Tomb Museum
(nán yuè wáng mù) 南越王汉墓
Also known as the 'Museum of the Western Han Dynasty of the Southern Yue King's Tomb'. The museum is built on the site of the tomb of the second ruler of the Southern Yue Kingdom dating back to 100 BC. The Southern Yue Kingdom is what the area around Guangzhou was called during the Han Dynasty (206-220 AD). It's an excellent museum with English explanations. More than 500 rare artefacts are on display.

Chen Clan Academy 陈氏书院/陈家词
(chén shì shū yuàn; chén jiā cí)
This academy of classical learning is housed in a large compound built between 1890 and 1894. The compound encloses 19 traditional-style buildings along with numerous courtyards, stone carvings and sculptures.

Liuhua Park (liúhuā gōngyuán) 流花公园
This enormous park on Renmin Beilu contains the largest artificial lake in the city. It was built in 1958, a product of the ill-fated Great Leap Forward. The entrance to the park is on Renmin Beilu.

Guangzhou Zoo
(guǎngzhōu dòngwùyuán) 广州动物园
The zoo was built in 1958 and is one of the better zoos you'll see in China, which is perhaps not saying much. It's on Xianlie Lu, north-east of the Mausoleum of the 72 Martyrs.

Guangdong Provincial Museum
(guǎngdōng shěng bówùguǎn)
广东省博物馆
The museum is on Yan'an 2-Lu on the south side of the Pearl River, and houses exhibitions of archaeological finds from Guangdong Province.

Zhongshan University
(zhōngshān dàxué) 中山大学
Also on Yan'an 2-Lu, the university houses the Lu Xun Museum *(lǔ xùn bówùguǎn)*. Lu Xun (1881-1936) was one of China's great modern writers. He was not a Communist though most of his books were banned by the Kuomintang. He taught at the university in 1927.

Sanyuanli *(sānyuánlǐ)* 三元里
In the area north of the railway station is the nondescript neighbourhood of Sanyuanli. Today, it's an area of factories and apartment blocks, which obscures the fact that this place was notable for its role in the first Opium War. A Chinese leaflet relates that:

In 1840, the British imperialists launched the Opium War against China. No sooner had the British invaders landed on the western outskirts of Guangzhou on 24 May 1841 than they started to burn, slaughter, rape and loot the local people. All this aroused Guangzhou people's great indignation. Holding high the great banner of anti-invasion, the heroic people of Sanyuanli together with the people from the nearby 103 villages took an oath to fight against the enemy at Sanyuan Old Temple. On 30 May, they lured the British troops to the place called Niulangang where they used hoes, swords and spears as weapons and annihilated over 200 British invaders armed with rifles and cannons. Finally the British troops were forced to withdraw from the Guangzhou area.

A little-visited monument *(kàngyīng jìniàn bēi)* commemorates the struggle that took place at Sanyuanli. You pass Sanyuanli on your way from Guangzhou to Baiyun Airport.

Horse Racing Track *(pǎo mǎ chǎng)*
跑马场
That most bourgeois of capitalist activities, gambling, has staged a comeback in Guangzhou with the opening of the horse

racing track. Chairman Mao is no doubt doing somersaults in his grave. Races are held in the evening twice weekly during the racing season, which is winter, but the exact times are subject to change. The track is east of town along Huangpu Dadao.

Guangzhou Fair 中国出口商品交易会
(zhōngguó chūkǒu shāngpǐn jiāoyì huì)
Apart from the Chinese New Year, this is the biggest event in Guangzhou. The name implies that this is a fair with clowns and balloons for the kiddies. In fact, it's nothing of the kind. The Guangzhou Fair is otherwise known as the Chinese Export Commodities Fair and is mostly of interest to business people who want to conduct foreign trade with China. The fair aims to promote China's exports, although it is a good place to make business contacts which could be helpful later in China. The fair is held twice yearly, usually in April and October, in spring and autumn, each time for 20 days.

The fair takes place in the large exhibition hall across the street from the Dong Fang Hotel, near the intersection of Liuhua Lu and Renmin Beilu. During the rest of the year when there is no fair, the building sits unused. Unfortunately, the fair is not open to everybody who would like to attend. You must first receive an invitation from one of China's national foreign trade corporations (FTC).

Getting an invitation takes some effort. Those who have previously done business with an FTC should automatically receive an invitation. Those who have never done business with China should apply to China Travel Service (CTS) in Hong Kong. They need several days to process an application.

The Guangzhou Fair is important to travellers for one reason – accommodation becomes a real problem at that time and many hotels double the room prices. The fair is a very big event, and unless you are attending, Guangzhou would be a good place to avoid at that time. If you're staying in youth hostels, this should be less of a problem since few business people will stay in rock-bottom

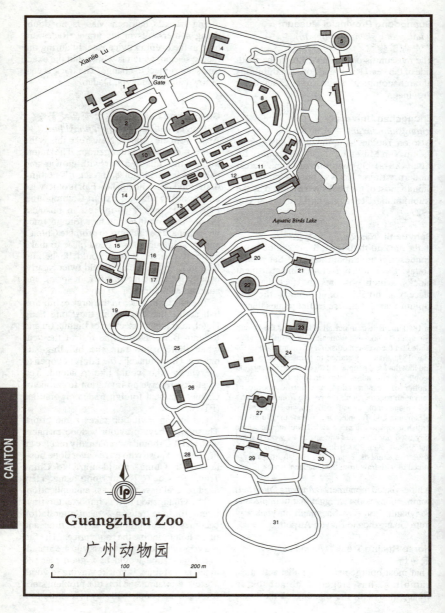

Xianlie Lu

Front Gate

Aquatic Birds Lake

CANTON

Guangzhou Zoo

广州动物园

0   100   200 m

1	Broadcasting Room 广播楼	17	Yak 牦牛
2	Baboon, Mandrill 猕猴	18	Lion Hill 狮子山
3	Gorilla 大猩猩	19	Hippopotamus 河马
4	Goldfish 金鱼	20	Restaurant 餐厅
5	Boa House 蟒蛇楼	21	Monkey Hill 猴子山
6	Snakes 蛇	22	Lesser Panda 小熊猫
7	Reptiles 爬行动物	23	Panda 大熊猫
8	Birds 鸟舍	24	Kangaroo 袋鼠
9	Smaller Animals 小动物	25	Mexican Dog 墨西哥狗
10	Gibbon 长臂猿	26	Asian Elephant 亚洲象
11	Lynx 山猫	27	Giraffe 长颈鹿
12	Bear 熊	28	Bactrian Camel 单峰驼
13	Leopard 豹	29	Zebra 斑马
14	Bear Hill 熊山	30	Bear 熊
15	Tiger Hill 虎山	31	Deer 鹿
16	Herbivores 食草动物		

accommodation. However, transport will be more crowded than usual during the fair.

Places to Stay – bottom end
For definition purposes, the bottom end in Guangzhou is anything costing under US$25.

Shamian Island Area Shamian Island remains a popular place to look for cheap hotels in reasonably pleasant and quiet surroundings. To get to them, take bus No 5 from Huanshi Xilu; the stop is on the opposite side of the road and just to the west of the railway station. The bus runs along Liu'ersan Lu on the northern boundary of the canal which separates Shamian Island from the rest of Guangzhou. Four footbridges connect Shamian Island to the city.

Near the massive White Swan Hotel is the *Guangzhou Youth Hostel* (☎ 8884298) (*guǎngzhōu qīngnián zhāodàisuǒ*) at 2 Shamian 4-Jie. By default, this place wins the title of 'backpackers' headquarters' in Guangzhou since there is almost nothing else in this price range open to foreigners. The hostel was gutted by fire in 1992 but has now been reopened with fancy decor and vastly inflated prices. The dormitories have just three beds per room and cost US$10 to US$14 per person. Double rooms are not cheap at all, costing from US$24 to US$32.

Other Zhongshan University has dormitories where foreigners can stay for US$3 per person, but rooms are often full. You will probably have to get there by taxi, which costs around US$2.

The only other place that has dormitories is the *CITS Hostel* (☎ 6664263) (*guólü zhāodàisuǒ*) right behind CITS on the east side of the railway station. A single costs US$11.50. The 'dormitories' in fact do not exist unless there are at least two foreigners staying in this place willing to share a room. If you're the only foreigner in the place, then you pay for the empty beds. The hostel really caters to locals and sees few foreigners, which is just as well since it's a fairly depressing place and the staff are hostile.

The staff at the CITS Hostel were very rude. They wouldn't give us a bed because there was already a Chinese in the room and 'Chinese and foreigners are not allowed to share a room'.

Railway Station Area Near the railway station is the *Zhanqian Hotel* (☎ 6670348) (*zhànqián jiǔdiàn*), 81 Zhanqian Lu. This place is a bargain (for Guangzhou at least) with twin rooms costing US$17.20. Even more amazing is that the staff are very friendly.

Just down the street is the *Leizhou Hotel* (☎ 6681688) (*léizhōu jiǔdiàn*) at 88 Zhanqian Lu. Rooms are priced between US$24 and US$41.

Also in the neighbourhood is the *Maoming Shihua Hotel* (☎ 6688388; fax 6682722) (*màomíng shi'ihuà bīnguǎn*), 101 Zhanqian Lu. Doubles here cost US$21 to US$25. In the very same building is the *Jinhuan Hotel* (☎ 6689510; fax 6662778) (*jīnhuán jiǔdiàn*) where doubles are US$26 to US$38.

Certainly one of the better deals in this neighbourhood is the *Friendship Hotel* (☎ 6679898; fax 6678653) (*yǒuyí bīnguǎn*) at 698 Renmin Beilu. On 'side B' of the hotel, doubles are US$20 and US$22 while 'side A' costs US$23 and US$26. The adjoining Apollo Fast Food Restaurant is a cheap place to eat.

Places to Stay – middle
For Guangzhou, the mid-range is defined as hotels where double rooms cost between US$26 and US$52.

Pearl River Area The *Shamian Hotel* (☎ 8888124; fax 8861068) (*shāmiàn bīnguǎn*), 50 Shamian Nanjie, is only a few steps to the east of the Guangzhou Youth Hostel on Shamian Island. Doubles with twin beds start at US$23.

On the east side of the Shamian Hotel is the *Pearl Inn* (☎ 8889238; fax 8861068) (*yèmíngzhū jiǔdiàn*), a fancy place known for its good restaurant, bar, sauna, disco and aggressive air-con. At the time of writing it was undergoing renovation, and when it reopens prices may well edge towards the upper end of mid-range.

On the corner of Shamian 4-Jie and Shamian Beijie is the *Victory Hotel* (☎ 8862622; fax 8862413) (*shènglì bīnguǎn*). There's a lack of English signs, but the hotel is easily identified – it looks like a seafood restaurant with big fish tanks outside. Standard/superior doubles cost US$28/31. Rooms in the luxurious new annexe are US$45/49.

The *Aiqun Hotel* (☎ 8866668; fax 8883519) (*àiqún dàjiǔdiàn*) is at 113 Yanjiang Xilu (on the corner with Changdi Lu). Opened in 1937 but fully refurbished, this grand old place overlooks the Pearl River. Given the high standards, prices are reasonable (for Guangzhou anyway) at US$35/46 for doubles/twins, or US$58 for a deluxe twin with riverfront view. The hotel seems to have restaurants tucked away in every corner – if you won't choke on the prices, check out the rooftop revolving restaurant.

The *Bai Gong Hotel* (☎ 8882313; fax 8889161) (*bái gōng jiǔdiàn*) is a pleasant and friendly place to stay though the staff speaks little English. It's near the river at 17 Renmin Nanlu. Singles (often full with long-term business travellers) are US$17, but you'll probably have to settle for a double costing US$25 or a suite priced at US$35. From the railway station, take bus No 31 and get off when you come to the river.

Across the street from the Bai Gong is the *New Asia Hotel* (☎ 8884722) (*xīnyà jiǔdiàn*), 10 Renmin Nanlu, where doubles are US$27 and twins are US$29. The hotel is a huge, elegant-looking place popular with Hong Kongers but rather few foreigners.

There is no English sign on the hotel and the staff's English-speaking ability consists of 'Hello', but it's not a bad place to stay.

Just to the south of the New Asia is the *Xinhua Hotel* (☎ 8882688) (*xīnhuá dàjiǔdiàn*) at 4 Renmin Nanlu. Another large, Chinese-speaking place geared towards the Hong Kong crowd, rooms are reasonably priced at US\$22/25 for doubles/twins.

The *GD Hotel* (☎ 8883601) (*guǎngdōng dàjiǔdiàn*) is at 294 Changdi Lu, one block north of the Aiqun Hotel and next to the palatial Furama Hotel. It's a large and attractive hotel with rooms for US\$24, US\$31 and US\$52. No one here speaks English so they prefer foreigners who speak Chinese.

Railway Station Area Zhanqian Lu has a large collection of hotels in the middle price range. One of the better deals is the *Sinochem Hotel* (☎ 6672288; fax 6674163) (*zhōnghuà dà jiǔdiàn*), 58 Zhanqian Lu. Doubles cost US\$33 to US\$36.

Also on Zhanqian Lu and just next door to the foregoing is the three-star *Overseas Chinese Hotel* (☎ 6663488) (*huáqiáo jiǔdiàn*). Doubles/twins are US\$48/57 but some travellers have gotten a discount by booking at CTS in Hong Kong.

Yet another place on Zhanqian Lu but closer to the railway station is the *New Mainland Hotel* (*xīn dàdì bīnguǎn*). Doubles in this cavernous place start at US\$45.

The *Liuhua Hotel* (☎ 6668800) (*liúhuā bīnguǎn)* is the large building directly opposite the railway station at 194 Huanshi Xilu. At one time this place was the lap of luxury in Guangzhou, but it seems to be going steadily downhill and much of the current clientele are cadres visiting Guangzhou 'on business'. The harried staff at reception speak little English. Standard double rooms range from US\$40 to US\$42. The cheaper rooms are on the ground floor and can be noisy – look the room over first before deciding on whether to stay here.

North-East Area The *Hua Shan Hotel* (☎ 7763868; fax 7760668) (*huá shān bīnguǎn*), 420 Huanshi Donglu, is certainly one of the best deals in this trendy neighbourhood. Singles, if you can get them, start at US\$17 while doubles are US\$29 and US\$35. The staff at reception seem to be very friendly though not much English is spoken.

Just on the east side of the Hua Shan Hotel is the *Guangdong Jinye Hotel* (☎ 7772888; fax 7787759) (*guǎngdōng jīnyè dàshà*), 422 Huanshi Donglu. Prices for standard doubles are US\$28 and US\$31, or you can pay US\$59 for a suite.

The *Hakkas Hotel* (☎ 7771688; fax 7770788) (*jiāyìng bīnguǎn*), 418 Huanshi Donglu, is aimed at the business traveller. Doubles/twins are US\$41/48.

Airport The *Airport Hotel* (☎ 6661700) (*báiyún jīchǎng bīnguǎn*) is right next to the main terminal and is an excellent place to stay. All rooms are air-con and reasonably clean.

Places to Stay – top end
Pearl River Area The *White Swan Hotel* (☎ 8886968; fax 8861188) (*báitiāné bīnguǎn*), 1 Shamian Nanjie, is one of the few hotels in China to boast a waterfall in the lobby. Other amenities include a pool, sauna, disco and a great location on Shamian Island. The hotel has played host to some of China's biggest big shots – the hotel's restaurant was a favourite haunt of Deng Xiaoping. The fancy trimmings don't come cheap – standard doubles are US\$80. Despite the luxuries, this place is not what it used to be. The hotel's formerly excellent in-house travel agency has shut down and there is better accommodation for the money in north-east Guangzhou.

If you're not wearing a necktie or high heels, you'll feel the glaring hostility from the staff – the management is trying to scare off backpackers who wander in to cash travellers' cheques, buy magazines, send faxes and so on. In the process, the hotel is also scaring off their guests.

The *Furama Hotel* (☎ 8863288; fax 8863388) (*fùlìhuá dàjiǔdiàn*), 316 Changdi Lu is a large and splashy place near the river. Rooms start at US\$43.

The *Guangzhou Hotel* (☎ 3338168; fax 3330791) *(guǎngzhōu bīnguǎn)* is at Haizhu (Sea Pearl) Square. Twins cost US$36 to US$47. Bus No 29 from Huanshi Xilu near the railway station goes past the hotel. Haizhu Square is a big roundabout which might be better named 'Change Money Square'.

Also on Haizhu Square is the *Hotel Landmark Canton* (☎ 3355988; fax 3336197) *(huáshà dàjiǔdiàn)*. Prices start at a breathtaking US$49 in economy class and range up to US$324 for a suite.

Railway Station Area The *Hotel Equatorial* (☎ 6672888; fax 6672582) *(guìdū jiǔdiàn)*, 931 Renmin Beilu, is a short walk from the railway station and offers plush doubles for US$48.

The *Guangdong Guesthouse* (☎ 333 2950; fax 3332911) *(guǎngdōng yíng bīnguǎn)*, 603 Jiefang Beilu, has standard/deluxe doubles for US$43/49. It's an exclusive-looking place with its own grounds and a wall around it. A sign by the lobby reminds you that 'proper attire' is required at all times. This place is actually about halfway between the railway station and the Pearl River, in a rather out-of-the-way location.

The *Dongfang Hotel* (☎ 6669900; fax 6681618) *(dōngfāng bīnguǎn)* at 120 Liuhua Lu near Jiefang Beilu and next to the China Hotel. One of the greatest attractions is the beautiful garden in the hotel's central courtyard where there are a number of gardenside restaurants. Singles/twins cost US$61/71. It's about a 15-minute walk from the railway station and bus No 31 runs right by.

Towering over the Dongfang Hotel is the gleaming *China Hotel* (☎ 6666888; fax 6677014) *(zhōngguó dàjiǔdiàn)* which boasts wall-to-wall marble, a disco and a bowling alley. Doubles are US$80.

North-East Area This is Guangzhou's exclusive neighbourhood. High-rise hotels and office blocks are being built here like mad. If there's any part of Guangzhou determined to mimic Hong Kong's skyscraper canyons, this is it.

The *Baiyun Hotel* (☎ 3333998; fax 3336498) *(báiyún bīnguǎn)*, 367 Huanshi Donglu, is one of the oldest (but still excellent) hotels in this part of town. Doubles are US$41.

Opposite the Baiyun Hotel is the *Garden Hotel* (☎ 3338989; fax 3350467) *(huāyuán jiǔdiàn)* at 368 Huanshi Donglu. This place positively drips with elegance and is, without a doubt, one of the most spectacular hotels in China. The hotel is topped by a revolving restaurant, and there's a snooker hall and a lobby large enough to park a jumbo-jet. Doubles start at US$87.

Also in the same neighbourhood is the *Ocean Hotel* (☎ 7765988) *(yuǎnyáng bīnguǎn)* 412 Huanshi Donglu. Doubles/twins start from US$41/44.

Immediately to the north-west of the Ocean Hotel is the *Holiday Inn* (☎ 7766999; fax 7753126) *(wénhuà jiàrì jiǔdiàn)*, 28 Guangming Lu. Doubles/twins cost US$55/65.

Yuehai Hotel (☎ 7779688; fax 7788364) *(yuèhǎi dàshà)* is to the north-east at 472 Haunshi Donglu. Standard doubles start at US$40 and fancier rooms are US$68 and US$72.

The *Cathay Hotel* (☎ 7753888; fax 7766606) *(guótài bīnguǎn)*, 376 Huanshi Donglu, is slightly cheaper than its neighbours at US$40 for a double and US$52 for a triple.

With a height of 63 storeys, the *Gitic Plaza Hotel* (☎ 3311888; fax 3311666) *(guǎngdōng guójì dàshà)* is the tallest building in China. Home of Guangzhou's first McDonald's, this building probably rates as a tourist attraction in itself. Double rooms start at US$67.

South-East Area This is Guangzhou's new development area. So far there aren't many hotels, but they are sprouting fast. Chief among them is the *Ramada Pearl Hotel* (☎ 7772988; fax 7767482) *(kǎixuán huáměidá jiǔdiàn)* at Guangzhou Dadao and Mingyue 1-Lu. Doubles cost US$51.

Places to Eat

The Chinese have a saying that to enjoy the best in life, one has to be 'born in Suzhou, live in Hangzhou, eat in Guangzhou and die in Liuzhou'. Suzhou is renowned for beautiful women, Hangzhou for scenery and Liuzhou for the finest wood for coffin-making. It's too late for me to be born in Suzhou, I don't like the weather in Hangzhou and I have no enthusiasm for dying in Liuzhou, but when it comes to eating, Guangzhou is a pretty good place to stuff your face.

Fast Food *Timmy's* (☎ 882012) *(tiān měi shí)* 382 Changdi Lu near the Aiqun Hotel, serves slightly modified Western fast food, including the familiar French fries, hot apple pie and ice cream in a cup. The hamburgers are an acquired taste but the fried chicken can compete with the best.

Fairwood Fast Food (dà kuàihuó) is indeed a branch of the Hong Kong instant food chain by the same name (which means 'big happy'). You'll know this place by the red plastic clown face by the door. As far as fast food goes, you could certainly do worse. There is a Fairwood in the basement of the Nam Fong International Plaza next to the Friendship Store on Huanshi Donglu.

Another place that serves a somewhat improved version of fast food is the *Friendship Cafe*, which is next to the Friendship Store and the Baiyun Hotel on Huanshi Donglu. The unfriendly menu is entirely in Chinese, except the word 'fast food' which is translated as 'hasty meals'.

The China Hotel's *Hasty Tasty Fast Food* shop (which opens on to Jiefang Beilu) should make you feel at home. It looks and tastes exactly like any Hong Kong or American fast-food oulet with banks of neon lights in the ceiling, laminex tables and food served in the finest paper and plastic packaging.

Kentucky Fried Chicken spreads its wings at 171 Changdi Lu near the Aiqun Hotel and the golden arches arrived in 1993 with the opening of *McDonald's* on the ground floor of the 63-storey Gitic Plaza Hotel. However, some old China hands recall the days of deprivation before eleven secret herbs 'n spices and Big Macs made their debut in Guangzhou:

It was a hot and steamy summer afternoon. I was sitting in Hasty Tasty, Guangzhou's premier fast-food restaurant, enjoying the air-con and sipping a large Coke with ice. As I sat there contemplating where I would go next in this sizzling weather, a foreign tourist stepped up to the counter. His name was George.

George's wife was sitting at a table by the door. She wore a purple jumpsuit, gaudy fake jewellery, horn-rimmed sunglasses and enough perfume to be a fire hazard. Her hair – flaming orange and held rigid by hair spray – looked like two jiao worth of cotton candy. She was carefully explaining to her two children how she would break both their arms if they didn't shut up and stop fighting with each other.

As George approached the counter, the waitress grinned at him. Perhaps she did that to all the customers, or perhaps it had something to do with the way George was dressed – in pink shorts, a flowered shirt and a white sunhat embroidered with a picture of a fish and the words 'Sea World'.

'May I take your order?' the waitress said. George looked relieved, obviously pleased that the waitress could speak English. 'Excuse me, I don't want to order anything right now, but could you tell me where's the nearest McDonald's'.

'Sorry sir', the waitress replied, 'we don't have McDonald's in Guangzhou. I have never eaten there. But they have in Hong Kong – I saw on television'.

You might as well have hit him with a freight train. Shock, horror, disbelief – you could see it in his face. George turned his back on the waitress without saying another word and trudged fearfully towards the table where his wife and two charming children were sitting.

'Well George', she bellowed, 'where's the McDonald's?'

'They haven't got one here', he answered coarsely. Immediately the two kids started yelling 'We want a Big Mac!'

'Shut up!' George explained. 'We have to go back to Hong Kong!' I could see he was starting to panic. He slung his big camera over his shoulder, grabbed a shopping bag full of tourist junk purchased at the Friendship Store, and headed out the door with his wife and two children behind him. I watched from the window as they flagged down a taxi, and wondered if they were indeed heading for Hong Kong.

Chinese Food On Shamian Island, most budget travellers head for *Li Qin Restaurant (lì qún yǐn shídiàn)* on Shamian Dajie near the Victory Hotel – distinguished by a large tree growing right inside the restaurant and out through the roof. Prices are very low and the food is excellent. The owner's daughter is obsessed with playing cards – if you can play too, you should have an instant friend and a formidable opponent.

The *Pearl Inn (yèmíngzhū jiǔdiàn)* is just to your right as you face the Shamian Hotel on Shamian Nanjie. They have good, cheap dim sum breakfast and lunches on the ground-floor restaurant. There is also a coffee shop serving Western breakfasts.

Also on Shamian Island is the *Victory Restaurant*, attached to the Victory Hotel. Prices are amazingly reasonable for such a high standard of service. Good Chinese food, but seafood can be expensive. An English menu is available. Near the new annexe of the Victory Hotel is the even more expensive *Sea Dragon Restaurant (hǎilóng yúgǎn)*.

Lucy's Bar & Cafe (lùsī kāfēi shì) occupies a prime piece of real estate on Shamian Island near the river. Unfortunately, every restaurant located in this building has gone bust within a year, so we can only hope that Lucy has better luck. The cafe is open in the evening.

There are a couple of good places close to the riverfront. Foremost is the *Datong* (☎ 8888988) *(dàtóng jiǔjiā)* at 63 Yanjiang Xilu, just around the corner from Renmin Lu. The restaurant occupies an entire eight-storey building overlooking the river. Specialties of the house are crisp fried chicken and roast suckling pig. The crisp-roasted pig skin is a favourite here and it's a great place for morning dim sum.

Close to the Datong Restaurant is the *Yan Yan Restaurant* (☎ 8885967) *(rénrén càiguǎn)*, 28-32 Xihao 2-Lu, a side street which runs east from Renmin Lu. (Look for the pedestrian overpass which goes over Renmin Lu up from the intersection with Yanjiang Lu. The steps of the overpass lead down into a side street and the restaurant is opposite them.) The Yan Yan is easily recognisable by the fish tanks at the entrance. Get your turtles, catfish and roast suckling pig here. It also has great air-con.

The *Aiqun Hotel* has a great restaurant on

the 14th floor. Besides the food, it's worth coming up here just for the views overlooking the Pearl River.

Over near the railway station are heaps of places to eat. Within the Zhanqian Hotel at 81 Zhanqian Lu is the *Chuan Caiguan* which dishes out cheap but excellent Sichuan food. However, you can forget about English menus in this place.

One of the city's best-known restaurants is the *Guangzhou* (☎ 8888388) *(guǎngzhōu jiǔjiā)*, 2 Wenchang Nanlu near the intersection with Dishipu Lu. It boasts a 70-year history and in the 1930s came to be known as the 'first house in Guangzhou'. Its kitchens were staffed by the city's best chefs and the restaurant was frequented by the most important people of the day. The four storeys of dining halls and private rooms are built around a central garden courtyard, where potted shrubs, flowers and landscape paintings are intended to give the feeling (at least to the people in the dingy ground-floor rooms) of 'eating in a landscape'. Specialities of the house include shark fin soup with shredded chicken, chopped crabmeat balls and braised dove. It does tend to be expensive and reservations are sometimes necessary.

The *Muslim Restaurant* (☎ 8888991) *(huímín fàndiàn)* is at 325 Zhongshan 6-Lu, on the corner with Renmin Lu. Look for the Arabic letters above the front entrance. It's an OK place, but go upstairs since the ground floor is dingy.

North of Zhongshan Lu is Dongfeng Lu, which runs east-west across the city. At 202 Xiaobei Lu is the *North Garden Restaurant* (☎ 3330087) *(běiyuán jiǔjiā)*. This is another of Guangzhou's 'famous houses' – a measure of its success being the number of cars and tourist buses parked outside. Specialties of the house include barbecued chicken liver, steamed chicken in huadiao wine, stewed fish head with vegetables, fried boneless chicken (could be a first for China) and stewed duck legs in oyster sauce. Good value.

In the west of Guangzhou, the *Panxi* (☎ 8815718) *(bànxī jiǔjiā)*, 151 Longjin

Xilu, is the biggest restaurant in the city. It's noted for its dumplings, stewed turtle, roast pork, chicken in tea leaves and a crabmeat-sharkfin consommé. Its famed dim sum is served from about 5 to 9.30 am, at noon and again at night. Dim sum includes fried dumplings with shrimp, chicken gizzards, pork and mushrooms – even shark fin dumplings! You can try crispy fried egg rolls stuffed with chicken, shrimp, pork, bamboo shoots and mushrooms. Monkey brains are steamed with ginger, scallions and rice wine, and then steamed again with crab roe, eggs and lotus blossoms.

In the same general direction is the *Taotaoju* (☎ 8885769) *(táotáojū)*, 288 Xiuli 2-Lu. Originally built as a private academy in the 17th century, it was turned into a restaurant in the late 19th century. Tao Tao was the name of the proprietor's wife. Dim sum is the specialty here; you choose sweet and savoury snacks from the selection on trolleys that are wheeled around the restaurant. Tea is the preferred beverage and is said to be made with Guangzhou's best water – brought in from the Nine Dragon Well in the White Cloud Hills.

Beijing Lu has two of Guangzhou's 'famous' restaurants. The *Wild Animals Restaurant (yěwèixiāng fàndiàn)* at No 247 is where you can feast on dogs, cats, deer, bear paws and snake. Once upon a time they even served tiger.

Highly recommended is the *Taipingguan* (☎ 3332938) *(tàipíngguǎn cānfīng* at 344 Beijing Lu, which serves both Western and Chinese food. Zhou Enlai fancied their roast pigeon.

The *South Garden Restaurant* (☎ 4449211) *(nányuán jiǔjiā)* is at 142 Qianjin Lu and the menu features chicken in honey and oyster sauce or pigeon in plum sauce. Qianjin Lu is on the south side of the Pearl River. To get to it you have to cross Haizhu Bridge and go down Jiangnan Dadao. Qianjin Lu branches off to the east.

Just to the west of Renmin Lu at 43 Jianglan Lu is the *Snake Restaurant* (☎ 8883811) *(shé cānguǎn)*, with the snakes

Location of Snake Restaurant

蛇餐馆

Not to Scale

on display in the window. The restaurant was originally known as the 'Snake King Moon' and has a history of 80 years. To get to the restaurant you have to walk down Heping Lu which runs west from Renmin Lu. After a few minutes turn right into Jianglan Lu and follow it around to the restaurant on the left-hand side. Creative snake recipes include fricasseed assorted snake and cat meats, snake breast meat stuffed with shelled shrimp, stir-fried colourful shredded snakes, and braised snake slices with chicken liver.

The Chinese believe that snake meat is effective in curing diseases. It is supposed to be good for dispelling wind, promoting blood circulation, useful in treating anaemia, rheumatism, arthritis and asthenia (abnormal loss of strength). Snake gall bladder is supposed to be effective in dispelling wind, promoting blood circulation, dissolving phlegm and soothing one's breathing. Way back in the 1320s the Franciscan friar Odoric visited China and commented on the snake-eating habits of the southern Chinese: 'There be monstrous great serpents likewise which are taken by the inhabitants and eaten. A solemn feast among them with serpents is thought nothing of'.

Bakeries One of the great delights of Guangzhou is that you can get decent bread and pastries for breakfast or snacks. The

Victory Bakery next to the Victory Hotel on Shamian Island is just one of many good places to start.

Cheap Eats Small government-owned dumpling (*jiǎozi*) restaurants are cheap and the food is usually good, but the service leaves a lot to be desired. Before you get your food you must pay the cashier and obtain tickets which you take to the cook. Especially when they are busy, customers tend to be ignored, so if you want something to eat you have to be aggressive. Just watch how the Chinese do it. Join the push and shove match, or else come back later in the off-peak hours.

Innumerable street stalls are open at night in the vicinity of the Aiqun Hotel. If you walk around the streets, and particularly along Changdi Lu on the north side of the hotel, you'll find sidewalk stalls dishing up frogs, toads and tortoises. At your merest whim these will be summarily executed, thrown in the wok and fried. It's a bit like eating in an abattoir, but at least there's no doubt about the freshness.

Adequate but mundane food is served in the little restaurants in Zhanqian Lu, a lane which runs alongside the Liuhua Hotel. A few of these places are marginally better than the others. Look around until you see something you like. Some of the restaurateurs have an aggravating habit of trying to snatch you off the street and charge ridiculous prices.

Vegetarian The *Caigenxiang Vegetarian Restaurant* (☎ 3344363) (*càigēnxiāng sùshíguǎn*), 167 Zhongshan 6-Lu, is one of the few places in Guangzhou where you don't have to worry about accidentally ordering dogs, cats or monkey brains.

Beer Guangzhou's local brew is Zhujiang (Pearl River) Beer. Tsingtao is available everywhere, though the draft is said to be much better when not in bottles. San Miguel has a brewery in Guangzhou.

Entertainment
Karaoke has taken over the nightlife scene in China and you won't have any trouble finding it. The Guangzhou Youth Hostel is probably the only hotel in Guangzhou that does not have a karaoke lounge, but maybe it will by the time you read this.

If you're looking for a pub that appeals to Western notions of nightlife, it's worth checking out *Red Ants* which is in Guangzhou Dadao opposite the Ramada Pearl Hotel. This place might be described as Guangzhou's first serious attempt to clone a Hong Kong-style bar. Beer is served in kegs (dirt cheap) and the place can even get rowdy on Saturday nights. The PBS shut down the place once, but it has re-opened and become a major attraction for foreigners. But pray that the management doesn't decide to install a karaoke machine.

Things to Buy
The intersection of Beijing Lu and Zhongshan Lu is the top shopping area in the city. Here many excellent shops spread out along both streets. Another street that demands your attention is the bottom part of that long loop street (see map) in the southwest part of the city. I can't tell you the name of the street because it changes every few blocks. The section north of Shamian Island (near the Guangzhou Restaurant) is called Dishipu Lu. As you walk east from there the name changes to Xiajiu Lu, then Shangjiu Lu and finally Dade Lu. Whatever you want to call it, it's an excellent street for walking and shopping. The downtown section of Jiefang Lu is also good.

Department Stores Guangzhou's department stores have certainly changed over the past decade. Visitors from the 1980s recall finding everyday consumer goods for sale such as jackhammers, lathes, anti-aircraft spotlights and 10,000-V transformers. These days, you're more likely to find video tape players, electric guitars and Nintendo.

Guangzhou's main department store is the Nanfang (*nánfáng dàshà*) at 49 Yanjiang 1-Lu, just to the east and opposite the main entrance to the Cultural Park. You can also enter the store from the Yanjiang Lu side by the Pearl River.

On the corner of Beijing Lu and Xihu Lu is the Guangzhou Department Store (*guǎngzhōu bǎihuò dàlóu*). The other main store in town is the Dongshan Department Store (*dōngshān bǎihuò dàlóu*), just south of Zhongshan 1-Lu and north of Dongshanhu Park.

Friendship Stores There are two Friendship Stores in Guangzhou. The main one is next to the Baiyun Hotel on Huanshi Donglu. It's adjacent to the Friendship Cafe. This store has a particularly good supermarket, so if you have a craving for Cadbury chocolate bars or Swiss cheese, this is the place to come.

The other Friendship Store is next to the China Hotel on the corner of Liuhua Lu and Jiefang Beilu. Both Friendship Stores accept all main credit cards and can arrange shipment of goods back to your country.

Shopping Malls Guangzhou's first true shopping mall is Nam Fong International Plaza (*nánfāng guójì guǎngchǎng*) immediately to the east of the Friendship Store on Huanshi Donglu. There is a decent Hong Kong-style supermarket here, but the mall is heavily geared towards luxury items like jewellery, perfume, lipstick and the latest fashions.

Down Jackets If you're heading to north China in winter and don't already have a good down jacket, get one in Guangzhou. Your life depends on it!

Down jackets are a bargain in China. With all the ducks and geese that the Cantonese eat, they have to do something with all those feathers. You can pick up a decent down jacket for around US$25 at (*gōngnóng fúzhuāng chǎng*) 310 Zhongshan 4-Lu, on the north side of the street and east of Beijing Lu and the Children's Park. This store also sells top-quality down sleeping bags.

Always check zippers when you buy clothing in China. Good down jackets should

have some sort of elastic around the inside of the sleeves near the wrists. Otherwise the cold will travel up to your armpits. Make sure that the jacket has a hood.

Antiques The Friendship Stores have antique sections, but prices are high so don't expect to find a bargain. Only antiques which have been cleared for sale to foreigners may be taken out of the country. When you buy an item which is more than 100 years old it will come with an official red wax seal attached – this seal does not necessarily indicate that the item is an antique! You'll also get a receipt of sale which you must show to customs when you leave the country, otherwise the antique will be confiscated. Imitation antiques are sold everywhere. Some museum shops sell replicas of pieces on exhibit.

Another place that plugs these wares is the touristy Guangzhou Antique Shop (☎ 3334229) at 146 and 162 Wende Beilu.

Arts & Crafts Brushes, paints and other art materials may be worth checking as a lot of this stuff is being imported by Western countries, so you should be able to pick it up cheaper at the source.

Scroll paintings are sold everywhere and are invariably expensive, partly because the material on which the painting is done is expensive. There are many street artists in China who often sit on the sidewalk making on-the-spot drawings and paintings and selling them to passers-by.

Beautiful kites are sold in China and are worth getting, just to hang on your wall. Paper rubbings of stone inscriptions are cheap and make nice wall hangings when framed. Papercuts are sold everywhere and some are exquisite. Jade and ivory jewellery is commonly sold in China, but watch out for fakes. Countries such as Australia and the USA prohibit the importation of ivory.

The Jiangnan Native Product Store at 399 Zhongshan 4-Lu has a good selection of bamboo and baskets and the Guangzhou Arts & Crafts Market is conveniently located at

284 Changdi Dama Lu, near the Aiqun Hotel.

No prizes for guessing the specialty at the Guangzhou Pottery Store, 151 Zhongshan 5-Lu.

Books, Posters & Magazines The gift shops at major hotels might seem like a strange place to shop for books, but they have a decent collection of English-language maps, books and foreign magazines such as *Time*, *Newsweek*, *Far Eastern Economic Review* and the *Economist*. You can find lower prices in Guangzhou's Chinese bookstores, but the foreign magazines are priced the same everywhere. The Holiday Inn seems to have one of the better bookshops in town.

The Foreign Language Bookstore at 326 Beijing Lu has mostly textbooks and some notable English classics, but it's slim pickings if you'd like some contemporary blockbusters. The Classical Bookstore at 338 Beijing Lu specialises in pre-1949 Chinese string-bound editions.

The main Chinese bookstore in the city is the Xinhua Bookstore at 336 Beijing Lu. It has a good collection of maps, often better than those you can buy on the street. The maps are mostly in Chinese characters though some have both Chinese characters and pinyin. It also has lots of wall posters as well as reproductions of Chinese paintings.

Stamps Some travellers seem to think they can buy stamps cheaply in China and sell them for a profit at home, but it rarely works out that way. Nevertheless, China produces some beautiful stamps, and if you're a collector, it's worth checking out. The Guangzhou Stamp Company is at 151 Huanshi Xilu, west of the railway station.

Getting There & Away

Air To give pilots a challenge, Guangzhou's Baiyun Airport is right next to the White Cloud Hills, Guangzhou's only mountains. It's 12 km north of the city centre. The facilities are pretty grotty, but a new airport is

under construction with a projected opening date sometime in 1997.

Airline Offices In Guangzhou, CAAC is at 181 Huanshi Lu, to your left as you come out of the railway station. They have separate telephone numbers for domestic (☎ 6662969) and international (☎ 6661803). You can also book air tickets at the travel agencies in the White Swan and China hotels. The office is open 8 am to 8 pm daily. There is an inexpensive bus that runs directly from the CAAC office to Baiyun Airport and back again.

International Flights There are at least four daily flights (usually more) from Hong Kong on CAAC and Dragonair for US$85. A return fare is exactly double. The flight takes 35 minutes.

There are direct flights between Guangzhou and a number of other foreign cities including: Bangkok, Hanoi, Jakarta, Kuala Lumpur, Manila, Melbourne, Penang, Singapore, Surabaya and Sydney.

Singapore Airlines (☎ 3358886) is in Room 1056, Garden Tower, Garden Hotel, 368 Huanshi Donglu. Malaysian Airline System (☎ 3358828) is also in the Garden Hotel, Shop M04-05.

Domestic Flights Check the CAAC timetable for current listings. Domestic flights with airfares (in brackets) from Guangzhou are as follows:

Destination	Fare
Baotou	US$180
Beihai	US$54
Beijing	US$170
Changchun	US$250
Changde	US$68
Changsha	US$50
Changzhou	US$106
Chengdu	US$116
Chongqing	US$102
Dalian	US$195
Dandong	US$243
Fuzhou	US$61
Guilin	US$52
Guiyang	US$73
Haikou	US$56
Hangzhou	US$94

CANTON

ion44444444

Harbin	US$269
Hengyang	US$36
Huangshan	US$80
Huangyan	US$97
Jilin	US$259
Ji'nan	US$143
Kunming	US$99
Lanzhou	US$179
Lianyungang	US$135
Liuzhou	US$45
Luoyang	US$120
Meixian	US$52
Mudanjiang	US$290
Nanchang	US$55
Nanjing	US$106
Nanning	US$49
Ningbo	US$100
Qingdao	US$161
Qiqihar	US$280
Sanya	US$64
Shanghai	US$108
Shantou	US$61
Shashi	US$78
Shenyang	US$226
Shijiazhuang	US$158
Taiyuan	US$148
Tianjin	US$170
Ürümqi	US$332
Wenzhou	US$109
Wuhan	US$75
Xiamen	US$50
Xi'an	US$132
Xiangfan	US$103
Xining	US$186
Yantai	US$181
Yichang	US$80
Yiwu	US$96
Zhanjiang	US$61
Zhengzhou	US$116

Bus Buses ply both international and domestic routes. A small sampling of what's on offer would include the following:

To/From Macau If you want to go directly from Macau, Kee Kwan Motors, across the street from the Floating Casino, sells bus tickets to Guangzhou. One bus takes you to the border at Zhuhai while a second bus takes you from there to Guangzhou four hours later. The trip takes about five hours in all. On weekdays, buy your ticket the evening before departure.

This international bus is not necessarily the best way to make this journey. Having to get off the Macau bus, go through immigra-

tion and customs, wait for all your fellow passengers (and their enormous luggage), and then boarding another bus is a time-wasting and confusing exercise. It's usually faster to cross the Macau-Zhuhai border by foot and catch a minibus from Zhuhai to Guangzhou. In Macau, bus No 3 runs between the Jetfoil Pier and the China border, via the Hotel Lisboa, Avenida Almeida Ribeiro and the Floating Casino.

To/From Shenzhen Privately owned air-con minibuses are lined up opposite the Shenzhen Railway Station near the Hong Kong border. The fare is posted on a sign where the minibuses line up, and at the time of writing was US$5. The drivers in Shenzhen often ask for Hong Kong dollars but will reluctantly accept yuan. Keep a calculator handy to see which works out cheaper. The trip takes five hours.

From Guangzhou to Shenzhen, minibuses operate from a bus station in front of the Liuhua Hotel, which is across the street from the Guangzhou Railway Station. The east side of the bus station (closest to the Liuhua Hotel) is where the big government-run buses are. These are cheaper but slower and less comfortable. On the west side of this bus station is where you get the minibuses.

To/From Zhuhai From the Zhuhai Bus Station, which is to the west of the customs building, you can catch buses to Guangzhou and other parts of Guangdong Province.

From Guangzhou, buses to Zhuhai depart from the bus station across the street from the railway station, west of the Liuhua Hotel. There are two kinds of buses – minibuses and government-run buses. The minibuses are preferable and cost US$4. The trip takes at least four hours.

To/From Guilin & Yangshuo You can get a bus ticket without problems from a booth in the forecourt to the left of the main railway station. A sleeper costs US$16 and leaves at 6 pm. A free minibus will take you from the railway station area to the long-distance bus station which is slightly out of town. You get a tour of bus stations until the bus is full. The trip is not very comfortable and takes 15 hours, but you can get off at Yangshuo if you don't want to go all the way to Guilin.

Train Guangzhou is also blessed with an international and domestic train service. Getting sleepers on the domestic routes can be difficult.

To/From Hong Kong The express train between Hong Kong and Guangzhou is comfortable and convenient. The train covers the 182-km route in 2½ hours. However, it is much cheaper to take a local train to Shenzhen and then another local train to Guangzhou.

Departures are from the Hunghom KCR Station in Kowloon. You complete Immigration exit formalities at the station before boarding the train. To reach the Hunghom KCR Station from Tsimshatsui, take green minibus No 6 from Hankow Rd (south side of Peking Rd).

Timetables change, but the current departure times from Hong Kong are at 7.50 and 8.35 am and 12.25 and 2.10 pm. From Guangzhou, departures to Hong Kong are at 8.15 and 10 am and 4.13 and 6 pm. In Guangzhou Station, Hong Kong trains go from the end of the station, not from the main station building.

In Hong Kong, tickets can be booked up to seven days before departure at CTS or the Hunghom KCR Station for US$23.50. Children aged five through nine are charged US$11.70. Return tickets are also sold, but only seven to 30 days before departure.

In Guangzhou, CITS sells railway tickets but *not* for same-day departure. Same-day tickets can be bought to your right as you enter the railway station on the 1st floor of the 'Express Departure Area'.

You're allowed to take bicycles on the express train, and these are stowed in the freight car.

To/From Shenzhen The local hard-seat train from Shenzhen to Guangzhou is cheap and reasonably fast, but there are often long queues for tickets and seats can be difficult to come by at peak times. Hard seats (the Chinese equivalent of 2nd class) are US$6.60. Soft seat (1st class) cost US$8.60, and these are only available on the express train. There are many trains everyday from Shenzhen to Guangzhou, but the schedules change so often that they're hardly worth quoting here. The trip takes between 2½ and three hours.

The local hard-seat trains from Shenzhen all terminate at the new East Station. It may be nice and new, but it's also a long way from anywhere. Just follow the crowd to take a bus or minibus to the main railway station. The soft-seat express trains all go to the main Guangzhou Railway Station.

In Guangzhou, you can buy railway tickets from CITS several days in advance. Otherwise, you can join the queues at the railway station.

Whatever you do, be careful near the railway station. The whole area is a den of thieves – everything from pickpockets to bag slitters and purse snatchers. There are people selling black market (Chinese price) tickets outside the station, but the tickets are printed in Chinese so be sure you know what you're buying.

To/From Beijing Trains head north from Guangzhou to Beijing, Shanghai and every province in the country except Hainan Island and Tibet. Sleepers can be booked several days in advance at CITS in Guangzhou (east side of the railway station). You can also book domestic railway tickets at CTS in Hong Kong for more than double the price! Hard-seat fares to Beijing are US$31 while hard-sleeper is US$51 and soft-sleeper costs US$92. The fastest express trains to Beijing take 33 hours (if on time), but most trains require 36 hours or more.

Honeymoon Train You don't have to be on your honeymoon to take advantage of it, but this luxury train is geared towards those with a fair bit of money and some holiday time. Catering mostly to Hong Kongers and foreigners, the honeymoon train is a luxury hotel on wheels. The train heads westwards from Guangzhou to Foshan, Sanshui, Zhaoqing and Maoming before turning back. You can get off at Maoming and continue on if you like, though that somewhat defeats the purpose (three days of luxurious revelry).

The cost for a three-day excursion is US$362 for two people (price is the same for one person in case you want to have a honeymoon by yourself). Everything is included – food, accommodation, tour guide, etc – but you must supply your own honeymoon partner. Evening entertainment includes dancing and a karaoke bar.

For further information, contact the Guangdong Sanmao Railway Company (☎ 7765139 ext 0163 or 0169), 374 Huanshi Donglu, just on the east side of the Garden Hotel. The schedule is subject to change but should run about once weekly, probably more often during summer.

In Future A new high-speed railway is being constructed between Hong Kong and Guangzhou which should reduce the trip to perhaps an hour or so. A new railway line is also under construction from Guangzhou to the Zhuhai Special Economic Zone near Macau. Yet another railway line is being built up the east coast with the goal of connecting Guangzhou with Fujian Province. Don't expect to be making use of all these marvellous new additions to the Chinese railway system for a long while. Perhaps these lines will be open when we publish the next edition of this book...or the edition after that.

Boat Guangzhou is the major port on China's southern coast, offering high-speed catamaran services or slower overnight ferries to a number of destinations.

To/From Hong Kong There are two types of ships plying the route between Hong Kong and Guangzhou: jetcat (jet-powered catamaran) and a slow, overnight ferry.

The jetcat (named *Liwanhu*) takes three hours from Hong Kong to Guangzhou. It departs Hong Kong once daily from China Hong Kong City, Tsimshatsui at 8.15 am and costs US$25 on weekdays or US$30 on weekends and public holidays. In Guangzhou, departures are from Zhoutouzui Wharf at 1 pm. Tickets can be bought at the wharf and some major hotels if you give them enough advance notice. All tickets cost US$3 less in China than in Hong Kong.

There is also a hovercraft departing Hong Kong at 9 am, but this only goes as far as the port of Huangpu, 24 km east of Guangzhou. This is not so convenient, so try to avoid getting on this one by mistake. On the rare chance you find yourself in Huangpu, the hovercraft returns to Hong Kong at 2.45 pm. From Hong Kong it costs US$23, and from Guangzhou it's US$20.

The Pearl River Shipping Company runs two overnight ferries between Hong Kong and Guangzhou – the *Tianhu* and the *Xinghu*. This is an excellent way to get to Guangzhou from Hong Kong and saves you the cost of one night's accommodation. The ships are clean, fully air-con, and have comfortable beds. One ship departs Hong Kong daily from China Hong Kong City in Tsimshatsui at 9 pm and arrives in Guangzhou the following morning at 6 am, but you cannot disembark until 7 am. In Guangzhou the other ship departs at 9 pm and arrives in Hong Kong at 6 am. There is no service on the 31st day of the month. The ships have good restaurants, and especially recommended are the dim sum breakfasts available at 6 am.

Ferry tickets to Guangzhou can be bought cheaply in China Hong Kong City. You can also buy them at CTS for an extra US$3 service fee.

Second class has dormitory beds, which are quite comfortable – the biggest problem might be noisy neighbours. A 1st class ticket gets you a bed in a four-person cabin with private bath. Special class is a two-person cabin with bath. VIP class is like your own little hotel room.

Tickets purchased in Guangzhou are slightly cheaper than those bought in Hong Kong because China has no departure tax on ships. On holidays there is an extra US$1.70 charge.

	Class Status	From Hong Kong	From Guangzhou
Special	2-bed cabin	US$33	US$30
1st	2-bed cabin	US$29	US$26
2nd	4-bed cabin	US$25	US$21
3rd	dormitory	US$19	US$16
Child	-	US$12	US$9

Bus No 31 (not trolley bus No 31) will drop you off near Houde Lu in Guangzhou, which leads to Zhoutouzui Wharf (see map). To get from the wharf to the railway station, walk up to the main road, cross to the other side and take bus No 31 all the way to the station.

To/From Macau There is a direct overnight ferry between Macau and Guangzhou. There are two ships which run on alternate days, the *Dongshanhu* and the *Xiangshanhu*.

In Macau, departures are from the pier near the Floating Casino (*not* the Jetfoil Pier). The boat leaves Macau at 8.30 pm and arrives in Guangzhou the next morning at 7.30 am. Fares are M$94 in 2nd class, M$125 in 1st class and special class costs M$176. There is an extra M$7.40 charge on holidays.

In Guangzhou, departures are from Zhoutouzui Wharf. Fares are exactly the same as in Macau. From Guangzhou, the boat departs at 8.30 pm.

To/From Wuzhou/Yangshuo You can purchase a combination boat/bus ticket costing US$6.20 to make an overnight trip from Guangzhou to Yangshuo via Wuzhou. The boat has dormitory accommodation and is reasonably comfortable. The boat departs Dashatou Wharf in Guangzhou daily at 12.30 pm and terminates at Wuzhou, where you pick up the bus.

From Wuzhou you can return to Hong Kong directly by ship. These depart Wuzhou at 7.30 am on odd-numbered dates and take 10 hours.

To/From Hainan Boats to Haikou (Hainan Island) depart daily at 9 am from Guangzhou's Zhoutouzui Wharf and the trip takes 25 hours. Starting from 2nd class and moving down-market, prices are US$9, US$10, US$12, US$16, US$17 and US$20.

There are also daily boats to Sanya on Hainan Island, departing Zhoutouzui Wharf at 10 pm. Prices are nearly the same as the Haikou boat.

To/From Shanghai Third class costs US$52 and 2nd class is US$80. In Shanghai, you can book tickets at CITS.

To/From Xiamen Boats run between Guangzhou and Xiamen (Fujian Province) approximately once a week. Departures are from Guangzhou's Zhoutouzui Wharf at 8 am.

To/From Wenzhou Wenzhou (Zhejiang Province) has boats to/from Guangzhou about once weekly. In Guangzhou, departures are from Zhoutouzui Wharf at 8 am.

Getting Around

Guangzhou proper extends for 60 sq km, with most of the interesting sights scattered throughout, so seeing the place on foot is impractical. Just the walk from the railway station to the youth hostel on Shamian Island is about six km – good exercise but not recommended for beginning each day's sightseeing.

Bus Guangzhou has an extensive network of motor and electric trolley buses which will get you just about anywhere you want to go. The problem is that they are almost always packed. Once an empty bus pulls in at a stop, a battle for seats ensues and a passive crowd of Chinese suddenly turns into a stampeding herd.

Even more aggravating is the tedious speed at which buses move, accentuated by the drivers' peculiar habit of turning off their motors and letting the bus roll to the next stop. You just have to be patient. Never expect anything to move rapidly and allow lots of time to get to the railway station to catch your train. Sometimes you may find you'll give up and walk. One consolation is that buses are cheap – you'll rarely pay more than two jiao per trip.

When boarding a bus, point to where you want to go on a map so that the conductor

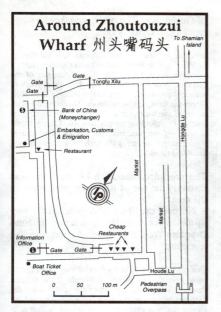

Around Zhoutouzui Wharf 州头嘴码头

To Shamian Island

Gate
Gate
Gate
Tongfu Xilu

Bank of China
(Moneychanger)

Embarkation, Customs
& Emigration

Restaurant

Hongde Lu

Market

Market

Cheap
Restaurants

Information
Office

Gate   Gate

Boat Ticket
Office

Houde Lu

Pedestrian
Overpass

0   50   100 m

the railway station to the Baiyun and Garden hotels.

No 5

Starting from the main railway station, this bus takes a similar route to No 31, but instead of crossing Renmin Bridge it carries on along Liu'ersan Lu, which runs by the northern side of the canal separating the city from Shamian Island. Get off here and walk across the small bridge to the island.

Taxi Taxis are available from the main hotels 24 hours a day. You can also catch a taxi outside the railway station or hail one in the street – a first for China. Demand for taxis is great, particularly during the peak hours: from 8 to 9 am and during lunch and dinner hours.

Taxis are equipped with meters and drivers use them unless you've negotiated a set fee in advance. The cost of a taxi varies depending on what type of vehicle it is. The cost per km (after flagfall) is displayed on a little sticker on the right rear window. For the cheapest taxis, the sticker displays the number 1.60. Flagfall for these taxis is Y6 which takes you one km, after which you are charged at the rate of Y1.60 for every additional km, though the meter clicks Y0.80 every half-km interval. The taxis marked Y2.00 cost Y7.20 at flagfall and Y2 per km with the meter clicking Y1 every half-km. In the Y1.60 taxis, a trip from the railway station to Shamian Island would cost around Y12.

Taxis can be hired for a single trip or chartered on an hourly or daily basis. The latter is worth considering if you've got the money or if you're in a group which can split the cost. If you hire for a set period of time, negotiate the fee in advance and make it clear which currency you will pay with.

Minibus Minibuses seating 15 to 20 people ply the streets on set routes. If you can find out where they're going, they're a good way to avoid the crowded buses. The front window usually displays a sign with the destination written in Chinese characters.

Bicycle Shamian Island has at least two

(who is seated near the door) will be able to sell you the right ticket. They usually tell you where you have to get off. In the early days of individual travel to China it was common for Chinese to offer their seats to foreigners. Sorry, but the novelty has worn off and these days you'll stand like everybody else.

Good Chinese maps of the city with bus routes are sold by hawkers outside the railway station and at some of the tourist hotel bookshops. Get one! There are too many bus routes to list here, but a few of the important routes are:

No 31

Runs along Gongye Dadao Bei, east of Zhoutouzui Wharf, crosses Renmin Bridge and goes straight up Renmin Lu to the main railway station at the north of the city.

No 30

Runs from the main railway station eastwards along Huanshi Lu before turning down Nonglin Xia Lu to terminate in the far east of the city. This is a convenient bus to take if you want to go from

CANTON

places to rent bicycles – finding bikes for rent elsewhere in the city takes luck. The Happy Bike Rental Station is opposite the White Swan Hotel and across the road from the Guangzhou Youth Hostel.

The Guangzhou Youth Hostel rents bicycles to its guests. A Y100 deposit is required unless you leave your passport. Bicycle theft is a problem, so you'd be wise to buy a cable lock (widely available) and try to leave the bike only in designated bicycle parks where it will be watched by attendants.

Around Guangzhou

WHITE CLOUD HILLS (báiyún shān)
白云山

The White Cloud Hills, in the north-eastern suburbs of Guangzhou, are an offshoot of Dayu Ling, the chief mountain range of Guangdong Province. The hills were once dotted with temples and monasteries, though no buildings of any historical significance remain. The hills are popular with the local people who come here to admire the views and slurp cups of tea. The Cloudy Rock Teahouse by a small waterfall on the hillside is recommended if you want to do the same.

At the southern foot of the hills is **Lu Lake**, also called Golden Liquid Lake, which was built for water storage in 1958 and is now used as a park.

The highest peak in the White Cloud Hills is **Star Touching Hill** (mōxīng líng). At 382 metres it's considerably shorter than Hong Kong's famed Victoria Peak (554 metres), but anything higher than a sandcastle is a mountain in the Pearl River delta area. On a clear day, you can see a panorama of the city – the Xiqiao Hills to one side, the North River and the Fayuan Hills on the other side, and the sweep of the Pearl River. Unfortunately, clear days are becoming a rarity in Guangzhou.

The Chinese rate the evening view from **Cheng Precipice** as one of the eight sights of Guangzhou. The precipice takes its name from a Qin Dynasty tale.

It is said that the first Qin Emperor, Qin Shi Huang, heard of a herb which would confer immortality on whoever ate it. Cheng On Kee, a minister of the emperor, was dispatched to find it. Five years of wandering brought Cheng to the White Cloud Hills where the herb grew in profusion. On eating the herb, he found that the rest of it disappeared. In dismay and fearful of returning empty-handed, Cheng threw himself off the precipice, but having been assured immortality from eating the herb, he was caught by a stork and taken to heaven.

The precipice, named in his memory, was formerly the site of the oldest monastery in the area.

North of the Cheng Precipice, on the way up to Star Touching Hill, you'll pass the **Nine Dragons Well**, the origins of which are also legendary.

One story goes that Guangzhou officials worshipped twice yearly and in times of drought at the Dragon Emperor Temple that existed on the spot. During the 18th century, the governor of Guangzhou visited the temple during a drought. As he prayed he saw nine small boys dancing in front of the temple, but they vanished when he rose from his knees. A spring bubbled forth from where he had knelt. A monk at the temple informed the amazed governor that these boys were in fact nine dragons sent to advise the governor that his prayers had been heard in heaven and the spring became known as the Nine Dragons Well.

Getting There & Away

The White Cloud Hills are about 15 km from Guangzhou and makes a good half-day excursion. Express buses leave from Guangwei Lu, a little street running off Zhongshan 5-Lu to the west of the Children's Park, about every 15 minutes. The trip takes between 30 and 60 minutes, depending on traffic. There is also a cable car from the bottom of the hill.

NANHU AMUSEMENT PARK
(nánhú lèyuán) 南湖乐园

As the name implies, this is geared for children rather than adults. However, even if you're no longer a toddler, this is still one way to kill half a day. Aside from the roller

CANTON

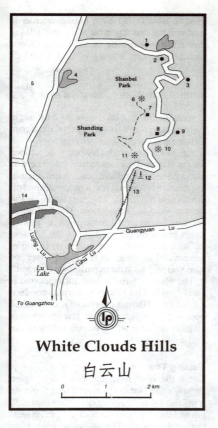

1	Liaoyang Clinic 疗养院
2	Mingzhu Building 明珠楼
3	White Cloud Billowing Pines 白云松涛
4	Dajinzhong Reservoir 大金钟水库
5	Nanfang Amusement Park 南方乐园
6	Star Touching Peak 摩星岭
7	Shanzhuang Inn 山庄旅舍
8	Twin River Villa 双溪别墅
9	Dripping Water Crag 滴水岩
10	Southern Sky First Peak 天南第一峰
11	Cheng Precipice 白云晚望
12	Nengren Temple 能仁寺
13	Cable Car 白云索道
14	Jingtai Hollow 景泰坑

White Clouds Hills

白云山

coaster, water slide, dodgem cars, skating rink and go-carts, the park has a tree-shaded lake and a good restaurant.

The park is north-east of the city in an area of rolling hills and is a good place to escape the crowds and noise of Guangzhou. However, avoid this place on weekends when it is packed.

Getting There & Away

Getting to Nanhu is easy. Air-con minibuses depart from near the main entrance of the railway station and go directly there.

Another amusement park nearer to Guangzhou is called Dongfang Leyuan, but it's not nearly as pleasant or scenic as Nanhu.

LOTUS MOUNTAIN (liánhuā shān) 莲花山
This interesting and exotic place is only 46 km to the south-east of Guangzhou and makes an excellent full-day trip. The name Lotus Mountain might conjure up images of some holy mountain like Emeishan or Huangshan. In fact, it's nothing like that.

Lotus Mountain is an old quarry site. Most people wouldn't think of a quarry as being attractive, but this place is an exception. The stonecutting ceased several hundred years ago and the cliffs have sufficiently eroded to a state where it looks almost natural.

Attempts to dress up the area by building pagodas, pavilions and stone steps have made the area into a sort of gigantic rock garden. Dense vegetation and good views of the Pearl River add to the effect. Overall, most of the buildings fit in well with the

CANTON

scenery and there are some nice walks. If only someone could persuade Chinese tourists to stop filling up the lotus ponds and gorges with bottles, drink cans and plastic bags, the area might become more popular with Westerners.

However, Lotus Mountain is now a popular summer weekend stop-off for tour boats from Hong Kong, which means that it would be best to visit on weekdays or during the low season (winter).

There is one good restaurant on the mountain in the Lotus Mansion (*liánhuā lóu*). It's doubtful that you'd want to spend the night here, but there is one hotel, the Lotus Mountain Villa (*liánhuā shānzhuāng*).

Getting There & Away

You can get there by either bus or boat, but the boat is more interesting. The once-daily boat leaves Guangzhou at 8 am and takes about 2½ hours to reach Lotus Mountain, departing for Guangzhou at 4 pm. That gives you about five hours on the mountain, which I found was about right for a relaxing hike and picnic.

The boat leaves from the Tianzi Pier (*tiānzì mǎtóu*) on Yanjiang Lu, one block east of Haizhu Square and the Haizhu Bridge. It's not a bad idea to buy a ticket one day in advance. There are mahjong tables on the boat and you won't have any trouble finding partners if you want to participate.

Buses depart from the railway station area in Guangzhou. In theory the bus should be faster than the boat, but with Guangzhou's traffic jams it works out about the same. Soft drinks are available on the boat, but no food.

The major hotels in Guangzhou also run tours to Lotus Mountain, though this will cost considerably more than doing it yourself.

There are fast boats direct from Hong Kong (2½ hours, US$23) which run at touristy times like weekends, summer holidays and public holidays. For the latest schedule, inquire at CKS (*zhūjiāng kèyùn*) in Kowloon's China Hong Kong City Ferry Terminal. It also looks like they take all the fun out of the trip. I saw several of these tour groups, usually led by a young woman in uniform holding up a big flag and talking through a megaphone as the tourist troops marched in step leaving behind a trail of rubbish.

JINSHA PARK (*jīnshātān dùjià cūn*)
金沙滩度假村

If you like cruising on riverboats, you might enjoy having a look upstream from Guangzhou.

Jinsha Park is gradually being developed into a standard Chinese carnival. There is also a picnic ground and beach with a changing room, a restaurant and a place selling soft drinks near the beach. The river is muddy but cleaner than in Guangzhou. The full name for this place in Chinese means 'golden sands beach holiday village' – the Chinese do have a tendency to exaggerate. If you're determined to swim in the Pearl River, be sure you've had your hepatitis vaccination.

The place where the boat turns around is Jinxi (*jīnxī*). The village is a small community of no particular interest in itself, but the boat trip is pleasant. Few foreign visitors come here, but it will give you a view of life in the countryside.

Getting There & Away

Catch the boat from the No 1 ferry pier, opposite the Nanfang Department Store on Yanjiang 1-Lu. Morning departure is at 9.30 am and there is a second boat at 4 pm (at least during summer). The morning boat from Guangzhou will drop you off at Jinshan Park about noon and continues upstream, returning at 3 pm. Jinxi is the last stop. After a lunch break the boat is turned around and returns to Guangzhou.

CONGHUA HOT SPRINGS
(*cōnghuà wēnquán*) 从化温泉

The springs are 85 km north-east of Guangzhou in a pleasant forested valley with a river flowing through it. Twelve springs have been found with temperatures varying from 30°C to 40°C, the highest being over 70°C.

Foreigners come here to enjoy the comfort of soaking in hot water during Guangzhou's chilly winter. The Chinese come here because they believe the hot springs can cure everything: arthritis, dermatitis, migraine headaches, high blood pressure, constipation, impotency, the lot. One tourist leaflet even claims relief for 'fatigue of the cerebral cortex' and gynaecological disease.

Unfortunately, there are no longer any outdoor pools. The water is piped into the private bathrooms of nearby hotels, so you'll have to enjoy the water without the benefit of natural scenery. Nevertheless, Conghua is a pleasant place to visit.

Information
CTS For whatever it's worth, CTS has an office in the CTS Travel Hotel. CITS also has plans to open a branch in Conghua to cash in on the free-spending tourist hordes from Hong Kong.

Places to Stay
Judging by the amount of hotel construction going on, the Chinese appear to be developing a hot springs Disneyland. Depending on how you feel about CTS, you can try the *CTS Travel Hotel (lüyóu bīnguǎn)* which is just next to the Happy Forever Restaurant. The *Wenquan Binguan* charges US$33 to US$41 for a double. Other choices include the *Hot Springs Hotel (wēnquán dàjiǔdiàn)* and *Guangdong Hot Springs Guesthouse (guǎngdōng wēnquán bīnguǎn)*.

Touts representing smaller private hotels meet arriving buses – it might be worth talking to them. Prices range around US$10 to US$20 for a double.

Getting There & Away
Buses to Conghua depart all day from the long-distance bus station on Huanshi Xilu near Guangzhou East Railway Station. Probably more convenient are the buses departing from the Huangsha Bus Station on Huangsha Dadao near Shamian Island. Some buses go directly to the hot springs, but most of the buses terminate in the town of Conghua, an ugly place 16 km from the hot springs. In that case, you have to catch another bus (20 minutes) to the hot springs *(wēnquán)*.

The one-way trip takes three hours, or more depending on traffic. From Huangsha Station, there are two departures directly to the hot springs at 7.35 and 10.35 am; departures to Conghua town are at 8, 9 and 10 am, 1.40, 2.30, 3.30, 4, 4.30, 5 and 5.30 pm.

The place is thick with bodies at the weekend, so try to avoid going then. If you do go on a weekend or holiday, buy a return ticket to Guangzhou on arrival because the buses fill up fast at those times.

FOSHAN *(fóshān)* 佛山
Just 28 km south-west of Guangzhou is the town of Foshan (Buddha Hill).

The story goes that a monk travelling through the area enshrined three statues of Buddha on a hilltop. After the monk left, the shrine collapsed and the statues disappeared. Hundreds of years later, during the Tang Dynasty (618 AD-907), the Buddha figurines were suddenly rediscovered, a new temple was built on the hill and the town was renamed.

Whether or not the story is true, from about the 10th century onwards the town became a well-known religious centre and, because of its location in the north of the Pearl River delta with the Fen River flowing through it, and its proximity to Guangzhou, Foshan was ideally placed to thrive as a market town and trade centre.

Since the 10th or 11th century, Foshan has been notable as one of the four main handicraft centres of old China. The other three were Zhuxian in Henan Province, Jingdezhen in Jiangxi and Hankou in Hebei. The nearby town of Shiwan (which is now just an extension of Foshan) became famous for its pottery, and the village of Nanpu (which is now a suburb of Foshan) developed the art of metal casting. Silk weaving and papercutting also became important industries and now Foshan papercuts are a commonly sold tourist souvenir in China.

Foshan has been devoured by urbanisation complete with heavy traffic, factories and ugly buildings – no respite here from Guangzhou. However, it is smaller, a bit

CANTON

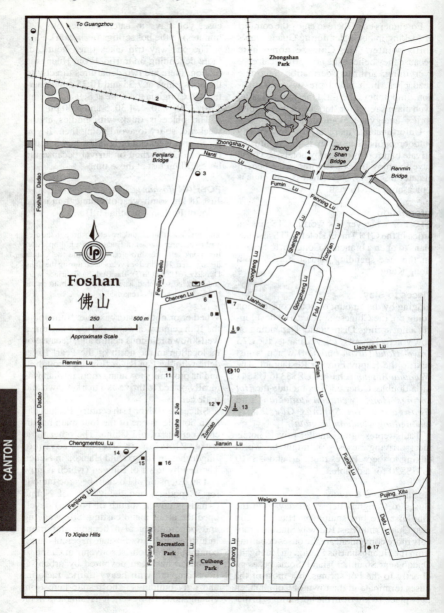

1	Buses to Guangzhou & Xiqiao Hills 广佛公共汽车站
2	Railway Station 火车站
3	Long-Distance Bus Station 长途汽车站
4	Renmin Athletic Field 人民体育场
5	Post Office 邮电局
6	Pearl River Hotel 珠江大酒店
7	Rotating Palace Hotel 旋宫酒店
8	Overseas Chinese Hotel 华侨大厦
9	Renshou Pagoda 仁寿寺
10	Bank of China & New Stadium 中国银行/新广场
11	Foshan Electronic Hotel 电子宾馆
12	Rose Restaurant 玫瑰酒家
13	Ancestors' Temple 祖庙
14	Minibus Stop to Xiqiao Hills 往西樵山车站
15	Golden City Hotel 金城大酒店
16	Foshan Hotel & CITS 佛山宾馆
17	City Hall & Public Security 市政府/佛市公安局

easier to get around. The city is worth a little bit of your time, but not much. The chief reason for coming is to visit a couple of odd temples. It's convenient to stop here on the way to the scenic Xiqiao Hills (which *are* worth visiting).

Information

CITS (☎ 223338) is in the Foshan Hotel at 75 Fenjiang Nanlu. CTS (☎ 223828) is in the Overseas Chinese Hotel at 14 Zumiao Lu.

Ancestors' Temple (*zǔ miào*) 祖庙

Foshan's only real tourist attraction, the Ancestors' Temple, is attracting large tour groups from Hong Kong and elsewhere. Recognising the opportunity, several hotels and restaurants have sprouted in the neighbourhood, but the temple grounds are still quiet and peaceful.

At the southern end of Zumiao Lu, the original temple was built during the Song Dynasty in the latter part of the 11th century, and was used by workers in the metal-smelting trade for worshipping their ancestors. It was destroyed by fire at the end of the Yuan Dynasty in the mid-1300s and was rebuilt at the beginning of the Ming Dynasty during the reign of the first Ming Emperor Hong Wu. The Ancestors' Temple was converted into a Taoist temple because the emperor worshipped a Taoist god.

The temple has been developed through renovations and additions in the Ming and Qing dynasties. The structure is built entirely of interlocking wooden beams, with no nails or other metal used at all. It is roofed with coloured tiles made in Shiwan.

The main hall contains a 2500-kg bronze statue of a god known as the Northern Emperor (Beidi). He's also known as the Black Emperor (Heidi) and rules over water and all its inhabitants, especially fish, turtles and snakes. Since South China was prone to floods, people often tried to appease Beidi by honouring him with temples and carvings of turtles and snakes. In the courtyard is a pool containing a large statue of a turtle with a serpent crawling over it, into which the Chinese throw one, two and five-fen notes, plus the odd drink can.

The temple also has an interesting collection of ornate weapons used on ceremonial occasions during the imperial days. The Foshan Museum is in the temple grounds, as is the Foshan Antique Store and an arts & crafts store. The temple is open daily from 8.30 am to 4.30 pm.

Renshou Pagoda (*rénshòu sì*) 仁寿寺

The name means 'benevolent longevity', but that's about all you can learn about this pagoda. You can admire the structure from the outside, but the doors seem to be permanently locked and there are no resident monks or worshippers. The pagoda is just

CANTON

south of the Rotating Palace Hotel on Zumiao Lu.

Places to Stay

About the cheapest in town is the *Pearl River Hotel* (☎ 287512) *(zhū jiāng dàjiǔdiàn)* which has doubles for US$21 and US$26. It's on Qinren Lu in the centre of town, across the street from the post office.

Around the corner and just opposite Renshou Pagoda is the *Overseas Chinese Hotel* (☎ 223828; fax 227702) *(huáqiáo dàshà)*, 14 Zumiao Lu. Singles cost US$23 and US$34 while doubles start at US$33.

Rotating Palace Hotel (☎ 285622) *(xuá ngōng jiǔdiàn)*, is in the centre of town on the corner of Zumiao Lu and Lianhua Lu. A double room costs US$46. The hotel doesn't rotate but the rooftop restaurant does, and even if you don't eat there, you can pay a visit to the 16th floor for a sweeping view of Foshan's haze and industrial smokestacks.

Foshan Electronic Hotel (☎ 288998; fax 225781) *(diànzi bīnguǎn)*, 101 Renmin Lu, has doubles ranging from US$37 to US$50. This 19-storey building is readily identified by a large red 'FEG' on the roof (Foshan Electronic Group). The hotel features receptionists who giggle uncontrollably at every foreigner who approaches the front desk while the FEG's colourful brochure explains '...the solicitous and attentive service by the desk girls makes the guest feeling warmth at home'.

The *Golden City Hotel* (☎ 357228; fax 353924) *(jīnchéng dàjiǔdiàn)*, 48 Fenjiang Nanlu, is pleasant enough, though the location at a noisy intersection is not especially aesthetic. Doubles are US$48 to US$57 while suites start from US$91 and go to US$356.

The *Foshan Hotel* (☎ 287923) *(fóshān bīnguǎn)*, 75 Fenjiang Nanlu, is the home to CITS. Singles are US$17 though these seem to be permanently 'all full'. Doubles are US$38 and US$62.

Places to Eat

The *Rose Restaurant* on Zumiao Lu just opposite the entrance to the Ancestors' Temple is one of the better places in town.

Hotel restaurants serve their usual excellent and pricey food. The brochure of the *Foshan Hotel Restaurant* also provides some food for thought:

For the purpose of constantly excavating, developing and researching the Chinese nationality's food cultwe, Fushan Hotel Restaurant chooses the best cream, keeps the style of palace cuisine and add the Cantonese flavour on the besis of Man-Han Banquet to solemnly present the 'Selection of Man-Han Banquet' and 'Small Man-Han Banquet' for all personalities and various circles. These banquet will make the guests to enjoy the flavour of Palace and emporor's banquet on 90's tast the fine product of Chinese cuisine art.

Getting There & Away

Air There is a little-used airport seven km north-west of the city. Unless you charter your own flight, you aren't likely to arrive this way.

Bus The easiest way to Foshan is to catch one of the numerous minibuses at the Huangsha Bus Station on Huangsha Dadao (just west of Shamian Island and Liu'ersan Lu). The slower local minibuses take over an hour while minibuses using the expressway take about 45 minutes.

You can catch a bus at the terminal on Huangsha Dadao, one block to the west of Shamian Island. From the White Swan Hotel you can walk to the terminal in less than five minutes.

You can also catch buses to Foshan departing from the bus terminal next to the Liuhua Hotel, near the railway station.

The bus from Guangzhou heads into Foshan from the north. First stop is Foshan Railway Station.

Train Taking the train from Guangzhou to Foshan (30 minutes) might seem like a good way to beat the maddening traffic. However, the time you waste organising the ticket at Guangzhou's chaotic railway station and waiting for the train will more than make up for what you waste sitting on the bus in a traffic jam. Still, it's worth considering the train if you're heading west, because the line from Guangzhou passes through Foshan, then continues westwards to Sanshui, Zhaoqing, Maoming and Zhanjiang (the gateway to Hainan Island).

The schedule will doubtless change, but at the time of writing there were six departures daily from Guangzhou at 7.25, 8.30 and 11 am, 2.10, 6.10 and 6.45 pm. Going the other way, departures from Foshan Railway Station are at 7.14 and 9.40 am, 12.39, 4.55, 5.38 and 7.06 pm. Westbound trains depart Foshan for Sanshui at 6.50 and 10.30 am, 12.40 and 3.45 pm.

For the busy business traveller, there are now direct express trains to/from Hong Kong. These cost US$25 and take three hours to make the journey. Currently, there are two trains daily, departing Kowloon's Hunghom KCR Station at 4.28 and 6.10 pm. Going the other way, departures from Foshan are at 11.50 am and 1.32 pm.

Getting Around

Motorcycle Taxi You won't have to look too hard for the two-wheeled taxis – they will be looking for you. Motorcycle drivers wearing red safety helmets greet minibuses arriving from Guangzhou and practically kidnap disembarking passengers. There are no meters and fare is strictly by negotiation. The drivers assume that every foreigner wants to head immediately for the Ancestors' Temple. If that's not where you want to go, make that clear straight away.

Pedicab There aren't too many of these, but you will see them about town. Foshan's pedicabs are really designed for hauling freight – there are no seats, just a cargo area behind the driver. Fares are negotiable.

XIQIAO HILLS (xīqiáo shān) 西樵山

If you're tired of Guangzhou's filthy air and traffic jams, these hills are well worth visiting. Just 68 km south-west of Guangzhou, Xiqiao Hills can be visited as a long day trip or a pleasant overnighter. Seventy-two peaks (basically hills) make up the area, the highest rising to a mighty 345 metres. There are 36

caves, 32 springs, 28 waterfalls and 21 crags. A number of tacky tourist facilities have been built, including a luxury hotel, kiosks, kiddie mini-train and paddle boats on Baiyun Lake. Despite these intrusions, the area offers pleasant walks and is an excellent retreat provided you avoid weekends and holidays. It's popular with Chinese tourists, but foreigners of any kind are rare.

At the foot of the hills is the bustling market town of Xiqiao, where the main attraction is the busy river port area. The hills themselves are protected in a large park and, unusually, there is no admission charge (yet). Around the upper levels of the hills are scattered several centuries-old villages, but don't expect to find ancient China here. Most of the area is made accessible by stone paths. You can cheat your way to the top by taking the cable car, but don't count on it since it's often not in operation.

Places to Stay

Most travellers do this as a day trip from Guangzhou, but within the park itself is the *Xiqiao Hills Hotel* (☎ 686799; fax 682292). It's luxurious enough, reflected in the price of US$44 for a double. Cheaper rooms in Xiqiao may be available, but foreigners are herded into the expensive places.

Getting There & Away

On Zhongshan 8-Lu near Zhujiang Bridge in west Guangzhou is a small bus station (*guǎngfó chēzhàn*) where you can catch minibuses to Xiqiao. All the minibuses run via Foshan and you can also catch them there. None of the minibuses go into the park itself, but let you off at the archway (*páifáng*) which marks the entrance.

ZHAOQING (zhàoqìng) 肇庆

Zhàoqìng, 110 km west of Guangzhou on the Xi River, is bounded to the south by the river and to the north by the immense Seven Star Crags Park.

For almost 1000 years people have been coming to Zhaoqing to scribble graffiti on its cliffs or inside its caves – often poems or

CANTON

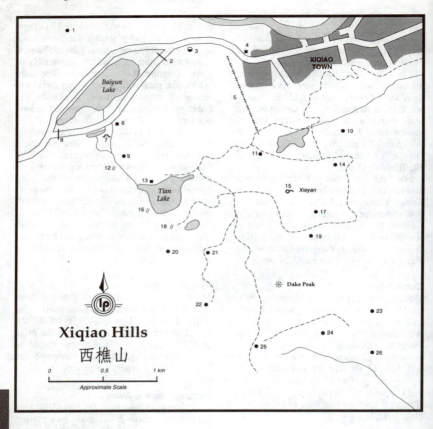

Xiqiao Hills
西樵山

0   0.5   1 km
Approximate Scale

essays describing how much they liked the rock formations they were drawing on.

If you're going to Guilin or Yangshuo, you could easily give this place a miss, but it's fair to say that Zhaoqing is one of the most beautiful places in the Pearl River delta region.

Zhaoqing is a small place and much of it can be seen on foot.

Seven Star Crags (*qī xīng yán*) 七星岩
Zhaoqing's premier attraction, the Seven Star Crags is a group of limestone towers – a peculiar geological formation abundant in the paddy fields of Guilin and Yangshuo. Legend has it that the crags were actually seven stars that fell from the sky to form a pattern resembling the Big Dipper. In keeping with their celestial origin each has been given an exotic name like 'Hill Slope' and 'Toad'. The artificial lakes were built in 1955.

The crags are in a large park on the north side of town. Hire a bicycle and head off along the paths away from the lake. Old villages, duck ponds, door gods, buffalo swimming in ponds, strange pavilions and caves can all be found.

1	Xingtou Village 杏头村	14	Baishan Village 白山村
2	East Archway 东门牌坊	15	Xieyan Spring 蟹眼泉
3	Minibuses to Guangzhou 往广州小公共汽车站	16	Youchuihong Waterfall 右垂虹瀑
4	Xiqiao Hotel 西樵饭店	17	Wuye Well 无叶井
5	Cable Car 缆车	18	Zuochuihong Waterfall 左垂虹瀑
6	Xiqiao Hills Hotel 西樵山大酒店	19	Biyun Village 碧云村
7	Baiyun Cave & Kuiguang Hall 白云洞/奎光楼	20	Yunduan Village 云端村
8	West Archway 西门牌坊	21	Dishui Crag 滴水岩
9	Yuanquan Fairy House 云泉仙馆	22	Yunlu Village 云路村
10	Jade Crag Pearl Waterfall 玉岩珠瀑	23	Heaven's Bed (Tianchuangge) 天窗格
11	Shipai Village 石牌村	24	Donggu Rock 冬菇石
12	Water Flies 1000 Metres (waterfall) 飞流千尺	25	Sifang Bamboo Grove 四方竹园
13	Tianhu Hotel/Restaurant 天湖饭店	26	Shiyan Crag 石燕岩

Chongxi Pagoda *(chóngxī tǎ)* 崇禧塔

This nine-storey pagoda on Tajiao Lu in the south-east was in a sad state after the Cultural Revolution, but was restored in the 1980s. On the opposite bank of the river are two similar pagodas. Tajiao Lu, a quiet riverside street, has interesting old houses.

Yuejiang Temple *(yuèjiāng lóu)* 阅江楼

This is a restored temple about a 30-minute walk from the Chongxi Pagoda, just back from the waterfront at the eastern end of Zheng Donglu.

Plum Monastery *(méi ān)* 梅庵

This small monastery by a lake is in the western part of town off Zheng Xilu.

Dinghushan *(dǐnghú shān)* 鼎湖山

This is one of the best scenic spots in Guangdong. Apart from its streams, brooks, pools, hills and trees, the mountain is noted for the Qingyuan Temple, built towards the end of the Ming Dynasty.

Dinghushan can be visited as a day trip from Zhaoqing, but there are hotels on the mountain costing US$19.

Dinghushan is 20 km east of Zhaoqing along the Guangzhou-Zhaoqing highway. Take any highway bus heading towards Guangzhou and get off at the Dinghushan junction. Then walk or flag down a minibus to go the last two km up the mountain.

Places to Stay

Many budget travellers stay at the *Huata Hotel* (☎ 232423) *(huātǎ jiǔdiàn)*, 5 Gongnong Beilu. Doubles with shared bath are US$9, or US$14 with private bath. Carpeting makes it US$19, or you can bask in luxury for US$28 and US$33.

The *Duanzhou Hotel* (☎ 233215) *(duānzhōu dàjiǔdiàn)*, 77 Tianning Beilu, is certainly one of the better deals in town. Although it looks frightfully expensive on the outside, singles/doubles cost US$10/17.

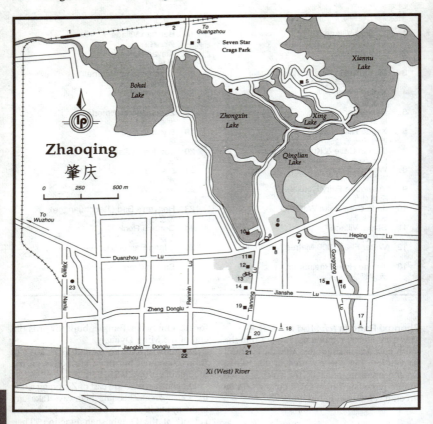

Xinhua Hotel (☎ 22574) *(xīnhuá lǚdiàn)* on Tianning Beilu is just behind Xinhua Bookstore (everybody in Zhaoqing is getting into the hotel business!). Rooms start at US$12.

Another reasonable alternative is the *Holiday Hotel* (☎ 221688; fax 221898) *(jiàrì jiǔdiàn)* at the southern end of Tianning Beilu. Singles/doubles are US$24/31.

The *Xinghuwan Songyuan* (☎ 227521) is a collection of three hotels right in Seven Star Crag Park. On the north side is the *Bohailou Hotel (bōhǎilóu)*, attractive and quiet but not as pleasant as the other two. More towards

the centre of the park is the *Xingyan Hotel (xīngyán bīnguǎn)* and just to the west of that is the very pleasant *Songtao Hotel* (☎ 224412) *(sōngtāo bīnguǎn)*. Double rooms cost US$15, US$22, US$29 and US$34, and a room for four persons is US$43.

Also in the lake, but not quite as nice, is the *Huguang Hotel* (☎ 224904, 224905) *(húguāng jiǔdiàn)*. Rooms are US$23, US$26 and US$27. The hotel is just inside the main gate on Duanzhou Lu.

The *Yuehai Hotel (yuèhǎi dàshà)* on Jiangbin Donglu and Tianning Nanlu does doubles for US$26.

1   Main Railway Station
    肇庆火车站
2   Seven Star Crags Railway Station
    七星岩火车站
3   Bohailou Hotel
    波海楼
4   Songtao Hotel
    松涛滨馆
5   Xingyan Hotel
    星岩宾馆
6   Star Lake Amusement Park
    星湖游乐园
7   Long-Distance Bus Station
    市汽车站
8   Star Lake Hotel
    星湖大厦
9   Local Bus Station
    公共汽车站
10 Huguang Hotel
    湖光酒店
11 Huaqiao Hotel
    华侨大厦
12 Duanzhou Hotel
    端州大酒店
13 Bicycle Rentals
    租自行车店
14 Xinhua Hotel & Bookstore
    新华旅店/新华书店
15 Jinye Hotel
    金叶大厦
16 Huata Hotel
    花塔酒店
17 Chongxi Pagoda
    崇禧塔
18 Yuejiang Temple
    阅江楼
19 Holiday Hotel
    假日酒店
20 Yuehai Hotel
    粤海大厦
21 Floating Restaurant
    海鲜舫
22 Passenger Ferry Terminal
    肇庆港客运站
23 Plum Monastery
    梅庵

doubles and triples are US$51, US$75 and US$103 respectively, or check out the presidential suite for US$625.

The *Star Lake Hotel* (☎ 221188) (*xīnghú dàshà*), 37 Duanzhou 4-Lu, is a multistorey glass high-rise that looks ridiculously out of place in a town noted for its parks, lakes and hills. All this gaudiness costs US$48, US$52 or US$57.

Places to Eat
One can only hope that the Sungs and the Jesuits ate somewhat better. There's nothing remarkable to be had here. The bus station has a cheap, tolerable restaurant and there are cheap restaurants along Duanzhou Lu and Tianning Lu. There is a *Floating Restaurant* (*hǎixiān fǎng*) on the river which serves seafood and attracts Hong Kongers.

Getting There & Away
Bus There are buses to Zhaoqing from

Jinye Hotel (☎ 221338; fax 221368) (*jīnyè dàshà*) is at the southern end of Gongnong Beilu. Doubles cost from US$24 to US$31, with suites available for US$84 and US$101.

Huaqiao Hotel (☎ 232952) (*huáqiáo dàshà*), 90 Tianning Beilu, has an excellent location but prices to make you pause. Singles,

Around Zhaoqing
肇庆郊区

0   1   2 km

Bohai Lake
Seven Star Crags
Dong Lake
Zhongxin Lake
Qinglian Lake
GAOYAO COUNTY
Huguang Lake
ZHAOQING CITY
To Dinghushan
Flowery Pagoda
Yuejiang Tower
Xi (West) River

CANTON

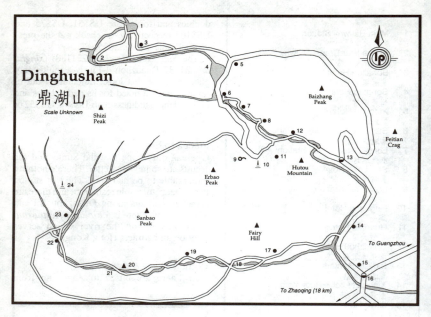

Dinghushan

鼎湖山

Scale Unknown

1	**Heaven Lake** 天湖	13	**Bus Station** 鼎湖山汽车站
2	**Cliff-face Plank Path** 连天栈道	14	**Archway** 牌楼
3	**No 1 Hydroelectric Station** 水电一站	15	**Kengkou Store** 坑口商店
4	**Grass Pond** 草塘	16	**Kengkou Bus Station** 坑口汽车站
5	**No 2 Hydroelectric Station** 水电二站	17	**Crane Viewing Pavilion** 望鹤亭
6	**Twin Rainbow Bridge** 双虹飞堑	18	**Ping Lake** 平湖
7	**Tingpu Pavilion** 听瀑亭	19	**Lion's Roar Rock** 狮吼石
8	**Sun Yatsen Swimming Area** 孙中山游泳处	20	**Pearl Mouth Mountain** 含珠洞
9	**Gulong Spring** 古龙泉	21	**White Goose Pond** 白鹅潭
10	**Qingyun Temple** 庆云寺	22	**Leaping Dragon Pool** 跃龙潭
11	**Tea Flower Pavilion** 花茶阁	23	**Leaping Dragon Nunnery** 跃龙庵
12	**Half Mountain Pavilion** 半山亭	24	**White Cloud Temple** 白云寺

CANTON

Guangzhou's long-distance bus station on Huanshi Xilu. There are half a dozen buses a day and the trip takes about 2½ hours. Try to avoid returning to Guangzhou on a weekend afternoon as traffic jams are common on this road.

Privately run minibuses operate between Zhaoqing and Guangzhou. In Zhaoqing the minibus ticket office is inside the main gate of the Seven Star Crags Park.

Train Be careful – there are two railway stations in Zhaoqing. All trains stop at the main railway station (*zhàoqìng huǒchē zhàn*) but only train Nos 351 and 356 make a stop at the Seven Star Crags Railway Station (*qīxīngyán huǒchē zhàn*). If you get into a taxi and say you want to go to the railway station, drivers will automatically assume you mean the main railway station.

Trains from Guangzhou cost US$3 hard-seat and take two to three hours. All trains also stop at Foshan. Train Nos 69 and 70 connect Zhaoqing and Shenzhen – you do not need to get off at Guangzhou if you wish to go straight through.

Boat The dock and ticket office for boats to Wuzhou and Guangzhou is at 3 Jiangbin Donglu, just west of the intersection with Renmin Nanlu. It appears that only lower-class boat tickets can be bought here since Zhaoqing is an intermediate stop. Boats to Wuzhou and Guangzhou depart in the early

evening. From Zhaoqing to Wuzhou takes around 12 hours. From Zhaoqing to Guangzhou is a 10-hour trip. The boat is not popular because it's so slow. In Guangzhou, departures are from Dashatou Wharf.

In the tourist season (basically summer and holidays), there are direct boats to and from Hong Kong. There are two boats, the Xijiang which is an overnight ferry taking 12 hours, and the Duanzhouhu which is a high-speed catamaran taking five hours. The Xijiang departs Hong Kong on odd-numbered dates at 7.30 pm, and departs Zhaoqing on even-numbered dates at 7 pm. The Duanzhouhu departs Hong Kong on odd-numbered dates at 7.45 am and departs Zhaoqing on even-numbered dates at 2 pm. Fares are as follows:

Xijiang (overnight ferry)

Class	From HK	From Zhaoqing
Special A	US$80	-
Special B	US$47	-
1st	US$41	US$37
2nd	US$37	US$33
3rd	US$30	US$26

Duanzhouhu (catamaran)

Class	From HK	From Zhaoqing
Special	US$40	US$34
1st	US$37	US$33

Getting Around

The local bus station is on Duanzhou Lu, a few minutes' walk east of the intersection with Tianning Lu. Bus No 1 runs to the ferry

CANTON

Train Schedule

Train No	From	To	Depart	Arrive
351	Guangzhou	Zhaoqing	7.25 am	9.51 am
69	Guangzhou	Zhaoqing	11.07 am	1.20 pm
353	Guangzhou	Zhaoqing	4.45 pm	7.43 pm
355	Guangzhou	Zhaoqing	7.00 pm	9.25 pm
352	Zhaoqing	Guangzhou	7.15 am	9.56 am
354	Zhaoqing	Guangzhou	10.12 am	12.50 pm
70	Zhaoqing	Guangzhou	2.25 pm	4.30 pm
356	Zhaoqing	Guangzhou	5.45 pm	8.22 pm
282/283	Zhanjiang	Zhaoqing	6.30 pm	3.59 am
281/284	Zhaoqing	Zhanjiang	11.59 pm	10.20 am

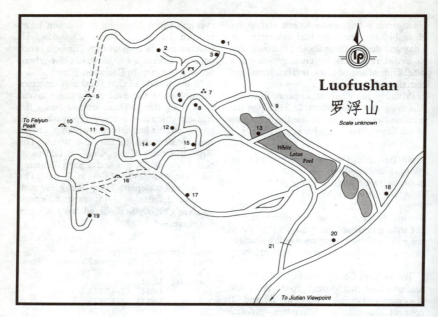

1	Yuanshuai Building 元帅楼	12	Taoyuan Cave Heaven 桃源洞天
2	Shishan Pavilion 狮山亭	13	Huxin Pavilion 湖心亭
3	Zhuming Cave Heaven 朱明洞天	14	Feilai Rock 飞来石
4	Liandan Picnic Area 炼丹灶	15	Penglai Path 蓬莱径
5	Hudie Cave 蝴蝶洞	16	Penglai Fairy Cave 蓬莱仙洞
6	Dongpo Pavilion 东坡亭	17	Fanjue Pavilion 梵觉亭
7	Chongxu Ancient Site 冲虚古观	18	Zhuyun Pavilion 驻云亭
8	Xiyao Pool 洗药池	19	Kuangxin Pavilion 旷心亭
9	Huixian Bridge 会仙桥	20	Meihua Pavilion 梅花亭
10	Quanyuan Cave 泉源洞	21	Luofushan Gate 罗浮山门楼
11	Yiluxuan 遗履轩		

CANTON

dock on the Xi River. Bus Nos 4 and 5 go to the Plum Monastery.

The railway station is well out of town near the north-west corner of the lake. Taxis and minibuses into town are cheap.

Next to walking, the best way to get around Zhaoqing is by bicycle. There is a hire place diagonally opposite the main entrance to the Seven Star Crags, and another south of the Duanzhou Hotel. They ask exorbitant fees if you have a foreign face, but will accept US$2 per day.

LUOFUSHAN (luófúshān) 罗浮山

Possibly the best sight in Guangdong Province, Luofushan (Catch Fortune Mountain) is one of China's principal Taoist sites. It's also the place where the third patriarch of Buddhism wrote poems, and the mountainside is appropriately dressed for the occasion with temples. However, you need not have any interest in Buddhism or Taoism to enjoy the fine scenery. Luofushan presents a dramatic face, rising sharply from the plains to an elevation of 1281 metres. Silver pheasants breed on the mountain.

Despite Luofushan's enchanting scenery and religious appeal, surprisingly few Hong Kongers have ever heard of the place. Most residents of Guangzhou have been there at least once, but the mountain has yet to make it on the international tour circuit. Perhaps that alone is a good reason to visit.

Getting There & Away

Luofushan is approximately 100 km east of Guangzhou, and about the same distance north of Hong Kong. The easiest approach is from Guangzhou where there are early morning buses to the mountain from the main bus station (near Guangzhou Railway Station).

Coming from the direction of Shenzhen, it is possible to reach Luofushan by making a number of transfers, but this is advised only if you can speak some Chinese. First take the train to Shitan. When exiting the railway station at Shitan, turn left and walk nearly one km to reach the main road where you get buses to Zengcheng (22 km north of Shitan). Zengcheng is on a major east-west highway, and you can get buses or minibuses to Changning which is six km from Luofushan. From Changning there are many minibuses going the remaining distance to the mountain.

Many Guangzhou travel agents are willing to book a car or minibus for a group, with fees starting at US$100 for a full day-trip. This isn't too outrageous if split between four or more travellers.

CANTON

Shenzhen 深圳

'The mountains are high and the emperor is far away', says an ancient Chinese proverb, meaning that life can be relatively free if one keeps far enough away from the central government. Shenzhen is more than 2300 km from Beijing but within sight of Hong Kong, and a living example of the wisdom of this ancient proverb. Like citizens of Hong Kong, Shenzhen residents want only one thing from Beijing – to be left alone.

Shenzhen is a border town with Hong Kong and officially labelled a Special Economic Zone (SEZ). The Shenzhen SEZ came into existence in 1980. Three other SEZs were established at the same time: Zhuhai (near Macau), Shantou in the eastern part of Guangdong Province and Xiamen in Fujian Province.

But it soon became apparent that Shenzhen's location gave it major advantages over the others. Hong Kong investors can easily slip across the border to keep an eye on the factories they have set up in Shenzhen to exploit China's cheap land and labour. Hong Kong tourists find it cheap and convenient to make weekend excursions to the new luxury resorts that have sprung up in Shenzhen. These resorts were also built by Hong Kong investors. A maximum tax rate of 15% and a minimum of bureaucratic hassles (at least by Chinese standards) makes Shenzhen an attractive place to invest.

Another attraction is its open policy on housing. In China everybody needs a permit, called a *hukou*, to establish where they can live. Legally changing your place of residence is a

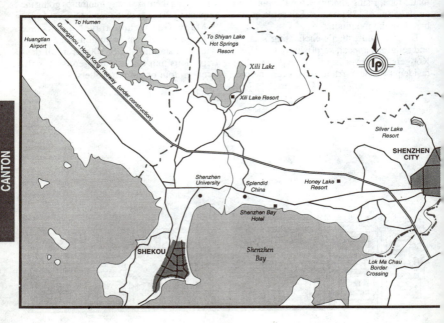

difficult procedure in bureaucratic China, but anyone who buys a flat in Shenzhen can live there. Taking advantage of this, many Hong Kongers bought flats in Shenzhen's new high-rises and moved their relatives to the border area where they could be easily visited. Taking advantage of the fact that housing costs in Shenzhen are only about a third of the price in Hong Kong, many Hong Kongers have also moved to Shenzhen and commute daily across the border.

Shenzhen even benefits from Hong Kong's waste. Many old taxis and buses were given or sold for scrap to Shenzhen where they now make up the bulk of the public transport. This accounts for the large number of vehicles in Shenzhen with the steering wheel on the right-hand side. It's also the reason why so many vehicles in Shenzhen look like they belong in the wrecking yard.

When travellers take the train from Hong Kong to China, the first view they get of the People's Republic of China (PRC) is Shenzhen. For some, it's a dramatic entrance. For others, it's an anti-climax. With its towering skyscrapers Shenzhen looks so much like Hong Kong that you'll wonder if you didn't accidentally get on the wrong train.

After passing through customs most travellers board the first train for Guangzhou, only stopping in Shenzhen long enough to change money and use the toilet. This is a pity, because Shenzhen is worth exploring, even if only for a day. True, the Chinese are trying to make Shenzhen into another Manhattan, but they haven't really succeeded, at least not yet.

As the first and most important of China's SEZs, Shenzhen has received the closest possible scrutiny from Beijing. During the first few years of operation, it was deemed a failure, especially by hardline Communist

Sanzhoutian
Reservoir

Xiaomeisha
Beach Resort

Wutong Peak
(944 m)

Shenzhen
Reservoir

Mirs
Bay

HONG
KONG

Wu
rder
ssing

Wenjindu
Border
Crossing

**Shenzhen Special
Economic Zone**

深圳市经济特区

0   2.5   5 km

CANTON

opponents of economic reform. Amongst the problems cited was the tendency for Shenzhen to attract imported goods which were then smuggled to other parts of China. There was also the ceaseless black marketeering in foreign currency (still a popular profession). Yet another problem was that the Chinese government discovered that its own enterprises didn't (and still don't) compete very well against more efficient private companies.

In late 1992, China's leaders had a rude reminder of how free-market capitalism can clash with socialist attempts at central planning. When the decision was made to establish China's second stock market in Shenzhen (the first is in Shanghai), it soon became obvious that not enough shares would be issued to meet demand. The government's answer was to issue applications to perspective shareholders, but these too fell short of demand. Amidst rumours that cadres were withholding the applications so that only they could buy shares, riots broke out which were quelled with swift brutality. Hong Kong reporters trying to cover the riots were detained by the police and threatened. Thus did the leadership in Beijing demonstrate how much it knows about governing a free-market enclave. Hong Kongers – with their eyes on 1997 – took note.

Few today would call Shenzhen a failure – on the contrary, it's a boomtown. While an economic growth rate of 10% is considered very fast, Shenzhen has chalked up an incredible average of 45% in recent years!

Shenzhen's population is booming too, not from births but from immigration. While hardly anyone wanted to live in Shenzhen when it was first designated a SEZ, today the government has to fight to keep people out. Access to the SEZ is restricted – Chinese citizens need a special permit to visit Shenzhen, though foreigners can visit by simply showing a passport. Indeed, Shenzhen experiences the same problem that Hong Kong has with illegal immigrants. To stem the human tide, an electrified fence has been installed around the SEZ. Nevertheless, the population of three million is growing by an incredible 20% a year. At this breakneck speed, Shenzhen will soon be one of China's largest cities – it is already one of the most important economically.

It's not hard to understand why the immigrants keep coming. Typical salaries in Shenzhen are nearly five times the national average. Of course, the cost of living is also much higher than elsewhere in China (almost as high as Hong Kong), but employment in Shenzhen is relatively easy to find. There is no doubt that Shenzhen residents are economically better off than other Chinese.

Shenzhen is very much a bold experiment. The Chinese are learning from their experience in Shenzhen just how a modern capitalist economy works. It's true that Shenzhen is not the real China – it's what China would be if it were not Communist.

ORIENTATION

The name 'Shenzhen' refers to three places: Shenzhen City (opposite the Hong Kong border crossing at Lo Wu); Shenzhen Special Economic Zone (SEZ); and Shenzhen County, which extends several km north of the SEZ. Most of the hotels, restaurants and shopping centres are in Shenzhen City, along Renmin Nanlu, Jianshe Lu and Shennan Lu.

In the western area of the SEZ is the port of Shekou where you can get a hoverferry to Hong Kong. Shenzhen University is also in the west, as are the holiday resorts of Shenzhen Bay and Honey Lake. The main attraction in the eastern part of the zone is the beach at Xiaomeisha.

The northern part of the SEZ is walled off from the rest of China by an electrified fence to prevent smuggling and to keep back the hoards of people trying to emigrate illegally into Shenzhen and Hong Kong. There is a checkpoint when you leave the SEZ. You don't need your passport to leave but you will need it to get back in, so don't leave it in your hotel if you decide to make a day trip outside Shenzhen.

INFORMATION
Tourist Office

CITS (☎ 2229403) has two offices. The most convenient is on the 1st floor of the new railway station, but the main office is at 2 Chuanbu Jie, just west of Heping Lu.

Post & Telecommunications

The GPO is at the north end of Jianshe Lu and is often packed out – a great place to practice sumo wrestling. Telecommunications is in a separate building on Shennan Donglu (see map), but many hotels now offer IDD service right from your room. Rates to Hong Kong are very cheap.

For direct dialling to Shenzhen, the area code is ☎ 0755.

Public Security

The Foreign Affairs Office of the Public Security Bureau (☎ 5572114) is on the west end of Jiefang Lu, on the north side of the street.

Money

Hotels change money or you can do it right at the border crossing from Hong Kong. There is also a large Bank of China at 23 Jianshe Lu.

Although Hong Kong is supposed to revert to China in 1997, it seems that Hong Kong has taken over Shenzhen – while Chinese yuan is the legal currency of Shenzhen, Hong Kong dollars is the real one. Upmarket hotels only accept Hong Kong dollars but might take Chinese money after much argument. After all, why should the Chinese accept their own currency? Mid-range hotels will accept Chinese money, though the staff might scowl.

It is much the same story in restaurants and some supermarkets. Expensive places ask for Hong Kong dollars, while down at the lower end yuan is OK. But even street vendors may ask you for Hong Kong dollars, at least if you have a foreign face!

Note the current exchange rates when you enter China and keep a calculator handy. Some places give you a better deal when you pay in Hong Kong dollars, but often the opposite is true. You need that calculator to figure out which currency gives you the best value.

Invariably, moneychangers will approach you on the street and yell *gāngbì* (Hong Kong dollars). Like elsewhere in China, most are swindlers.

If you have an Electronic Teller Card (ETC) from Hong Kong, you can use it to withdraw cash from the Hong Kong & Shanghai Bank, which has an auto-teller machine on the south-west corner of Cunfeng Lu and Renmin Nanlu, adjacent to the Century Plaza Hotel.

Maps

Chinese character maps of Shenzhen are widely available from stalls near the railway station and elsewhere. English-language maps of Shenzhen are only readily available in Hong Kong.

Laundry

There is a laundry (sign in English!) on the north side of the Overseas Chinese Hotel on Heping Lu.

SHENZHEN CITY (shēnzhèn shì) 深圳市

There isn't much in Shenzhen City to see, but it's still an interesting place to explore. The urban area near the border is a good place for walking. Most visitors spend their time exploring the shopping arcades and restaurants along Renmin Nanlu and Jianshe Lu.

SPLENDID CHINA
(jǐnxiù zhōnghuá) 锦绣中华

This is the mainland's answer to Taiwan's Window on China. The tourist brochure for Splendid China says 'visit all of China in one day'. You get to see Beijing's Forbidden City, the Great Wall, Tibet's Potala Palace, the Shaolin Temple, the gardens of Suzhou, the rock formations of Guilin, the Tianshan Mountains of Xinjiang, the Stone Forest in Yunnan, Huangguoshu Waterfall and even some sights in Taiwan. The catch is that everything is reduced to one-fifthteenth of life size.

Some foreigners find the place intriguing; others call it a 'bad Disneyland without the rides'. The Chinese are crazy about the place

CANTON

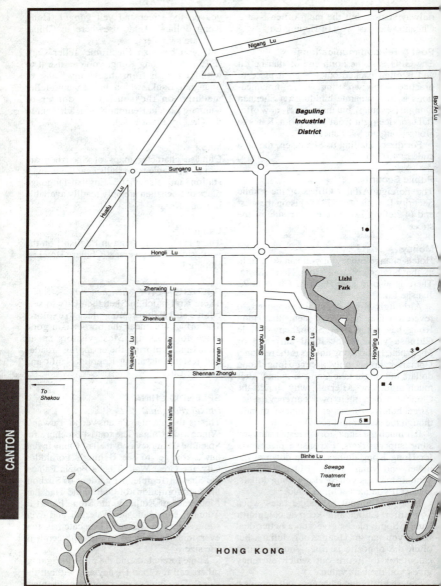

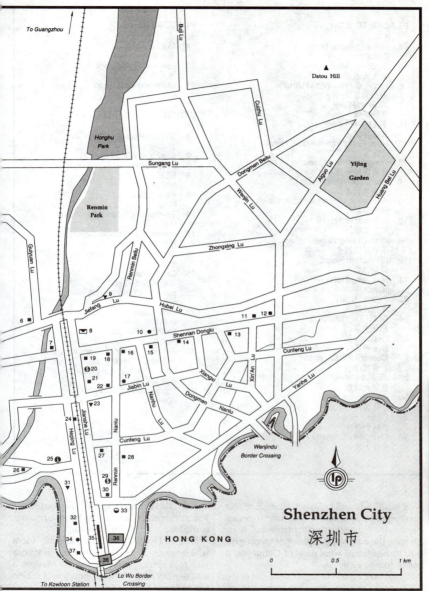

To Guangzhou

Datou Hill

Buji Lu

Ciuzhu Lu

Dongmen Beilu

Aiguo Lu

Yijing
Garden

Huang Bei Lu

Honghu
Park

Sungang Lu

Weijin Lu

Renmin
Park

Zhongxing Lu

Guiyuan Lu

Renmin Beilu

9

Jiefang Lu

Hubei Lu

11   12

6

8

10

Shennan Donglu

13

7

14

Cunfeng Lu

19   18

16   15

Xianxi Lu

Xin'An Lu

20

21   17

Jiabin Lu

22

Dongmen Nanlu

Yanhe Lu

23

Nanhu Lu

Nanlu

24

Jianshe Lu

Cunfeng Lu

Wenjindu
Border Crossing

25

27   28

26

Renmin

29

30

31

CANTON

Shenzhen City
深圳市

32

33

34   35   36   HONG KONG

37

38

0   0.5   1 km

To Kowloon Station

Lo Wu Border
Crossing

PLACES TO STAY

4 Hotel Oriental Regent
晶都酒店
5 Binjiang Hotel
宾江大酒店
6 Hubei & New World Hotels
湖北宾馆/新世界宾馆
7 Yatwah Hotel
日华宾馆
11 Jingpeng Hotel
京鹏宾馆
12 Nam Fong International Hotel
南方国际大酒店
13 Tung Nam International Hotel
东南国际大酒店
14 Far East Grand Hotel
远东大酒店
15 Airlines & Guangdong Hotels
航空酒店
16 Oriental Hotel
东方酒店
18 Wah Chung Hotel
华中国际酒店
19 Shenzhen Hotel
深圳酒店
21 Nanyang Hotel
南洋酒店
22 Petrel Hotel
海燕大酒店
24 Shen Tieh Building
深铁大厦
26 Heping Hotel
和平酒店
27 Century Plaza Hotel
新都酒店
28 Jinghu Hotel
京湖大酒店
30 Shangri-La Hotel
香格里拉大酒店
32 Forum Hotel
富临大酒店
37 Overseas Chinese Hotel
华侨大厦

PLACES TO EAT

9 McDonald's
麦当劳
23 Pan Hsi Restaurant
泮溪酒家
31 Fairwood Fast Food
大快活

OTHER

1 Xinhua Bookstore
新华书店
2 Shenzhen City Hall
深圳市政府
3 PSB
公安局外事科
8 Post Office
邮局
10 Telecommunications Building
电信大楼
17 International Trade Centre
国贸大厦
20 Bank of China (large)
中国银行
25 CITS Main Office
中国国际旅行社
29 Bank of China (small)
中国银行
33 Minibuses
小公共汽车站
34 Laundry Service
洗衣店
35 Railway Station & Dragon Inn
火车站/港龙大酒店
36 Lowu Commercial Plaza
罗湖商业城
38 Immigration & Customs
联检大楼

– on weekends and holidays, Hong Kongers converge on Splendid China like it was a carnival – in fact, that's just what it is. Despite the circus atmosphere, it might give you some idea of what parts of China you'd really like to visit.

Splendid China is in the western end of the SEZ, near Shenzhen Bay. From the railway station there are frequent minibuses. If you're entering Shenzhen by hoverferry, you could take a taxi from Shekou.

CTS in Hong Kong books full-day tours which take in Splendid China, along with a visit to a kindergarten, Dongmen Market, a traditional Hakka village, lunch and return trip to Hong Kong.

CHINA FOLK CULTURE VILLAGES
(zhōngguó mínsú wénhuà cūn)
中国民俗文化村

Adjacent to the previously mentioned Splendid China, the China Folk Culture Villages seeks to do the same thing – give you a chance to see all of China in one day. In this case, rather than admiring miniaturised temples and mountains, you get to see full-sized ethnic minorities. To add to the effect, there are over 20 re-creations of minority villages including a cave, Lama Temple, drum tower, rattan bridge and a statue of Guanyin (Kuanyin), the Goddess of Mercy. Just to remind you of China's claim to Taiwan, the 'Gaoshan' (high mountain) minority was invented to represent Taiwan's 10 aboriginal tribes. However, as yet there are no representatives of Hong Kong's gwailo minority – could be an employment opportunity here.

OVERSEAS CHINESE TOWN
(huáqiáo chéng) 华侨城

This is not really meant to be a tourist attraction, but rather a residential area for upper crust Overseas Chinese investors who operate businesses in Shenzhen. There are some factories in this district too, but they are not the dirty, smoke-belching type. The official name for this place is the 'Overseas Chinese Town Economic Development Area' and it covers some five sq km of which only half is yet developed.

CTS (Hong Kong branch) has invested heavily in this place, and there is an Overseas Chinese Town CTS branch office (☎ 6601163). If you're interested in coming here to invest or speculate in real estate (a popular Hong Kong activity) this is the office to contact.

The main interest for lower to middle income travellers is to see how the other half lives and perhaps make use of the newly built shopping centres. The Overseas Chinese Town is to the north of Splendid China.

PLACES TO STAY – BOTTOM END

There is some good news and some bad news. The good news is that in Shenzhen you can get a much larger and more luxurious room than you could in Hong Kong for the same amount of money. In Shenzhen you can find a large deluxe double room with air-con, TV and private bath for less than US$40. In Hong Kong, this level of accommodation would cost three times as much.

The bad news for budget travellers is that there is nothing really cheap. Virtually every hotel demands Hong Kong dollars or else tacks a heavy penalty if you want to pay in Chinese yuan. In Shenzhen, 'bottom-end' means any hotel costing under US$40 for a double. Of course, there are some very cheap places for Chinese only and it will be impossible to persuade them to take you unless you have special permission from the Public Security Bureau. Your best course of action is to find two or three other travellers to share with you. Remember, this situation occurs often in China, though Shenzhen is more expensive than the rest of the country. Many hotels charge 10% extra on weekends.

A lot of hotels in Shenzhen have a nasty habit of wanting to hold your passport as security, even though you pay for a room in advance. Since most can't read English, you could easily give them an old expired passport if you have one. Otherwise, just tell the staff you need your passport to cash travellers' cheques – they usually accept this though they may require a US$10 deposit instead.

The *Binjiang Hotel (bīnjiāng dàjiǔdiàn)* on Hongling Lu is one of the better deals in town and very popular with locals. Double rooms start at US$22, US$29 and US$34.

The *Yat Wah Hotel (rìhuá bīnguǎn)* has a good location on the north-west corner of Shennan Lu and Heping Lu, just to the west of the railroad tracks. The outside looks a bit tattered, but the interior is alright. Room prices are US$22, US$25 and US$31, plus an additional 10% on weekends. This is one of the cheapest places in Shenzhen that will accept foreigners.

The *Jing Peng Hotel* (☎ 2227190) *(jīngpéng bīnguǎn)* is an elegant-looking place that offers good value for money.

Doubles with twin beds are US$33 and US$40. Triples are US$40 and US$48 while suites are US$76. The hotel has its own billiard room, restaurant, gift shop and karaoke bar.

The *Jinghu Hotel (jīnghú dàjiǔdiàn)* has no English sign but is easy to find and centrally located south of Renmin Nanlu just south of Cunfeng Lu. Singles/doubles are US$21/40 but the single rooms seem to be permanently 'all full'.

The *Shen Tieh Building* (☎ 5584248) *(shēntiě dàxià)* on Heping Lu is good value when not full (as it often is). Double rooms are US$27 and US$40.

Relatively good value is offered by the *Oriental Hotel* (☎ 2234118; fax 2234123) *(dōngfāng jiǔdiàn)*, 136 Shennan Donglu. Singles/doubles cost US$29/38 and triples are US$45. There is an additional 10% surcharge.

Also recommended is the *Heping Hotel* (☎ 2252111, 2228149) *(hépíng jiǔdiàn)*, 63 Chuanbu Jie, near CITS. Comfortable doubles/triples start at US$34/41. There is an added 10% service charge on weekends though this buys you no extra service.

The *Shenzhen Hotel* (☎ 2238000; fax 2222284) *(shēnzhèn jiǔdiàn)* at 156 Shennan Donglu has doubles for US$38 and US$43. This is a tasteful and friendly place and not bad value for money by Shenzhen standards.

Nearby at 140 Shennan Donglu is the *Wah Chung Hotel* (☎ 2238060) *(huázhōng guójì jiǔdiàn)*. Spacious doubles cost US$40 and US$48 and a triple room is US$49. There is a 10% service charge and rooms cost 10% more on weekends.

The *Nanyang Hotel* (☎ 2224968) *(nányáng jiǔdiàn)* has doubles for US$37 and triples for US$45. This reasonably luxurious hotel is well known for its disco. It's on Jianshe Lu, north of Jiabin Lu.

The oddly-named *Petrel Hotel* (☎ 2232828; fax 2221398) *(hǎiyàn dàjiǔdiàn)* on Jiabin Lu is a 29-storey tower offering reasonably-priced doubles for US$36, US$49 and US$62 plus 10% service charge. The only thing that has me wondering about the place is the name. As the hotel's brochure clearly explains, 'Petrel hover at sea of the red sun shine upon'.

The *Hubei Hotel* (☎ 5573272) *(húběi bīnguǎn)* and adjacent *New World Hotel (xīn shìjiè bīnguǎn)* are on the corner of Jiefang Lu and Guiyuan Lu. Both were under renovation at the time of writing but appeared to be decent mid-range hotels. They are near McDonald's, if that's a consideration.

PLACES TO STAY – MIDDLE

In Shenzhen, 'mid-range' would be defined as a hotel costing between US$39 and US$58.

The *Overseas Chinese Hotel* (☎ 5573811) *(huáqiáo dàshà)* looks run-down but costs US$41 for a double. Its one real advantage is the location on Heping Lu which is very close to the railway station.

For a convenient location, you can hardly beat the *Dragon Inn* (☎ 2229228; fax 2205664) *(gǎnglóng dàjiǔdiàn)* which is on the ground floor of the railway station. It's relatively impressive for a railway station hotel in China. Doubles are US$43 to US$51 and suites are US$82 to US$93.

The *Airlines Hotel* (☎ 2237999; fax 2237866) *(hángkōng dàjiǔdiàn)*, 130 Shennan Donglu, has doubles/twins for US$45/52. It's modern, clean and ruthlessly air-con.

The *Bamboo Garden Hotel* (☎ 5533138; fax 5534835) *(zhúyuán bīnguǎn)* is a little inconveniently located at Dongmen Beilu near the intersection with Aiguo Lu. However, it is a luxurious place and is known for its excellent restaurant. Many tour groups make a lunch stop here, though lately they are being pulled away by new restaurants near Splendid China. You can book rooms from the Hong Kong office (☎ 3674127). Doubles cost US$46.

Guangdong Hotel (☎ 5895108; fax 5769381) *(yuèhǎi jiǔdiàn)* is a sparkling glass-and-concrete edifice on Shennan Donglu. Rooms cost US$54, US$61, US$62 and US$76 plus 10%.

In the same neighbourhood is the *Far East Grand Hotel* (☎ 2205369; fax 2200239) *(yuǎndōng dàjiǔdiàn)*, 104 Shennan Donglu.

Singles are US$49 and doubles are US$64 and US$68 plus 10%.

Nearby is the *Tung Nam Hotel (dōngnán guójì dàjiǔdiàn)* on Shennan Donglu with doubles for US$48.

PLACES TO STAY – TOP END

Nam Fong International Hotel (☎ 2256728; fax 2256936) *(nánfāng guójì dàjiǔdiàn)* is an upmarket place on the eastern end of Shennan Donglu. Doubles cost US$55, US$62 and US$68. There is a 10% service charge.

If you want to go 1st class, the *Century Plaza Hotel* (☎ 2220888; fax 2234060) *(xīndū jiǔdiàn)* has it all. The hotel has a good spot on Cunfeng Lu, between Jianshe Lu and Renmin Nanlu. You can also make reservations in Hong Kong (☎ 8680638). Standard/deluxe doubles are US$90. There is an additional 10% surcharge.

The *Forum Hotel* (☎ 5586333; fax 5561700) *(fùlín dàjiǔdiàn)* is at 67 Heping Lu, just to the west of the railway station. This place positively radiates luxury and has prices to match. Doubles cost a cool US$89 and US$101.

One of the newest places in town is the high-rise *Hotel Oriental Regent* (☎ 2247000; fax 2247290) *(jīngdū jiǔdiàn)* on the south-east corner of Shennan Zhonglu and Hongling Lu. This place has got everything from marble floors to perfumed toilet paper. Double rooms come in three standards costing US$72, US$81 and US$88.

The *Shangri-La Hotel* (☎ 2230888; fax 2239878) *(xiānggé lǐlā dàjiǔdiàn)* faces the railway station and is topped by a revolving restaurant. Doubles cost US$106, US$121 and US$155 plus 10%.

Resort Villages

Although the Shenzhen SEZ was originally meant to attract high-technology manufacturing, one of its chief sources of foreign exchange are the luxurious resorts outside the city. These places defy description, but are a bit like Club Méditerranée, Disneyland, old European castles and Hong Kong's Ocean Park all rolled into one. They offer discos, saunas, swimming pools, golf courses, horseback riding, roller coasters, supermarkets, palaces, castles, Chinese pavilions, statues and monorails, not to mention luxury hotels. The huge (and surprisingly cheap) dim sum restaurants become nightclubs in the evening, with Las Vegas-style floor shows.

The resorts are flooded on the weekends, so avoid visiting them unless you consider watching the crowd one of the amusements.

Weekday prices are about US$40 to US$55 for a double, which often includes a free breakfast and transportation to and from the Shenzhen border crossing (railway station area). They often throw in free use of their other facilities (sauna, disco, swimming pool) or offer sizeable discounts to hotel guests. They usually give a discount in their shopping centres if you stay at the resort.

You can book directly through the hotels or the resorts' Hong Kong offices. Hong Kong travel agents, including CTS, can tell you about special package deals that the hotels won't bother to mention. Well-known resorts include:

Honey Lake Resort (☎ 7745061; fax 7745045) *(xiāngmì hú dùjià cūn)* is west of Shenzhen City. It's known for its amusement park, a miniature version of Disneyland called 'China Happy City' *(zhōngguó yúlè chéng)* which is complete with monorail, roller coaster and castles. Despite the name this resort doesn't seem to be much more than a duck pond. Doubles cost US$27 to US$48 on weekdays. Contact the two Hong Kong booking offices (☎ 7989288, 8656210) for bookings. Hotel guests receive a 20% discount in the restaurant, amusement park, sauna and other facilities.

Shenzhen Bay Hotel (☎ 6600111; fax 6600139) *(shēnzhèn wān dàjiǔdiàn)*, Overseas Chinese Town, is on the beach and has good views across the bay to the New Territories. On weekdays doubles cost US$55 to US$73. Its Hong Kong booking office (☎ 3693368) is in the New World Office Building, Tsimshatsui. Hotel guests have free use of the swimming pool, night club shows and other facilities. Guests also receive a discount at the shopping centre.

Shiyan Lake Hot Springs Resort (☎ 9960143) *(shíyán hú wēnquán dùjià cūn)* is five km to the north-west of Shenzhen outside the SEZ. There are

CANTON

good country club facilities here. Doubles range from US$37 to US$52 on weekdays.

Silver Lake Resort Camp (☎ 2222827; fax 2242622) *(yín hú lùyóu zhōngxīn)* is very close to Shenzhen City but is not as nice as the other resorts. Doubles range from US$36 to US$54 on weekdays.

Xiaomeisha Beach Resort (☎ 5550000) *(xiǎoméishā dàjiǔdiàn)* is the most beautiful of all. It's on the east side of the SEZ on the shore of Mirs Bay and has the best beach in Shenzhen. Doubles cost US$37 to US$55 which includes breakfast and a 20% discount on other meals. Weekend rates are higher.

Xili Lake Resort (☎ 6660022; fax 6660521) *(xīlì hú)* has a nice lakeside view and good facilities. Doubles range from US$32 to US$52 on weekdays.

PLACES TO EAT

For the backpacker on a budget, Shenzhen is no picnic. There are the usual assortment of cheap noodle shops in side alleys but self-catering seems the logical alternative as grocery stores, supermarkets, bakeries and fruit stalls appear on almost every corner.

Dim sum breakfast and lunch is available in all but the scruffiest hotels. Usually the dim sum restaurants are on the 2nd or 3rd floor rather than by the lobby. Prices are slightly lower than in Hong Kong. You'll have to pay in Hong Kong dollars in the nicer hotels but you may get away with Chinese yuan elsewhere.

The *Oriental Hotel*, on the corner of Renmin Nanlu and Shennan Donglu, has a Western-style restaurant on the ground floor. You have to pay in Hong Kong dollars, but prices are about as cheap as you can find in Shenzhen if you need Western food.

One of Shenzhen's best restaurants is the *Pan Hsi Restaurant* (☎ 2238081) *(bànxī jiǔjiā)* 33 Jianshe Lu.

Shenzhen is the site of China's first *McDonald's*, a major tourist attraction which draws Chinese from all over the country. A second McDonald's has been built in the west end of town and more are sure to follow, but you might want to visit the original site for historical reasons. It's on the north side of Jiefang Lu (see map).

Fairwood Fast Food (dà kuàihuó) offers Hong Kong-style fast food and charges Hong Kong dollars. Not bad though. The restaurant is on the west side of Heping Lu just north of the towering Forum Hotel.

On the north-east corner of Jiabin Lu and Renmin Nanlu is the International Trade Centre *(guómào dàshà)* which has no English sign, but is easily recognised by its mammoth high-rise topped with a *Revolving Restaurant* (☎ 2251464) *(xuánzhuǎng cāntīng)*. Though not the cheapest restaurant in town, you can't beat the view. The ground-floor lobby is often flooded with Chinese tourists taking photos of each other standing in front of the fountains. There is a supermarket and several good shops on the 3rd and 4th floors by the fountains (not in the high-rise section).

ENTERTAINMENT

Hong Kongers and Shenzhen's trendsetters love nightlife, which consists largely of eating, drinking and watching floor shows in huge Cantonese restaurants. As in Hong Kong, karaoke has taken over and pushed the discos out of business. Western tastes are not catered for, so you can forget about Hong Kong-style pubs with darts and live bands.

GETTING THERE & AWAY
Air

Shenzhen's new Huangtian Airport is rapidly becoming one of China's busiest. Presently, there are flights to Beihai, Beijing, Changchun, Changsha, Chengdu, Chongqing, Dalian, Fuzhou, Guilin, Guiyang, Haikou, Hangzhou, Harbin, Kunming, Lanzhou, Meixian, Nanchang, Nanjing, Nanning, Ningbo, Qingdao, Shanghai, Shantou, Shenyang, Taiyuan, Tianjin, Ürümqi, Wenzhou, Wuhan, Xi'an, Xiamen, Yantai and Zhanjiang.

Shenzhen officials harbour ambitions to make Huangtian into an international airport. Plans call for setting up a separate customs and immigration terminal for China-bound passengers and Hong Kong-bound passengers. In the meantime, many Hong Kongers step across the border into Shenzhen to take advantage of the relatively cheap domestic flights. For example, flying from Shenzhen to Beijing saves US$89 as opposed to a straight Hong Kong-Beijing flight. Of course, those savings are reduced somewhat when you factor in the cost of getting from Hong Kong to Shenzhen's airport.

You can purchase air tickets at the Airlines Hotel *(hángkōng dàjiŭdiàn)* at 130 Shennan Donglu in downtown Shenzhen.

Bus

From Hong Kong, there is a bus service to Shenzhen run by Citybus (☎ 7363888) and by Motor Transport Company of Guangdong & Hong Kong Ltd at the Canton Rd Bus Terminus. For most travellers, buses are not a good option unless you are on a tour. For information and tickets, contact CTS.

There are long-distance buses to Fuzhou, Xiamen and other coastal cities departing from the Overseas Chinese Travel Service *(huáqiáo lüyóu bù)*, next to the Overseas Chinese Hotel on Heping Lu.

Minibus

There are frequent minibuses running between Guangzhou and Shenzhen. In Guangzhou, buses depart from next to the Liuhua Hotel, across the street from the railway station. In Shenzhen, departures are just to the east of the railway station next to the Hong Kong border crossing. The fare is US$6 and the ride takes five hours.

Train

The Kowloon-Canton Railway (KCR) offers the fastest and most convenient transport to Shenzhen from Hong Kong. Trains to the border crossing at Lo Wu begin from the Hunghom Station in Tsimshatsui East. Unless you want to walk to Hunghom, it's easiest to take the MTR to the Kowloon Tong Station, then change to the KCR. There are frequent departures throughout the day and the trains start running at 6.05 am. The fare from Hunghom Station to Lo Wu is HK$27. The last train from Hunghom to Lo Wu is at 9.45 pm (there are trains departing until 11.20 pm which do *not* go all the way to Lo

Wu). The border closes at 11 pm and reopens at 7 am. Hunghom to Lo Wu is 34 km and the trip takes 37 minutes. Avoid taking this train on weekends when it's packed to overflowing and the stampede at the border crossing is a horror.

There are frequent local trains running between Guangzhou and Shenzhen and the journey takes about three hours. Touristprice hard-seat is US$3 and soft-seat US$6. The trains are often packed and there are long queues at the ticket windows. Foreigners have to go to the 2nd floor to purchase tickets.

Car

It is possible to drive across the Hong Kong-Shenzhen border, but I don't know why anyone would want to given the convenience of public transport and the risks of driving in China. The border crossing is at Man Kam To on the Hong Kong side and is called Wenjindu on the Chinese side. Another border crossing was opened at Lok Ma Chau in 1991.

On my first night in Shenzhen I saw a collision between a Shenzhen taxi and a car driven by a Hong Kong tourist. No one was seriously injured, but both cars were badly damaged. The accident occurred in front of my hotel at 7 pm. The police were called and the drivers were told to stay by their vehicles until the police arrived. By 11 pm the police had still not arrived. The Hong Kong tourist checked into my hotel and the taxi driver went home. The next morning I got up at 7 am and the police still hadn't come and the Hong Kong tourist and the taxi driver were playing mahjong together next to their wrecked vehicles. I ate breakfast then checked out of my hotel at 9 am. The police were still nowhere to be seen.

Boat

Hoverferries run between Hong Kong and Shekou, Shenzhen's port on the west side of town. Departures are from ferry terminal at China Hong Kong City on Canton Rd in Tsimshatsui, Kowloon, and also from the Macau Ferry Pier on Hong Kong Island. The fare from Hong Kong is US$13, but from China it is US$10. The journey takes one hour and the schedule is currently as follows:

Kowloon – Shekou

From Kowloon	From Shekou
7.50 am	9.05 am
10.15 am	2.30 pm
3.30 pm	5.00 pm

Hong Kong Island – Shekou

From Hong Kong	From Shekou
8.20 am	8.15 am
9.30 am	10.45 am
2.00 pm	3.15 pm
4.30 pm	4.45 pm

There is a jetcat (jet-powered catamaran) daily from Macau to Shekou. It departs Macau at 8.30 am and arrives at 10 am. The cost is M$79.

There are five daily jetcats running between Shekou and Zhuhai SEZ (north of Macau).

GETTING AROUND
To/From the Airport

There are shuttle buses between the airport and the Airlines Hotel (*hángkōng dàjiǔdiàn*) at 130 Shennan Donglu in downtown Shenzhen. Minibuses and taxis also add to the choices, but remember that in Shenzhen's traffic, getting to the airport can take a considerable amount of time.

If you want to travel directly between the airport and Hong Kong, there is now a rapid boat service (jet-powered catamaran) taking two hours to complete the journey. The sole ticketing agent in Hong Kong is the branch office of CTS (☎ 7361863) in Kowloon's China Hong Kong City Ferry Terminal on Canton Rd. In Shenzhen, you can purchase tickets right at the airport. The price is steep and based on season (what is the high season for visiting an airport?): high/low season deck class costs US$27/21; super-deck class is US$53/40; a VIP cabin costs US$320/243 but at that price why not charter a helicopter? Currently, there are six sailings daily as follows:

Hong Kong – Huangtian Airport

From Hong Kong	From Shenzhen
7.30 am	9.00 am
9.00 am	10.30 am
10.30 am	noon
1.00 pm	2.30 pm
2.30 pm	4.00 pm
4.00 pm	5.15 pm

Getting to Huangtian Airport by bus from Hong Kong is also possible. Citybus No 505 costs US$18 and tickets can be bought from CTS in Hong Kong. Another place selling these tickets is MTR Travel Services Centres. The following MTR stations also sell these tickets: Admiralty, Causeway Bay, Central, Kwun Tong, Mongkok, Taikoo, Tsimshatsui and Tsuen Wan. The schedule is very limited and subject to change, so ring Citybus (☎ 7363888) to inquire about changes. Currently, departures from Hong Kong are in the morning only at 7.45, 8, 9.15, 9.30 and 9.45 am.

Bus & Minibus

Shenzhen has some of the best public transport in China. The city bus is OK. It's also cheap and not as crowded as elsewhere in China.

The minibuses are faster. These are privately run and cheap, but if you can't read the destination in Chinese characters, you will need help. To get to the resorts, take a minibus from the railway station area in Shenzhen. These are operated by the hotels and only accept payment in Hong Kong dollars. The privately run minibuses that run up and down Shennan Lu are cheaper and accept payment in yuan, but you'll have to find out which minibus goes where.

Taxi

Taxis are abundant but not so cheap because their drivers have been spoilt by free-spending tourists. There are no meters so negotiate the fare before you get in. Make sure you understand which currency is being negotiated – drivers will usually ask for payment in Hong Kong dollars.

SHEKOU (*shékǒu*) 蛇口

A rapidly growing port city at the western end of the Shenzhen SEZ, Shekou is of only minor interest to tourists. There are many factories here, and north of the city is Shenzhen University. Because of the facto-

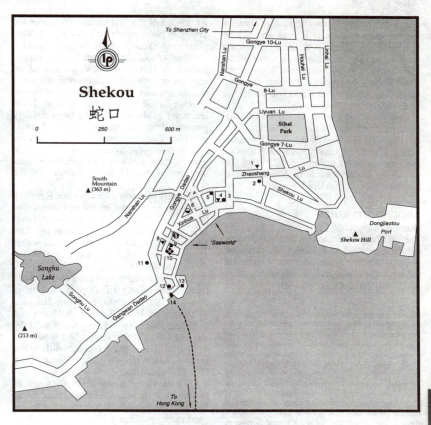

1	Bin Bin Restaurant 宾彬酒家	8	Shanghai Restaurant 上海酒家
2	Light Industrial Products Arcade 上海轻工业品总汇	9	Nanshan Hotel 南山宾馆
3	Friendship Store 友宜商场	10	Shopping Centre 购物中心
4	Beijing Restaurant 北京餐厅	11	Cultural Relics Exhibition Hall 文物展览馆
5	Qianlong Hotel 潜龙宾馆	12	Guanhai (Seaview) Tower 观海楼
6	Bus Station 汽车站	13	Nanhai Hotel 南海酒店
7	Bank of China 中国银行	14	Passenger Wharf 蛇口港客运站

ries, many business travellers come here, so for that reason there is a posh and pricey Nanhai Hotel. There is a direct hoverferry service linking Shekou to Hong Kong Island and Kowloon. From Shenzhen City, you can reach Shekou by minibus. Perhaps the most interesting thing about Shekou is its name, which means 'snake's mouth'.

The *Nanhai Hotel* (☎ 6692888; fax 6692440) *(nánhǎi jiǔdiàn)* in Shekou is a top-flight hotel where doubles cost a breath-taking US$80 to US$123. Other places to stay are nearly as expensive, including the *Qianlong Hotel (qiánlóng bīnguǎn)* and *Nanshan Hotel (nánshān bīnguǎn)*.

AROUND SHENZHEN

Humen *(hǔmén)* 虎门

The small city of Humen on the Pearl River is only of interest to history buffs with a particular curiosity for the Opium Wars that directly led to Hong Kong's creation as a British colony. According to one Chinese leaflet:

Humen was the place where the Chinese people captured and burned the opium dumped into China by the British and American merchants in the 1830s. It was also the outpost for the Chinese fight against the war on opium. In 1839, Lin Zexu, the then imperial envoy of the Qing government, resolutely put a ban on opium smoking and the trade of opium. Supported by the broad masses of the people, Lin Zexu forced the British and American opium mongers to hand over 20,285 cases of opium...and burned all of them at Humen Beach, Dongguang County. This just action showed the strong will of the Chinese people in resisting imperialist aggression...

At the end of the first Opium War, after the Treaty of Nanking, there was a British Supplementary Treaty of the Bogue, signed 8 October 1843. The **Bogue Forts** *(shājiǎo pàotái)* at Humen is now the site of an impressive museum which commemorates the destruction of the surrendered opium which sparked the first Opium War. There are many exhibits, including large artillery pieces and other relics and the actual ponds in which Commissioner Lin Zexu had the opium destroyed. When the new museum opened, there was a special exhibition commemorating the 150th anniversary of the war.

The only problem with this place is getting there. No buses go directly to Humen, but buses and minibuses travelling from Shenzhen to Guangzhou go right by. You could ask to be let off at the Humen access road, and then get a taxi, hitch or walk the five km into town.

At least on paper, there are daily ferries from Hong Kong to Taiping, which is almost walking distance from Humen. These depart Hong Kong at 8.45 am and 2.20 pm, returning to Hong Kong at 11.50 am and 4.50 pm. However, you'd be wise to inquire about the current schedule at the ferry ticket office in China Hong Kong City in Tsimshatsui.

CTS in Hong Kong arranges tours to Humen, but these cater to the Hong Kong and local market, which means the guides are Cantonese-speaking only.

CANTON

Zhuhai 珠海

From any hilltop in Macau, you can gaze to the north and see a mass of modern buildings just across the border in China. This is the Zhuhai Special Economic Zone (SEZ). Like the Shenzhen SEZ, Zhuhai was built from the floor up on what was farmland less than a decade ago. The areas near the beach have several high-class resort playgrounds catering to Chinese residents of Hong Kong and Macau as well as the occasional foreigner. Cadres also come to Zhuhai for 'meetings', usually returning to Beijing with a good suntan and a suitcase full of electronic goodies which can be sold for a profit up north.

Many travellers conclude that, having seen Shenzhen, they will bypass Zhuhai. This is a pity since Zhuhai has its own character and in many ways is more attractive than Shenzhen.

However, Zhuhai is changing, and the speed of development is almost frightening. Travellers from the 1980s (even *late* 1980s) remember Zhuhai as a small agricultural town with a few rural industries and a quiet beach. Nowadays, high-rise hotels, factories and workers' flats have crowded out the few remaining farms and half of the beach has been paved over to make way for a new waterfront freeway.

Be that as it may, Zhuhai is more laid-back than Shenzhen, much cleaner than Guangzhou and definitely cheaper than Macau. True, it's not the real China, but since the real China puts many people off, that might be no great loss. If you're looking for a pleasant getaway from Hong Kong and Macau but with all the modern conveniences, Zhuhai might be the place for you. Zhuhai is so close to the border that a visit can be arranged as a day trip from Macau, and you can see many of the sights just travelling by foot. The more adventurous can use Zhuhai as a stepping stone to Guangzhou and beyond.

ORIENTATION
Zhuhai City is a municipality and SEZ which is divided into three main areas. The area nearest the Macau border is called Gongbei and is the main tourist area with lots of hotels, restaurants and shops. To the northeast is Jida, the eastern area which includes Zhuhai Harbour (*jiǔzhōu gǎng*). The Jida area has some large resort hotels, a reasonable beach and at least one beautiful mountain with walking paths winding between the boulders.

Finally, the northernmost section of the city is called Xiangzhou. There isn't much to see here. Xiangzhou is mostly an area of worker flats, factories and shops catering to the local Chinese population. It is for this – an everyday glimpse of China's burgeoning entrepreneurial class – that travellers may find it interesting.

Maps of Zhuhai are widely available from bookstalls and hotel gift shops. These are all in Chinese characters but have bus routes and are useful for getting around. There are no useful English maps. The map entitled *Map of Macau & Zhuhai* published by Universal Publications of Hong Kong only covers the Xiangzhou area of Zhuhai, which isn't much use since most travellers stay in Gongbei.

INFORMATION
Tourist Office
CTS (☎ 885777) is at 4 Shuiwan Lu, opposite the Gongbei Palace Hotel.

Public Security
The Public Security Bureau (PSB) (☎ 222459) is in the Xiangzhou district on the south-west corner of Anping Lu and Kangning Lu.

Money
The big resort hotels like Hong Kong dollars and will usually only accept Chinese money at a punitive rate.

There are black-market moneychangers at the border offering high rates for Hong Kong

433

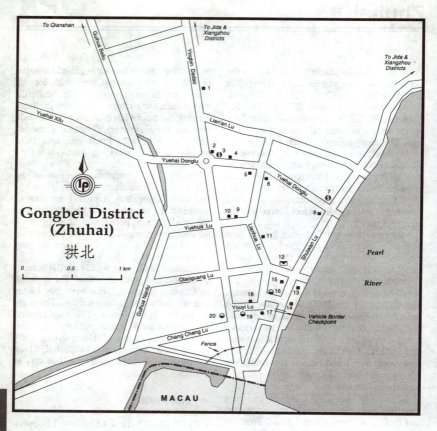

Gongbei District (Zhuhai)

拱北

0   0.5   1 km

MACAU

dollars. It's best to ignore them unless you want to get ripped off.

The Bank of China is a gleaming new building next to the towering Yindo Hotel on the corner of Yuehai Lu and Yingbin Dadao. You can also change money in most hotels, but another good place in Gongbei is the Nan Tung Bank on the corner of Yuehai Donglu and Shuiwan Lu. There is an official moneychanger at the Macau border entry/exit station.

Post & Telecommunications

The most useful post office is on Qiaoguang

Lu. You can make IDD calls from your own room in most hotels. The area code for Zhuhai is 0756.

THINGS TO SEE

Most visitors start their exploration of Zhuhai from the area near the Macau border. It's worth taking a look at the **Gongbei Market** on Yuehua Lu, next to the Overseas Chinese Hotel. It's reasonably clean and not nearly as exotic as the Qingping Market in Guangzhou – they keep the dog meat hidden when the tour buses come through.

The **beach** is the top attraction during the

1	Huaqiao Hotel 华侨宾馆	11	Lianhua Hotel 莲花大厦
2	Yindo Hotel 银都酒店	12	Post Office 邮店局
3	Bank of China 中国银行	13	Gongbei Palace Hotel 拱北宾馆
4	Zhuhai Quzhao Hotel 拱北大厦	14	Jiuzhou Hotel 九洲酒店
5	Good World Hotel 好世界酒店	15	Traffic Hotel 交通大厦
6	Guangdong Hotel 粤海酒店	16	Bus Station & Yongtong Hotel 长途汽车站/永通酒店
7	Nan Tung Bank 南通银行	17	Customs & Immigration 海关
8	Popoko Hotel 步步高大酒店	18	Friendship Hotel 友谊酒店
9	Overseas Chinese Hotel 华侨大酒店	19	Local Bus Station 拱北公共汽车总站
10	Gongbei Market 拱北市场	20	Minibus Station 小车出租点

summer months. The nicest stretch of beach is in the **Zhuhai Holiday Resort** at the south end of the Jida district and west of Jiuzhou Harbour. The walk along the coastline from Gongbei to this beach is very pleasant, and be sure to wander around the resort itself. You can't say it's not a beautiful place, though the statue of Mickey Mouse waving hello doesn't quite fit in with my idea of an idyllic beach resort. The Chinese apparently don't agree: carloads come to this place just to get their picture taken standing next to Mickey.

West of Haibin Park is an area called **Shijingshan Tourist Centre** (*shíjĭngshān lǚyóu zhōngxīn*). The tourist centre itself is no big deal, just some gardens, an artificial lake, a supermarket and shops selling tourist junk. However, if you go inside the centre, head towards the back and you'll find some stone steps going uphill. Follow them up and you'll quickly find yourself in a forest with big granite boulders all around. Keep climbing to the top of the ridge and be rewarded with outstanding views of Zhuhai City, Zhongshan and Macau.

On the south side of Shijingshan Tourist Centre is **Jiuzhou Cheng**. From the outside,

you'll probably think it's some kind of restored Ming Dynasty village. Inside, you'll find that it's a fashionable shopping centre where everything is priced in Hong Kong dollars.

On the south side of Jiuzhou Cheng is the **Zhuhai Resort** (*zhūhǎi bīnguǎn*), another playground for rich Hong Kongers and cadres attending 'meetings'. It's worth stopping for a brief look.

There are several other interesting things to see in the area north of Zhuhai City in Zhongshan County. See the Around Zhuhai section later.

PLACES TO STAY – BOTTOM END

While there are no cheap dormitories which accept foreigners, accommodation in Zhuhai is relatively inexpensive – at least it's cheaper than Shenzhen. It would probably be best to avoid Zhuhai on weekends and holidays when throngs of Hong Kong and Macau tourists flood across the border and hotels are full. On the other hand, if you're looking for nightlife, the hotel discos should be jumping on Saturday night.

Living it up in Zhuhai for one night before crossing the border into Macau, where hotels

CANTON

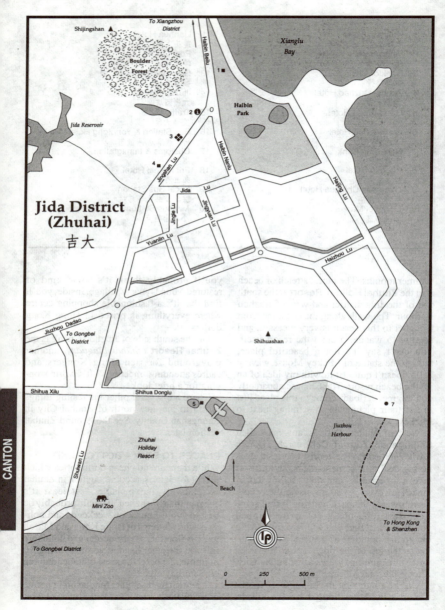

CANTON

Jida District (Zhuhai) 吉大

Shijingshan

To Xiangzhou District

Boulder Forest

Xianglu Bay

Jida Reservoir

Haibin Beilu

Haibin Park

Haibin Nanlu

Jingshan Lu

Jingyuan Lu

Jida Lu

Jingyuan Lu

Haijing Lu

Yuanlin Lu

Haizhou Lu

Jiuzhou Dadao

To Gongbei District

Shihuashan

Shihua Xilu

Shihua Donglu

Shuiwan Lu

Zhuhai Holiday Resort

Jiuzhou Harbour

Beach

Mini Zoo

To Gongbei District

To Hong Kong & Shenzhen

0   250   500 m

1	Jiari Hotel
	假日酒店
2	Shijingshan Tourist Centre
	石景山旅游中心
3	Jiuzhou Cheng (shopping mall)
	九洲城
4	Zhuhai Hotel
	珠海宾馆
5	ZHR Hotel
	珠海度假村
6	Mickey Mouse Statue
	米老鼠
7	Jiuzhou Harbour Passenger Terminal
	九洲港客运站

and meals cost at least double, is a good way to end a trip to China.

PLACES TO STAY – MIDDLE

The *Friendship Hotel* (☎ 886683) (*yǒuyí jiǔdiàn*), 2 Youyi Lu (Friendship St) is near the border gate between Lianhua Lu and Yingbin Dadao. Doubles cost US$18 to US$22, and you must leave a refundable US$10 deposit to ensure that you don't run off with the TV or toilet.

Lianhua Hotel (☎ 885637) (*liánhuā dàshà*), 13 Lianhua Lu, is in the heart of Zhuhai's liveliest market district. The hotel has no English sign on the door but is easy enough to find. Singles/doubles are US$12/20.

The *Traffic Hotel* (☎ 884474) (*jiāotōng dàshà*) at 1 Shuimen Lu does doubles for US$20.

Just opposite the border gate and in the same building as the long-distance bus station is the new *Yongtong Hotel* (☎ 888887) (*yǒngtōng jiǔdiàn*). Singles/doubles are US$31/33.

A little further from the border is the *Overseas Chinese Hotel* (☎ 885183) (*huáqiáo dàjiǔdiàn*), on the north side of Yuehua Lu between Yingbin Dadao and Lianhua Lu, right next to the Zhuhai Market. Doubles are US$18 to US$23.

The *Huaqiao Hotel* (☎ 885123) (*huáqiáo bīnguǎn*) on Yingbin Dadao, one block north of Yuehai Donglu, has double rooms for

US$27 and US$32. The in-house restaurant is excellent.

The *Popoko Hotel* (☎ 886628) (*bùbùgāo dàjiǔdiàn*) is at 2 Yuehai Donglu, is on the corner with Shuiwan Lu near the waterfront. Double rooms start at US$34.

Tucked away in the forested grounds of Haibin Park is the quiet (except on weekends) *Jiari Hotel* (☎ 333277) (*jiàrì jiǔdiàn*). Double rooms are US$31 to US$52. Haibin Park is in the Jida district north-east of Gongbei, within walking distance of the Shijingshan Tourist Centre and luxurious Zhuhai Hotel.

Zhuhai Quzhao Hotel (☎ 886256) (*gǒngběi dàshà*) on Yuehai Donglu looks palatial on the outside, but has double rooms as low as US$31. Nevertheless, it does not seem to be popular, possibly because of the unfriendly staff.

PLACES TO STAY – TOP END

Good World Hotel (☎ 880222) (*hǎo shìjiè jiǔdiàn*), 82 Lianhua Lu, is a fine place at the lower end of top-end accommodation. Deluxe doubles are US$43. There is a 10% surcharge with another 10% on weekends or 20% on major holidays.

The *Gongbei Palace Hotel* (☎ 886833; fax 885686) (*gǒngběi bīnguǎn*) is the most luxurious place close to the border. It's by the waterfront on Shuiwan Lu near Qiaoguang Lu, about a one-minute walk from the border crossing. Among the facilities are a disco, video-game arcade, sauna and swimming pool (including water slide). Unfortunately, the 'beach' is just for looking – it's too rocky for swimming. The hotel runs bus tours of the surrounding area. Singles/doubles are US$55/65, but for the same price you can get a villa. There is an additional 15% service charge. At least these prices keep out the riff-raff.

Adjacent to the Gongbei Palace is the *Jiuzhou Hotel* (☎ 886851) (*jiǔzhōu jiǔdiàn*). Once known as a budget hotel, it has moved upmarket with doubles starting at US$35 and skyrocketting to US$62 for cushier rooms. It's on the waterfront on Shuiwan Lu near

CANTON

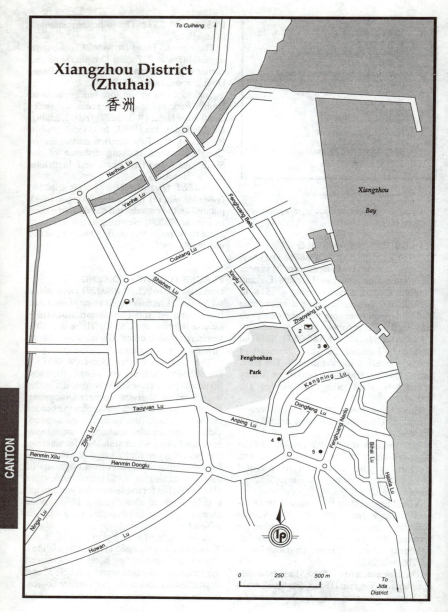

Xiangzhou District (Zhuhai)
香洲

Xiangzhou Bay

To Cuiheng

Nanhua Lu

Yanhe Lu

Fenghuang Beilu

Cuixiang Lu

Shishan Lu

Xingfu Lu

Zhaoyang Lu

Fengboshan Park

Kangning Lu

Taoyuan Lu

Anping Lu

Dongfeng Lu

Zijing Lu

Fenghuang Nanlu

Bihai Lu

Haibia Lu

Renmin Xilu

Renmin Donglu

Ningbu Lu

Huwan Lu

0   250   500 m

To Jida District

1	Bus Station
	汽车站
2	Post Office
	邮局
3	Martyrs' Mausoleum
	烈士陵园
4	PSB
	公安局
5	City Hall
	市政府

Qiaoguang Lu and south of the Gongbei Palace Hotel, a stone's throw from the border.

Guangdong Hotel (☎ 889115; fax 885063) *(yuèhǎi jiǔdiàn)*, 34 Yuehai Donglu, is a flashy place where standard doubles cost US$53 and deluxe doubles/twins are US$54/57. There is a 15% surcharge and Hong Kong dollars are definitely favoured.

The ultra-modern *Yindo Hotel* (☎ 883388; fax 883311) *(yíndū jiǔdiàn)* is a gleaming glass and steel high-rise dominating Zhuhai's skyline. Amenities include a bowling alley and miniature golf course. Standard twins start at US$59 with somewhat cosier rooms priced at US$69, US$78 and US$88. Or you can rent the presidential suite for a mere US$1180. There is a 15% surcharge plus 10% more on weekends and 20% more on holidays. The hotel is on the corner of Yuehai Lu and Yingbin Dadao.

The *Zhuhai Holiday Resort* (☎ 332038; fax 332036) *(zhūhǎi dùjià cūn)* or *ZHR* is a five-star resort with the best beach in Zhuhai and amenities such as a bowling alley, roller rink, tennis courts, club house, go-cart racing, horse riding, camel riding, disco, karaoke, video-game parlour and sauna. This is a place to wrap yourself in luxury if you can afford it and don't mind the fact that it doesn't look or feel much like traditional China. The resort is on the shoreline north-east of Gongbei near Jiuzhou Harbour. Single rooms in the main hotel start from US$47, but a villa for two people is a better deal at US$40. There is a 15% surcharge.

The *Zhuhai Hotel* (☎ 333718; fax 332339) *(zhūhǎi bīnguǎn)* is another playground for the upper crust. However, it lacks the benefits of a beach, which means it doesn't, in my opinion, warrant the expense. Nevertheless, it caters to every whim and has a sauna, tennis courts, billiard room, swimming pool, nightclub and even mahjong rooms. Double rooms cost US$49, US$75 and US$85, while villas start at US$125. There is also a 15% surcharge. Children under 12 are free if sharing the same accommodation. You can book in Macau (☎ 552275).

PLACES TO EAT

The area near the Macau border crossing has the most of everything – restaurants, bakeries, night markets and street vendors. It also has the most pickpockets! Little kids who approach you as beggars will sometimes try to relieve you of your wallet. They work in groups and practically glue themselves to foreigners. Their mothers can be equally aggressive.

Hang on to your wallet and you'll find plenty to spend your money on. Right near the border crossing is *Maxim's* (☎ 885209) at 4 Lianhua Lu, the Hong Kong fast-food chain famous for its cakes. It's a good place to catch a quick breakfast. You'll see many other restaurants around the border area.

The north-east corner of Youyi Lu and Yingbin Dadao has a good collection of street vendors and sidewalk restaurants, particularly in the evening.

If you haven't already made the discovery, dim sum restaurants are to be found in most hotels, usually on the 2nd or 3rd floors. Prices are low. I really liked the dim sum restaurant on the 2nd floor of the *Huaqiao Hotel* on Yingbin Dadao (north of Yuehai Donglu).

The 8th floor of the *Friendship Hotel* has a small, pleasant and cheap restaurant with good views of the harbour. The menu is in Chinese only but the staff are friendly, so you can always point.

THINGS TO BUY

By Chinese standards, Zhuhai is considered a great place to shop. Foreigners will probably be less impressed – nearby Macau and

CANTON

Hong Kong offer greater variety and usually lower prices. However, for goods made in China, Zhuhai offers competitive prices and a good selection.

Jiuzhou Cheng is an exclusive shopping mall next to the Zhuhai Hotel on Jingshan Lu in the Jida district. Obviously not for the local people, everything is priced in Hong Kong dollars. The mall looks like an ancient Chinese palace from the outside. Inside, you'll find numerous shops, well-manicured gardens, fountains, pavilions and fish ponds. The shops sell many imported goods such as electrical appliances, pharmaceuticals and stereos, though increasingly this stuff is being made in China. It's open from 10 am to 6 pm. One good thing about this place is the supermarket. You can stock up on imported Hong Kong delicacies such as Watson's Cola and No Frills Dried Lemon Peel.

GETTING THERE & AWAY
To/From Macau
Simply walk across the border. In Macau, bus Nos 3 and 5 lead to the Barrier Gate, from where you make the crossing on foot. The Macau-Zhuhai border is open from 7 am to 9 pm.

To/From Guangzhou
Buses to Zhuhai depart from the bus station across the street from the railway station, west of the Liuhua Hotel. The large government buses are cheaper, but less frequent, slower and more crowded. Minibuses from this station are air-con, cost US$4 and leave according to a posted schedule. Unscheduled minibuses cost US$3 and cruise in front of the station in a circular direction (south on Renmin Beilu then back on Zhanqian Lu) looking for passengers.

Going the other way, buses from Zhuhai to Guangzhou depart from the main bus terminal on Youyi Lu, directly opposite the customs building (the border checkpoint). The minibus station is also on Youyi Lu, one block to the west of the customs building.

To/From Hong Kong
Jetcats between Zhuhai and Hong Kong do the trip in about 70 minutes. Departure times are 7.45 and 11 am and 2.30 pm. Boats depart from the ferry terminal at China Hong Kong City on Canton Rd in Tsimshatsui, and cost US$20 on weekdays and US$22 on weekends.

Going the other way, departures are from Jiuzhou Harbour (jiǔzhōu gǎng) in Zhuhai at 9.30 am, 1 and 4.45 pm. Even when you buy the ticket in Zhuhai, you must pay in Hong Kong dollars! If you argue long enough and loud enough, the staff will eventually allow you to pay in Chinese money after tacking on an extra 50% 'service charge' which likely goes into their own pockets. In Zhuhai, the official fare is supposed to be US$15.

To/From Shenzhen
A high-speed ferry operates between the port of Shekou in Shenzhen and Jiuzhou Harbour in Zhuhai. There are five departures daily in each direction. From Shenzhen, the first boat is at 9 am and the last at 4.30 pm. From Zhuhai, first departure is 8.20 am and the last at 3 pm. Despite the fact that this is a domestic service, foreigners must pay in HK dollars or US dollars! The fare for the fast boats is US$14, but the staff on the Zhuhai side seem to inexplicably add an extra US$3 for themselves above the ticket price! If you argue, they tell you to swim.

GETTING AROUND
Bus & Minibus
Zhuhai has a decent public transport system. The routes are clearly shown on the Zhuhai city map and you shouldn't have any trouble figuring it out. You might have to stand, but the buses aren't nearly as packed-out as in Guangzhou.

Even better is the minibus system. You'll never have to wait more than 30 seconds for one of these to come along. To flag one down, just wave and they will come screeching to a halt regardless of other traffic behind them. Minibuses will stop in the public bus stops and most other places, but cannot stop in major intersections.

On minibuses, the destination is written in Chinese characters and displayed on the windshield. Even if you can't read Chinese it hardly matters because there are only two basic routes. One route runs along Shuiwan Lu by the waterfront. The other route goes up Yingbin Dadao and terminates in Xiangzhou. Actually, there are variations of these routes, but all you have to do is tell the driver where you want to go (before you get in). If he doesn't go there, he'll just wave you off and drive away. If you can't pronounce the Chinese, point to it on a map or write it down.

The fare for minibuses is US$0.50 for any destination within the city limits.

Taxi

You are most likely to use taxis to shuttle between your hotel and the boats at Jiuzhou Harbour. Zhuhai taxis have no meters and fares are strictly by negotiation. Drivers typically try to charge foreigners double. A fair price from the Macau border to Jiuzhou Harbour is around US$4, but given China's inflation, it's best to first ask a neutral bystander (try the desk clerks at your hotel) what the current fare is.

Around Zhuhai

North of Zhuhai City is Zhongshan County, where the south is among the more interesting places to visit. By starting in the morning, you can travel by minibus and visit all of these places in one day and be back in Zhuhai in time for dinner.

A quick look at the map makes it clear that the logical way to do this is to make a loop trip. Starting from Gongbei, take a minibus along the coast to the former residence of Dr Sun Yatsen, then up to Zhongshan City, southward again to the Zhongshan Hot Springs and back to Gongbei.

SUN YATSEN'S RESIDENCE
(*sūn zhōngshān gùjū*) 孙中山故居
China's most famous revolutionary, Dr Sun

Yatsen was born in a house on this site on 12 November 1866. That house was torn down after a new home was built in 1892. This second house is still standing and open to the public. The site also has a museum, but the Chinese have turned the place into something of a circus.

Dr Sun dedicated his life to the overthrow of the corrupt and brutal Qing (Manchu) Dynasty. His goal was to do away with dynasties altogether and establish a Chinese republic based on Western democratic principles. He organised several uprisings, all of which failed. As a result, he spent much of his life in exile because of a price on his head. There is no doubt that he would have faced a horrible death by torture if the emperor had succeeded in capturing him.

When the actual revolution came in 1911, Dr Sun wasn't in China. Still, there is no denying his role as a major organiser and instigator of the revolution. Sun Yatsen is widely regarded as the father of his country and has been deified by both the Communist Party and the Nationalists in Taiwan. He briefly served as the first president of the Republic of China. He died in 1925 from liver cancer at the age of 59. His wife was Soong Chingling, the sister of Soong Mayling (Madame Chiang Kaishek).

Dr Sun's house is in the village of Cuiheng, north of the city limits of Zhuhai. There are frequent minibuses to Cuiheng departing from Gongbei near the border checkpoint.

Just before you reach the Zhuhai City limits, you pass Pearl Land (*zhēnzhū lèyuán*), another Chinese amusement park, which isn't worth stopping for unless you're really into roller coasters.

In Cuiheng there are two hotels – the huge Cuiheng Hotel (*cuìhēng bīnguǎn*) and the smaller Cuiheng Jiudian.

ZHONGSHAN CITY
(*zhōngshān shì*) 中山市
The administrative centre of the county by the same name, Zhongshan City is also known as Shiqi. It's an industrial city so hardly a main tourist attraction. Still, you

CANTON

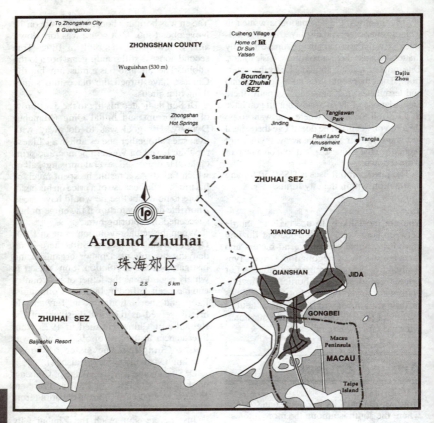

Around Zhuhai
珠海郊区

CANTON

must pass through here if doing the loop trip from Zhuhai to Zhongshan Hot Springs and back to Zhuhai. The city is worth perhaps 45 minutes of time to walk around.

The one and only scenic spot in town is **Zhongshan Park** which is pleasantly forested and dominated by a large hill *(yāndūn shān)* topped with a pagoda. It's visible from most parts of the city so it's easy to find. It's nice and quiet in the park (except on Sunday) and a climb to the top of the pagoda will reward you with a sweeping view of the city's factories and air pollution. Perhaps this

explains why the English translation of the hill's name is 'smokey mound'.

There is a large **Sun Yatsen Memorial Hall** *(sūn zhōngshān jìniàn táng)* on Sunwen Zhonglu to the east of Zhongshan Park. The car park is often jammed with tour buses from Macau, though there is nothing special about this place. The most worthwhile sight is the old, rusting MIG fighter parked on the lawn, a relic of the Korean War.

Apart from the pagoda in Zhongshan Park, the other dominant feature on the skyline of Zhongshan City is the Fu Hua

Hotel, a huge golden building topped with a revolving restaurant. The hotel has a disco, sauna, bowling alley, billiard room and swimming pool. You might be curious as to why anybody would build this stunning resort hotel in the middle of an industrial wasteland such as Zhongshan City. I asked numerous Hong Kongers this question and the answer was always the same – everyone is here on business.

Places to Stay

Should you be so taken with Zhongshan City that you want to stay, a relatively cheap place accepting foreigners is the *Tiecheng* ('Iron City') *Hotel* (☎ 873803; fax 871103) *(tiěchéng jiǔdiàn)* at Zhongshan Lu and Sunwen Xilu. Doubles are US$28 to US$30.

Perhaps a better deal is the new *Xiangshan Hotel* (☎ 874567; fax 874929) *(xiāngshān jiǔdiàn)* at 1 Xiangshan Dajie. Agreeable doubles are US$27.

Moving upwards in price is the prosaically-named *Zhongshan Building* (☎ 873838; fax 871133), 3 Fuhua Dao. Rooms with twin beds are US$35 to US$48.

Across the street is the *International Hotel* (☎ 874788; fax 874736) *(guójì jiǔdiàn)*, 1 Zhongshan Lu, where doubles/twins cost US$57/62.

Top of the line is the *Fu Hua Hotel* (☎ 861338; fax 861862) *(fùhuá jiǔdiàn)*, which has doubles/twins for US$57/62. If you want to spend your honeymoon here, there are honeymoon suites for US$93 and the presidential suite goes for a trifling US$878. On weekends and holidays there is an additional 10% surcharge.

Most likely, you won't want to stay in Zhongshan City unless you decide to open a factory there.

Places to Eat

In addition to the usual abundance of cheap noodle shops, elegant seafood dining is available at the *Jumbo Floating Restaurant* *(zhēnbǎo hǎixiān fǎng)* which floats on the Qi River.

Fast food has made its debut in Zhongshan City. *Timmy's (tiān měi shí)* on Zhongshan

Lu (south of Sunwen Xilu) can satisfy a sudden attack of uncontrollable lust for French fries, hamburgers and milkshakes.

Getting There & Away

Bus & Minibus All buses running between Guangzhou and Zhuhai pass through Zhongshan. The quickest way out of town is to catch a minibus from the carpark of the Tiecheng Hotel.

Boat Because of its importance as a manufacturing centre, frequent high-speed catamarans ply the route directly between Zhongshan and Hong Kong in just one hour and 45 minutes. Tourists seldom make use of this route, but if you're sick of Zhongshan and just want out, this is one quick way to make an exit. Fares are modest at US$19. The schedule is currently as follows:

From Hong Kong	From Zhongshan
7.30 am	7.45 am
7.45 am	9.30 am
8.40 am	11.15 am
9.30 am	11.45 am
11.00 am	1.00 pm
1.00 pm	3.00 pm
1.15 pm	4.15 pm
2.00 pm	4.45 pm
2.30 pm	5.00 pm
5.00 pm	10.30 pm

ZHONGSHAN HOT SPRINGS

(zhōngshān wēnquán) 中山温泉

On the way back to Gongbei, it's easy to make a stop-off at this hot springs resort north of the Zhuhai City limits. The hot springs are not such a big attraction – they are piped into the hotel. In the past, the area was known for its pleasant countryside, but this has recently been replaced by factories and worker flats.

Aside from the mineral baths, the resort is famous for its golf course. Just how much longer before the golf course also becomes an industrial park is open to speculation. The first professional golf championship ever held in China, the 1988 Dunhill Cup Pacific, took place here. Nowadays you'll have

CANTON

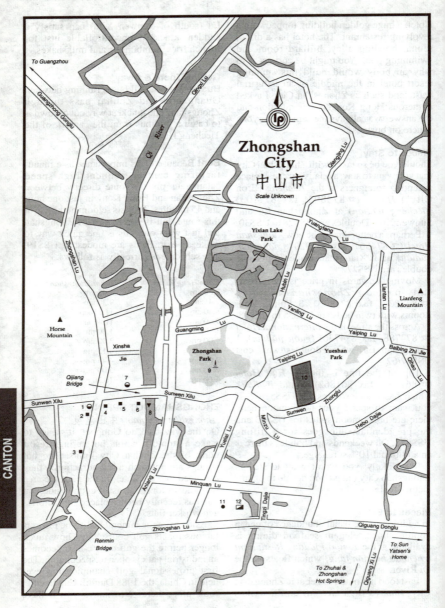

Zhongshan City

中山市

Scale Unknown

To Guangzhou

Guangzhong Gonglu

Qi River

Qingxi Lu

Qiangjing Lu

Yuangteng Lu

Yixian Lake Park

Hubin Lu

Zhongshan Lu

Yanling Lu

Lianfeng Mountain

Lianfen Lu

Yaiping Lu

Horse Mountain

Guangming Lu

Baibing Zhi Jie

Xinsha Jie

Zhongshan Park

9

Taiping Lu

Yueshan Park

Qiao Lu

Qijiang Bridge

7

10

Sunwen Xilu

Zhonglu

Sunwen

1

2

4

5

6

8

Minsu Lu

Hebo Dajie

3

Anlang Lu

Yuelai Lu

Minquan Lu

Tingzi Dajie

11

12

Zhongshan Lu

Qiguang Donglu

Renmin Bridge

To Sun Yatsen's Home

To Zhuhai & Zhongshan Hot Springs

Qiguang Xi Lu

CANTON

1	Minibuses to Zhuhai 开往拱北的小汽车
2	Tiecheng Hotel 铁城酒店
3	Xiangshan Hotel & Timmy's Fast Food 香山酒店/添美食
4	International Hotel 国际酒店
5	Zhongshan Building (Hotel) 中山大厦
6	Fu Hua Hotel 富华酒店
7	Bus Station 汽车站
8	Jumbo Floating Restaurant 珍宝海鲜舫
9	Pagoda 烟墩山宝塔
10	Sun Yatsen Memorial Hall 孙中山纪念堂
11	Renmin Athletic Field 人民体育场
12	Swimming Pool 游泳池

trouble distinguishing the sand traps from the waste dumps.

Thanks to the rapidly deteriorating environment, prices at the hotel have stayed reasonable for such plush amenities. The Zhongshan Hot Springs Hotel (☎ 683888; fax 683333) charges US$25 to US$57.

A minibus drops you by the entrance to the resort, then it's nearly a half-km walk to the hotel. For US$0.50 you can hire someone to carry you on the back of a bicycle. You won't have to look for them as they'll be looking for you. To get back to Gongbei, flag down any minibus you see passing the resort entrance.

LINGDING ISLAND
(nèi língdīng dǎo) 内伶仃岛

This little island is supposed to be Zhuhai's answer to Macau. Rather than see all that revenue from the slot machines and dice going into Macau's pocket, Zhuhai has decided to launch a gambling resort of its own. To entice customers, Hong Kong residents will be permitted to visit the island without a visa, but there's been no word yet on whether or not foreigners will enjoy the right to a visa-free visit.

Not that it matters much. The whole project has been long on rhetoric and short on action.

Getting There & Away

Direct ferries from Hong Kong to Lingding Island are supposed to be in operation and CTS is the ticket agent – unfortunately, no one at CTS knows anything about it. Since the island is midway between Shenzhen and Zhuhai, plenty of ferries pass by but none stop. For the moment, the only way to reach the island is to charter a boat. Some have managed to do this from Cheung Chau in Hong Kong, rather than from Zhuhai.

I confess that I haven't been to Lingding Island, and probably won't bother going until a regular ferry service begins. Meanwhile, Zhuhai officials confidently predict that this island will soon be the next Las Vegas. If so, don't forget that you read it here first.

Glossary

amah – domestic servant

cheongsam – formal tight-fitting dress with a revealing slit up the side, often worn at weddings and by restaurant hostesses

congee – watery rice porridge

dai pai dong – street market where finger-pointing is a necessary part of ordering food

dragon boat – a very long and narrow rowboat used in races on Dragon Boat Day

fleecy – sweet, cold drink, usually with mung beans or fruit

fungshui – geomancy, the art of manipulating the environment to blow away bad spirits

gam bei – 'cheers' or 'bottoms up', literally 'dry glass'

ganmao – the common cold, often referred to as the 'China Syndrome'

godown – warehouse

gongfu (kungfu) – traditional Chinese martial arts

gwailo – literally 'ghost person' and interpreted as 'foreign devil', but now a term of both ridicule and endearment

Hakka – northern Chinese who migrated south; much noted for their eclectic cooking style

hong – large company

hukou – permit designating where one is to live

joss – luck, fortune

joss sticks – incense

junk – traditional Chinese fishing boat, but the term has been expanded to included most small to medium-sized Chinese boats

kaido – a small to medium-sized ferry

lo lun chai – mixed vegetable dish

mai dan – the bill or cheque in a restaurant

muntjak – barking deers found in Hong Kong

oolong – high grade Chinese tea, partially fermented

qigong – gongfu (kungfu) meditation

sampan – a motorised launch which can only accommodate a few people and too small to go on the open sea

shroff – cashier

snake – a smuggler of illegal immigrants

taijiquan – formerly spelt 'taichichuan', this is a form of slow motion shadow boxing

taipan – big boss of a large company

triciclos – three-wheeled bicycles (pedicabs) favoured in Macau

vila – a guesthouse in Macau (also known as a hospedaria or pensao)

walla walla – a motorised launch used as a water taxi and capable of short runs on the open sea

wushu – martial arts

yum cha – dim sum meal, literally 'drink tea'

CANTON

Index

ABBREVIATIONS

Kowloon – Kow
Hong Kong Island – HKI
The New Territories – NT

Outlying Islands – OI
Macau Peninsula – MP
Macau Islands – MI

Guangzhou – Guang
Shenzhen – Shen
Zhuhai – Zhu

MAPS

Aberdeen (HKI) 181
Around Victoria Peak (HKI) 172
Around Zhoutouzi Wharf
  (Guang) 401
Around Zhuhai (Zhu) 442

Central Macau (MP) 292-293
Cheung Chau (OI) 221
Coloane Island (MI) 311
Coloane Village (MI) 313

Dinghushan (Guang) 414
Discovery Bay (OI) 241

Foshan (Guang) 406

Gongbei District (Zhu) 434
Guangzhou (Canton) 372-373
Guangzhou Zoo (Guang) 386

Hong Kong 14-15
  Districts 19
  Kowloon-Canton Railway 127
  Light Rail Transit (opposite
    page 128)
  Mass Transit Railway 125
  Public Bus Routes 124
  Youth Hostel 86
Hong Kong Central (HKI) 168-
169
Hong Kong Island 164-165
Hong Kong, Macau &
  Guangzhou 9

Hunghom (Kow) 141

Jida District (Zhu) 436

Kowloon 136
  Kowloon City Restaurants 151

Lamma Island (OI) 226
Lan Kwai Fong (HKI) 190
Lantau Island (OI) 232-233
Location of Snake Restaurant
  (Guang) 393
Luofushan (Guang) 416

Macau 254
Macau Peninsula 286-287
Ma Wan (NT) 204
Ma Wui Hall (HKI) 182
Memorial Garden to the Martyrs
  (Guang) 378
Mongkok (Kow) 143
Mui Wo (Silvermine Bay) (OI)
  236

New Territories 200-201

Pearl River Delta (Guang) 317
Peasant Movement Institute Plan
  (Guang) 377
Peng Chau (OI) 246
Ping Chau (NT) 216
Poi Toi Island (OI) 250

Shamian Island (Guang) 381
Shatin (NT) 212
Shekou (Shen) 431
Shenzhen City 422-423
Shenzhen Special Economic
  Zone 418-419
Stanley (HKI) 178

Taipa Island (MI) 306
Taipa Village (MI) 308
Tai Po (NT) 209
Tap Mun Chau (NT) 215
Tsimshatsui (Kow) 138-139
Tsuen Wan (NT) 202-203
Tuen Mun (NT) 206
Tung Lung Chau (OI) 249

Wanchai-Causeway Bay
(HKI) 174
White Cloud Hills (Guang) 403

Xiangzhou District (Zhu) 438
Xiqiao Hills (Guang) 410

Yuexiu Park (Guang) 383
Yung Shue Wan (OI) 227

Zhaoqing (Guang) 412
  Around Zhaoqing (Guang) 413
Zhongshan City (Zhu) 444

TEXT

Map references are in **bold** type

A-Ma Temple (Ma Kok Miu)
  (MP) 291, 295
Aberdeen (HKI) 180-182, **181**
acupuncture 71-72 see also
  herbal medicine
Amah Rock (NT) 213

Ancestors' Temple (Guang) 407
Apliu St (Kow) 144-145

Bank of China Building (HKI)
  166
banquets 91
bargaining 46, 265-266, 333
Barra Hill (MP) 295
Barrier Gate (MP) 296-297

Big Wave Bay Beach (HKI) 177
billiards & snooker 77
Bird Market (Kow) 142
Birthday of Lord Buddha
  Festival 52
bowling 77
Bright Filial Piety Temple
  (Guang) 379
Buddhism 31-32

Buddhist Western Monastery (NT) 199
Bun Festival 223

Camoes Grotto & Gardens (MP) 285-289
canoeing 77
car rental 130
Cat St Galleries (HKI) 170
Causeway Bay (HKI) 175-176
Causeway Bay Sports Ground (HKI) 176-177
Cenotaph (HKI) 163
Central (HKI) 163-167, **168-169**
Central Market (HKI) 166
Central Plaza (HKI) 173
Chapel of St Francis Xavier (MI) 312
Che Kung Miu Temple (NT) 211
Chen Clan Academy (Guang) 384
Cheng Precipice (Guang) 402
Cheoc Van Beach (MI) 312
Cheung Chau (OI) 220-226, **221**
Cheung Chau Bun Festival 52
Cheung Chau Typhoon Shelter (OI) 220
Cheung Chau Village (OI) 220
Cheung Po Tsai Cave (OI) 222-223
Cheung Sha Beach (OI) 239
Cheung Yeung Festival 53-54
Chi Ma Wan (OI) 240
Chiang Kaishek 318-319, 376
China Folk Culture Villages (Shen) 425
China International Travel Service (CITS) 335
China Travel Service (CTS) 335-336
Chinese gods 35
Chinese (Lunar) New Year 50-51
Chinese opera 26-27
Chinese University of Hong Kong (NT) 26
Chinese zodiac 28
Ching Chung Koon (Green Pine) Temple (NT) 205
Ching Ming Festival 51
Chinnery, George 256, 289
Chongxi Pagoda (Guang) 411
Chuk Lam Sim Yuen Temples (NT) 199-202
Chungking Mansions (Kow) 145-149
Clearwater Bay (NT) 213
Clock Tower (Kow) 134
Coloane Island (MI) 310, **311**
Coloane Park (MI) 310-312

Coloane Village (MI) 312, **313**
computer clubs 77-78
Confucianism 33-34
Conghua Hot Springs (Guang) 404-405
cricket 78
Cultural Park (Guang) 382
cycling 78, 130

Deep Water Bay (HKI) 179
Deng Xiaoping 321
Dinghushan (Guang) 411, **414**
Discovery Bay (OI) 240-242, **241**
Dr Sun Yatsen 290-291, 318-319, 441
Dragon Boat Festival 52

electronic mail 59
Elliot, Captain Charles 12-13

Fa Peng Knoll (OI) 222
Fan Lau (OI) 239
Fanling (NT) 208
fishing 78
Five Genies Temple (Guang) 379
Floating Casino (MP) 303
fortune tellers 28-29
Foshan (Guang) 405-409, **406**
Four-Faced Buddha Shrine (MI) 309
Fung Ping Shan Museum (HKI) 171
Fung Ying Sin Kwun Temple (NT) 208
fungshui (geomancy) 29-30

Ghost Month Festival 53
golf 78-79
Gongbei District (Zhu) **434**
Gongbei Market (Zhu) 434
Government House (HKI) 166-167
Government House (MP) 296
Governor's Residence (MP) 296
grand prix 277-278
Guangdong Provincial Museum (Guang) 385
Guangzhou (Canton) 371-417, **372-373**
    accommodation 357-358
    books & magazines 342-346
    entertainment 363-364, 394
    food & drinks 358-363
    getting around 369-370, 400-402
    getting there & away 366-368, 396-400
    health 348-353
    history 316-319

language 323
    places to eat 391-394
    places to stay 387-390
    safety 353-354
    shopping 364, 394-396
    work 354-356
Guangzhou Fair (Guang) 385-387
Guangzhou Zoo (Guang) 384
Guia Lighthouse (MP) 291

Hac Sa Beach (MI) 312-313
Hac Sa Sports & Recreation Park (MI) 313
Haichuang Park (Guang) 382
hakka (people) 25
handball 79
Happy Valley (HKI) 177
Hebe Haven (NT) 214
herbal medicine 69-71
hiking 79-80
Hollywood Rd (HKI) 170
Hong Kong **14-15**
    accommodation 85-89
    books & magazines 61-64
    entertainment 99-102
    food & drinks 89-98
    getting around 123-133
    getting there & away 113-122
    health 65-73
    history 12-18
    language 36
    safety 73-74
    shopping 102
    work 75-76
Hong Kong & Shanghai Bank Building (HKI) 163-166
Hong Kong Arts Centre (HKI) 175
Hong Kong Coliseum (Kow) 61
Hong Kong Consumer Council (Kow) 49
Hong Kong Convention & Exhibition Centre (HKI) 175
Hong Kong Cultural Centre (Kow) 60-61, 134
Hong Kong Information Services Department (HKI) 48-49
Hong Kong Island 163-197, **164-165**
    entertainment 190-195
    places to eat 184-190
    places to stay 182-184
    shopping 195-197
Hong Kong Museum of Art (Kow) 134
Hong Kong Park (HKI) 167
Hong Kong Railway Museum (NT) 210

Hong Kong Science Museum (Kow) 140
Hong Kong Stadium (HKI) 61
Hong Kong Trail (HKI) 173
Hong Kong University (HKI) 26, 171
Hong Kong University of Science & Technology (NT) 26
horse racing 80
horseback riding 80
Huaisheng Mosque (Guang) 379-380
Humen (Shen) 432
Hung Shing Ye Beach (OI) 228-229
Hunghom (Kow) 140, **141**

Jade Market (Kow) 140-141
Jai-Alai Casino (MP) 304
Jardine Matheson 176 see also Noon-Day Gun
Jinsha Park (Guang) 404
Joao Ferreira do Amaral 258
Jorge Alvares Statue (MP) 285

Kam Pek Casino (MP) 303-304
Kam Tin (NT) 207-208
karaoke 101
karting 80
Kartodrome (MI) 309
Kat Hing Wai Village (NT) 207-208
Kau-O Village (MI) 314
Kingsway Hotel Casino (MP) 304
Kowloon 134-162, **136, 151**
    entertainment 157
    places to eat 153,157-159
    places to stay 145-153
    shopping 159-162
Kowloon Mosque (Kow) 137
Kowloon Park (Kow) 135
Kuanyin's Birthday 51
Kun Iam Temple (MI) 296
Kun Iam Temple (MP) 307
Kun Iam Temple (Coloane Village) 312
Kwun Yum Wan Beach (OI) 222

Laichikok Amusement Park (Kow) 144
Lamma (OI) 226-231, **226**
Lan Kwai Fong District (HKI) 166, 190-193, **190**
Lantau (OI) 231-245, **232-233**
Lantau Peak (OI) 238
Lantau Tea Gardens (OI) 238
Lantau Trail (OI) 238-239

Lantern Festival 51
Laufaushan (NT) 207
lawn bowling 80
Leal Senado (MP) 285
Lei Cheng Uk Museum (Kow) 144
Lei Yue Mun Village (Kow) 145
Li Yuen St (HKI) 166
Lingding Island (Zhu) 445
lion dances 26
Lisboa Casino (MP) 303
Liu'ersan Lu (Guang) 380
Liuhua Park (Guang) 384
Lo So Shing Beach (OI) 229
Lord MacLehose 204
Lotus Mountain (Guang) 403-404
Lotus Temple (Lin Fong Miu) (MP) 296
Lou Lim Loc Gardens (MP) 290
Lu Lake (Guang) 402
Luis de Camoes 256
Luis de Camoes Museum (MP) 285
Luofushan (Guang) **416**, 417

Ma On Shan (NT) 214
Ma Wan (NT) **204**, 205
Macau **254**
    accommodation 272-273
    books & magazines 270-271
    entertainment 274-277
    food & drinks 273-274
    getting around 281-284
    getting there & away 279-280
    history 254-258
    language 262-263
    religion 262
Macau, Central 285-291, **292-293**
Macau Islands 305-314
    getting there & away 305
Macau Jockey Club (MI) 308-309
Macau Peninsula 285-304, **286-287**
    entertainment 302-304
    places to eat 300-302
    places to stay 297-300
Macau-Seac Tin Hau Temple (MP) 297
Macau, the North 296-297
Macau, the South 291-296
Macau University (MI) 307
Maclehose Trail (NT) 204-205
mahjong 101
Mai Po Marsh (NT) 207
Maidens' Festival 53
Man Mo Temple (HKI) 170
Man Mo Temple (NT) 210

Man Wa Lane (HKI) 170
Mandarin Oriental Hotel Casino (MP) 304
Mao Zedong 320-321
Maritime Museum (MP) 295
martial arts 31 see also taijiquan
Mausoleum of the 72 Martyrs (Guang) 377
Memorial Garden to the Martyrs (Guang) 376-377, **378**
Memorial of Yellow Flowers (Guang) 377
Mid-Autumn (Moon) Festival 53
Military Museum (MP) 291
Miu Fat Monastery (NT) 207
Mo Tat Wan Beach (OI) 229
Mohammedan Tomb (Guang) 380
Mongkok (Kow) 142, **143**
Monte Fort (MP) 290
Monument to the Martyrs of the Shaji Massacre (Guang) 382
Mt Stenhouse (OI) 229
Mui Wo (Silvermine Bay) (OI) 235, **236**
Museum of Chinese Historical Relics (HKI) 175
Museum of History (Kow) 137

Nanhu Amusement Park (Guang) 402-403
Nathan Rd (Kow) 135
New Kowloon (Kow) 142-145
New Territories 198-217, **200-201**
    places to eat 217
    places to stay 216-217
New World Hotel (Kow) 137
Ngong Ping (OI) 237-239
Nine Dragons Well (Guang) 402
Noon-Day Gun (HKI) 175-176
noticeboards 346-347

Ocean Banner Monastery (Guang) 382
Ocean Park (HKI) 179-180
Ocean Terminal (Kow) 135
Old Protestant Cemetery (MP) 289
opium wars & treaties 13-16
Orchid Park (Guang) 384
Our Lady of Carmel Church (MI) 308
Outlying Islands 218-251
    accommodation 219
    getting there & away 219-220
    information 219
Overseas Chinese Town (Shen) 425

overseas reps
  Chinese overseas reps 336-337
  Hong Kong overseas reps 48
  Macau overseas reps 266-267

Pak Tai Temple (OI) 220-222
Pak Tam Chung (NT) 214
parachuting 80-81
paragliding 81
Pat Sin Leng Nature Trail (NT) 210
Patten, Governor Christopher 18
Peak Galleria (HKI) 171
Pearl River (Guang) **317**, 380
Peasant Movement Institute (Guang) 376, **377**
Peng Chau (OI) 245-248, **246**
Penha Church (MP) 296
Peninsula Hotel (Kow) 135
Penny's Bay (OI) 242
Ping Chau (NT) 215-216, **216**
pinyin 323-324
Plover Cove Reservoir (NT) 210
Plum Monastery (Guang) 411
Po Lin Monastery (OI) 237
Poi Toi (OI) 250-251, **250**
Police Museum (HKI) 175
Possession St (HKI) 170
Pou Tai Un Temple (MI) 307
Promenade, the (Kow) 140
Public Security Bureau (PSB) 337, 371

Qigong 31
Qingping Market (Guang) 380
Quarry Bay (HKI) 177
Queen Elizabeth Stadium (HKI) 61

Renshou Pagoda (Guang) 407-408
Repulse Bay (HKI) 179
rickshaw 132
running 81

Sai Kung Peninsula (NT) 213-214
Sai Kung Town (NT) 214
Sam Seng Temple (MI) 312
Sam Tung Uk Museum (NT) 202
Sanyuanli (Guang) 385
sauna & massage 81-82
scuba diving 82
Sculpture of the Five Rams (Guang) 384
Seven Star Crags (Guang) 410
Sham Wan Beach (OI) 229
Shamian Island (Guang) 380-382, **381**

Shatin (NT) 211-213, **212**
Shatin New Town Plaza (NT) 213
Shatin Racecourse (NT) 211
Shek Kong Airfield (NT) 208
Shek O (HKI) 177
Shek Pai Wan Beach (OI) 229
Shek Pik Reservoir (OI) 239
Shekou (Shen) 430-432, **431**
Shenzhen 418-432
  getting around 430
  getting there & away 428-430
  places to eat 428
  places to stay 425
Shenzhen City (Shen) 421, **422-423**
Sheung Shui (NT) 208
Sheung Wan (HKI) 170-171
Shui Tau Village (NT) 208
Sino-British Joint Declaration 17
skating 82
soccer 82
Sok Kwu Wan (OI) 229
Southern Yue Tomb Museum (Guang) 384
Space Museum (Kow) 134-135
Splendid China (Shen) 421-424
squash 82
St Augustine Church (MP) 291
St Dominic's Church (MP) 285
St Lazarus Church (MP) 291
St Michael Cemetery (MP) 290
St Paul's Ruins (MP) 289-290
St Stephen's Beach (HKI) 179
Stanley (HKI) 177-179, **178**
Stanley Market (HKI) 177
Star House (Kow) 135
Star Touching Hill (Guang) 402
Statue Square (HKI) 163
Sun Yatsen Memorial Hall (Guang) 377-378
Sun Yatsen Memorial Home (MP) 290-291
Sun Yatsen Monument (Guang) 384
Sun Yatsen's Residence (Zhu) 441
Sung (Song) Dynasty Village (Kow) 144
swimming 83

Tai Kwai Wan Beach (OI) 222
Tai Mo Shan (NT) 202-204
Tai O (OI) 239
Tai Ping Carpet Factory (NT) 210
Tai Po (NT) 208-210
Tai Po Kau (NT) **209**, 210
taijiquan 30

Taipa House Museum (MI) 307-308
Taipa Island (MI) 305-310, **306**
Taipa Village (MI) 307-308, **308**
Tam Kong Temple (MI) 312
tankas (people) 25
Taoism 32-33
Tap Mun Chau (NT) 215
Temple of the Six Banyan Trees (Guang) 378
Temple St (Kow) 141-142
Ten Thousand Buddha Monastery (NT) 211
tennis 83
Tiger Balm Gardens (HKI) 176-177
Tin Hau Festival 51-52
Tin Hau Temple (Causeway Bay) 176
Tin Hau Temple (Coloane Village) 312
Tin Hau Temple (Stanley) 179
Tin Hau Temple (Yaumatei) 141
tipping 46, 265, 333
Tolo Harbour (NT) 215
Tong Fuk (OI) 239
tourist offices
  Chinese tourist offices 334-337
  Hong Kong tourist offices 47-48
  Macau tourist offices 266
Trappist Haven Monastery (OI) 235-237
triads 74
Tsimshatsui (Kow) 134-137, **138-139**
Tsimshatsui Eas (Kow) 137-140
Tsuen Wan (NT) 199-202, **203**
Tsuen Wan Plaza (NT) 202
Tsui Museum of Art (HKI) 166
Tuen Mun (NT) 205-207, **206**
Tung Choi St (Kow) 142
Tung Chung (OI) 240
Tung Chung Battery (OI) 240
Tung Chung Fort (OI) 240
Tung Lung Chau (OI) 249-250, **249**
Tung Wan Beach (OI) 222
Tung Wan Tsai Beach (OI) 222
Typhoon Shelter (HKI) 175
typhoons 20-21

United Chinese Cemetery (MI) 309

Vasco da Gama Garden (MP) 291
Victoria Park (HKI) 176

Victoria Peak (HKI) 171-173, **172**
visas
  Chinese visas 329-330
  Hong Kong visas 42-43
  Macau visas 264

Wanchai (HKI) 173-175, **174**
war & revolution 16
waterskiing 84
Water World (HKI) 180
Western Market (HKI) 170
Whampoa Gardens (Kow) 140
White Cloud Hills (Guang) 402, **403**
windsurfing 84

Wong Tai Sin Temple (Kow) 142-144

Xavier, Francis 256
Xiqiao Hills (Guang) 409

yachting 84-85
Yam O Wan (OI) 242
Yaumatei (Kow) 140-142
Yuejiang Temple (Guang) 411
Yuen Long (NT) 207
Yuen Yuen Institute (NT) 199
Yuexiu Park (Guang) 382-384, **383**
Yung Shue Wan (OI) **227**, 227-228

Zhaoqing (Guang) 409-417, **412**
Zhenhai Tower (Guang) 384
Zhongshan City (Zhu) 441-443, **444**
Zhongshan County (Zhu) 441-445
Zhongshan Hot Springs (Zhu) 443-445
Zhongshan Park (Zhu) 442
Zhongshan University (Guang) 385
Zhuhai 433-445, **442**
  getting around 440-441
  getting there & away 440
  places to eat 439
  places to stay 435-439
Zhuhai Holiday Resort (Zhu) 435

PLANET TALK
Lonely Planet's FREE quarterly newsletter

We love hearing from you and think you'd like to hear from us.

When...*is the right time to see reindeer in Finland?*
Where...*can you hear the best palm-wine music in Ghana?*
How...*do you get from Asunción to Areguá by steam train?*
What...*is the best way to see India?*

For the answer to these and many other questions read PLANET TALK.

Every issue is packed with up-to-date travel news and advice including:

- *a letter from Lonely Planet founders Tony and Maureen Wheeler*
- *travel diary from a Lonely Planet author - find out what it's really like out on the road*
- *feature article on an important and topical travel issue*
- *a selection of recent letters from our readers*
- *the latest travel news from all over the world*
- *details on Lonely Planet's new and forthcoming releases*

To join our mailing list contact any Lonely Planet office (address below).

LONELY PLANET PUBLICATIONS
Australia: PO Box 617, Hawthorn 3122, Victoria (tel: 03-819 1877)
USA: Embarcadero West, 155 Filbert St, Suite 251, Oakland, CA 94607 (tel: 510-893 8555)
TOLL FREE: (800) 275-8555
UK: 10 Barley Mow Passage, Chiswick, London W4 4PH (tel: 0181-742 3161)
France: 71 bis rue du Cardinal Lemoine – 75005 Paris (tel: 1-46 34 00 58)

Also available: Lonely Planet T-shirts. 100% heavyweight cotton (S, M, L, XL)

Guides to North-East Asia

Beijing - city guide
Beijing is the hub of a vast nation. This guide will help travellers to find the best this ancient and fascinating city has to offer.

North-East Asia on a shoestring
Concise information for independent low-budget travel in China, Hong Kong, Japan, Macau, North Korea, South Korea, Taiwan and Mongolia.

China - a travel survival kit
This book is the recognised authority for independent travellers in the People's Republic. With essential tips for avoiding pitfalls, and comprehensive practical information, it will help you to discover the real China.

Japan - a travel survival kit
Japan combines modern cities and remote wilderness areas, sophisticated technology and ancient tradition. This guide tells you how to find the Japan that many visitors never see.

Korea - a travel survival kit
South Korea is one of the great undiscovered destinations, with its mountains, ancient temples and lively modern cities. This guide also includes a chapter on reclusive North Korea.

Mongolia - a travel survival kit
Mongolia is truly a destination for the adventurous. This guide gives visitors the first real opportunity to explore this remote but newly accessible country.

Seoul - city guide
It is easy to explore Seoul's ancient royal palaces and bustling market places with this comprehensive guide packed with vital information for leisure and business travellers alike.

Taiwan - a travel survival kit
Traditional Chinese ways survive in prosperous Taiwan. This guide has Chinese script and pinyin throughout.

Tibet - a travel survival kit
The fabled mountain-land of Tibet is slowly becoming accessible to travellers. This guide has full details on this remote and fascinating region, including the border crossing to Nepal.

Tokyo - city guide
Tokyo is a dynamic metropolis and one of the world's leading arbiters of taste and style. This guide will help you to explore the many sides of Tokyo, the modern Japanese miracle rolled into a single fascinating, sometimes startling package.

Also available:
Cantonese phrasebook, *Mandarin Chinese* phrasebook, *Korean* phrasebook, *Tibet* phrasebook, and *Japanese* phrasebook.

Lonely Planet Guidebooks

Lonely Planet guidebooks cover every accessible part of Asia as well as Australia, the Pacific, South America, Africa, the Middle East, Europe and parts of North America. There are five series: *travel survival kits*, covering a country for a range of budgets; *shoestring guides* with compact information for low-budget travel in a major region; *walking guides*; *city guides* and *phrasebooks*.

Australia & the Pacific
Australia
Australian phrasebook
Bushwalking in Australia
Islands of Australia's Great Barrier Reef
Outback Australia
Fiji
Fijian phrasebook
Melbourne city guide
Micronesia
New Caledonia
New South Wales
New Zealand
Tramping in New Zealand
Papua New Guinea
Bushwalking in Papua New Guinea
Papua New Guinea phrasebook
Rarotonga & the Cook Islands
Samoa
Solomon Islands
Sydney city guide
Tahiti & French Polynesia
Tonga
Vanuatu
Victoria
Western Australia

South-East Asia
Bali & Lombok
Bangkok city guide
Cambodia
Indonesia
Indonesia phrasebook
Laos
Malaysia, Singapore & Brunei
Myanmar (Burma)
Burmese phrasebook
Philippines
Pilipino phrasebook
Singapore city guide
South-East Asia on a shoestring
Thailand
Thai phrasebook
Vietnam
Vietnamese phrasebook

Middle East
Arab Gulf States
Egypt & the Sudan
Arabic (Egyptian) phrasebook
Iran
Israel
Jordan & Syria
Middle East
Turkey
Turkish phrasebook
Trekking in Turkey
Yemen

North-East Asia
China
Beijing city guide
Cantonese phrasebook
Mandarin Chinese phrasebook
Hong Kong, Macau & Canton
Japan
Japanese phrasebook
Korea
Korean phrasebook
Mongolia
North-East Asia on a shoestring
Seoul city guide
Taiwan
Tibet
Tibet phrasebook
Tokyo city guide

Indian Ocean
Madagascar & Comoros
Maldives & Islands of the East Indian Ocean
Mauritius, Réunion & Seychelles

Mail Order

Lonely Planet guidebooks are distributed worldwide. They are also available by mail order from Lonely Planet, so if you have difficulty finding a title please write to us. US and Canadian residents should write to Embarcadero West, 155 Filbert St, Suite 251, Oakland CA 94607, USA; European residents should write to 10 Barley Mow Passage, Chiswick, London W4 4PH; and residents of other countries to PO Box 617, Hawthorn, Victoria 3122, Australia.

Indian Subcontinent
Bangladesh
India
Hindi/Urdu phrasebook
Trekking in the Indian Himalaya
Karakoram Highway
Kashmir, Ladakh & Zanskar
Nepal
Trekking in the Nepal Himalaya
Nepali phrasebook
Pakistan
Sri Lanka
Sri Lanka phrasebook

Africa
Africa on a shoestring
Central Africa
East Africa
Trekking in East Africa
Kenya
Swahili phrasebook
Morocco
Arabic (Moroccan) phrasebook
North Africa
South Africa, Lesotho & Swaziland
Zimbabwe, Botswana & Namibia
West Africa

Europe
Baltic States & Kaliningrad
Britain
Central Europe on a shoestring
Central Europe phrasebook
Czech & Slovak Republics
Dublin city guide
Eastern Europe on a shoestring
Eastern Europe phrasebook
Finland
France
Greece
Hungary
Iceland, Greenland & the Faroe Islands
Ireland
Italy
Mediterranean Europe on a shoestring
Mediterranean Europe phrasebook
Poland
Prague city guide
Scandinavian & Baltic Europe on a shoestring
Scandinavian Europe phrasebook
Switzerland
Trekking in Spain
Trekking in Greece
USSR
Russian phrasebook
Vienna city guide
Western Europe on a shoestring
Western Europe phrasebook

Central America & the Caribbean
Baja California
Central America on a shoestring
Costa Rica
Eastern Caribbean
Guatemala, Belize & Yucatán: La Ruta Maya
Mexico

North America
Alaska
Backpacking in Alaska
Canada
Hawaii

South America
Argentina, Uruguay & Paraguay
Bolivia
Brazil
Brazilian phrasebook
Chile & Easter Island
Colombia
Ecuador & the Galápagos Islands
Latin American Spanish phrasebook
Peru
Quechua phrasebook
South America on a shoestring
Trekking in the Patagonian Andes
Venezuela

The Lonely Planet Story

Lonely Planet published its first book in 1973 in response to the numerous 'How did you do it?' questions Maureen and Tony Wheeler were asked after driving, bussing, hitching, sailing and railing their way from England to Australia.

Written at a kitchen table and hand collated, trimmed and stapled, *Across Asia on the Cheap* became an instant local bestseller, inspiring thoughts of another book.

Eighteen months in South-East Asia resulted in their second guide, *South-East Asia on a shoestring*, which they put together in a backstreet Chinese hotel in Singapore in 1975. The 'yellow bible' as it quickly became known to backpackers around the world, soon became *the* guide to the region. It has sold well over half a million copies and is now in its 8th edition, still retaining its familiar yellow cover.

Today there are over 140 Lonely Planet titles in print – books that have that same adventurous approach to travel as those early guides; books that 'assume you know how to get your luggage off the carousel' as one reviewer put it.

Although Lonely Planet initially specialised in guides to Asia, they now cover most regions of the world, including the Pacific, South America, Africa, the Middle East and Europe. The list of *walking guides* and *phrasebooks* (for 'unusual' languages such as Quechua, Swahili, Nepali and Egyptian Arabic) is also growing rapidly.

The emphasis continues to be on travel for independent travellers. Tony and Maureen still travel for several months of each year and play an active part in the writing, updating and quality control of Lonely Planet's guides.

They have been joined by over 50 authors, 110 staff – mainly editors, cartographers & designers – at our office in Melbourne, Australia, at our US office in Oakland, California and at our European office in Paris; another five at our office in London handle sales for Britain, Europe and Africa. Travellers themselves also make a valuable contribution to the guides through the feedback we receive in thousands of letters each year.

The people at Lonely Planet strongly believe that travellers can make a positive contribution to the countries they visit, both through their appreciation of the countries' culture, wildlife and natural features, and through the money they spend. In addition, the company makes a direct contribution to the countries and regions it covers. Since 1986 a percentage of the income from each book has been donated to ventures such as famine relief in Africa; aid projects in India; agricultural projects in Central America; Greenpeace's efforts to halt French nuclear testing in the Pacific; and Amnesty International. In 1994 over $100,000 was donated to such causes.

Lonely Planet's basic travel philosophy is summed up in Tony Wheeler's comment, 'Don't worry about whether your trip will work out. Just go!'.